International Finance
Management, Markets, and Institutions

James C. Baker
Kent State University

PRENTICE HALL   Upper Saddle River, New Jersey 07458

Acquisitions Editor: Paul Donnelly
Associate Editor: Gladys Soto
Editorial Assistant: MaryBeth Sanok
Editor-in-Chief: James Boyd
Marketing Manager: Patrick Lynch
Managing Editor: Dee Josephson
Production Coordinator: Maureen Wilson
Manufacturing Buyer: Diane Peirano
Manufacturing Supervisor: Arnold Vila
Manufacturing Manager: Vincent Scelta
Composition: Maryland Composition
Cover image: Creator/Source

Copyright © 1998 by Prentice-Hall, Inc.
A Simon & Schuster Company
Upper Saddle River, NJ 07458

Library of Congress Cataloging-in-Publication Data
Baker, James Calvin
    International finance : management, markets, and institutions / by
James C. Baker.
        p.   cm.
    Includes bibliographical references and index.
    ISBN 0-02-305891-9
    1. International business enterprises—Finance.   2. International
finance.   I. Title.
HG4027.5.B35   1998
658.15′99—dc21   97-23781
                                                          CIP

Prentice-Hall International (UK) Limited, *London*
Prentice-Hall of Australia Pty. Limited, *Sydney*
Prentice-Hall Canada Inc., *Toronto*
Prentice-Hall Hispanoamericana, S.A., *Mexico*
Prentice-Hall of India Private Limited, *New Delhi*
Prentice-Hall of Japan, Inc., *Tokyo*
Simon & Schuster Asia Pte. Ltd., *Singapore*
Editora Prentice-Hall do Brasil, Ltda., *Rio de Janeiro*

Printed in the United States of America
10 9 8 7 6 5 4 3

To my mother, Lillian Adams, and the memory of my father,
Clyde Baker, who made it all possible

About the Author

James C. Baker is Professor of Finance and International Business at Kent State University where he has taught since 1971. He has M.B.A. and D.B.A. degrees in International Business from Indiana University and has held full-time appointments at the University of Maryland and San Francisco State University as well as part-time appointments at George Washington University, University of Hawaii, Catholic University in Puerto Rico, Madrid Business School in Spain, and Hiram College. He was international financial adviser at Federal Deposit Insurance Corporation from 1975–77. His teaching and research specialties are international financial management, international financial institutions and markets, international banking, and international business.

His books include *International Business Expansion into Less-Developed Countries*—a definitive study of the International Finance Corporation, *Foreign Influence in Korean Banking* (with Y. D. Euh), *International Business Classics* (with Donald Howard and J. K. Ryans), *International Bank Regulation,* and *The German Stock Markets*—the only English-language study of these markets. His articles have appeared in such journals as *Accounting and Business Research, The Banker, California Management Review, Columbia Journal of World Business, International Journal of Finance, International Trade Journal, Journal of Business Ethics, Journal of World Trade Law,* and *Managerial Finance.*

Dr. Baker currently serves on the editorial review boards of *Advances in Competitiveness Research, Global Finance and Business Review, Journal of Asia-Pacific Business, Journal of Emerging Markets, Journal of Global Business,* and *Multinational Business Review.* He serves as Membership Committee Chair for the Academy of International Business and on the Globalization Committee of the Financial Management Association International. His next project is a study of agencies that facilitate and encourage foreign direct investment in developing countries, e.g., Multilateral Investment Guarantee Agency (MIGA) and International Centre for Settlement of Investment Disputes (ICSID).

Brief Contents

Contents

PART VI: SHORT-TERM CAPITAL MANAGEMENT OF INTERNATIONAL OPERATIONS   389

Preface

In 1963, the term "multinational corporation" (MNC) became a household term after a cover story about the institution in *Business Week*. In the following three decades, global business prospered as a result of the need for poor countries to develop, the end of the cold war and breakup of the Union of Soviet Socialist Republics, privatization of business and banking, and the burgeoning economic power of the global triad—Asia, the United States, and Europe. The latter phenomenon has created a market of nearly a billion people and, if East Europe and Latin America become part of the triad, the global economic village is even larger. The world is becoming more and more a borderless world for economic transactions as a result of GATT negotiations to reduce trade restrictions, the continuing move by the European Union toward a true United States of Europe with one currency, and trading arrangements such as the North American Free Trade Agreement uniting Canada, the United States, and Mexico into one large trading bloc.

Business operations in this borderless world need to be financed and managed with more attention to the most current methods available to financial managers. It is the purpose of this book to offer coverage of the most up-to-date methods for financial management of the international firms that carry out cross-border operations in this borderless world. The major emphasis is on instruction of undergraduate and beginning level MBA students.

Strategies of *International Finance: Management, Markets, and Institutions*

To achieve this purpose, a number of strategies have been formulated. First, the discussion of the book deals with management of the finance function from the viewpoint of the chief financial officer of the MNC. Second, the sources of funds to finance these MNCs are examined. Third, the markets for the financial instruments used to finance the MNC or to hedge its various risks are analyzed. Major concepts, analytical methods, and applications are incorporated.

International Finance: Management, Markets, and Institutions is organized into seven major areas. In Part I, Introduction, the student is introduced to international business finance and the cultural variables of international business that affect the international finance function. A birdseye view of international finance is presented. The chapter concludes with a discussion of readings highly recommended for the student of international finance.

Part II covers the global environment of business finance. The major topics include the international monetary system, the balance of payments, foreign exchange, the management of foreign exchange risk, and the measurement and management of political risk.

Planning for foreign investment and operations is the topic of Part III. The major areas covered are foreign direct investments, capital budgeting, cost of capital, financial structure of the MNC, and planning and organization of the international finance function.

The focus of Part IV is on the role of banks in global finance. International banks play a major role in the development and nurturing of MNC operations. Thus, the functions of international banks are examined.

Part V is a discussion and analysis of the non-bank financial institutions and international financial markets that represent an inventory of financial resources for the MNC. The latter coverage includes treatment of financial derivatives used in hedging financial risks, including exchange-traded and over-the-counter derivatives.

The day-to-day management of international financial operations is examined in Part VI. The coverage includes working capital management; accounting, control and auditing of international operations; and taxation of these operations.

The book concludes with coverage of special issues in chapter 18 that affect the financial management of MNCs. This chapter is devoted to payment systems, global custody, and settlement of cross-border transactions, activities that are becoming more and more important in global finance as we approach the 21st century.

Distinctive Characteristics of the Book

International Finance: Management, Markets, and Institutions has incorporated some distinctive characteristics. First, the book is shorter in length and number of chapters than most books in international business finance. Most books in this area have seven to ten or more chapters and are difficult to complete in one semester. Second, the book emphasizes the role of the chief financial officer (CFO) of the MNC and contains several caselets that examine CFOs and financial institutions' executives in real-life situations. Third, coverage of the three major foreign exchange exposures are treated in one chapter. Fourth, major functions of international banks are covered in one chapter. Fifth, an inventory of financial resources has been constructed in Part V, with an analysis of major sources of financing and hedging for MNCs. Finally, the area of global custody and settlement is covered in chapter 18. These areas have become more important for international firms and investors during the past decade.

Pedagogical Materials

The book includes a number of pedagogical aids to enhance the learning process by students. These include the following:

1. 33 management applications (brief cases) that cover examples of techniques, institutions, functions, and personalities in international financial management;

2. key objectives and terms to be learned in each chapter that are listed at the beginning of each chapter;

3. study aids placed throughout each chapter that suggest to the student additional readings or problems to facilitate his/her critical thinking and understanding of the material;

4. end-of-chapter lists of additional readings, discussion questions, and problem exercises;

5. a glossary of terms of significance to the area of international financial management;

6. a comprehensive Instructor's Manual that contains solutions to end-of-chapter discussion questions and problems as well as chapter outlines and synopses; overhead transparency masters; test banks of true/false, multiple choice, and essay questions and answers; and other sources of information of value to the instructor using this textbook.

Guidelines for the Instructor

The book is designed to be a less-rigorous examination of international business finance for undergraduate and beginning MBA students. It can be used as a textbook for the upper-level undergraduate international business finance course or as a supplement for an advanced financial management course, using the sections that discuss financial management concepts, such as Parts II, III, and VI. It can be used as a supplement for the financial institutions and markets course using Parts IV and V. It can also be used as a supplement for an International Business course whose primary textbook is trade- or marketing-oriented.

Recommended Readings

Several outside readings can be recommended for a course in global finance that will supplement the textbook and classroom experience for students. Most of the materials discussed in this section should be found in any university library.

Before international finance periodicals are recommended, it must be noted that the subject of culture should be among the background subjects covered by a student of global finance. Unfortunately, few students are required to take an introductory course in international business in which the subject of cultural variables in international business is covered. The student can develop sufficient background in cultural aspects by reading just two books: *The Cultural Environment of International Business* by Terpstra and David and *The Silent Language* by Edward Hall.[1]

Several international business periodicals of a general nature are helpful, including: (1) *Journal of International Business Studies,* the quarterly refereed journal of the Academy of International Business, that occasionally contains excellent scholarly material on such subjects as foreign investment theory and empirical studies on various functional aspects of international financial management; (2) *Management International Review,* a refereed scholarly general international business journal with occasional pieces on international financial management; (3) *Journal of World Business,* formerly *Columbia Journal of World Business,* a quarterly refereed journal covering international business issues; (4) *International Trade Journal,* the refereed journal of the International Trade and Finance Association, covers international trade and finance issues bordering on the theoretical that have economic implications; (5) *The International Executive,* a bimonthly refereed journal aimed at advancement and dissemination of research in the field of international business.

In addition to these scholarly periodicals, some other more general publications are mentioned for their value to scholars in international business and finance. These include *The Economist* and *Business Week,* two weeklies containing some international business material. *Fortune* and *Business* are two periodicals published less frequently than weekly that have occasional case studies of MNCs and their operations. Finally, daily business newspapers such as the *Wall Street Journal, Investor's Business Daily,* and the *Financial Times* contain valuable information about international financial markets and news of international business that is very current.

Journals and periodicals devoted to international finance topics can be divided between those that are practice oriented and those that are scholarly in nature. Among

---

[1] Vern Terpstra and Keith David, *The Cultural Environment of International Business* (Cincinnati, OH: South-Western, 1991) and Edward T. Hall, *The Silent Language* (New York: Doubleday & Co., 1959).

the former, *Euromoney,* subtitled *The Journal for International Money and Capital Markets,* should be singled out for its valuable material. This monthly periodical contains many articles on international financial institutions and markets and material about the personalities and issues in the field of international finance.

Other practical periodicals include: (1) *International Financial Law Review,* a monthly magazine that examines the technical and regulatory side of international finance; (2) *International Currency Review,* a bimonthly periodical devoted to analyses of leading currencies that can be used by MNC management; and (3) *Global Finance,* a monthly magazine, covering the major issues in international finance.

A number of scholarly journals have been published during the past few years, including the following: (1) *Journal of International Money and Finance,* the most rigorous of the international finance refereed journals, is devoted to highly theoretical research in this area; (2) *Global Finance Journal,* a refereed journal devoted to high-level international financial management issues; (3) *Journal of International Financial Management and Accounting,* a refereed journal that examines research in international financial management and accounting; (4) *Journal of Multinational Financial Management,* another refereed journal devoted to international financial management issues; (5) *International Review of Economics and Finance,* a quarterly refereed journal; (6) *Multinational Finance Journal,* the quarterly publication of the Multinational Finance Society.

A few books that are closely related to the international finance area fill important niches and are important reference works. These include: (1) John Pippenger, *Fundamentals of International Finance* (Englewood Cliffs, NJ: Prentice Hall, 1984), a book that concentrates on the international financial economics underlying much of international financial management. This book could be used as a supplement in the international financial management course; (2) J. Orlin Grabbe, *International Financial Markets* (Englewood Cliffs, NJ: Prentice-Hall, 1996), a book that specializes in the narrow aspect of international financial markets and their operations; (3) Bruno Solnik, *International Investments* (Reading, MA: Addison-Wesley, 1996) is a book similar to those by Grabbe, Evans, and Madura et al. in that it can be used as a supplement in an international financial management course, but Solnik concentrates on the investment side of international financial markets; (4) Ian H. Giddy, *Global Financial Markets* (Lexington, MA: D.C. Heath & Co., 1994), covers international financial markets; (5) international finance casebooks that can be used as supplements in an international financial management course, particularly the second edition of Gunter Dufey and Ian H. Giddy, *Cases in International Finance* (Reading, MA: Addison-Wesley, 1993); Harvey A. Poniachek, *Cases in International Finance* (New York: John Wiley, 1993), and W. Carl. Kester and Timothy A. Luehrman, *Case Problems in International Finance* (New York: McGraw-Hill, 1993).

Finally, several publications are available as research data tools for the international finance scholar. Among these are (1) *International Financial Statistics,* a monthly publication of the International Monetary Fund (IMF) that includes several types of statistical data about the international financial aspects of member countries of the IMF; (2) *Balance of Payments Yearbook,* a publication of the IMF that includes periodical information regarding the balance of payments of IMF member countries; (3) *The Dow Jones Guide to the World Stock Market,* a reference book that includes information on the 2,500 biggest stocks in 20 of the key equity markets around the globe that make up the Dow Jones World Stock Index.

Acknowledgments

This book is the result of teaching international financial management for 25 years. My interest in this topic was sparked by Lee Nehrt in his first graduate course, International Finance, at Indiana University in 1962. During the ensuing years, I have used all major texts in the field and owe a debt of gratitude to their authors, including Zwick and Zenoff, Eiteman/Stonehill/Moffett, Shapiro, Madura, Abdullah, Eng/Lees/Mauer, Kim/Kim, Butler, and others. Their concepts and discussion of the issues in this field have broadened my knowledge of the area.

My visits to several international financial institutions have resulted in contacts and materials that have been invaluable in formulating parts of the book. These include: Chicago Mercantile Exchange, Chicago Board of Trade, World Bank, International Monetary Fund, London International Financial Futures Exchange, Amsterdam Stock Exchange, London Stock Exchange, Madrid Stock Exchange, the German stock exchanges, stock exchanges in Zurich and Geneva, and several Edge Act banks in the United States. In addition, my visits to MNCs, such as Goodyear, Rubbermaid, Sherwin-Williams, BP, Timken, Babcock-Wilcox, and others, for discussion with their financial executives, as well as to foreign exchange trading rooms in Chicago and Cleveland have brought me in contact with many generous executives whose assistance has embellished several areas of this book.

I have had several doctoral students who have sharpened my conceptual knowledge of various areas of international finance and they should be acknowledged. They include Raj Aggarwal, Thomas Stuhldreher, Ezra Byler, Andrea DeMaskey, M. Anaam Hashmi, Sharif Ahkam, Daniel Borgia, David Rayome, and William Roberts. These and others have kept the juices flowing with the continuation of their research.

Many of the topical areas in this book have been sharpened by the many students who have taken the numerous courses and seminars in the areas of international financial management, international financial markets, and international banking which I have given during the past 25 years at the University of Maryland, San Francisco State University, Kent State University, Catholic University of Puerto Rico, University of Hawaii, George Washington University, Madrid Business School, and the Kent State University Geneva Semester program. These students have kept me current in this fast moving field.

Numerous reviews of international financial management research that I have done have furnished examples of financing techniques as the papers were published. Such journals include *Journal of International Business Studies, Global Finance Journal, Multinational Business Review, Journal of Emerging Markets, Global Finance and Business Review,* and *Journal of Asia-Pacific Business*. In addition, publications such as *Euromoney* and *Global Finance* have furnished real-world examples of many operations in this area.

I owe deep gratitude to the various reviewers of several drafts of the manuscript. These include Shirley Love of Idaho State University, Swapen Sen of Michigan Technological University, John M. Simms, Jr., of the University of North Carolina-Greensboro, Inayat U. Mangla of Western Michigan University, A. Sam Ghanty of University of Wisconsin-Green Bay, Michael E. Solt of San Jose State University, Ravi Vaidyanathan of Northeastern State University, Keqian Bi of the University of San Francisco, and Mark A. White of the University of Virginia. Their suggestions have im-

proved this book in many ways and I am forever grateful for the time they spent improving the manuscript.

In addition to the major reviewers, numerous other people have assisted me in the preparation of this book. Teresa Cohan of Simon & Schuster guided the various drafts to reviewers and was very cooperative in the methodical process resulting in a final product. Paul Donnelly of Prentice-Hall was instrumental in pushing the project along to completion. Mary Beth Sanok of Simon Schuster/Prentice-Hall took the project down the homestretch. Helen Powers and Gladys Soto were meticulous in their editorial work on the final draft. The editing that they performed greatly improved the final product. I am grateful to Apple Computer Corporation for the simplicity of its Powerbook 160 that facilitated the editing of several drafts of the manuscript. I owe much to Bruce Campbell, a Kent State University doctoral student, who offered much assistance in the problem solutions and test bank for the *Instructor's Manual* during a time of his own family loss. Susan Edwards, another Kent State University doctoral student, has been helpful in various aspects of this project. I am grateful to those who gave permission to include items in this text. They are listed elsewhere.

Finally, I am grateful to my wife, Jean, who sacrificed several vacations during the past three years while I worked on the book, and to my son, Jeff, who kept the grass mowed, the leaves raked, and the snow off the walks and driveway and, thus, freed up my time. I must acknowledge Dr. Delos Cosgrove and his team of cardiac surgeons at the Cleveland Clinic who repaired my aortic valve during the early stage of the manuscript and whose results kept me healthy for the remainder of the project.

Reworking various drafts of the book has removed many errors and brought confidence that it is free from mistakes. However, gremlins always manage to subvert such a feeling. I will appreciate any comments, corrections, or suggestions from any reader. Until then, I accept the responsibility for any and all errors that have not been corrected.

James C. Baker
Kent, Ohio, U.S.A.

PART

Introduction

This book is devoted to a discussion of business finance practiced in a borderless world by multinational corporations. The cross-border operations of these companies are carried out as though no national borders exist. It is the author's desire to introduce students to this borderless world of global finance and elicit such an interest in this area that students will continue to examine the world of finance using this text and other references.

The first chapter introduces the student to a number of topics in the field of international business finance. The gains from trade in goods and services and comparative advantage are discussed to show the need for foreign exchange. The reasons to study this topic are covered. In addition, cultural variables are discussed. The topics involving international trade and cultural concepts are included because many students take an international financial management course without an introductory course in international business. The environment of international finance is covered as is the orientation of the book and a discussion of selected literature available to the student to facilitate his/her understanding of this field.

Introduction to International Business Finance

Major Objectives of Chapter 1

(1) To introduce the student to the environmental differences encountered by the manager of the international finance function in a multinational corporation, (2) to present the outline of the book, and (3) to introduce the student to selected major items in the literature of international financial management.

Key terms to be learned in chapter 1:

- self-reference criterion
- foreign exchange risk
- interest rate risk
- credit risk
- contagion risk
- operations risk
- absolute advantage

- silent languages
- political risk
- settlement risk
- market risk
- mercantilism
- comparative advantage

Introduction to the International Finance Function

Financial management is one of the major business functions. Every business enterprise must implement financial management at some time in its operations. To a firm that produces and sells a product or service, financial management is as important as the management of marketing, human resources, and production. Thus, business students must take one or more courses in financial management in these core areas.

THE GAINS FROM TRADE IN GOODS AND SERVICES

This textbook assumes that the student has had a basic economics course or two and, thus, has some background in the reasons for international trade. However, a brief basic review of the theory of comparative advantage and cultural aspects is provided to enhance the student's basic understanding of some fundamental principles of interna-

tional financial management. Without international trade among nations, foreign currency would be unnecessary and an international currency exchange would not be needed. The theory of comparative advantage clearly explains why countries should enter into international trade. Cultural differences do exist in international business relationships that affect the implementation of the international financial management function. These subjects are discussed in the following sections.

Comparative Advantage

In 1776 in *The Wealth of Nations*, Adam Smith argued that trade was not a zero-sum game as the mercantilists had argued. A nation could use its superior manufacturing ability to produce a good and, thereby, could have an absolute advantage in the production of that good. Countries that had such an absolute advantage could specialize in the production of that good and trade it to other countries for the product in which they specialized. In other words, a country has an absolute advantage in a product if it is more efficient than any other nation in the production of that good.

Adam Smith claimed that free market forces will determine the direction, volume, and composition of international trade. In such an environment, each nation should specialize in producing those goods that it can make most efficiently and trade those goods to pay for imports that other nations can make more efficiently. In such an environment, each country may have an absolute advantage in the production of the goods it exports.

It can be shown that gains from trade can result even when a country may have an absolute advantage in any two goods it trades. The theory of comparative advantage, developed by Ricardo,[1] can be used to show that a basis for trade still exists in such cases if one nation has a lesser absolute disadvantage in the production of two goods with respect to another nation. Many believe that trade depends on absolute advantage. The theory of comparative advantage shows that absolute advantage has nothing to do with the pattern of trade. Only comparative advantage matters.

Suppose that two countries, United States and Russia, each produce soybeans and vodka with the following output per unit of input:

| | *Output Per Unit of Input* | |
Product	*United States*	*Russia*
Bushels of soybeans	20	10
Cases of vodka	4	5

In the United States, 20 bushels of soybeans can be produced with 1 unit of input, whereas 4 cases of vodka can be produced with 1 unit of input. In Russia, 10 bushels of soybeans can be produced with 1 unit of input while 5 cases of vodka can be produced with 1 unit of input. The United States has an absolute advantage in wheat (20 to 10 or 2 to 1) while Russia has an absolute advantage in vodka (5 to 4 or 1.25 to 1).

Without trade, each country may produce some of each product since consumer demand exists for each. Suppose that each country devotes half its resources to the production of soybeans and half to the production of vodka. Each country must consume what it produces. The United States would be able to produce 10 bushels of soybeans

[1] David Ricardo, "The Principles of Political Economy and Taxation," in *International Trade Theory: Hume to Ohlin* ed. William R. Allen (New York: Random House, 1965), pp. 62–7.

and 2 cases of vodka (point A in Figure 1–1). Russia would be able to produce 5 bushels of soybeans and 2.5 cases of vodka (point B in Figure 1–1). Without trade, the combined production of both countries would be 15 bushels of soybeans and 4.5 cases of vodka. If each country were to specialize in producing the good in which it has an absolute advantage and then trade with the other for the good the country does not have, the United States could produce 20 bushels of soybeans and Russia could produce 5 cases of vodka. Thus, with specialization and trade, production of both goods would be increased by 5 bushels of soybeans and .5 case of vodka.

Both nations can gain from trading the products in which they have an absolute advantage against the other country. But suppose one country has an absolute advantage in both products. Can trade still be beneficial? Under the theory of comparative advantage, suppose the terms of trade between Russia and the United States in soybeans and vodka are as follows:

| | *Output Per Unit of Input* | |
Commodity	*United States*	*Russia*
Bushels of soybeans	25	10
Cases of vodka	6	5

FIGURE 1–1 Absolute Advantage

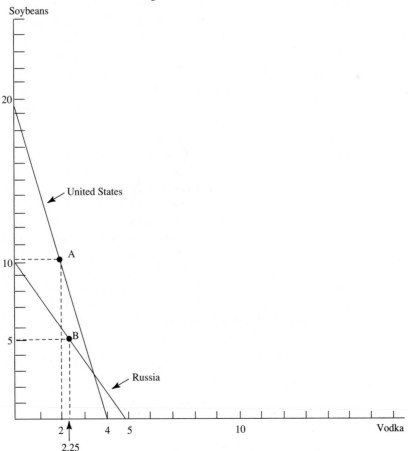

If no trade exists between the two countries, 25 bushels of soybeans will be exchanged in the United States for 6 cases of vodka while 10 bushels of soybeans will be traded for 5 cases of vodka in Russia. The United States has an absolute advantage in both soybeans and vodka. Why should the United States trade with Russia when it has an absolute advantage in both goods? Although the United States has an absolute advantage in both goods, it has a comparative advantage in the production of soybeans. It can produce 2.5 times as much soybeans as Russia but only 1.2 times as much vodka. The United States is comparatively more efficient at producing soybeans than it is at producing vodka. Assuming no specialization and trade and that each country uses half its resources to produce each good, total production of soybeans will be 17.5 bushels (12.5 bushels in the United States and 5 bushels in Russia). Total production of vodka will be 5.5 cases (3 in the United States and 2.5 in Russia).

Since the United States has a comparative advantage in soybeans, gains will result from trade if: (1) the United States specializes in soybeans and exports this product to Russia, and (2) Russia specializes in vodka and exports that product to the United States. The net result of this policy will be a general rise in the living standards of both countries.

Suppose, according to the 25/6 and 10/5 terms of trade in the United States and Russia, respectively, that the United States specializes in soybeans and Russia specializes in vodka. The U.S. exportable surplus is 25 bushels of soybeans gained by shifting its inputs to soybeans, and Russia will have a surplus of 5 cases of vodka to export. A straight exchange of 25 bushels of soybeans for 5 cases of vodka would result in better terms of trade for soybean producers than they could get domestically where they could get 6 cases of vodka for 25 bushels of soybeans. U.S. soybean producers could get 6 cases of vodka if they used their resources to produce vodka themselves. The United States would not trade at a price of 25 bushels of soybeans for 5 cases of vodka, but the Russians would be better off at these 25/5 terms of trade. However, for trade to occur, both the Americans and the Russians must be willing to trade.

Russian vodka producers have to give 5 cases of vodka for 10 bushels of soybeans at home, the equivalent of 12.5 cases of vodka for 25 bushels of soybeans. The two countries might decide on an exchange rate somewhere between these two extremes for the international market to work, e.g., 8 cases of vodka for 25 bushels of soybeans.

The gains from specialization and international trade can be shown by examining the opportunity costs in each country. In Russia, the opportunity cost of obtaining more soybeans would be vodka foregone. If the Russians specialize in soybeans, they would give up 5 cases of vodka for 10 bushels of soybeans, or .5 unit of vodka per bushel of soybeans. If they specialize in vodka, they will give up 10 bushels of soybeans for 5 cases of vodka, or 2 units of soybeans for 1 unit of vodka. In the United States, if only soybeans are produced, Americans will give up 6 cases of vodka for 25 bushels of soybeans. The opportunity cost is 6/25 cases of vodka per bushel of soybeans. If Americans produce only vodka, they would get 6 cases of vodka but give up 25 bushels of soybeans. The opportunity cost would be 4.16 bushels for 1 case of vodka. The lowest opportunity cost can be shown as follows:

	Lowest Opportunity Cost	
Commodity	*United States*	*Russia*
Soybeans	× (6/25 vs. 1/2)	
Vodka		× (2.00 vs. 4.16)

Each country may want to produce domestically and consume some of each good. The United States may give up some soybeans for vodka, but the opportunity cost of 4.16 bushels of soybeans for a case of vodka is a steep cost. The Russians may want some soybeans for vodka and will have to give up .5 case of vodka for a bushel of soybeans. These steep costs create an opportunity to specialize in one of the goods and trade at some cost between the original terms of trade of 6/25 and 1/2 for vodka and 4.16 and 2.00 for soybeans, respectively. The new terms of trade will be set somewhere between the original terms at, let's assume, 8 cases of vodka for 25 bushels of soybeans, i.e., 1 case of vodka for 3.13 bushels of soybeans, or .32 case of vodka for 1 bushel of soybeans.

To demonstrate the gains from specialization and international trade, the following example is offered. Let's say that Americans want two cases of vodka. They would have to give up 6.26 bushels of soybeans in trade, leaving them with 18.74 bushels of soybeans but with 2 cases of vodka. If the United States does not trade, it must give up 8.33 bushels of soybeans to produce the 2 cases of vodka. Thus, it would have 16.67 bushels of soybeans and 2 cases of vodka. With trade, the United States has gained 2.07 bushels of soybeans for consumption (18.74 bushels − 16.67 bushels = 2.07 bushels). On the Russian side, the Russians want to consume 5 bushels of soybeans but will have to give up 2.5 cases of vodka without trade. With trade, Russia, according to the new terms of trade of 8 cases of vodka for 25 bushels of soybeans, will have to give up 1.6 cases of vodka for 5 bushels of soybeans. Russia will then have 3.4 cases of vodka left for domestic consumption and 5 bushels of soybeans. Russia will have .9 of a case of vodka more with specialization and trade than it would have had without trade (3.4 cases − 2.5 cases = 0.9 case). Thus, with specialization and international trade at the new terms of trade, the United States gains 2.07 bushels of soybeans for domestic consumption and Russia gains .9 of a case of vodka for domestic consumption. The gains after specialization and trade are shown in Figure 1–2 at the new international terms of trade.

REASONS TO STUDY GLOBAL FINANCE

Financial management is studied for several reasons. First, management must determine the amount of short-term funds needed by the firm for day-to-day operations. These funds are required to finance accounts receivables, if the firm sells products or services on account, and to finance inventories of finished or semifinished goods or raw materials.

Second, projects must be evaluated for their long-term profitability. Thus, a number of methods can be used for evaluating or ranking projects that require long-term financing. Among these are the accounting rate of return, the pay-back period, and discounted cash flow methods such as net present value and the internal rate of return.

Third, the most appropriate methods of funding these short- and long-term operations must be determined. Thus, the appropriate financial instruments and markets must be identified. The appropriate maturities of debt instruments must be determined. The cost of these types of capital must be weighed against their benefits.

Finally, the different risks of doing business must be measured and managed, taking into consideration the risk threshold of the firm and its management. Such risks include those caused by fluctuations in interest rates (the price of money) and credit risk (the risk that the firm will not generate sufficient cash flows to remain solvent). Management may use the futures and options markets to hedge these risks.

Multinational corporations (MNCs) face other risks besides fluctuations in interest rates and credit risk. A number of these are described in Figure 1–3. Banking firms face still more specific risks. These are discussed more fully in chapter 9.

	Output Per Unit of Input	
Commodity	*United States*	*Russia*
Bushels of soybeans	25	10
Cases of vodka	6	5

	Production and Consumption without Trade	
Commodity	*United States*	*Russia*
Bushels of soybeans	16.67	5.0
Cases of vodka	2.00	2.5

	Production with Specialization and Trade	
Commodity	*United States*	*Russia*
Bushels of soybeans	18.74	5.0
Cases of vodka	2.00	3.4

	Increase in Consumption from Specialization and Trade	
Commodity	*United States*	*Russia*
Bushels of soybeans	2.07	0
Cases of vodka	0	0.9

FIGURE 1–2 Comparative Advantage Gains from Trade

It is useful to examine some of the most cited cases involving the impact of these risks on MNCs and international banks. Foreign exchange risk occurred in the case of Bankhaus Herstatt in 1974 when this small German private bank became overextended in foreign exchange trading and was closed by German banking authorities. Unfortunately for many large international banks trading with Herstatt, the bank was closed after these banks had paid their side of the transactions but before they could be repaid by Herstatt. Thus, this case is cited as the definitive example of settlement risk in the foreign exchange market.

Other international banking operations have been the victims of risk encountered in such operations. Barings Bank PLC, the 300-year-old British merchant bank, failed in 1995 because of market risk caused by unauthorized trading in derivatives by one employee of the bank. The Bank for Credit and Commerce International (BCCI), a

FIGURE 1–3 Risks Faced by Global Firms

1. **Foreign exchange risk:** the risk losses caused by fluctuations in the foreign exchange rate between the time a transaction is entered and it is settled
2. **Political risk:** the risk of losses because of foreign government action that causes currency inconvertibility, expropriation of foreign investment, interference with contractual terms, or damage from violence
3. **Interest rate risk:** the risk of loss in market value of securities because of interest rate fluctuations
4. **Credit risk:** the risk of loss because of nonpayment of a contractual commitment by a counterparty to a transaction
5. **Settlement risk:** risk of loss on a transaction during the settlement period

Pakistani-based bank with worldwide operations, is an example of operations risk. Its management stole millions, perhaps billions, of dollars from the bank, laundered drug and illegal weapons money, faked loans, and hid losses from bank regulators over a long period of time. Global standards for risk-based capital were imposed by global banking regulators as a result of the BCCI fraud. Finally, the credit risk stemming from the 1982 sovereign loan crisis when Mexico and other less-developed countries (LDCs) defaulted on their large borrowings from the international banking system caused many large banks to retreat from the international lending business.

A number of specific cases can be cited where MNCs have encountered some of these risks. The expropriation of all foreign companies in Cuba by the Castro government in the late 1950s, foreign electric utilities by the Argentinian and Brazilian governments in the 1960s, and foreign copper companies by the Chilean government in the 1970s are examples of the operations risk facing foreign firms in many LDCs. Caterpillar Company encountered a decline in earnings in 1995 because of the appreciation of the U.S. dollar—an example of exposure to foreign exchange risk. Holiday Inns/Occidental Petroleum had construction halted in the Republic of Morocco in 1972 because unilateral action by the Moroccan government created an operations risk, in this case, interference with contract provisions.

Finally, some risks are global in nature. Contagion risk is the risk that a securities market decline in one country will spread to another, causing serious market losses, or that the failure of one large financial institution will lead to the failure of others. The 1984 failure of Continental Illinois Bank in Chicago was effectively remedied by U.S. Federal Bank authorities who were afraid that if they did not bail out Continental Bank the failure of many other banks would occur. The 1987 stock market collapse at the New York Stock Exchange did spread to other markets around the world, causing global securities market losses.

THE MOST FUNDAMENTAL AND POWERFUL CONCEPTS

The study of international financial management has at its core two fundamental and powerful concepts: (1) that the primary objective of the multinational corporation is still the same primary objective of any firm, i.e., to maximize shareholder wealth, and (2) that foreign exchange, or foreign currency, must be used to obtain foreign goods, services, or securities. The major objective of the firm that all financial management textbooks stress is maximization of shareholder wealth. All of the strategies, techniques, and methodologies discussed in this textbook, which differ from those covered in the basic financial management textbook, are directed at achieving this basic goal: to maximize shareholder wealth. From that standpoint, international financial management does not differ from generic financial management.

However, the concept of foreign exchange does distinguish international financial management from the practice of domestic financial management—the general subject of most basic financial management textbooks. To purchase foreign goods, services, or financial instruments or invest in foreign securities, an individual, private company, or government must have foreign exchange. Foreign goods, services, and securities must be purchased with foreign exchange. Thus, an understanding of the foreign exchange market, the pricing of foreign exchange, and the management of exposure to the risk of loss from foreign exchange fluctuations is important. This subject matter will be an underlying and fundamental concept in all areas of this textbook.

THE ENVIRONMENT OF MULTINATIONAL BUSINESS

Global finance is a subset of international business. Students should have some familiarity with this field before studying the more specific area of global finance. International business was practiced before the time of the Phoenicians. Traders carried their wares across national borders for thousands of years. For centuries Indians transported goods from India to the African continent by means of the Indian Ocean. Before Germany was carved up as a result of the reparations agreements after World War I, the country was home to at least 23 *Börsen*, or securities exchanges. These financial markets evolved from crossroads markets where traders had met for centuries to trade specie (hard currency) as well as produce and commodities. The large East and West India Trading Companies, based in the Netherlands, fostered international trade by sending ships to Africa and the Far East to bring back spices and other commodities. Their securities were among the first to be traded on an exchange floor and provided the basis for the formation of the Amsterdam Stock Exchange in the sixteenth century. The explorers from Portugal, Spain, and other European countries exploited raw materials, commodities, and precious metals found in other countries of the world. It was these adventurers who opened Japan to the outside world.

However, international trade did not begin to grow significantly until after World War I. The British Commonwealth had been a world power with its member countries circling the globe. The United States began to exploit international trade after its military success in World War I. The Federal Reserve System recognized this international movement in 1919 when it authorized American banks to establish Edge Act banks, wholly owned subsidiaries that devoted at least 90 percent of their business to the assistance of U.S. customers with export-import trade and international credit.[2]

This global business trend was slowed by the worldwide depression of the 1930s and by World War II and its aftermath. However, in the early 1960s, international trade and investment began to grow. Reconstruction had been completed after the war. Less-developed countries began to plan their economic growth. For example, the South Korean government implemented its first five-year economic plan in 1962. By the 1990s, *chaebol* (large Korean business firms) had gained leadership positions in many industries, Korean products began to show up on store shelves around the world, and its stock market had become one of the ten busiest in terms of volume.

Many large business firms in several countries moved from being companies that merely exported products to foreign countries or extracted minerals from foreign countries to organizations that carried on production and performed services in several countries. In 1963, *Business Week* printed a cover article about the "multinational company," (MNC). Although the term had been used previously, this article gave official status to the term. The MNC was defined as a company with operations in two or more countries that made its decisions concerning manufacturing and financial issues based on the alternatives faced by the firm anywhere in the world.

Since then other more complex versions of the international company have been suggested, including the transnational corporation (TNC) or enterprise (TNE). The TNC or TNE is an MNC whose managerial cadre and share ownership are also international. Many MNCs are trending toward this type of business organization.

Thus, as Shapiro[3] and others have pointed out, an evolutionary process created the MNC. Companies initially moved into international business and cross-border ac-

---

[2] Peter S. Rose, *Commercial Bank Management* (Homewood, IL: Richard D. Irwin, 1991), p. 570; James C. Baker and Miles G. Bradford, *American Banking Abroad: Edge Act Companies and Multinational Banking* (New York: Praeger, 1974).

[3] Alan Shapiro, *Multinational Financial Management* (Boston: Allyn Bacon, 1993), p. 6.

tivities as raw materials seekers, then as market seekers, and, finally, as cost minimizers. As raw materials seekers, early British, Dutch, French, and Belgian businessmen formed the East India Company, Hudson's Bay Trading Company, and Union Miniere Haut-Katanga, among others, to explore for raw materials. The East India Company was instrumental in the formation of the Amsterdam Stock Exchange, perhaps the world's first stock market, when its shares were issued to the public. These companies formed multinational oil and mining companies, the forerunners of today's British Petroleum, Exxon, International Nickel, and Anaconda and Kennecott Copper Companies.

As market seekers, many companies invested abroad to create new markets for their products, and later, services. Before World War II, Colt Firearms, Coca-Cola, Philips Lamp, and Imperial Chemical Industries invested overseas. This was primarily a one-way flow of funds and, for a few decades after World War II, it was mostly from the United States to Europe. After the Japanese made inroads in the market share of several industries, foreign investment grew significantly everywhere except Africa.

Cost minimizing companies moved operations to locations where manufacturing could be done for the least cost possible. Foreign direct investment moved to Hong Kong, Taiwan, and Ireland. Examples of companies searching for low-cost production included Texas Instruments, Atari, Zenith, and other electronics companies. American auto manufacturers moved engine assembly operations to maquiladoras, small, low-cost firms located in Mexico near the U.S. border. The newly independent East European countries have become host to the next wave of cost minimization with their move to privatization and numerous joint ventures such as that of General Electric and Tungsram in Hungary. The equity swaps carried out by some industries have been attempts to minimize the cost of joint projects by some companies. Examples include the Ford/Mazda arrangement to build the Ford Probe and General Motors/Suzuki arrangement to build the Geo line of cars.

The futurist and author of *Megatrends*, John Naisbitt examined the growth of worldwide capital in the mid-1980s in a study for Klynveld Main Goerdeler for its merger with the global accounting firm, Peat Marwick.[4] He found that nearly all companies, no matter what size, will resort to raising capital anywhere in the world. Furthermore, he predicted that capital with a national identity would become extinct, with dollars, yen, marks, and sterling becoming commodities in a global financial market.

THE OBJECTIVE OF THIS BOOK

Given the growth of multinational corporate activities, international financial transactions, the advent of new international financial instruments and markets, and the volatility of the global financial markets and their inherent riskiness—ensuing from forces generated by economic decisions and political policies of nations, firms, and individuals—the objective of this book is to present a discussion of the field of international financial management of MNCs in such an environment. The information presented is based on the principle of a borderless world as described by Kenichi Ohmae. He hypothesized a rapidly emerging world of business with an interlinked economy. It would be bigger than a continent and comprised of a triad consisting of the United States, Europe, and Japan, joined by smaller economies such as those in Taiwan, Korea, Singapore, and Hong Kong. This is a system sufficiently powerful to chew up consumers and corporations, and from a bureaucrat's viewpoint, it will be a borderless world.[5]

---

[4] Frank C. Taylor, "Going Global," *World* 21 (July–September 1987): 8.

[5] Kenichi Ohmae, *The Borderless World* (New York: Harper Business, 1990).

Ohmae reminds us that boundaries are quite apparent on a political map. However, in a competitive global economy, such boundaries will no longer be present.[6] These borders will have been erased by the increasingly speedy flow of information among nations and companies. Monopolies will no longer be possible or they will be difficult to maintain. Products will have become universal in their value and demand. Ford Motor Company has already produced the World Car—the Ford Contour or the Mercury Mystique—and it has been copied by many other competitors.

Ohmae's thesis is that the emerging consumer does not care about the country of origin or country of residence. The consumer does not care that a British sneaker produced by Reebok, now a U.S. company, was made in Korea, or that a German sneaker by Adidas was made in Taiwan, or that a French ski by Rossignol was made in Spain. The product's quality, price, design, value, and appeal are the important characteristics to the consumer. Essentially, the major financial consideration is to maximize shareholder's wealth or share prices based on income made by appealing to such consumers. In nonfinancial terms, this major financial objective can be paraphrased: to produce high-quality, low-cost products that offer real value to consumers, i.e., a shift to a greater emphasis on marketing and production.

In the world of financial services, international finance has moved to the institutional investor level and away from the retail level. Many retail financial services originate in foreign countries, and the investments stemming from these services are made across borders. Money has become a global product because of foreign exchange markets, international money and capital markets, and other integrated trading markets. The MNC must operate in such an environment, and its financial managers will be subject to such a world.

In fact, Ohmae's global triad of Europe, Japan, and the United States, whose currencies have become the most significant means of payment, has certainly become the operational mode in the past few years. In light of the declining dollar during the early to mid-1990s, the yen has become more acceptable in international commerce.[7] Since 1970 it has increased in value nearly 225 percent against the dollar, although it began to depreciate against the dollar in 1995 because of a series of economic problems in Japan. More of the world's central banks are holding yen in their foreign currency reserves. Until 1995 foreigners had been investing heavily in Japan's financial markets. Trade had been more and more denominated in yen rather than dollars. Japanese monetary and fiscal policy had become more important as a factor to be analyzed in international markets. For example, a rug merchant in Turkey with an outlet near the country's largest mosque accepts the yen just as readily as he does the dollar. A tour guide in Hungary would rather take yen than dollars. Cashiers at David Jones Australia Private Ltd., the premier retailer in Australia, accept yen as well as U.S. and Australian dollars.

These global activities in yen may have been slowed drastically by the 1995 financial problems in Japan. Because of a number of economic changes in Japan, including a recession and dramatic declines in the value of real estate and other assets held by Japanese investors, the Japanese banking system suffered greatly in 1995. The government refused major assistance to this sector. As a result, in July–August 1995, the dollar and other major currencies began to appreciate significantly against the yen. However, it still remains an important global currency.

Naisbitt also predicted the formation of a computerized global transaction clearing system and a world securities commission to control cross-border securities transactions. Furthermore, he suggested in his study that corporations will become their own

[6] Kenichi Ohmae, "Managing in a Borderless World," *Harvard Business Review* 67 (May–June 1989): 152–61.
[7] Quentin Hardy, "Yen Gains Acceptance for Global Use," *Wall Street Journal*, 18 May 1993, p. A2.

international bankers and their top executives will be more financially oriented than marketing oriented. Whether these changes are desirable remains to be seen.

The management of these global companies became more complex as international business became more important in the 1970s and 1980s. A particular function of business enterprise, financial management, became extremely complex and significant by the 1990s. Some analysts, such as Naisbitt, have suggested that financial management will become the driving force in the international company of the future. The information on financial management in the global company presented in this textbook will help prepare students for the future.

The Borderless World and the Real World

The reference to the borderless world of international business stemming from Ohmae's writings must be tempered with the practice used by many countries of protectionism and trade barriers to enhance their nationalistic tendencies. Despite the advantages of international trade based on the theory of comparative advantage and the concept of a borderless world advanced by Kenichi Ohmae, most countries practice some form of mercantilism. Mercantilism is an economic philosophy that states that a government will improve the welfare of its citizenry by promulgating laws and regulations designed to restrict the inflow of foreign goods and services, and that wealth can be increased from the promotion of the nation's exports. Thus, exports will be promoted and imports will be restricted by government policies.

A prime example of the practice of mercantilism can be found in Asia. State-directed capitalism and protectionism have been practiced for decades by Japan. Their model has been exported to other countries in the region. The first of these was Korea with Malaysia and China also adopting mercantilistic policies. These countries have practiced protectionism under the guise of complex wholesale and retail marketing systems.

Other countries have also practiced such trade policies. The members of the European Union resort to a host of product standards that actually restrict trade among the member countries. Many of the emerging or transitional economies such as those of East and Central Europe often barter their goods with other nations because of the inconvertibility of many of their currencies. Even the United States has prohibited the importation of products such as Argentinian beef under the guise of administrative restrictions resulting from the danger of spreading anthrax, a cattle disease not seen in Argentina for many decades, and Asian sugar to protect the sugar beet farmers in southern United States. Until these trade barriers are reduced or eliminated, the borderless world will remain a testable hypothesis.

CULTURAL VARIABLES OF INTERNATIONAL BUSINESS

Before the focus turns to international finance in the MNC, another major difference between domestic and international business should be discussed. Cultural variables of international business represent one of the most serious problems facing the international manager, especially the expatriate manager—the one who actually lives and works abroad. Generally, coverage of cultural variables in international business is emphasized in the introductory international business course. However, many programs do not require such a course as a prerequisite to the international financial management course. Since an understanding of cultural variables is an important ingredient to international business, the student should be exposed to it at this point.

Research has shown that of the six most significant reasons why expatriate managers fail in their overseas assignments, the two most important are (1) the inability of the manager to cope with the foreign environment and (2) the inability of the man-

ager's spouse and/or family to cope with the foreign environment.[8] Recent research indicates that overseas failure is still caused primarily by the inability of the expatriate manager's spouse to adjust to a new environment.[9]

A major cause of the problems faced by the international manager is culture. The culture, customs, and attitudes of foreign countries have become focal points of the global marketplace. Many overseas blunders in international trade, marketing, and investment have been caused by management decisions and practices that were not based on a consideration of cultural differences.[10]

Culture is "the combination of behavioral characteristics, habits, skills, arts, instruments, and institutions that have been developed, acquired, accumulated, or adapted by a certain people."[11] Several authors have discussed culture in the context of international business. James Lee held that people from a given geographic area or country will refer to and identify with their own cultural values. He referred to this phenomenon as "self-reference criterion" (SRC) and believes that international managers must be aware of the cultural differences of other peoples.[12] SRC is practiced, for example, by the company towns set up by American and British oil companies in Saudi Arabia that are small representative communities for American and British employees with all the comforts of home. Wadia developed a concept of culture and said it is that which separates humans from nonhumans.[13] Kluckhohn and Kelby defined culture as "the historically created designs for living, explicit and implicit, rational, irrational and nonrational, which exist at any given time as potential guides for the behavior of man."[14] Hall developed a set of differing variables found in most cultures that affect international business.[15] These were the silent languages of time, space, material possessions, friendship patterns, and agreements. For example, people in different cultures place different meanings on the concept of time. In the United States, for example, a delay in responding to a business communication could mean a large backlog, poor organization, or a technical problem. To the person waiting for the response, it could mean the matter has a low priority. In other countries, long delays may be part of the cultural behavior of the people. In Ethiopia, the time a decision requires is directly proportional to its importance. In the Arab East, more important people get faster service from less important people and vice versa. In India, appointments are scheduled depending on the type of business. If the appointment is with a government official, the appointment is made for a particular hour. If the appointment is with a private business, it is made for either morning or afternoon. If the appointment is with a village official, it is made for a particular day.

The language of friendship differs from one country to another. An American finds friends next door and among those with whom he works. In other countries,

---

[8] John M. Ivancevich, "A Study of American Expatriate On-the-Job Performance Failures," *Washington Business Review* 28 (Winter 1969): 42–9.

[9] Kurt Sandholtz, "Executives' Spouses Face Tough Adjustments Overseas," *National Business Employment Weekly* 5 (June 8, 1986): 9–10.

[10] See, for example, David A. Ricks, *Big Business Blunders: Mistakes in Multinational Marketing* (Homewood, IL: Dow Jones-Irwin, 1983).

[11] James C. Baker, John K. Ryans, Jr., and Donald G. Howard, eds., *International Business Classics* (Lexington, MA: Lexington Books, 1988), p. 73.

[12] James A. Lee, "Cultural Analysis in Overseas Operations," *Harvard Business Review* 44 (March–April 1966): 106–14.

[13] Maneck S. Wadia, "The Concept of Culture," *Journal of Retailing* 41 (Spring 1965): 21–9, 55.

[14] Clyde Kluckhohn and William Kelby, "The Concept of Culture," in *The Science of Man in World Crisis* ed. Ralph Linton (New York: Columbia University Press, 1945), p. 97.

[15] Edward T. Hall, "The Silent Language in Overseas Business," *Harvard Business Review* 38 (May–June 1960): 87–96.

friendships take longer to form but go much deeper, last longer, and involve real obligations.

The language of agreements is based on cultural differences as well. Rules may be spelled out technically as in laws or regulations, i.e., in the United States. Moral practices are mutually agreed on and taught to the young as a set of principles. Informal customs may be practiced to which everyone conforms without being able to state the exact rules. In some countries, a verbal agreement is more binding than a written contract. The western legalistic nature of the latter method is actually demeaning in some cultures.

Most of these cultural variables have an impact on marketing or administrative decision making. Companies must exercise care in the use of color in international marketing. In Iran, blue is for mourning, but in Japan, mourners wear white. Purple symbolizes death in Latin America, whereas black is associated with death in the United States. The use of symbols also is important in many countries. The shape of packaging is important in many countries because a certain shape may have implied symbolism.

Cultural variables affect some areas of international finance. In chapter 7 we will see that culture may be a key determinant of optimal capital structures of foreign firms when capital budgeting and cost of capital are discussed. The organizational structures of banks in other countries may be affected by the culture of those countries. Payment terms, taxation of foreign profits, and the use of certain types of financial institutions may be affected and determined by cultural aspects in other countries. No matter what area of international business is practiced, local culture must be taken into consideration. Firms are more successful in their international operations if they act as though they are not in a vacuum. Research shows that the number of American expatriate managers will increase rapidly in the next five years from the 40,000 currently working overseas, and international search firms will look for executives with international backgrounds as well as cross-cultural and multilingual skills.[16]

The Environment of International Finance

The field of international finance has become extremely important during the past twenty-five years. The growth of multinational corporate and banking operations on a global basis has been phenomenal. The revolution in global business has fostered the development of the Eurocurrency market—a stateless pool of funds approaching $5 trillion used to fund working capital operations of international companies as well as to make long-term funds available in the form of Eurocredits, Eurobonds, and other long-term securities.

GROWTH OF GLOBAL FINANCIAL FIRMS

Nonfinancial MNCs have grown significantly during the past twenty-five years. This growth has necessitated a concomitant growth in the financial firms—banks, insurance companies, and securities firms—that facilitate the financing of nonfinancial MNCs. The following five tables offer a view of such growth. Table 1–1 shows the ten largest nonfinancial corporations in the world, ranked by market value. These firms are dominated by Japanese and U.S. firms. Table 1–2 shows the ten largest banks in the world, ranked by asset size. All but one of these banks are Japanese. In fact, twenty-seven banks are larger than the largest U.S. bank, Citicorp, when ranked by assets. Table 1–3 shows the ten largest securities firms, ranked by total capital. These firms are domi-

---

[16] Lori Ioannou, "Cultivating the New Expatriate Executive," *International Business* 7 (July 1994): 40–50.

TABLE 1–1. The World's Ten Largest Public Nonfinancial Corporations
(ranked by market value)* (millions U.S.$ December 31, 1994)

Rank	Company (Country)	Market Value	Fiscal 1994 Sales
1	NTT (Japan)	$133,249	$ 67,024
2	Royal Dutch/Shell (Netherlands/U.K.)	108,643	97,848
3	General Electric (U.S.)	99,939	60,109
4	Exxon (U.S.)	90,062	101,459
5	AT&T (U.S.)	83,464	75,094
6	Coca-Cola (U.S.)	83,180	16,172
7	Toyota Motor (Japan)	78,127	93,843
8	Fuji Bank (Japan)**	70,754	552,432
9	Industrial Bank of Japan (Japan)**	69,978	425,863
10	Mitsubishi Bank (Japan)**	68,385	500,399

* Market value refers to the market value of the companies' shares.

** Considered industrial companies in Japan because of their industrial company investments.

Source: Adapted from ''World Business,'' *Wall Street Journal,* 2 October 1995, p. R32. Reprinted with permission.

nated by U.S. companies. Table 1–4 shows the ten largest private insurance companies in the world, ranked by total assets. These firms are dominated by Japanese insurers. Finally, Table 1–5 shows growth rates by country for the 100 largest banks, 50 largest insurers, and 25 largest securities firms in the world for 1994 compared with 1993. German and U.S. banks had the highest asset growth. Italian, British, and German banks had the highest capital growth. Net income growth was highest for U.K. banks. U.K. insurance companies had the highest asset growth. U.S. securities firms had the highest capital growth, while Japanese securities firms had the highest net income growth.

Foreign firms and banks have increased investment in the United States to the point that Americans have become concerned that major industries will be taken over. The U.S. tire industry can be cited as such an example. Bridgestone, a Japanese producer, has merged with and effectively taken over Firestone. Continental Gummi, a

TABLE 1–2. The World's Ten Largest Banks
(ranked by total assets) (millions U.S.$ December 31, 1995)

Rank	Bank (Country)	Assets	Capital
1	Dai-Ichi Kangyo Bank (Japan)	$520,335	$ 38,310
2	Fuji Bank (Japan)	518,101	55,550
3	Sumitomo Bank (Japan)	510,272	45,901
4	Sakura Bank (Japan)	508,736	41,403
5	Sanwa Bank (Japan)	506,416	41,913
6	Mitsubishi Bank (Japan)	471,968	34,160
7	Norinchukin Bank (Japan)	443,708	93,433
8	Industrial Bank (Japan)	397,057	256,842
9	Deutsche Bank (Germany)	365,774	45,608
10	Mitsubishi Trust & Banking (Japan)	333,858	11,452

Source: Adapted from ''World Business,'' *Wall Street Journal,* 2 October 1995, p. R33. Reprinted with permission.

TABLE 1–3. The World's Ten Largest Securities Firms
(ranked by total capital) (millions U.S.$ December 31, 1994)

Rank	Company (Country)	Capital	Assets
1	Nomura Securities (Japan)	$20,936	$ 84,150
2	Goldman Sachs (U.S.)	18,591	64,675
3	Salomon (U.S.)	15,774*	111,906
4	Merrill Lynch (U.S.)	14,544	97,436
5	Morgan Stanley (U.S.)	12,310	60,552
6	Daiwa Securities (Japan)	12,245	38,200
7	Lehman Brothers Holdings (U.S.)	11,643	61,840
8	Nikko Securities (Japan)	11,322	27,042
9	Yamaichi Securities (Japan)	9,813	29,051
10	Dean Witter, Discover (U.S.)	9,001	28,383

* Excludes $3.0 billion of collateralized mortgage obligations.

Source: Adapted from ''World Business,'' *Wall Street Journal,* 2 October 1995, p. R33. Reprinted with permission.

German tire manufacturer, has taken over General Tire. The U.S. Congress has proposed laws to limit such foreign investment at the same time that trade liberalization measures, such as the North American Free Trade Agreement, combining the markets of Canada, the United States, and Mexico, have been approved.

FOREIGN EXCHANGE MARKETS

The world's foreign exchange markets have become extremely important in recent years, especially for treasurers of U.S. global companies, since the advent of floating exchange rates in 1973 and the initiation of formal accounting rules by the Financial Accounting Standards Board. Its FASB-8, a very controversial accounting rule dealing with foreign currency translation, was replaced by the more sweeping FASB-52, a U.S.

TABLE 1–4. The World's Ten Largest Insurance Firms
(ranked by total assets) (millions U.S.$ December 31, 1995)

Rank	Company (Country)	Assets	Capital
1	Nippon Life (Japan)	$348,579	$ 4,164
2	Zenkyoren (Japan)	247,700	3,551
3	Dai-Ichi Mutual Life (Japan)	245,926	3,412
4	Sumitomo Life (Japan)	214,835	3,067
5	Prudential Insurance (U.S.)	211,902	11,711
6	Allianz Holding (Germany)	164,601	13,759
7	Compagnie UAP (France)	160,376	17,369
8	Meiji Mutual Life (Japan)	148,640	2,498
9	Axa* (France)	145,031	13,470
10	Metropolitan Life (U.S.)	131,177	8,285

* Includes consolidation of Equitable Companies.

Source: Adapted from ''World Business,'' *Wall Street Journal,* 2 October 1995, p. R32. Reprinted with permission.

TABLE 1–5. Growth Rates by Countries (1994 compared to 1993)
(largest 100 banks, 50 insurers, and 25 securities firms)

	Asset Growth	Capital Growth	Net Income Growth	Revenue Growth	Growth of Capital/Assets
Banks					
France	2.2%	−4.0%	1.0%	−14.3%	−6.2%
Germany	10.9	18.6	9.7	7.5	7.7
Italy	5.2	25.9	−36.5	−5.6	20.7
Japan	1.0	3.6	−19.0	−10.9	2.6
United Kingdom	3.4	19.1	50.7	−3.9	15.7
United States	11.9	8.2	14.8	4.7	−3.7
Others	12.7	10.4	−0.2	−0.9	−2.3
Top 100 Average	6.8%	9.7%	−2.5%	−4.1%	2.9%
Insurers					
Japan	8.0%	−11.0%	−8.4%	4.2%	−19.0%
United Kingdom	11.9	−22.4	−4.7	2.0	−34.3
United States	4.2	−0.5	0.4	−0.5	−4.7
Others	9.0	−2.0	5.7	2.5	−11.0
Top 50 Average	7.3%	−5.7%	−0.4%	1.7%	−13.0%
Securities Firms					
Japan	−2.2%	−3.3%	99.9%	10.5%	−1.1%
United States	2.0	22.5	−17.8	6.1	20.5
Others	15.0	12.0	46.8	43.4	−3.0
Top 25 Average	2.6%	11.1%	39.4%	14.7%	8.5%

Source: From "World Business," *Wall Street Journal,* 2 October 1995, p. R33. Reprinted with permission.

accounting standard that called for translation of foreign financial statements using a functional currency and for translation gains or losses to be reported in a special stockholders' equity account.

The decline of the U.S. dollar on world currency markets during the years 1985–87, 1992, and 1994–95 affected many sectors of American life, including mortgage rates, the cost of overseas travel, and the price of foreign investments. After 1987, the rise in the dollar fostered a large increase in foreign investment in the United States, particularly in real estate and acquisitions of American companies.

During the foreign currency crisis of August 1992, the declining dollar encouraged government intervention on a broad scale and may have caused the demise of a planned European monetary union under the Maastricht Treaty, a treaty that is designed to unite the European Community member countries into one monetary system operating eventually with only one currency. Volume in daily worldwide foreign exchange trading reached $1 trillion in fall 1992. The ensuing volatility nearly resulted in a meltdown of the currency markets, and the volatility in this market and in debt markets fostered the growth of a large number of derivative financial instruments that international companies now use to hedge foreign exchange and interest rate risk.

The international currency attack of summer 1992, centered in Europe, presented several implications for the future of multinational business. Currency speculators attacked a number of European currencies including the British pound, French franc, Swedish kroner, Finnish markka, Spanish peseta, and Italian lira. First, an immediate problem stemmed from the chaos in the foreign exchange markets. The price information function of the marketplace in foreign currencies did not operate efficiently. A senior currency trader at Chase Manhattan Bank said that people tried to get prices and could not find them in the marketplace.[17] This problem is discussed in more detail in chapter 3.

Another implication stemming from the currency speculation of 1992 is that the goal of monetary union, advocated before the crisis by the European Community (EC),[18] may have been slowed or, perhaps, ended. The EC members were to vote for monetary unity by ratifying the Maastricht Treaty. Instead, some members withheld votes, some voted against the treaty, and some withdrew from the EC's Exchange Rate Mechanism (ERM), e.g., Great Britain and Italy, at least temporarily. This upheaval in the ERM resulted in turbulent foreign exchange trading—estimated at $1 trillion per day. This turbulence is discussed in more detail in chapter 2.

Third, the 1992 currency speculation presented some dire implications for U.S. companies operating in Europe. Most considered it a short-term phenomenon. Some reassessed their pricing structures while others considered changes and realignments of the currencies in which they were operating. The uncertainty generated by the crisis disrupted planning by many companies, especially international trade and investment strategies. For some, a foreign exchange crisis, such as that in 1992 that nearly brought down the European Monetary System, can increase their risk and change their decision about an optimum manufacturing site overseas.[19]

Finally, some currency analysts have questioned the fixed exchange rate system used by the EC members in the ERM. The ERM was essentially a target zone exchange rate system in the European Union. Monetary authorities pledged to keep the exchange rate with a particular foreign currency or, in this case, basket of currencies, within given margins around a central parity. Such target zones blend the advantages of fixed exchange rates with flexible exchange rate systems. The European currencies that remained in the ERM remained fixed against each member's currency after the currency volatility of 1992 but with wider bands. Analysts have predicted that EC members will have trouble maintaining their fixed rates with each other while keeping interest rates stable and relatively high, especially in Germany. In short, some have said that the EC must resort to floating rates with each other.[20] In fact, the German Bundesbank, the nation's central bank, lowered Germany's interest rates in mid-September 1992 for the first time in five years.[21] Most currency analysts predicted that the single European currency and a European monetary union would never come to pass as a result of the 1992 currency problems in European exchange markets. As will be

---

[17] Randall Smith, "European Exchange-Rate Chaos Is Bedlam for Currency Traders at Chase Manhattan," *Wall Street Journal*, 17 September 1992, p. C1.

[18] On January 1, 1993, the European Community (EC) officially changed its name to the European Union (EU). These terms will be used interchangeably in this book. In addition, in January 1994, the EU membership increased from twelve to fifteen nations.

[19] "U.S. Executives Say Uncertainty Is Their Biggest Worry for Now," *Wall Street Journal*, 17 September 1992, p. A7.

[20] Alan A. Walters and Steve H. Hanke, "End of the Exchange Peg," *Wall Street Journal*, 18 September 1992, p. A10.

[21] Bill Javetski et al., "Europe's Money Mess," *Business Week* (September 28, 1992): 30.

shown in chapter 2, since global currency rates were pegged and fixed by the 1944 Bretton Woods, New Hampshire, meeting that established the International Monetary Fund, several currency "fiascoes" have occurred and most were focused on pegged systems of foreign exchange rates.

Since individuals and companies cannot carry on international transactions in trade and investment without foreign currencies, a well-functioning foreign exchange market is essential to such multinational business. Thus, foreign exchange and its marketplace is an essential ingredient of this book.

MANAGEMENT APPLICATION NO. 1

Gerhard Liener, Chief Financial Officer, Daimler-Benz

Just as there are two views of Daimler-Benz's landmark New York Stock Exchange listing, there are two views of the deal's negotiator, finance chief Gerhard Liener. Some analysts see the October 5 [1993] listing as a desperate attempt to raise capital. Others, including investors who pushed the company's shares to a 52-week high of DM 771 ($482) before it fell back to around DM 760 on the day of the listing, view Daimler-Benz's actions as a bold move by a company determined to face its problems.

Critics say the 62-year-old Liener, who has a passion for tennis, golf, and classical music, is a fine numbers cruncher but too often defers to more aggressive but not more visionary board executives. "Because he has not insisted on a decent return from the company's divisions, he was forced to break ranks with other German companies and compromise over this listing," says one London-based analyst, referring to separate talks with the Securities and Exchange Commission that Liener initiated last winter after a group of German blue-chip companies failed to win a waiver for relatively lax German accounting rules.

Indeed, three-year operating results that Daimler published last month to reconcile less transparent German accounting with US standards were anemic. Daimler-Benz recorded a net loss of DM 949 million for the first half of 1993, rather than the DM 168 million profit that German methods allowed. The SEC compromise forced the company to publish annual results for its four main operating units (Deutsche Aerospace, Debis, AEG, and Mercedes-Benz) and to disclose unencumbered equity.

Daimler notes that it is at least spared the burden of quarterly reports and segment reporting for the 30 businesses in which it is active. But other horrified German financial officers vow their companies have no intention of following Daimler's lead. "A lot of people are angry with us," acknowledges Liener, an economist who speaks four languages, "mainly because they have no choice now but to follow." An analyst agrees that with a long recession likely in Germany, other German companies will expand overseas and will need access to US capital. "Liener has scored a major publicity coup," he says.

Most analysts believe that Daimler's long-term prospects are good and applaud Liener's harvest of capital markets. Since the 27-year Daimler veteran received his current title in 1989, he has overseen stock listings in Tokyo, London, Paris, and Vienna, launched the first asset-backed credit for a German company, and set up the first multi-currency loan facility with a yen component for a German company.

Daimler-Benz is making a commitment to the United States. It has announced plans for a $300 million four-wheel-drive vehicle plant in Alabama and has said it hopes US investors will eventually hold 10% of its shares. Analysts expect Daimler to boost its capital soon through a roughly $500 million US stock issue.

Source: David Lanchner, "Chief Financial Officer of the Month," *Global Finance* 7 (October 1993): 55. Reprinted with permission.

THE CHIEF FINANCIAL OFFICER OF AN MNC

The chief financial officer (CFO) of an MNC wears many hats. As we shall see in the following chapters, the CFO is responsible for not only managing the financial resources of the firm, but he/she is responsible for obtaining these resources on a global basis. Thus, knowledge of financial instruments, institutions, and markets is essential to this objective. In addition to the markets for such mundane securities as stocks and bonds, the markets for risk management instruments such as derivatives must be mastered. This includes the "plain vanilla" types such as exchange-traded futures and options in addition to the OTC-traded interest rate and currency swaps and newer exotic derivatives based on indexes and other underlying instruments. The CFO must be able to hire and supervise the experts who will arrange exotic trade financing deals, Eurocurrency financing, and foreign exchange trades, including forward market contracts. Thus, he/she is the (1) chief funding officer, chief manager of funds, and, thus, becomes

---

MANAGEMENT APPLICATION NO. 2

Jerome B. York, Chief Financial Officer, IBM

Employees seeing Jerome B. York joining IBM might be forgiven for updating their resumés. York, who last May was named chief financial officer and senior vice president, came to the troubled computer giant from Chrysler. As that company's CFO, he directed a $3 billion cost reduction program that included sizable layoffs.

Already, York has helped fashion IBM's plan to cut a dramatic $7 billion from annual operating costs over three years—in part by shedding 35,000 jobs. The Memphis native, who holds an MBA from the University of Michigan and a master's in structural engineering from Massachusetts Institute of Technology, arrived at the cuts figure by analyzing IBM's competitors. "We looked at approximately 50 companies that are in the information technology industry," says York. "We picked those exhibiting the best performance in terms of profit returned to shareholders. We said our goal would be to get the same weighted return for our shareholders."

Whether the cuts will be IBM's last, as the company's new chairman, Louis Gerstner, claims, or just the latest in a series of changes and cuts totaling $28 billion over the past eight years, remains to be seen. "If our gross margins continue to deteriorate," says York, "we may determine that we need to get more costs out."

While corporate downsizing isn't everyone's idea of fun, it's all part of York's job. "In the old days, cost reduction meant every department being given a 5%, across-the-board budget task. Now, in a lot of industries faced with stiff international competition, including our own, 5% is just not enough. This has led to a lot of new business redesigns."

York says today's CFO is much more than a numbers cruncher. "The modern CFO has become a participant in the planning process," he says, adding: "Today a CFO has to be highly attuned to customer satisfaction, employee morale, and product quality. You cannot just view cost structure in a vacuum. For example, IBM could cut $7 billion one heck of a lot quicker than 1996 [as announced], but we would run some customer and quality risks. There's no such thing as a riskless business, but the name of the game is taking intelligent risks."

So has this veteran of Chrysler, Delta Truck Body, and Baker Industries become a kind of fiscal Mr Fixit, who will move from IBM to another troubled industry? "No," laughs York. "I'm 55 years old. It's quite conceivable that I'll retire at IBM."

Source: Dave Lindorff, "Chief Financial Officer of the Month," *Global Finance* 7 (September 1993): 35. Reprinted with permission.

involved in long-term foreign investment, capital budgeting, and cost of capital issues, (2) chief financial flows officer, (3) chief of accounting and reporting of foreign operations, (4) chief comptroller and foreign operations performance evaluator, and (5) chief global tax manager. Management Applications 1–3 show representative examples of leading CFOs.

MANAGEMENT APPLICATION NO. 3

Steve Key, Chief Financial Officer, ConAgra

Steve Key, the CFO at ConAgra, has been quick to see the value of flexible income preferred securities [FLIPS]. In late January the Omaha-based food company launched its third issue, for $250 million, bringing the total that it has raised through FLIPS to a potential $525 million since Wall Street created this new wrinkle in corporate finance last year [1994]. FLIPS, like MIPS—monthly income preferred securities—are treated much like equity by rating agencies, so they don't burden a balance sheet with debt. But the tax man sees them as debt, so interest payments are tax-deductible to the issuer.

FLIPS are designed to be more flexible than MIPS because they can be "flipped" to a debt instrument with nearly identical terms.

"Given the complexity of the Internal Revenue Code, it's nice to have flexibility," says Key, who notes FLIPS are a less costly way to raise capital than common stock.

"Steve is exceptionally creative," says Herb Wreschner, a Smith Barney banker who structured ConAgra's FLIPS. "He starts out saying, 'Here's the traditional way. Now, how do we improve on it?' Steve saw early on that FLIPS could be used to lower the cost of capital and provide financial flexibility."

Key, whose wife, Sharon, is a Presbyterian minister and former opera singer, has run ConAgra's finances for three years. After receiving an MBA from Cornell, he went to work for the Arthur Young accounting firm in 1969 and was a managing partner of its New York office when he left in 1991.

At that time, ConAgra's extremely decentralized structure had made the company quick and entrepreneurial. But since its divisions operated independently, it was unable to exploit its size to lower capital costs. "We needed a CFO who was very knowledgeable about financing large ventures and who could interface with all our different businesses," says ConAgra chairman and CEO Philip Fletcher. "Steve's dealing[s] with a broad range of clients over time gave him the experience we thought was necessary."

Says Key: "ConAgra has gone from a nearly bankrupt company with $400 million in sales in 1974 to $25 billion today, largely through acquisitions, which is my forte." Indeed, Key has personally negotiated about 20 of the 100 buyouts ConAgra has completed since he arrived, including the acquisitions of National Foods and Universal Frozen Foods.

Getting along with the heads of ConAgra's six operating divisions is a major challenge. "They are all strong personalities and all very different. The ability to interrelate with these guys is not a small demand," says a former consultant who knows ConAgra well. Key makes it work with a combination of charm and financial savvy. "We don't force ourselves on the operating officers, but they frequently invite Steve in when they are discussing acquisitions or their capital needs," says Fletcher.

The operating officers appreciate Key's willingness to stand back and support operations, rather than step in and control them. "We are trying to serve two masters," says Key. "We are trying to do an effective job at the corporate level, but at [the] same time we have a boss, and that's ConAgra's 211 profit centers. Our job is to help them do their job easier, with fewer resources."

Source: Michael Fraser, "Chief Financial Officer of the Month," *Global Finance* 9 (February 1995): 33. Reprinted with permission.

Additional Readings

Baker, James C., John K. Ryans, Jr., and Donald G. Howard, eds. *International Business Classics.* Lexington, MA: Lexington Books, 1988.

Eiteman, David K., Arthur I. Stonehill, and Michael H. Moffett. *Multinational Business Finance.* Reading, MA: Addison-Wesley, 1992.

Eng, Maximo, Francis A. Lees, and Laurence J. Mauer. *Global Finance.* New York: Harper-Collins College Publishers, 1995.

Hall, Edward T. *The Silent Language.* New York: Doubleday & Co., 1959.

Kim, Suk H., and Seung H. Kim. *Global Corporate Finance: Text & Cases.* Cambridge, MA: Blackwell Publishers, 1996.

Lee, James A. "Cultural Analysis in Overseas Operations." *Harvard Business Review* 44 (March-April 1966):106–114.

Ohmae, Kenichi. *The Borderless World.* New York: Harper Business, 1990.

Ricks, David A. *Big Business Blunders: Mistakes in Multinational Marketing.* Homewood, IL: Dow Jones-Irwin, 1983.

Shapiro, Alan. *Multinational Financial Management.* Boston: Allyn Bacon, 1996.

Terpstra, Vern, and Keith David. *The Cultural Environment of International Business.* Cincinnati, OH: South-Western, 1991.

Wadia, Maneck S. "The Concept of Culture." *Journal of Retailing* 41 (Spring 1965):21–9, 55.

Discussion Questions

1. Why is global finance important?
2. Discuss the importance of the theory of comparative advantage.
3. How does the environment differ between domestic business and multinational business?
4. What distinguishes an MNC from a transnational corporation? Compile a list of companies that exemplify each.
5. What is the self-reference criterion?
6. Discuss the silent language of international business.
7. Why is culture important in international business? What is culture?
8. Become familiar with one major international finance periodical and write a one-page essay about its importance.

Problems

1. Compile a list of the twenty-five largest companies worldwide by asset size; the twenty-five largest banks worldwide by asset size; the ten largest investment banking firms and the ten largest stock exchanges by trading volume; and the ten largest cross-border company mergers by dollar size of the transaction. (A useful source is the mid-summer international issue of *Forbes* or the annual "World Business" issue of the *Wall Street Journal* published in September.
2. Write an abstract of one analysis of a major currency and one analysis of a minor, or exotic, currency reported in the *International Currency Review.*
3. Become familiar with the publication *Euromoney* by listing the most interesting article to you in any issue from the past two years.
4. Write a book review of any book written during the past ten years on international financial markets.
5. Compile a list of incidents you can think of in which an American student at your university has practiced the self-reference criterion.

6. Compile a list of examples of U.S. companies that, when dealing internationally, experienced embarrassments because of misunderstandings associated with cultural differences or language misuses.

7. Suppose that two countries, the United States and Spain, each produce two products: bagels and sherry. The United States has an absolute advantage in the production of each good. For one unit of factor input, the United States can produce either twenty-five bagels or fifteen bottles of sherry. For one unit of factor input, Spain can produce either fifteen bagels or three bottles of sherry. According to the theory of comparative advantage, can production be increased if the United States specializes in one of these products, Spain specializes in the other product, and they trade their products with each other? If production cannot be increased in this manner, why not?

PART

II

The Global Business Finance Environment

The MNC operates in a complex environment involving an international monetary system that has changed drastically several times during the past century or more. Within this system of central banks, private banks, and other financial institutions, the firm must have access to foreign exchange if it is to operate in the international arena. In order to buy foreign goods, invest abroad, or operate in a foreign country, the firm must have foreign exchange. Foreign exchange is traded within the monetary system by a vast interbank network that handles more than $1 trillion per day. These traders have operated in a variety of international monetary systems. The history of these international monetary systems and the present situation is discussed in chapter 2. This chapter also includes a detailed discussion of the international balance of payments including its importance, what information it contains, and government policies designed to cope with disequilibrium situations in some areas of the balance of payments.

Because most international business transactions have a lag between the time they are entered into and the time when they are finally settled, the foreign exchange rate—the domestic price of foreign money—may fluctuate in the marketplace. The firm, thus, is subject to losses when it takes delivery of foreign exchange to set-

tle the transaction. Therefore, the firm must measure and manage this exposure to the risk of loss in foreign exchange operations. Foreign exchange and its role in international business are discussed in chapter 3. The measurement and management of foreign exchange risk are covered in chapter 4.

When trading with a foreign firm or individual or making direct investments in plants and equipment in a foreign country, the firm is subject to political risk. These risks arise from political actions in the form of decrees, administrative actions, laws, and other pronouncements by the host government. They may take the form of restrictions on the convertibility of currency; expropriation of the foreign investor's property; interference with contractual obligations; or violence from civil war, coups, insurrections, or regional violence or terrorism. These risks and their management, as well as investment insurance are the subjects of chapter 5.

2

The International Monetary System and the Balance of Payments

---

Major Objectives of Chapter 2

(1) To analyze the evolution of today's international monetary system and (2) to understand the mechanics and meaning of the balance of payments.

Key terms to be learned in chapter 2:

- gold standard
- Bretton Woods
- special drawing rights
- managed floating system
- European Monetary System
- Ecu
- Plaza Accord
- Forex market intervention
- balance of payments
- current account
- official reserves account
- interest equalization tax
- mandatory controls program

- gold exchange standard
- adjustable peg system
- Smithsonian Agreement
- Jamaica Agreement
- exchange rate mechanism
- Maastricht Treaty
- Louvre Accord
- target-zone arrangement
- unilateral transfer
- capital account
- trade balance
- voluntary controls program
- Office of Foreign Direct Investment

Introduction

Cross-border transactions in trade and investment must operate in a global environment that is rationally organized. This environment is called the international monetary system. Within this system, individuals, banks, companies, and governments must be able to exchange foreign currencies in order to purchase goods, services, and investments. A rational system for clearing and settling these transactions must be placed

into operation. Before 1880, global trade and investment were settled by a relatively small number of firms and banks. However, industrial development in Europe and the United States in the late nineteenth century necessitated a more formal way of settling imbalances in the balance of payments between nations.

International Monetary Systems

THE GOLD STANDARD

The major trading nations, primarily the British Commonwealth countries and the United States, entered into the first so-called international monetary system—the gold standard. The society of international trading nations practiced the gold standard from about 1880 to 1914. A majority of countries used this system to settle their international transactions balances. Gold standard currencies were valued in terms of a gold equivalent. For example, one ounce of gold was valued at U.S.$20.67 and all other currencies were linked to the dollar in a system of fixed exchange rates. Thus, the gold standard resulted in a system of fixed exchange rates among participating nations. Such stable exchange rates were considered a necessity to increasing trade among gold standard nations.

The quantity theory of money was the foundation of the gold standard. It is expressed in the equation $MV = PQ$, where M is the money stock, V is the velocity of that money stock circulating in the economy, P is the price of goods, and Q is the quantity of goods produced by the economy. In a gold standard economy, if the country had a deficit in trade with the rest of the world, the result would be an outflow of gold to settle the deficit. This would cause M to fall and, thus, P would fall. The decline in prices would make the country's exports less expensive to the rest of the world and they would increase. The resulting surplus would cause an inflow of gold, M would increase, P would increase, exports would fall, and the cycle would continue from disequilibrium to equilibrium to disequilibrium, and so forth.

A number of problems emerged with the gold standard. This monetary system assumed that the major settling currencies, namely the pound sterling and the dollar, were backed by gold. Gold is a finite commodity. Its supply is limited, but international trade had expanded after the Industrial Revolution. Although the period was one of stability and growth—a major argument espoused by those who advocate a return to the gold standard, this environment may have been more a result of the absence of wars or serious global economic shocks, although the recession at the beginning of the twentieth century was quite severe in the United States.

World War I caused a severe shock to the system and the United States and Great Britain went off the gold standard. The former returned to the gold standard in 1919 and became even more prominent in world trade than Great Britain. Inflation in Europe, especially in Germany, during the 1920s prohibited restoration of the gold standard because differential inflation among the world's trading nations made it difficult to determine appropriate exchange rates. Finally, the United States went off the standard in 1933 as the Great Depression and the retaliation against the Smoot-Hawley Tariff, enacted by the U.S. government, led to a virtual halt in global trade. The depression resulted in a severe contraction of international trade and investment. Nations allowed their currencies to depreciate as a means to solve their international balance of payments deficits, and this movement led to global currency instability, further eroding the usefulness of the gold standard.

THE GOLD EXCHANGE STANDARD

From 1925 to 1931, a gold exchange standard was attempted by the major trading partners. Essentially this was a modification of the gold standard in which the dollar and the pound sterling were used along with gold to settle international imbalances. However, the pound sterling was ruled inconvertible in 1931, leading to a run on U.S. gold and a drop of 15 percent in U.S. holdings of the metal. The depression in the United States and the subsequent passage of the Smoot-Hawley Tariff led to the retaliation and currency instability mentioned previously. The global depression brought an end to the gold exchange standard as global economic problems were converted into political problems and the resulting World War II.

Many in the field of international finance still advocate a return to the gold standard. The usefulness of gold as a store of value still continues. Gold bugs recommend that every individual portfolio should contain at least 10 percent of its value in gold or some equivalent such as shares of gold producers or certificates backed by the commodity. The Chairman of the Federal Reserve Board, Alan Greenspan, uses the price of gold as an indicator of inflationary pressures in his formulation of monetary policy.

THE BRETTON WOODS SYSTEM

As World War II came to an end, the founders of the new United Nations believed international financial institutions were needed to assist the reconstruction of war-torn countries and the economic development of the poor nations as well as to replace the earlier international monetary systems. World trade and investment once again grew worldwide and the currency system needed a reorganization. The world powers met in 1944 at Bretton Woods, New Hampshire, a resort in the Mount Washington area to contemplate the establishment of institutions designed to achieve these objectives.

Two multilateral financial institutions were established at Bretton Woods. The International Bank for Reconstruction and Development, known today as the World Bank, was formed to furnish loans to nations for reconstruction of war damages and to assist in economic development with funds for social overhead capital projects such as dams, ports, and other social infrastructure. The International Monetary Fund (IMF) was established to pool international reserves of members that could be loaned on a short-term basis to those members with temporary balance of payments imbalances. A new international monetary system linking currencies to a new system was also enacted—the Bretton Woods System. The most instrumental personality of the Bretton Woods meeting was a British economist, John Maynard Keynes, whose vision of an orderly world monetary system came to fruition in the form of the IMF.

The new system revalued gold to U.S.$35 per ounce of gold, or $1 = 1/35 ounce of gold. All currencies were then linked to the dollar by exchange rates fixed at some par value. Essentially this was an adjustable peg system with parity set within a band of plus or minus 1 percent of par, i.e., the par is the peg and rates could be adjusted within this narrow band. Thus, currencies could be traded in the foreign exchange market but only within a very narrow range. If a currency's foreign exchange rate began to float near or slightly above the ceiling, the central bank of that currency had to be prepared to sell reserves into the market so that the increased supply would cause the rate to fall. If the rate fell to the floor, 1 percent below par, the central bank had to buy the currency with other foreign exchange so that the rate would increase back toward par. Another rule enacted by the IMF and approved by member countries held that changes in a country's currency beyond the plus or minus 1 percent from par had to be approved by the IMF.

This system was a modification of the gold exchange standard and was appropriate for the 1950s. But when the U.S. balance of payments deficits of the late 1950s and throughout the 1960s led to speculation in the currency markets that the dollar would be devalued, the demand for gold increased. The Japanese yen, German mark, and Swiss franc were pressured to revalue. Currency analysts stated that such a revaluation could have stabilized the system but these nations said the dollar should be devalued. No nation at that time wanted to drastically change its currency beyond the narrow band around par and certainly not by the amounts advocated at that time.

Richard Nixon, while campaigning for president of the United States in 1968, advocated that the Bretton Woods international monetary system in which the major reserve currencies were backed by gold be replaced by essentially a dollar standard. In other words, the United States Treasury Department should not buy and sell gold on demand. In 1969, President Nixon unofficially closed the so-called gold door to purchases of sales of U.S. gold. One of the cornerstones of this era was the official currency swap by central banks. Deficits in the U.S. balance of payments were settled by currency swaps of dollars held by foreign central banks for other currencies.

The IMF created special drawing rights (SDRs) in 1969. These are international reserve assets allocated to IMF members to supplement existing reserve assets. The IMF has made six allocations of SDRs since 1970 totaling SDR 21.4 billion. Each nation had their subscriptions of reserves and gold to the IMF supplemented by SDRs. Although SDRs have not yet reached their potential and were at first traded between central banks, banks now issue SDR-denominated deposits and make loans denominated in SDRs. They are used as a unit of account in bonds and other assets. The value of an SDR is set daily as the weighted average value of five major currencies: the U.S. dollar, German (deutsche) mark, French franc, Japanese yen, and British pound. The basket of currencies is revised every five years. As of August 28, 1995, the value of one SDR was U.S.$1.49553.[1] Effective January 1, 1996, the value of the SDR was set according to the sum of the values of each of the five currencies, as follows:

Currency	Value
U.S. dollar	0.582
Deutsche mark	0.446
Japanese yen	27.200
French franc	0.813
British pound	0.105

thus making the weights of each currency as follows: 39 percent for the U.S. dollar, 21 percent for the deutsche Mark, 18 percent for the Japanese yen, and 11 percent each for the French franc and the British pound.[2]

The measures did not stop the speculation built up by the continual U.S. balance of payments deficits and the slow erosion of U.S. international reserves and diminishing value of the dollar. By summer 1971, an international monetary crisis was in full bloom. The United States had some $88 billion in short-term liquid liabilities owed to foreigners as a result of the balance of payments deficits. However, the U.S. official gold supply had fallen to less than $12 billion, at the official value of gold at that time—$35 per ounce of gold. This condition is dramatically described in Figure 2–1, which

---

[1] "International Reserve Asset Also Serves as Unit of Account," *IMF Survey* 24 (September 1995): 20–2.

[2] "IMF Calculates New Currency Amounts for SDR Valuation Basket," *IMF Survey* 25 (January 22, 1996): 35.

shows the period from about 1950 until 1971. The declining line at the bottom of the figure shows U.S. official reserve assets, primarily gold, falling to about $12 billion. The upper lines show U.S. liquid liabilities to all foreigners rising almost exponentially during the 1970–71 period to more than $88 billion. Some of the gold had to be held to back domestic greenbacks. Of the $88 billion in short-term liquid liabilities held by foreigners, some 50 percent was held by foreign central banks. This amount was fairly safe given the ability of the Federal Reserve Board and the U.S. Treasury Department to negotiate with these central banks. Another 25 percent was held by foreign multinational companies. These firms were predictable in that they would probably not exchange these liabilities for international reserves. The final 25 percent was in the hands of foreign speculators, Middle Eastern sheiks, and other unknown elements. This $22

FIGURE 2–1 Short-term Liquid Liabilities vs. U.S. Official Reserves (1950–71)

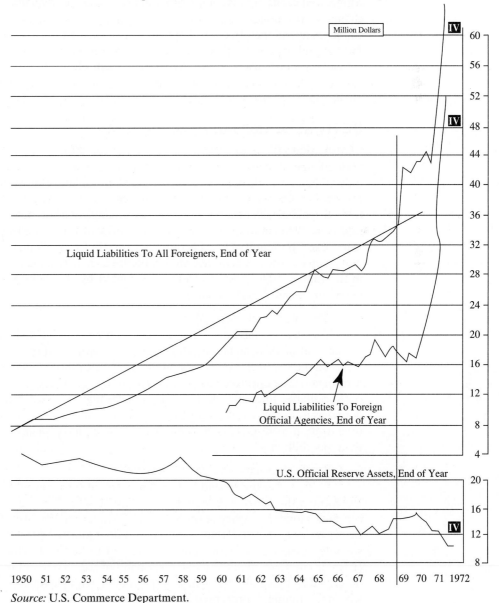

Source: U.S. Commerce Department.

billion in debt could be presented to the U.S. government in return for gold, thus depleting the entire U.S. reserve. President Nixon, on August 15, 1971, recognized the possibility that the U.S. gold supply could be wiped out by such uncontrollable factors, and he officially announced that the United States would no longer buy or sell official gold on demand. The world had officially gone off a gold standard and onto a dollar standard instead.

The United States, without permission from the IMF or, for that matter, the U.S. Congress, devalued the dollar by more than 8.5 percent by increasing the official price of gold from $35 per ounce to $38. President Nixon became the first Republican president to devalue the U.S. currency. At a meeting at the end of 1971 of the major central banks at the Smithsonian Institution in Washington, D.C., the Smithsonian Agreement was reached. This agreement resulted in a number of changes in the international monetary system. The major currencies were realigned with the dollar devaluation coupled with revaluations of most of the other major currencies by a like amount, resulting in a change in the dollar vis-à-vis the major currencies by as much as 16 percent. Many countries abandoned fixed exchange rates, including the British pound. Germany and Switzerland applied legal controls over their currencies. The original IMF-set band of ±1 percent of par was widened to ±2.25 percent of par. In 1972, the U.S. trade deficit nearly tripled from 1971, and speculative flows of currencies continued, resulting in the international monetary crisis of February 1973.

THE FLOATING EXCHANGE RATE SYSTEM

In response to this crisis, President Nixon devalued the dollar again, this time by more than 10.5 percent. In March 1973, the major currencies began to float against each other. This new international monetary system replaced the system of fixed exchange rates with a managed, or "dirty," floating system, i.e., exchange rates were flexible or floated against each other in the foreign exchange market, but governments could still intervene in the markets to keep currency prices from going too high or too low. The European Community (EC) currencies were still fixed in value against each other and moved up or down as demonstrated in Figure 2–2. This concept is known as the "snake in the tunnel." The basic concept represented by this managed floating system has been, for the most part, in place since 1973.

Jamaica Agreement of 1976

The system has been fine tuned a number of times since 1973. The Jamaica Agreement of 1976, signed by IMF members, formalized the floating rate system that replaced the Bretton Woods System. Floating rates were declared acceptable and IMF members were permitted to trade in the foreign exchange (forex) markets to balance out speculative fluctuations of their currencies that were unwarranted. Gold was abandoned as a reserve asset. Total IMF quotas that member countries contributed to the organization were increased to $41 billion. They have since been increased to more than $180 billion.

The European Monetary System

In 1979 after the second U.S. dollar devaluation, eight of the nine members of the EC formed the European Monetary System (EMS). This was the first step toward a common monetary policy in the EC. The EMS members agreed to fix their exchange rates against each other's currencies and to float jointly against outside currencies, in a so-called target zone arrangement, referred to as the Exchange Rate Mechanism (ERM). The EMS dictated a narrower band of ±2.25 percent of par. Currencies were described as being like the snake in the tunnel, with currency rates going up or down within the tunnel, represented by the upper and lower limits of the band, but in a tun-

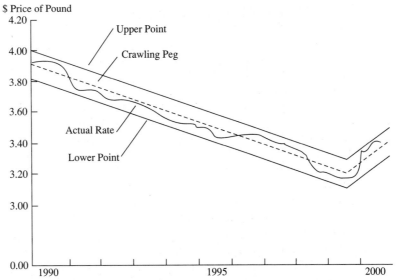

FIGURE 2–2 The Snake in the Tunnel European Union Members

nel that seemed to be sloped upward because of the tendency of these currencies to revalue against other major currencies. An example of the snake in the tunnel is shown in Figure 2–2. In practice, some EMS members have practiced larger ranges of 6 to 15 percent. Spain joined the EMS in 1989, the United Kingdom joined in 1990 with a range of 6 percent plus or minus par value but withdrew in 1992, and Portugal joined in 1992. Sweden, Norway, Finland, and Austria were scheduled to join in 1995; however, all but Finland had joined by early 1996.

The EC model of monetary integration and union has at its center the issue of supranational versus national power. Some countries, or national powers, will gain sovereignty and others will lose it by accepting the principles of a supranational power such as the EC. For example, suppose that Great Britain encounters a weak housing market and would benefit from lower interest rates. The central European monetary authority might fear that inflation is more dangerous and will keep rates high, thus further harming the British housing market.

The EMS was given three objectives by the EC. They are (1) to create a zone of monetary stability in Europe, (2) to control inflation by monetary discipline, and (3) to coordinate exchange rate policies against non-EC currencies such as the dollar and the yen. The tools with which the EMS achieves these objectives are the European currency unit (Ecu) and the exchange rate mechanism (ERM). The Ecu is a market basket of EC currencies that serves as the unit of account for the EMS. The share of each country's currency in the Ecu depends on the country's relative economic weight within the EC. The German mark is the most important currency in the Ecu, representing some 30 percent of its value. The ERM requires each EC currency to be fixed against each other on a bilateral basis, as mentioned previously, and to float against the currencies of non-EC countries within the boundaries set by the EMS. The Ecu rates for the EMS countries are shown along with those of non-ERM members in Table 2–1.

The Ecu is used to denominate some deposits and loans in the Eurocurrency market. Securities denominated in Ecus have been issued in Germany, Switzerland, France, Belgium, the Netherlands, Luxembourg, and the United Kingdom. Ecu loans have been made to both MNCs and governments.

TABLE 2–1.   EMS European Currency Unit Rates

EMS European Currency Unit Rates

Oct. 11	Ecu Cen. Rates	Rate Against Ecu	Change on Day	% ± from Cen. Rate	% Spread v Weakeast	Div. Ind.
Netherlands	2.15214	2.09693	+0.00303	−2.57	5.83	19
Belgium	39.3960	38.5247	+0.0501	−2.21	5.45	16
Germany	1.91007	1.87192	+0.00281	−2.00	5.21	20
Austria	13.4383	13.1730	+0.0205	−1.97	5.19	14
Denmark	7.28580	7.26466	+0.00087	−0.29	3.41	2
Spain	162.493	162.090	−0.141	−0.25	3.37	2
Portugal	195.792	196.550	−0.012	0.39	2.72	−3
France	6.40608	6.53655	−0.02123	2.04	1.06	−17
Ireland	0.792214	0.816878	−0.000184	3.11	0.00	−21
Non-ERM Members						
Greece	292.867	307.974	+0.468	5.16	−1.94	—
Italy	2106.15	2114.76	−6.38	0.41	2.69	—
UK	0.786652	0.834991	+0.001081	6.14	−2.86	—

Ecu central rates set by the European Commission. Currencies are in descending relative strength.

Percentage changes are for Ecu; a positive change denotes a weak currency. Divergence shows the ratio between two spreads: the percentage difference between the actual market and Ecu central rates for a currency, and the maximum permitted percentage deviation of the currency's market rate from its Ecu central rate.

(17/9/92) Sterling and Italian Lira suspended from ERM. Adjustment calculated by the *Financial Times.*
Source: Financial Times, 12 October 1995, p. 27.

The ERM was made the focal point when the EC countries, as part of Single Market 1992, formulated the Maastricht Treaty that proposed a single European currency and central bank by 1999. However, before the treaty could be fully ratified, speculative pressure in the forex markets hit the British pound and the Italian lira. Forex traders sold these currencies and bought marks, believing that the pound and the lira would have to be realigned within the ERM. Both countries exited from the ERM on September 17, 1992, when they were not willing to maintain their currencies within their ERM bands. The currency crisis, resulting in a trillion dollar per day trading volume, caused a crisis in the markets and the possible, certainly temporary, demise of the ERM.[3] Denmark voted against ratification of the Maastricht Treaty. A watered down version, applying to Denmark, was approved in 1993. The French approved the Maastricht Treaty by a narrow margin in 1992. The ERM may survive but the Maastricht objectives will be delayed. National monetary sovereignty is difficult to relinquish.

However, some claim that the ERM has been relatively successful. A leading French monetary authority believes the system has been underrated. In a 1995 interview, he stated that seven of the ERM currencies had not been realigned among themselves in more than eight years and that ten of the fifteen EU currencies are still

---

[3] The term "currency crisis" is used here and throughout this book to illustrate a period when speculation in the foreign exchange markets in a currency or currencies renders the attacked currency exchange rate unstable and nearly undefendable by major country monetary authorities. Such crises can stem from a number of economic events including increases in interest rates, stock market declines, increase in uncertainty, bank panics, decline of economic activity, and sharp changes in prices.

TABLE 2–2. Composition of the European Currency Unit

Currency	Weight (%)
Drachma (Greece)	0.7
Escudo (Portugal)	0.8
Franc (Belgium/Luxembourg)	8.1
Franc (France)	19.3
Guilder (Netherlands)	9.6
Krone (Denmark)	2.5
Lira (Italy)	9.7
Mark (Germany)	30.4
Peseta (Spain)	5.2
Pound sterling (Britain)	12.6
Pound (Ireland)	1.1

Source: Suk K. Kim and Seung H. Kim, *Global Corporate Finance* (Miami, FL: Kolb Publishing Co., 1993), p. 90.

members of the ERM. He projects that the Maastricht Treaty will go into effect on January 1, 1999.[4]

Other Problems Even if the monetary problems are alleviated, other problems arise in the move to a single currency by the EU. The name of the currency is an issue. The Maastricht Treaty decreed that the currency's name would be the Ecu. The French approved this because the country used a coin by this name hundreds of years ago. The Germans did not like the term because they would say "ein Ecu" and German pronunciation of this term sounds like "eine Kuh," or cow. In October, 1995, the committee of the European Union (EU) charged with selecting a name for the single currency settled on "Euro" for the new money and, in late 1995, the EU adopted this name for its single currency. Second, the present Ecu is based on a trade-weighted basket of European currencies, some of which have declined more than 30 percent in recent years. Table 2–2 lists the composition of the Ecu by country. Third, the currency design is an issue. Some countries want a national symbol on the Ecus the individual countries will issue. Even the size of the currency is at issue. The French franc bill is larger than the German mark bill. At least ten different designs have been proposed. With fifteen nations currently members of the EU—Finland, Austria, and Sweden joined the original twelve in 1995, these issues may take years to resolve.

The Maastricht Treaty stipulates five economic criteria that EU member nations must meet before they can join the planned monetary union. Meeting these criteria may be very difficult or impossible for some EU members to meet before the January 1, 1999, deadline for a single monetary system. These criteria are

1. annual inflation: it must not exceed that of the three best-performing nations by more than 1.5 percent;

---

[4] "Lord Trichet of Maastricht," *Euromoney* (December 1995): 48-50. Lord Jean-Claude Trichet was Director of the French Treasury from 1988 to 1993 and then became Governor of the Banque de France, the French central bank.

Country	Inflation	Budget Deficit	Debt	Interest Rates	Exchange Rate	Outlook
Austria	X		X	X	X	Deficit is problem, but surmountable
Belgium	X			X	X	Debt at over 130% of GDP is chronic
Denmark	X	X		X	X	Debt and political will are obstacles
Finland	X			X		Should make it
France	X		X	X	X	Must cut budget deficit
Germany	X		X	X	X	Should sail in, barring public backlash
Greece						No chance of making it
Ireland	X	X		X	X	On course to make it
Italy						No hope, unless rules are bent
Luxembourg	X	X	X	na	X	Top of the class
Netherlands	X			X	X	Government debt at 80% is too high
Portugal					X	Virtually no hope
Spain					X	Almost no chance
Sweden	X					Major debt and deficit troubles
United Kingdom	X		X	X		Could make it—if it wants to

Source: Philip Moore, "Beyond the Shadow of EMU," *Euromoney* (March 1996): 73.

FIGURE 2–3 European Union Members Whether They Have Met Maastricht Criteria Toward Monetary Union (X Signifies Compliance)

2. public sector budget deficit: it must not exceed 3 percent of gross domestic product;

3. public sector debt: it must not exceed 60 percent of gross domestic product;

4. long-term interest rates: they must not exceed those of the three nations with the best inflation performance by more than 2 percentage points;

5. the exchange rate: it has to be kept within normal bands of Europe's Exchange Rate Mechanism for the previous two years.

The record for each of the fifteen EU member nations toward meeting these five criteria for monetary union in 1999 is shown in Figure 2–3.

Based on the information shown in Figure 2–3, a number of EU countries will have trouble meeting these criteria. In 1995, Greece, Italy, Portugal, Spain, and Sweden were not able to meet the criteria. However, the Maastricht Treaty requires a monetary union if as few as only two countries meet the criteria. EU officials do not want to delay the beginning of the monetary union beyond 1999, having already formed the European Monetary Institute in Frankfurt, the forerunner of a unified central bank. Some say that a strict reading of the Maastricht Treaty might produce a monetary union of only Germany and Luxembourg.[5]

---

[5] Charles Goldsmith, "EU Warns Delays Could Hurt Plan For One Currency," *Wall Street Journal* 26 September 1995, p. C19.

The possible lesson of the 1992 EMS crisis may be the vulnerability of pegged exchange rates.[6] The EMS had become a model for viable pegged exchange rate systems. Most cases of speculative currency attacks occurred in developing countries that had limited foreign exchange reserves and imposed capital controls to maintain pegged systems. The near collapse of the ERM demonstrates how a currency attack may be made in the foreign exchange market where easy access to foreign exchange reserves exists and where capital mobility is much freer. Nations that practice a fixed exchange rate system cannot have free capital flows and maintain sovereignty over their monetary policy.

The Plaza Accord

A number of accords or agreements were negotiated among the leading central bank officials during the 1980s because of perceived instability in the price of the U.S. dollar on foreign exchange markets. These agreements were meant to be a sign to the markets that the major countries desired to confirm either an upward or downward direction in the price of the U.S. dollar. The first of these agreements was the Plaza Accord.

The Plaza Accord was an agreement of finance ministers and central bank governors of the Group of Five (G-5) countries signed at the Plaza Hotel in New York on September 22, 1985. The United States, Japan, Germany, France, and Great Britain agreed to a joint strategy that stressed that further orderly appreciation of the main nondollar currencies against the dollar would be desirable. This strategy was agreed to because the dollar had risen to nearly all-time highs against other major currencies in March 1985. For example, the pound had fallen to $1.05. But the G-5 nations did not believe the dollar had fallen sufficiently to reverse the growing U.S. trade deficit.

The dollar had declined 13 percent from its February high until the time of the Plaza Accord. Immediately after the G-5 countries announced their policy, the dollar declined 4.29 percent against the world's leading currencies. During the next two years, the dollar continued to depreciate against the major currencies and, by 1987, it had fallen to the same price where it had started in 1981 when the Reagan administration had announced it would not intervene in the forex markets.

The Louvre Accord

In fear that the dollar might fall too far, the Group of Five finance ministers met at the Louvre in Paris in February 1987 and reached a new agreement known as the Louvre Accord. The ministers agreed that exchange rates had been realigned suffi-

---

STUDY AID

The Exchange Rate Mechanism (ERM) is the heart of the European Community's monetary system whose objective is a central monetary authority for Europe and a single currency. It is a system within which the members' currencies are fixed on each other but float against currencies outside the ERM. By now, you should be familiar with the various currency systems and with the Maastricht Treaty criteria that member countries must meet by 1999. Think through the discussion questions at the end of the chapter to become familiar with the international issues raised by the ERM and examine the international business literature to see if more EU members have achieved any additional Maastricht criteria.

---

[6] Mathias Zurlinden, "The Vulnerability of Pegged Exchange Rates: The British Pound in the ERM," *Federal Reserve Bank of St. Louis Review* 75 (September/October 1993): 41–56.

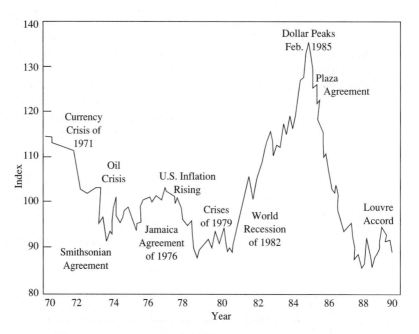

Source: Fifteen-country nominal exchange rate index of the U.S. dollar, Morgan Guaranty, *World Financial Markets*, various issues. 1980–1982 = 100.

FIGURE 2–4 U.S. Dollar Movement Under Floating Exchange Rates (1970–90)

ciently in the past and, further, pledged support to the stability of forex rates around the current levels by intervention in the markets. At the time of the meeting, the dollar had fallen to a range of ¥150 to 155 to the dollar. The dollar continued to decline, but the rate of decline slowed and, by the following year, the dollar decline had ended. Figure 2–4 contains a graph showing the U.S. dollar exchange rate during the 1970s and 1980s under floating rates indexed against the currencies of fifteen major countries.

The Currency Attack of 1992

During the summer of 1992, the forex markets nearly ground to a halt. The problems stemmed from the attempts in Europe to initiate steps toward a single monetary authority and currency. The ERM fixed EC currencies at some par value with each other in a target zone arrangement and permitted them to float against non-EC members' currencies. West Germany had absorbed East Germany and all the country's economic problems. The German money supply increased dramatically. The Bundesbank decided to keep German interest rates high to dampen the expected inflation at the same time that the U.S. government was cutting interest rates to help the economy out of its recession. Investors sold dollars and bought marks, pushing the mark higher and the dollar lower in the forex markets. Finland and Sweden, although not then members of the EC, had their currencies tied to the European Monetary System (EMS).

Forex traders mounted speculative pressure on the British pound and the Italian lira, selling these currencies and purchasing marks. These countries needed to increase their interest rates in order to avoid devaluation within the fixed rate system of the ERM. Thus, the pound and the lira fell below their required par values vis-à-vis other EC currencies and the mark rose in value.

Finland temporarily removed its currency, the markka, from the EMS, allowing it to float toward a planned 15 percent devaluation. Sweden had strong trade ties to Finland and did not want this relationship to result in a devaluation of the Swedish krona. Speculators then focused on the Swedish krona, as well as the pound. Sweden raised its

marginal interest rates from 16 to 24 percent on September 8, 1992, and then to 75 percent the next day, and finally to 500 percent, the country's largest single increase in more than 300 years. Sweden's central bank held against the currency speculation but at great cost. Although the Finnish currency devalued 15 percent by the end of one week while the krona had devalued only 1 percent, by the end of 1992, the krona was allowed to float and the market devalued the currency by 35 percent.[7]

Great Britain spent more than $15 billion to support the pound and increased interest rates to 12 percent and then to 15 percent. The intervention did not work. Great Britain had to withdraw from the ERM, lowered interest rates back to 10 percent, and floated the pound. All of this occurred in one day. Italy also pulled out of the ERM. Speculation turned to the French franc, but Germany and France bought francs to support the ERM. These moves stopped the speculative binge in the global markets, which were on the verge of total instability. EMS members were estimated to have intervened in the foreign exchange markets with a total of $100 billion, with half of that by the German Bundesbank. These central banks lost $4–6 billion in foreign exchange intervention during the period.[8]

This crisis occurred at the time when EC members were starting to consider final ratification of the Maastricht Treaty, which proposed a single monetary authority and currency in the EC by 1999. Denmark voted against the treaty and raised their overnight rates to as high as 500 percent. Currency trading exceeded $1 trillion per day and the long-term in the forex market—if one could obtain bid/ask prices—amounted to as little as five minutes or less. By fall 1992, the worst was over and the market finally stabilized after the German Bundesbank loosened its monetary policy ever so slightly. The episode considerably slowed the move toward monetary union.

The 1994–95 Dollar Crisis

During 1994, the U.S. dollar consistently fell against most major currencies. The dollar declined against the Japanese yen by 10 percent between February and the end of June 1994. The dollar declined about 8 percent against the deutsche Mark during this time period, falling to DM 1.59 by the first of July 1994. During June 1994, the dollar hit an historical low against the Japanese yen, falling below ¥100 to the dollar and constantly hovering around ¥100 to the dollar during that summer. On July 4, 1994, during intraday trading, the dollar fell to ¥98.54.

After mid-year 1994, the dollar continued to fall against the yen and the mark. On November 1, 1994, the dollar was quoted at DM 1.4953. Against the Japanese yen, the dollar was quoted on that day at ¥96.65. Thus, in the four months since July, the dollar had fallen by another 6 percent against the mark and by nearly 2 percent against the yen. At least one central bank intervention had been attempted during this period, but the dollar continued to decline against these two major currencies. The prediction at that time was that there would be a further decline in the dollar.

Much of the reason for the prediction that the dollar might continue to decline stemmed from the chronic U.S. current account deficit in the balance of payments. These deficits had totaled $1.025 trillion since 1984. The IMF had forecast that the U.S. current account deficit would continue to worsen, increasing to $166 billion in 1995 from $109 billion in 1993.[9] In addition, the increasing U.S. budget deficit added to the decline in the dollar.

[7] Charles E. Maxwell, *Financial Markets and Institutions: The Global View* (St. Paul, MN: West Publishing Co., 1994), p. 105.

[8] Frederic S. Mishkin, *Financial Markets, Institutions, and Money* (New York: HarperCollins, 1995), p. 594.

[9] Peter Norman, "Chastened Traders Yearn for Trend," *Financial Times*, 2 June 1994, p. 1 of the *Financial Times* Survey on Foreign Exchange.

Several reasons were advanced for the dollar's decline. Although the U.S. Federal Reserve Board increased short-term interest rates on four different occasions during the first half of 1994, speculators, investors, and economists believed U.S. short-term rates were still too low and expected them to be further increased. The world was awash with dollars caused by decades of U.S. trade deficits that oversupplied the world with hundreds of billions of dollars. The global appetite for U.S. securities may have declined since the Japanese cut their foreign securities holdings because of their recession and U.S. investors bought more foreign securities. When the dollar declined from ¥100 to ¥95, a Japanese investor in U.S. bonds needed a 5 percent higher yield to compensate for the 5 percent decline in foreign exchange—a result of the interest rate parity theory discussed in chapter 3.

The business firms had traded several currencies for German marks since many of these companies believed the German economy would strengthen. It was believed that interest rates would probably not be cut by German monetary authorities and an improving economy would present a better investor market. Japan had economic and political problems during the past few years so it might have been more difficult to get the Japanese government to liberalize imports or reduce taxes to stimulate the economy. The Group of Seven (G-7) central bankers were divided over foreign exchange market intervention during the first half of 1994, and some of their interventions, e.g., June 24, 1994, were poorly executed, lacking in surprise, and came at times when the dollar was not headed in a direction the G-7 nations wanted to push it. Finally, the U.S. government sent mixed signals to currency traders. Some in the Clinton administration supported a falling dollar because exports would be less expensive to the rest of the world and imports would be relatively more expensive to Americans, thus reducing the trade deficit and increasing manufacturing income. Others in the U.S. government wanted the dollar to rise in value since a declining dollar means inflation from higher priced imports and higher long-term interest rates because of the decline in bond prices resulting from investors' moving their funds from U.S. securities to foreign stocks and bonds.

The import-induced inflation argument can be refuted. At the time of the 1994 currency crisis, the United States imported more from Canada and Mexico than it did from Japan and Germany. Against the Canadian dollar and the Mexican peso, the U.S. dollar appreciated. Japan absorbed only 15.6 percent of U.S. foreign trade while Canada took 20 percent of U.S. trade, and the dollar appreciated 10.9 percent against the Canadian dollar from May 1993 to May 1994. The dollar increased 5 percent against an average of Europe's currencies from May 1993 to May 1994, by 1 percent against the Mexican peso, and 8.9 percent against all other Latin American currencies during the same time period. The real danger of the dollar falling too far is that investments in other countries have returns equal to those in the United States without the currency risk. This may cause interest rates to rise in the United States as a result of declining foreign investment and, thus, the dollar will fall even further. However, the increase in interest rates may also lead to an automatic stabilization of the value of the dollar. The effect of rising interest rates may reduce the possibility of a vicious cycle.

A Possible Solution to Currency Speculation   It was suggested previously that one major reason for the falling dollar in 1994 was speculation among currency traders. James Tobin, the Nobel laureate economist at Yale University repeated a proposal he made fifteen years earlier in the United Nation's 1994 *Human Development Report*. He suggested a small tax on international currency transactions.[10] Volume in the foreign

---

[10] Gene Koretz, "Economic Trends: Would a Tax on Currency Speculators Calm the Markets?" *Business Week* (July 11, 1994): 30.

exchange markets amounts to $1 trillion every day. The ratio of foreign exchange traded to that actually needed for international trade and investments has been estimated by the author to be about 30–1. If total international trade is about $6 trillion and total international direct and portfolio investment is $4 trillion, as some have estimated, then annual foreign exchange trading volume of $260–300 trillion produces a ratio of $26–30 of foreign exchange traded for every $1 of trade and investment. Tobin believes a 0.05% tax would produce $150 billion in annual revenues. A tax one-tenth that size could still produce $15 billion in revenues, to be used to supplement the economic development work of organizations such as the World Bank and the United Nations.

The Falling Dollar and Its Impact

During the past 20–25 years, the general trend of the dollar has been downward, primarily against the German mark and the Japanese yen. Against many other currencies with which the United States has major trading relationships, e.g., Canada, Mexico, Great Britain, France, the U.S. dollar has generally appreciated. The dollar bought ¥100 in mid-1994, down from ¥360 in 1969. Several reasons have been cited for this decline. Basically, Americans have lived beyond their means, borrowing much abroad and buying more from the rest of the world than they sell, especially from the Japanese. The rest of the world has a glut of dollars and simple economic principles of supply and demand dictate a falling dollar.

Although a decline in the dollar reduces the cost of U.S. exports to the rest of the world, it has several adverse effects on the United States. A declining dollar raises the price of imports and Americans have always had a high propensity to import. Americans find value in much of what is imported, either in quality or in price. Higher import prices also lead to price increases by domestic producers who do not fear loss of markets to foreign competitors. All of this may lead to inflation.

A declining dollar also may cause higher interest rates. The U.S. government budget deficits have added up to more than $5 trillion U.S. debt, some 16–18 percent of which has to be financed by foreign investors. As the dollar declines, foreign investors stop buying U.S. Treasury bonds because they will be paid back in devalued dollars. Bond prices decline and interest rates increase, leading to higher interest rates on mortgage, car, and consumer loans, as well as higher interest payments by the U.S. government.

Explanation for the Falling Dollar   In 1994, the dollar fell 11 percent relative to the Japanese yen, 9 percent relative to the German mark, and 6 percent relative to the British pound.[11] The dollar declined despite the fact that the U.S. economy was stronger than the Japanese or European economies. U.S. gross domestic product grew, unemployment decreased, productivity increased, and corporate profits rose.

The currency crisis became multinational in scope in early 1995. The dollar continued to decline, and, on March 7, 1995, it closed at historical lows against the German mark and Japanese yen. During that day, the dollar fell to ¥89.85 and DM 1.3675 in intraday trading. In Europe, the currencies of Great Britain, France, Sweden, Spain, Italy, and Portugal fell to record lows against the mark. From 1992 to 1995, the Spanish peseta lost 25 percent of its value against the mark, including a 7 percent devaluation by the Spanish government on March 5, 1995.

Economists usually blame a declining dollar on a current account deficit, i.e., an excess of U.S. expenditures for imports of goods and services over receipts from exports. However, the answer probably lies in the size and composition of U.S. capital ex-

---

[11] Charles Wolf, Jr., "The Dollar Depreciation Mystery," *Wall Street Journal*, 10 February 1995, p. A8.

ports. U.S. capital exports and imports for investment in short- and long-term investments have been among the world's largest. U.S. investors, individual and institutional, have poured large amounts of funds into international and emerging market global equity funds, mostly mutual or open-end funds, but some are closed-end investment companies. These are investment companies that either have no limit to the number of shares they can issue (open-end or mutual funds) or they have an amount of shares issued and outstanding as authorized by shareholders (closed-end investment companies).

U.S. capital exports are more responsive to foreign exchange rate fluctuations than to interest rate changes.[12] However, much of the capital imports are foreign bank loans to U.S. banks and are more sensitive to interest rate fluctuations. Thus, the impact from the dollar exchange rate is greater on capital exports than on capital imports. Both U.S. capital exports and imports have been the largest of any country in the world, and the net deficit in these items has financed the U.S. current account deficit in recent years. If U.S. capital exports remain large, the dollar may continue to decline. As foreign securities markets become less attractive, U.S. capital exports may begin to decline in the future and the dollar may begin to appreciate. It may be that these capital exports from the United States for investments, for example, in the emerging markets of the less-developed countries (LDCs), are the result of reverse capital flight, i.e., previous capital flight from those countries now returning home. Capital may have a preferred habitat, i.e., its own home.

In light of such international financial market crises such as in Mexico, discussed in the next section, the following scenario may take place. U.S. capital exports may decline, American portfolio investments abroad will be repatriated, and the net inflow will more than offset the current account deficit. Because of the falling dollar from 1994 to 1995, U.S. merchandise exports increased and, therefore, the dollar had a tendency to become stronger.

This major economic issue, the falling dollar, that faced the United States and its citizenry again emphasized the importance of foreign exchange and the forex market. This was an important public policy issue: whether to permit the dollar to continue to decline against the German mark and the Japanese yen—while it apparently was rising against most other currencies—or to increase interest rates in an attempt to boost the price of the dollar. Higher nominal interest rates lead to a decline in consumer spending and business investment and possible higher unemployment. Whichever way this issue was treated by the U.S. government and other leading central banks, the resulting policy significantly affected U.S. multinational companies.

A 1995–96 Postcript on the U.S. Dollar   Having reached a near historical low against the German mark of DM 1.3438 on March 8, 1995 and an all-time historical low against the Japanese yen of ¥79.75 on April 19, 1995, the dollar began to stabilize against both currencies in April and May 1995. The Federal Reserve Bank of New York had intervened by buying dollars in a number of markets in April 1995, at the same time that the Group of Three (G-3)—Germany, Japan, and the United States—agreed to coordinate their currency market intervention. Germany and Japan also agreed to stimulate their economies—Germany by reducing interest rates and Japan with fiscal measures. The U.S. Congress began to deliberate government spending cuts in an attempt to reduce the budget deficit.

The G-3 established a policy that included targeting the dollar/yen exchange rate at 100–113 and keeping it in the bottom half of that range. The dollar/mark target rate

---

[12] Ibid.

was set at a range of 1.49–1.72 with emphasis on the 1.45–1.65 range.[13] On May 31, 1995, the Group of Ten (G-10) countries intervened on behalf of the dollar. The dollar traded in a narrow range against the yen and the mark during June. During the third quarter, the dollar appreciated against most currencies and reached a 1995 high of ¥111 to the dollar, a 39 percent increase in the U.S. dollar since the low in mid-April 1995.[14] By April 1996, the U.S. dollar had risen to ¥108 or 35 percent from its low one year earlier. This was the highest level in the dollar against the yen since 1994. The dollar had risen 9 percent against the German mark.

The strength in the dollar caused U.S. businessmen to worry about the effect on U.S. exports. Several companies have reported that earnings declined in the second half of 1996 because of a decline in exports. A stronger dollar may also cause a decline in U.S. global competitiveness. Daimler-Benz forecast that the reduction in its work-force and the shift of production overseas will be enhanced by the stronger dollar so that the company will achieve its breakeven point (DM 1.35/$) in terms of exchange rates by 1997. Japanese automakers also cut costs during the decline of the dollar, enabling these companies to achieve large profit margins. With the stronger dollar, Japanese companies can sell cars for lower prices in the United States, thus increasing market share.

However, the stronger dollar has encouraged foreign purchases of U.S. Treasury securities. Nearly 72 percent of all Treasury securities were purchased by foreign investors in 1995. As inflation fears have increased in the United States, interest rates have risen. The lower bond prices could result in a sell-off of these securities, causing even higher interest rates during an election year. Thus, the stronger dollar has both short-term and long-term implications for the U.S. economy.

Analysts estimated, after the interventions of spring 1995, that the new target ranges established by G-3 might be sustainable for two years.[15] They did not see the U.S. trade deficit as a problem because the direction was down and it amounted to only 2 percent of the U.S. GDP, compared with, for example, 6 percent for Australia. In addition, U.S. reserves were growing globally at a rate of $60–65 billion per year because of the growth of imports around the world, thus enabling the United States to continue to run trade deficits without much effect on the dollar exchange rate.

Finally, the G-7 (Canada, France, Germany, Great Britain, Italy, Japan, and the United States) monetary authorities met in October 1995.[16] Their joint statement after this meeting reaffirmed their commitment to cooperate closely in the foreign exchange markets. This agreement meant to many currency analysts that the G-7 would support the dollar. Others, such as Carl Weinberg of High Frequency Economics, an economic consulting firm, believed that the G-7 would not buy dollars and that foreign exchange traders would sell dollars without the support. The G-7 countries also met in April 1996 and reconfirmed their concern for a rising dollar but decided not to intervene at that time.

The 1994–95 Mexican Peso Crisis

The Mexican government had granted its central bank more autonomy and had improved its monetary policy before 1994. Monetary growth and inflation slowed dramatically after 1992. However, political turmoil in 1994 caused foreign capital inflows

[13] Joan Ogden, "Wow! The Incredible Rising Dollar Scenario: Dollar Soars, Global Economy Takes Off, Markets Move," *Global Finance* 9 (September 1995): 34.

[14] Peter R. Fisher, "Treasury and Federal Reserve Foreign Exchange Operations: April-June 1995," published by the Federal Reserve Board of Governors, Washington, D.C.

[15] Ogden, "Wow! The Incredible Rising Dollar Scenario," 34–5.

[16] Bill Montague, "G7's Dollar Policy Moves into Spotlight," *USA Today*, 9 October 1995, p. B1.

into Mexico to slow, and the country's official reserves declined. A flight from pesos ensued since domestic investors did not want to hold the Mexican currency. The country did not have a history of price stability and, thus, the credibility of its central bank declined.

During the last few days of 1994 and early days of 1995, the value of the Mexican peso fell by as much as 45 percent. This currency crisis came a year after the debate on the North American Free Trade Agreement (NAFTA) and caused some in the newly formed Republican majority in the U.S. Congress to question whether NAFTA should be shelved. A new president started a six-year term in Mexico but inherited the economic problems of the retiring president. The crisis drastically affected the Mexican Bolsa where share prices fell precipitously and then spread to Brazil and Argentina where stock prices fell. Although economic deterioration had preceded the peso collapse by years, the catalyst was the $45 billion in mutual fund cash that Mexico had attracted from the rest of the world, primarily the United States, in the early 1990s. When the peso collapsed, fund managers pulled out much of these funds from the Mexican economy and the Mexico City Stock Exchange. This action exacerbated the peso devaluation.[17]

The Clinton administration asked the U.S. Congress to approve a $40 billion loan guarantee package to alleviate the Mexican financial crisis. Since polls in the United States showed that the American public did not support such a plan, congressional leaders would not introduce legislation to support the guarantee package. Instead, the Clinton administration marshalled a $49.8 billion loan guarantee package by using $20 billion of guarantees from the U.S. Treasury's Exchange Stabilization Fund (funds normally used to support the dollar) coupled with additional assistance from the IMF and the Bank for International Settlements.[18] The IMF provided $10 billion in five-year loans in addition to $7.8 billion in credit already promised Mexico by the IMF. Other nations advanced $10 billion in short-term credit through the Bank for International Settlements. In addition, Canada pledged $1 billion as did other Latin American nations. Finally, the U.S. Federal Reserve System made available $4.5–6.0 billion in short-term loans until the promised longer term treasury financing was advanced. This bailout package may have reached a total of $53 billion or more. It represented one of the largest socializations of market risk in global history.

This program encouraged the Mexican government to incorporate an economic policy mix including tightened monetary policy to shore up the peso, aggressive deregulation, and tax cutting to create opportunities for mid- and small-sized entrepreneurs, including strict targets for money supply, domestic credit, fiscal spending, and foreign borrowing. The loan guarantees from the United States and the IMF are backed by oil export revenues held by the New York Federal Reserve Bank as collateral.

This crisis, according to the *Wall Street Journal*, presents an instructional case about the discipline of international financial markets.[19] Much of the capital flight from Mexico was comprised of funds invested in mutual funds. On-line investors with a computer modem can withdraw their money from these investments very quickly.

The case of the Mexican devaluation and bailout has caused some students of international monetary systems to call for an early warning system that can detect problems in developing economies before they drastically affect the economy. The IMF, along with the United States and Bank for International Settlements, may have come

---

[17] William Glasgall, "Welcome to the New World Order of Finance," *Business Week* (February 13, 1995): 38.

[18] Dean Foust, Susan B. Garland, Douglas Harbrecht, and Richard S. Dunham, "Anatomy of A Rescue Mission," *Business Week* (February 13, 1995): 32–4.

[19] "Asleep on Mexico," *Wall Street Journal*, 28 December 1994, p. A10.

to Mexico's rescue at the last moment but some wondered where these institutions and countries were in mid-1994 before the deteriorating Mexican economy turned into a crisis situation.

Some global financial analysts suggest that the Mexican peso collapse is an excellent case in support of the multilateral safety net proposed by the G-7 at Halifax, Nova Scotia. When the global debt crisis began in Mexico in 1982, the banks that had loaned large amounts of funds to LDCs did not have to mark these loans to market on a daily basis. The mutual funds that moved large amounts of investment capital into the emerging markets did mark to market and their managers measured the risk almost minute by minute. Without the global aid to support the peso, an international liquidity crisis might well have happened because international banks might have ceased lending to LDCs and called loans to these countries, which might have caused liquidity to dry up on a global basis. A multilateral safety net, much like the Federal Reserve rediscount window in the United States, could alleviate such crises much quicker than aid marshalled by any one country.

One proposed model suggests that the IMF could become a global Securities and Exchange Commission that would require governments to provide current information regarding their financial condition.[20] With increased globalization of financial markets, especially in the emerging nations, investors need to know whether or not countries receiving international capital are concealing dangerous financial secrets. Two-thirds of the world's governments are subject to little or no monitoring of their economic condition by external authorities. The IMF itself has contributed to the lack of financial disclosure among most of the world's nations in that it has never declassified the loan documents and accompanying internal analyses required in loans by the IMF to its member nations.

Reasons for the 1995 Global Currency Crisis

Some of the possible reasons for the global currency crisis have been discussed previously, including the Mexican peso crisis and the persistent current account deficits in the U.S. balance of payments. These and other causes have been suggested by currency analysts.[21] The Mexican currency crisis caused global money managers to reduce the value of currencies and securities by selling their investments denominated in the currencies of economies with heavy foreign debt and weak financial systems. Japanese and German monetary authorities became nervous about the U.S. Federal Reserve System, believing that it would not raise interest rates at that time, thus permitting inflation to increase.

In Europe, as global money bought German marks, the German Bundesbank showed its displeasure with the American bailout of Mexico. Currency traders sold the currencies of Great Britain, Spain, Portugal, Greece, Sweden, and Italy because these countries maintained budget deficits. The proposed European monetary union, hurt in the 1992 crisis, was damaged even further. In Japan, interest rates were forecast to rise and the country suffered an earthquake in Kobe that cost $200 billion in damages, making it necessary to slow the recycling of its $146 billion annual trade surplus to conserve cash. Thus, the yen rose to historical highs against the dollar.

In March 1995, foreign currency analysts were worried about the dollar. The dollar's status as the major reserve currency had declined greatly and some said that the German mark would replace the dollar as the currency of choice for nations that hold their extra currency in dollars. In 1975, 80 percent of foreign currency reserves around

---

[20] Dean Foust, "What the IMF Needs is a Good Alarm System," *Business Week* (February 20, 1995): 55.

[21] William Glasgall, Bill Javetski, Rose Brady, and Robert Neff, "Hot Money," *Business Week* (March 20, 1995): 46–50.

the world were in dollars. That figure declined to 60 percent in 1995.[22] Many international traders and investors wanted the dollar supported by central bank intervention.

Persistent U.S. trade deficits represent a major reason why currency analysts worry about the U.S. dollar. For example, the U.S. trade deficit in 1995 was about $111 billion. Other analysts look at other factors when examining the trade deficit. They believe the downward trend in the magnitude is good as well as the fact that the U.S. trade deficit is only about 2 percent of the GDP. This is favorable when compared with, for example, Australia's trade deficit, which is 6 percent of the GDP. In addition, dollar reserves are growing by about $60–65 billion per year in light of a 10 percent growth rate in global imports. Therefore, the United States should be able to run trade deficits without adversely affecting the dollar.[23]

Foreign Exchange Market Intervention

The current floating rate system (dirty or managed system) is subject to government intervention in the forex market. Governments have intervened actively in the foreign exchange markets since the advent of the flexible exchange system in 1973. In fact, the Gold Reserve Act of 1934 gives the U.S. Treasury Department primary responsibility for U.S. foreign exchange operations through its Exchange Stabilization Fund.

Foreign exchange operations by governments may be either unsterilized or sterilized transactions. Unsterilized foreign exchange operations involve changes in the monetary base while sterilized operations do not. For example, the Federal Reserve could acquire foreign exchange in an unsterilized purchase by using newly created base money, e.g., bank reserves or currency. Such a foreign exchange purchase would be an expansionary monetary policy action because it would result in an increase of the monetary base. A foreign exchange purchase would be sterilized if the Federal Reserve offset its effect on the monetary base by selling an equivalent amount of dollar-denominated securities. Since the Federal Reserve controls the monetary base, it can determine whether a foreign exchange operation will be sterilized. In most cases, the Federal Reserve sterilizes its foreign currency operations.[24]

The intervention is implemented through the major central banks as they buy or sell large amounts of foreign exchange to reduce rate volatility or change the direction of currency prices. For example, in 1978, the Carter administration attempted to manipulate the price of the dollar upward by buying $30 billion in the market. In October 1978, the dollar index was at 100. After the Carter intervention, the dollar index rose to only 101.7 by October 1980. The intervention had little impact on the price of the dollar.

Central bank intervention to reduce exchange rate volatility is implemented for three reasons. First, volatility may restrict international investment flows. Exchange rate volatility adds risk to the required rate of return on foreign investment projects and may reduce the profitability of such projects. Second, exchange rate volatility may reduce international trade because it creates uncertainty about international trade profitability. Third, exchange rate volatility may cause the riskiness of a nation's financial markets to increase and the prices of assets traded in these markets may become more volatile.

Central bank intervention in the foreign exchange markets may increase or reduce exchange rate volatility or it may have no effect at all. Empirical evidence has been cited that finds that such intervention does not generally reduce exchange rate

---

[22] David Wessel, "What If the Dollar Doesn't Stay on Top?" *Wall Street Journal*, 20 March 1995, p. A1.

[23] Ogden, "Wow! The Incredible Rising Dollar Scenario," 35.

[24] J. Alfred Broaddus, Jr. and Marvin Goodfriend, "Foreign Exchange Operations and the Federal Reserve," *1995 Annual Report* (Richmond, VA: Federal Reserve Bank of Richmond, 1996), p. 11.

volatility. In fact, intervention typically has little effect on foreign exchange rate volatility and has been found to increase it.[25]

Some believe that intervention does have its merits. The Institute for International Economics (IIE), a think tank based in Washington, D.C., produced a study that stated that intervention in the foreign exchange markets is effective as a policy tool to determine how a nation's macroeconomic policy is held by the market.[26] A study by Kathryn Dominguez and Jeffrey Frankel found that intervention was not a viable tool in the 1960s when currencies were convertible into other currencies at some fixed exchange rate. After 1973 and the advent of floating rates, intervention was seen as a way to find out what the market thought about policies formulated and implemented by governments. By surveying a large amount of empirical research, the authors also found that the freely floating exchange market did not necessarily function in an optimal way.[27]

In fact, on three occasions during the twentieth century, external pressures led to the breakup of a fixed rate monetary system: the international gold standard in the 1930s, the Bretton Woods system in the 1970s, and the exit of countries from the exchange rate mechanism of the European Community during the currency crisis in 1992. These breakups were followed by monetary systems that imposed some degree of exchange rate flexibility followed soon by the advocacy of a new fixed rate regime. Pegged exchange rate systems do seem to be attractive, especially to countries that have problems maintaining financial stability.

The currency crisis, or dollar crisis, of 1994–95 demonstrated an example of a proposed intervention to signal a change in monetary policy. Some members of the U.S. Federal Reserve Board advocated increasing interest rates to fight inflation that might be exacerbated by a falling dollar. Others in this debate think the falling dollar will lead to increased exports, falling trade deficits, and a growing U.S. economy.

Other attempts by central bankers to intervene in the foreign exchange markets have shown mixed results.[28] The Plaza Accord in 1985 demonstrated an attempt on the part of the G-5 countries to manage the dollar and is presented as evidence that intervention works. However, the dollar had begun to decline six months before the Plaza meeting and its rate of decline was as rapid before intervention as the decline after intervention. Some analysts believed the decline in the dollar after the Plaza Accord was attributed to a tighter monetary policy in Japan and a decline in the price of oil that caused a rise in the mark and the yen. Germany and Japan were more dependent on oil imports than was the United States.

The Louvre Agreement to stabilize the dollar in 1987 is offered as evidence that intervention is not effective. Within two months of the Louvre intervention, the dollar had dropped 5 percent and new target ranges for the dollar had to be established by the G-7 nations. Stability in the dollar during the next six months was attributed more to a tighter monetary policy in the United States resulting in relatively higher U.S. interest rates.

Essentially, central banks do not have sufficient global clout to contribute effectively in foreign exchange market intervention. Most central banks only conduct intervention through domestic institutions. Many central banks only use offshore markets

---

[25] Catherine Bonser-Neal, "Does Central Bank Intervention Stabilize Foreign Exchange Rates?" *Federal Reserve Bank of Kansas City Economic Review* 81 (First Quarter 1996): 43–57.

[26] John Starrels, "Study Examines Effectiveness of Foreign Exchange Market Intervention," *IMF Survey* 22 (March 22, 1993): 82–3.

[27] Ibid., 82.

[28] Martin Feldstein, "Let the Market Decide," *The Economist* (December 3, 1988): 22.

TABLE 2–3. Official Foreign Exchange Reserves[1] (billions U.S.$)

Items	1990	1991	1992	1993	1994	Amounts Outstanding At End of 1994
Changes, At Current Exchange Rates						
Total of which:	123.7	45.8	23.9	100.7	146.7	1,108.2
Industrial countries	82.1	−24.3	−25.9	27.6	56.7	515.6
Asian NIEs[2]	11.7	19.5	15.5	20.6	30.4	225.1
Other LDCs	37.2	54.7	32.9	48.3	53.7	340.7
Changes, At Constant Exchange Rates[3]						
Total	88.7	44.0	45.1	105.0	106.3	1,108.2
Dollar reserves of which held:	47.4	29.8	52.8	69.8	91.0	679.3
In the United States	29.9	22.3	32.8	79.0	34.5	453.2
With banks outside the United States[4]	4.6	5.8	9.2	1.1	31.7	124.6
Unallocated	12.9	1.7	10.8	−10.3	24.8	101.5
Nondollar reserves	41.3	14.2	−7.7	35.2	15.3	428.9
of which held with banks[4]	16.3	−29.2	−6.9	6.6	1.7	109.9

[1] Excluding official Ecu holdings.

[2] NIE = newly industrialized economies, e.g., South Korea.

[3] Partly estimated.

[4] Deposits by official monetary institutions with banks reporting to the BIS.

Source: Bank for International Settlements, *65th Annual Report,* 1 April 1994–31 March 1995, p. 128.

for commercial activities. Their principal motive for intervention is to signal forthcoming monetary policy. They do not wish to be misinterpreted and, thus, the best place to signal their intent is in the domestic market. Most domestic banks keep in touch with what central banks are doing, not so much for forex intervention activity, but to derive indirect benefits such as information about future monetary policy direction.

In addition to central bank intervention, the executive branches of some nations maintain so-called stabilization reserves to be used for currency market intervention. For example, the United States maintained a $40 billion fund for such intervention. However, half of this was committed to the Mexico bailout in early 1995. The foreign exchange market perception of this decision was that this weakened the ability of the United States to intervene in supporting the dollar. The dollar fell even further as a result.

When the daily volume in global forex markets of $1 trillion or more is considered, the relatively small currency reserves held by central banks seem too small to be very effective. Total official foreign exchange reserves for all reporting countries is shown in Table 2–3. Total reserves available for all purposes amounted to $1,108.2 billion at the end of 1994.

It should be noted that exchange volume is a flow and country reserves are stocks. The very high daily volume that is reported is composed of multiple transactions in the same amount of currency, some in the form of derivatives and hedges, i.e., forward transactions, and some of these transactions cancel each other out. Thus, intervention may still be desirable and effective for the signals being sent by the national authorities.

The forex market interventions of this period may have been an attempt to emphasize the importance of the exchange rate in policy determination and to signal pos-

sible future changes in domestic monetary policy, especially in the United States. Most empirical studies have shown that sterilized intervention (official intervention in forex markets that leaves the money supply unchanged) alone has an effect on the long-run value of the exchange rate, but it may have a short-run effect, i.e., to signal some monetary policy change, such as fighting inflation with interest rate increases.[29] Long-run implementation by the domestic authorities of sound monetary and fiscal policies may be the best method to avoid wide swings in a country's currency.[30]

Review of Proposals for International Monetary Accord

Several proposals have been made by monetary analysts, economists, and think tanks for programs designed to insure harmony in the international monetary system. Some have advocated a return to the fixed rate system but with wider bands around currency par values. Others who advocate a return to fixed rates think a crawling peg would be better than the current system. Governments would occasionally peg the value of their currencies, fixing them at some value for some period of time. Others believe the solution would result from a more extensive use of SDRs, denominating more securities in them, or actually having nations settle their balance of payments imbalances with them. Some believe a freely floating exchange rate system with no government intervention would be better than the present system. Intervention has seldom been successful, at least for the longer term.

Some economists desire a return to the gold standard. Those who advocate this position are usually known as "gold bugs," who see gold as a magic potion that can automatically solve the disequilibria prevalent among trading nations. This position has a small minority of advocates. Others believe that a system of multiple exchange rates—one official rate that the government uses, another rate for necessary imports, another rate for luxury goods, such as many Latin American nations have practiced—would benefit the international monetary system. This currency regime has not helped Latin America very much. Finally, many monetary economists believe that basic economic changes in the industrialized nations coupled with more international cooperation will improve the system.

When considering these proposals for their merit, it is helpful to compare the positions of the major economic players in the early 1970s with those of today's players. When a floating rate regime was being considered in 1972–73, those who desired this system the most were central bankers of the nations that faced drastic changes in their currencies, especially devaluations. They believed the fixed rate system demanded too much discipline over their domestic economies, especially in controlling inflation and interest rates, two very strong determinants of exchange rates. Those who did not want a floating rate system were primarily the executives of MNCs who thought they could not cope with exchange rates that changed frequently.

These positions have almost completely reversed today. The MNCs have learned how to measure and manage their exposure to risk of foreign exchange rate fluctuations with a variety of market and internal strategies and tactics. Although the cost has been high, as discussed in chapter 4, international firms have coped well with a world of floating exchange rates.

Meanwhile, many nations want to return to fixed exchange rates. Governments had difficulty managing their domestic economies. The result has been that monetary and fiscal policies often become transmitted to the foreign exchange markets, which

---

[29] Michael W. Klein and Eric S. Rosengren, "Foreign Exchange Intervention as a Signal of Monetary Policy," *New England Economic Review* (May/June 1991): 39–50.

[30] Feldstein, "Let the Market Decide," 24.

make the necessary changes in rates in a more nonpolitical manner. Many nations have been able to relax economic policies. Under a fixed rate system, policies such as monetary, wage, and price controls require more discipline on the part of the government.

However, many developing countries have found the benefits of floating rates to outweigh the disadvantages.[31] Some thirty-three developing and former Union of Soviet Socialist Republics countries have adopted floating rate systems. These nations have diverse economic structures and relatively simple financial systems but have been able to operate effectively with floating rate systems. Their economic indicators have performed better in most cases after adopting floating rate mechanisms. The key factor that seems to insure that floating rate systems do better in these countries is the adoption of conservative monetary and fiscal policies that result in macroeconomic stability. The periodic crises discussed previously will be fewer and less severe if governments maintain monetary and fiscal policies that are conservative and tightly enforced. The state of the art of currency stabilization is just that, an art, and either a fixed rate system or a floating rate system may demand more discipline than most governments are willing to endure.

Pros and Cons of Floating Exchange Rates

Floating or flexible foreign exchange rates have several advantages. First, each country can follow macroeconomic policies independent of the policies of other countries. To maintain fixed rates, countries have to share a common inflation experience. Suppose that the United States' inflation rate is growing faster than the German government desires. If the United States chooses 8 percent inflation and Germany only 3 percent, the dollar will steadily depreciate against the deutsche Mark. Second, floating rates allow for an orderly adjustment to differing inflation rates.

Flexible foreign exchange rates also have a number of disadvantages. First, they are not as good as fixed rates in providing international discipline on the inflationary policies of other countries. By maintaining fixed exchange rates to the dollar, for example, each country's inflation rate becomes anchored to the dollar. Thus, other countries will follow the policy established for the dollar. Second, flexible rates may be subject to destabilizing speculation, as was the case in the September 1992 currency markets because of the ERM breakdown. Speculative foreign exchange trading causes rates to be more volatile than they might be without speculation.

The era of floating exchange rates has offered the international community some important lessons.[32] Floating rates have not precluded high interest rates in countries that overspend on military programs or domestic projects. Floating rates have not eased monetary policy by the provision of an automatic corrective mechanism, even in countries such as Japan with high savings rates. Flexible exchange rates have not pro-

---

STUDY AID

By now, you should have an understanding of why nations intervene in the foreign exchange markets. You should also be aware of the degree of success such interventions achieve. Examine articles in *The Economist, Business Week, International Currency Review*, and *Euromoney* to find episodes of foreign exchange market interventions by national authorities.

---

[31] Peter J. Quirk and Hernán Cortés-Douglas, "The Experience with Floating Rates," *Finance & Development* 30 (June 1993): 28–31.

[32] Wayne Angell, "As Good as Gold," *Wall Street Journal* 22 July 1994, p. A10.

vided restrained monetary policies for countries with low savings rates and chronic balance of trade deficits, such as the United States.

SUMMARY OF ALTERNATIVE EXCHANGE RATE SYSTEMS

At the current time, the global monetary system is one of floating exchange rates that are occasionally managed or manipulated by governments. However, at the same time, several systems can be found in practice. First, when the foreign exchange markets are not being manipulated by central banks, the market is a freely floating one with supply and demand forces determining rates, i.e., a clean float.

Second, a managed floating rate system is practiced when governments do attempt to manipulate one or more currencies, i.e., a dirty float. Intervention is sometimes attempted to smooth out daily changes in rates or, as in Japan, it is a resort to unofficial pegging of rates when the Japanese resist revaluations by pegging the currency through market manipulation.

Third, some countries practice a target-zone arrangement in which a group of nations set target zones that each attempts to maintain while floating their currencies against the rest of the world. The EMS in the European Union is such a system in which fixed rates are agreed to among the members but each nation's currency is permitted to float against nonmember currencies.

Fourth, some countries still practice a fixed rate system, such as the Bretton Woods System, where a nation's currency is pegged against some major currency such as the dollar. For example, the Barbados dollar is fixed against the U.S. dollar as are some two dozen other currencies. The Barbadian dollar changes against other currencies as the U.S. dollar floats against them but never changes vis-à-vis the U.S. dollar at 2.03 Barbadian dollars/U.S. dollar. After the breakup of the Union of Soviet Socialist Republics and the independence of many of these countries, seven of the newly independent nations pegged their currencies to the Russian ruble, which floats in the international currency markets but with strong management by the Russian government. Three countries, Chile, Colombia, and Madagascar adjust their currency values according to the changes in a set of economic indicators. Figure 2-5 lists the currency values of most of the world's nations as of May 24, 1996. The value for each nation's currency is vis-à-vis the U.S. dollar. This chart is found each week in the *Wall Street Journal* and can be used to define each nation's currency and its relationship to the U.S. dollar. Thus, our current international monetary system is a hybrid of all of the systems described here.[33]

The Balance of Payments

Each nation publishes, in various degrees of complexity, a set of financial reports that demonstrate the economic status of the country. These include gross domestic product, gross national product, national income, personal income, and the balance on international transactions, i.e., the balance of payments. It is this latter document that is relevant to students of international economics and commerce.[34]

---

[33] For a good historical perspective, see Michael D. Bordo, "The Gold Standard, Bretton Woods and Other Monetary Regimes: A Historical Appraisal," *Federal Reserve Bank of St. Louis Review* (March/April 1993): 123–91.

[34] Three publications are valuable for balance of payments analysis. They are (1) the annual June issue of *The Survey of Current Business*, the U.S. Commerce Department monthly publication, which is devoted to a detailed analysis of the preceding year's U.S. Balance of Payments; (2) the *Balance of Payments Yearbook*, published by the International Monetary Fund, presents periodical balance of payments for IMF member countries; (3) the *Balance of Payments Manual*, published by the IMF, provides guidance to member countries on how balance of payments and related data on the international investment position are compiled.

World Value of the Dollar

The table below, compiled by Bank of America, gives the rates of exchange for the U.S. dollar against various currencies as of Friday May 24, 1996. Unless otherwise noted, all rates listed are middle rates of interbank bid and asked quotes, and are expressed in foreign currency units per one U.S. dollar. The rates are indicative and aren't based on, nor intended to be used as a basis for, particular transactions.

BankAmerica International doesn't trade in all the listed foreign currencies.

Country (Currency)	Value 5/24	Value 5/17	Country (Currency)	Value 5/24	Value 5/17	Country (Currency)	Value 5/24	Value 5/17
Afghanistan (Afghani -c)	4750.00	4750.00	Germany (Mark)	1.5415	1.595	Oman, Sultanate of (Rial)	0.385	0.385
Albania (Lek)	99.49	99.34	Ghana (Cedi)	1622.50	1620.50	Pakistan (Rupee -8)	34.7153	34.8369
Algeria (Dinar)	55.2683	55.0945	Gibraltar (Pound *)	1.5141	1.5142	Panama (Balboa)	1.00	1.00
Andorra (Pesela)	128.46	127.77	Greece (Drachma)	244.04	242.57	Papua N.G. (Kina)	1.287	1.2895
Andorra (Franc)	5.2165	5.1813	Greenland (Danish Krone)	5.9525	5.9205	Paraguay (Guarani -d)	2040.00	2040.00
Angola (Readjust Kwanza)	31784.00	31784.00	Grenada (E Caribbean $)	2.70	2.70	Peru (New Sol -d)	2.411	2.412
Antigua (E Caribbean $)	2.70	2.70	Guadeloupe (Franc)	5.2165	5.1813	Philippines (Peso)	26.185	26.175
Argentina (Peso)	0.9999	0.9997	Guam (U.S. $)	1.00	1.00	Pitcairn Island (N.Z.Dollar)	1.4615	1.4561
Aruba (Florin)	1.79	1.79	Guatemala (Quetzal)	6.0615	6.0638	Poland (Zloty -o)	2.693	2.6685
Australia (Australia Dollar)	1.2653	1.2491	Guinea Bissau (Peso)	18036.00	18036.00	Portugal (Escudo)	158.28	157.18
Austria (Schilling)	10.8395	10.775	Guinea Rep (Franc)	997.00	997.00	Puerto Rico (U.S. $)	1.00	1.00
Azerbaijan (Manat -9)	4376.00	4376.00	Guyana (Dollar)	138.90	138.90	Qatar (Riyal)	3.6395	3.6395
Bahamas (Dollar)	1.00	1.00	Haiti (Gourde)	16.176	16.176	Repub of Macedonia (Denar -4)	40.4952	40.3737
Bahrain (Dinar)	0.377	0.377	Honduras Rep (Lempira -d)	10.87	10.87	Republic of Yemen (Rial -a-6)	140.00	140.00
Bangladesh (Taka)	41.911	41.911	Hong Kong (Dollar)	7.7358	7.7365	Reunion, Ile de la (Franc)	5.2165	5.1813
Barbados (Dollar)	2.0113	2.0113	Hungary (Forint)	152.81	152.22	Romania (Leu)	2946.00	2933.00
Belgium (Franc)	31.69	31.43	Iceland (Krona)	67.67	67.23	Rwanda (Franc)	220.00	220.00
Belize (Dollar)	2.00	2.00	India (Rupee -m)	35.095	35.055	Saint Christopher (E Caribbean $)	2.70	2.70
Benin (C.F.A. Franc)	521.65	518.13	Indonesia (Ruplah)	2330.50	2329.50	Saint Helena (Pound Sterling *)	1.5141	1.5142
Bermuda (Dollar)	1.00	1.00	Iran (Rial -o)	3000.00	3000.00	Saint Lucia (E Caribbean $)	2.70	2.70
Bhutan (Ngulfrum)	35.095	35.055	Iraq (Dinar -o-7)	0.3109	0.3109	Saint Pierre (Franc)	5.2165	5.1813
Bolivia (Boliviano -o)	5.06	5.06	Iraq (Dinar -m-7)	1000.00	1000.00	Saint Vincent (E Caribbean $)	2.70	2.70
Bolivia (Boliviano -f)	5.07	5.07	Ireland (Punt *)	1.562	1.562	Samoa, American (U.S. $)	1.00	1.00
Botswana (Pula)	3.368	3.3557	Israel (New Shekel)	3.271	3.254	Samoa, Western (Tala)	2.445	2.4372
Bouvet Island (Norwegian Krone)	6.599	6.5785	Italy (Lira)	1560.65	1550.63	San Marino (Lira)	1560.65	1550.63
Brazil (Real)	0.9999	0.9987	Ivory Coast (C.F.A. Franc)	521.65	518.13	San Tome & Principe (Dobra)	2127.10	1985.65
Brunet (Dollar)	1.4093	1.408	Jamaica (Dollar -o)	37.75	37.75	Saudi Arabia (Riyal)	3.7503	3.7503
Bulgaria (Lev)	137.25	108.46	Japan (Yen)	106.975	106.575	Senegal (C.F.A. Franc)	521.65	518.13
Burkina Faso (C.F.A. Franc)	521.65	518.13	Jordan (Dinar)	0.709	0.709	Seychelles (Rupee)	5.035	5.0666
Burma (Kyal)	5.9217	5.9588	Kenya (Shilling)	58.20	58.20	Sierra Leone (Leone)	840.00	840.00
Burundi (Franc)	285.9553	287.7497	Kirlbati (Australia Dollar)	1.2653	1.2491	Singapore (Dollar)	1.4093	1.408
Cambodia (Riel)	2300.00	2300.00	Korea, North (Won)	2.15	2.15	Slovak (Koruna)	31.089	30.948
Cameroon (C.F.A. Franc)	521.65	518.13	Korea, South (Won)	780.90	778.70	Slovenia (Tolar)	138.58	136.43
Canada (Dollar)	1.3754	1.3696	Kuwait (Dinar)	0.302	0.3001	Solomon Islands (Solomon Dollar)	3.5348	3.5323
Cape Verde Isl (Escudo)	82.97	82.97	Laos, People DR (Kip)	920.00	920.00	Somali Rep (Shilling -d)	2620.00	2620.00
Cayman Islands (Dollar)	0.8282	0.8282	Latvia (Lat)	0.56	0.55	South Africa (Rand -c)	4.35	4.3375
Centrl African Rp (C.F.A. Franc)	521.65	518.13	Lebanon (Pound)	1575.00	1578.00	Spain (Peseta)	128.46	127.77
Chad (C.F.A. Franc)	521.65	518.13	Lesotho (Maloti)	4.35	4.3375	Sri Lanka (Rupee)	52.693	54.80
Chile (Peso -m)	406.59	406.50	Liberia (Dollar)	1.00	1.00	Sudan Rep (Pound -c)	980.00	980.00
Chile (Peso -o)	451.30	449.97	Libya (Dinar)	0.3555	0.3555	Sudan Rep (Dinar)	98.00	98.00
China (Renminbi Yuan)	8.3267	8.3293	Liechtenstein (Franc)	1.2637	1.2542	Surinam (Guilder)	410.00	410.00
Colombia (Peso -o)	1068.90	1066.575	Lithuania (Litas)	4.00	4.00	Swaziland (Lilangeni)	4.35	4.3375
Commwlth Ind Sts (s Rouble -m)	5005.00	4995.00	Luxembourg (Lux. Franc)	31.69	31.43	Sweden (Krona)	6.3885	6.7495
Comoros (Franc)	391.2375	388.5975	Macao (Pataca)	7.991	7.9918	Switzerland (Franc)	1.2637	1.2542
Congo, People Rp (C.F.A. Franc)	521.65	518.13	Madagascar DR (Franc)	3800.00	3800.00	Syria (Pound)	41.95	41.95
Costa Rica (Colon)	204.915	204.42	Malawi (Kwacha)	15.33	15.335	Taiwan (Dollar -m)	27.05	26.96
Croatia (Kuna)	5.5406	5.5285	Malaysia (Ringgit)	2.4914	2.4887	Tanzania (Shilling)	575.00	570.00
Cuba (Peso)	1.00	1.00	Maldive (Rulfiyaa)	11.77	11.77	Thailand (Baht)	25.3125	25.2845
Cyprus (Pound*)	2.102	2.1068	Mali Rep (C.F.A. Franc)	521.65	518.13	Togo, Rep (C.F.A. Franc)	521.65	518.13
Czech (Koruna -2)	27.696	27.547	Malta (Lira *)	2.7226	2.7347	Tonga Islands (Pa'anga)	1.2237	1.2185
Denmark (Danish Krone)	5.9525	5.9205	Martinique (Franc)	5.2165	5.1813	Trinidad & Tobago (Dollar)	5.735	5.735
Djibouti (Djibouti Franc)	160.00	160.00	Mauritania (Ouguiya)	137.30	137.30	Tunisia (Dinar)	0.9895	0.98
Domina (E Caribbean $)	2.70	2.70	Mauritius (Rupee)	19.595	19.465	Turkey (Lira)	78423.00	77634.50
Dominican Rep (Peso -d)	14.10	14.10	Mexico (New Peso)	7.39	7.425	Turks & Caicos (U.S. $)	1.00	1.00
Ecuador (Sucre -o)	3125.00	3143.00	Monaco (Franc)	5.2165	5.1813	Tuvalu (Australia Dollar)	1.2653	1.2491
Ecuador (Sucre -d)	3125.00	3116.00	Mongolia (Tugrik -o)	466.67	466.67	Uganda (Shilling -l)	1018.00	1017.00
Egypt (Pound)	3.3945	3.3945	Montserrat (E Caribbean $)	2.70	2.70	Ukraine (Karbovanet)	185400.00	184200.00
El Salvador (Colon -d)	8.77	8.755	Morocco (Dirham)	8.842	8.805	United Arab Emir (Dirham)	3.671	3.671
Equatorial Guinea (C.F.A. Franc)	521.65	518.13	Mozambique (Metical)	11140.50	11140.50	United Kingdom (Pound Sterling *)	1.5141	1.5142
Estonia (Kroon)	12.35	12.28	Namibia (Rand -c)	4.35	4.3375	Uruguay (Peso Uruguayo -m)	7.73	7.73
Ethiopia (Birr -o)	6.29	6.29	Nauru Island (Australia Dollar)	1.2653	1.2491	Vanuatu (Vatu)	111.05	109.88
Faeroe Islands (Danish Krone)	5.9525	5.9205	Nepal (Rupee)	56.025	56.025	Vatican City (Lira)	1560.65	1550.63
Falkland Islands (Pound *)	1.5141	1.5142	Netherlands (Guilder)	1.7243	1.7098	Venezuela (Bolivar -d-1)	470.625	466.625
Fiji (Dollar)	1.4017	1.3972	Netherlands Ant'les (Guilder)	1.79	1.79	Vietnam (Dong -o)	10960.00	10960.00
Finland (Markka)	4.7475	4.741	New Zealand (N.Z.Dollar)	1.4615	1.4561	Virgin Is, Br (U.S. $)	1.00	1.00
France (Franc)	5.2165	5.1813	Nicaragua (Gold Cordoba)	8.2931	8.2931	Virgin Is, US (U.S. $)	1.00	1.00
French Guiana (Franc)	5.2165	5.1813	Niger Rep (C.F.A. Franc)	521.65	518.13	Yugoslavia (New Dinar -3)	5.02	5.04
Franch Pacific Isl (C.F.P. Franc)	94.8454	94.2054	Nigeria (Naira -o)	22.00	22.00	Zaire Rep (New Zaire)	26221.31	25448.36
Gabon (C.F.A. Franc)	521.65	518.13	Nigeria (Naira -m)	80.75	80.75	Zambia (Kwacha)	1242.50	1242.50
Gambia (Dalasi)	9.925	9.90	Norway (Norwegian Krone)	6.599	6.5785	Zimbabwe (Dollar)	9.825	9.825

* U.S. dollars per National Currency unit. (a) Free market central bank rate. (b) Floating rate. (c) Commercial rate. (d) Free market rate. (e) Controlled. (f) Financial rate. (g) Preferential rate. (h) Nonessential imports. (i) Floating tourist rate. (j) Public transaction rate. (k) Agricultural products. (l) Priority rate. (m) Market rate. (n) Essential imports. (o) Official rate. (p) Exports. (n.a.) Not available.

(1) Venezuela, 11 December 1995: Bolivar devalued by approx 41%. (2) Czech. 28 February 1996: Fluctuation band widened for fixing the Crown to 15% from 1% (3) Yugoslavia, 26 November 1995: New Dinar devalued by approx 69.7%. (4) , 26 May 1995: Exchange rate now being quoted for Macedonia. (5) Angola, 3 July 1995: New currency called the Readjusted Kwanza introduced. (6) Republic of Yemen, 7 January 1996: Official Riyal exchange rate abolished. (7) Iraq, 17 November 1995: Market and Official rates now quoted for Iraq (8) Pakistan, 30 October 1995: Rupee devalued by approx 7%. (9) Azerbaijan, 31 August 1995: Exchange rate now being quoted for Azerbaijan.

SOURCE: *The Wall Street Journal*, May 28, 1996, p. B14. Reprinted by permission.

FIGURE 2–5 National Currency Values (May 24, 1996)

The balance of payments is a statistical compilation of all economic transactions between the home country and all other nations for a given period of time, usually one calendar year. If a transaction meets these criteria, it is an entry within the balance of payments. If it does not, the transaction is outside the balance of payments. For example, if an American flies to Spain on Delta Airlines, the airline ticket is not within the balance of payments because the transaction is between American citizens. If, however, the American flies to Spain on Iberia Airlines, the transaction would be entered in the balance of payments since it is a transaction between an American citizen and Iberia, a Spanish airline. In short, the balance of payments measures a country's payments to and its receipts from other countries.

As will be shown in the following sections, the balance of payments is an important document. The data published in the balance of payments has, however, caused a great deal of consternation to government officials in some countries, including the United States. It is alleged that two things worried President John F. Kennedy more than anything else: nuclear holocaust and the balance of payments. It seems strange to put these two items in the same category but trying to alleviate problems in the balance of payments by public policy could cause a national leader to think in this manner.

Balance of payments data are useful in a number of ways. Such data demonstrate the healthiness of a country's currency. Long-term currency movements and exchange rate changes can be predicted from the analysis of such data. Some of the data reports information about the exportation and importation of goods and services. The exportation of these items provides a supply of foreign exchange while the importation of them provides demand for foreign exchange. It is the interaction of the supply of foreign exchange and the demand for foreign exchange that creates the foreign exchange rate—the domestic price of foreign money, at some equilibrium demand and supply, the classical supply/demand schedule.

The data in the balance of payments helps in the forecast of a country's market potential in the short run. A country with a serious deficit, such as the United States, is not likely to import as much as if it has a surplus. The balance of payments data show pressure on the country's foreign exchange rate and the potential for gains and losses for a firm trading or investing in that country. Finally, continuing deficits may signal future government controls on outgoing capital movements, e.g., dividends, management fees, interest payments, or royalties to foreign firms and investors.

ECONOMIC IMPACTS ON THE BALANCE OF PAYMENTS

Several economic forces may have an impact on the balance of payments of a specific nation. Among these economic factors are the inflation rate, real growth in gross national product (GNP), interest rates, and the spot exchange rate (or current rate for exchanges of currency that day). For example, inflation may lead to price level increases, which make domestic goods and services relatively too expensive for nondomestic buyers. Exports will become less competitive and imports will become more attractive to domestic consumers. As exports decline and imports rise, the balance of trade sector in the balance of payments may become negative, and if this trade deficit is not balanced by capital inflows, the basic balance of the balance of payments may be in deficit. The basic balance is essentially the balance of all current and capital account items including merchandise exports and imports, travel and transportation, current investment income inflows and outflows, and private long-term investment inflows and outflows.

High rates of growth in GNP tend to cause consumers to import more goods and services from abroad. Higher GNP pushes personal income up and if, as in the United States, consumers have a high propensity to import because of relatively higher incomes, imports may increase faster than exports, causing a dampening effect on the balance of payments. Lower GNP will usually result in lower imports of goods and services.

Interest rates influence foreign investments in money and capital market instruments in a given country. If a country has high real interest rates relative to other countries, it will experience high inflows of funds for investment in financial instruments, as was the case in Germany in 1994. When real interest rates decline in a country, as in the United States during 1992–94, capital outflows occur and the basic balance deficit may increase. Expectations about the level of future interest rates may also have an impact on investment flows into and out of a country.

Spot exchange rates influence the relative cost of imports vis-à-vis domestic goods and the relative cost of exports vis-à-vis foreign goods in importing countries. Relatively high exchange rates of the foreign currency compared to the domestic currency discourage imports and encourage exports, as in the case of the United States and Japan. The dollar has declined against the yen, making Japanese goods less attractive to U.S. consumers and U.S. goods and services more attractive to Japanese consumers. If the domestic currency appreciates against the foreign currency, export prices to foreigners will be less attractive and import prices to domestic citizens will be more attractive.

SOME BALANCE OF PAYMENTS CONCEPTS

The balance of payments of every country is basically alike in characteristics. However, some countries have a very simplistic format while others, such as the United States, have a very complex format. To examine the differences among countries, the IMF's *Balance of Payments Yearbook* should be consulted. This is a collection of the periodical balance of payments of the IMF member countries during each calendar year.

All transactions that require a payment to a foreign citizen or government, i.e., imports of goods and services, are entered in the balance of payments accounts as a debit item with a negative ($-$) sign. All transactions that result in a payment from foreign countries, i.e., exports of goods and services, are entered as a credit item with a positive ($+$) sign.

Essentially, the balance of payments is based on a double entry bookkeeping system. Every transaction enters the balance of payments accounts twice, once as a credit and once as a debit. For example, suppose that the British auto manufacturer Jaguar, although owned by Ford, an American company, ships a car to an American dealer, for $60,000. This import represents a payment by an American citizen to a foreign citizen and is entered as a debit in the balance of payments accounts. However, Jaguar Car Company may open a bank account and deposit the $60,000. This transaction will be entered as a credit of $60,000 in the balance of payments accounts since it is the purchase of a service by a foreign citizen from a domestic citizen. This deposit may further be loaned by the U.S. bank to another bank overseas in the Eurocurrency interbank market. Such a transaction, a payment by a U.S. citizen to a foreign citizen, is entered in the balance of payments accounts as a debit of $60,000. The Eurobank may then lend the funds to an electric utility company in the United States so that this company can pay its social security liability to the U.S. government (or any other bill), and this transaction will be entered in the balance of payments accounts as a credit of $60,000 since it is a payment by a foreign citizen to a domestic citizen.

More Balance of Payments Entry Examples[35]

Assume that Kaufmann's Department Store in the United States imports $500,000 of men's sport jackets from Colombia in 1994 and has to pay for the jackets 30 days after the shipment has been received. This transaction has two components: an import and a 30-day loan. The import is a current account debit. The loan is a short-term capital credit. If Kaufmann's pays the Colombian exporter directly while borrowing from an off-shore bank, say one in Panama, the import and the loan represent two different transactions and a double entry in the balance of payments is made for each. The following entries are made:

1. the import and payment:

	Debits	Credits
Imports	$500,000	
Short-term claims on foreigners		$500,000

2. loan:

	Debits	Credits
Short-term liabilities to foreigners		$500,000
Short-term claims on foreigners	$500,000	

The loan by the Panamanian bank is a short-term capital inflow and, therefore, a credit. The cash is paid to an account owned by Kaufmann's, a U.S. importer, and, being a short-term capital outflow, is a debit. When Kaufmann's repays the Panamanian bank with interest of 8 percent per year, or 0.67 percent for 30 days, it makes a payment of $503,350. This transaction is entered in the balance of payments as follows:

3. repayment of the loan:

	Debits	Credits
Short-term liabilities to foreigners	$500,000	
Interest	3,350	
Short-term claims on foreigners		$503,350

The repayment of the loan eliminates the $500,000 of foreign short-term capital inflow while the interest is debited to services in the current account.

Suppose another scenario in which Glaxo Holdings PLC, a British pharmaceuticals producer, makes a decision to build a production plant in the United States for manufacture of a new arthritis drug. It buys an existing plant from Squibb Products for $50 million. Glaxo then purchases $25 million of equipment and machinery from a British manufacturer and sends it to the new plant. It sells $75 million of its stock on the U.S. capital market in New York in the form of American Depositary Receipts (ADRs). The following balance of payments entries are made:

4. direct investment in the United States by a foreign company:

	Debits	Credits
Direct investment		$50 million
Short-term claims on foreigners	$50 million	
Direct investment		25 million
Imports	25 million	
Long-term portfolio investment	75 million	
Short-term claims on foreigners		75 million

---

[35] This example is based on a discussion of this topic in George Feiger and Bertrand Jacquillat, *International Finance: Text and Cases* (Boston, MA: Allyn and Bacon, 1982), pp. 100–2.

The foreign direct investment in the purchase of a plant by Glaxo, a foreign company, in the United States is a credit in the capital account and U.S. citizens own $50 million in short-term claims on foreigners. In addition, $25 million of direct investment is used to pay for the import, a current account debit item, of $25 million of equipment and machinery from a foreign manufacturer. The issue of Glaxo ADRs represents stock actually issued and deposited in a bank depository overseas and reduces an account held overseas by a U.S. bank.

One account in the balance of payments seems to violate the principle that every debit has an offsetting credit and vice versa. This is the unilateral transfer account or unrequited transfers, an account found in the current account of the balance of payments. The major accounts are discussed in the next section. Unrequited transfers may be private or public. These are payments that are outflows of funds, or debit items, for which no offsetting credit item appears to exist. Private unilateral or unrequited transfers are primarily pension payments, either private or social security payments, that are sent to foreign residents who lived and worked in the United States and who have retired and moved back to their home countries. Technically, the offsetting credit items for unrequited transfers occurred earlier when these foreign residents may have worked for companies that manufactured export items. Public, or official, unrequited transfers are economic or military assistance exports made to foreign countries in the form of government-to-government grants. Other examples of unilateral transfers include contributions by the American Jewish community to institutions in Israel and by Irish-Americans who contribute to the Irish Republican Army.

Another underlying principle is that the balance of payments is always in balance. Analyses and commentaries often discuss imbalances, surpluses or deficits, in the balance of payments. This is not accurate. The deficits, for example, in the U.S. balance of payments, or the surpluses, for example, in the Japanese balance of payments, are surpluses or deficits in certain parts of the balance of payments. The bottom line of a country's balance of payments has been adjusted by various entries so that no imbalance—surplus or deficit—exists.

The Major Accounts

The balance of payments is composed of three major sections: the current account, the capital account, and the official reserves account. Figure 2–6 provides a general outline of the balance of payments. The current account entries are for those transactions that take place and are settled during the period of the balance of payments, generally the calendar year. Capital account entries are for those transactions that have a longer time horizon, such as direct and portfolio investments by one country's companies in another country. Official reserve account entries show the change in the nation's official reserves as a result of what occurs in the current and capital accounts.

FIGURE 2–6 Balance of Payments Accounts

- Current Account
  Merchandise trade
  Service trade
  Unilateral transfers
- Capital Account
  Long-term capital flows
  Short-term capital flows
  Statistical discrepancies
- Official Reserves Account
  Official reserve assets
  Foreign official assets

Nation's RECEIPTS less its PAYMENTS equals the Nation's BALANCE OF PAYMENTS[1]

EXPORTS of Merchandise	IMPORTS of Merchandise
	Balance of Trade
Services	Services
	Balance of Goods and Services
Private and government aid	Private and government aid
	Balance on Current Account
CAPITAL INFLOWS	CAPITAL OUTFLOWS
From	From
Investment	Investment
Government borrowing	Government lending
Long-term private borrowing	Long-term private lending
	Basic Balance[2]
Short-term private borrowing	Short-term private lending
Liquid	Liquid
Nonliquid	Nonliquid
	Official Settlements Balance
SALES of Reserves	PURCHASES of Reserves

[1] Each balance in this table is a cumulative measure of all the items above it.

[2] The basic balance is also known as the balance on current and long-term capital account.

Source: Anthony M. Solomon, "Toward a More Resilient International Financial System," *Federal Reserve Bank of Minneapolis Quarterly Review* 7 (Summer 1983): 7.

FIGURE 2–7 The Balance of Payments

Another way of looking at the balance of payments is to examine the three sections in more detail. Figure 2-7 shows that a nation's receipts less its payments equals the nation's balance of payments. The settlement account entries are those that affect the imbalance on current and capital account, the so-called basic balance, and that will eventually bring the balance of payments of one nation into equilibrium with the rest of the world.

Perhaps the most important section in the balance of payments is the balance of trade, the net balance of exports and imports of merchandise trade. When a surplus or deficit is mentioned, it is the balance of trade to which the commentator is most often referring. In the U.S. balance of payments, for example, net merchandise trade was in surplus for all of the twentieth century, until 1971.

Since 1971, when the balance of trade was −$2.7 billion, it has been in deficit almost every year. The U.S. trade deficit in 1994 was $166.1 billion, up 25 percent from the 1993 trade deficit of $132.6 billion, which was 38 percent higher than the deficit in 1992. The 1992 deficit amounted to $96.1 billion, up 30 percent from the trade deficit of $73.8 billion in 1991. It was the threat of a trade deficit that forced President Nixon to devalue the dollar and officially close the gold door on August 15, 1971, and it was the $6.4 billion U.S. trade deficit in 1972 that led him to devalue the dollar again in early 1973.

In the world of perfect competition in which only two nations trade a single good with each other, the balance of payments of a nation will reflect only a current account balance composed of the trade balance. It is only when the global economy becomes sufficiently complex that nations settle their trade imbalances with long-term loans or when investment is placed abroad that the capital account is needed to reflect these long-term capital flows. Mature debtor nations will have extensive capital account transactions.

TABLE 2–4. U.S. Balance of Payments Year-ends 1991, 1992, 1993, and 1994 (millions of U.S.$)

	1991	1992	1993	1994
Exports of goods, services, and income	708,489	731,373	755,533	838,820
Merchandise, excluding military	416,937	440,361	456,866	502,485
Services	164,260	176,563	184,811	198,716
Income receipts on investments	127,292	114,449	113,856	137,619
Imports of goods, services, and income	− 723,388	− 767,217	− 827,312	− 954,304
Merchandise, excluding military	− 490,739	− 536,458	− 589,441	− 668,584
Service	− 118,378	− 120,850	− 127,961	− 138,829
Income payments on investments	− 114,272	− 109,109	− 109,910	146,891
Unilateral transfers	6,575	− 32,042	− 32,117	35,761
U.S. assets abroad, net (increase/capital outflow [−])	− 59,974	− 61,510	− 147,898	− 125,851
U.S. official reserve assets, net	5,763	3,901	− 1,379	5,346
U.S. government assets, other than official reserve assets, net	2,905	− 1,652	− 306	− 322
U.S. private assets, net	− 68,643	− 63,759	− 146,213	− 130,875
Foreign assets in the U.S., net (increase/capital inflow [+])	83,439	146,504	230,698	291,365
Foreign official assets, net	17,564	40,858	71,681	39,409
Other foreign assets, net	65,875	105,646	159,017	251,956
Allocations of special drawing rights				
Statistical discrepancy	− 15,140	− 17,108	21,096	− 14,269
Memorandum:				
Balance on current account	− 8,324	− 67,886	− 103,896	− 151,245

Source: Survey of Current Business, 73–4 (June 1993, June 1994, June 1995).

Prior to the 1971 U.S. trade deficit, the trade balance was almost always in surplus and was considered a cushion for the capital account, which was generally in deficit, since U.S. direct and U.S. portfolio foreign investments exceeded foreign investment in the United States. When the balance of payments is said to be in surplus or deficit, it is the balance on current and capital account that is actually in surplus or deficit. This is also referred to as the basic balance, i.e., the balance on current and capital account. Such a balance is an indicator of longer term trends, especially with regard to the size of a nation's reserves.

For many nations, their current account may be in disequilibrium but the capital account disequilibrium may offset the current account deviation from equilibrium. For example, Japan has generally had a large current account surplus because of that country's large merchandise trade surplus. However, the surplus is used to invest large amounts in foreign countries in plant and equipment, real estate, and other investments. Thus, their capital account may run a large deficit. The United States has generally run a large current account deficit because of the deficit in the trade balance. However, because the United States is considered a safe haven economy, i.e., a nation with little political risk, large inflows of foreign investments create a surplus in the capital account of the U.S. balance of payments.

The official settlements balance measures the amount of governmental funds needed to finance payments flows. It is the amount in the balance of payments still remaining in either surplus or deficit after all private short-term and long-term transactions have been settled. At this point in the balance of payments, any imbalance will be settled at the official (government) level by movements of international reserves be-

tween central banks or other official agencies or by government accounts receivables or payables being increased or decreased.

To understand the balance of payments principles, it is useful to look at the U.S. balance of payments for 1991–94, as shown in Table 2–4. The United States for some time has consistently run large deficits in merchandise trade and in the current account. Some analysts believe that the United States can run a current account deficit because the emerging LDCs are short of dollars. In fact, nonoil-exporting countries such as South Korea, Taiwan, and some in Latin America have been running large trade surpluses with the United States but reinvesting these proceeds in U.S. securities. In 1993, these countries acquired $32 billion of U.S. international reserves from their surpluses as well as $45 billion of long-term U.S. securities, not to mention a large part of the $165 billion of short-term securities sold overseas.[36] This may explain why U.S. government policy has not been too strict on these countries with regard to the U.S. trade deficit with them.

U.S. GOVERNMENT BALANCE OF PAYMENTS POLICY—HISTORICAL LESSONS

Most countries put off or downplay balance of payments policy. This was especially so before the advent of flexible exchange rates. If a currency needed its par value changed, most governments delayed this decision, or if they did change the par value of their currency, they did not make a sufficient change. For example, if a currency was overpriced and needed to be devalued, most countries would delay the decision until speculative pressures built up in the forex markets. When the country finally devalued, the devaluation was generally not enough to bring the currency back into total equilibrium.

A devaluation causes a nation's exports to be relatively lower priced compared with other nations' goods. Imports will be relatively more expensive. Thus, exports will increase, imports should decline, and the trade balance will improve. However, an increase in net exports increases national income, the money supply will increase, costs will increase, and prices of exports will increase commensurately unless the devaluing nation implements some type of economic policy designed to keep prices down, either by tighter monetary policy or by fiscal policy that calls for reduced government spending and/or higher taxes. Most countries find such domestic policies difficult to implement because of political reasons. The result is higher prices for exports, trade deficits, and an overpriced currency.

The United States has been a good example of this problem. Throughout the 1950s and 1960s, the U.S. balance of trade was in surplus but flows of funds to foreign countries for direct and portfolio investment and foreign economic assistance from the U.S. government resulted in a basic balance deficit, i.e., a deficit in the current and cap-

---

STUDY AID

By now you should be familiar with the basic accounting concepts of a nation's international balance of payments. This document has some of the elements of a balance sheet, e.g., static measurements, and some of the elements of an income statement, e.g., cash flows. Some of the problems at the end of this chapter will demonstrate the format and placement of certain economic transactions between one nation and the rest of the world.

---

[36] "Emerging Nations Can't Get Enough Greenbacks," *Business Week* (April 4, 1994): 28.

ital account. Economists have advocated that the basic balance deficits (small by today's standards) furnished needed liquidity for the rest of the world, especially the wartorn countries of Europe and the developing nations. This was said to be a small price to pay to reconstruct the world and would contribute to economic growth in the United States in the long term.

Various U.S. administrations promoted various plans to alleviate the basic balance deficits. The Eisenhower administration thought the problem lay in foreign aid distributed by the United States to LDCs. The Kennedy administration demonstrated that this was not the problem because most U.S. bilateral aid was tied to the purchase of U.S. exports of agricultural supplies and other goods to LDCs. In fact, the Johnson administration later tied nearly 95 percent of U.S. aid to the purchase of U.S. goods and services. Under such a policy, each reduction of $1.00 in foreign aid would actually reduce U.S. exports by $0.95.

The Interest Equalization Tax

The Kennedy administration proposed the first restrictions on private long-term capital flows. In 1963, it proposed legislation to enact an interest equalization tax (IET) on foreign portfolio investments. Although U.S. companies were investing heavily in plant and equipment overseas, especially in western Europe, President Kennedy, always the consummate politician, believed that restrictions on these flows might hurt his political organization. However, Americans had also begun to invest in foreign stocks and bonds to a greater degree during the early 1960s. More information about foreign investments was forthcoming and the returns on foreign securities were higher than on comparable U.S. securities, with commensurate risk. The deficit in net foreign portfolio investments in the balance of payments seemed to increase at an increasing rate during that time. Thus, a tax on these investments was proposed in 1963.

The debate in Congress lasted nearly nine months. By the time the IET was passed in 1964, Lyndon Johnson was president. This law imposed an effective 15 percent tax on Americans' purchases of foreign stocks and bonds. It was believed this tax would reduce the effective return on foreign securities and make them less acceptable to American investors. The tax, like the wartime telephone tax, was to be a temporary tax with a two-year life before being reconsidered by Congress. This tax lasted ten years and was effectively abolished in 1974 when the Nixon administration did not request that it be renewed.

It is unclear how much the IET alleviated the U.S. balance of payments basic balance deficit. From 1960 through 1963, the purchases of foreign securities by Americans nearly doubled. In the first year of IET, such securities declined by nearly 40 percent but rose in the second year of the tax when investors found loopholes in the law. These loopholes were closed in 1966 and foreign securities purchases by Americans declined that year by more than 35 percent. However in 1967, U.S. investors nearly tripled their purchases of foreign securities and continued at the 1967 level of more than $1.2 billion each year during 1968 and 1969. The law was tightened in 1970 and purchases of foreign securities declined dramatically for 1970 and 1971. However, foreign purchases of U.S. securities increased dramatically during this period, particularly in the 1968–71 period and the U.S. government relaxed its emphasis on the IET. It is fairly clear that one major financial market was formed because of the IET. The Eurobond market was spawned with the 1963 issue by the Italian company Autostrade of a 5.5 percent Eurobond issue denominated in U.S. dollars, a new debt instrument that shifted international market activity from New York to London to avoid the extra cost imposed by the IET.

Voluntary Controls Programs

The Johnson administration recommended several measures to alleviate the balance of payments problems. One suggestion was to impose a $100 visa fee. The travel and transportation account in the current account of the U.S. balance of payments, the so-called T & T account, had consistently had a $1–2 billion net deficit since more Americans traveled overseas during that period than foreigners traveled to the United States. This was quickly discarded as a potential policy because, among other reasons, the U.S. Government had encouraged Americans to travel abroad for educational objectives under the Fulbright Grant Program. A $100 visa expense would discourage many Americans from traveling overseas.

The Johnson administration placed its emphasis on the capital account. First, U.S. foreign aid was tied even tighter to the purchase of American goods. At one time, 95 percent of U.S. economic assistance was tied to the purchase of U.S. exports of goods and services. Second and most important, President Johnson believed an important outflow item in the balance of payments was foreign direct investment by U.S. business firms and banks. Johnson did not have the fears of loss of political support from restricting these investments as did President Kennedy. Thus, the Voluntary Controls Program (VCP) was made operative in 1965.

The VCP restricted flows of foreign direct investment by U.S. companies. The program effectively singled out 600 U.S. companies doing the bulk of international trade and investment and requested that they voluntarily improve their own balance of payments. In other words, if the U.S. company exported, it should export more. If it imported, it should import less. If it invested abroad, it should invest less. In fact, a formula was adopted that limited U.S. foreign direct investment by companies to a small increase or no increase over the average of the preceding two or three years. It should have increased dividends or interest payments from the foreign operation to the parent company. The program also asked U.S. banks to reduce their movements of funds abroad and to remit more funds back to the parent bank.

The results of the VCP at first were not very effective. U.S. direct investment abroad increased in 1966 to $3.7 billion from $3.5 billion in 1965. In 1967, the U.S. government increased the number of firms asked to participate in the program to 900—those companies that did the vast bulk of international business. These companies were essentially told that if they did not voluntarily control their international outflows of funds, a mandatory program would be implemented. By the end of 1967, this voluntary program appeared to be ineffective.

Mandatory Controls Program

By the end of 1967, the Johnson administration believed that the VCP had not worked. The basic balance deficit had nearly doubled from $1.7 billion to $3.3 billion. Thus, the U.S. government initiated the mandatory controls program (MCP) on January 1, 1968. To facilitate this program, the Office of Foreign Direct Investment (OFDI) was established in the U.S. Department of Commerce. The world was divided into three sets of countries. U.S. companies were restricted in their foreign direct investments abroad depending on the set of countries in which their overseas operations were located. A U.S. company could transfer no funds for direct investment to subsidiaries located in continental western Europe, where most of the foreign subsidiaries with the highest growth rates were located. A U.S. company could invest an amount which was 105 percent of the annual average of their 1965–67 investments in LDCs. The third group of countries represented nations politically close to the United States, such as Great Britain, Brazil, and other leading LDCs. U.S. company direct investment was limited to 65 percent of the 1965–67 annual average. Each company investing overseas had to furnish data to the OFDI to show their compliance with the law.

In spite of the intentions of the program, U.S. direct investment abroad increased to $3.3 billion in 1969, $4.4 billion in 1970, and $4.8 billion in 1971. The program may have slowed the flow of funds for FDI but it did not reduce these flows. The mandatory controls program and the IET were abolished by the Nixon administration but only after the two dollar devaluations, the global realignment of currency values, and the establishment of a new international monetary system built on floating exchange rates.

Policies Since Mandatory Controls

Since the 1970s when the interest equalization tax and the mandatory controls program were abolished, the U.S. government has relied on interest rate controls by the Federal Reserve System designed to keep interest rates relatively high, in the guise of fighting inflation, and promotion of U.S. exports by opening up new markets overseas. High merchandise trade deficits and current account deficits have been tolerated. Occasional foreign exchange market interventions have been orchestrated by the G-7 central banks. Foreign exchange market intervention and its relative futility are discussed in chapter 3. The major result from these U.S. policies seems to have been a large increase in the global supply of dollars. This, coupled with recessions in major trading partners of the U.S. and a large U.S. federal budget deficit has caused a general decline in the value of the U.S. dollar since 1985.

Summary and Conclusions

An overview of the international monetary system and its history has been presented in this chapter. The world has moved from a relatively simple gold standard that used gold, then pound sterling and dollars, to settle international transactions to a system of flexible exchange rates with occasional government intervention in a foreign exchange market handled by international banks trading $1 trillion of currency every day. This market is discussed in detail in chapter 3.

The accounting for transactions of the world's nations is presented in the balance of payments of each of these nations. This economic accounting system was discussed in this chapter. Government policies designed to bring these accounts into equilibrium were discussed and demonstrated the frustration on the part of many national governments resulting from conflicts among price stability, rising national income, and falling unemployment—all at the same time.

Finally, the relationship between the balance of payments and the foreign exchange market is quite important. The former was examined in this chapter and the latter is discussed in the next chapter. The balance of payments contains those transactions that are credit items and that result in a supply of foreign exchange and debit items that result in a demand for foreign exchange. In the foreign exchange market, the price of foreign money (the foreign exchange rate) is determined by the intersection in a demand-supply schedule of the demand for foreign exchange and the supply of foreign exchange at some given quantity of foreign exchange demanded and supplied. This simple relationship is at the heart of foreign exchange. International trade and investment cannot be accomplished without foreign exchange. This relationship and the foreign exchange market and the role of banks is discussed in chapter 3 while theories for determination of foreign exchange rates for future delivery are also

discussed in chapter 3. In addition, the exposure to various types of foreign exchange risk, its measurement, and management by MNCs are examined in chapter 4.

Additional Readings

Balance of Payments Yearbook. Washington, D.C.: International Monetary Fund, any year.

Bean, Charles R. "Economic and Monetary Union in Europe." *The Journal of Economic Perspectives* (Fall 1992): 31–52.

Bordo, Michael D. "The Gold Standard, Bretton Woods and Other Monetary Regimes: A Historical Appraisal," *Review of the Federal Reserve Bank of St. Louis* 75 (March/April 1993): 123–91.

Coombs, Charles A. *The Arena of International Finance.* New York: John Wiley & Sons, 1976.

Dominguez, Kathryn M., and Jeffrey A. Frankel. *Does Foreign Exchange Intervention Work?* Washington, D.C.: Institute of International Economics, 1993.

Krieger, Andrew (with Edward Claflin). *The Money Bazaar.* New York: Times Books, 1992.

Neely, Christopher J. "Realignments of Target Zone Exchange Rate Systems: What Do We Know?" *Federal Reserve Bank of St. Louis Review* 76 (September/October 1994): 23–34.

Svensson, Lars E.O. "The Simplest Test of Target Zone Credibility." *IMF Staff Papers.* September 1991, pp. 655–65.

Yoichi, Funabashi. *Managing the Dollar: From the Plaza to the Louvre.* Washington, D.C.: Institute of International Economics, 1989.

Zurlinden, Mathias, "The Vulnerability of Pegged Exchange Rates: The British Pound in the ERM." *Federal Reserve Bank of St. Louis Review* 75 (September/October 1993): 41–56.

Discussion Questions

1. Compare and contrast the gold standard and the gold exchange standard.
2. What happened at Bretton Woods, New Hampshire? What were the intentions of this conference?
3. Country spokespersons have advocated a return to a fixed exchange rate global system. Discuss their reasons for a return to this international monetary system.
4. Discuss the reasons for the currency crisis of 1992.
5. What caused the dollar crisis of 1994–95? What recommendations would you have made to solve that "crisis"?
6. Briefly describe the various exchange rate systems in effect around the world. Give examples of each.
7. Define the balance of payments.
8. What does the balance of payments tell analysts?
9. Analyze the various economic impacts on the balance of payments and their effects.
10. The goal of the U.S. balance of payments policy from 1960 to 1975 was to avoid devaluation of the dollar. Discuss some of the policies implemented to solve the U.S. balance of payments problems.
11. What was the interest equalization tax? What did it equalize? Was it effective?
12. How would you solve the persistent trade, current account, and basic balance deficits in the U.S. balance of payments?
13. Suppose that foreign exchange rates between Great Britain and Germany are irrevocably fixed. What will be the relationship between British interest rates and German interest rates? Why? What will be the result if one country incurs much higher inflation than the other country does?

14. Comment on the following statement:

> Losses from foreign exchange intervention can be explained by attempts of a central bank to maintain an exchange rate when its country's equilibrium level experiences a change. The central bank is able to influence the exchange rate for a period of time. However, market forces eventually force an adjustment and the central bank realizes a loss.

15. Comment on the following statement:

> From the *Financial Times*, June 25, 1994: "Up to 17 central banks, led by the Fed, bought in excess of $3bn(£1.95bn) three days after the dollar had fallen briefly below ¥100, a post-1945 low. The dollar initially rallied on the intervention, climbing to ¥101.8 and DM 1.61, but then fell back to ¥100.9 and DM 1.5972 by the London close. It closed in New York at ¥100.525 and DM 1.584, below the levels at which the central banks first intervened."

Problems

1. Assume the following international transactions:
   a. a Japanese company increases its bank deposit in a California bank by $1,000,000;
   b. the Algerians buy $5,000,000 worth of Canadian wheat;
   c. an Ohio manufacturer ships $5,000,000 worth of electric motors to England;
   d. an American retiree purchases a condominium on the Costa del Sol in Spain for $3,500,000;
   e. Caterpillar Company remits $4,000,000 in dividends from its European subsidiary to the parent company in Peoria;
   f. Korean Airlines buys a new Boeing 777 jet airplane, including parts, from the Seattle plant for $140,000,000;
   g. Honda Company in Marysville, Ohio, declares a $10,000,000 dividend to its parent headquarters in Japan;
   h. Daimler-Benz builds a $100,000,000 auto manufacturing plant in Virginia;
   i. the U.S. government gives $30,000,000 in foreign aid to Rwanda;
   j. Japanese carmakers export 1 million cars at $20,000 each, landed value in the United States, to U.S. car dealers.

   Prepare a balance of payments using these transactions and show the net merchandise trade balance, the balance on current account, the basic balance, and the international settlements balance.

2. If the basic balance in the U.S. balance of payments is in deficit by $40 billion and $20 billion of short-term liquid funds flow into the country during 1995, what can the U.S. government do to balance the remaining deficit? Be specific.

3. Consult the IMF publication, *Balance of Payments Yearbook*. Select the balance of payments of a nation not your own and write a three-page analysis of why the basic balance of payments is in deficit or surplus.

4. Assume the following merchandise trade transactions by Americans with foreign companies:
   a. U.S. department stores import $20 million of finished mens' suits from South American countries;
   b. Champion Company in Toledo, Ohio, exports $10 million of spark plugs to African auto repair shops;
   c. DeBeers Ltd. of South Africa ships $100 million of diamonds to New York diamond merchants;
   d. McDonnell-Douglas ships $500 million worth of MD-80 airliners to European airlines;
   e. American farmers ship $50 million of wheat to Russia;
   f. Ford Motor Company ships $50 million of engines from its Mexican plant to its German manufacturing subsidiary;

g. RJR-Nabisco ships $50 million of cigarettes from its U.S. plant to Spanish tobacco shops;

h. Timken Company ships $50 million of tapered roller bearings from its Canton, Ohio, plant to manufacturers in England;

i. IBM ships $50 million of laptop computers from its Sindelfingen, Germany, plant to retail stores in Hong Kong.

Using this data, calculate the net merchandise trade balance of the United States.

3

The Foreign Exchange Market, Forecasting Exchange Rates, and Parity Relationships

---

Major Objectives of Chapter 3

(1) To present an overview of the foreign exchange market, (2) to discuss the function of forecasting foreign exchange rates, and (3) to examine the five important relationships, i.e., theories to explain future exchange rates.

Key terms to be learned in chapter 3:

- direct exchange rate
- forward rate
- cross rates
- international Fisher effect
- forward-spot relation
- indirect exchange rate
- discount
- purchasing power parity
- interest rate parity
- Bankhaus Herstatt
- premium
- Fisher effect
- covered interest

Introduction

The life blood of international trade and investment is foreign exchange. Foreign exchange, or forex, is foreign money. No foreign transaction is possible without foreign exchange, in some form or another. The amount of foreign exchange sloshing around the world is difficult to measure but it has been estimated that more than $1 trillion is

traded daily in the foreign exchange markets. In September 1992, when the European Monetary System nearly collapsed, approximately $1 trillion of foreign exchange was traded each day. When an American shops at Macy's, the Gap, or K-Mart, many of the products offered are foreign made. Although the American buys these goods with dollars, the original purchase by the American department store requires foreign exchange. When an American buys a Japanese built Honda or Toyota automobile, the original purchase by the importer required foreign exchange. When Japanese security dealers buy U.S. Treasury bonds, foreign exchange is required. Oil is priced and traded in dollars; thus, any foreign country importing oil must obtain dollars in the foreign exchange market.

The focus in this chapter is on three major areas: the foreign exchange market, forecasting foreign exchange rates, and the parity relationships between spot and future exchange rates presented in theory. In the first part of this chapter, the organization and nature of the foreign exchange market and the role of its major institutions, international banks, will be examined. The discussion will move to the mechanics of foreign exchange trading and how spot and forward exchange rates are determined.

The foreign exchange market is considered the largest global financial market and, perhaps, the most efficient one. Volume traded in the market and the depth of trading has much to do with this supposition. For example, the total international trade in goods and services on an annual basis is approximately $4.5 trillion. Another $1–1.5 trillion per year can be added to this total for foreign direct investment by all countries. The global volume for portfolio investment transactions, such as equities, bonds, and derivatives, probably amounts to $1–2 trillion per year. Thus, total international commercial transactions on an annual basis amount to as much as $8 trillion per year. If annual foreign exchange market volume amounts to as much as $250–300 trillion or more, the ratio of foreign exchange traded to the amount actually needed for international transactions may be as high as 30–1. Foreign exchange dealers, when queried by banking regulators as to why this ratio is so high, suggesting it should be closer to a 1:1 ratio, justify such trading volume by stating that the liquidity furnished by a 30:1 ratio is necessary for the presence of an orderly and viable market where exchange rates are stable and volatility is minimal.

Foreign Exchange Markets

THE ROLE OF COMMERCIAL BANKS

Large international commercial banks play a major role in the global foreign exchange markets. Banks globally trade as much as 94–95 percent of all foreign exchange. Foreign currency is traded in two different prices: spot rate, the current price being quoted at any time during the trading day, and the forward rate. The forward rate is the price of currency for delivery at some specific time in the future, and this price and the spot rate are set by market forces in the foreign exchange market.

Of all foreign exchange traded in the interbank foreign exchange market, 70 percent is traded at the spot rate; the remainder is traded at some forward rate. The 5–6 percent of foreign exchange not traded on the foreign exchange market is traded in the form of currency futures contracts on organized futures exchanges such as the International Monetary Market at the Chicago Mercantile Exchange or the London International Financial Futures Exchange. A discussion of the specific role of commercial banks in the foreign exchange markets is included in chapter 10.

The World as a Marketplace

The foreign exchange market, the world's largest financial market, is almost a 24-hour market. As one foreign exchange trading center closes, another opens. These marketplaces overlap. For example, when it is 3:00 P.M. in Tokyo, it is 2:00 P.M. in Hong Kong. When it is 3:00 P.M. in Hong Kong, it is 1:00 P.M. in Singapore. When it is 3:00 P.M. in Singapore, it is noon in Bahrain. When it is 3:00 P.M. in Bahrain, it is noon in Frankfurt and Zurich and 11:00 A.M. in London. When it is 3:00 P.M. in London, it is 10:00 A.M. in New York. When it is 3:00 P.M. in New York, it is noon in Los Angeles. When it is 3:00 P.M. in Los Angeles, it is 9:00 A.M. the next day in Sydney, Australia. Nearly two-thirds of foreign exchange trading takes place in London, New York, and Tokyo. In the morning when New York and London markets are open, foreign exchange trading is at its heaviest. Senior traders may have Reuters screens in their homes so that they are able to trade throughout the night. A map of the major international financial markets is shown in Figure 3–1 with time zones included for each major market.

The European forex markets usually open around 8:30–9:00 A.M., with the London market opening at about the same time, even when the London market is one hour behind the Continent. Market-makers open the day with relatively moderate currency exposures that they have remaining from the previous day. Opening quotations are usually based on closing rates of the previous time zone but may be updated by quotations from banks established in the country of the currencies being quoted. European markets tend to be less volatile than the New York or Far Eastern markets after the European markets have closed for the day.

After the market-maker has heard some quotes in this manner, he/she will establish his/her own buying and selling quotations for a currency. These quotations are to trade a certain volume of foreign exchange, based on the various limits set by the market-maker's bank. These limits are discussed in chapter 10.

Transactions in foreign exchange in the interbank market are executed on a good-faith basis. Trades are made by telephone or by other electronic means with written

FIGURE 3–1 Major International Financial Centers with Trading Time Zones

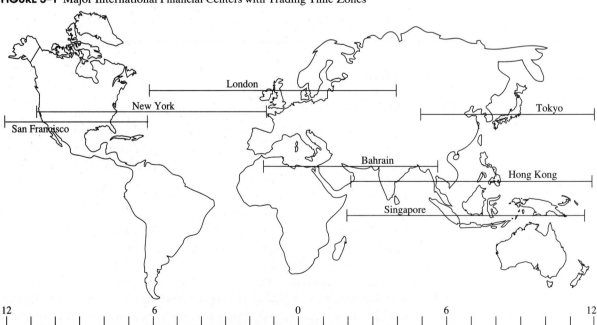

Hours Difference from Greenwich Mean Time

confirmations to follow later in the day. Traders operate on the principle of *meum pactum*, or "my word is my bond." Foreign exchange trading is so fast and furious that traders would not be able to operate efficiently if they did not trade under this principle. Mistakes in trading do occur. Incorrect direction of trades is noted on the trade slips. Incorrect price or volume information may be noted. Incorrect payment instructions are occasionally exchanged by traders. These mistakes must be corrected by written confirmation as soon as possible.

The most notorious example of the settlement risk occurring in foreign exchange trading is the case of the Bankhaus Herstatt. Herstatt was a Cologne, Germany-based private bank that received funds for massive foreign exchange trades from large New York banks, in 1974, but did not deliver the currency against those liabilities before the German banking authorities permanently closed the bank. The risk that arose from such a transaction is now commonly referred to as "Herstatt risk." This will be discussed in more detail later.

Foreign exchange trading by banks is highly concentrated. Twenty banks worldwide handle half of all forex business. A representation of the international network for forex trading is presented in Figure 3–2.

The Spot Market

Typical foreign exchange transactions involve trades of one currency for another in the spot or cash market, or forward transactions. Spot transactions involve today's

FIGURE 3–2 Structure of Foreign Exchange Markets

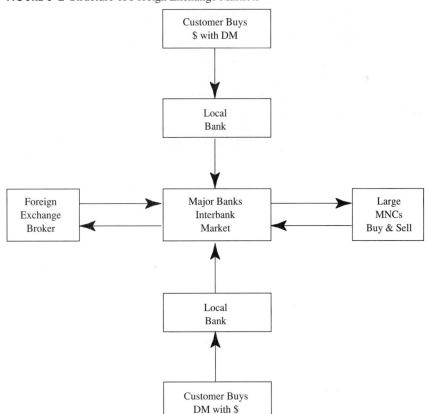

Source: K. Alec Chrystal, "A Guide to Foreign Exchange Markets," *Bulletin Federal Reserve Bank of St. Louis* (March 1984): 9.

prices of currency and delivery of the currency within two business days, except for Canadian dollars, which must be delivered within one day. Forward transactions are those that involve the purchase or sale of foreign currency for delivery at some fixed future date with the rate fixed at the time of sale. Settlement is not made until the currency is delivered by the seller at the fixed future date. Forward transactions will be discussed in a subsequent section.

The following example is representative of a spot forex transaction. Company A has £100,000 and needs dollars. Company B has dollars and needs £100,000. The companies buy and sell these currencies through a foreign exchange dealer, a bank, which trades from its own position. If the dealer has a long position in a currency, it means he has bought more of that currency than he has sold. If he has a short position in a given currency, he has sold more of it than he has purchased. Company A might even approach its own bank. This bank would deduct the dollars from the company's bank account. The smaller bank would then contact a large money center bank with which it has regular dealings and maintains a correspondent account, instructing the large bank to make the required transfer to a designated foreign account. The large bank deducts the amount from the small bank's correspondent account. No currency actually changes hands. The various accounts are all credited or debited electronically. The large bank contacts its foreign branch, correspondent, or other bank wishing to trade dollars for pound sterling.

The forex department of a bank or other dealer buys and sells currencies for its own account and will have different balances of forex at different times. It keeps working balances that it uses to satisfy the demands of its customers in any one currency. Forex brokers, as shown in Figure 3–2, are located in major money centers and work independently, on behalf of banks, or as intermediaries in forex trading between banks. The organization of a bank's foreign exchange trading department is shown in Figure 3–3. As this figure shows, banks interact in the foreign exchange and money markets. Each bank that houses a foreign exchange trading desk and a money market desk controls these trading units from the perspective of bank management, having formulated and implemented management controls, which will be discussed later. Each bank trading room has a foreign exchange and money market manager who is responsible for the traders on each desk. Each trading desk usually has chief foreign exchange and money market dealers and a number of other broker/dealers in each of the respective markets.

FIGURE 3–3 Foreign Exchange Dealing Department

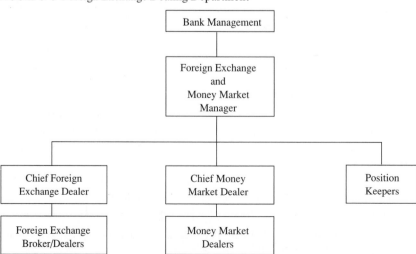

Each trading bank has position keepers, shown at the bottom right in Figure 3–3. These traders maintain positions in foreign exchange or money market instruments entered by the bank for its own account. These traders communicate with the chief dealers and desk managers to maintain positions in individual currencies or money market instruments within the controls set by bank management.

Direct and Indirect Quotations

Spot rates for major currencies are published in the *Wall Street Journal* and the *London Financial Times*. Currency quotations for a particular day are shown in Table 3–1. This table also shows forward rates for a few major currencies. Forward rates will be discussed later in this chapter. Table 3–1 shows each currency expressed in either the U.S. dollar equivalent—or direct exchange rate, or in foreign currency relative to the dollar—the indirect exchange rate. Most currencies are quoted indirectly, i.e., DM 1.5285 per dollar. This method is also referred to as European terms. The pound sterling is quoted directly, i.e., $1.5030 per dollar, or in American terms. The latter quotation is a convention of the forex markets. Traders refer to British pounds as "cable," stemming from the days when trading with London dealers was done via transatlantic cable.[1] If one has the indirect quotation for a currency, the direct quotation may be found by taking the reciprocal of the indirect quotation, e.g., 1 divided by the indirect quotation. If the direct quotation is known, the indirect quotation may be found by dividing 1 by the direct quotation. Direct and indirect quotations for major currencies are shown in Table 3–2. To measure the change in spot rates over time in indirect rates, the following equation is used:

$$\% \Delta \text{ in spot rate} = (\text{beginning rate} - \text{end rate}) \div \text{ending rate} \times 100$$

To measure the change in spot rates over time in direct rates, the following equation is used:

$$\% \Delta \text{ in spot rate} = (\text{end rate} - \text{beginning rate}) \div \text{beginning rate} \times 100$$

A Spot Exchange Transaction

Tracing through an example of a spot transaction, suppose that a German firm takes 10,000,000 German marks (DM) to a bank and requests conversion to dollars. The bank establishes the price it will buy the marks, the bid price, by contacting other

---

MANAGEMENT APPLICATION NO. 4

Example of a Spot Transaction

Assume that on Wednesday, January 10, the XYZ Company, a U.S. manufacturer, must make a payment for tools ordered from Germany. The invoice shows that the payment due is 50,000 deutsche Marks (DM). Three steps are involved. First, XYZ Company calls the foreign exchange department of its bank and requests the foreign exchange rate for purchasing DM 50,000. Second, the bank tells XYZ Company that the current spot rate for DM is 1.4910. Therefore, the bank will sell DM 50,000 to XYZ in exchange for U.S.$33,534.54 (DM 50,000/1.4910). The transaction is valued for two business days later on Friday, January 12. That is, a spot transaction exchange rate is good for two business days. Third, on Friday, January 12, the bank will deliver DM 50,000 to XYZ Company's supplier in Germany and XYZ Company will deliver U.S.$33,534.54 to the bank.

---

[1]Andrew Krieger (with Edward Claflin), *The Money Bazaar* (New York: Times Books, 1992), p. 29.

TABLE 3–1.   Currency Quotations (May 2, 1996)

Currency Trading
Exchange Rates
Thursday, May 2, 1996

The New York foreign exchange selling rates below apply to trading among banks in amounts of $1 million and more, as quoted at 3 P.M. Eastern time by Dow Jones Telerate Inc. and other sources. Retail transactions provide fewer units of foreign currency per dollar.

Country	U.S. $ equiv.		Currency per U.S. $	
	Thu	Wed	Thu	Wed
Argentina (Peso)	1.0012	1.0012	.9988	.9988
Australia (Dollar)	.7973	.7900	1.2542	1.2658
Austria (Schilling)	.09282	.09269	10.773	10.789
Bahrain (Dinar)	2.6525	2.6525	.3770	.3770
Belgium (Franc)	.03176	.03170	31.486	31.546
Brazil (Real)	1.0089	1.0089	.9912	.9912
Britain (Pound)	1.5030	1.4925	.6653	.6700
30-Day Forward	1.5022	1.4917	.6657	.6704
90-Day Forward	1.5011	1.4905	.6662	.6709
180-Day Forward	1.4997	1.4892	.6668	.6715
Canada (Dollar)	.7339	.7346	1.3625	1.3613
30-Day Forward	.7344	.7350	1.3617	1.3606
90-Day Forward	.7351	.7357	1.3604	1.3593
180-Day Forward	.7359	.7365	1.3589	1.3578
Chile (Peso)	.002458	.002455	406.85	407.35
China (Renminbi)	.1198	.1198	8.3501	8.3501
Colombia (Peso)	.0009671	.0009709	1034.00	1030.00
Czech. Rep. (Koruna)				
Commercial rate	.03597	.03603	27.800	27.753
Denmark (Krone)	.1694	.1690	5.9032	5.9170
Ecuador (Sucre)				
Floating rate	.0003265	.0003265	3063.00	3063.00
Finland (Markka)	.2078	.2062	4.8120	4.8496
France (Franc)	.1938	.1928	5.1610	5.1875
30-Day Forward	.1940	.1930	5.1540	5.1805
90-Day Forward	.1946	.1936	5.1395	5.1663
180-Day Forward	.1954	.1944	5.1171	5.1436
Germany (Mark)	.6542	.6510	1.5285	1.5360
30-Day Forward	.6554	.6522	1.5259	1.5333
90-Day Forward	.6579	.6547	1.5199	1.5275
180-Day Forward	.6620	.6587	1.5105	1.5182
Greece (Drachma)	.004113	.004091	243.11	244.43
Hong Kong (Dollar)	.1293	.1293	7.7358	7.7363
Hungary (Forint)	.006610	.006627	151.28	150.89
India (Rupee)	.02890	.02881	34.600	34.705
Indonesia (Ruplah)	.0004293	.0004295	2329.25	2328.50
Ireland (Punt)	1.5569	1.5487	.6423	.6457
Israel (Shekel)	.3118	.3124	3.2075	3.2015
Italy (Lira)	.0006394	.0006390	1564.00	1565.00

(cont.)

TABLE 3–1.   *(cont.)*

Country	U.S. $ equiv.		Currency per U.S. $	
	Thu	Wed	Thu	Wed
Japan (Yen)	.009579	.009494	104.40	105.33
30-Day Forward	.009622	.009537	103.92	104.86
90-Day Forward	.009697	.009611	103.12	104.05
180-Day Forward	.009813	.009724	101.90	102.84
Jordan (Dinar)	1.4104	1.4065	.7090	.7110
Kuwait (Dinar)	3.3333	3.3333	.3000	.3000
Lebanon (Pound)	.0006331	.0006329	1579.50	1580.00
Malaysia (Ringgit)	.4009	.4012	2.4943	2.4923
Malta (Lira)	2.6144	2.7360	.3825	.3655
Mexico (Peso)				
Floating rate	.1339	.1350	7.4700	7.4075
Netherland (Guilder)	.5854	.5820	1.7082	1.7182
New Zealand (Dollar)	.6895	.6851	1.4503	1.4596
Norway (Krone)	.1521	.1519	6.5727	6.5843
Pakistan (Rupee)	.02910	.02910	34.370	34.370
Peru (new Sol)	.4237	.4237	2.3601	2.3601
Philippines (Peso)	.03820	.03821	26.180	26.170
Poland (Zloty)	.3753	.3753	2.6645	2.6645
Portugal (Escudo)	.006367	.006354	157.07	157.37
Russia (Ruble)[a]	.0002019	.0002019	4954.00	4954.00
Saudi Arabia (Riyal)	.2666	.2666	3.7505	3.7505
Singapore (Dollar)	.7110	.7110	1.4065	1.4065
Slovak Rep. (Koruna)	.03258	.03285	30.689	30.446
South Africa (Rand)	.2292	.2303	4.3625	4.3425
South Korea (Won)	.001285	.001285	778.25	778.15
Spain (Peseta)	.007836	.007836	127.62	127.61
Sweden (Krona)	.1458	.1462	6.8599	6.8420
Switzerland (Franc)	.8039	.7997	1.2440	1.2505
30-Day Forward	.8063	.8020	1.2403	1.2469
90-Day Forward	.8111	.8070	1.2329	1.2391
180-Day Forward	.8189	.8145	1.2211	1.2277
Taiwan (Dollar)	.03681	.03681	27.169	27.169
Thailand (Baht)	.03957	.03960	25.270	25.250
Turkey (Lira)	.00001334	.00001344	74989.00	74421.50
United Arab (Dirham)	.2723	.2723	3.6725	3.6725
Uruguay (New Peso)				
Financial	.1311	.1311	7.6300	7.6300
Venezuela (Bolivar)[b]	.002174	.002198	460.00	455.00
Brady Rate	.002169	.002174	461.00	460.00
SDR	1.4457	1.4456	.6917	.6917
Ecu	1.2274	1.2241		

Special Drawing Rights (SDR) are based on exchange rates for the U.S., German, British, French, and Japanese currencies.

European Currency Unit (Ecu) is based on a basket of community currencies.

[a] fixing, Moscow Interbank Currency Exchange.

[b] Change to market rate effective Apr. 22.

Source: Wall Street Journal, 3 May 1996, p. C14. Reprinted with permission.

TABLE 3–2. Direct and Indirect Currency Quotations (May 2, 1996)

Direct Quotes	Indirect Quotes
British £ = $1.5030	$ = £0.6653
Canadian $ = $0.7339	$ = C$1.3625
German DM = $0.6542	$ = DM 1.5285
French Fr = $0.1938	$ = Fr 5.1610
Japanese ¥ = $0.009579	$ = ¥ 104.40
Mexican peso = $0.1339	$ = Ps 7.4700

Source: Wall Street Journal, 3 May 1996, p. C23.

banks to determine the market price for the marks. The bid price quoted the German firm is $0.6333/DM. The German firm accepts this price and agrees to exchange the marks for dollars at this price. The bank must deliver $6,333,000 (DM 10,000,000 × 0.6333) to the German firm. On the same day, a U.S. firm needs DM 10,000,000 to pay French suppliers. The bank agrees to sell the marks it has accumulated at $0.6343/DM—the ask price. The U.S. firm pays $6,343,000 for DM 10,000,000. No specific commission or fee is charged by the bank. The spread between the bid and ask prices is the cost of the transactions. The bank charged more than it paid on the transactions for a round-trip profit of $10,000. The organization of a foreign exchange department of a large bank was shown in Figure 3–3 and the flow chart for a typical foreign exchange transaction is shown in Figure 3–4.

In Figure 3–4, a typical foreign exchange transaction begins with a customer, which may be an individual, a company, or another bank. The customer enters the trade with the bank's dealing department, essentially shown in Figure 3–3. The bank's dealing department transacts the foreign exchange trade with another bank's dealing department. The bank confirms the transaction with the customer, usually by phone, and the customer approves the confirmation. A trading ticket, showing the details of the transaction—quantity of which currency at the transacted price and maturity of any forward rate agreements—is forwarded by the dealing department to the bank's oper-

FIGURE 3–4 Flow Chart for a Typical Foreign Exchange Transaction

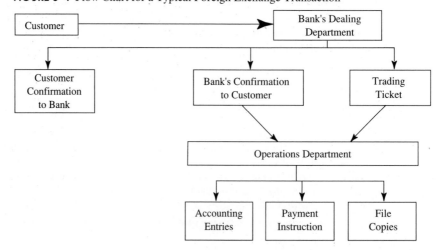

ations department, the so-called back room, where appropriate accounting entries, payment instruction, and file copies are recorded.

It is important for firms to know how much the percentage spread is. This is the cost of the transaction and can be compared with other means of obtaining the currency, such as borrowing in the local currency market. To find the percentage spread, the following equation is used:

$$(\text{Ask price} - \text{bid price})/\text{ask price} \times 100$$

$$\text{or}$$

$$(A - B)/A \times 100$$

In the dollar/DM example, the percentage spread is as follows:

$$[(0.6343 - 0.6333) \div 0.6343] \times 100 = 0.15765\%$$

One should also consider this transaction from the bank's perspective. This relatively small percentage spread must cover the bank's cost of operations, overhead, assumed risk, and profit margin. Thus, banks make money in the foreign exchange market not on profit margin but on volume.

Certain price quotation conventions are followed by traders in the foreign exchange markets. For example, the Swiss franc is quoted in Table 3–1 as trading spot on May 2, 1996, at 1.2440 to the dollar. If an exporter asked a foreign exchange trader for a quote on the Swiss franc, he would be given a quote of 40, the last two digits of the quotation, meaning the dealer's ask price is 1.2440 Swiss francs to the dollar. The dealer assumes the exporter knows the rest of the quote, or the "handle." Or the dealer might offer a quote of 40–45, meaning 1.2440–1.2445 to the dollar, the bid and ask prices for Swiss francs showing the spread between where the dealer wants to buy and sell dollars for Swiss francs. The price might be quoted on a Reuters screen in the trading room as 1.2440/45, or Sfr 1.2445 if the exporter is buying and Sfr 1.2440 if he/she is selling.

The exporter might also ask for a quote on a specific amount of Swiss francs. He might ask for a quote, for example, on 20 Swiss francs, meaning Sfr 20 million. If the dealer were to offer a quote of 40–45 for Sfr 20 million, he is offering to sell the exporter Sfr 20 million at 1.2445 to the dollar, or he will buy Sfr 20 million from the exporter at 1.2440 to the dollar. The dealer assumes that the deal is for spot Swiss francs, meaning delivery will take place in two banking days. If the exporter agrees to buy Sfr 20 million at this price, the dealer enters the "fill" or the price at which the order is filled on his trading sheet. The confirmation is generated later by the operations room of the bank, as shown in Figure 3–3, and the parties have committed to deliver the respective currencies. The market operates on a good-faith basis, i.e., because transactions are entered by phone or electronic communication with written confirmations and payments to follow, parties rely on each other to make payments or delivery.

Good faith does not always work in the foreign exchange market. Suppose that a mistake is made. A dealer in Bank 1 commits to buy deutsche Marks from a dealer at Bank 2. The dealer in Bank 2 enters a buy on his trading sheet, i.e., the opposite transaction from that desired by the dealer in Bank 1. Since confirmations do not follow until sometime later, probably the next day, the mistake is not immediately noticed. Dealers try to work out such mistakes amicably. When this fails, the dealer at Bank 1 may not do business again with the dealer at Bank 2. In 1974, Bankhaus Herstatt, a relatively small bank in Germany failed because of excessive foreign exchange trading. This bank had correspondent relations for trading purposes with many international banks. In this case, confirmations did not follow the trading done just before the collapse and several leading banks lost large amounts of money because Herstatt did not make delivery on these trades. This case is used by foreign exchange traders and bank

TABLE 3–3.   Key Currency Cross Rates (August 5, 1994)

	Dollar	Pound	SFranc	Guilder	Peso	Yen	Lira	D-Mark	FFranc	CdnDlr
Canada	1.3625	2.0478	1.0953	.79762	.18240	.01305	.00087	.89140	.26400	
France	5.1610	7.7570	4.1487	3.0213	.69090	.04943	.00330	3.3765		3.7879
Germany	1.5285	2.2973	1.2287	.89480	.20462	.01464	.00098		.29616	1.1218
Italy	1564.0	2350.7	1257.2	915.58	209.37	14.981		1023.2	303.04	1147.9
Japan	104.4	156.91	83.923	61.117	13.976		.06675	68.302	20.229	76.624
Mexico	7.4700	11.227	6.0048	4.3730		.07155	.00478	4.8871	1.4474	5.4826
Netherlands	1.7082	2.5674	1.3732		.22867	.01636	.00109	1.1176	.33098	1.2537
Switzerland	1.2440	1.8697		.72825	.16653	.01192	.00080	.81387	.24104	.91303
U.K.	.66534		.53484	.38950	.08907	.00637	.00043	.43529	.12892	.48832
U.S.		1.5030	.80386	.58541	.13387	.00958	.00064	.65424	.19376	.73394

Source: Wall Street Journal, 3 May 1996, p. C14. Reprinted with permission.

regulators as the watershed example of systemic risk among banks in foreign exchange trading, resulting from the so-called Herstatt risk, or settlement risk.

Cross Rates for Foreign Currency

In some cases, it is necessary to transact foreign exchange trades using cross rates. Some pairs of currencies may have little or no trading volume so their relationship to a third currency must be determined. This is referred to as a cross rate. Since foreign exchange is generally quoted against the dollar, suppose that a U.S. company is operating in British pounds and in Swiss francs and must hedge, let us say, Swiss-owned assets in Great Britain. Exchange rates can be quoted for Swiss francs against the dollar and for British pounds against the dollar but it is necessary to know the rate for Swiss francs against the British pound. From Table 3–1, we find that £1 = \$1.5030 and Sfr 1 = \$0.8039. To find the £/Sfr rate, solve the following equation: \$1.5030/\$0.8039 = £1 = Sfr 1.8696. Essentially, the equation for calculating these or any other cross rates is as follows:

$$\text{Sfr/£} = \text{\$/Sfr} \times \text{\$/£}$$

Cross rates for other currencies can be found by using information from the \$-denominated quotes in the *Wall Street Journal*. They are also precalculated and quoted daily in the *Wall Street Journal*. An example is shown in Table 3–3.

Arbitrage

With the exception of a very small percentage, foreign exchange is traded in the interbank system of a borderless world. These banks do not operate on the floor of an organized market place. They are connected by telephone and other electronic means. Yet forex rates for any given currency tend to be relatively uniform at any moment in time. This uniformity is the result of arbitrage, the process of buying and selling the same commodity in different markets—buying in markets where the price is low and selling in markets where it is high. The result will be a narrowing of the prices in different markets, theoretically to a uniform price. Assume the following information about the deutsche Mark:

	Bank 1	Bank 2
Bid price for DM	\$0.50	\$0.52
Ask price for DM	0.51	0.53

An arbitrageur will buy deutsche Marks from Bank 1 at \$0.51 and will sell to Bank 2 at \$0.52. The arbitrageur makes a profit until Bank 1 raises and Bank 2 lowers the price

of deutsche Marks to the same exchange rate. Theoretically, this process will return the prices to an equilibrium price instantaneously. In practice, it usually takes longer. The market for some currencies may not be free. For example, official market prices as well as gray or black market prices prevail in many LDCs because of foreign exchange controls. In these markets, price differences remain for a long time because no legal means is possible to take advantage of or to arbitrage these differences.

Triangular Arbitrage   Traders can perform arbitrage with simultaneous purchases and sales of foreign exchange in different markets by means of triangular arbitrage.[2] Assuming away bid-offer spreads, suppose the following: sterling trades at $1.80 in London and the mark is quoted at DM 2.20/$ in Frankfurt. The implied sterling/mark cross rate[3] is, therefore, DM 3.96/£ (or [£/1.80]/[DM/.4545]). Arbitrage opportunities arise whenever any of these three rates get out of line. If the pound were less than $1.80 in New York, say $1.75, with the other rates unchanged, it would pay to buy sterling in New York, sell it for marks, and sell the marks for dollars in Frankfurt. In New York, the pound is undervalued against the dollar and/or the dollar is overvalued against pound sterling. Starting with $1,750, the trader could sell it for £1,000 in New York; then sell the £1,000 for DM 3,960 in London at the sterling/mark cross rate of DM 3.96/£; then sell the DM 3,960 in Frankfurt at DM 2.20/$ for $1,800. The arbitrage profit is $50, which was earned because the rates were out of line from the original cross rate. Arbitrageurs in New York, however, will quickly notice the ability to make a profit and will buy sterling until the gap between the pound and dollar is closed and the cross rates restored.

Forward Exchange Market

Foreign exchange is also traded for future delivery in the forward exchange market. A forward rate for a currency is established by dealing banks and is the rate to be paid for delivery of specific currency at some future date. The forward rate is established at the time the parties enter into the contract. Payment and delivery are made at maturity of the forward contract. As shown in Table 3–1, forward rates are usually quoted for 30, 90, and 180 days, but a forward quotation can be obtained for almost any date in the future. A Society Bank trader once quoted an 11-year forward rate to one customer.

Forward exchange contracts are used to reduce the risk that foreign exchange rate fluctuations will adversely affect transactions that will be settled in the future. For example, assume that a U.S. importer needs DM 2 million in 90 days to pay for goods imported from Germany. Suppose the spot rate is $0.49/DM. The market is quoting a 90-day forward rate of $0.50, i.e., deutsche Marks for delivery in 90 days are selling for $0.50/DM. The importer enters into a forward contract with its banks to deliver $1 million for deutsche Marks in 90 days. This is a firm commitment and locks in a price. If the price of deutsche Marks were to rise to $0.52/DM in 90 days, the importer would need to exchange $1,040,000, or $40,000 more for the deutsche Marks if he had not entered into a forward exchange contract. See Figure 3–5 for an example of a dealing bank's forward exchange contract.

Or suppose that an American Jaguar dealer expects to import ten Jaguar motor cars 90 days from now. The Jaguar Motor Car Company quotes a price for the ten cars with spare parts at £335,570, or $500,000 at the spot rate of $1.49. The current forward

---

[2] Roger M. Kubarych, *Foreign Exchange Markets in the United States* (New York: Federal Reserve Bank of New York, 1983), p. 19.

[3] Cross rates are quotations for rates between third currencies—such as the number of marks per pound sterling. They are discussed in the previous section and an example is shown in Table 3–3.

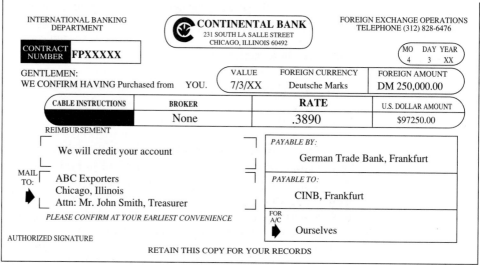

Rates are for illustrative purposes only and do not indicate current market rates.

FIGURE 3–5 Forward Exchange Contract

rate quoted for 90 days is $1.4867/£. The importer can buy £335,570 forward for 90 days at this price. In 90 days, the importer will have to deliver $498,892. Suppose, however, that the pound appreciates to $1.60 during the 90 days, the result of a massive oil discovery in the North Sea. The cars would have cost the importer almost $537,000 if he had not purchased £ sterling forward. He actually "saved" more than $1,000 on the original contract but avoided a loss of $37,000. As will be discussed subsequently, if interest rate parity holds, he could have entered into a money market transaction involving the spot rate and achieved the same result.

Forward rates are quoted at a discount from or a premium to the spot rate. If the forward rate is less than the spot rate, the forward rate is at a discount from the spot rate. If the forward rate is higher than the spot rate, the forward rate is at a premium to the spot rate. The information in Table 3–4 shows forward rates for the Canadian dollar and the Japanese yen for May 2, 1996.

TABLE 3–4. **Forward Rates**		
	Canadian $	*Japanese ¥*
Spot	$0.7256	$0.009648
30 days	0.7244	0.009661
90 days	0.7224	0.009695
180 days	0.7191	0.009750
	Discount	Premium

Source: Wall Street Journal, 22 April 1994, p. C6.

To determine the percentage discount or premium for forward exchange, the following equation can be used:

FOR A DIRECT QUOTE

$$[(\text{Forward price} - \text{spot price}) \div \text{spot price}] \times (360 \div N) \times 100$$

FOR AN INDIRECT QUOTE

$$[(\text{Spot price} - \text{forward price}) \div \text{forward price}] \times (360 \div N) \times 100$$

where N is the number of days to future delivery in the contract.

In Table 3–4, the Canadian dollar trades at a discount from spot, while the Japanese yen trades at a premium. To find the percentage discount that the Canadian dollar is selling forward for 180 days, the following equation is solved for the forward rate premium or discount at an indirect quote:

$$[(0.7191 - 0.7256) \div 0.7256] \times (360 \div 180) \times 100 = \text{forward discount for C\$}$$
$$180 \text{ days forward} = -1.79\%$$

To find the percentage premium that yen is trading forward for 180 days, the following equation is solved:

$$[(0.009750 - 0.009648) \div 0.009648] \times (360 \div 180) \times 100 =$$
$$\text{forward premium for ¥ 180 days forward} = +2.11\%$$

The determinants of the size of the forward premium or discount include relative interest rates between countries. Differences in interest rates between countries move forward rates to either premiums or discounts from the spot exchange rate. In addition, expected changes in macroeconomic activity, i.e., growth in gross domestic product, and expected inflation rates also will have an impact on forward exchange rates.

Forward contracts can be tailored to the needs of customers and, for example, can be contracted for maturities that range from a few days to several years. Such rates are negotiated between market rate standard forward contract maturities of 30, 90, 180 days, etc. The parties to forward contracts can be hedgers, speculators, or arbitrageurs.

MANAGEMENT APPLICATION NO. 5

A Forward Contract

Assume that on Wednesday, January 10, XYZ Company, a U.S. manufacturer, signs a purchase order to buy a machine from a supplier in Italy. The invoice is for 250,000,000 Italian lira (L). The payment is due June 10. XYZ Company first calls the foreign exchange department at its bank and requests the rate to purchase L250,000,000 for value June 10. The bank tells XYZ Company that the current rate to purchase lira is 1610 per U.S. dollar and the forward points for June 10 are L25 premium. Therefore, the forward rate for June is L1635/U.S.$(1610 + 25). The bank agrees to sell L250,000,000 to XYZ Company for value June 10 at a rate of L1635 in exchange for U.S.$152,905.20 (L250,000,000/L1635 = U.S.$152,905.20). On June 10, the bank delivers L250,000,000 to XYZ Company's supplier and XYZ delivers U.S.$152,905.20 to the bank. This transaction is completed at the rate agreed to on January 10 regardless of any movements that may have occurred in the meantime between the Italian lira and the U.S. dollar.

Forward Contract with a Maturity Window

Occasionally, a company deals with a foreign firm that may be late in making payments in the future. The firm receiving payment may not want to lock in a forward rate that will obligate it to deliver foreign currency on a specific date. The receiving firm may choose to enter into a forward contract with a maturity window. For example, suppose that XYZ Company, a U.S. manufacturer, receives a purchase order from a customer in England on Wednesday, January 10. The invoice is for £50,000 and payment is due on June 10. XYZ Company calls the foreign exchange department at its bank and requests the rate to sell £50,000 for a maturity window of June 10 through July 9. The bank tells XYZ Company that the current spot rate is $1.5530 per pound sterling and the forward points are 80 discount. Therefore, the forward rate is $1.5450 ($1.5530 − $0.0080 = $1.5450). The bank agrees to buy £50,000 from XYZ Company at a rate of $1.5450 and, in exchange, the bank will pay $77,250 to XYZ Company. The deal is valued for a maturity window of June 10 through July 9. At anytime between June 10 and July 9, XYZ Company can deliver to the bank £50,000 and in return will receive U.S.$77,250 (£50,000 × $1.5450).

A Maturity Swap

Suppose in the preceding example, on July 7, two days before its forward contract with a maturity window matures, XYZ Company realizes that it will not be able to deliver the £50,000 as agreed to in the contract with its bank because its customer is late in making payment. However, the customer promises that payment will be made on August 10. XYZ Company wishes to swap out of its contract with the bank, i.e., change it to another maturity. As mentioned earlier, about 30 percent of all bank foreign exchange trading is for a swap of a forward contract from one maturity to another. XYZ Company calls the foreign exchange department of its bank and requests to swap out of the existing contract—the agreement to sell £50,000 to the bank at a rate of $1.5450. XYZ Company requests a new value date of August 10. The bank tells XYZ Company that the current spot rate is $1.5520 and that the forward points for August 10 are 18 discount. Therefore, the forward rate is $1.5502 ($1.5520 − $0.0018 = $1.5502).

The bank agrees to sell £50,000 to XYZ Company for value July 9 in exchange for $77,600 (£50,000 × $1.5520). This enables XYZ Company to meet its obligation under the original contract. The bank also agrees to buy back £50,000 from XYZ Company on August 10 and, in exchange, will deliver to XYZ Company $77,510 (£50,000 × $1.5502 = $77,510). On July 9, XYZ Company owes the bank a net amount of $350. This is calculated as follows:

1. Original forward contract valued July 9: the bank buys £50,000 at $1.5450 and sells to XYZ Company $77,250;

2. New spot contract valued July 9: the bank sells £50,000 at $1.5520 and buys from XYZ Company $77,600;

3. The net difference, therefore, is $77,600 − 77,250 = $350.

On August 10, XYZ Company delivers £50,000 to the bank and the bank delivers $77,510 to the XYZ Company. The swap of forward rate maturities has cost the XYZ Company $350 but might have cost even more, depending on foreign exchange rate fluctuations, if no action on the original forward contract had been taken.

Traders' Quotations

Traders have certain conventions in making quotations for foreign exchange transactions. For example, in Table 3–5, the outright basis for prices of the deutsche Mark vis-à-vis the dollar is shown for spot and 30-, 90-, and 180-day forward rates. The bank's bid and ask prices are shown. The column labeled "Points" shows the difference

TABLE 3–5. DM Quotations Against the U.S.$

Basis	Bid	Ask	Points
Spot	DM 1.7870	DM 1.7882	1.7870/12
30-day forward	1.7841	1.7855	29/27
90-day forward	1.7778	1.7795	92/87
180-day forward	1.7692	1.7714	178/168

in basis points from the bid to the ask price in spot, and the difference between bid prices from spot to each of the forward rates and for ask prices from spot to each of the forward rates. For example, if the bid price is DM 1.7870/$ and the ask price is DM 1.7882/$, under the Points column, the quotation would be 1.7870/12, or the ask price is 12 basis points higher than the bid price. For the 30-day forward contract, the bid price is DM 1.7841/$ and the ask price is DM 1.7855/$. In the Points column, the quotation is 29/27, meaning the 30-day forward bid rate is 29 basis points less than the spot bid rate and the 30-day forward rate is 27 basis points less than the spot ask rate. For these quotations, a smaller ask number means the deutsche Mark is trading at a premium to the dollar, or the dollar is trading at a discount to the deutsche Mark. In other words, the forward market holds that the DM is appreciating in value against the dollar. For DM forward 180 days, the Points column quotation is 178/168. The 180-day forward bid rate is 178 basis points less than spot bid price and the 180-day forward ask rate is 168 basis points less than the spot ask price. These quotations state that the dollar will buy fewer DM in the future.

At the same time, the Canadian dollar exchange rate against the U.S. dollar is shown to be trading forward at a discount against spot foreign exchange, as shown in Table 3–6. In these traders' quotations, the relationship of the "points" is consistent with maintaining a widening bid-ask spread as time increases; if the bid points are greater than ask points, we subtract them, and vice versa.

FOREIGN EXCHANGE RATE DETERMINATION

Foreign exchange rates are determined by a number of factors, all operating in the foreign exchange market. Among these are expectations, speculative efficiency, speculator characteristics, and the relation between interest rates and inflation rates from country to country. The expectation theory essentially states that rational expectations are generally self-fulfilling. These expectations can stem from what traders think other traders are thinking. If consumers, for example, think prices will rise in the future, they will behave as though prices will increase, will spend on consumption goods rather than save, and this behavior will drive prices up, and, lo and behold, in the future prices will

TABLE 3–6. C$ Quotations Against the U.S.$

Basis	Bid	Ask	Points
Spot	1.3411	1.3426	1.3411/15
30-day forward	1.3426	1.3442	15/16
90-day forward	1.3453	1.3473	42/47
180-day forward	1.3499	1.3525	88/99

increase, fulfilling the market expectations. The speculative efficiency hypothesis states that the forward rate *t* periods from now is the best unbiased predictor of the spot rate *t* periods from now. Thus, it is rational to expect that future spot rates will be the same as forward rates. Underlying this hypothesis is the notion that market variables exist that embody the sum total of the market's information about the future.

For periods up to 90 days, it has been shown by some empirical research that the forward rate is a good predictor of the future spot rate. However, forward rates have not been good predictors of future spot rates, e.g., in the early 1980s. In order to satisfy the interest rate parity, as discussed later, the forward rate depends on the structure of nominal interest rates. In the context of calling the forward rate a "forecast or predictor," this fact needs to be acknowledged despite the empirical evidence.

MANAGEMENT APPLICATION NO. 6

Foreign Exchange Traders' Quotations

A trader in New York would quote the following rates to buy or sell Swiss francs in the spot, 1-month, 3-month, 6-month, and 12-month markets:

$0.3969/74   9/11   21/24   32/46   53/70.

These quotes would equal the following outright rates:

Maturity	Buy	Sell
Spot	$.3969	$.3974
1-month forward	.3978	.3985
3-month forward	.3990	.3998
6-month forward	.4001	.4020
12-month forward	.4022	.4044

A trader in Zurich would give these quotes to a Swiss company wishing to buy U.S. dollars. The rates that follow are exactly the same as those given in New York in the previous example; except that they are the indirect quotations:

Sfr 2.5164/95   70/57   151/132   288/201   436/332

In outright terms, those rates would be

Maturity	Buy $	Sell $
Spot	2.5164	2.5195
1-month forward	2.5094	2.5138
3-month forward	2.5013	2.5063
6-month forward	2.4876	2.4994
12-month forward	2.4728	2.4893

Thus, for a spot quotation, the first number is always a bid for the denominator currency and the second is the ask for the denominator currency. In this example, the denominator currency is the dollar. For the points quotation, if the first number is smaller, it is always added to the spot rate. This implies that the denominator currency is at a premium and, if the first number of the points quotation is larger, it is always subtracted from the spot rate, meaning that the denominator currency is trading at a discount from the spot rate. Such a quotation system always works regardless of whether the foreign exchange quotation is a direct quote, indirect quote, American terms, European terms, or any other quotation.

STUDY AID

The concepts discussed in this chapter to this point include how foreign exchange spot and forward rates are quoted and how they and cross rates are used by international firms and traders. Be familiar with where to find daily information about foreign exchange rates. These concepts will underlay discussion about foreign exchange rate determination and forecasting, currency futures, and currency options in succeeding sections of this book.

Finally, speculator characteristics help determine foreign exchange rates. Among these are (1) risk neutrality, i.e., the notion that the amount of money won is not worth less than the amount of money lost, (2) full information, i.e., the speculator is able to predict future spot prices in the forward market with more success when he has full information, and (3) the speculator's wealth is constrained and the possibility exists of ultimate ruin.

The decline of the U.S. dollar to historical lows in early 1995 is an example of the effect of speculation on the determination of foreign currency rates. At that time, U.S. economic fundamentals did not warrant such a drop in the market value of the dollar.[4] During the 1990s, U.S. business productivity had risen at a strong annual rate of 2.1 percent. Corporate operating profits were at their highest level in 20 years. Inflation was quite low, as shown by the 0.9 percent increase in unit labor costs in 1994. Although the U.S. government budget and trade deficits from 1980 to 1995 had increased, the percentage of U.S. debt as a ratio to gross domestic product compared with most other industrialized nations was lower. The U.S. stock market was up 40 percent in the 1990s while that of Japan was down 45 percent.

Thus, the 1994–95 decline in the dollar could not be fully explained by economic fundamentals. The psychology of the foreign exchange market caused much of the decline. Political events in the United States, including a congressional defeat of a balanced budget amendment to the U.S. Constitution and the 1994 elections, which signaled a national desire for tax cuts, triggered a mindset among currency traders that the dollar should not be the major global reserve currency. Apparently traders perceive that these political actions will not reduce the budget and trade deficits and, thus, nominal interest rates and inflation may increase and the dollar should, therefore, remain weak.

The market may have decided that the German mark will be the major global reserve currency. Germany has exercised caution and conservativism in the formulation of its monetary and fiscal policy. One threat to this possibility may stem from the heavy burden of incorporating the East German economy. Germans, for example, are constantly reminded by the government and the economic press of the tremendous inflation suffered by the country in the early 1920s. From 1921 to late 1923, inflation was so high in Germany that the exchange rate during this period went from 4 Reichsmarks to the U.S. dollar to 4.2 trillion Reichsmarks to the dollar.[5] Thus, the heavy burden of acquiring a nearly bankrupt East Germany could increase inflationary pressures in Germany as a whole. Table 3–7 shows the gradual but very dramatic effect of inflation during the 1921 to 1923 period on the German currency.

The Expectation Theory and the Asset-Market Model of Forex Rates

Exchange rates, as mentioned earlier, may be determined by the expectations of economic participants. Several examples can be cited to demonstrate this theory. In the 1960s and 1970s, during the Vietnam War, a number of incidents caused growth rates to drop. These incidents included inflation, a shaken political system in the United States, President Johnson's retirement, President Nixon's resignation, and the loss of confidence by the people in Presidents Ford and Carter. In 1980, however, the dollar appreciated because of the Reagan Presidency and supply side economics, the tax cut in the early 1980s, and a good political climate, which attracted capital to the United States. In 1985, growth declined and foreign assets became more attractive. Foreigners

---

[4] Christopher Farrell, "The Dollar Doesn't Deserve This Thumping," *Business Week* (March 20, 1995):51.

[5] Gustav Stolper, *German Economy, 1870–1940, Issues and Trends* (New York: Reynal & Hitchcock, 1940), p. 151.

TABLE 3-7. Effect of Inflation on Dollar Quotations in German Marks (monthly average rates) (1914–1923)	
Date	*DM/U.S.$*
July 1914	4.2
January 1919	8.9
July 1919	14.0
January 1920	64.8
July 1920	39.5
January 1921	64.9
July 1921	76.7
January 1922	191.8
July 1922	493.2
January 1923	17,972.0
July 1923	353,412.0
August 1923	4,620,455.0
September 1923	98,860,000.0
October 1923	25,260,208,000.0
November 1923	4,200,000,000,000.0

Source: Gustave Stolper, *German Economy, 1870–1940, Issues and Trends* (New York: Reynal & Hitchcock, 1940), p. 151, and revised version in James C. Baker, *The German Stock Market: Its Operations, Problems, and Prospects* (New York: Praeger Publishers, 1970), p. 11.

perceived that the United States wanted the dollar to drop and they sold U.S. assets. In Mexico, in 1985, after an earthquake, property was expropriated by the government, private sector confidence declined, capital flight occurred, and the peso fell 30 percent. These expectations in the United States and Mexico all had an impact on currency rates for the dollar and the peso.

The Equilibrium Approach to Exchange Rates

The foreign exchange currency market clears, i.e., supply and demand are equated, through price adjustments. Real disturbances to the supply of or demand for goods, currencies in this case, cause changes in their relative prices, including the real exchange rate. Repeated shocks in supply and demand create a correlation between changes in real and nominal exchange rates.

Several policy implications stem from these occurrences. First, exchange rates do not cause changes in relative prices but are a part of the process through which changes occur in equilibrium. Second, the correlation between nominal and real foreign exchange rates is not exploitable by government. Intervention to change nominal rates will fail. Third, no simple relation exists between changes in exchange rates and changes in international competitiveness or employment. Fourth, no simple relation exists between exchange rates and the current account balance. Trade deficits do not cause currency depreciation, nor does currency depreciation by itself help reduce a trade deficit. After 1971, when President Nixon devalued the dollar, the U.S. trade deficit nearly tripled in 1972. The U.S. experience since 1985 is another similar example.

It is important to note that government should not invoke protectionist policies on the trade of goods or financial assets as a response to changes in foreign exchange

rates. The issue is not undervalued or overvalued currencies. Real exchange rates are only reflections of underlying market conditions and government policies. The policies carried out by the Mexican Government in the mid-1970s and the concomitant market conditions led to the capital flight and massive devaluations of the Mexican peso.

FOREIGN EXCHANGE MARKET REGULATIONS

Few regulations are imposed on the foreign exchange markets and the trading process. Most of the regulations are aimed at banks in their trading operations so that another Herstatt failure can be avoided. Restrictions on foreign exchange trading would have an adverse impact on international trade and investment flows.

The few foreign exchange market regulations are divided into those that are broad and global and those that are imposed by a nation against trading within that country. The former are formulated and implemented by international agencies such as the International Monetary Fund (IMF), discussed in chapter 2, and the Bank for International Settlements, discussed in chapter 9, and represent agreements that stem from changes in the world economy. For example, the central bank of a particular country may regulate the exchange value of its own currency but this regulation will be formulated in cooperation with the relevant parties that are members of the IMF or of G-5, the Group of Five, etc.

Those regulations affecting the foreign exchange market for a country's currency within the home country are formulated because of political pressures from some group within the country's economy or because of the desire by the local government to change certain economic parameters. For example, in late 1993, the new Russian Federation prohibited the use of foreign currency in that country. This regulation had effects on several other currencies.

Other countries have also restricted foreign exchange operations in their countries, for example, Sweden, which restricted currency outflows until 1989. These restrictions usually are ultimately abolished because the economy of the country imposing the restriction improves sufficiently to remove such restrictions, or pressure may be brought, as in Italy in preparation for the Single Market Europe in 1992.

FORECASTING FOREIGN EXCHANGE RATES

The foreign exchange dealer constantly attempts to anticipate market trends, whether he is trading for his own account as a speculation or an investment or hedging for a customer. He must analyze all of the economic factors discussed in chapter 2 concerning the balance of payments of countries whose currency he is trading, as well as interest rates, inflation, and politico-economic factors. Market psychology must be analyzed. What are the expectations of traders in the current market? It is quite obvious that the secret to success in the foreign exchange market, whether one is a dealer, speculator, investor, or hedger, is to forecast foreign exchange rates and to forecast them well.

What makes a good forecast? To be successful, a forecast should be on the correct side of the forward rate. According to Table 3–1, the yen/dollar rate on May 2, 1996, was ¥104.40/$. It was reported in the *Wall Street Journal* that the 180-day forward rate on that day was ¥101.90/$, i.e., the yen was forecast by the forward market to appreciate a little further against the dollar over the next six months. Suppose that a Japanese company requests a 1-year forecast for the yen because of a transaction to be entered into now but settled in one year. The 12-month forward rate quoted by the company's bank is ¥102/$. The Japanese trader, looking at a $10 million transaction, wants more precision in the forecast and asks two different currency analysts to forecast the yen 12 months ahead. Mr. Andrews submits a forecast of ¥93/$. Ms. Brown

submits a forecast of ¥102/$. The future spot rate realized in the market 12 months from the May 2, 1996, quotation was ¥100/$. The Japanese company uses currency forecasts to help it decide whether to cover dollars payable with a forward contract or wait 12 months and sell dollars in the spot market.

These forecasts can be analyzed by calculating the forecast errors from the realized foreign exchange spot rate. Mr. Andrews forecast a rate of ¥93 with an error of 7 percent from the realized spot rate of ¥100. Ms. Brown's forecast error from the realized spot rate was only 3 percent. Her forecast is closer to the forecast spot but this is not the important factor. Her forecast is in excess of the realized spot rate. If her forecast were followed, the Japanese firm would wait and sell dollars in the spot market in 12 months, or it would take a long position in dollars. Since the future realized spot rate of ¥100 is less than the forward rate at which dollars could be sold (¥102/$), the firm would receive ¥100 million rather than ¥102 million for the $10 million. If the firm followed Mr. Andrew's forecast, the Japanese company would sell dollars forward or take a short position in dollars. The firm would then sell dollars at the forward rate of ¥102/$ rather than wait and receive ¥100/$. The forward contract would yield ¥2 million more than the uncovered position.

From this example, it is clear that the most important criterion is to be on the correct side of the forward rate. The size of the forecast error is not useful, although a hedger may have an indifference point that is somewhere between forecast error rates. More importantly, Mr. Andrews was on the correct side of the forward rate.

Forex Forecasting Methods

Future spot rates can be forecast using five different methods. These are (1) balance of payments, (2) forward rate, (3) economic models, (4) lead indicators, and (5) technical analysis. The balance of payment forecast uses a country's balance of payments and the trends in the current and capital accounts to forecast the supply of and demand for foreign exchange at some future spot rate. While this method offers a comprehensive solution to forecasting, it is costly and time-consuming. The use of the forward rate to be an indicator of the future spot rate will be discussed in the section on parity relationships. Although this method is relatively sound for forecast periods up to 90 days, it has been found to be a poor indicator of the future spot rate. Economic models such as purchasing power parity and interest rate parity will also be discussed later in this chapter. The ease of using, for example, purchasing power parity is that differentials in inflation rates between countries can be forecast easily but these models are relatively weak for short-term forecasting. The use of lead indicators such as the ratio of official reserves to imports and changes in official reserves as a percent of the money supply are advantageous in that their data inputs are relatively easy to collect and update but such methods may not furnish much of an early warning. These methods may not always work equally well for revaluation and devaluation. Finally, technical analysis incorporates market data such as prices and relies on extrapolations of these data. Moving averages can be modeled into computer programs to detect trends. Technical analysis is generally easy to implement at relatively low costs. But since many companies use such methodology, beating the market becomes difficult.

Evaluation of Forex Forecasts

Firms must decide which forecasters are best when they pay top money to hire them as consultants. How can forex forecasts be evaluated? It has been suggested that the forecaster must be on the right side of the forecast. However, such a determination may take up to a year or more. In the meantime, the performance of forex forecasters must be evaluated. Determination of the forecast error by incorporating the following

equation, as discussed previously, is one method: forecast error = predicted exchange rate/actual exchange rate.

One analyst has distinguished between accurate forecasts and correct forecasts.[6] Accurate forecasts are a measure of the size of errors, as follows:

$$\text{Forecast error} = \text{predicted exchange rate} - \text{actual exchange rate}$$

Exchange rate forecasts have been found to be less accurate than forward rate predictions by the market. Such market forward rates have been found to be less than accurate when measured by the mean square error (MSE), as follows:

$$\text{MSE} = 1/n \sum_{1}^{n} (\text{forecast} - \text{actual})^2$$

The professional services were found to be better than forward market predictions in producing correct forecasts.[7] Such results were found by ignoring the magnitude of forecast errors and concentrating on the times when the correct direction of the currency movement was forecast. This can be demonstrated by letting S_p and S_a be the predicted and actual spot exchange rates, respectively, and F the lagged forward rate. $(S_p - F)$ is the forecaster's bias, while $(S_a - F)$ is the market's error. The forecast is correct if both the forecaster's bias and the market's error have the same sign, either both positive or both negative. Users of such forecasts who would have hedged all or nothing of the currency amount would have made money but they would have had to take risks.

Selected Foreign Exchange Forecasting Methods

Several forecasting methods are practiced by foreign exchange market professionals in addition to the rate determination theories discussed in the next major section. Traders, for example, make informed judgements and intuitive estimates of forex rates. These are good in the absence of other methods and as a supplement. Trends are observed closely in such data as balance of payments and the internal economic activity of a nation. Helpful literature includes the *Quarterly Country Reports* published by *The Economist* and the bimonthly analyses contained in *International Currency Reviews*. The interest rate parity, discussed later in this chapter, is best for the short-term, i.e., 3 months to 1 year forward. The future spot rate estimate is based on the current forward rate. The purchasing power parity theory, discussed in a subsequent section, is best for the longer run. The longer the term, the smaller the percentage error will be with this method. Essentially, this theory holds that changes in exchange rates parallel differences in rates of inflation. Finally, various econometric models can be used to forecast future exchange rates. These models include Box-Jenkins, a form of time series using moving averages, and decomposition theory in which several factors affecting exchange rates are decomposed, or collapsed, resulting in fewer parameters than were present at first. These are usually best for the intermediate term, i.e., less than a year to about three to five years. These methods consist of computerized models of national economies often linked together by equations that represent the foreign sector.

CENTRAL BANK INTERVENTION

In chapter 2, the current international foreign exchange rate regime was discussed. Exchange rates are permitted to fluctuate freely in the marketplace. However, rates do

---

[6] R. M. Levich, "Evaluating the Performance of the Forecasters," in *The Management of Foreign Exchange Risk* ed. Richard Ensor (London: Euromoney Publications, 1982), pp. 121–34.

[7] Ian H. Giddy, *Global Financial Markets* (Lexington, MA: D.C. Heath, 1994), p. 161.

not fluctuate freely at all times. The system is called a dirty, or managed, floating rate regime. Central banks can and occasionally do intervene in the foreign exchange market to keep a currency's value from rising or declining more. Central bank intervention is likely to be either ineffectual or irresponsible, as discussed in chapter 2. In October 1978, the Carter administration intervened in the foreign exchange market because the dollar was believed to be too low in price. A total of $30 billion was bought in the market in an attempt to move the dollar up. At that time, the U.S. dollar index was 100. Two years later, after this massive intervention, the index had risen to only 101.7. On February 27, 1985, West European central bankers telephoned banks in Frankfurt, Milan, and other financial centers, ordering the sale of hundreds of millions of dollars because the dollar was thought to be too high. The U.S. Federal Reserve Bank in New York joined the action and markets panicked. The dollar declined 5 percent that day. Shortly afterward, the dollar rose until signs of the U.S. economic downturn appeared in March.

Exchange rates are determined by real economic variables such as relative prices, national incomes, and interest rates between and among countries. Exchange rates in turn determine magnitudes and direction of the flow of goods, services, and capital among countries. Intervention in the forex markets may temporarily influence the movement of exchange rates but unless the underlying market-generated supply and demand forces change, the impact of intervention will be swamped by these market forces.

Intervention seldom has the apparent intended effect, i.e., changing the foreign exchange rate up or down. Some 17 central banks intervened in the forex markets on June 24, 1994, to support the dollar by purchasing $3 billion in the forex markets. U.S. monetary authorities furnished $1.56 billion of this amount. The dollar continued to fall. The action was too little and probably too late because the market had already anticipated the intervention. Officials at the Federal Reserve Bank of New York conceded that the action was a failure.[8] And during the first week of November 1994, the Federal Reserve intervened with $2 billion of foreign exchange to keep the dollar from falling further against the mark and the yen. The move did not work because the dollar continued to decline.

On the other hand, U.S. monetary authorities intervened three times during April–May 1995, after the dollar fell to a historical low against the yen and near-historical low against the mark. Afterward, the dollar began to stabilize and, for example, rose 35 percent against the yen during the summer of 1995. It may be true that traders had believed the dollar had fallen far enough and worked to turn the market around. However, evidence exists that these interventions served as a catalyst.

As mentioned in chapter 2, the intervention sometimes is intended to signal a change in monetary policy in a major country. This usually works in the short-run but has little long-term effect, especially if policy does not change. Economic indicators usually prevail to move the market in the intended direction, or the action of speculators and traders in general will have their intended effect, i.e., to move a given currency in the direction they wish it to go. Thus, intervention is usually a lot of hot air from central banks fueled with more currency trading volume.

---

[8] Gary Rosenberger, "New York Fed Concedes June 24 Move To Bolster Dollar Was Seen as a Failure," *Wall Street Journal*, 8 August 1994, p. C15.

Theories of Foreign Exchange Rate Determination

We have discussed the efficient exchange markets and market equilibrium determinants of foreign exchange rates. Five other theories are very important in the determination of foreign exchange rates.[9] These are the theory of purchasing power parity (PPP), the Fisher effect, the international Fisher effect, the theory of interest rate parity (IRP), and the forward rate as the unbiased predictor of the future spot rate. These theories and their synthesis will be discussed in the following sections.

PURCHASING POWER PARITY

Purchasing power parity (PPP) means that exchange rates change to make equivalent values in each currency equal in purchasing power. Stated in a weaker form, PPP holds that the rate of appreciation or depreciation between the currencies of two countries is related to rates of inflation in each country. In the long-run, PPP holds that exchange rates between any two currencies should equate the prices of identical baskets of goods and services in the two respective countries. In Figure 3–6, purchasing power parity relative to equilibrium can be shown. In this diagram, the vertical axis represents percentage appreciation or depreciation of the foreign currency relative to the home

FIGURE 3–6 Purchasing Power Parity and Equilibrium

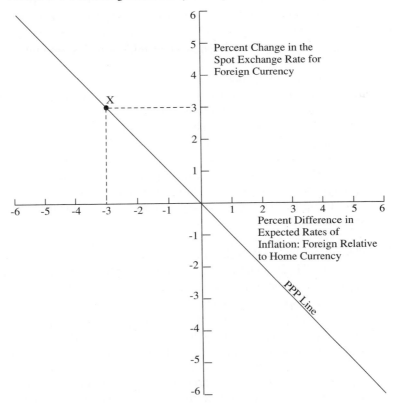

---

[9] For a good discussion and tutorial of the interrelationship among these five theories, see Carl B. McGowan, Jr. and Henry W. Collier, "Foreign Exchange Rate Parity Conditions: A Pedagogical Note," *Financial Practice and Education* 3 (Spring/Summer, 1993): 77–83.

currency. The horizontal axis represents the rate of inflation in the foreign country relative to the home country as a percentage higher or lower. The diagonal line shows the equilibrium position between a change in the exchange rate and the inflation rate. Any point on this line is an equilibrium between the inflation rate and the foreign exchange rate at a given time. For example, point X on this line represents an equilibrium point where inflation in Germany is 3 percent lower than in the home country, the United States. Thus, relative PPP would predict the German mark to appreciate 3 percent per annum with respect to the U.S. dollar.

In 1990, *The Economist* tested PPP by using a Big Mac hamburger made by McDonald's.[10] This product is almost identical in quality because of rigorous standards imposed by the company in the more than 50 countries in which it operates. In four major U.S. cities, the Big Mac averaged $2.25, whereas in Tokyo, the sandwich cost ¥380, then the equivalent of about $2.81. This test implied that the dollar was approximately 20 percent undervalued against the yen. On a Big Mac PPP basis, the dollar should have bought ¥169 on the foreign exchange market—the yen price of a Big Mac divided by the dollar price. At the time of the survey, the dollar was valued at ¥135. The dollar, in this test, was undervalued against almost all other currencies. Presumably, for the PPP to work using the Big Mac, barriers to trade could not exist and labor, rent, and other significant costs would have to be the same at all 15,000 McDonald's stores worldwide.

Another example using the principle of PPP may be found in the markets for the stock of Daimler-Benz (DB), the German auto manufacturer. DB shares are quoted on the Frankfurt Stock Exchange. American depository receipts (ADRs)—shares of foreign companies traded in the United States and discussed in chapter 12—for DB have been traded on the New York Stock Exchange for the past two years. Before being listed on the New York Stock Exchange, Daimler-Benz ADRs were traded over-the-counter in the United States. The DB ADRs represent 1/10 share of the Frankfurt traded stock. On September 14, 1995, DB shares were quoted on the Frankfurt Stock Exchange at DM 745.50. The spot exchange rate that day was DM 1.4870/U.S.$1. Thus, the dollar price of the Frankfurt shares was $501.34. The DB ADR was quoted in New York at $50.50. Since 10 ADRs = 1 Frankfurt share, then 10 ADRs in New York were trading for $505.00, or $4.66 more than the Frankfurt shares. A case might be made that the U.S. dollar is overvalued since these two prices have the same underlying security, the DB shares, and, thus, arbitrage is possible. However, some of this premium may not be explained by PPP because, as discussed in chapter 12, some of an ADR's price represents a premium for the convenience and safety factors represented by this instrument.

Another way to show the effects of PPP can be seen in the data from a survey of 209 nations by the World Bank.[11] The data shows that per capita income in the United States is $24,750, placing U.S. workers seventh among the world's nations, versus the leader, Switzerland, with a per capita income of $36,410. However, if per capita incomes are measured by living standards and PPP calculations are used to smooth out the effects of currency swings and different price levels, the adjusted per capita incomes places the United States in second place with a figure of $24,750 behind the leader, Luxembourg, with an adjusted per capita income of $29,510, but ahead of Japan with $21,090 and Germany with $20,980.

PPP has also been referred to as the law of one price. For example, assume that gold sells for $400 per ounce in the United States and for £250 per ounce in Great

---

[10] "Big MacCurrencies," *The Economist Yearbook, 1992 Concise Edition* (Reading, MA: Addison-Wesley 1993), p. 209.

[11] "Plenty of Bang for the Buck," *Business Week* (January 16, 1995): 24.

Britain. The law of one price sets an exchange rate of $400 = S(t)£250, or S(t) = $1.60/£, where S(t) = the current exchange rate. Essentially, PPP holds that a currency should be able to buy the same basket of goods both at home and abroad, assuming it is costless to move goods between countries and no impediments to trade exist, such as tariffs and quotas. First, however, the prices must be converted to a common currency. Once converted, the prices of comparable products from any two countries should be the same. After converting pounds into dollars, for example, a bottle of Laphroaig, James Bond's favorite Scotch, bought in London should cost the same as a bottle of Laphroaig bought in New York City. So in theory, markets enforce the law of one price. In practice, the law does not always hold because of transportation costs, tariffs, quotas, or other market hindrances.

Assume the following:

Country A	Country B

$$\text{new CPI/old CPI} = \text{new CPI/old CPI}$$

$$R_t/R_0 = P_d/P_f$$

where

R = domestic price of foreign exchange, t = periods into the future, and 0 = at present

P_d = domestic price index

P_f = foreign price index

Both price indices should have the same base period, 0, and both should use the same weights, i.e., CPI, consumer price index, or WPI, wholesale price index. Thus, a change in the exchange rate from one period to another should equal the change in the relative purchasing power of two different currencies. For example, if during the next two years, prices are expected to increase 115 percent in Argentina and only 15 percent in the United States, then in T + 2, the dollar price of the Argentinian peso will be half what it is now, according to PPP.

Another use of PPP is to forecast the appreciation or depreciation of a specific currency.[12] A business firm that may be contemplating building a factory in a foreign country must look far into the future to evaluate the viability of the investment. The value of the dollar is a key factor in the decision. A large rise in the value of the dollar, say, five years from now could sharply reduce the value of profits remitted to the parent firm five years from now.

Assume the following case. Suppose that the U.S. price level is currently 115 and that of Germany is 110, both having the same base year when their respective price levels were 100. The initial value of the German mark is $0.6250. According to PPP, the value of the mark should rise to $0.6534. The relevant formula to determine this rate is

$$\text{Forward rate/spot rate} = \text{index}_{\text{Dom}}/\text{index}_{\text{For}}$$

or

$$\$0.625 \times (115 \div 110) = \$0.6534, \text{ or an appreciation of } 4.54\%$$

---

[12] See, for example, Craig S. Hakkio, "Is Purchasing Power Parity a Useful Guide to the Dollar?" *Federal Reserve Bank of Kansas City Economic Review* 77 (Third Quarter 1992): p. 36–51.

If the German price level at the present time is 121, while the U.S. price level remains at 115, then the mark should fall to $0.5940, or by 4.96 percent.

PPP has been shown empirically to be useful in the long-term. It also has short-run benefits although research has found it to be less useful in the short-run. When deviations from PPP between two countries are large, one of the currencies is most likely to move toward PPP in the short-run. Short-run differences are usually not large, however, in the PPP between any two countries.

THE FISHER EFFECT

The Fisher effect holds that the level of nominal interest rates in a given country is related both to the real return on assets that investors require and to the expected rate of inflation. The real return on assets is equalized across national boundaries from one country to another. In other words, currencies with high rates of inflation should bear higher nominal interest rates than should currencies with lower rates of inflation. Funds will flow to the country with a higher nominal interest rate differential until returns become equalized by the effects of arbitrage. Simply put, if the required real return is 3 percent and expected inflation is 10 percent, then the nominal rate should be 13 percent, or, actually, a little higher. The formula for this determination is as follows:

$$1 + \text{nominal rate} = (1 + \text{real rate})(1 + \text{expected inflation})$$

or

$$1 + r = (1 + a)(1 + i)$$

or

$$r = a + i + ai$$

or

$$\text{approximately } a + i$$

where a = required real rate of return and i = expected rate of inflation. To be exact, in the example just mentioned, if the required real return is 3 percent and expected inflation is 10 percent, then

$$r = 0.03 + 0.10 + (0.03 \times 0.10)$$

or

$$r = 0.1330, \text{ or } 13.3 \text{ percent}$$

THE INTERNATIONAL FISHER EFFECT

The international Fisher effect holds that differences in the rate of appreciation or depreciation between currencies is related to the nominal interest rates between the countries of these currencies. Essentially, the currency of a country with low interest rates is expected to appreciate relative to a currency of a country with high interest rates, and the currency of a country with high interest rates is expected to depreciate relative to a currency of a country with low interest rates. It has been suggested that if the law of one price holds for real rates of return in two different countries and no government intervention is practiced, then interest rate differentials should reflect inflation differentials and, thus, the international Fisher relation or effect holds. The relevant equation for the international Fisher effect assuming PPP and Fisher effect is

$$S_{t+1}/S = (1 + r_h)/(1 + r_f)$$

where r_h = home country interest rate

r_f = foreign country interest rate

S = current spot foreign exchange rate

S_{t+1} = future spot foreign exchange rate

For example, if the 1-year rate of interest is 4 percent on Swiss franc Treasury bills and 7 percent on U.S. Treasury bills and if the current exchange rate, or spot rate, is Sf 1 = $0.63, what is the expected future spot rate in one year, acc

$$F/\$0.63 = 1.07/1.04$$

or

$$F = \$0.6482$$

If changes in the expectations of future U.S. inflation cause the expected future spot foreign exchange rate of the Swiss franc to the dollar to rise to $0.70, what should happen to U.S. interest rates, according to the international Fisher effect? The answer is

$$0.70/0.63 = (1 + r_h) \div 1.04$$

or

$$r_d = 15.56\%, \text{ the U.S. expected interest rate}$$

INTEREST RATE PARITY

The theory of interest rate parity (IRP) holds that differences in nominal interest rates between currencies determine the premiums or discounts on currencies in the forward foreign exchange market. In other words, the difference in the national interest rates for securities of similar risk and maturity should be equal to, but opposite in sign to, the forward exchange rate discount or premium for the foreign currency, assuming away transactions costs and taxes on any gains. High interest rates in a country are offset by forward discounts and low interest rates in a country are offset by forward premiums.

On July 1, 1994, the foreign exchange rate between the Japanese yen and the U.S. dollar closed at an historical low dollar price of ¥98.54 to the dollar, or $0.010148 per yen. If the interest rate on the one year Treasury bill (T bill) is 4 percent in the United States and 3 percent in Japan, what should the one year forward be for the yen versus the dollar, according to IRP?

Mathematically speaking, the formula for an approximate IRP is

$$r_h - r_f = (F - S)/S \times 360/n$$

where r_h = the home country interest rate

r_f = the foreign country interest rate

F = the forward exchange rate

S = the spot, or current exchange rate

n = the number of days until the forward contract

This formula furnishes an approximate forward rate:

$$0.04 - 0.03 = (F - \$0.010148)/\$0.010148$$

or

$$F = \$0.010249$$

The answer using the international Fisher effect formula will be slightly different. That formula, using the same notations as in the IRP formula above, is

$$F/S = (1 + r_h)/(1 + r_f)$$

Thus, this formula furnishes a more exact answer:

$$F/\$0.010148 = 1.04/1.03$$

or

$$F = \$0.010247$$

The theory of IRP holds that a relationship exists between the forward exchange rate and the current spot exchange rate. In fact, it has been empirically tested and proved by some research that, up to 90 days, the 90-day forward exchange rate is the best indicator of the future spot exchange rate, i.e., its expected value. In other words, as will be discussed later, the 90-day forward rate is an unbiased predictor of the 90-day future spot exchange rate.

Covered Interest Arbitrage: Using a Money Market Hedge

In a situation where IRP does not hold, profitable covered interest arbitrage may be possible. The arbitrageur recognizes the imbalance by investing in whichever currency offers higher returns on a covered basis. See Figure 3–7 for a description of IRP and covered interest arbitrage in the money and foreign exchange markets.

Figure 3–7 assumes that IRP holds. In other words, the CFO of a Japanese company will need $1 million to pay for a U.S.-made computer in 180 days. The spot rate for yen versus the dollar is ¥100/$. The U.S. T bill rate is 4.00 percent per annum while the Japanese T bill rate is 3.00 percent per annum. Given IRP and these interest rates, the 180-day forward foreign exchange rate quoted in the market by the CFO's banker is ¥99.5098/$.

The Japanese CFO has two alternatives. He can convert ¥100,000,000 at the spot rate, receive $1 million, invest in U.S. T bills at 4.00 percent, and receive $1,020,000 in principal and interest in 180 days. He will have sufficient funds, risk-free, to pay for the

FIGURE 3–7 IRP and Covered Interest Arbitrage

U.S. T Bill Rate = 4.00% Per Annum
(2.00% per 180 days)

Start $1,000,000 — Times 1.02 → $1,020,000

Dollar Money Market

S = Times ¥100/$ 180 days   Divide F₁₈₀ = ¥99.5098

Yen Money Market

¥100,000,000 — Times 1.015 → ¥101,500,000

Japanese T Bill Rate = 3% Per Annum
(1.50% per 180 days)

S = spot rate; F = forward rate

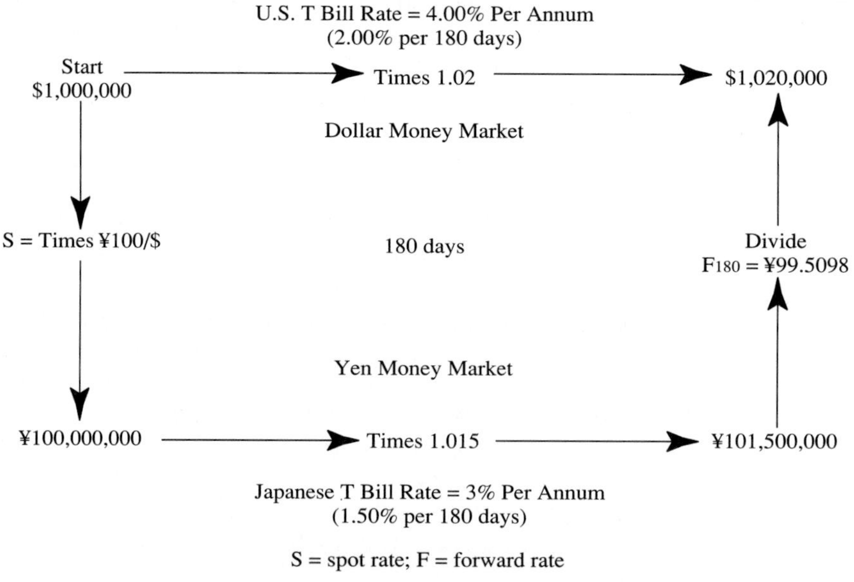

computer and will have made some additional interest income. Or he could invest the ¥100,000,000 in Japanese T bills at the 3.00 percent market rate, receive ¥101,500,000 in 180 days, and, given IRP, convert these funds at what will be the future spot rate, now the 180-day forward rate, of ¥99.5098/$, and receive $1,020,000. Thus, he is indifferent between the two alternatives.

In the real world, the future spot rate sometimes will be different from the current forward rate, especially for periods longer than 90 days. However, arbitrageurs will work to bring exchange rates into equilibrium, given interest rate differentials and the underlying mechanics of the IRP. Certainly, little or no difference will exist in these alternatives up to 90 days, and, given the relative efficiency and liquidity of the global foreign exchange market, very little difference will exist for 180 days forward.

Let us examine one more example of covered interest arbitrage. Assume that on July 1, interest rates in the United States are 6 percent and in the United Kingdom, they are 10 percent, i.e., the differential is 4 percent. The spot foreign exchange rate is $1.72/£. If the IRP holds, one-year forward rates for the pound *should be* selling at a 4 percent discount in terms of dollars. Thus, the one-year forward rate should be

$$r_h - r_f = (F - S)/S$$

or

$$0.06 - 0.10 = (F - \$1.72)/\$1.72$$

or

$$(1.72)(-0.04) = F - 1.72$$

or

$$\$1.72 - 0.0688$$

or

$$F = \$1.6512$$

On July 1, a trader buys £50,000 at $1.72 for $86,000. In the forward market, she hedges the spot transaction, which is to be held for one year to pay for a commercial transaction, by selling £55,000 at $1.67, the forward market quotation on that day. She bought £50,000 worth of U.K. CDs paying 10 percent p.a., or £5,000 p.a. (£50,000 × 0.10) interest income. One year later, she collected the principal and interest on the CDs, £55,000, and delivered £55,000 against the one-year-old forward position. This transaction nets her, assuming away taxes and transaction costs, $91,850 (£55,000 × $1.67), for a profit on the transaction of $5,850 ($91,850 − 86,000). If IRP had held in this case and the future spot rate had been $1.6575, the 4 percent discount from the original spot price, this trader would have netted $91,162.50 (£55,000 × $1.6575). The basis changed during the year and she made a profit. However, she could have lost money on this covered arbitrage had the pound rallied and ended higher than $1.72.

It should be understood that one cannot make a profit or incur a loss on covered interest arbitrage. A return greater than that available in the domestic market can be locked in. In a hedging example such as the one described, opportunity gains and losses are possible.

Finally, interest rate parity and equilibrium is demonstrated in Figure 3–8. The vertical axis represents the percentage difference between foreign and domestic interest rates while the horizontal axis shows the forward premium or discount on the foreign currency. The diagonal interest rate parity line represents the equilibrium position. This diagram ignores transaction costs that, if considered, might cause the equilibrium line to be a narrow band. Point A shows one possible equilibrium position, where a −3 percent interest differential on foreign currency securities would be offset by a 3 percent premium on forward foreign exchange.

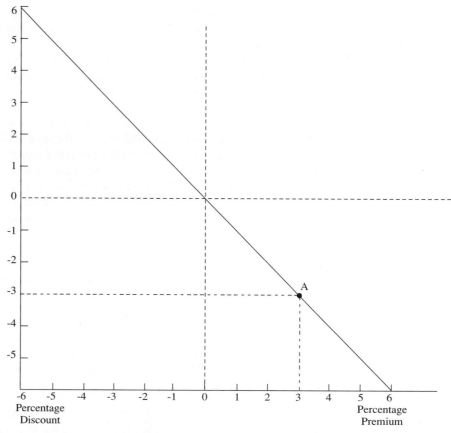

Percentage Difference Between
Foreign and Domestic Interest Rates

FIGURE 3–8 Interest Rate Parity and Equilibrium

Discount or Premium Equal to the Interest Rate Difference

IRP asserts that the discount or premium in the forward foreign exchange market, i.e., percentage difference, is equal to the difference in interest rates between the two countries whose forward rates are quoted, but in the opposite sign. Assume that the one-year interest rate is 5 percent in the United States and 10 percent in France. The French franc (Ffr) should sell at a 5 percent discount. If the spot rate on Ffr is Ffr 1 = \$0.1500, then the one-year forward rate on Ffr should be approximately 5 percent lower, or \$0.1425, given the IRP formula

$$r_\$ - f_{Ffr} = (\text{Fwd} - \text{spot})/\text{spot},$$

i.e., the forward rate can be approximated by means of the following formula:

$$0.05 - 0.10 = (\text{Fwd} - 0.15)/0.15$$
$$-0.0075 = \text{Fwd} - 0.15$$
$$\text{Fwd} = \$0.1425$$

or using the IRP formula given above, the forward rate should be exactly \$0.1432.

Another example: ignoring bid-ask spreads, if the following interest rates are assumed: Euro \$ = 15 percent and Euro £ = 10 percent and the spot exchange rate for pound sterling is presently £1 = \$2.20, then what should the twelve-month forward for-

eign exchange rate be? The following equation to find the approximate forward rate is used:

$$(1 + i_h)/(1 + i_f) = (F - S)/S$$

where i_h = the nominal interest rate at home
i_f = the nominal interest rate in the foreign country
F = the forward rate
S = the spot rate

Solving for F, the forward rate, we obtain the following:

$$0.15 - 0.10 = (F - \$2.20) \div \$2.20$$
$$0.05 = (F - 2.20) \div 2.20$$
$$0.11 = F - 2.20 \rightarrow F = \$2.31$$

Thus, the twelve-month forward foreign exchange rate is expected to be $2.31, which is a twelve-month forward premium, in terms of pound sterling, equal to the 5 percent interest differential. Suppose the actual forward rate is not $2.31, but $2.35. Arbitrageurs could buy £ sterling spot, then invest and sell £ sterling forward for dollars, since the future price of the dollar is lower than that implied by the interest parity relation. The spot rate will rise and the forward rate will decline. This arbitrage will bring the forward premium back in line with the interest differential.

THE FORWARD-SPOT RELATIONSHIP

This theorem holds that the premiums or discounts on currencies in the forward market are related to the rate of currency appreciation or depreciation anticipated over the life of a forward contract. In other words, the forward rate is an unbiased predictor of the future spot rate. If the foreign exchange market quotes a 5 percent premium on a foreign currency, the future spot exchange rate for that maturity should appreciate by 5 percent between now and the maturity date. If the foreign exchange market quotes a

---

MANAGEMENT APPLICATION NO. 7

Interest Rate Parity in Practice

A U.S.-based investor would like to maximize his risk-free return on $100,000, which he has available for a one-year period. Euromarket deposit rates are: U.S. dollar—7 percent and U.K. pound—12 percent. The pound has the highest return, but an uncovered investment would run the risk of devaluation. To eliminate that risk, the investor can enter into a one-year swap. The market rates are:

	Spot	*1-Year*
	(Sell)*	(Buy)*
U.K. pound	$2.35	$2.2451

Using the formula given above to approximate the forward rate, the investor has two choices: invest in dollars at 7 percent and receive $107,000 after one year, or buy pounds spot at the bank's selling rate getting £42,553, which he then invests at 12 percent receiving £47,659 at the end of the period. When he converts those pounds back to dollars through a one-year forward contract, he will end up with $107,000, assuming the interest rate parity theory holds.

---

*Spot selling and one-year buying exchange rates are used in the example because the investor must assume that his bank will sell sterling to him at his bank's selling rate and buy from him forward at the bank's buying rate.

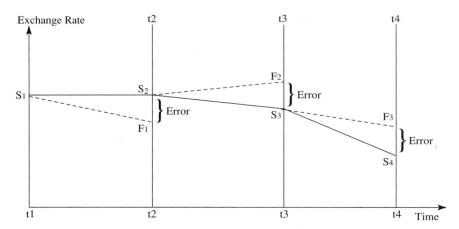

FIGURE 3–9 Forward Rate as an Unbiased Predictor of Future Spot Rate

5 percent discount on a foreign currency, the future spot exchange rate for that maturity should depreciate by 5 percent between now and the maturity date.

This relationship has been empirically tested successfully by some studies and generally holds best for forward maturities up to 90 days. However, other studies have found forward exchange rates to be poor indicators of future spot rates. Unexpected news may influence spot rates and, thus, cause the relationship to fail.[13] For periods of more than 180 days, this relationship does not hold very well, if at all. The forward rate as an unbiased predictor of the future spot rate is demonstrated in Figure 3–9. If this theorem holds, according to this diagram, the expected value of the future spot rate at time 2 equals the present forward rate for time 2 delivery, available at time 1, the present, or $E(S_2) = F_1$.

SUMMARY OF THE EQUILIBRIUM FRAMEWORK

In summary, five key equilibrium economic relationships furnish the foundation of the global foreign exchange market. These are purchasing power parity, the Fisher effect, the international Fisher effect, interest rate parity, and the forward rate as an unbiased estimate of the future spot rate. To reiterate, purchasing power parity states that the ratio of forward to spot rates equals the ratio of domestic to foreign inflation rates. The Fisher effect for a single country states that the nominal interest rate equals the real interest rate plus the expected inflation rate. The international Fisher effect suggests the ratio of forward to spot rates equals the ratio of interest rates of domestic to foreign countries. Interest rate parity theory states the forward exchange rate premium or discount equals the interest rate differential, i.e., the interest rate parity, but will also be of opposite signs. Finally, the unbiased forward rate theory states the forward exchange rate premium or discount equals the expected rate of change of the future exchange rate. These international parity relationships are depicted in Figure 3–10 and are at the heart of all international financial management issues, including analysis of the firm's foreign exchange exposure, currency forecasting, and decisions about which currency to use when borrowing or lending.

Finally, the question must be asked: if the market is so efficient that prices reflect all current and past information, then why should a firm buy any of the many foreign exchange forecasting services available? Several reasons can be cited in the real world

---

[13] Maximo V. Eng, Francis A. Lees, and Laurence J. Mauer, *Global Finance* (New York: Harper Collins, 1995), p. 112.

Intergrated International Exchange Rate Parity Conditions

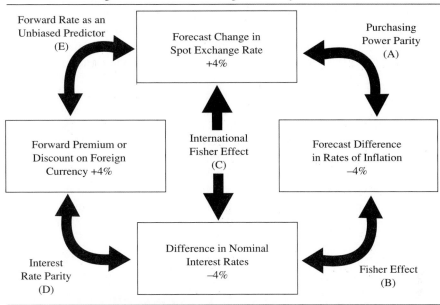

Parity relations are for any percent change in rates or difference in rates. This
example simply uses 4% for illustrative purposes.

Source: David K. Eiteman, Arthur I. Stonehill, and Michael H. Moffett, *Multinational Business Finance* (Boston: Addison-Wesley, 1995), p. 147. Reprinted with permission.

FIGURE 3–10 International Parity Relations

of global finance and business. Some services do manage to beat the market at certain times. Evidence that some of these services consistently out-forecast the market is not a sign that the market is inefficient. The difference between the forward rate and a forecast rate may include transaction costs. Thus, no abnormal return may exist from using this forecast. If the difference is a risk premium, then returns from such forecasts are merely normal compensation for bearing the risk.

Services are generally not free. Some economic departments of large banks offer free forecasts to corporate customers, perhaps as loss leaders, but professional forecasters usually charge large fees. If profits from foreign exchange trading reflect speculation, then forecasters cannot earn abnormal returns from their forecasts. Returns to forecasters with superior results might be considerably large but no evidence has been found that abnormally large profits have been made by professional forecasting services. However, if someone developed a model that consistently outperformed other forecasters, would that forecaster tell anyone else how the feat was accomplished? Finally, another rationale may exist for purchasing forex forecasts. If decisions based on the forecast turn out badly, the firm can blame "outsiders" instead of the firm's treasury staffers, who are not supposed to be as smart as forex traders.

Summary and Conclusions

International companies cannot trade or invest abroad without foreign exchange. It is the life blood of global business operations. Trading in national currencies has become the busiest financial market with a trillion dollars of foreign exchange being traded every day.

Commercial banks play a major role in the foreign exchange markets. The vast bulk of forex trading is carried out in the global banking system with transactions in spot currency prices as well as for future delivery. A small amount of foreign exchange transactions, mostly for speculation, is executed on organized futures exchanges such as the Chicago Mercantile Exchange and the London International Financial Futures Exchange.

Foreign exchange rates must be forecast by banks and MNCs so that the future prices of currency can be determined in order to facilitate international trade and investment transactions to be executed in the future. A number of theories can be used to forecast the future price of foreign currency. These include the purchasing power parity theory, Fisher effect, international Fisher effect, interest rate parity, and forward-spot relationship. These theories have been empirically tested. Some research has shown these theories to hold while other research has shown them to be weak forecasters of the future spot rate. The jury is out on this issue.

MANAGEMENT APPLICATION NO. 8

Interest Rate Parity in Practice

If a U.S.-based trader in Eurocurrency deposits is asked to quote on a DM 10,000,000 6-month deposit by one of his corporate accounts, he would go through the following calculations, assuming that he wished to quote competitively:

6-month Eurodollar deposit, or bid, rate	7.5%
Spot deutsche Mark exchange rate (buy)*	$0.4238
6-month deutsche Mark forward rate (sell)*	$0.4293

The trader calculates that he will sell his customer's marks at spot for $4,238,000 and place the dollars on deposit for six months at 7.5 percent. In six months time, he will receive $4,555,850 in principal and interest. The trader, protecting himself, will sell the $4,555,850 forward for deutsche Marks for delivery in six months; at today's forward rate he would receive DM 10,612,276 in six months. To quote a competitive interest rate for the mark deposit, the trader would calculate

$$[(10,612,276 - 10,000,000) \div 10,000,000] \times (360 \div 182**) = 12.1\%$$

He would bid 12.1 percent for the 6-month Euro-DM deposit.

---

*The trader will take marks on deposit from his customer and sell them to the market at the market's buying rate. In six months, he will buy them back at the market's selling rate.

**Normally the actual number of days is used.

STUDY AID

Determination of foreign exchange spot and future spot rates are at the heart of foreign exchange exposure management, discussed in the next chapter, and to making payment for present and future international transactions. The basic theories that facilitate the determination of these rates and their relationships are depicted in Figure 3–10. These relationships are at the heart of nearly every international financial transaction made by MNCs. Become familiar with the theories and their implications. Problems at the end of this chapter will facilitate this understanding.

Additional Readings

Coninx, Raymond G.F. *Foreign Exchange Today*. New York: John Wiley & Sons, 1978.

Copeland, Lawrence S. *Exchange Rates and International Finance*. Reading, MA: Addison-Wesley, 1989.

Crump, Norman. *The ABC of the Foreign Exchanges*. London: Macmillan & Co., Ltd., 1958.

Krieger, Andrew (with Edward Claflin). *The Money Bazaar*. New York: Times Books, 1992.

McGowan, Carl B., Jr., and Henry W. Collier. "Foreign Exchange Rate Parity Conditions: A Pedagogical Note." *Financial Practice and Education* 3 (Spring/Summer, 1993). 77–83.

Rhim, Jong C., Mohammed F. Khayum, and Yong H. Kim. "Causes of Deviations from Purchasing Power Parity." *Multinational Business Review* 4 (Spring 1996): 112–21.

Discussion Questions

1. Discuss the role of banks in the foreign exchange markets.
2. What are the major centers of the global foreign exchange market?
3. How does arbitrage work? What is its purpose?
4. Central banks occasionally intervene in foreign exchange markets. Discuss the purposes of such intervention. How effective is intervention?
5. Describe and discuss one model for forecasting foreign exchange rates.
6. How do banks make profits in the foreign exchange market?
7. Why has the volume of foreign exchange trading increased so much in the last decade?
8. Why is the volume of foreign exchange trading such a high multiple of the total of international trade and investment?
9. Compare and contrast the expectation theory and the equilibrium approach to foreign exchange rates.
10. How does purchasing power parity work?
11. Discuss in detail interest rate parity.
12. Please define and relate interest rate parity, purchasing power parity, the Fisher effect, the international Fisher effect, and the forward-spot relationship.
13. How many bilateral exchange rates can be created using 30 currencies?
14. The following are bid-ask spot prices quoted by three banks for Italian lira against the U.S. dollar simultaneously by telephone:

Bank 1	1557–1559
Bank 2	1560–1562
Bank 3	1558–1562

    Are these quotations reasonable? Does an arbitrage opportunity exist?
15. A French company knows that it will have to pay 10 million Swiss francs in three months. The current spot exchange rate is Ffr 4.14/Sfr. The 3-month forward rate is Ffr 4.16/Sfr. The treasurer is worried that the French franc will depreciate in the next few weeks. What action can be taken? Three months later, the spot exchange rate turned out to be Ffr 4.25/Sfr. Was your decision a wise decision?

Problems

1. An investor wishes to buy French francs spot at $0.1080/Ffr and sell French francs forward for 180 days at $0.1086/Ffr.
   a. What is the premium on 180-day French francs as a percentage?

2. Suppose the spot quotation on the German mark is $0.3302–10 and the spot quotation on the French franc is $0.1180–90. Compute the percentage bid-ask spreads on the German mark and the French franc.

3. Show using a diagram the relationships among the five international exchange rate parity conditions, given the following data: countries are Japan and the United States; inflation rates expected in Japan = 3 percent, in the United States = 6 percent; the yen sells at a 3 percent premium against the dollar, and interest rates on comparable securities are 3 percent in Japan and 6 percent in the United States.

4. Describe using a diagram the concept of covered interest arbitrage.

5. Two countries, the United States and England, produce only one good, wheat. Suppose the price of wheat in the United States is $3.25 and in England it is £1.35.
   a. According to the law of one price, what should the $:£ spot exchange rate be?
   b. Suppose the price of wheat over the next year is expected to rise to $3.50 in the United States and to £1.60 in England. What should the one-year $:£ forward rate be?
   c. If the U.S. government imposes a tariff of $0.50 per bushel on wheat imported from England, what is the maximum possible change in the spot exchange rate that could occur?

6. Given the following spot and forward quotations, calculate the forward discount or premium as a percentage at an annual rate on the German mark. Remember, a positive sign means at a premium and a negative sign means at a discount.

	Spot (DM/$)	*Forward (DM/$)*	*Days Forward*
a.	1.6545	1.6600	30
b.	1.6545	1.6700	90
c.	1.6545	1.7200	180

    30 days forward _____

    90 days forward _____

    180 days forward _____

7. Suppose that on January 1, the cost of borrowing Mexican pesos for one year is 20 percent. During the year, U.S. inflation is 4 percent and Mexican inflation is 15 percent. At the same time, the exchange rate changes from Ps 3,000/$ on January 1 to Ps 3,400/$ on December 31. What is the real interest cost as a percentage for an American who borrows Mexican pesos, changes them for dollars, and one year later uses dollars to repay the peso loan?

8. Assume the following facts:
   a. the current spot rate = Sfr 1.2355/$
   b. U.S. 1-year T bill rate = 4 percent
   c. Swiss 1-year government security rate = 6 percent

   Using the Fisher effect and interest rate parity, forecast the future spot rate one year from today for the Swiss franc.

9. Suppose that in Japan the interest rate is 8 percent and inflation is expected to be 3 percent. Meanwhile, the expected inflation rate in France is 12 percent, and the English interest rate is 14 percent. To the nearest whole number, what is the best estimate of the one-year forward exchange premium (discount) at which the pound will be selling relative to the French franc?

10. In September 1992, the U.S. dollar hit an all-time low, at that time, against the German mark. What has happened since then to the dollar against the mark and why?

11. Assume that the interest rate paid by an American borrower on a ten-year foreign bond is 10 percent if the bond is sold in Denmark and 7 percent if the bond is sold in the Netherlands. Will the expected inflation rate in the Netherlands likely be higher than the expected inflation rate in Denmark? Will the Danish kroner be expected to increase in value against the Dutch guilder?

12. If the foreign exchange rates are $1 = 1.65 German marks and $1.50 = 1£, what is the exchange rate for German marks vs. £ sterling?

13. Suppose the Argentinian peso devalues by 50 percent against the dollar. What is the percentage appreciation of the dollar against the Argentinian peso?

14. The inflation rate in Great Britain is expected to be 4 percent per year, and the inflation rate in France is expected to be 6 percent per year. If the current spot rate is £1 = Ffr 12.50, what is the expected spot rate in two years?

15. If the dollar appreciates by 100 percent against the Kenyan shilling, how much has the Kenyan shilling devalued against the dollar?

16. Assume the pound sterling is worth Ffr 8.3347 in Paris and Sfr 2.0556 in Zurich. Can British arbitrageurs make profits on these cross rates? If so, show how. What would be the eventual outcome on exchange rates in Paris and Zurich given such arbitrage? How would any transaction cost affect French franc prices for Swiss francs in Paris?

17. If the Belgian franc is $0.03251 on the spot market and the 180-day forward rate is $0.0324, what is the annualized interest rate in the United States over the next 6 months when the annualized interest rate in Belgium is 6 percent.

18. Suppose that 90-day interest rates (annualized) in Japan and the United States are 5 percent and 7 percent, respectively. If the spot rate is ¥100/$ and the 90-day forward rate is ¥96/$, where would you invest? Where would you borrow? Does an arbitrage opportunity exist?

19. Assume the following facts; a foreign exchange trader in New York quotes the following rates to buy or sell German marks in the spot, 1-month, 3-month, and 6-month markets:

    .6679/83   0/0   5/8   18/21.

    Construct the buying and selling foreign exchange rates that these quotations represent for spot, 1-month, 3-month, and 6-month periods.

20. If a bank currently quotes spot rates of DM 1.5249–1.5255/US$ and Bfr 31.2280–31.2340/US$, what would the bank's bid price be for the Belgian franc in terms of German marks?

21. The French franc is quoted as Ffr/$ = 5.1524–30. The German mark is quoted as DM/$ = 1.5249–53. What is the implicit cross rate Ffr/DM quotation?

CHAPTER 4

The Management of Foreign Exchange Rate Exposure

Major Objectives of Chapter 4

(1) To discuss the management of foreign exchange risk, and (2) to discuss ways to reduce this exposure.

Key terms to be learned in chapter 4:

- economic exposure
- transaction exposure
- exposure management

- translation exposure
- leads and lags
- multilateral netting

Introduction

The focus of this chapter is on the management of foreign exchange risk and methods available to the firm for reducing this risk—the risk of being exposed to fluctuations in the foreign exchange rate, or the domestic price of foreign currency. The various types of exchange exposure risk—translation, transaction, and economic—will be analyzed. The concluding part of the chapter will examine methodologies that MNCs can use to manage their currency risk and the organization of their foreign exchange exposure management function.

Foreign Exchange Exposures

Most companies with international operations find their business activity and financial statements affected by changes in foreign exchange rates of currencies in which they are dealing. These changes can occur in a very short time when foreign exchange markets are volatile, especially under a floating rate system. Thus, the risk that these for-

eign exchange fluctuations will adversely affect a company's profitability is a concern to multinational management. Each company must decide whether it can absorb a loss occasioned by adverse exchange rate changes. The average movement of exchange rates is approximately 10 percent annually. Thus, changes in excess of this average movement may be determined by a company to be adverse and, thus, pose a risk to the company's profits. The tools available to management of MNCs to measure and manage this risk will be discussed in the following sections.

The international financial manager of the MNC is concerned with three different types of exposure to losses from foreign exchange fluctuations. These are translation exposure, transaction exposure, and economic exposure.

TRANSLATION EXPOSURE

Translation exposure results from reporting consolidated worldwide operations according to preset accounting rules. The accounting method may result in some impact from exchange rate fluctuations on a company's recorded economic situation. The U.S. accounting standards FASB-8 and FASB-52, developed by the U.S. Financial Accounting Standards Board, are representative of preset rules governing translation of foreign currencies by U.S. companies. These rules will be discussed in more detail later in chapter 16.

The impact of translation exposure is on the financial statements of the firm. Translation exposure is measured by the net total of exposed assets less exposed liabilities on the balance sheet. Any foreign currency assets and liabilities are regarded as exposed if the company plans to translate these accounts into the parent currency at the current rate. The current rate is the exchange rate in effect at the time the accounts are closed for the purpose of reporting the foreign accounts back to the consolidated accounts of the parent firm. Any accounts translated at the historical rate are not considered to be exposed to foreign currency changes. The historical rate is the exchange rate that was in effect at the time the asset, liability, or equity item was entered into the company's accounts. Which rate is used—current or historical—will depend on the accounting rule used.

FASB-8

Before 1975, U.S. firms could translate their foreign accounts in a number of methods. Some firms used a current/noncurrent method in which all current assets and liabilities were translated at the current rate and all noncurrent assets and liabilities were translated at the historical rate. Other firms used the monetary/nonmonetary approach in which all monetary assets and liabilities were translated at the current rate and all nonmonetary assets and liabilities were translated at the historical rate. Most European firms used the current rate method in which all balance sheet items were translated at the current rate. Refer to chapter 16 and the section on accounting for translation gains and losses for examples of the application of FASB-8.

The major problem created by the ability of firms to translate their foreign accounts in a variety of methods is that investment analysts incurred problems in comparing companies, especially those in the same industry that might be using different translation methods. In other words, this was similar to comparing apples with oranges. Thus, the new Financial Accounting Standards Board (FASB), which had replaced the Accounting Principles Board, held hearings and solicited position papers from companies for opinions on FASB-8, a new accounting standard concerned with foreign currency translation.

The new standard was approved and put into effect in 1975–76. U.S. firms were

required to translate foreign accounts into the dollar and report all gains or losses from these translations into the income statement on a quarterly basis. The temporal approach was to be used in translating accounts. The temporal approach approximated the monetary/nonmonetary approach.

Problems arose immediately from the use of this standard. One problem stemmed from the use of the temporal approach. For example, inventories, a nonmonetary asset, were translated at the historical rate, whereas accounts payable, the liability that generally finances inventory and a monetary liability, was translated at the current rate. Plant and equipment, a nonmonetary asset, was translated at the historical rate, whereas long-term debt, a monetary liability that generally is used to finance plant and equipment, was translated at the current rate. Because of these anomalies, a firm operating in an appreciating currency country such as Germany might show losses after translation of the accounts of a profitable operation. A firm operating in a depreciating currency country such as Argentina might show gains after translation of the accounts of a losing operation. Second, these gains and losses were reported quarterly and some firms reported "yo-yo" earnings, up one quarter and down the next, as a result of FASB-8. Finally, the new standard did not address such problems as operating in a hyperinflation country or reporting gains or losses from forward currency market transactions, which a firm might engage in because it needed to hedge its foreign currency exposure.

FASB-52

In 1980, FASB held hearings and solicited letters of transmittal from U.S. business firms on a new foreign currency translation method, FASB-52. In 1981, the new standard was enacted and replaced FASB-8.[1] FASB-52 required U.S. companies to translate all foreign currency accounts except equity at the current rate. All translation gains or losses would be included in a new shareholders' equity account, the cumulative translation adjustment account (CTA). FASB-52 requires companies to translate foreign accounts into a functional currency and offers a number of tests to the firm to assist in selecting the functional currency. This currency can be the dollar but can also be the local currency or some third country currency. In addition, the new standard requires firms to treat hyperinflation in the affiliate's host country by translating the accounts into the dollar and reporting them under FASB-8 rules, if the cumulative inflation in the country of operations amounts to 100 percent or more over a 3-year period.

Gains and losses on foreign currency translation will continue to accumulate in the CTA until the company is merged into another firm or is dissolved by ending business operations. The CTA can be hedged by the use of forward currency contracts. Refer to Figures 16–6 and 16–7 in chapter 16 for examples of the application of FASB-8 and FASB-52 to the balance sheet and income statement of the overseas subsidiary of a U.S. company. The major differences between the two accounting standards are shown: (1) use of current and historical rates under FASB-8 and the current rate under FASB-52, and (2) accounting for exchange rate changes in the income statement under FASB-8 and in the cumulative translation account under FASB-52.

TRANSACTION EXPOSURE

Transaction exposure results from changes in exchange rates after transactions are initiated, but before they are settled, e.g., acquiring assets or incurring liabilities denomi-

---

[1] Laurence J. Mauer, "MNCs Gain New Freedom Under FAS 52 Flexibility," *Management Accounting* 65 (December 1983): 30–3.

nated in foreign currencies, borrowing or lending funds denominated in foreign currencies, or purchasing or selling on credit of goods and services where prices are stated in foreign currencies. The impact from transaction exposure is on the firm's future contractual cash flows.

Several transactions can lead to transactions exposure. These may include accounts payable or receivable in foreign currency, nonrecorded commitments to pay or to accept payment in foreign currency, debt payments or commitments to accept loan repayments in foreign currency, anticipated payments from foreign subsidiaries, and unperformed forward exchange contracts.

Four major methods are available to the firm in the management of transactions exposure. These are: hedging in the forward market, using a money market hedge, the use of a proxy currency such as SDRs or Ecus, and hedging in the derivatives market with currency futures contracts or currency options. These markets and instruments will be discussed in chapters 12–14.

ECONOMIC EXPOSURE

Economic exposure measures the amount of potential gain or loss in the value of the firm from exchange rate fluctuations, i.e., the value of the firm may change because of exchange rate fluctuations that alter sales volume, prices, or cost. The total impact of economic exposure is on the overall value of the firm.[2]

Economic exposure can be managed by changing company policies regarding diversification of various operations. First, economic exposure can be reduced by diversifying sales, either by products or by country. Second, the diversification of production factors of input can reduce economic exposure. In other words, the firm can buy commodities or semifinished inventory from different countries. Third, economic exposure can be reduced by the diversification of production locations. The firm should locate in different countries. The auto industry and companies such as IBM have adopted this strategy. Fourth, the firm can reduce economic exposure by diversification of its funding operations. By using different currencies in financing its operations, the risk of economic exposure can be reduced.

SUMMARY

The fundamental method for reducing currency exposure, other than the use of forward, futures, or options market transactions is the managerial decision to operate in a given currency by managing the firm's assets and liabilities. The objectives of management should be, when operating in a country with an appreciating currency, to increase monetary assets and reduce monetary liabilities, and, when operating in a country with

---

STUDY AID

By now, you should be familiar with the various foreign currency translation methods and, particularly, FASB-8 and FASB-52, as practiced in the United States since 1975. Familiarize yourself with the differences in these two accounting standards. You should be able to solve Problem No. 5.

---

[2] See Sharif N. Ahkam, "A Model for the Evaluation of and Response to Economic Exposure Risk by Multinational Companies," in *Managerial Finance* (special issue on "Risk Management in Global Finance"), ed. James C. Baker 21 (1995): 7–22.

	Monetary Assets	Monetary Liabilities
Appreciating Currency	Increase	Decrease
Depreciating Currency	Decrease	Increase

Subject to the requirements of
     1. Working capital and financing availability
     2. Corporate debt ratio considerations
     3. Other costs of these changes

FIGURE 4–1 Reducing Currency Exposure Management Objectives

a depreciating currency, to increase monetary liabilities and reduce monetary assets. These objectives are shown in Figure 4–1.

Foreign Exchange Management Issues

Given the firm must manage translation, transaction, and economic exposures, a number of questions must be answered by the international financial manager. For example, what is the appropriate definition of exposure for a given operation? Given FASB-52 has successfully replaced FASB-8 as the foreign currency translation standard for U.S. companies, can these companies ignore translation exposure? How much should a company hedge translation vs. transaction exposure? When is exposure material, i.e., how large is the exposure and potential impact on the company's profit? How much can the exchange rate change? Generally, the longer the time period, the greater the risk with foreign exchange rates. When does a policy of not hedging become speculation?

One problem for many U.S. companies is that top management does not understand or contribute sufficiently to foreign exchange policies and the difficult decisions that must be made in this area of international finance. This may be an organizational problem, i.e., should the firm centralize or decentralize the foreign exchange function? Should the firm use a committee approach or designate an individual for foreign exchange management responsibility?

Other managerial issues include managerial philosophy. For example, is the firm speculating when it trades in the forward market? Or should the firm speculate? How can the firm forecast currency rates? How can management function without credible currency forecasts? The MNC financial manager may become bogged down by his past decisions and has little time to improve the state-of-the-art. The ultimate question becomes: how long is the lack of improvement going to last?

Given an analysis of these questions, top management of companies exposed to currency risk should develop an effective strategy for managing this risk. Such a strategy should begin with at least three steps. First, company management should determine what exactly is at risk. To do this requires an understanding of what foreign exchange risk is, including the degree of volatility in foreign exchange rates. For exam-

ple, during the period of 18 months beginning in late 1994, the Mexican peso devalued 60 percent against the dollar in a three-month period, the U.S. dollar rose 35 percent against the Japanese yen and fell more than 20 percent against the German mark and the Swiss franc, the Canadian dollar fell 12 percent against the U.S. dollar, the Italian lira devalued 30 percent against the German mark, and the South African rand and Brazilian real devalued 10 percent against the U.S. dollar. Second, top management should identify the objectives of the company's foreign exchange risk management program. These objectives may include hedging of specific transactions and reducing fluctuations in translated profits. A company may even include speculation in foreign currencies as one of its objectives. Third, top management should design policies that will achieve these objectives. These stages should lead to an exchange risk management model designed to enhance market value of the firm in line with the goal of maximizing the value of shareholders' stake in the firm. This foreign exchange exposure management model underlies the following discussion of the organization and implementation of currency risk management in the MNC.

Organizing for Foreign Exchange Management

THE ISSUE OF CENTRALIZATION VS. DECENTRALIZATION

Centralized currency exposure management requires centralization of exposure itself. The centralized management of decentralized exposure manifests itself in two ways. First, a central hedging unit, operating in its own name and for its own account, can hedge positions that it does not have and that are positions of the various operating affiliates of the company. This method is classified as being centralized. Second, the central hedging unit can merely provide guidance or issue hedging instructions to the operating affiliates. They, in turn, do the hedging. This method is classified as being decentralized. In some cases, the central hedging unit will implement some variation of both of these methods when it acts as an advisory unit and hedges for the account of the affiliates. Serious weaknesses can be found in both approaches.

Advantages of Centralization

Centralization of foreign currency exposure hedging has a number of advantages. First, the home office has a global view of the company's exposure. Second, centralization results in fewer cross-conversions of currencies. These are situations in which one operating affiliate buys one currency that another unit has to sell at the same time. Third, centralization facilitates the pooling of foreign currencies so that better prices on conversions, deposits, and borrowing can be obtained. Finally, policy issues can be resolved at higher levels when hedging is centralized. Expertise is in short supply at lower levels of the firm.

Advantages of Decentralization

Decentralization of the exposure management function has some advantages. It permits more management levels to take part in hedging decisions, and decisions can be made in the environment of the financial markets of the individual currencies. Operating managers in the foreign environment are under pressure to respond to forex changes and have more access to local financial data. On the other hand, the advantages do not outweigh the disadvantages of decentralization.

Singer Company was an early pioneer of foreign exchange exposure management and practiced a mix of centralization and decentralization in operationalizing this function. Periodically, usually monthly, Singer would hold meetings at headquarters of all of its foreign operations managers. The degree of foreign currency exposure was measured during these meetings with input by the foreign managers. Decisions about the

amount of exposure to hedge would be made during these meetings. Thus, information relevant to the decision making was presented by managers in the field. Then, central management made the decisions about which tools to use in hedging the exposure.

Another U.S. company, Dexter Corporation, an industrial conglomerate that derives 50 percent of its revenues from abroad, established a centralized European treasury operation in Brussels in 1991. Before that time, the company had given local management responsibility over currency risk management. The company gained a competitive advantage by having the ability to pull exposure information and hedging responsibility into one location, especially in light of the ERM volatility in the early 1990s.[3]

The transition economies of Eastern Europe and the former Union of Soviet Socialist Republics present examples in which centralization of foreign currency management is important. The currencies of these economies are generally inconvertible into major currencies. This presents a serious problem for foreign investors wishing to participate in these countries. Financial investments into these countries has been facilitated by investment bankers that have sponsored funds for investment in Russia and Eastern Europe. These include Pictet, a Swiss private bank, and Cazenove, whose funds can be purchased in Dublin, London, and Luxembourg. Other leading banks such as Kleinwort Benson of the United Kingdom have managed equity investments in these transition economies.[4] Firms wishing to invest in these nations should centralize their foreign currency management and operate through such funds.

THE EXPOSURE MANAGEMENT FUNCTION

The strategies and organization of the exposure management function are discussed in the following sections.[5] First, the causes of currency fluctuations, discussed previously, need to be reiterated. These are caused by different inflation rates in different countries, which lead to different price levels in traded goods. Different demand management policies by governments cause trade surpluses or deficits. Different money supply policies and interest levels attract funds from easy money and low exchange rate centers to tight money and high rate centers. Other capital movements, such as the investment of former OPEC (Organization of Petroleum Exporting Countries) surpluses or the transfer by individuals of their liquid assets to politically safe countries lead to currency changes. And the foreign exchange traders speculate on all of these economic phenomena, causing even greater volatility in the foreign exchange markets.

Thus, firms must implement exchange risk management strategies and organize and control their exposure management functions. The firm can adopt any of three distinct exchange risk management strategies. The firm's management can adopt an extremely conservative policy by hedging all currency exposure. Second, management can adopt an extremely easygoing policy. The firm can resort to self-insurance, hedging none of the exposure. Before the advent of floating exchange rates, Hoover Company, for example, did not hedge its exposure to the British pound. After each pound devaluation, Hoover incurred large foreign currency losses because of its heavy ex-

---

[3] Nilly Ostro-Landau, "European Currency Convulsions," *International Business* (December 1995–January 1996): 22.

[4] Nicholas Denton and Richard Lapper, "Privatization Lures Cash to Russia," *Financial Times* (November 28, 1994): 15.

[5] For a discussion of exposure management, see, for example, James C. Baker and Raj Aggarwal, "Foreign Exchange Risk in Multinational Companies," *The Business Graduate* (U.K.) 14 (January 1984): 25–9; and James C. Baker, "Evolutionary Change in MNC Foreign Exchange Risk Management," *Baylor Business Studies* 12 (May, June, July 1981): 23–33.

Internal	*External*
Netting	Forward contracts
Leading and lagging	Money market hedge
Matching	Factoring
Asset/liability management	Discounting
Operational policies	Government insurance schemes
Constraints	*Constraints*
Adequate number of subsidiaries	Nonexistence of forward and spot markets in certain currencies
Degree of centralization of firm	
Political control over transfer prices, netting, and tax avoidance	Nonavailability of and limited access to local and offshore money markets
Customer and supplier reaction	Government regulation and control over spot, forward, and money markets
Degree of flexibility of operations	

Source: J.B. Holland, *International Financial Management* (Oxford, England: Basil Blackwell, 1986), p. 80.

FIGURE 4–2 Techniques of Foreign Exchange Risk Management

posed operations in the United Kingdom. Finally, the firm may adopt an intermediate policy of hedging some of the exposure and self-insuring the remainder.

Tactical Tools for Exposure Reduction

Several tools of a tactical nature can be used by most MNC CFOs to reduce foreign exchange exposure. These methods can be implemented from within the firm, i.e., internal techniques, or they may be available from sources external to the firm. See Figure 4–2 for a listing of these techniques and any constraints that may face the firm in their use. Figure 4–2 shows foreign exchange exposure management tools that are internal, i.e., those that a firm can adopt for use within the firm, and those that are available outside the firm from financial markets, commercial banks, and government agencies. These tools of exposure management are discussed in the following sections.

Figure 4–2 also presents the constraints for using either internal or external techniques that are incurred by financial management. For example, the firm must have an adequate number of subsidiaries to carry out techniques such as netting in order to take advantage of economies of scale. The degree of centralization of the firm may also restrict the use of some techniques. If the firm is highly decentralized, leading and lagging is difficult to implement. Netting requires some degree of decentralization since a regional netting center is required. Some countries do not have viable spot or forward exchange markets or prohibit the use of forward rate agreements. Money markets may be nonexistent for foreign firms in low-income countries. Financial markets may be tightly regulated by local governments because of foreign exchange shortages.

One of the most often used methods is to buy or sell currency in the forward exchange market, providing that the forward costs are reasonable or that such transactions are legally permitted. The firm may also tighten credit in order to reduce local receivables and develop disposable cash. All cash and marketable securities can be reduced to a minimum level by converting such items into plant and equipment or inventory or preferably into a cash transfer to the parent company, if transfers are permitted. Collection of receivables denominated in hard currency can be delayed. The firm can increase the importation of soft currency goods or change suppliers or source points. Local currency can be borrowed, although the firm should minimize the amount of cash retained. A simple offset may not help. The payment of accounts payable may

Strategy

Increase local currency assets (DM)	Decrease local currency liabilities
Decrease foreign currency assets (e.g., £s)	Increase foreign currency liabilities

Tactics

External

Buy local currency forward	Reduce local currency borrowings
Increase local currency cash and marketable securities	Accelerate payment of local currency accounts payable
Loosen local currency credit terms	Reduce imports of goods paid for in local currency
Tighten credit given in depreciating foreign currency	Invoice imports in foreign currency
Invoice exports in local currency (to depreciating foreign currency countries)	

Internal

Accelerate collection of receivables from parent and other units (Lead)	Delay dividends and fees to parent
	Delay payments to other (foreign) units (Lag)

Spot rate is DM 3.75/£. Three-month forward rate is DM 3.73/£. Thus: expect more pounds to the DM in three months or expect fewer DMs to the pound in three months.

Source: J.B. Holland, *International Financial Management*, (Oxford, England: Basil Blackwell, 1986), p. 76.

FIGURE 4–3 Strategy for a Subsidiary in Appreciating Currency Country (e.g., German subsidiary of a British firm)

FIGURE 4–4 Strategy for a Subsidiary in Depreciating Currency Country (e.g., French subsidiary of a British company)

Strategy

Decrease local currency (Ffr) assets	Increase local currency liabilities
Increase foreign currency (e.g., £s) assets	Decrease foreign currency liabilities

Tactics

External

Sell local currency forward (M)	Increase local currency borrowings (M)
Reduce local currency cash and marketable securities (M)	Delays accounts payable in local currency (CS)
Tighten credit in local foreign currency (CS)	Invoice imports in depreciating local currency (CS)
Loosen credit in appreciating foreign currency (CS)	
Invoice exports in appreciating foreign currency (CS)	

Internal

Slow down collection from parent and other units (Lag)	Accelerate payments of dividends and fees to parent
	Accelerate payments to parent and other foreign affiliates (Lead)

M = financial and foreign exchange market actions; CS = customer and supplier actions.

Spot rate is Ffr 9.5/£. Three-month forward rate is Ffr 9.8/£. Thus: expect more francs to the pound in 3 months or expect fewer pounds to the franc in 3 months.

Source: J.B. Holland, *International Financial Management*, (Oxford, England: Basil Blackwell, 1986), p. 77.

be delayed and purchase discounts may be ignored. Remittance of fees and dividends to the parent or to other affiliates may be accelerated. The settlement of intersubsidiary accounts payable may be accelerated.

Examples of the use of external and internal foreign exchange exposure management tools are shown in Figures 4–3 and 4–4. In Figure 4–3, an opportunistic strategy is shown for a firm whose subsidiary is operating in a country with an appreciating currency. The tactics shown should facilitate the implementation of a strategy that entails increasing local currency assets, decreasing local currency liabilities, decreasing foreign currency assets, and increasing foreign currency liabilities. Figure 4–4 presents a potential strategy for a firm whose subsidiary has operations in a country with a depreciating currency in which techniques are required for a strategy that includes decreasing local currency assets, increasing foreign currency assets, increasing local currency liabilities, and decreasing foreign currency liabilities.

Selected Forex Exposure Reduction Techniques

The two primary external techniques of foreign exchange exposure risk reduction, shown in Figure 4–3, forward market operations and money market hedges, have been discussed in detail elsewhere. Some discussion of two primary techniques that the firm can use in internal operations to reduce forex exposure merit discussion. These techniques are netting, particularly multilateral netting, and leads and lags.

Netting   Netting is the process whereby two or more affiliated companies that have reciprocal sales and purchases with each other choose to pay or to receive only the offsetting difference on a specific date. Multilateral currency netting is netting by affiliated companies located in different countries. The typical funds flows of an international company are shown in Figure 4–5. Multilateral netting requires some decentralization of the MNC by locating a regional netting center abroad. This regional operation can be referred to as a multicurrency management center and is a form of decentralization because some financial decisions regarding foreign exchange payments will be made in this location. The new funds flow arrangement is shown in Figure 4–6. The function of multilateral netting is demonstrated by comparing Figures 4–7 and 4–8. In Figure 4–7, the company has operations with payments and receipts in four different countries in which the U.S. dollar, Belgian franc, French franc, and Italian lira are used to settle payments among the four affiliates. In Figure 4–8, the employment of a netting center has reduced total receipts and payments drastically.

The benefits of multilateral netting are manifold. Bank transfer charges can be

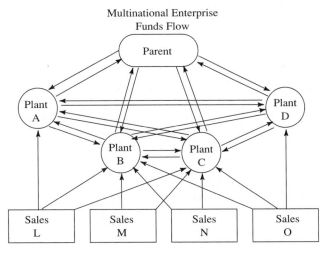

FIGURE 4–5 Typical Funds Flow of an MNC

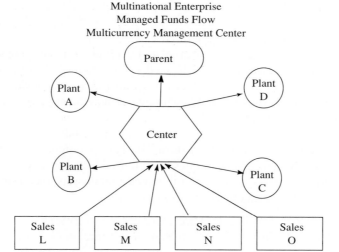

FIGURE 4–6 MNC Funds Flow with a Netting Center

	Paying Affiliates				
	United States	*Belgium*	*France*	*Italy*	*Total Receipts*
United States		300	400	500	1,200
Belgium	400		200	300	900
France	500	300		100	900
Italy	600	500	200		1,300
Total Payments	**1,500**	**1,100**	**800**	**900**	**4,300**

FIGURE 4–7 Multilateral International Payments Matrix Without Multilateral Netting

FIGURE 4–8 Multilateral International Payments Matrix with Multilateral Netting

	Net Payments			
	Payment	*Receipt*	*Net Payment*	*Net Receipt*
United States	1,500	1,200	300	—
Belgium	1,100	900	200	—
France	800	900	—	100
Italy	900	1,300	—	400

drastically reduced as can other foreign exchange-related expenses such as the purchase of foreign exchange, the opportunity costs of float, and cable charges. Double conversions of currencies are eliminated as is the float on transfers. The settlement process is simplified, and information is centralized. Multilateral netting provides discipline and better control. International cash and exposure management are facilitated.

A netting system has certain requirements. A central information and control point, the multicurrency management center, has to be established. A common currency of denomination must be chosen. Management of the netting center needs a thorough knowledge of foreign exchange markets as well as of banking and financial regulations.

Finally, intercompany netting, especially on a multilateral basis, needs certain types of information. The firm must have information regarding the amount and currencies of funds flows and knowledge of the origins and destinations of funds flows. The timing of these flows must be known, and the average size of payments is required. The per unit costs involved in sending funds between any two points must also be known.

Leads and Lags   The leading and lagging hedging technique will reduce foreign exchange exposure when receivables are delayed and payables are accelerated in an appreciating currency and when receivables are accelerated and payables are delayed in a depreciating currency. Other forms of funds flows such as management fees, dividends, and loan payments can also be used in the leading and lagging technique.

Leading and lagging has some limitations. The working capital needs of the local subsidiary must be considered before payments from the unit are accelerated. Local government regulations with regard to foreign exchange must also be considered. Some countries impose a maximum number of days in which payments can be slowed or accelerated. Management must be careful, especially in LDCs, when considering the initiation of such a policy against another firm. If the local firm is a government-owned principal supplier to the firm using leading and lagging, political problems may arise. See Figure 4–9 for a description of the leading and lagging hedging technique. The company in Figure 4–9, under normal situations, receives a year-end annual dividend from

FIGURE 4–9 Leading and Lagging

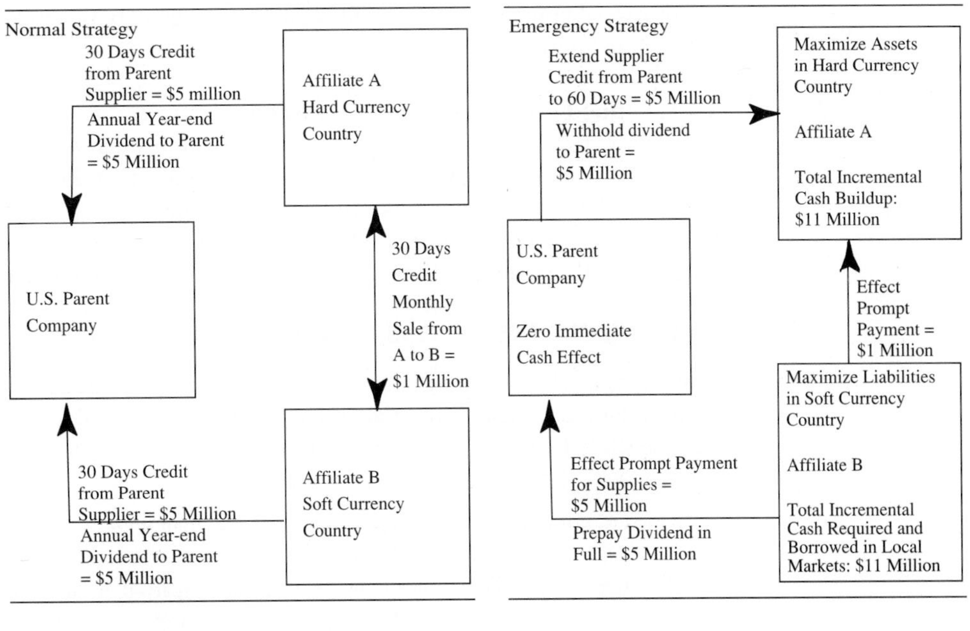

A Spanish company has an outstanding 6-month export receivable in the amount of $1 million on August 5, 1994. It borrows this amount for 6 months at 10% p.a.

a. It then sells $1 million spot against Spanish pesetas at Pta 129.84   Pta 129,840,000
  that yields
  ($1 million × 129.84)

b. Interest earned on 6 months Pta time deposit   Pta 6,492,000
  (Pta 129,840,000 × 10% × 6/12)

c. Gross Pta income (a + b)   Pta 136,332,000

d. Interest expense on dollars = $50,000 ($1 million × 10% × 6/12)   Pta 6,600,000
  Since this will be paid at the end of 6 months, it is brought forward
  against pesetas at Pta 132.00 (6 months forward rate) at a cost of

e. Net pretax revenue at end of transact (c − d)   Pta 129,732,000

Had it sold the dollars forward originally at the six months forward rate of Pta 130.92, the net receipt at maturity would have been Pta 130,920,000 ($1 million × 130.92).

Source: Based on Andreas R. Prindl, *Foreign Exchange Risk* (New York: John Wiley, 1976), p. 76.

FIGURE 4–10 Hedging Export Proceeds by Borrowing Same Currency

its affiliate in a hard currency country and gives thirty days credit for supplies to this affiliate. It gives the same treatment to its affiliate in a soft currency country. However, the company resorts to an emergency strategy when currency rates adversely affect its profitability if operations are continued under its normal strategy. A leading-lagging policy is implemented in which the company extends credit to the hard currency affiliate to sixty days and requires the affiliate to delay payment of its annual dividend. The effect will be to maximize assets in the hard currency country. At the same time, prompt payment for supplies is requested from the soft currency country affiliate and the dividend is prepaid, thus maximizing liabilities in the soft currency country.

Foreign Currency Loans

Hedging Export Proceeds   An exporter that invoices in a currency other than its own and that is forecast to weaken (or depreciate) can borrow in the same foreign currency for the maturity of the outstanding receivable and can sell the loan proceeds spot for its own currency.[6] The borrowing can be repaid at maturity by receipt of that currency. This transaction will reduce the gross borrowing cost. For example, assume the information shown in Figure 4–10; under the IRP, this technique approximates the cost of a forward contract. Some additional costs such as bank spreads or local reserve requirements may result in cost differentials.

Discounting Foreign Currency Receivables   In countries where no restrictions are placed on foreign currency borrowings, foreign currency receivables can be discounted.[7] The example shown in Figure 4–11 is based on the same example used in Figure 4–9. The discounting bank applies a combination of the domestic rate and the net cost/yield of the swap transaction, which may be affected by minimum reserve requirements and, thus, the discount rate may deviate from Euromarket rates.

ORGANIZING THE EXPOSURE MANAGEMENT FUNCTION

Any organization, whether a global firm or a function such as the management of foreign exchange exposure and risk, must begin with some objective.[8] It is preferable that the objective be stated formally but many firms—even *Fortune 500* companies—oper-

---

[6] Andreas R. Prindl, *Foreign Exchange Risk* (New York: John Wiley, 1976), p. 76.

[7] Ibid., p. 77.

[8] This section draws on the research found in Baker and Aggarwal, *Business Graduate*.

In the same Spanish company example, the exporter has received $1 million of discountable 6-month trade bills drawn on the importer.

a. These are discounted at 8% p.a. at a net interest cost of $40,000, leaving a dollar principal amount of $960,000

b. The dollar proceeds are sold at spot at Pta 129.84 yielding ..... Pta 124,646,400

c. Assuming again that the primary purpose of the transaction was to reduce or eliminate the currency risk and the funds are not needed for local purposes, they could be placed in a 6-month peseta time deposit at 5% p.a. This would yield interest of ..... Pta 3,116,160

Net pretax revenue   Pta 127,762,560

Lines for such transactions can be set up with the company's bank in advance and generally carry a commitment fee.

Source: Based on Andreas R. Prindl, *Foreign Exchange Risk* (New York: John Wiley, 1976), p. 77.

FIGURE 4–11 Discounting Foreign Currency Receivables

ate with no stated objectives. With regard to the management of foreign exchange risk, the exchange risk manager should identify the types of exposure to be monitored. The management objectives with respect to these exposure measures should be stated and guidance should be offered in the resolution of conflicts among the objectives.

In order to facilitate formulation of foreign exchange management objectives, the firm should identify the responsibility of exchange risk managers for input into long-term operating decisions that shape the firm's exchange risk threshold. This includes explicitly identifying and stating any constraints on the purpose and level of exposure management techniques, especially with regard to forward exchange market contracts, as identified in Figure 4–2. And the firm should adopt a methodology for evaluation and control of exchange risk management operations.

Exchange Risk Management Philosophy

In order to formulate the objectives of this function, the firm may be wise to adopt a philosophy concerning exchange risk management. This step may not be as complex as it sounds. The foreign exchange risk philosophy of an MNC may be to simply minimize forex losses or to cover every exposure, if possible, e.g., Caterpillar S.A. in Switzerland. Or the firm's philosophy may be complex, e.g., to reduce adverse effects from exchange exposure on cash. Or it may be somewhere between simple and complex. The philosophy practiced by Chemetron's management with regard to foreign operations mandates local managers to make a profit, manage efficiently, but leave the exposure problem to an exposure management team trained to operate in this area.

Other companies have evolved a set of foreign exchange risk management objectives over years of experience. Volvo, for example, fully covers exchange risks in order to maintain high liquidity, the latter a typical objective of auto manufacturers. Dow Chemical's managerial approach is one of flexibility. The company does more than just hedge and, on occasion, does its own trading in the foreign exchange market. Dow may even speculate on interest or foreign exchange rates. Company treasurers are oriented to a consolidated balance sheet, treat cash as a commodity or product, and believe profits should be made on it.

Organization of the Forex Risk Management Function

Companies have organized their foreign exchange exposure management function in various ways. DuPont has centralized the control of exposure management but maintains field input. Caterpillar uses an inhouse exchange trader. Diamond Shamrock created an exposure control committee with authority for financial decisions responsible for management of translation exposure. At Ely Lilly, the company organized exposure management around the function of multilateral netting with a regional netting

MNCs organize their foreign exchange management function in various ways. Search through business literature for examples of how international companies implement this function. Distinguish between those that centralize and those that decentralize foreign exchange management and evaluate the success of each managerial type.

center in London. The center notifies affiliates eight days prior to settlement. Affiliates then have four days to iron out communications with each other before they are then notified which will be net receivors and which net payors. Transfers are made on the settlement date and the London netting center buys or sells currencies forward to hedge the net amounts to be settled. Eastman Kodak uses surveillance to track currencies 18–24 hours a day. The exposure team continuously monitors currencies and adjusts forward positions overnight as conditions warrant. The function is centralized at headquarters and is managed by a five member exchange staff supervised by an international financial resources committee.

Control of the Forex Management Function

A management function may be initiated with very well-formulated objectives and have very good organization. If a system to evaluate and control the function is not implemented, the firm may not be able to identify problems in the management of foreign exchange risk. Some companies have given top priority to control of this function. At Union Carbide, top management holds periodic dialogues with operating management to determine and measure noncontractual cash flows. TRW has implemented a simple reporting system. The risk management function gets the same data that company accountants receive but on the twentieth day after closing the books on overseas operations. Most of the work and all of the analysis is done at headquarters and evaluation is accomplished by comparing the cost of borrowing with income from a subsequent investment. A determination is then made about how much is saved in reported foreign exchange losses by borrowing vs. doing nothing. Intercompany receivables and payables are eliminated. This leaves only translation/transaction exposure to be managed and this is covered by borrowing in the Eurocurrency market. Chemetron and Volvo both monitor foreign exchange positions monthly. At Chemetron, the system keys off data assembled monthly on current and forecast exposures of each foreign operation. Thus, companies have organized their forex risk management function in a variety of ways, depending on the management philosophy and risk threshold of top management.

Summary and Conclusions

A number of risks face banks and MNCs dealing in foreign exchange. Credit, transfer, and systemic risks affect banks. This has been especially so since the 1974 failure of Bankhaus Herstatt, a relatively small German privately-held bank that had large correspondent relationships with many large international banks.

MNCs also face translation, transaction, and economic exposure to foreign exchange rate fluctuations. Translation risk arises from reporting foreign operations denominated in foreign currency to the parent firm and translating these earnings into the

domestic currency according to preset accounting rules. Gains or losses may be incurred by these accounting procedures when the foreign currency operations are translated into the domestic currency at some exchange rate. Transaction risk arises when foreign exchange rates change after a transaction has been initiated but before it has been completely executed. Economic risk arises when the value of the firm changes because of exchange rate fluctuations that impact sales volume, prices, or costs.

Several tools are available to MNCs to hedge these exposure risks. They include the use of forward market contracts, multilateral netting, leads and lags, money market hedges, as well as a number of internal tactical techniques such as increasing or decreasing local borrowings, invoicing in foreign currencies, and changing the flow of dividends from foreign affiliates. Organization *and* control of the foreign exchange management function by the MNC is very important.

Additional Readings

Baker, James C., and Raj Aggarwal. "Foreign Exchange Risk in Multinational Companies." *The Business Graduate* (U.K.) 14 (January 1984): 25–9.

Brankovic, M., and J. Madura. "Effect of FASB Statement No. 52 on Profitability Ratios." *International Journal of Accounting Education and Research* 25 (1990): 19–28.

Garner, C. Kent, and Alan C. Shapiro. "A Practical Method of Assessing Foreign Exchange Risk." *Midland Corporate Finance Journal* (Fall 1984): 6–17.

Gill, C. W. "Foreign Exchange Exposures Under FASB 8 and 52." *The CPA Journal* 52 (1982): 24–31.

Griffin, P. A. "Management's Preferences for FASB Statement No. 52: Predictive Ability Results." *Abacus* 19 (1983): 130–8.

Khoury, Sarkis J., and K. Hung Chan. "Hedging Foreign Exchange Risk: Selecting the Optimal Tool." *Midland Corporate Finance Journal.* (Winter 1988): 40–52.

Miller, R. P., and N. N. Strauss. "SFAS No. 52: The FASB Tackles Foreign Currency Translation." *Corporate Accounting/Financial Manager/Small Business Controller* 1 (1983): 3–17.

Ndubizu, G. A. "Earnings Volatility and the Corporate Adoption Decision on FASB Statement No. 52: An Empirical Analysis." *Advances in International Accounting* 3 (1990): n.a.

Soenen, Luc A. "When Foreign Exchange Hedging Doesn't Help." *Journal of Cash Management* 11 (1991): 58–62.

Statement of Financial Accounting Standards No. 8 (Stamford, CT: Financial Accounting Standards Board, October 1975).

Statement of Financial Accounting Standards No. 52 (Stamford, CT: Financial Accounting Standards Board, December 1981).

Discussion Questions

1. Compare and contrast the three types of foreign exchange exposure risk.
2. The foreign exchange management function may be centralized or decentralized within the multinational firm. What are the advantages of centralization? What are the advantages of decentralization?
3. What is netting? How does bilateral netting differ from multilateral netting?
4. Discuss the ways by which MNCs measure *and* manage their foreign exchange risk.
5. How should the foreign exchange risk management function be organized?

Problems

1. Hoechst Chemical Company of Germany is negotiating a contract to supply a U.S. firm with chemical supplies at a dollar price fixed for one year. What should Hoechst do?

2. Niagra Machinery Company exports a significant amount of its bottle-washing equipment to Latin American countries and has been very reliable with its shipments. The dollar has appreciated greatly against the Argentinian peso during the past few years. Should Niagra reduce or stop its shipments to Argentina? What advice would you give the company?

3. Construct an international payments netting matrix without multilateral netting that includes company operations in the United States, Germany, Great Britain, and Spain with the United States operation making the following payments in dollar equivalents: (1) 600 to the German firm, 750 to the British unit, and 900 to the Spanish firm; (2) the German firm makes payments of 450 to the U.S. firm, 450 to the British firm, and 750 to the Spanish firm; (3) the British firm makes payments of 600 to the U.S. firm, 300 to the German firm, and 150 to the Spanish firm; and (4) the Spanish firm makes payments of 750 to the U.S. firm, 450 to the German firm, and 150 to the British firm.

4. Assume the facts in Problem #3 and that the U.S. parent firm has established a multilateral netting center in Europe. Construct a multilateral international payments netting matrix and show the changes in net payments and net receipts for the four operations.

5. Assume the following balance sheet for the German subsidiary of a U.S. MNC:

Balance Sheet
Hans Schuler AG
Year Ending December 31, 1995

Account	DM Amount
Cash	100
Accounts Receivable	600
Inventory	400
Fixed Assets	500
Total Assets	**DM 1,600**
Accounts Payable	400
Notes Payable	600
Long-Term Debt	300
Translation-Gain (Loss)	
Net Worth	300
Total Liabilities and Net Worth	**DM 1,600**

Assume the exchange rate at the beginning of the year is DM 1.4925 = $1 and, at the end of the year, it is DM 1.6667. Construct the balance sheet for this company in dollars assuming FASB-52 is used and that the dollar is the functional currency. What would be the effect of this currency change on the parent firm's financial statements if FASB-8 were still in effect?

5

Political Risk in Global Financial Management

Major Objectives of Chapter 5

To examine the various types of political risk facing the MNC and the methods available to the firm to manage or insure against such risks.

Key terms to be learned in chapter 5

- political risk
- expropriation
- FCIA
- MIGA
- ICSID
- BERI
- OPIC
- transition economies

Introduction

The MNC operates in a wide variety of political environments. These environments include private enterprise as we know it. Some host countries practice a system of private enterprise, e.g., Germany, where the national or local governments own a significant amount of enterprise. Some practice a type of private enterprise where the central government formulates and implements economic plans that control much of primary, secondary, and tertiary economic enterprise, e.g., Korea. In other countries, the MNC operates within a very controlled or socialistic system, as in many less-developed countries (LDCs). For example, the government of Tanzania controls much of economic activity in that country and, as a result of this and other problems, usually ranks at or near the bottom of most political risk rankings. Before the demise of communism in the now-defunct Union of Soviet Socialist Republics and its satellite nations in Eastern Europe, international companies operating in those countries encountered a great deal of political risk. These countries have adopted policies encouraging privatization during the past few years but much of the political riskiness of operating in countries in the beginning stages of the adoption of capitalism still affects foreign investment in these countries.

121

The political risk that companies encounter when investing in a foreign country must be analyzed, measured, and managed. These risks stem from government responses to external and internal changes in the national economy and to external and internal changes in the national social structure. The local government's response is manifest in the form of acts, policies, laws, decrees, regulations, and administrative pronouncements that affect the foreign enterprise in three major areas: (1) transfer risks—the risk that the foreign affiliate will be restricted in remittance of earnings or repatriation of capital to the parent firm, (2) operations risks—that, for example, the local government will require the foreign affiliate to hire mostly local nationals or to operate in a restricted manner, and (3) ownership-control risks—that the foreign affiliate might be expropriated or nationalized by the local government. The government response mentioned above is formulated by local standards and cultures including leadership styles, ideology, the way in which power is exercised, and traditions in administration and institutions in general.

Types of Political Risks

Companies, thus, will encounter political risk (PR) with most of their foreign investments, no matter how economically sound the host government. PR affects company operations and profits as a result of government action in the form of laws, decrees, policies, actions, and regulations and is manifest in several ways. The discussion here will concentrate on four types of political risk: (1) violence from war, revolution, coups, and insurrection; (2) inconvertibility of local currency or other restrictions on its use by foreign investors; (3) interference with contract obligations; and (4) expropriation of private property.

VIOLENCE OR WAR

MNCs have encountered violence from civil war, insurrection, coups, and terrorism in many countries. At any one time, some type of organized violence, stemming from the ultimate failure of national governments, or factions within a country, to negotiate a peaceful settlement of some political dispute may be found in as many as ten or more countries of the world. For example, in 1994, civil war was prominent in Bosnia, with Serbians, Moslems, and Bosnians engaged in a bloody war. United Nations troops have been assigned to Somalia to protect the public from factions fighting in a long civil war. Terrorism has been prevalent in the Philippines, Sri Lanka, and even countries such as India and Pakistan. The Irish Republican Army conflict in Northern Ireland, in opposition to the presence of British troops there, has resorted to terrorist bombings in London. Terrorism has also been at the center of the bombing of jet liners. Even the United States is not immune to terrorist attacks. Terrorists were responsible for the 1993 World Trade Center bombing in New York City and may have been the underlying cause for the bombing of the Federal Building in Oklahoma City, Oklahoma, and a train derailment in Arizona in 1995. Armed conflict has been prevalent in several African nations, including Liberia, Burundi, Chad, and Rwanda.

CURRENCY RESTRICTIONS

If a firm has made direct investments in plant and equipment in a foreign country, it will need to make periodical payments back to the parent company or to an affiliated company in the home or some third country. A major objective of the parent firm should

be to participate in the profits of the foreign subsidiary. Thus, foreign exchange will be needed to remit profits back to the headquarters firm. The foreign subsidiary may need to make interest and/or principal payments on a loan to the parent firm or to an affiliate in a third country. Other funds flows may require foreign exchange. These flows may be manifest in the form of management fees paid by the subsidiary to the parent, royalties on licensing agreements between the parent and subsidiary firms, or transfer payments for parts or other inventory.

The flow of profits from foreign subsidiaries to the parent firm may be restricted or blocked entirely by the host government. Thus, dividend payments, management fees, royalties on licensing agreements, subsidiary loan payments, and other transfers of funds may be restricted or blocked by foreign exchange regulations implemented by the host government. This action by the local government generates political risk.

The use of foreign exchange by a foreign firm may be restricted, thus hindering its ability to make any of these funds flows. Most developing countries have laws restricting the use of foreign exchange by their citizens. In fact, in some of these countries, foreign exchange may be limited for use by only the most sensitive economic sectors. Usually, if the foreign firm produces goods that will be exported and will, therefore, produce foreign exchange, restrictions against such firms will be light. However, in some of these countries, the use of foreign exchange may be licensed by the government. When such a system is incorporated, corruption and bribing of public officials may be prevalent.

CONTRACT INTERFERENCE

Contracts between foreign investors and local firms, or even host state government agencies, may be interfered with or repudiated by host government action. Contract interference may result for many reasons. For example, when the Korean jetliner 007 was shot down by a Soviet military plane, the Canadian Government severed cultural exchanges temporarily with the U.S.S.R. A tour of Canada by a Moscow circus was cancelled—a result of this suspension of cultural relations. The contract between Canadian tourism officials and the circus was repudiated by national government action. Another example of government interference with a contract occurred when a Scandinavian contractor who had half completed a deep water port in West Africa had his construction contract repudiated by the local government because a relative of a government official decided to develop a competing port further down the coast and had the local laws and regulations swung his way to eliminate competition. This loss was covered by political risk insurance.

A contract may be interfered with in very subtle ways. In one small-scale lobstering operation in Africa, a U.S. company had a franchise to catch lobster—on condition that the government inspector could fly with each payload from a local fishing area to the packing plant in a third country's principal city. This arrangement was satisfactory at first because the government inspector was a small person. He was subsequently replaced with a man the size of a professional football player. The extra weight caused the payload to become unprofitable and the entire operation had to be shut down. This was essentially an interference with a contract caused by a political action. The investor had purchased political risk insurance and the loss was covered.

An external governmental action can also cause problems for contract performance. The invasion of Kuwait that led to Desert Storm caused on-demand bonds to be called. These bonds are required to be put up by foreign construction companies to guarantee performance on construction projects. The U.S.-imposed embargo against Iraq also led to the cancellation of performance bonds.

Contract Disputes

Contract disputes often arise between parties to an investment project. Many of these are based on the cultural differences between the investors, especially if one investor is from an industrialized country and the other is from a LDC. Some of these disputes do arise from political risk inherent in the country. Such disputes must be settled so that they do not interfere with the terms of the contract or so that one of the parties does not repudiate the contract.

Most such disputes arise in contracts between private parties. These may be settled either amicably by the parties involved or the dispute may be settled by the judicial system of one of the parties in the dispute. Many of these disputes are settled by arbitration or conciliation, usually by a private group such as the American Arbitration Association, similar types of arbitration agencies in Japan and Korea, or by the facilities of the International Chamber of Commerce.

ICSID An increasing number of contract disputes have arisen between foreign investors and host state governments where contracts for foreign investment projects may be necessary between such parties. This is especially so in LDCs. An affiliate of the World Bank, the International Centre for Settlement of Investment Disputes (ICSID), was established in 1966 to facilitate settlement of such disputes.[1] ICSID exercises a very narrow jurisdiction over contract disputes that arise between foreign investors from nations whose government has ratified the ICSID Convention and host state governments that have also ratified the ICSID Convention. Once such a dispute arises, if the parties agree to ICSID intervention, a panel of from one to three experts is appointed with the agreement of the parties to the dispute and ICSID. This arbitration panel then deliberates over the dispute in meetings facilitated by ICSID. The parties, once they have initiated an ICSID arbitration, must agree to follow the deliberations through to their conclusion, no matter which party wins. At the end of ICSID's fiscal year 1995, 134 nations were signatory members of the organization and 119 of these had ratified the ICSID Convention.

One of the first cases in which ICSID was involved concerned a dispute between Holiday Inn and the Republic of Morocco.[2] Holiday Inn and Occidental Petroleum had entered into a contract with the Republic of Morocco to build four motels in that country. Moroccan subsidiaries were established by Holiday Inn in order to facilitate payment by the Moroccan government. Because of alleged acts by the Moroccan Government, Holiday Inn stopped construction. A dispute arose, both the investor's home country and Morocco had ratified the ICSID Convention, an ICSID arbitration was triggered, and an arbitration panel was appointed. In the ICSID proceedings, the claimants argued that the unilateral action by the Moroccan government was contrary to the terms of the basic agreement between the parties but also violated the character of ICSID principles. The dispute was finally settled several years later.

ICSID's case history has shown mixed success.[3] A total of 27 cases have been brought to ICSID since its inception through the end of its fiscal year 1993. Of these, 16 cases have come to a conclusion and 9 have ended in final awards. A number of cases have been settled amicably by the parties or dropped altogether. At the end of fiscal

---

[1] James C. Baker and Lois Yoder, "ICSID Arbitration and the U.S. Multinational Corporation: An Alternative Dispute Resolution Method for International Business," *Journal of International Arbitration* 5 (December 1988): 81–95.

[2] Georges R. Delaume, "ICSID Tribunals and Provisional Measures—A Review of the Cases," *ICSID Review Foreign Investment Law Journal* 1 (Fall 1986): 392–3.

[3] This information was obtained from several ICSID annual reports.

year 1994, only three cases were still pending outcomes. In a few, the finding has been appealed and, in some, one of the parties has withdrawn from ICSIDs jurisdiction. Thus, ICSID has had mixed results with this facility. Its narrow jurisdiction and the small case history of results coupled with its relative obscurity and lack of familiarity among MNCs has diminished its true potential. As more and more foreign investment projects involve contracts between foreign investors and agencies of host state governments, ICSID's services will become more significant.

Russia and other former Soviet countries represent one area of the world of business that may require more arbitration of the type that ICSID facilitates. The legal system in these countries has not developed to the extent that, for example, contract terms may be relied upon by foreign business firms that invest in these countries. Foreign parties to contracts with local businesses in that part of the world have had problems not only in the reliance upon contract terms, but also the enforcement of these terms.

EXPROPRIATION

Governments have the sovereign right to expropriate, or take over, property that is privately owned. Even in the United States, governments have the right of eminent domain to expropriate private property for government use—to build a city street or sewer system, to build a park or a government building, to form a lake above a dam from which hydroelectric power will be generated, to expand an airport, or for a variety of other reasons.

In some cases, government expropriation may be compensated. The compensation may be either partial or full. In some cases, the takeover may be accomplished by creeping nationalization in the form of laws requiring that a certain percentage of workers or executives be local citizens. In some regions, foreign investment is restricted to a finite period of time. For example, in the Andean Pact countries, the Andean Foreign Investment Code requires that foreign investment be divested within fifteen years after it is made. Such a requirement will mandate a different strategy toward foreign investment in these countries because the life of such investment cannot be considered for more than a relatively short period of time. Much new investment in plant and equipment takes years longer to mature and become profitable.

A number of examples can be cited in which foreign investment was expropriated and the action in some cases was a surprise while in others it came as a relief to the parent company. In the early 1970s, drastic change in the government of Chile created an antagonistic environment in which foreign investment, especially the copper companies, became highly resented. The Chilean government finally took over the copper companies, primarily U.S.-owned, under the guise that these companies had not paid their fair share of income taxes. It is probable in this country where tax payments were involuntary and not well enforced that the copper companies paid a higher amount of taxes owed than did Chilean companies.

In the 1950s and 1960s, electric utilities in Latin American countries were, in many cases, owned by foreign companies, such as ITT Corporation of the United States. Two economic problems were present in some of these cases, especially in Brazil and Argentina. Population growth required expansion and modernization of these electric utilities. Investment funds had to come from profits. However, the national governments in question would not allow the foreign owners to charge higher rates because of the political problems higher costs to consumers would produce. Thus, the plants were not modernized, could not keep up with the demand, and became losing operations. When they were eventually expropriated, the top management of parent foreign companies such as ITT gave a sigh of relief. They were happy to have these losing operations taken over by the host governments, as were the Mexican banks when they were taken over by the Mexican government in the 1980s.

Evaluation of Political Risk

Many firms, banks, and government agencies measure and analyze the political riskiness of countries. A wide variety of methodologies are used by the source of these evaluations and many of them rank countries by some type of index.[4] Some evaluations are country-specific and entail a very comprehensive analysis. In the following sections, the discussion will, first, concentrate on the information useful in analyzing the PR of specific countries and, second, cover the leading PR rankings, Business Environmental Risk Index (BERI), the *Euromoney* country risk ranking, the *Institutional Investor* country risk ranking, Frost and Sullivan's Political Risk Services, and others.

ANALYSIS AND MEASUREMENT OF POLITICAL RISK

The international firm can use one of these country risk ranking methods but when projects are considered in specific countries, management needs more than a simple ranking to make the investment decision. Political riskiness of the country or countries wherein the proposed project(s) is located must be identified and analyzed. One of the complex problems is identification of specific political risk. The risks need to be analyzed and the firm needs to identify what types of risk threaten the viability of the company's operations in that country.[5] Analysis of PR can be implemented as a process. First, management should consider all major risks that might be of crucial significance to the firm on a country-by-country or project-by-project basis. Second, the risks should be ranked accordingly and a systematic assessment should be made of the likelihood of these political risks actually occurring. Third, the firm should formulate a list of potential political risks that it might face in each country in which it has significant operations. At this point, the risk threshold at which top management should be warned should be identified. Corporate management should only be concerned with political risks that threaten the firm's viability in each country. Little attention should be paid to the remainder of the risks.[6]

Thus, the question is raised: what types of risk threaten the viability of operations? Such risks can be separated into three types: (1) those that reduce the company's capability to produce or market below the level needed to maintain viable operations and are not a direct result of government policies, e.g., war, insurrection, or other forms of violence; (2) government imposed restrictions, e.g., expropriation, tariff cutbacks, or price controls; and (3) government imposed restrictions that affect the remittance of profits or the repatriation of capital, e.g., export restrictions, devaluations, or other foreign exchange controls.

POLITICAL RISK RATING SERVICES

MNCs have available a number of services that rate the political riskiness of countries and that rank countries according to this risk. Among the major PR rating services are BERI (Business Environmental Risk Index), the *Euromoney* Country Risk Rankings,

---

[4] See, for example, James C. Baker and M. Anaam Hashmi, "Political Risk Management: Steering Clear of Risky Business," *Risk Management* 35 (October 1988): 40–7; Baker and Hashmi, "Political Risk Assessment Methods: Expectations and Practices of Multinational Companies," *The International Trade Journal* 3 (Winter 1988): 187–202; and E. Dichtl and H. C. Koalmayr, "Country Risk Ratings," *Management International Review* 26 (1988): 4–11.

[5] Conrad E. Pearson, "A Model for Identifying Political Risk," *Planning Review* (January 1982): 24–6, 39.

[6] See S. Prakash Sethi and K.A.N. Luther, "Political Risk Analysis and Direct Foreign Investment: Some Problems of Definition and Measurement," *California Management Review* 28 (Winter 1986): 57–68, for a comprehensive treatment of problems involved in political risk analysis.

the *Institutional Investor* Country Risk Rankings, and Frost and Sullivan's Political Risk Service. These will be discussed in more detail in the following sections.

Business Environmental Risk Index

The Business Environmental Risk Index (BERI) was developed by Frederick Haner, a former business professor at the University of Delaware, as a way to rank countries by their riskiness.[7] This quarterly index was begun in 1972 and covers business risks in forty-five countries. The higher the rating of a country, the lower is its riskiness for foreign investment. The index is formulated from subjective and quantitative inputs from a wide variety of panel members, originally about 100, recruited by Haner and located in the countries rated by the system. Some of these are close acquaintances of the founder of BERI and some of the material input into the index has been criticized as being anecdotal. This panel assesses countries each quarter and rates each factor on a scale of zero to four, zero indicating unacceptable conditions for investment in that country, one signifying poor conditions, two signifying acceptable or average conditions, three being above average, and four meaning superior conditions exist in the country being assessed.

The panelists rate fifteen factors that affect the business climate. These factors include political stability, balance of payments, bureaucratic delays, and long-term credit availability. At any rate, several leading firms have used the BERI as input into their foreign investment decision process.

Companies use the BERI analysis as a tool to verify and supplement information from other sources in making decisions about many international operations including the following.[8]

1. to evaluate expansion projects and new investment possibilities;

2. to decide whether, and where, to conclude licensing and trade agreements;

3. to appraise management performance in different parts of the world where local factors may make the performance of one manager seem better than that of a manager in another country.

Euromoney

One of the more respected country risk rating systems is that computed and published periodically in *Euromoney*, a monthly magazine with headquarters in London that covers global money and capital markets and financial institutions. This country risk assessment method utilizes nine categories that encompass the broad areas of analytical indicators, debt indicators, and access to international finance. The nine categories utilized in the *Euromoney* formula include economic data (25 percent weighting), political risk (25 percent), debt indicators (10 percent), debt in default or being rescheduled (10 percent), credit ratings (10 percent), and access to bank finance, access to short-term finance, access to international bond and syndicated loan markets, and access to and discount on forfeiting (each weighted 5 percent). The highest weighted items are economic data, taken from the *Euromoney* global economic projections for the current year, and political risk, accomplished by a *Euromoney* survey of risk analysts, risk insurance brokers, and bank credit officers who give countries a score of zero to ten, ten meaning no risk of nonpayment and zero indicating that no chance of payment exists.

Table 5–1 shows how the *Euromoney* weighting formula works in a comparison of two countries ranked in March 1994: the United States ranked No. 1 with a weighted score of 96.74 and Republic of Korea ranked No. 27 with a weighted score of 78.57. The

---

[7] Roy Hill, "Which Countries are Best for Investment?" *International Management* (August 1974): 12–5.

[8] Ibid.

TABLE 5-1. The *Euromoney* Weighted System United States vs. Republic of Korea

		Analytical Indicators		Debt Indicators			Access to International Finance			
	Total	Economic Performance	Political Risk	Debt Indicators	Debt in Default or Rescheduled	Credit Ratings	Access to Bank Lending	Access to Short-term Finance	Access to Capital Markets	Discount on Forfeiting
Weighting	100.00	25.00	25.00	10.00	10.00	10.00	5.00	5.00	5.00	5.00
United States	96.74	25.00	21.74	10.00	10.00	10.00	5.00	5.00	5.00	5.00
Rep. of Korea	78.57	19.99	21.74	9.66	10.00	6.92	0.14	2.50	3.50	4.11

United States had a perfect rating in eight of the nine factors. Only in political risk does the United States fall short of a perfect score. *Euromoney* gave it a score of 87 (21.74/ 25) in political riskiness, primarily because of the performance of the Clinton administration and uncertainty about congressional elections. Korea was near perfect in debt indicators and perfect in debt in default. Its access to bank lending was given a rating of nearly zero and all other indicators were rated only fair by *Euromoney*.

The *Euromoney* formula[9] results in ranking of 170 countries from highest risk to lowest. The rankings are formulated as follows: the different scores for each category are calculated into the weighted scores as follows: the highest figure in each category receives the full mark for the weighting. The lowest receives zero. The score for other figures is calculated proportionately according to the formula:

$$\text{final score} = [\text{weighting} \div (\text{maximum figure} - \text{minimum figure})]$$
$$\times (\text{intermediate figure} - \text{minimum figure})$$

See Table 5–2 for a listing of the top 25 countries and the lowest 25 countries ranked by the *Euromoney* model.

Institutional Investor

Another leading country risk ranking is published by *Institutional Investor*, a monthly magazine that covers all areas of finance. The *Institutional Investor* Country Risk Rankings are based on ratings provided by leading international banks. A sample of 75–100 international banks is queried and bankers grade each country on a scale of 0 to 100, or from lowest rank in terms of country risk to highest rank. Zero, thus, is least credit worthy while 100 is most credit worthy. The sample is updated every six months and published in *Institutional Investor*. Banks are not permitted to rate their home countries. The individual responses are weighted, using an *Institutional Investor* formula that properly gives more weight to responses from banks with the largest worldwide exposure and the most sophisticated country analysis systems. See Table 5–3 for the country ranking according to *Institutional Investor*.

Frost and Sullivan's Political Risk Services

Frost and Sullivan (F&S) is a property insurer and its political risk service is typical of a private insurer's methodology in rating country risk. F&S regularly monitors some 85 countries by surveying its global network of 250 country specialists. F&S considers such risk factors as repatriation restrictions on international business, payment delays facing exporters to that country, government policy related to fiscal and monetary expansion, and governmental foreign borrowing.[10] F&S gives each country rated a financial transfer risk grade ranging from A+—countries such as Germany, Japan, United Kingdom, and the United States receive this grade—to D—Brazil and Sudan

---

[9] The Euromoney Country Risk Method," *Euromoney* (September 1993): 366.

[10] "Political and Financial Risk," *Bankers Monthly* CV (June 1988): 12.

TABLE 5–2.   Top and Bottom 25 Countries Ranked by *Euromoney* (March 1994)

COUNTRY RISK RANKINGS 1993

Rank			Country	Total (weighting) 100	Analytical Indicators		Debt Indicators			Access to International Finance			
March 94	Sept 93	March 93			Economic Performance 25	Political Risk 25	Debt Indicators 10	Debt in Default or Rescheduled 10	Credit Ratings 10	Access to Bank Lending 5	Access to Short-term Finance 5	Access to Capital Markets 5	Discount on Forfeiting 5
1	1	2	United States	96.74	25.00	21.74	10.00	10.00	10.00	5.00	5.00	5.00	5.00
2	8	6	Austria	96.66	22.38	24.28	10.00	10.00	10.00	5.00	5.00	5.00	5.00
3	3	3	Luxembourg	96.49	22.58	23.91	10.00	10.00	10.00	5.00	5.00	5.00	5.00
4	6	5	Canada	96.46	22.94	23.91	10.00	10.00	9.62	5.00	5.00	5.00	5.00
5	7	8	Netherlands	96.38	22.10	24.28	10.00	10.00	10.00	5.00	5.00	5.00	5.00
6	4	11	Switzerland	95.73	21.41	25.00	10.00	10.00	10.00	5.00	5.00	5.00	4.32
7	5	4	France	95.55	21.28	24.28	10.00	10.00	10.00	5.00	5.00	5.00	5.00
8	9	9	Denmark	95.38	22.64	23.55	10.00	10.00	9.23	5.00	5.00	5.00	4.96
9	13	13	Germany	95.21	20.57	24.64	10.00	10.00	10.00	5.00	5.00	5.00	5.00
10	12	10	Singapore	94.39	24.19	22.26	10.00	10.00	9.23	5.00	3.75	5.00	4.96
11	11	12	Norway	94.27	22.94	22.46	10.00	10.00	9.62	5.00	5.00	5.00	4.26
12	10	7	United Kingdom	94.20	22.64	21.56	10.00	10.00	10.00	5.00	5.00	5.00	5.00
13	2	1	Japan	93.80	20.66	23.14	10.00	10.00	10.00	5.00	5.00	5.00	5.00
14	14	15	Belgium	91.98	19.56	23.19	10.00	10.00	9.23	5.00	5.00	5.00	5.00
15	15	16	Taiwan	91.67	23.83	22.83	10.00	10.00	9.23	5.00	2.50	4.00	4.28
16	19	18	Sweden	90.97	20.36	22.46	10.00	10.00	8.85	5.00	5.00	5.00	4.30
17	16	17	Australia	90.18	18.47	23.25	10.00	10.00	8.46	5.00	5.00	5.00	5.00
18	17	19	New Zealand	88.56	18.04	22.83	10.00	10.00	7.69	5.00	5.00	5.00	5.00
19	18	14	Spain	88.23	18.47	22.00	10.00	10.00	8.46	5.00	5.00	5.00	4.30
20	20	20	Ireland	88.09	19.90	20.54	10.00	10.00	7.69	5.00	5.00	5.00	4.96
21	23	23	Italy	87.65	18.51	22.46	10.00	10.00	7.69	5.00	5.00	4.00	4.98
22	21	24	Finland	87.52	18.77	21.38	10.00	10.00	8.08	5.00	5.00	5.00	4.30
23	25	26	Portugal	84.99	18.54	20.83	9.04	10.00	7.31	5.00	5.00	5.00	4.28
24	22	22	Hong Kong	82.31	19.72	20.71	10.00	10.00	6.15	5.00	3.00	4.00	3.73
25	24	21	Iceland	82.16	16.09	20.69	10.00	10.00	6.15	5.00	5.00	5.00	4.24

TABLE 5-2. (cont.)

COUNTRY RISK RANKINGS 1993

Rank			Country	Total (weighting) 100	Analytical Indicators		Debt Indicators		Credit Ratings 10	Access to International Finance			
March 94	Sept 93	March 93			Economic Performance 25	Political Risk 25	Debt Indicators 10	Debt in Default or Rescheduled 10		Access to Bank Lending 5	Access to Short-term Finance 5	Access to Capital Markets 5	Discount on Forfeiting 5
140	145	137	Mauritania	25.81	2.98	5.62	7.21	10.00	0.00	0.00	0.00	0.00	0.00
141	143	147	Angola	25.61	2.76	3.37	8.23	10.00	0.00	0.00	0.25	1.00	0.00
142	115	121	Macedonia	25.53	10.72	3.80	0.00	10.00	0.00	0.00	0.50	0.50	0.00
143	166	161	Liberia	24.72	0.00	3.97	10.00	10.00	0.00	0.00	0.25	0.50	0.00
144	163	157	Tajikistan	24.16	8.94	4.23	0.00	10.00	0.00	0.00	0.50	0.50	0.00
145	139	148	Belarus	23.75	6.45	5.80	0.00	10.00	0.00	0.00	0.50	1.00	0.00
146	157	166	Zaire	23.44	2.53	1.78	8.38	10.00	0.00	0.00	0.25	0.50	0.00
147	168	168	Sudan	23.11	2.83	2.68	7.35	10.00	0.00	0.00	0.25	0.00	0.00
148	160	159	Moldova	22.89	7.55	4.35	0.00	10.00	0.00	0.00	0.50	0.50	0.00
149	146	142	Ukraine	22.73	6.16	5.07	0.00	10.00	0.00	0.00	0.50	1.00	0.00
150	158	162	Mozambique	22.60	6.40	3.38	3.12	9.35	0.00	0.09	0.25	0.00	0.00
151	151	156	Georgia	22.07	7.45	3.62	0.00	10.00	0.00	0.00	1.00	0.00	0.00
152	123	113	Rwanda	22.01	0.00	3.04	8.97	10.00	0.00	0.00	0.00	0.00	0.00
153	147	145	Mongolia	21.60	4.17	6.93	0.00	10.00	0.00	0.00	0.00	0.50	0.00
154	165	158	Azerbaijan	20.71	5.86	4.35	0.00	10.00	0.00	0.00	0.50	0.00	0.00
155	162	164	Cambodia	19.78	4.47	4.06	0.00	10.00	0.00	0.00	0.25	1.00	0.00
156	119	119	Antigua & Barbuda	19.42	0.00	8.42	0.00	10.00	0.00	0.00	0.00	1.00	0.00
157	155	151	Korea, North	19.02	2.09	5.43	0.00	10.00	0.00	0.00	1.50	0.00	0.00
158	152	146	Sierra Leone	18.97	0.00	3.04	7.52	8.41	0.00	0.00	0.00	0.00	0.00
159	134	125	Guinea-Bissau	18.53	0.00	4.23	4.55	9.75	0.00	0.00	0.00	0.00	0.00
160	167	163	Nicaragua	18.30	4.02	5.43	0.00	7.59	0.00	0.00	0.25	1.00	0.00
161	156	154	Guyana	17.80	0.00	6.70	0.53	9.32	0.00	0.00	0.25	1.00	0.00
162	159	165	Armenia	17.77	5.46	1.81	0.00	10.00	0.00	0.00	0.50	0.00	0.00
163	150	138	Sao Tome and Principe	16.83	0.00	3.80	3.33	9.70	0.00	0.00	0.00	0.00	0.00
164	164	160	Iraq	16.04	2.68	2.11	0.00	10.00	0.00	0.00	1.25	0.00	0.00
165	169	167	Somalia	15.24	2.38	2.54	0.32	10.00	0.00	0.00	0.00	0.00	0.00
166	161	153	Afghanistan	14.87	0.00	3.62	0.00	10.00	0.00	0.00	0.25	1.00	0.00
167	170	169	Cuba	10.52	5.81	3.21	0.00	0.00	0.00	0.00	1.50	0.00	0.00

Source: "Country Risk Rankings 1993," *Euromoney* (March 1994):178, 180.

TABLE 5–3. Country Credit Ratings *Institutional Investor* (March 1994)

Rank Sept. 1993	Rank March 1994	Country	Institutional Investor Credit Rating	Six-month Change	One-year Change	Rank Sept. 1993	Rank March 1994	Country	Institutional Investor Credit Rating	Six-month Change	One-year Change
1	1	Switzerland	92.2	0.2	0.2	41	42	Mexico	46.9	1.3	1.7
2	2	Japan	91.0	−0.7	0.0	43	43	Hungary	46.1	1.3	1.8
4	3	United States	89.7	0.5	1.1	44	44	Botswana	45.7	1.0	4.6
3	4	Germany	89.4	−0.4	−0.9	42	45	Turkey	45.6	0.5	0.3
5	5	Netherlands	88.4	−0.4	−0.8	46	46	Israel	43.4	2.9	3.8
6	6	France	88.2	0.0	0.6	45	47	Mauritius	43.3	2.3	4.9
7	7	United Kingdom	86.0	0.6	1.4	48	48	Tunisia	42.9	2.6	4.1
8	8	Austria	85.6	0.3	0.3	47	49	Colombia	42.4	2.0	3.6
9	9	Luxembourg	84.6	0.0	0.1	49	50	India	40.0	1.6	1.4
10	10	Canada	81.9	−0.1	−0.1	50	51	South Africa	38.9	0.7	−0.9
11	11	Singapore	81.4	0.5	1.2	51	52	Venezuela	37.6	0.0	−1.0
13	12	Taiwan	79.0	0.9	0.5	52	53	Barbados	37.3	2.1	1.5
12	13*	Belgium	78.8	−1.0	−1.5	53	54	Uruguay	36.0	1.8	2.3
13	14*	Norway	78.8	0.7	1.7	54	55	Morocco	35.8	2.4	3.6
15	15	Denmark	77.8	1.1	2.5	55	56	Argentina	35.6	3.0	5.1
16	16	Spain	74.7	−0.5	−1.1	61	57	Slovenia	33.4	4.8	10.8
17	17	Sweden	74.5	0.1	−0.7	56	58	Papua New Guinea	32.8	0.4	0.4
18	18	Italy	72.6	−0.9	−2.5	57	59	Slovakia	31.6	1.0	0.6
19	19	Ireland	70.7	0.7	1.3	58	60	Trinidad & Tobago	30.8	1.4	1.2
20	20	Finland	69.9	0.5	0.3	64	61*	Philippines	30.5	2.5	3.4
21	21	South Korea	69.5	0.6	0.9	62	62*	Poland	30.5	1.9	3.6
22	22	Australia	68.9	0.8	1.0	67	63	Egypt	29.8	2.3	2.7
23	23	Portugal	67.3	0.6	1.2						
25	24	Malaysia	66.6	1.8	2.7						

TABLE 5-3. *(cont.)*

Rank Sept. 1993	Rank March 1994	Country	Institutional Investor Credit Rating	Six-month Change	One-year Change
81	82	Ecuador	22.5	1.2	1.7
85	83*	Panama	22.1	1.2	1.7
83	84*	Jordan	22.1	1.0	1.1
88	85	Vietnam	21.9	2.4	4.4
90	86	Dominican Republic	21.0	1.8	2.5
86	87	Senegal	20.9	0.8	0.9
84	88	Estonia	20.7	−0.2	−0.7
97	89	Guatemala	20.1	2.0	1.3
95	90	Bangladesh	20.0	1.3	0.7
89	91*	Bulgaria	19.8	0.3	0.9
102	92*	Lebanon	19.8	2.7	5.7
81	93	Cameroon	19.7	−1.6	−2.1
87	94	Latvia	19.6	−0.4	0.1
94	95	Bolivia	19.5	0.8	1.4
91	96	Nigeria	18.6	−0.5	−1.7
93	97	Lithuania	18.4	−0.6	−0.5
92	98	Russia	18.1	−0.9	−2.1
98	99	Kazakhstan	17.7	0.1	1.9
109	100	Peru	17.5	2.5	3.6
101	101	Malawi	17.4	0.1	1.2
107	102	El Salvador	17.3	2.0	2.1
99	103	Burkina Faso	17.2	−0.3	—
103	104	Benin	16.8	−0.1	—
107	105	Mali	16.7	1.4	—
104	106	Côte d'Ivoire	16.4	0.2	−0.3
106	107	Honduras	16.2	0.6	0.5
105	108*	Congo	15.5	−0.3	0.3
100	109*	Belarus	15.5	−2.0	−1.9
—	110	Togo	15.4	—	—
96	111	Ukraine	15.1	−3.1	−3.1
110	112	Uzbekistan	14.3	−0.1	−0.2
111	113	Tanzania	13.9	−0.1	1.0
114	114	Myanmar	13.3	0.3	0.9
116	115*	Zambia	13.1	0.7	1.4
111	116*	Guinea	13.1	−0.9	—
113	117	Croatia	12.8	−0.8	−1.4
115	118	Angola	10.7	−1.9	−3.0
120	119	Ethiopia	10.6	0.8	2.1
118	120**	Albania	10.3	−0.2	−0.8
121	121	Mozambique	10.3	0.6	1.9
123	122	Uganda	10.1	1.7	2.8
119	123	Afghanistan	9.9	−0.4	—
122	124	Nicaragua	9.1	0.4	0.8
117	125	Georgia	8.9	−2.8	—
128	126	Grenada	8.5	1.0	1.2
127	127	Cuba	7.9	0.2	−0.3
125	128	Haiti	7.5	−0.5	0.2
130	129*	Sierra Leone	7.2	0.6	0.5
129	130*	Iraq	7.2	0.0	−0.2
126	131	Zaire	6.9	−0.8	−1.9
124	132	Yugoslavia	6.6	−1.7	−3.4
131	133	North Korea	6.5	0.2	−0.8
133	134	Sudan	6.1	0.4	−0.9
132	135	Liberia	6.0	0.0	0.0
		Global average rating	36.7	0.6	−0.1

* Order determined by actual results before rounding.

** Actual tie.

Source: "Institutional Investor's 1994 Country Credit Ratings," *Institutional Investor* 28 (March 1994): 88, 91.

usually carry this grade—and presents a five-year average for debt service expressed as a percent of exports.

Other Political Risk Services

A number of other PR rating services are available to MNCs. The Global Risk Forecaster, a set of six to eight individual country analyses, is published monthly in *International Business*. These forecasts are published by Political Risk Services, based in Syracuse, New York, and cover eighteen months and five years while rating a country's financial transfers, direct investments, and export market. A short country sketch is also offered.

The World Political Risk Forecasts (WPRF) place emphasis on political and economic conditions that cause general concerns for all of the business operations within a given country. These forecasts emphasize regime change, political turmoil, expropriation, and repatriation restrictions.

The Political System Stability Index (PSSI) is a sophisticated approach that creates a number of indexes using such variables as GNP growth per capita, riots, and ethnolinguistic fractionalization. Ordinal rankings of countries are offered according to prosperity in the system.

Summary

The *Euromoney* and *Institutional Investor* rankings will generally be about the same. While individual countries may not be ranked exactly alike, usually the top ten or fifteen countries will appear in the highest positions of each service while the lowest ten or fifteen countries will nearly always be in the lowest section of each set of ratings. As mentioned previously, other rating services offer country risk rankings to MNCs. These include Business International Corporation, the World Political Risk Forecasts, as well as many banks, government agencies, and international insurance companies.

The financial manager of the MNC, when contemplating a foreign investment project, should not rely too heavily on these standardized risk ratings for quick-fix solutions of the question in which country should a proposed foreign investment be made.[11] Like the weekly college football and basketball rankings, any unranked team can defeat any ranked team on a given day. These ratings do not include the indepth analysis necessary for locating a successful investment. Individual countries must be analyzed in detail and the degree of risk, different for different countries, must be measured and compared with the risk threshold of the firm. Companies, banks, and government agencies use their own models to measure political or country risk. Representative data used in these models are presented in Figure 5–1.

STUDY AID

The *Euromoney* country risk rating system is one of the most important political risk evaluation models and the discussion earlier and the information shown in Table 5–2 should enable you to simulate your own country risk evaluation. Select a developing country and, using the *Euromoney* model, do your own rating based on information you find in the *Economist Quarterly Country Reports, International Financial Statistics,* or *International Currency Review,* all of which may be found in your library.

---

[11] Pravin Banker, "You're the Best Judge of Foreign Risks," *Harvard Business Review* 61 (March–April 1983): 157.

Statistics Frequently Used by Banks in Evaluating Country Risk

I. Internal Economy
  A. GNP per capita
    1. absolute
    2. rate of growth
  B. Inflation rate
  C. Money supply growth
  D. Net budget position
II. External Economy
  A. Balance of payments
    1. trade balance
      a. exports and export growth
      b. imports and import growth
    2. current account balance
    3. long-term capital flows
  B. External ratios
    1. debt service ratio (debt principal and interest-to-exports)
    2. reserves-to-imports ratio
  C. International reserves

Outline of Typical Qualitative Country Evaluation Report

I. Economics
  A. Background
    1. natural resources
    2. demographics
    3. other
  B. Current indicators
    1. internal
      a. GNP
      b. inflation
      c. government budget
      d. consumption
      e. investment
    2. external
      a. trade account
      b. current account
      c. capital account and/or foreign debt analysis
      d. other
          i. export diversity
         ii. import compressibility
        iii. main trading partners
  C. Long-run indicators
    1. managerial capability
    2. investment in human capital
    3. long-run projections
      a. internal economic indicators
      b. external economic indicators
II. Politics
  A. Stability
    1. type of government
    2. orderliness of political successions
    3. homogeneity of the populace
  B. External relations
    1. quality of relationships with major trading partners
    2. quality of relationships with the United States
  C. Long-run social and political trends

FIGURE 5-1 Country Risk Analysis Model Data

Management of Political Risk

Once political risks are measured and individual countries are ranked and the decision to invest abroad is made by the firm, the investment can be implemented. Once the project is on stream, political risks inherent to the host country must be managed. The firm can manage political risks in three ways: avoidance, reduction or shifting of the risk, and postcommitment practices. These will be discussed in the following sections.

AVOIDANCE

One simple form of political risk management is to simply avoid it. Some companies will not invest in any LDC where the least amount of PR may be present. Direct investment will only be made in countries with friendly governments and business systems similar to the investor's home country. Of course, where risk is low or nonexistent, profits may not be overwhelming. Such investments do not require a premium for risk to be applied to project analysis models such as capital budgeting.

REDUCTION OR SHIFTING OF RISK

The investing company can reduce or shift the risk. For example, the firm can implement a financial structure (debt-to-equity ratio) for the foreign project that shifts the risk to local creditors or shareholders. Contracts between foreign investors and local interests can be designed to reduce the riskiness of a project. For example, a "force majeure" clause can be included in such contracts that triggers repudiation or a revision of terms if some type of violence such as civil war, insurrection, or a coup breaks out in the host country. In a certain narrow class of investments where contracts are between foreign investors and host state governments, arbitration provisions may be written into contracts that trigger the facilities of ICSID (the International Centre for Settlement of Investment Disputes) if the foreign investor is from a nation that has signed the ICSID Convention and if the host state government is an ICSID Convention signatory.[12]

POSTCOMMITMENT PRACTICES

Finally, the firm can manage PR by resorting to certain practices after the investment has been committed. These include employment and ownership practices, modification of the firm's operating structure, and diversification.

First, a foreign investor can modify employment in the foreign project or its ownership in ways that will reduce political risks such as expropriation. If a majority of the employees, and particularly top management, are local nationals or if local ownership is significant in the project, the host government will have less incentive to nationalize the project. The former Kaiser Companies, with overseas operations in aluminum, cement, steel, and gypsum mostly located in LDCs, resorted to minority interests in these foreign operations. These were mostly extractive type industries and quite sensitive to foreign interference. The Kaiser operations were generally quite successful pursuing such an ownership strategy.

MNCs can enter into joint ventures with foreign investors.[13] However, research has shown that successful joint ventures depend on the type of foreign investor. Expropriation has been eight to ten times greater for 50–50 joint ventures between U.S.

---

[12] Baker and Yoder, *Journal of International Arbitration* 5: 81–95.

[13] *Insurance Decisions: Unsettling Risks in Stable Nations*, pamphlet published by INA Company, date n/a, pp. 8–9.

MNCs and host governments or other foreign MNCs than for wholly-owned U.S. subsidiaries. On the other hand, joint ventures between U.S. MNCs and local private parties have had a very low takeover incidence.

Occasionally, if the U.S. MNC has well-developed technology expertise, the local government may not bother it.[14] IBM, for example, has never had foreign investment expropriated. Local governments often pass over firms such as IBM when nationalizing foreign investments. One South American government nationalized the majority of U.S. investments but did not expropriate a pharmaceutical plant whose production technology had been kept secret in the company's New York headquarters. However, technology prowess did not keep Chilean copper mines or OPEC countries' oil refineries, once owned by U.S. companies, from being nationalized.

Second, the firm may resort to an operating structure designed to reduce PR. For example, its organization can emphasize operations that result in exports and inflow of foreign exchange into the host country. The project's operating structure can be designed to respect the local environment and encourage management to cooperate as closely as possible with local government.

Third, the firm can reduce political risk by diversification practices. The firm can locate operations in a number of countries in which the riskiness varies. Financing can be diversified so that foreign exchange risk can be reduced. Sources of factors of production can be diversified so that if political actions interfere with operations in one country, operations in other countries will continue. The project can sell into a number of countries so that if blocked funds result in nonpayment of invoices in one country, the foreign project will be able to get funds out of the other countries.

SUMMARY

Companies must work at being good citizens in foreign countries. They must do business as "local companies." If they borrow from local banks, they may demonstrate to local governments that they have concern for the local economy. Sourcing supplies locally may have a similar effect. A high level of local borrowing and accounts payable provides substantial local leverage against takeover.

Banks and Political Risk Management

Most big international banks practice some type of PR management. The predominant method used by these banks consists of an annual review of all countries they do business with and the estimation of their riskiness with some type of grading schedule. Chemical Bank, for example, forecasts conditions over their exposure period. Their review examines cross-border financing as well as domestic currency lending. The bank sets country limits for each product they market. Some of these limits are as narrow as intraday. Citibank, for example, sends people into the field to analyze the problems on a personal basis. The bank uses a country-by-country basis in its PR analyses. Chase Manhattan sets country limits during three annual meetings in New York, London, and Hong Kong. Line officers are held accountable for the PR analysis. Most banks, when setting country limits because of PR, consider the following factors:[15]

1. current business cycle conditions;
2. long-term growth potential, tempered by size constraints;

---

[14] Ibid., pp. 9–10.

[15] Jack Lowenstein, "How to Rate a State," *Euromoney* (September 1992): 63.

3. key concepts of volatility, including GDP growth, inflation, and trade balances;
4. political/social factors, including income distribution, political stability, and the consistency of economic policies;
5. other broad measures of transfer risk, including legal issues.

Although many banks, companies, and government agencies use scientific methods to evaluate PR, for most it is a matter of subjective judgement. ANZ Bank, for example, uses an 8-point grade risk matrix that measures a country's PR by how well the bank's management understands the country. Countries in the Indian subcontinent get higher limits from ANZ than they might get from other banks because ANZ is quite familiar with this geographical region.

Political Risk Insurance

In addition to the active management of PR by the firm, business activities can be insured against this type risk. PR insurance can be purchased from government agencies or private property/casualty insurers. The activities covered can be distinguished between those that are trade-related, usually one-shot transactions, and those that are property-related, i.e., direct investments, which happen more often and are on-going operations.

The firm can choose from three sources of PR insurer. These are: government sponsored programs, private financial service organizations that offer trade-related protection, and private property centered insurers. Of course, the firm has a fourth choice, its management may choose to insure the foreign investment itself, depending on the risk threshold of the firm's management.

GOVERNMENT SPONSORED PROGRAMS

First, government sponsored programs used are operated either by a single national government and their service is considered bilateral, or they are multinational in character and their service is considered multilateral. A bilateral operation is one that is operated by one country and only that country's citizens, natural or corporate, are eligible for assistance. A multilateral agency is one owned and operated by a number of countries and assists citizens from more than one country. Examples of U.S. bilateral providers of PR insurance are FCIA (Foreign Credit Insurance Association) and OPIC (Overseas Private Insurance Corporation). MIGA (Multilateral Insurance Guarantee Agency) is an example of a multilateral provider of PR insurance.

FCIA

FCIA (Foreign Credit Insurance Association) is a consortium of sixty or so private U.S. insurance companies in the marine, casualty, and fire insurance fields that insures exporters against nonpayment by overseas customers. It was established in the early 1960s during the Kennedy Administration, which encouraged this cooperative effort of private insurers. With FCIA insurance of trade credits, exporters can then obtain better credit from banks; thus, more bank financing of international trade is encouraged and more exporters will become involved in international trade.

The FCIA supplements the programs of the U.S. Export-Import Bank by offering a variety of programs designed to protect a U.S. exporter against the failure of an overseas customer to pay, thus supporting the exporter's penetration of higher risk markets. The FCIA covers commercial risks while the U.S. Export-Import Bank covers political risks that may be inherent in the transaction. As covered in chapter 9, the

Export-Import Bank actually guarantees trade credit, a service that is somewhat different from insuring those trade credits. FCIA is considered bilateral since it is an American institution offering trade insurance for U.S. exporters only.

OPIC

OPIC (Overseas Private Investment Corporation) was created by the U.S. Congress in 1969 and began operations in 1971 as a self-sustaining U.S. government agency whose services assist U.S. investors operating in 140 developing nations and emerging economies. OPIC has supported $60 billion in foreign investment and $27 billion in U.S. exports, while assisting the creation of 100,000 American jobs since its inception. In fiscal year 1995, OPIC issued a total of $8.6 billion of political risk insurance, compared with $2.8 billion in fiscal 1993. In addition, OPIC advanced $1.8 billion in project financing loans and guarantees.

OPIC's primary objective is to stimulate U.S. private investment in LDCs by providing insurance against PR and financial services in the form of loan guarantees, direct loans, and preinvestment assistance. It also provides investor services including advisory services, computer assisted project/investor matching, country and regional information, and investment missions. The impetus for such an agency was furnished by the expropriation of property owned by U.S. citizens by the Castro government after the Cuban Revolution in 1958. Such property was not insured against PR.

OPIC's guaranty and insurance obligations are backed by the full faith and credit of the U.S. government, as well as OPIC's own reserves. The agency's loan guarantees range in size from $10 million to $75 million, but have been as high as $200 million. In fact, the OPIC ceiling on both project financing and risk insurance has been increased to $200 million per project. OPIC insurance is also available for exporters to cover their losses of physical assets or bank accounts as a result of confiscation, political violence, contractual disputes, or wrongful calling of bid.[16]

OPIC offers insurance to U.S. investors with projects in the LDCs against political risks of expropriation, inconvertibility of currency, and violence from war, revolution, insurrection, and civil strife. In a few cases, OPIC has offered coverage against abrogation of contractual rights. A few LDCs, such as India, have agencies similar to OPIC. These agencies often become political in the achievement of their objectives. Investment, thus, may be directed to certain regional areas for political purposes. Some PR programs available in other industrialized nations base eligibility on the company's domicile rather than on nationality of ownership, as is true of OPIC.[17]

One advantage of OPIC coverage is the length of its policy terms. It can offer twenty-year terms, while most private PR insurers offer only three-year terms. However, OPIC's objectives assigned to it by the U.S. Congress may be in conflict. OPIC is required to give preference to the poorest countries and to consider effects of its programs on "respect for human rights and fundamental freedoms." But it is also required to insure projects that further the "balance of payments and employment objectives of the United States."[18] Agency officials have complete discretion in balancing these two objectives. The People's Republic of China and Chile have received OPIC insured foreign investments and both of these countries have histories of human rights violations. OPIC has been quite successful and, since it is self-sustaining, it is mostly exempt from Congressional annual reviews.

Most of OPIC's activity until 1990 focused on Central America and the

---

[16] Lori Ioannou, "Clinton's Third World Investment Emissary," *International Business* (December 1994): 34.

[17] Marina von Neumann Whitman, "Political and Other Risk Insurance: Eximbank, OPIC and MIGA, Part II," *Middle East Executive Reports* 11 (March 1988): 23–5.

[18] Frank Howard, "Overseas-Risk Agency Mistakes Girth for Growth," *Wall Street Journal*, 19 September 1985, p. 26.

TABLE 5–4. OPIC Project Financing and Risk Insurance Largest Amounts (1994–95)

U.S. Company/Project Company	*Country of Investment*	*Project*	*OPIC Financing*
Edison Mission Energy/ Paiton Energy	Indonesia	Coal-fired power plant	$200 million
U.S. West/Russian Telecom Development	Russia	Telecom joint venture	200 million
GTE and AT&T Int'l/ CTI Companîa de Teléfonos	Argentina	Cellular phone services	200 million
Energy Initiatives Termobarranquilla	Colombia	Gas-fired power plant	150 million
Citibank	Russia	On-lending facility	100 million

U.S. Company	*Country of Investment*	*Project*	*OPIC Insurance*
CMS International	Morocco	Coal-fired power plant	$200 million
Edison Mission Energy	Indonesia	Coal-fired power plant	200 million
Enron	Turkey	Gas-fired power plant	200 million
Magma Power	Philippines	Geothermal power plant	200 million
Union Carbide	Kuwait	Petrochemical	200 million

Source: Ellen Leander, "OPIC Financing is a Company's Best Bet," *Global Finance* 10 (March 1996):46.

Caribbean, although since then, it has begun to insure projects in Eastern Europe to a greater extent. OPIC also makes indirect investment loans, ranging from $1.5 to 2 million.[19] Some insurance was offered U.S. businesses against expropriation losses in the Soviet Union. U.S. investors planned to buy $250 million of minority interests in the old Soviet military industry, with losses from political violence and currency problems covered by OPIC.[20]

It is useful to examine some of OPIC's recent cases in order to understand better its operations.[21] In fiscal year 1992, OPIC issued $3.4 billion in new investment insurance to support 105 projects in 38 countries. Furthermore, the agency committed $274.6 million in loans and loan guaranties in support of seventeen projects in sixteen countries. OPIC made a $35 million loan guaranty and committed insurance to support K&M Engineering and Consulting Corporation and Chase Manhattan Bank investments in the construction and operation of a 90-megawatt natural gas-fired, steam injection electric power plant. OPIC insured the participation of Costanera Power Corporation, a subsidiary of PSI Resources, in the privatization of a 1,260-megawatt power generation facility in Argentina. In East Africa, OPIC made a $15 million investment guaranty to assist Tanruss Investment Ltd. in the construction and operation of an international business hotel in Dar es Salaam, Tanzania. OPIC's largest customers for both project financing and risk insurance for the 1994–95 period are shown in Table 5–4.

---

[19] "OPIC Gives a Leg Up," *D & B Reports* 38 (No. 3): 44, 63.

[20] K. Bradsher, "U.S. Plans to Insure Soviet Deal: Agency Will Cover American Investors," *New York Times*, 12 November 1991, p. 1.

[21] Overseas Private Investment Corporation, *Annual Report 1992*.

One of the problems with bilateral government agencies such as OPIC is that they sometimes adhere to their own political agendas. For example, OPIC canceled its political risk policy that covered a multimillion dollar investment by Freeport McMoran Copper and Gold Inc. in a huge gold mining project in Irian Jaya, Indonesia. The coverage was withdrawn after a contract dispute arose between Freeport McMoran and OPIC over environmental concerns. Although the dispute is now pending arbitration, the project is in jeopardy because of the loss of political risk insurance coverage.

MIGA

MIGA (Multilateral Investment Guarantee Agency) is an affiliate of the World Bank and, although proposed in 1951, was not established until 1985. It was patterned after the Inter-Arab Investment Guarantee Corporation, an Arab world multilateral investment insurer of Arab investments in Arab countries. MIGA officially began operations in 1988 with the major objective to encourage the flow of FDI into LDCs. It does this by issuing guarantees against noncommercial risks in a member country on private investment that flows from other member countries and by carrying out other appropriate activities promoting FDI into LDCs, such as insurance and coinsurance. MIGA had 152 signatory members in 1995, and 128 of these had fulfilled all membership requirements.

MIGA offers insurance against four major political risks: currency transfer, expropriation, war and civil disturbances, and breach of contract caused by the host government. In addition, it can act as a reinsurer. Reinsurance is the act of insuring by contracting to transfer in whole or in part a risk or contingent liability already covered under an existing contract.

MIGA's structure and mode of operations offers foreign investors advantages over bilateral agencies such as OPIC. Its coverage is more comprehensive, broad, and flexible than that offered by most national systems or private market insurers. It offers coverage against more types of risk than do other agencies. Its coverage can be more extensive in terms of amount and length of coverage. MIGA also carries out several supporting and service functions including research, provision of information and policy advice for member countries, as well as cooperative projects with other economic development institutions, such as the Foreign Investment Advisory Service (FIAS), a division of the International Finance Corporation (IFC).[22] MIGA, for example, has cooperated with FIAS in the indentification of several policy measures that have retarded foreign investment flows in some LDCs and has evaluated the investment policy and institutional framework for investment promotion in other countries.[23] MIGA has also held investment promotion conferences in Ghana and Hungary in 1990 and in Jamaica and Pakistan in 1991. The Pakistan conference may have generated as much as $600 million in new FDI.

MIGA has been quite successful in its early period of operations. By the end of fiscal year 1994, it had issued 101 insurance coverage contracts—applications for insurance coverage totaled more than 900 in fiscal years 1993 and 1994 alone—for investments in more than thirty host countries. Approved coverage totaled $1,244.8 million and involved FDI amounting to $6.16 billion, investment that generated more than 11,000 new jobs.[24]

Some of MIGA's insured projects are worth mentioning to illustrate the diverse

---

[22] IFC will be discussed in more detail in chapter 11.

[23] *MIGA Annual Report 1992* (Washington, D.C.: Multilateral Investment Guarantee Agency, 1992)

[24] James C. Baker, "Global Foreign Investment Insurance: The Case of MIGA with Comparisons to OPIC and Private Insurance," *Managerial Finance* 21 (1995): 32.

TABLE 5–5.   MIGA Guarantee Activities Fiscal Year 1990–95

	FY90	FY91	FY92	FY93	FY94	FY95	Cumulative Total
Number of guarantees	4	11	21	27	38	54	155
Maximum contingent liability (million U.S.$)	132	59	313	374	372	672	1,922
Aggregate direct investment facilitate (billion U.S.$)	1.0	0.9	1.0	1.9	1.3	2.5	8.6
Jobs generated in host countries	2,700	3,680	2,920	1,720	7,800	8,884	27,704

Source: MIGA Annual Report 1994 (Washington, D.C.: Multilateral Investment Guarantee Agency, 1994), p. 17, and *MIGA Annual Report 1995* (Washington, D.C.: Multilateral Investment Guarantee Agency, 1995), p. 15.

nature of this agency. During fiscal year 1991–92, MIGA guaranteed a Citibank branch in Turkey against currency transfer and expropriation. The coverage amounted to $20 million. Two projects in Poland, which were joint ventures of the U.S. Coca-Cola Export Corporation and a Norwegian company, were covered against currency transfer and civil disturbance for $16 million. During fiscal year 1992–93, MIGA insured $50 million in each of three projects. One of these was for a cement plant investment by Ciments Francais, a French company in the Czech Republic. One guarantee was issued to International Paper Investments to assist the privatization of a Polish company. The third guarantee was made for a Mobil Corporation project in Saudi Arabia. During fiscal year 1993–94, MIGA issued guarantees totaling $40 million to Newmont Mining Corporation of the United States against risks of expropriation and violence for a $150 million gold ore processing venture at a mine in Uzbekistan.

An indicator of the success of MIGA's operations and recognition by foreign investors is shown by the rising number of applications for MIGA coverage in the past few years. In fiscal year 1992, 302 applications for insurance from MIGA were made by foreign investors, an increase of more than one-third from the previous year. In fiscal year 1993, applications increased by 81 percent from the year before, to 546 registrations. MIGA should have a growing and well-diversified portfolio of investment insurance coverage issued for years to come. Table 5–5 shows selected MIGA operations for the 1990–95 period.

PRIVATE PROPERTY-CENTERED INSURANCE

Private market coverage for political risks is available from such multinational insurance companies as American International Group (AIG), the Chubb Group, the Insurance Company of North America (INA), and others. Lloyd's of London is well-known for its reinsurance coverage. Private investment insurance coverage is generally devoted to projects in the least risky LDCs and information about such coverage is strictly confidential. Private coverage is available for both commercial and political risk. MIGA covers risks of the latter kind only. The portfolios of these private insurers are usually large and diversified because one major loss can wipe out 1–2 years' premiums. Therefore, political risks are covered by a relatively few private insurers.

Some private insurers offer diverse types of coverage although they cannot offer the broad range and financial coverage that a multilateral government agency can offer. INA, a leading U.S. property-casualty insurance conglomerate, can offer coverage such as the following: expropriation and nationalization insurance, importation and ex-

portation insurance, service contract deterioration and repudiation insurance, on-de- mand guarantee insurance, and currency inconvertibility insurance.

IMPLICATIONS

Investment insurance is available for a wide variety of risks, both commercial and po- litical. Some of this coverage is bilateral while in the case of MIGA it is multilateral. Some is for short periods of time and some can be obtained for periods of ten years or longer and various transactions can be covered. Earlier in this chapter, some examples of the types of risk that might be covered were discussed. In the case of the suspension of cultural relations between Canada and Russia because of the Korean jetliner 007 dis- aster, the losses from this political action had not been covered by investment insur- ance. In the case of the losses from the projects in Africa—the deep water port and the lobster operation—both projects had been covered by investment insurance against political risks and both were caused by political actions, therefore, the losses were cov- ered. MNC financial management should be aware of such investment insurance, what types of risk can be covered, for how long, and how much the coverage costs. Self-in- surance can be very expensive, as discovered by those companies expropriated after the Castro Revolution.

Political Risk in Transition Economies

During the 1990s, the Union of Soviet Socialist Republics (U.S.S.R.) broke up into sev- eral countries making the transition from communist regimes to market economies. The countries in eastern Europe have also begun this transition. These transition economies have special problems that pose political risks to foreign investors. Most of these countries have encountered economic turmoil. National currencies have lost a great deal of their value and cannot be readily converted into major currencies. The practice of administered pricing under communist governments has resulted in infla- tion and reduced the purchasing power of the population in these countries.

The move to market economies has fostered a move to privatization of much of the formerly state-owned enterprises. To encourage foreign investment, local govern- ments have encouraged joint ventures between foreign investors and large local com- panies. In many of these countries, local officials have had to resist the tendency to return to centralized planning. Foreign ownership and control of local firms has been resisted by some of these governments. Privatization of the many former state-owned enterprises in these countries, estimated at more than 45,000 in Russia alone,[25] is nec-

---

[25] Alan M. Rugman and Richard M. Hodgetts, *International Business: A Strategic Management Approach* (New York: McGraw-Hill, 1995), p. 561.

essary if price controls are lifted in the attempt to stimulate economic recovery in these nations.

Centrally planned economies have very specific problems. In addition to the fact that central governments have owned and controlled the major factors of production including labor, the infrastructure in these economies is underdeveloped. The transformation from a state-controlled economy to a market economy is a difficult process. Telecommunications systems are not up-to-date and in some countries, especially Russia, telephone lines were "bugged" by the state; many of these systems have had to be rewired. Acceptable accounting systems were nonexistent. Pricing policies to increase market share are unknown to officials of these countries, since markets for their goods are uncommon and competition may be unknown. Many former state officials, familiar with administered pricing systems, have little knowledge that a firm can cut prices to increase sales. Property rights in these economies may be poorly defined. Incorrect setting of foreign exchange rates for their currencies exacerbates the problem.

Germany is a specific example where a state-controlled country, East Germany, has created economic problems for West Germany after the reunification of the two countries. The debt that Germany has incurred in order to absorb a weak economy has created significant inflation in that country for the first time in many years. For example, BASF, the large German chemical company, was an early investor in East Germany. The former communist officials did not cooperate with plant modernization, the telephone system had to be rewired, employees left the plant before the end of the working day because their buses left early, and customers of the acquired plant—such as Russia—could not pay their bills. Although BASF believes the East German investment will eventually pay off and the cost of labor is cheap, the company will probably not buy another East German plant.[26]

The People's Republic of China (China) is a vast country with a very large population. It is seen as a major global economic force in years to come and a major trading partner of the United States. However, several problems that present political risks for foreign investors are found in this transition economy. Some foreign joint ventures have had trouble in China in the past because of low-quality local producers, poor technology, poorly trained workforce, unreliable local sources of productive factors, and weak infrastructure.[27] In addition, the United States and China have escalated the dispute over piracy of intellectual property by Chinese business to a trade war in 1996 involving trade sanctions by both countries against the other's imported goods. Red tape resulting from the burgeoning bureaucracy in China leads to delays in starting new businesses, and bribery of government officials is also not unheard of.

In summary, many of the new transition economies of China, Eastern Europe, and the former U.S.S.R. present a host of political risks to foreign investors. These include the major risks of currency inconvertibility, contract interference, and nationalization of investments, as well as commercial risks resulting from lack of free market experience, business know-how, technology, and infrastructure. Nearly one-third of the countries in the bottom twenty-five ranked by *Euromoney* in Table 5–2 are transition economies. Foreign investors are needed to move these nations from transition economies to emerging markets. In order to promote foreign investment, all of the tools discussed in this chapter will need to be employed.

---

[26] "Investing in Eastern Europe: The Money Pit," *The Economist*, 22 June 1991, pp. 74–5.

[27] "Joint Ventures in China: Foreign Companies find it Hard to Invest Successfully," *The Economist*, 6 August 1994, pp. 56–7.

Summary and Conclusions

When a MNC operates in a foreign country, no matter how sophisticated the host country is, political risks may be encountered. These risks can affect the transfer of earnings or capital back to the parent firm. They can affect internal operations of the foreign affiliate when local laws require a certain number of local nationals to be hired by the foreign subsidiary. They can affect ownership of the foreign affiliate if the local government expropriates or nationalizes the affiliate.

These risks must be analyzed, measured, and managed by the international firm. When business firms want to invest in a foreign country or banks want to lend to a foreign country, such organizations must assess both the economic performance and the socio-political agenda that created the economic performance. To measure one and not the other is senseless. Thus, both business firms and banks are beginning to synthesize their approaches to PR measurement.[28] Many measurement methodologies are available from econometric to subjective. However, country risk assessment is not yet a mathematical science.

A number of agencies and private entities are available to assist the MNC in the function of country, or political, risk assessment. World Bank agencies, such as the multilateral international institutions ICSID and MIGA, can assist in the settlement of contract disputes or can insure foreign investment if certain conditions are present. Some nations have established bilateral agencies to insure foreign investments made by citizens of the home country. OPIC in the United States is an example of such an agency. Several insurance companies offer private foreign investment insurance, including Alexander and Alexander, AIG, and INA. Trade credit insurance covering political risks is also available from agencies such as the Foreign Credit Insurance Association in the United States.

Several companies offer systems that evaluate and rank countries according to their political riskiness. These include the systems developed by *Euromoney* and *Institutional Investor*, BERI, and companies such as Frost & Sullivan and Political Risk Services.

Companies have available methods for management of political risks. Besides avoiding such risks altogether, they can reduce or shift political risks by changes in their financial structure, diversification of international investments, and contract design. They can resort to postcommitment practices such as employment practices and modification of the firm's operating structure.

Companies operating in foreign environments must recognize that cultural differences in these areas create political risks. These risks may adversely affect their international operations, as they did when foreign companies were expropriated by the Castro Regime after the Cuban Revolution and as they do now with foreign investors in the transition economies of East Europe, Russia, and China. The cost to manage or insure political risks may be much less than the cost of doing nothing.

Additional Readings

August, Ray, *International Business Law: Text, Cases, and Readings.* Englewood Cliffs, NJ: Prentice-Hall, 1993, pp. 103–12.

Baker, James C. "Global Foreign Investment Insurance: The Case of MIGA with Comparisons to OPIC and Private Insurance." *Managerial Finance* 21 (June 1995): 23–39.

---

[28] Fred Snow, "Understanding Country Risk," working paper, Kent State University, Kent, OH, December 10, 1991, pp. 15–16.

Baker, James C., and M. Anaam Hashmi. "Political Risk Management: Steering Clear of Risky Business." *Risk Management* 35 (October 1988): 40–7.

Baker, James C., and Lois Yoder. "ICSID Arbitration and the U.S. Multinational Corporation: An Alternative Dispute Resolution Method for International Business." *Journal of International Arbitration* 5 (December 1988): 81–95.

Caporaso, James A. "International Relations Theory and Multilateralism: The Search for Foundations." *International Organization* 46 (No. 3, 1992): 599–632.

Shihata, F.I. *Towards A Greater Depoliticization of Investment Disputes: The Roles of ICSID and MIGA.* Washington, D.C.: World Bank, 1992.

Discussion Questions

1. Discuss the four major types of political risk.
2. What is ICSID and what does it do?
3. What are some of the qualitative questions asked by political analysts when measuring the political risk of a country? What are some of the quantitative questions asked by these political analysts?
4. What are the differences in the formats of the BERI, *Euromoney*, and *Institutional Investor* systems for ranking countries according to their political riskiness?
5. What is the difference between the insurance of and the management of political risk?
6. Discuss three ways to manage political risk.
7. Why are banks so interested in political, or country, risk?
8. What is the difference between insurance offered by FCIA and by OPIC?
9. How does the MIGA program differ from the OPIC program?
10. What are the principal differences between government sponsored investment insurance programs and those that are offered by private insurance companies?

Problems

1. Select a less developed country and assess its political risk.
2. Present a report on any three projects that the Multilateral Investment Guarantee Agency has covered with its investment insurance.
3. Prepare a list of investment disputes whose settlement has been facilitated by (1) the American Arbitration Association, (2) the International Chamber of Commerce facilities, and (3) the International Centre for Settlement of Investment Disputes.
4. Write to any of the following for information brochures on their political risk insurance programs: Foreign Credit Insurance Association, U.S. Export-Import Bank, Overseas Private Investment Company, Multilateral Investment Guarantee Agency, or any large multinational property casualty insurance company.
5. The president of an LDC asks you to evaluate the following proposed policies:
   a. an expansion of M1 to keep interest rates from rising and to stimulate economic growth;
   b. an increase in minimum wages to raise the income of the poor;
   c. the imposition of quotas on imports to protect local manufacturers;
   d. increased income taxes to boost revenues and reduce the deficit;
   e. fixing of the exchange rate to keep the cost of imports of necessities down.

   What are the potential consequences of each policy? Will they achieve their objectives?
6. Examine the most recent country rankings in *Euromoney*. Explain the differences among the top ten countries ranked. Then explain why the bottom ten countries are ranked as they are.
7. Follow up on Problem No. 6 by explaining the differences between the top ten ranked countries and the bottom ten ranked countries.

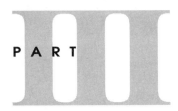

PART III

Planning for Foreign Investment and Operations

This section is devoted to the planning function for foreign investment and operations. Foreign direct investment (FDI) plays a very important role in international business and in global business development. The global triad—the United States, the European Community (EC), and Japan—has become increasingly important in world trade for the past decade or so. In addition, studies by agencies such as the United Nations Centre for Transnational Corporations have found that these three regional blocks have also become extremely important foreign investment targets. In the 1990s, the German mark, the focal currency of the EC, and the Japanese yen have challenged the U.S. dollar as the major reserve currency for the community of nations. The FDI decision to locate in a foreign country, no matter in which major currency, remains one of the most important decisions for MNC management.

The first major step in locating operations abroad is to decide whether to go abroad and if so, where to invest. Foreign investments must be analyzed. In chapter 6, some reasons for foreign investment and for the business form known as the multinational corporation will be discussed. The foreign investment decision will be presented as a process.

Once the decision has been made to invest in a foreign country, the project, the focus of the foreign investment decision process, must be analyzed. The typical financial methodology for analyzing a given project is capital budgeting. Thus, in chapter 7, capital budgeting, as it pertains to foreign projects, will be discussed. Techniques for ranking projects as well as relevant cash flows of these projects will be included. Since the cost of capital of a project is an instrumental part of the capital budgeting process, especially when discounted cash flow methodology is used, the chapter will also examine the role of the cost of capital in MNCs. And, since the cost of capital is often determined by the optimal capital structure of the company, some of the research on what is, in fact, an optimal capital structure for an MNC is included in the discussion.

Finally, in chapter 8, it is assumed that the foreign investment decision has been made, the capital budgeting technique has been adopted, and the project has been found to be economically feasible. Foreign operations will have to be initiated and the international operations of the firm organized. Some of the strategy of overseas operations and methods for organizing overseas direct investment or licensing operations will be discussed. The discussion will focus on forecasting overall financial needs of the project as well as the formulation of international business objectives. Organization of the international finance function will also be covered.

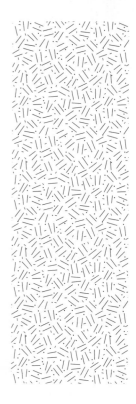

Foreign Direct Investment

Major Objectives of Chapter 6

(1) To examine the benefits of foreign direct investment, (2) to analyze major theories of foreign direct investment, and (3) to discuss various approaches of foreign investment by MNCs.

Key terms to be learned in chapter 6:

- foreign direct investment
- internalization theory
- decision tree analysis
- premium for risk
- range of estimates

- product life cycle
- eclectic theory
- licensing
- entry strategies
- competitive advantage of nations

Introduction

The discussion in this chapter is devoted to foreign investment. However, trade between and among nations preceded foreign investment and one must understand the basic theories of international trade. An understanding of trade theory is introduced in a basic economics course. However, the theory of comparative trade was discussed in chapter 1 and should be reviewed. Major theories of foreign investment are discussed in the appendix to this chapter. This discussion is more important for graduate level courses and is optional for undergraduate courses.

Although the focus in the chapter is on foreign investment, other strategies for entry into the foreign marketplace are available to the MNC. The international firm may franchise operations overseas, as McDonald's, Wendy's, Kentucky Fried Chicken, and other fast-food restaurants have done. Intermediaries such as export management companies, export trading companies, and Webb-Pomerene associations may be used, especially by U.S. firms. Export management companies and export trading companies are agent middlemen that take possession of a firm's merchandise and export it in return for a commission. These firms service companies that have a product to export but do not have the information, experience, or staff to handle an export sales department. Webb-Pomerene associations are combines of U.S. firms that are exempt from U.S.

TABLE 6–1. Global Foreign Direct Investment (1981–93 inflows and outflows) (billions U.S.$)								
	1981–85	*1986–90*	*1988*	*1989*	*1990*	*1991*	*1992*	*1993*
Annual Average								
Developed Countries								
Inflows	37	130	131	168	176	121	102	109
Outflows	47	163	162	212	222	185	162	181
Developing Countries								
Inflows	13	25	28	27	31	39	51	80
Outflows	1	6	6	10	10	7	9	14

Source: Frances Williams, "Global Business a Fact of Life," *Financial Times,* 31 August 1994, p. 4.

antitrust laws and can combine their marketing efforts. Firms can implement continuing strategies for foreign entry by expanding their market at home and abroad, by expanding their production and service at home and abroad, and, finally, by direct investment in facilities abroad.

Foreign direct investment (FDI) has played an increasingly important role in world economic development during the past few decades. FDI grew significantly during the last half of the 1980s, rising at an annual rate of 29 percent, three times faster than the increase in world trade. The global stock of FDI amounted to $2.1 trillion in 1993.[1] This foreign investment was owned by 37,000 parent companies with more than 200,000 foreign affiliates. In 1993, worldwide flows of FDI amounted to $195 billion, up from $171 billion in 1992, an increase of nearly 12 percent. Flows in 1993 to less-developed countries (LDCs) amounted to $64 billion, nearly twice the 1991 level.

FDI was dominated in the 1980s by the United States, accounting at that time for about half of the total stock of FDI. Since then, the EU and Japan have increased significantly their FDI flows and the EU stock now equals that of the United States with the Japanese forecast to catch up in 5–10 years. These three blocks now account for 81 percent of global FDI, compared with a 47 percent share of global exports.[2] In fact, the group of five industrialized countries increased FDI flows tremendously among themselves during the early part of the 1980s. The rate of increase of FDI into the United States was 105 percent, 40 percent for Japan, 31 percent for Germany, 29 percent for France, and 21 percent for Great Britain.[3] The latter country is the most popular investment destination in the EU and the second biggest investor worldwide. Table 6–1 shows inflows and outflows of FDI for the 1981–93 period. In 1993, U.S. direct investment abroad amounted to $548.6 billion. Of this amount, 17.6 percent was invested in Great Britain, 12.8 percent in Canada, 6.8 percent in Germany, 6.0 percent in Switzerland, 5.7 percent in Japan, 5.1 percent in Bermuda, 4.3 percent in France, 3.6 percent in the Netherlands, 3.4 percent in Australia, and 3.1 percent in Brazil.[4]

---

[1] Frances Williams, "Global Investment Surges After Two Years of Decline," *The Financial Times* (August 31, 1994): 14.

[2] Ibid.

[3] John Plender, "No Foreign Capital, Please," *Financial Times* (May 16, 1988): 22.

[4] Jeff Dionise, "BizFacts," *Akron Beacon Journal* (January 9, 1995): D1.

BENEFITS OF FOREIGN DIRECT INVESTMENT

Host countries derive several benefits from FDI.[5] These include the following:

1. additional equity capital from whose profits yield tax revenues;

2. transfer of patented technologies;

3. access to scarce managerial skills;

4. creation of new jobs;

5. access to overseas market networks and marketing expertise;

6. reduced flight of domestic capital abroad;

7. more rigorous appraisal of investment proposals, which reduces the number of inappropriate or nonfeasible projects;

8. diffusion of improved techniques and better business practices;

9. long-term commitment to successful completion of FDI projects;

10. a catalyst for associated lending for specific projects, thus increasing the availability of external funding.

Much of the impetus for FDI by the United States in West Europe came from the Single Market 1992 planned by the European Union (EU).[6] The directive to have a single market for companies located in the EU by the end of 1992 created a fear among U.S. company management that they would be left out. If a company did not have a presence in the EU by the end of 1992, it was believed that "Fortress Europe" would keep them out. Fortress Europe was the term applied by some analysts of the EU who believed that the integration of the EU, by means of Single Market 1992, might result in increased restrictions on trade and investment by outsiders.

Several acquisitions can be cited that illustrate the desire of American companies to be in the EU before 1993.[7] Sara Lee Corporation bought Dim, the French hosiery maker. Ford purchased Jaguar, the British car maker for $2.5 billion. General Motors bought 50 percent of the Swedish car maker, Saab. Texas Instruments spent $1.2 billion in the southern region of Italy, with half of the investment subsidized by the Italians. Intel built a plant outside Dublin, Ireland, designed to employ 2,600 by the end of the century. Emerson Electric paid $450 million for Leroy-Somer, French maker of electric motors.

The United States became a fertile ground for foreign investment in the 1980s. The Reagan administration cut taxes early in the decade and tight monetary policy was implemented to bring inflation down. The result was a very strong U.S. dollar from 1981 to 1985 and relatively high real rates of interest on investments. Foreign holdings of all investments, direct and portfolio, tripled from 1980 to 1987 and reached $1.5 trillion in value.[8] These holdings included 20 percent of prime commercial real estate in

[5] Keith Marsden, "The Role of Foreign Direct Investment," Extract from FIAS background paper on the private investment climate in Sub-Saharan Africa at International Finance Corporation, Washington, D.C., August 1989.

[6] The terms, European Community and European Union, are used synonymously in this book. The latter is the most recent name given to the European regional grouping.

[7] Blanca Riemer, Jonathan Kapstein, Mark Maremont, John Rossant, et al. "America's New Rush to Europe," *Business Week* (March 26, 1990): 48–9.

[8] John Hillkirk, "USA 'Selling off our Real Wealth,'" *USA Today,* 28 July 1988, 1A.

New York City, 10 percent of the U.S. manufacturing base, which accounted for 7 percent of U.S. employment, 12.5 million acres of farmland in 49 states, along with acquisitions of CBS Records, Brooks Brothers, Ball Park Franks, and Smith-Corona Typewriters. From 1980 to 1987 in the United States, British investments increased 431 percent to $75 billion, Dutch investments increased 146 percent to $47 billion, Japanese investments increased 611 percent to $33 billion, Canadian investments rose 78 percent to $22 billion, German investments increased 158 percent to $20 billion, Swiss investments increased 180 percent to $14 billion, and French investments rose 176 percent to $10 billion.[9]

These investments in the EU and the United States are the forerunners of the next wave, probably of FDI in Japan. Given the strength of the yen, government policy toward selling into Japan, and the difficult distribution system in place there, the domestic demand for foreign products as well as the weak state of the economy may foster a surge of FDI into Japan. During the early 1980s when the U.S. dollar was strong, FDI into the United States increased. Investors must believe that a strong currency is commensurate with a strong economy, although other reasons may cause such increased FDI. At any rate, the MNC thrives on locating facilities in foreign countries. The expansion of global business, whether in the form of international trade or investment, is inherent in the multinational business firm.

For a firm to become multinational, it must make direct investments in foreign countries. Direct investments are those made for the purpose of controlling the investment, as compared with portfolio investments, which are made in stocks and bonds solely for income purposes. Direct investments usually consist of plant and equipment or a service outlet of some type. Thus, the foreign project venture must be analyzed for its feasibility. In this chapter, feasibility analysis will be discussed in terms of the input necessary. It is important also to examine and understand some of the major reasons or theories of FDI that have been formulated during the past three decades. The focus will then turn to some of the approaches to foreign investment analysis or to foreign investment decision making that are practiced by MNCs. But first, let us examine the area of FDI in LDCs, which provides the reasons for implementing the analysis and asking the questions that are posed in chapter 5.

FDI In LDCs

FDI is increasingly believed to be a strong factor in the economic development of LDCs. These countries receive only 30 percent of all foreign private investment; the remainder flows from one industrialized country to another. Even this figure may be suspect. For example, one analyst has estimated that FDI flows to LDCs in the 1980s never exceeded 15 percent of annual FDI flows to industrial countries.[10] A World Bank survey found that firms investing abroad were motivated by currency appreciation in the home country, increased real labor costs at home, attempts to gain access to major markets seeking competitive advantage by upgrading technology and improving industry reputation, and procurement of raw materials.[11] Is it any wonder that little FDI flows into LDCs?

---

[9] John Hillkirk, "Numbers Stir Debate On Capitol Hill," *USA Today,* 28 July 1988, 1B.

[10] Frank Vogl, "Foreign Investment: Myth and Reality," *Asian Finance* 16 (August 15, 1990): 33.

[11] Ibid.

TABLE 6-2. Selected Capital Flows to Developing Countries (millions 1993 U.S.$)

	1960s	*1970s*	*1980s*	*1991*	*1992*	*1993*
Net foreign direct investment	304	3,024	12,988	34,475	44,868	63,999
Portfolio investment	13	423	3,353	17,505	24,250	86,569
Net commercial bank lending	384	9,839	11,791	1,892	14,541	5,482
Grants and official debt flows	1,466	9,854	34,366	59,301	47,383	52,336
Total	**2,167**	**23,140**	**62,498**	**113,173**	**131,042**	**208,386**

Source: Joel Bergsman and Xiaofang Shen, ''Foreign Direct Investment in Developing Countries: Progress and Problems,'' *Finance & Development* 32 (December 1995):7.

Some regions of the developing world receive even less FDI. For example, in Africa, where private investment—domestic and foreign—is only 5 percent of gross domestic product (GDP), FDI is only 0.5 percent of GDP, or about one-third the level for all LDCs, itself a paltry amount. The global level of 1.5 percent of GDP flowing to LDCs is low. However, FDI flowing into LDCs in 1993 amounted to $64 billion, nearly twice the 1991 amount.[12] Thus, FDI is beginning to make some inroads into the developing countries. See Table 6–2 for a breakdown of selected capital flows to developing countries from the 1960s to 1993.

Most of the FDI flowing into developing countries was directed to countries in East Asia and the Pacific region. For example, 52 percent of FDI from industrialized nations to developing countries flowed to this region during the 1990–94 period. During this same period, Latin American countries received 29 percent of this FDI while 9 percent was aimed at Eastern Europe and Central Asia, 4 percent each to the regions of Middle East/North Africa and Sub-Saharan Africa, and 2 percent to South Asian nations.[13]

RESTRICTIONS ON FDI IN LDCS

If these benefits accrue to FDI, why is the level of FDI flows to LDCs so low, and even more appallingly low in regions such as Africa? Although the benefits are not difficult to identify, restrictions on FDI in many LDCs have been the name of the game. Ownership controls are often imposed on foreign investment projects, such as in the Andean Pact countries. The Andean Foreign Investment Code states that foreign investment is welcome, but it further states that such investment must be divested by its owners within fifteen years. Firms do invest in Andean Pact countries but they must operate with a short-term strategy, knowing that as soon as they go into the country, they must begin planning how to divest the project.

Bureaucratic snafus caused by red tape permeate the investment environment of many LDCs. Contract disputes often occur, local laws may mandate that a certain percentage of the project's employment must be local nationals, regardless of qualifications, and residency requirements may be imposed for expatriate employment. The local government may also make performance requirements mandatory, including local content laws. Exchange controls may be imposed in order to regulate an inadequate supply of foreign exchange. Such restrictions usually are combined with controls on the

---

[12] Joel Bergsman and Xiaofang Shen, "Foreign Direct Investment in Developing Countries: Progress and Problems," *Finance & Development* 32 (December 1995): 7.
[13] Ibid.

repatriation of capital. Local government may offer investment incentives, in the form of tax breaks or low-cost loans, which may distort the efficient allocation of resources into areas less desirable to the foreign investor. Tax policies may be formulated that discriminate against foreign firms. In a nutshell, the scale of the political and economic quagmire in the LDCs should not be underestimated.

The local government may formulate other policies that restrict the firm. These policies include price controls—restricting the firm from raising prices on its products in the face of severe inflation. Contractual obligations may not be respected by local investors because of government influence against foreign investors. Arbitrary government decisions may slow down operations.

These restrictions and government policies may all lead to financial restraints that impede the foreign firm from operating successfully. The foreign investor may not be able to obtain adequate investment funds. Financial regulations will slow down operations. Insufficient foreign exchange reserves make difficult or impossible the remittance of earnings, payment of interest on loans to the parent or to foreign financial institutions, and repatriation of capital. Finally, the public sector may crowd out local private enterprise from obtaining money and capital market funds.

In 1989, the World Bank surveyed 31 corporations in four of the most developed of the emerging economies, Hong Kong, Taiwan, Korea, and Singapore, to determine why FDI flows were so high in those countries. The factors mentioned by these firms that motivated their FDI decisions in those countries were the same as those mentioned previously, including currency appreciation in the home country, increased real labor costs at home, and attempts to gain access to major markets in their search for a competitive advantage by upgrading their technology and industry reputation. Actually, only the latter reason stemmed from a factor present in the four LDCs in which they were invested.[14] The best way to entice FDI seems to be a good economic environment with sound government policies in contrast to the restrictions found in many African nations.

BENEFITS TO INDUSTRIALIZED NATIONS FROM FDI

Some economic analysts have stated that FDI is beneficial to industrialized countries, especially those that have trade deficits, such as the United States. The argument holds that FDI boosts the competitiveness of U.S. foreign affiliates because of the increased capital spending and transfers of technology and expertise.[15] Studies by the U.S. Department of Commerce have found that such has not been the case in the United States. One such study found that U.S. affiliates of foreign companies have had a rising share of the merchandise trade deficit, hitting a high of 78 percent in 1989. A study at the Federal Reserve Bank of New York found that, in the four major industries of autos, steel, chemicals, and electronics, which have heavy foreign investment in the United States, trade deficits with the primary investing foreign countries amounted to 42 percent of the U.S. merchandise trade deficit. Many U.S. foreign affiliates were either set up to import merchandise goods from the home country or spend more than their domestic counterparts on capital goods, supplies, and components from the home country if involved in manufacturing.

Summary and Conclusions

One thing is clear concerning foreign direct investment. Most of FDI flows to industrialized countries. Many reasons can be cited why so little FDI flows to the devel-

---

14 Vogl, "Foreign Investment," 33.
15 Gene Koretz, "Will Direct Foreign Investment Help on the Trade Front?" *Business Week* (December 16, 1991).

oping world. One needs only to look at Africa with civil wars in Burundi, Chad, Liberia, Rwanda, and other countries to understand why FDI has been little encouraged to flow into that part of the world.[16]

Feasibility of Foreign Ventures

As mentioned in chapter 5, political risks often reduce or discourage the flow of FDI into many countries, most of which are the developing nations in need of more private investment, whether domestic or foreign. It is the LDCs in particular where foreign project proposals need to be highly scrutinized.

Foreign venture feasibility is a complex problem. The questions to be answered are many faceted. What happens to profits when they are earned abroad, taxed by a foreign government, divided with local partners, converted to the parent currency, and remitted across at least two borders? In order to answer this question, data must be analyzed from four areas of evaluation: politics, currency, taxes, and general conditions. The questions asked assume that the foreign investor is a U.S. firm. However, similar questions can be asked about a third country firm.

POLITICS

Several questions need to be asked about the politics of the host country. For example, is the host country politically stable? Or have swings occurred to the left or to the right? What kind of political alignments does the host country government have with the foreign investor's competition and/or potential partners? What has been the effect on project approvals and/or special incentives? How are relations between the host country government and the United States or among neighboring countries?

A U.S. firm contemplating foreign investment can derive answers to these questions from a broad variety of sources. Local business firms and banks can give information about the political climate. If diplomatic relations exist between the potential host country and the United States, then information can be obtained from country desk officers at the U.S. Departments of Commerce or State or from the U.S. Ambassador to the host country. Data about the business and economic environment can be found in the *Country Reports* published by *The Economist*. Other quantitative data can be found in *International Financial Statistics*, a monthly publication of the International Monetary Fund, which presents financial information on member countries.

CURRENCY

The currency of the host country and its condition is very important to the MNC contemplating an investment in that country. The MNC, once it has located an operation in that country will hope to have local currency on which the host government has placed few if any restrictions. Profits or interest on loans may need to be remitted to the parent firm. The parent firm may charge the subsidiary with management fees or transfer prices for goods or services exported to the foreign country. Raw materials or parts may need to be imported by the foreign subsidiary.

A number of questions about the local currency need to be answered. How stable is the exchange rate between the local currency and other foreign currencies? What degree of freedom does the firm have to convert local currency to foreign exchange? Do some elements in the national accounts, such as the trade balance, affect the outlook for the local currency? What is the value of the local currency in free markets and what

---

16 "Foreign Investment and the Triad." *The Economist* 320 (August 24, 1991): 57.

STUDY AID

Foreign direct investment takes place for many reasons. Some regions of the world elicit a great deal of interest from foreign investors while other regions are shunned by them. Select two regions of Africa, north, south, east, or west, one of which promotes foreign investment and one which has an economic environment restricting it. Compare and contrast these regions and show what the differences are by examining library resources such as the *Economist Quarterly Country Reports*.

are the possible losses from foreign exchange in the host country? In other words, will the MNC be exposed to the risk of loss in the local currency? What is the trend in the amount of foreign exchange circulating and its availability for capital and/or customer payment of invoices? These and other questions about the currency may be answered by international banks as well as reports in publications such as *International Currency Review*, a bimonthly review containing comprehensive analyses of various currencies.

TAXES

The MNC is faced with a myriad of taxes around the world. Taxes represent another cost of operations and the goal of the firm should be to reduce them wherever possible. A number of questions about taxation in the host country of the proposed investment need to be answered. What is the history of the rates and types of taxes in the host country? Does this country levy special taxes on foreigners? Is it possible to credit local taxes against the U.S. tax liability? Are import or export tariff problems and/or protectionism prevalent in the host country? Is the project eligible for special incentives or must it be modified? Does the parent firm have a corporate structure designed to reduce its exposure to taxation?

Taxation information about specific countries is available from a variety of sources. Price Waterhouse, Ernst and Whinney, and other large accounting firms have published country reports about business conditions and tax matters. *The Journal of Taxation, The International Tax Journal*, and other periodical journals occasionally publish articles about tax problems in foreign countries. Business International Corporation, a Geneva-headquartered international business information-gathering firm, publishes weekly and monthly reports about international operating problems such as international tax management.

GENERAL CONDITIONS

Finally, a firm contemplating an investment proposal in a foreign country should be aware of the general conditions in that country. The following questions are representative but not all inclusive concerning such conditions. For example, do payoffs to induce acceptance of a project or sale of the firm's products have an impact on company morale, profits, or ethics? What is the attitude in the host country toward Americans? Could the local weather have an adverse effect on personnel recruitment and compensation or do other dangers pose a threat to employees of the foreign investor, should the project be approved? Are good overseas communications facilities, especially the telephone, available in the host country? Does the host country have a businesslike environment, such as adherence to contracts or decision by tradition rather than logic? These are questions that are best answered by a good intelligence system put into place by the MNC.

The Foreign Investment Decision Process

Aharoni, whose doctoral work set the standards to be included in the discussion of this topic,[17] analyzed the foreign investment decision as a process. This simple, almost checklist, format can be used to explain how FDI happens in the real world. The foreign investment decision process is composed essentially of five steps. They are the initial decision to look abroad, the investigation process, the decision to invest abroad, project reviews and negotiations with home or host government agencies, and changes to the project through modifications. The foreign investment decision process as advanced by Aharoni is shown in Figure 6–1.

FIGURE 6–1 The Foreign Investment Decision Process

I. The Decision to Look Abroad
  A. Initiating forces
    1. drive of high-ranking executives
    2. outside proposals
    3. fear of losing a market
    4. the bandwagon effect
    5. strong competition from abroad
  B. Auxiliary forces
    1. markets for components and other products
    2. utilization of old machinery
    3. capitalization of know-how and spreading fixed costs
    4. indirect return to lost markets

II. The Investigation Process
  A. Risk and uncertainty
  B. Changes in perceived risk through investigation
  C. Size of market

III. The Decision to Invest
  A. Concept of commitment
  B. Creation of commitments during investigation
  C. Evolving set of constraints

IV. Reviews and Negotiations
  A. Bargaining with reviewing bodies
  B. Modifications and negotiations
    1. reduction of company's own capital investment
    2. search for local partners
    3. flexibility
    4. foreign government concessions, etc.

V. Changes through Repetition: The International Division
  A. The time element
  B. Organizational evolution
  C. Institutional forces
    1. changes in strategy
    2. roles
    3. information
  D. Attitudes toward risk and uncertainty
  E. Top management involvement

Source: Based on Yair Aharoni, *The Foreign Investment Decision* (Boston, MA: Harvard Business School, 1966).

---

[17] Yair Aharoni, *The Foreign Investment Decision* (Boston, MA: Harvard Business School, 1966).

THE DECISION TO LOOK ABROAD

The company's management makes the decision to look abroad for a foreign investment project by initiating forces—those forces that are imposed directly upon the firm—and auxiliary forces—forces that stem indirectly from some rather remotely related reason. Initiating forces include the drive of high-ranking executives toward international business, outside proposals from, for example, agencies such as the World Bank or government institutions such as the Desk Officers at the U.S. Departments of State or Commerce, the fear by a firm of losing a market, the bandwagon effect—everyone is doing it, so we had better do it—and strong competition from abroad.

Auxiliary forces that result in using capital equipment or funds for foreign projects may stem from some unrelated reason for doing the foreign project. The foreign project may create a market for components and other products made by the parent firm. Old machinery may be obsolete in the home country but may be useable in some LDC. Capitalization of know-how and spreading fixed costs can be accomplished by the FDI project. And the FDI project might lead to an indirect return to lost markets.

THE INVESTIGATION PROCESS

Once the decision is made to analyze potential foreign projects, the process then turns to an investigation of the proposal. Initially, some level of risk and uncertainty is generated by the project among top management. As the project is further analyzed, the firm will make changes in its perceived risk; usually, the more top management knows about the project and the host country, the less risk that management will perceive. The size of the market will be estimated during this marketing feasibility stage.

THE DECISION TO INVEST

The firm then decides to make the foreign investment. At this stage, the firm's management will conceive some commitment toward the project. During the investigation further commitments will still be created, including how much to invest, the size of the plant and its employment, and whether home office personnel will be sent to the overseas project. A set of constraints evolve including currency convertibility, profitability, and other operating characteristics.

REVIEWS AND NEGOTIATIONS

At this time, the firm has decided to commit some finite amount of resources to the project. It may then find it necessary to review the project with home and host country officials. Modifications in and negotiations about the project may be required. These may include a reduction in the company's own capital investment, the search for local partners, and foreign government concessions, e.g., tax holidays or abatements, and low-interest government loans, etc.

CHANGES THROUGH REPETITION

Finally, as the project progresses and the firm makes more and more foreign investments, changes will be made in its FDI analysis process. The firm may become more interested in the time element, i.e., how long a project will take to mature. An organizational structure that is more and more internationally oriented may evolve. Institutional forces may be formulated that will facilitate further foreign investment. These include changes in strategy, assignment of roles to top management so that their expertise can be utilized in FDI questions, and the development of an intelligence in-

ventory to assist in FDI analysis. Further repetitions in FDI will cause management's attitudes toward risk and uncertainty to be modified, enhancing the firm's ability to make better FDI decisions in the future. Finally, the firm's top management will become more involved in international business as more and more FDI is made. The Aharoni model is a simple framework for analyzing the foreign investment decision process but it has stood the test of time.

Approaches to Foreign Investment Analysis

Theories can be used to explain FDI. The process can be analyzed to show how FDI works. However, to understand how firms actually decide on a particular foreign investment project, it is useful to examine the approaches that firms actually use in deciding to invest abroad.[18]

GO/NO GO APPROACH

First, the approach can be a very simple one, much like the pay-back period method for long-term capital budgeting purposes. The firm can use a simple go/no go approach. Taking into consideration only one or two factors, the firm's management decides to accept or not accept the foreign project. This factor might be a particular piece of economic data about the market in the foreign country, or the availability of manpower there, or the firm might decide not to invest in a particular place because of the perceived business or political risk. This is a very simple approach and management does not have to resort to elaborate financial, marketing, or other types of analyses.

PREMIUM FOR RISK APPROACH

Second, a firm may use the premium for risk approach. This approach is actually used by 80 percent of international firms and requires that a lower return on investment be demanded for projects in industrialized nations and a higher one for LDCs; or the required returns may be ranked according to a country's investment climate. For example, suppose a firm determines that its weighted average cost of capital is 10 percent and that this figure is used as the firm's required rate of return on domestic projects. If a project is located in western Europe, the firm might use this same required rate of return. However, if the firm invests in a project in eastern Europe, because of the added riskiness in those countries, a premium for risk may be added to the 10 percent required rate of return, say 5 percent, making the required rate of return for the project 15 percent. If the firm locates a project in one of the less stable African countries, say Tanzania—usually ranked quite low in either the *Institutional Investor* or *Euromoney* country risk rankings—the firm may add a 10 percent premium for risk, making the required rate of return for that project 20 percent.

   The alternatives can be considered and, perhaps, a different discount factor can be used for each year, or different weights can be applied to the investment returns based on a rating scale. This is similar to the addition of a premium of risk to the discount factor in determining the net present value of a project in a capital budgeting problem, to be discussed in the following chapter. The major trouble with this approach is that a uniform degree of risk is assumed over the life of the project.

---

[18] Robert B. Stobaugh, Jr., "How to Analyze Foreign Investment Climates," *Harvard Business Review* 47 (September–October 1969): 100–8.

RANGE OF ESTIMATES APPROACH

Third, the range of estimates may be used to determine whether to invest in a foreign project. To apply this approach, the best estimates are made for the values of the various factors that will affect the project's profitability. Estimates are then made for cash flows or profits depending on the variation in these value estimates. In fact, the factors affecting a firm's profits can be distinguished by whether they are stable factors, ones that change only very slowly, e.g., income tax rates, depreciation allowance rates, tariff rates, the presence of foreign exchange controls, the availability of loan funds and their quantity and cost, or less stable factors, those whose variation can be volatile, e.g., the number of foreign exchange rate changes in recent years, the level of currency reserves, trends in the country's exports and imports, or the amount of variability in reserves.

PROBABILITY THEORY APPROACH

Finally, firms are turning to probability theory in risk analysis to determine whether to invest abroad. With the advent of better computers, software, and quantitative methodologies, management has found it easier to apply probability theories to foreign investment analysis. For example, an estimate can be made, using risk analysis, of the

FIGURE 6–2 Decision Tree Analysis in Foreign Investment

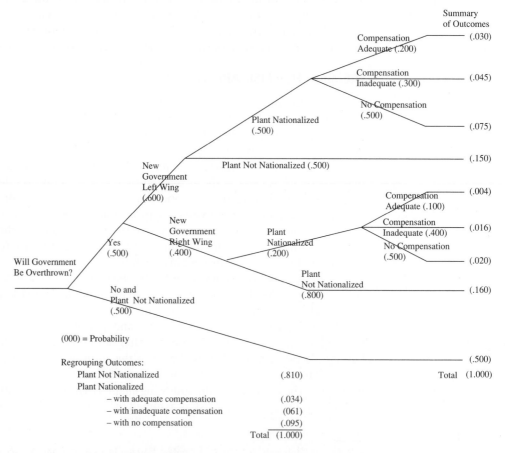

Source: Robert B. Stobaugh, Jr., "How to Analyze Foreign Investment Climates," *Harvard Business Review* 47 (September–October 1969):108. Reprinted with permission.

probable outcomes of various events, e.g., a 12-month estimate of the foreign exchange rate for the prospective country's currency. This estimate can begin as, for example, a 20 percent probability of devaluation. This probability can be further broken down to give us an estimate of the most and least likely amounts of the devaluation. For instance, the 20 percent chance of a devaluation can be further estimated at $p = .05$ of a 15 percent devaluation, $p = .10$ of a 20 percent devaluation, and $p = .05$ of a 25 percent devaluation.

A form of probability analysis, decision tree analysis, is shown in Figure 6–2 to examine the various possibilities at various stages of the effects of the overthrow of the government of a country in which a foreign subsidiary is located. The analysis by a firm with a subsidiary in that country begins with the 50–50 probability that a particular government will be overthrown. If it is overthrown, a 60 percent chance exists that the new government will be left wing, with a greater chance, if it is, that the firm's subsidiary will be nationalized. If the subsidiary is nationalized, analysis shows a 50 percent chance that no compensation will be given if the new government is left wing. The various estimated outcomes will all add up to 100 percent and the parent firm can make decisions based on the most likely outcome. This type analysis is helpful to MNC management in making decisions to make further investments in that country or how to manage the current political risk.

Licensing as an Alternative to FDI

The discussion to this point has assumed that the firm makes direct investment of funds in the foreign project. However, for a number of reasons, some firms wish to have a foreign presence but do not want to make direct investments. Perhaps the firm is not sufficiently knowledgeable about direct investments in foreign countries or has insufficient personnel familiar with international business. Maybe the firm's risk threshold is too high, or perhaps the firm has insufficient funds for direct investments. One alternative available to the firm is to license its patents, technical know-how, or processes to foreign firms, which will then manufacture and generally market the firm's product. The firm owning the technical know-how (the licensor) possesses something that he has reason to believe will be marketable to another firm (the licensee), in this case in a foreign country, from which both firms will profit. Thus, the licensor rents the know-how to the licensee for manufacture and marketing and, in return, the licensee remits a certain percentage of the revenues in the form of royalties to the licensor.

RISKS

Foreign licensing entails certain risks to the owner of the intangible property rights. The agreement demands much good faith about the quality of the product manufactured by the licensee and whether the latter will make a good faith effort to market the product. The benefits of these arrangements can be offset if the licensee infringes upon the licensor's intangible property rights by absconding with the patent or know-how underlying the manufacturing process.

These risks can be reduced by the provisions in the agreement between the licensor and the licensee. For example, a well-drafted agreement will contain controls concerning quality so that manufacturing standards will be maintained. It will insure that no antitrust laws are violated in the foreign country such as exclusive agreements. Financial considerations are important including how much down payment, how future payments are to be determined, etc. Legal provisions should be included in the agreement to insure that the licensor does not relinquish legal rights to intangible property rights.

Some procedures can be utilized that will maximize returns to the licensor. The agreement should identify who has responsibility for review and renewal of the agreement, and it should state when the agreement is to be reviewed. Evaluation techniques should be set forth in the agreement including a focus on past performance of revenue and future projections on revenue. New contract provisions might include statements about product additions or deletions, any changes in the royalty schedule, and possible expansion of the licensee's territory. This will insure that the licensee does not come into competition against the licensor.

Licensing can be a profitable means of entering a foreign market without making a direct investment. However, it can become a nightmare of entangling international litigation. A handful of large law firms in the United States and abroad concentrate their entire legal business on cases involving infringement of intangible property rights of blue-chip MNCs around the world.

Impact of FDI on MNCs' Competitive Advantage

Global strategy concerning the FDI after it has been made may have an impact on the competitive advantage of MNCs.[19] Some firms have free-standing subsidiaries that operate independently in the foreign location. For example, the Swiss company, Brown Boveri, and some U.S. MNCs such as General Motors have been organized in this manner and, thus, their competitive advantage was diminished and they lost market position to competitors.

Firms that have subsidiary operations in foreign countries may formulate and implement strategies that will increase their competitive advantage. The MNC can locate FDI in many other nations. The key, however, is for the parent to coordinate these widely dispersed activities. For example, Sony or Honda do not produce only in Japan, they locate manufacturing plants in the United States and Europe. Coordination of these operations can be achieved by either using the same brand name or sales approach or by choosing a separate brand or sales channel custom-tailored to the local needs.

Dispersing the operations in foreign countries requires FDI. Industries that resort to dispersion of FDI require lower transportation, communications, and storage costs than are encountered in a central location. The problems of a central location, discussed earlier, include exchange rate, political, and supply interruption risks, and these risks can be diversified by FDI dispersion. But it is important for the firm to coordinate these activities in order to maintain a competitive advantage.

Summary and Conclusions

Foreign direct investment (FDI) plays a vital role in international business. FDI is advantageous in the economic development of low-income countries. It furnishes an outlet for the resources of a MNC for further expansion, which may be profitable for any number of reasons. FDI is the catalyst that rationalizes the theory of comparative advantage and that brings nations together in sharing scarce economic resources.

Companies must make FDI decisions in order to become MNCs. Several theories have been advanced during the past thirty or so years and some of these have been empirically tested. They not only explain why FDI flows from one country to another but

---

[19] Michael E. Porter, *The Competitive Advantage of Nations* (New York: The Free Press, 1990), pp. 54–63.

they also are attempts to explain the rationale for multinational corporate operations. Some of the early theories, those advanced by Kindleberger, Hymer, Caves, and others, are extensions of economic theory and explain FDI by the deviations from perfect competition. More recent theories advanced by Buckley and Casson and by Dunning explain FDI as a method for moving intellectual property across borders or as the result of many eclectic foundations for the movement of FDI abroad. These theories are discussed in the following appendix.

A number of approaches to FDI have been used by firms. Decisions to invest abroad are sometimes made very simply as go/no go decisions or may involve very complex probability models. Finally, if the firm does not have the know-how or resources to send direct investment abroad, it can license a foreign firm to manufacture and market its product by permitting it to use intangible property rights such as patents or formulae.

Appendix: Theories of Foreign Investment

Economic theory has taught that countries should specialize in production that they do best, i.e., use the least factors of production. They should then trade such products to other nations with which they have a comparative advantage over the product in which those nations specialize. No foreign investment is made, only international trade is practiced in these specialized products. However, this theory is usually practiced in a world of perfect competition. In the real world, imperfections and other reasons exist that motivate firms to invest abroad.

Since 1960, scholars of international business or economics have formulated several theories to explain direct investment by foreign firms. In recent years, much of this literature has also been used to explain why firms become multinational. In the following sections, some of the major theories will be discussed.

FACTOR MARKET IMPERFECTIONS

During the 1960s, Kindleberger[20] and Hymer[21] were among the first to attempt to explain why firms invest abroad. These economists suggested that the major determinants of FDI stemmed from the imperfections in national and international product and factor markets. In a neoclassical world of perfect competition, no barriers to trade exist, information is costless, and no economies of scale are present. Thus, exporting will be the only form of international operations and locating overseas offers no advantage. However, in the real world, as we know, perfect competition does not exist and FDI does occur.

Hymer was one of the first to distinguish between portfolio and direct investment abroad. He noted that in the early part of the twentieth century the pattern of international investment did not conform with the expectations of portfolio investment theory. He suggested that direct investment took place for reasons other than interest rate differentials. Investors used direct investment for the purpose of gaining control of the enterprise for two reasons: (1) to ensure the safety of the investment, and (2) because the investor (or investing firm) had some type of advantage with which it wished to exploit that foreign market.

Kindleberger held that an investor must possess some advantage that would allow a direct investment to earn sufficient return to justify competing with firms in the

---

[20] Charles P. Kindleberger, *American Business Abroad* (New Haven, CT: Yale University Press, 1969).

[21] Stephen H. Hymer, *The International Operations of National Firms: A Study of Direct Foreign Investment* (Cambridge, MA: The MIT Press, 1976).

host country. Under conditions of perfect markets and factors, no one can possess an advantage that would justify direct investment. He then cites a number of imperfections that cause direct investment in an imperfect world.[22] For example, market imperfections may arise from the limited amounts of natural resources such as mineral deposits. Other imperfections may arise from the creation of competitive advantages from product differentiation practiced by oligopolistic firms. Governments may create market imperfections by imposing tariffs or nontariff trade barriers on imports.

The Advantage of Information

Caves[23] indicated that FDI tended to occur only in a few of many possible institutional forms and only within a few industries in developed countries. Caves agreed with Hymer and Kindleberger that, for FDI to occur, the firm investing abroad must have an advantage in information about its special asset to offset the information disadvantage of its alien status. In addition, it must also find production abroad preferable to any other means of obtaining income from the foreign market, such as exporting, licensing, or the establishment of a native producer. The MNC has the power to differentiate its products and can produce a stream of them at lower cost.

A Synthesis of Hypotheses

A number of hypotheses were formulated by Louis Calvet that were intended to explain foreign direct investment.[24] Calvet identified these hypotheses as (1) market equilibrium, (2) government imposed distortions, (3) market structure imperfections, and (4) market failure imperfection.

MARKET EQUILIBRIUM HYPOTHESIS

This hypothesis focuses on the short-term nature of disequilibria. Profit seeking firms and arbitrageurs cause FDI to flow abroad until a new equilibrium emerges. In other words, FDI flows from high labor cost countries to low labor cost countries in order to minimize cost. The result is a finite life for FDI.

GOVERNMENT-IMPOSED DISTORTIONS

This hypothesis holds that governments distort markets and create profit opportunities when they impose tariffs, import quotas, or legislate national tax systems that are different from those in other countries. A classic case can be found in the European Community where, first, U.S. firms moved large amounts of FDI to EC member countries and, second, where Japan has now become a large direct investor in order to get around the EC's trade barriers.

MARKET STRUCTURE IMPERFECTIONS

Under this hypothesis, firms have oligopoly power to interfere with market pricing mechanisms. These firms then set up barriers to entry with the creation of unique prod-

---

[22] Charles P. Kindleberger, *American Business Abroad.*

[23] Richard E. Caves, "International Corporations: The Industrial Economics of Foreign Investment," *Economica* 38 (February 1971): 1–27.

[24] Louis A. Calvet, "A Synthesis of Foreign Direct Investment Theories and Theories of the Multinational Firm," *Journal of International Business Studies* 7 (Spring/Summer 1981): 43–59.

ucts in the marketplace. In addition, such firms may display their interdependence by predicting and then emulating the actions of their competitors. Such actions have been explained by Vernon's product life cycle theory of FDI,[25] by Knickerbocker's follow the leader behavior,[26] and by Caves, mentioned previously.

MARKET FAILURE IMPERFECTIONS

Finally, Calvet hypothesized that markets fail because they depart from perfect market assumptions about production techniques and commodity properties. Existing knowledge—technology—should be available to other firms as a free good because of social efficiency. This creates a dilemma about how firms can be motivated to produce new knowledge if no property rights will be granted. Calvet held that the natural characteristics of knowledge favor its transfer within a single firm and, hence, FDI is justified over other alternatives of exploiting foreign markets when firms transfer their technology within the firm and across borders to their foreign affiliates.

Internalization

Buckley and Casson[27] developed a broader theory for the rationale of the MNC; they referred to this theory as internalization. The MNC consists of many interconnected activities such as marketing, research and development, finance, training, as well as production. Buckley and Casson held that these connections create a series of flows of intermediate products such as knowledge, expertise—the technology to which Calvet referred—as well as semiprocessed materials and tangible goods. The markets for these incomplete or intangible products are difficult to organize and such a problem is compounded when one deals with an intangible such as knowledge. An incentive is created for the firm that has produced this technology to bypass regular markets and *internalize* such transaction within the firm and, in the case of FDI, across national borders.

Buckley and Casson and, then, Buckley, have attempted to further refine their internalization theory. In 1985, they noted several advantages of internalization including: (1) the increased ability to control and plan production and, in particular, to coordinate flows of crucial inputs, (2) the exploitation of market power by discriminatory pricing, (3) the avoidance of bilateral market power, (4) the avoidance of uncertainties in the transfer of knowledge between parties, and (5) the avoidance of potential government intervention.[28] Buckley then explored the problems of empirically testing the internalization theory.[29] Different types of costs and demand conditions that arise in the internal and external markets have to be specified properly. The measurement of key variables and proxies presents a problem as does the introduction of dynamic elements into the theory.

---

[25] Raymond Vernon, "International Investment and International Trade in the Product Cycle," *Quarterly Journal of Economics* 30 (May 1966): 190–207.

[26] Frederick T. Knickerbocker, *Oligopolistic Reaction and Multinational Enterprise* (Boston, MA: Harvard University Press, 1973).

[27] Peter J. Buckley and Mark Casson, *The Future of the Multinational Enterprise* (New York: Holmes and Meiers, 1976).

[28] Peter J. Buckley and Mark Casson, *The Economic Theory of the Multinational Enterprise* (New York: St. Martin's Press, 1985).

[29] Peter J. Buckley, "The Limits of Explanation: Testing the Internalization Theory of the Multinational Enterprise," *Journal of International Business Studies* 6 (Summer 1980): 181–93.

Buckley then attempted to differentiate between internalization and market structure and internalization and competitive advantage.[30] He observed that some industries were relatively fixed and concentrated in structure and this characteristic encouraged these firms to diversify. Other industries were more open and their market structure was not so well developed; these industries encouraged internalization in order to overcome these imperfections in their market structure.

Eclecticism

John Dunning, a British economist, began in 1971 to identify market imperfections as the reason why companies invest abroad.[31] He related three predominant strands of FDI theory into his "eclectic" theory of international production.[32] The reasons why companies invest abroad are: (1) to exploit market potential, (2) to secure materials for manufacturing, and (3) to exploit a comparative advantage that they possess.

Dunning further refined his eclectic theory of international production in 1981.[33] A firm would engage in FDI if the following conditions were met: (1) the firm possesses some net ownership advantage over the competing firms in the local market, (2) it must be more beneficial for the firm to retain control of these advantages rather than leasing or licensing them to the local firms, and (3) it must be profitable for the enterprise to utilize these advantages in conjunction with at least some factor inputs (including natural resources) outside its home country, or, otherwise, foreign markets could be entirely served by exports.

Finally, Dunning defended his eclectic theory against several criticisms.[34] This defense centered on the general differences between most FDI theories concerned with the structural distortions of the market and transactional market failure. These structural distortions were concerned with government intervention that encouraged or discouraged FDI. Transactions gains in the face of such government distortion, Dunning held, could be realized from foreign exchange operations, enhanced arbitrage and leverage opportunities, and better coordination of financial decision making.

Dunning's eclectic theory has been critically examined by Itaki.[35] Itaki examined the theoretical redundancy of the "ownership advantage," the inseparability of the "ownership advantage" from the "location advantage," the conceptual ambiguity of the "location advantage," and the possible methodological dangers of a multifactor analysis under the three headings of the eclectic theory. His major conclusion was that further analysis should be conducted. He suggested that FDI theory should not be separated from international trade theory and that comparative advantage should be considered in any analysis of FDI theory.

---

[30] Peter J. Buckley, "Problems and Developments in the Core Theory of International Business," *Journal of International Business Studies* 21(Fourth Quarter 1990): 657–65.

[31] John H. Dunning, "Trade, Location of Economic Activity and the MNE: A Search for an Eclectic Approach," in *In the International Allocation of Economic Activity* Proceedings of a Nobel Symposium held at Stockholm, ed. Bertil Ohlin (London: Macmillan, 1971).

[32] John H. Dunning, "Explaining Changing Patterns of International Production: In Defence of the Eclectic Theory," *Oxford Bulletin of Economics and Statistics* 4 (November 1979): 269–95.

[33] John H. Dunning, *International Production and the Multinational Enterprise* (London: George Allen and Unwin, 1981).

[34] John H. Dunning, "The Eclectic Paradigm of International Production: A Restatement and Some Possible Extensions," *Journal of International Business Studies* 14 (Spring 1988): 1–31.

[35] Masahiko Itaki, "A Critical Assessment of the Eclectic Theory of the Multinational Enterprise," *Journal of International Business Studies* 22 (Third Quarter 1991): 445–60.

The Japanese School

Another explanation for FDI has been labeled the "Japanese School" approach. Kojima and Ozawa[36] suggested that the market cannot efficiently handle industrial adjustment in a global marketplace. They argued that government intervention be used to ensure a successful adjustment by encouraging trade and FDI, including acting as trade intermediaries and participating in new forms of FDI such as joint ventures, direct overseas loans, and plant exports and management.

The Theory of International Banking

The theories discussed in the previous sections primarily explain foreign direct investment by manufacturing and service-oriented MNCs. However, international banks are also corporations and invest in overseas banking units. Some of the previously mentioned theories explain the behavior of banks headquartered in particular countries in setting up branches or subsidiaries in foreign countries. The "follow the leader" and Dunning's eclectic theory of production are among those theories that explain why banks invest in operations in foreign countries.

However, other particular theories have been suggested to explain the international operations of banks.[37] These include the gravitational pull effect, i.e., banks go abroad in order to serve their domestic customers who have invested abroad.[38] Swiss National Bank in Chicago and Allgemeine Bank Nederland in New York are examples of foreign banks that have set up operations in the United States because Swiss and Dutch companies have U.S. operations. Another more general theory of international banking uses simple price theory principles to explain foreign bank expansion. For example, international retail banks use management technology and marketing know-how developed for domestic purposes at very low marginal cost abroad. This theory, advanced by Grubel,[39] is nearly identical to the theory developed by Kindleberger and discussed earlier.

Summary

Several theories have been advanced to explain why firms directly invest in operations abroad. In recent years, some of these theories have attempted to explain why firms become multinational in their operations. Many of these theories have not been empirically tested. Recently, some research has attempted to test some of these theories. For example, Doukas and Travlos[40] looked at the effect on stock prices of international acquisitions attempted by U.S. firms and found some evidence to support the internal-

---

[36] Kiyoshi Kojima and Terutomo Ozawa, "Micro- and Macro-Economic Models of Direct Foreign Investment: Toward a Synthesis," *Hitotsubashi Journal of Economics* 25 (June 1984): 1–20.

[37] Robert Z. Aliber, "International Banking: A Survey," *Journal of Money, Credit, and Banking* 16 (November 1984, Part 2): 661–712.

[38] Joel Metais, "The Multinationalization of the Large Commercial Banks: An Industrial Economics Approach," *Revue Economique* (May 1979): n.a.

[39] Herbert G. Grubel, "A Theory of Multinational Banking," *Banca Nazionale del Lavoro Quarterly Review* 123 (December 1977): 349–63.

[40] John Doukas and Nicholaos G. Travlos, "The Effect of Corporate Multinationalism on Shareholders' Wealth: Evidence From International Acquisitions," *Journal of Finance* 43 (December 1988): 1161–75.

If you have been assigned the appendix to this chapter, you should be familiar with the major theories that attempt to explain foreign direct investment or the multinational company. Examine closely the writings of Buckley and Casson concerning internalization and those of Dunning and his eclectic paradigm. Try to determine whether these concepts can be tested empirically and, if so, how.

---

ization theory. Other studies have been inconclusive in testing the Hymer-Kindleberger and Dunning theories. Buckley attempted to differentiate between internalization and market structure and internalization and competitive advantage.[41]

The field of international business is a relatively young field of study. The leading schools of thought on this subject are less than 40 years old. Explanations for the multinationalism of business enterprise are even younger. FDI will continue to grow as the borderless world grows smaller via the information superhighway.

These and other theories have been advanced to explain why FDI takes place and why firms become multinational enterprises. Whatever the explanations for FDI, it does take place and can be characterized as a process. This process will be discussed in more detail in the following chapter.

Additional Readings

Aharoni, Yair. *The Foreign Investment-Decision.* Boston, MA: Harvard Business School, 1966.

Aliber, Robert Z. "International Banking: A Survey." *Journal of Money, Credit, and Banking* 16 (November 1984, Part 2): 661–712.

Bergsman, Joel, and Xiaofang Shen. "Foreign Direct Investment in Developing Countries: Progress and Problems." *Finance & Development* 32 (December 1995): 6–8.

Buckley, Peter J., and Mark Casson. *The Future of the Multinational Enterprise.* New York: Holmes and Meiers, 1976.

Calvet, Louis A. "A Synthesis of Foreign Direct Investment Theories and Theories of the Multinational Firm." *Journal of International Business Studies* 7 (Spring/Summer 1981): 43–59.

Caves, Richard E. "International Corporations: The Industrial Economics of Foreign Investment." *Economica* 38 (February 1971): 1–27.

Dunning, John H. "The Eclectic Paradigm of International Production: A Restatement and Some Possible Extensions." *Journal of International Business Studies* 14 (Spring 1988): 1–31.

Dunning, John H. "Explaining Changing Patterns of International Production: In Defense of the Eclectic Theory." *Oxford Bulletin of Economics and Statistics* 4 (November 1979): 269–95.

Grosse, Robert. "The Theory of Foreign Direct Investment," *Essays in International Business* 3 (December 1981).

Hymer, Stephen H. *The International Operations of National Firms: A Study of Direct Foreign Investment.* Cambridge, MA: The MIT Press, 1976.

Kindleberger, Charles P. *American Business Abroad.* New Haven, CT: Yale University Press, 1969.

Knickerbocker, Frederick T. *Oligopolistic Reaction and Multinational Enterprise.* Boston, MA: Harvard University Press, 1973.

---

[41] Peter J. Buckley, *International Business Studies*, 657–65.

Rayome, David L., and James C. Baker. "Foreign Direct Investment: A Review and Analysis of the Literature." *International Trade Journal* 9 (Spring 1995): 3–38.

Stobaugh, Robert B., Jr. "How to Analyze Foreign Investment Climates." *Harvard Business Review* 47 (September–October 1969): 100–8.

Vernon, Raymond. "International Investment and International Trade in the Product Cycle." *Quarterly Journal of Economics* 30 (May 1966): 190–207.

Discussion Questions

1. What are the benefits to be derived from foreign direct investment?
2. Why has so little FDI flowed into the less-developed countries?
3. What major factors must be analyzed to determine the feasibility of a foreign venture?
4. What did Kindleberger, Hymer, and Caves contribute to the theory of foreign investment?
5. Calvet synthesized the major theories of FDI. Up to that point, discuss his synthesization of these theories.
6. What is the internalization theory? Is it valid?
7. Is Dunning's Eclectic Theory a theory? Why or why not?
8. What is the value of Aharoni's foreign investment decision process?
9. Discuss four major approaches used by firms to analyze foreign investment proposals.
10. What is licensing? How does it differ from FDI? What are some of the problems with licensing in international business?

Problems

1. Select one industrialized country and one developing country and write a brief foreign investment feasibility report for (1) a McDonald's restaurant, (2) a computer retail outlet, and (3) an automobile manufacturing plant.
2. Draft an Aharoni-type foreign investment decision process report for manufacturing a product of your choice in a country of your choice.
3. Report on the articles that have attempted to empirically test Dunning's eclectic theory and Buckley and Casson's internalization theory.
4. Choose three sub-Saharan African nations and show why they are not receptive to foreign private investment.
5. Compare and contrast three case studies of licensing of product manufacture in foreign countries by U.S. companies.

C H A P T E R

Long-Term Capital Management

Major Objectives of Chapter 7

(1) To examine the differences found in capital budgeting for international projects, (2) to examine the role of cost of capital in the international capital budgeting problem, and (3) to discuss the financial structure of MNCs.

Key terms to be learned in chapter 7:

- uncertainty absorption
- optimal financial structure
- adjusted present value
- multiple hurdle rate

Introduction

In chapter 6, MNC management decided whether to invest abroad and foreign investment projects were analyzed to enable the firm to decide whether to place such investment abroad. However, at the firm level, once the decision has been made to go abroad, projects must be analyzed for their economic feasibility. The firm generally may have an infinite amount of projects and a finite amount of capital. Capital must be rationed. If more than one project is found to be feasible, the projects must be ranked in some rational manner. The age-old equation of an infinite number of projects and a finite amount of capital must be solved. This capital budgeting requirement is endemic to all business firms, whether domestic or international.

The material in this chapter is predicated on the major objectives of the capital budgeting function. They are

1. establishment of a realistic firm financial standard or profit goal against which all projects can be compared and judged;

2. development of some mathematical criteria that can be used to rank projects according to their relative profitability and to permit them to be validly compared with the company standards.

In addition, the material covered in this chapter assumes that the student has a good background in capital budgeting techniques and methodology, thus, the analysis of each method is kept to a minimum.

This chapter addresses the capital budgeting function in international companies. The differences between capital budgeting for domestic projects and capital budgeting for foreign projects will be analyzed. Various methods for ranking and analyzing projects will be covered. Relevant cash flows from a foreign project will be identified. The discussion will turn to the cost of capital for MNCs. Cost of capital is a vital input in the discounted cash flow methods used in capital budgeting, and its relationship to the financial structure of the international firm will be addressed. First, however, it is helpful to examine the literature of capital budgeting in general and in MNCs specifically.

Capital Budgeting Literature

GENERAL LITERATURE

To understand the subject of capital budgeting, it is useful to examine selected items in the literature. The subject of capital budgeting was introduced to the finance literature in the writings of Dean[1] and Lutz and Lutz.[2] Bierman and Smidt[3] have produced a number of editions of a general treatise on capital budgeting techniques in which they analyze the four major techniques: pay-back period, accounting rate of return, net present value, and internal rate of return, and explain why they think the net present value method is the best.

INTERNATIONAL CAPITAL BUDGETING LITERATURE

A number of students of capital budgeting have made contributions about the application of this area to international business. Some of the major literature is presented in the following sections.

Bugnion

Capital budgeting was associated with international business for the first time in a 1965 article by J. R. Bugnion who discussed the differences in relevant cash flows in the capital budgeting process for multinational companies.[4] Bugnion demonstrated that capital budgeting theory, originally designed for domestic companies, was not directly applicable to international companies. He thought it vain to attempt a universal theory that would be equally applicable to all MNCs because he believed that no two international companies were identical.

One of Bugnion's contributions involved a method for determination of the cost of funds borrowed by a subsidiary from the parent company. The assumption underlying this methodology was, of course, that the affiliate borrowed from the parent and not from local or international money or capital markets.

Stonehill and Nathanson

Stonehill and Nathanson followed in 1968 with a treatise on how cash flows should be adjusted for risk when capital budgeting is implemented in the MNC.[5] The

---

[1] Joel Dean, *Capital Budgeting* (New York: Columbia University Press, 1951).

[2] Friedrich Lutz and Vera Lutz, *The Theory of Investment of the Firm* (Princeton, NJ: Princeton University Press, 1951).

[3] Harold Bierman, Jr. and Seymour Smidt, *The Capital Budgeting Decision* (New York: Macmillan, 1988).

[4] J. R. Bugnion, "Capital Budgeting and International Corporations," *Quarterly Journal of AIESEC International* 1 (November 1965): 30–54.

[5] Arthur Stonehill and Leonard Nathanson, "Capital Budgeting in the Multinational Company," *California Management Review* 11 (Summer 1968): 39–54.

objective of this study was the development of a better conceptual framework for evaluating foreign investments. The authors surveyed firms to determine what methods they were using to evaluate multinational investments. This study recommended that incremental cash inflows from the parent's viewpoint should include dividends, know-how payments, interest on loan repayments, export profits, intangible gains, and the "cash-out" value of the foreign affiliate using the time horizon for capital budgeting to reflect the value of reinvested earnings. Cash flows should be discounted by the parent's weighted average cost of capital under an optimal capital structure. Cash flows should be adjusted for risk by charging them with what the authors termed an "uncertainty absorption." Incremental cash flows from the viewpoint of the foreign affiliate should include net earnings after local taxes but before depreciation, interest, and know-how payments. Cash outflow should be measured in terms of the original investment in assets.

Shapiro

Shapiro discussed the role of the cost of capital in capital budgeting for the multinational corporation.[6] He agreed with Stonehill and Nathanson that project cash flows, rather than the discount rate, should be adjusted for risk. Tax factors and segmented capital market effects should also be incorporated by adjusting cash flows. His reasoning for this method was that the firm has more and better information concerning the effect of risk on future cash flows than on the required discount rate.

Baker

A number of studies dealing with the practices of MNCs were reported during the 1980s. Among these were the studies by Baker about the practices of U.S. and European companies during the period of 1978 and 1981.[7] In 1978, Baker studied 245 U.S. MNCs, all with sales in excess of $500 million and ranked in the *Fortune Directory of the 500 Largest U.S. Companies*. In 1980–81, the study was directed toward 190 firms among the top 200 European companies, ranked according to the *London Financial Times*. Personal interviews of top executives of several U.S. firms were made and confirmed much of the information derived from survey instruments. Firms were asked what capital budgeting method they used, how they accounted for risk in their computations, what major factors affected their capital budgeting decisions, and what major factors they used in estimating relevant cash flows for capital budgeting purposes.

Several conclusions were reached by these studies of U.S. and European firms. First, respondent firms formulated and implemented capital budgeting policies and practices according to acceptable financial literature, whether they were U.S. or European firms. Second, where large differences existed among the responses, such wide variations could be explained by differences in company philosophies, national tax laws, accounting practices, and cultural perceptions about inflation and risk. Third, both sets of firms, U.S. and European, showed a growing interest in the use of discounted cash flow methods; however, it was found that the pay-back period was still used by more U.S. *and* European firms than was any of the other capital budgeting methods. Fourth, subjective management judgement was found to be a contributing factor in the implementation of capital project evaluation by many of these companies.

[6] Alan Shapiro, "Capital Budgeting for the Multinational Corporation," *Financial Management* 7 (Spring 1978): 7–16.

[7] See, for example, James C. Baker, "Financial Policy in U.S. Multinational Companies' Capital Budgeting Techniques," *The Journal of Business of Seton Hall* 18 (December 1979): 13–7; James C. Baker, "Capital Budgeting in West European Companies," *Managerial Finance* (U.K.) 19 (1981): 3–10; James C. Baker, "Capital Budgeting in American and European Companies," *The Mid-Atlantic Journal of Business* 22 (Summer 1984): 15–28.

TABLE 7–1. Capital Budgeting Methods Used (percentage of N)

Method	(A) Substantial Usage U.S.	(A) Substantial Usage Europe	(B) Some Usage U.S.	(B) Some Usage Europe	No Usage U.S.	No Usage Europe	(A + B) Total Usage U.S.	(A + B) Total Usage Europe
Pay-back period	59	61	34	33	7	6	93	94
Internal rate of return	74	70	10	13	16	17	84	83
Net present value	37	41	34	22	29	37	71	63
Accounting rate of return	28	20	22	19	50	61	50	39
Profitability index	7	15	10	9	83	76	17	24
Other	14	5	3	—	83	95	17	5

$N = 68$ for U.S. firms' study; 57 for European firms' study.

Source: James C. Baker, "Capital Budgeting in American and European Companies," *The Mid-Atlantic Journal of Business* 22 (Summer 1984):19.

For example, some projects with positive net present values or internal rates of return in excess of the cost of capital were not accepted because top management did not like them and others with negative net present values or internal rates of return less than the cost of capital were accepted because they were acceptable to top management. And fifth, strategic considerations must be made. For example, it was found that some firms allocated capital to projects on the basis of very high internal rates of return or net present values, only to have the project fail in the long-run because the strategic and behavioral factors had not been considered. See Tables 7–1, 7–2, and 7–3 for selected results from these studies.

TABLE 7–2. Major Factors Affecting Capital Budgeting Decisions (percentage of N)

Factors	(A) Substantial Effect U.S.	(A) Substantial Effect Europe	(B) Little Effect U.S.	(B) Little Effect Europe	No Effect U.S.	No Effect Europe	(A + B) Having Effect U.S.	(A + B) Having Effect Europe
Prospects for remittance of profits to parent	84	59	10	22	6	19	94	81
Stability of exchange rate	53	29	38	43	9	28	91	72
Ability to repatriate capital	66	46	24	25	10	29	90	71
Inflation rate	50	38	38	43	12	19	88	81
Convertibility of foreign currency	65	46	24	22	12	32	88	68
Availability of investment guarantees	21	23	1	2	81	65	19	25

$N = 68$ for U.S. firms' study; 57 for European firms' study.

Source: James C. Baker, "Capital Budgeting in American and European Companies," *The Mid-Atlantic Journal of Business* 22 (Summer 1984):22.

Accounting Rate of Return

The accounting rate of return, or return on investment, ranks projects by the percentage rate of return found when dividing the returns from an investment by the total investment. These factors are merely book value items based on accounting data and, although the accounting rate of return is easy to calculate, it does not take the time value of money into consideration. One can compute the average income on book value in which the average book value—the investment divided by two—is considered and average income is proceeds less depreciation. Or one can simply divide average income by total original cost to find the rate of return. Neither method considers the timing of the cash proceeds.

Net Present Value

The net present value method ordinarily requires the input of two factors: the expected cash flows (CF) stemming from the project on an after-tax basis and a discount factor, k, normally the weighted average cost of capital (WACC), although technically this should be the marginal cost of capital at the source of funds. The CF are discounted by k back to a present value, NPV, which is compared with the initial investment, I_0. If the NPV is greater than I_0, the project is said to have a positive net present value and is economically feasible; that is, the project will be profitable for the firm. The normal NPV equation is as follows:

$$\text{NPV} = -I_0 + \Sigma\, X_i/(1 + k_0)^n + T_n/(1 + k)_n$$

where
NPV = net present value of project
$\quad I_0$ = initial investment
$\quad X_i$ = after-tax project cash flow in year i if all-equity
$\quad n$ = anticipated life of the project
$\quad k_0$ = weighted average cost of capital
$\quad T_n$ = terminal or salvage value in year n

The weighted average cost of capital, k_0 or WACC, is also commonly known as the required rate of return on an investment and is used to discount future cash flows to a net present value. It is the combination of the cost of equity capital and the after-tax cost of debt in relation to their respective weights in the firm's total capital.

Internal Rate of Return

Another discounted cash flow method for evaluating and/or ranking capital projects is the internal rate of return (IRR) method. In this method, the IRR is determined, and that rate will be used to discount the estimated project CF, C_t, to a present value equal to the initial investment, as in the following equation, where the internal rate of return of a project is found by solving for r, the internal rate of return

$$I - \sum_{t=1}^{n} C_t(1 + r)^t + T_n/(1 + r)^n = 0$$

or

$$\sum_{t=1}^{n} C_t(1 + r)^t + = I$$

C_0 is the outlay and is negative and the equation is solved by a trial-and-error procedure, or with a modern handheld calculator. The IRR, or r, is then compared with the project cost of capital, k, and if it is equal to or greater than k, the project is economically feasible and will add to the value of the firm. If IRR is less than k, the project should be turned down.

The IRR method has some shortcomings over the NPV method. For every change of sign in the estimated cash flows over the life of the project, it is mathemati-

cally possible to have another different IRR. In the real world, projects with lives longer than a few years may, indeed, have a period in which negative CF is the case. For example, planned maintenance or new investment may have to be added to the original project cost for some subsequent period. This problem can be solved because it is relatively simple to determine the most appropriate IRR. Until the advent of better electronic calculators, solution of the IRR problem was more difficult than for the NPV problem because of the need to interpolate between values.

The literature recommends the NPV method over the IRR method for a number of reasons.[10] The NPV method is simpler, easier, and more direct. If the company knows its cost of funds and can obtain additional funds from the market at this cost or can invest excess funds at this rate, then either NPV or IRR is appropriate to make the right decision. The IRR can be used to make correct capital budgeting decisions if the cost of capital is the same for all future periods. Such may not always hold, and the IRR rules are more complex than for NPV. A single investment, as mentioned earlier, may have more than one IRR. If a group of two or more mutually exclusive investments is considered, a direct comparison of their IRRs may not lead to the correct decision for the best alternative. Finally, it may be impossible to define the IRR for a cash flow series, whereas it is usually easier to interpret the cash flows using NPV.[11]

Adjusted Present Value

MNC financial management has found that all of the capital budgeting models discussed here need revisions for use in the real world. Some firms are using a discounted pay-back period, probably because the simple mechanics of the pay-back period are desirable but some attention to the time value of investment funds is also necessary. A number of tax differences from one country to another as well as various investment incentives such as accelerated depreciation, investment tax credits, or tax holidays have created a need to adjust the normal discounted cash flow models. One such model is the adjusted present value (APV). This model takes into consideration the differences from country to country in project risks and financial structure. These differences must be considered with different raw materials, production stages, and the stage of the project.[12]

The APV can be formulated as follows:[13]

APV = (PV of the capital outlays) + (PV of the remittable after-tax operating CF)
    + (PV of the tax savings from depreciation) + (PV of financial subsidies)
    + (PV of project contribution to corporate debt capacity)
    + (PV of other tax savings) + (PV of additional remittances)
    + (PV of residual plant and equipment)

The nature of the tax system and the tax rate can affect most of the individual PV terms in the APV model. For example, the terms concerning tax shields and interest subsidies are discounted at the before-tax cost of dollar debt. This reflects the relatively certain value of the cash flows because of tax shields and interest savings.

---

[10] Ibid., 109–10.

[11] Ibid., 110.

[12] See, for example, William R. Folks, Jr., and Raj Aggarwal, *International Dimensions of Financial Management* (Boston, MA: Kent Publishing Company, 1988): 224–7; and Alan C. Shapiro, *International Corporate Finance: Survey & Synthesis* (Tampa, FL: Financial Management Association, 1986); 49–51.

[13] Donald R. Lessard, "Evaluating Foreign Projects: An Adjusted Present Value Approach," in *International Financial Management: Theory and Application* ed. Donald R. Lessard (New York: John Wiley & Sons, 1985), pp. 570–84.

A Comparative Capital Budgeting Problem

The following project analysis comparatively demonstrates the capital budgeting methods just discussed. The following assumptions are made with regard to this project:

1. the investment is located in Germany and is denominated in German marks;

2. the project has an estimated life of 5 years;

3. the initial investment is DM 1.5 million ($1 million with an exchange rate of DM 1.5/$) and no additional investments are made during the life of the project;

4. the DM/$ future spot rates at the time of each dividend remittance are estimated, from the forward market, to be (based on a best estimates basis): (1) Year 1 DM 1.45/$; (2) Year 2 DM 1.40/$; (3) Year 3 DM 1.35/$; (4) Year 4 DM 1.30/$; (5) Year 5 DM 1.25/$;

5. the estimated net cash flows are after-tax (both German corporate income and dividend withholding taxes) dividends declared to the parent company from the foreign project and their probability is 100 percent; they are: Year 1—DM 145,000 ($100,000), Year 2—DM 280,000 ($200,000), Year 3—DM 405,000 ($300,000), Year 4—DM 390,000 ($300,000), and Year 5—DM 500,000 ($400,000);

6. the project's salvage value is DM 62,500 ($50,000);

7. the parent firm uses straight-line depreciation for domestic operations, but we assume that the foreign location does not allow depreciation;

8. the foreign country does not offer an investment tax credit;

9. the company's marginal corporate tax rate is 34 percent;

10. the parent company has excess foreign tax credits[14] and, thus, it is assumed that no U.S. tax liability will be owed on these dividend remittances;

11. the company's weighted average cost of capital is 6 percent;

12. working capital invested at the beginning of the project is recouped at the end of the project;

13. the flows are after all foreign taxes and represent dividends translated into dollars to the parent firm; project cash flows are considered from the parent firm viewpoint.

Investment	Cash Proceeds	Translated Dividends Remitted to Parent	Cumulative Cash Proceeds
Year 1 DM 1,500,000	DM 145,000	$100,000	$100,000
Year 2	DM 280,000	200,000	300,000
Year 3	DM 405,000	300,000	600,000
Year 4	DM 390,000	300,000	900,000
Year 5	DM 500,000	400,000	1,300,000

Pay-back period (Assumes returns remitted to parent as the relevant cash flows;)

Average proceeds remitted/year = $1,300,000/5

$$= \$260,000$$
$$PP = \$1,000,000/\$260,000 = 3.85 \text{ years}$$

Return on investment for remitted AT Dividends (Accounting rate of return assuming returns remitted to parent as the relevant cash flows.)

ROI = $260,000 (average proceeds per year)/$1,000,000
= 26%

Average return on book value=$260,000/($1,000,000/2)
= 52%

Net present value of remitted after-tax dividends (Assuming returns remitted to parent as the relevant cash flows.)

---

14 The foreign tax credit will be explained in chapter 17.

$-\$1,000,000 + \$100,000/(1 + .06) + \$200,000/$ $(1 + .06)^2 + \$300,000/(1 + .06)^3 + \$300,000/(1 + .06)^4$ $+ \$400,000/(1 + .06)^5 + \$50,000/(1 + .06)^5 = \$1,098,135$

Present value of future cash flows $-1,000,000 =$ $\$98,135$ Net present value of project at 6%

Internal rate of return on after-tax remitted dividends

$-\$1,000,000 - [\$100,000/(1 + r) + \$200,000/$ $(1 + r)^2 + \$300,000/(1 + r)^3 + \$300,000/(1 + r)^4$ $+ \$400,000/(1 + r)^5 + \$50,000/(1 + r)^5] = 0$

$$r = 8.81\%$$

The analysis of this project by the four leading capital budgeting methods shows the project, on a quantitative basis, to be a good project. The methods that do not consider the time value of money show the project to have a pay-back period of 3.85 years, less than the expected life of the project, and an accounting rate of return to be a relatively high 26 percent, or 52 percent, depending on whether we use total investment or average investment.

On a discounted cash flow basis, the project has a positive net present value and an internal rate of return of 8.81 percent, which is higher than the cost of capital of 6 percent. Since the problem considers the present value of capital outlays, residual plant and equipment, and remittable after-tax operating cash flows but gives no information about financial subsidies, other tax savings or foreign country depreciation laws, we can consider the adjusted present value to be identical to the net present value. Barring any qualitative factors that might be negative considerations, this project is acceptable by either simple quantitative analyses or discounted cash flow analyses.

CULTURAL PROBLEMS

In addition to the methodology used and the problems inherent with each type of capital budgeting, cultural differences result in problems of determination of the long-term value of a project. For example, the United States and Germany are both decidedly capitalistic economies. However, German firms tend to maximize the value of the firm while the primary objective of U.S. firms is to maximize shareholder wealth. The German objective concentrates on growth of assets and the balance sheet whereas the U.S. counterpart concentrates on the income statement, earnings per share, and short-term profit goals, coupled with risk reduction. Thus, discounted cash flow models with very long horizons are more useful to German firms while some type of pay-back period or accounting rate of return model may facilitate the shorter term outlook of American firms.

PROBLEMS WITH DISCOUNTED CASH FLOW MODELS

Discounted cash flow models pose a number of problems for MNCs in their evaluation of foreign projects. One of those problems has been alleviated with the modifications of the APV model, which adjusts for depreciation, investment tax credits, and other tax allowances. Another is the problem whether to consider the foreign project from the parent firm's perspective or from that of the local country. This problem is discussed in detail in the next section.

Estimating the factors needed to find the NPV or IRR of a project presents problems. Cash flows for any project are difficult to estimate, especially for long periods into the future. They are especially difficult to estimate when considered in a foreign currency environment where political risk, inflation, and economic policies may have a significant impact on the foreign project. In the world of global finance, companies have a great deal of difficulty in determining the cost of capital for the firm in general and for foreign projects specifically.

The estimation of foreign project cash flows also requires prowess in forecasting foreign exchange rates. Since the foreign project's net after-tax local earnings remitted

to the parent firm represent the relevant project returns, these returns will have to be exchanged from the foreign currency into the parent firm's currency. Timing of dividend remittances becomes very important. Thus, the parent firm must have personnel who are quite adept at forecasting foreign exchange rates in order to determine the optimum time for remittance of these earnings. The assignment of probabilities must be made to the forecasts of foreign exchange rates. Scenarios of forecast rates can involve most likely, average, and least likely exchange rate changes in forecast foreign currency cash flows. The problems of exchange rate forecasting, discussed in chapter 4, are all applicable in this process.

Research shows that MNCs identify various factors when estimating cash flows of foreign projects.[15] A significant number of firms have been found to consider the following to estimate project CF: translated profits after foreign taxes, translated profits after foreign and domestic taxes, translated profits or cash flows remitted to the parent firm, a combination of translated profits after all taxes and some amount to be reinvested with the balance to be remitted, and untranslated profits after foreign taxes, as shown in Table 7–3.

In addition, many MNC financial managers do not seem to be clear about their cost of capital. U.S. and European firms that use the NPV technique use various methods when discounting estimated CF.[16] These include cost of long-term capital companywide, cost of long-term debt companywide, cost of long-term debt in the local currency, cost of long-term and working capital companywide, cost of long-term capital in the local currency, and cost of long-term and working capital in the local currency (see Table 7–4).

Some firms seem confused about the methodology used in determining their cost of capital. When interviewed for a research project concerning this area, a company executive stated that the operating manual for the company suggested that the firm used a continuous discount factor—more mathematically appropriate than the normal discounting method—but no evidence was found that this company actually implemented this policy in practice. A large tire manufacturer stated that the capital asset pricing model was used to determine the firm's cost of equity funds. However, no evidence was found that this practice had actually been implemented by the firm. A large consumer

TABLE 7–4. Discount Rate Used by Firms When Employing Net Present Value Method (percentage of N)

	U.S. Firms	European Firms
Cost of long-term capital (companywide) (a)	42	26
Cost of long-term debt (companywide) (b)	6	20
Cost of long-term debt (local country) (b)	6	17
Cost of long-term and working capital (companywide) (a)	8	14
Cost of long-term capital (local country) (a)	4	9
Cost of long-term and working capital (local country) (a)	2	9
Other	35	29

(a) = average weighted cost; (b) = after-tax.

$N = 48$ for U.S. firms study; 35 for European firms' study.

Source: James C. Baker, "Capital Budgeting in American and European Companies," *The Mid-Atlantic Journal of Business* 22 (Summer 1984):20.

[15] Baker, *Mid-Atlantic Journal*, 15–28.
[16] Baker, ibid.

products firm used a discount rate that would produce a doubling of project value every 5 years. This objective just happened to be the company's major goal and was implemented, no matter what the firm's actual cost of capital really was. These problems do not stem from the models themselves but from the implementation of the models.

Parent or Local Perspective

A key question that faces international financial management is whether the project should be evaluated from the parent's perspective or from the local, i.e., project, perspective. In other words, should the cash flows be considered and discounted from the parent's or the project's perspective? If most or all of the investment funds were furnished from the parent, by means of equity and/or debt transfers, the project should be discounted by the parent firm's WACC, taking into consideration the risk threshold, inflation rate, and other factors relevant to the parent firm's currency. The relevant CF will be the dividends and other remittances from the foreign project to the parent on an after-tax basis and the discounted present value of the CF will be compared with the net initial investment furnished by the parent firm.

However, suppose that most or all of the investment funds are from sources external to the parent firm and in other currencies, including local currency. In this case, it is best to evaluate the project from a local or project perspective, taking into consideration the cost of the external funds, local inflation rates, and local risk factors. Most companies do evaluate foreign projects using a local perspective, although they may also use a parent perspective to insure that the project is appropriate for overall corporate objectives.

Management should analyze the effects of the investment on the parent firm's profits before and after the implementation of the project. The net benefits to the overall firm should be determined. Too often, foreign subsidiary managers will not take into consideration fully the benefits of their particular project to global MNC operations. For example, the foreign project may replace earnings from exports from the parent firm to the foreign affiliate or from another subsidiary to the foreign affiliate host of the investment project. The project may be profitable from a localized capital budgeting standpoint but may be unprofitable for the overall firm.

In general, it is conceptually correct to consider the impact of the foreign project on the MNC's consolidated cash flows. But if the project is unconsolidated or a standalone project, the perspective will be from the project's viewpoint. For example, the project may be in a LDC that has restricted dividend payments to foreign firms. The choice of the discount rate used for capital budgeting purposes may dictate from whose viewpoint the cash flows are considered. If the global WACC is used by the firm, the viewpoint will be from the parent's perspective. If the subsidiary uses the discount rate that relates to the cost of capital incurred by local competitors, the viewpoint will more than likely be from that of the subsidiary. Finally, the revenue/cost configuration for

the MNC may dictate the perspective. If the project is the result of the parent's licensing intangible property rights, the net benefit will be in the form of royalties from the foreign project to the parent firm. However, the foreign unit may consider these services as costs.

The Cost of Capital and Financial Structure

The cost of capital (k), as discussed previously, is important in the computation of both the net present value and the internal rate of return. It, as defined correctly, is the factor used to discount the estimated future cash flows of the foreign investment project. It is also the factor with which the internal rate of return is compared to determine whether the project is economically feasible. The cost of capital is defined as the minimum rate of return that a project must yield to be accepted by the firm. It is the required rate of return from a project. It has also been defined as the minimum before-tax real rate of return that must be generated from a project in order to pay the financing costs of the project after tax liabilities. Technically, the correct cost of capital for discounting purposes should be the marginal cost of capital at the source.

Oftentimes in the finance literature, the WACC is recommended as the best cost of capital because it permits a firm to use a single component cost as a hurdle rate. This takes into account the fact that low return projects may be accepted by a lower k while some projects with higher returns may be rejected. Lower return projects may be accepted because they can be financed with a lower cost capital, e.g., debt. Also if a firm accepts projects whose returns are higher than its WACC, it can increase the market value of its equity.[17]

The WACC is the cost of each type of capital—debt or equity—weighted by its proportion of the total amount of capital issued by the firm. It can be shown as follows:

$$k = [S/(B + S)] \ (k_e) + \ [B/(B + S)] \ (k_d)$$

where:
k = weighted average cost of capital
k_e = cost of equity
k_d = after-tax cost of debt
B = market value of the firm's debt
S = market value of the firm's equity

The underlined terms in this equation are the respective weights of equity and debt in the firm's total capital. By multiplying the left-hand term by k_e, the cost of equity, and the right-hand term by k_d, the cost of debt, k, the weighted average cost of capital is calculated. Thus, the firm's financial structure, its debt/equity ratio, is important to the determination of the company's cost of capital.

The cost of capital may differ from one country to another.[18] A number of reasons may explain these differences. Some of the differences may be explained by the variation in tax rates imposed against business firms in different countries. A higher tax rate may require a higher before-tax return in order to achieve an after-tax return objective by the investor. In some countries, higher savings rates result in lower returns to savers and, thus, lower expected real rates of return on investments. Such is true in

[17] Suk H. Kim and Seung H. Kim, *Global Corporate Finance: Text and Cases* (Miami, FL: Kolb Publishing Company, 1993), pp. 357–8.

[18] Robert N. McCauley and Steven A. Zimmer, "Explaining International Differences in the Cost of Capital," *FRBNY Quarterly Review* 14 (Summer 1989): 7–28.

Japan and to a limited extent in Germany. Differences in the rationing of credit in a country may create some difference in the local cost of capital. In Japan, interest rates on consumer loans are generally higher than those imposed on business loans. The perception by business firms in some countries, such as Japan and Germany, that lower risk attaches to the returns on business projects may cause savers to accept a lower real rate of return, thus lowering the cost of capital.

FACTORS THAT AFFECT AN AFFILIATE'S FINANCIAL STRUCTURE

In most cases, financial structure of foreign affiliates varies from one country to another. Some of the significant factors that can cause this variation include the affiliate's earnings, its exposure to country risk, the cost of debt, currency exchange rate fluctuations, and agency problems of the affiliate.[19] First, earnings may suffer because the affiliate may have to use debt for long-term operations as a result of low earnings. With low earnings, the affiliate may not be able to take advantage of tax breaks from the use of debt. Foreign tax credits are available to the parent firm for overseas earnings that are taxed locally. Tax rates vary greatly from one country to another, and may, thus, reduce the impact of the tax shield on debt.

Second, exposure to country risk, as discussed in detail in chapter 5, may reduce the use of equity in foreign investment projects in favor of debt because of the various political risks encountered in the local environment, including risk of currency inconvertibility, expropriation, interference with contract terms, and violence. Insurance against these country risks can be obtained from agencies such as the Multilateral Investment Guaranty Agency (MIGA), Overseas Private Investment Corporation (OPIC), if the investor is a U.S. firm, or from private insurance companies. Political risk insurance was discussed in chapter 5.

Third, the cost of debt varies from country to country. The affiliate may emphasize debt financing if local interest rates are low. In addition, foreign debt markets tend to be segmented causing the cost of debt to vary from country to country. Local debt may be the best form of capital if the local currency is under pressure to depreciate.

Fourth, exchange rate fluctuations may affect the financial structure. Affiliates generally are required to remit earnings when local currency is relatively strong vis-à-vis the parent's currency. This produces a higher value of funds remitted to the parent but also may deplete retained earnings in the affiliate, leaving it to increase the percentage of debt in its financial structure. When local currency is weak, the converse is true, earnings are retained locally, and less debt is used. Finally, if foreign operations are more decentralized and cannot be controlled adequately, this agency issue may cause the parent to require the increased remittance of earnings, leaving the affiliate with the need to fund its financial structure with more debt.

In addition to these factors affecting a foreign affiliate's financial structure, one study that surveyed 188 managers of foreign subsidiaries of U.S. firms found other factors to have a significant effect on determination of the foreign subsidiary's financial structure.[20] These include the age of the subsidiary, the ownership structure, and financial risk. Foreign affiliates that are located in a relatively low-risk environment have more debt in their financial structure than do subsidiaries that operate in a high-risk environment. Total asset turnover was also found by this study to be an important determinant of a foreign subsidiary's financial structure.

---

[19] Jeff Madura, *International Finance Perspectives* (Miami, FL: Kolb Publishing Company, 1993), pp. 166–8.
[20] Lawrence Peter Shao, Iftekhar Hasan, and Alan T. Shao, "Determinants of International Capital Structure for U.S. Foreign Subsidiaries," *Multinational Business Review* 3 (Fall 1995): 67–77.

OPTIMAL FINANCIAL STRUCTURE

The financial structure of a foreign project or foreign subsidiary owned by a MNC may be very important to the success of the enterprise. One of the unresolved issues in finance theory is whether an optimal financial structure exists. U.S. companies often act as though it does, especially if they are in the same industry, because of the similarity of financial structures of the firms in that industry. An optimal financial structure is defined as the ratio of total debt to total equity that satisfies the objectives of both the borrowing firm and its creditors, given the value systems found in their individual countries. For firms in the same industry, but domiciled in different countries, financial structures that are country norms may be more important.[21]

It is the practice in many countries including Germany, Japan, and Sweden, for firms to have high debt/equity ratios. These are countries where banks lend a great deal and private placements are more prevalent than public issues of equity and debt. This is the result of low shareholder interest, lack of institutional investors, low default risk, and a desirability for high leverage. Where these country norms exist, it is better for the MNC to require each subsidiary to use it as a financial structure norm.

Such a policy has several advantages. The use of a financial structure country norm might reduce the criticism that a foreign subsidiary operates with too much debt and not enough risk capital. The practice enables management to evaluate the return on equity relative to local competitors in the same industry. In countries where interest rates are high because of the scarcity of capital, the penalty paid will remind management that unless return on assets is higher than the local cost of capital, the firm will misallocate scarce domestic resources.

Studies in the 1970s found that optimal financial structures probably do exist, even in the United States.[22] In other words, financial structures in the countries studied were culture-bound rather than universal. The authors covered France, Japan, the Netherlands, Norway, and the United States. This study found that perceived business risk was not a universal determinant of a firm's financial structure, i.e., for firms in the same industry, industry type was not a determinant of debt/equity ratios. Business risk was perceived differently in different countries; thus, a cultural bias toward financial structure was found in the countries studied. Size of firm and ownership type, i.e., family-owned, widespread public ownership, etc., were also found not to be determinants of financial structures.

What follows from these studies is that what is being taught about the theory of financial structure is not widely understood nor is it used in practice by financial executives of MNCs. The descriptive material purporting to describe the actual behavior of firms was not confirmed by such research. Financial structures are largely determined by the local beliefs of financial executives and bankers in each country. In other words, financial structure determination is culture-bound rather than universal in nature.

COST OF CAPITAL ISSUES

The cost of capital is at the heart of the issues discussed in this chapter including discounted cash flow methods in capital budgeting and the effect of firms' financial structures on the cost of capital. A study by the author, which included a survey of 435 U.S. and European companies and interviews with several of these firms, found evidence of

---

[21] Arthur Stonehill and Thomas Stitzel, "Financial Structure and Multinational Corporations," *California Management Review* 12 (Fall 1969): 91–6.

[22] See, for example, Arthur Stonehill, Theo Beekhuisen, Richard Wright, Lee Remmers, et al. "Financial Goals and Debt Ratio Determinants: A Survey of Practice in Five Countries," *Financial Management* 4 (Autumn 1975): 27–41.

several problems in the determination and use of a firm's cost of capital.[23] WACC was most often used as a discount or hurdle rate although one company used a hurdle rate that is slightly less than its k and that if earned, will allow the firm to double operations and earnings every 5 years, the historical growth pattern of the firm. A number of firms acknowledged use of CAPM to measure their cost of equity although no evidence of its use was found. See Table 7–4 for survey results concerning what discount rate was used by those firms that used the net present value method. Table 7–4 shows that the respondents to the author's survey used several different rates to discount estimated cash flows to a net present value. They included the cost of long-term capital on a companywide basis, the cost of long-term debt on a companywide basis, the cost of long-term debt on a local country basis, the cost of long-term and working capital on a companywide basis, the cost of long-term capital on a local country basis, and the cost of long-term and working capital on a local country basis.

Firms were found to adjust for risk in capital budgeting methodology in a variety of ways: shortening the pay-back period, increasing the discount rate, lowering the estimated future cash flows, and increasing the accepted accounting rate of return. Other methods used included subjective management judgment, sensitivity analysis, assignment of probability distributions of estimated risk levels, simulation, linear programming, and critical path analysis (see Table 7–5). Some firms added a premium for risk to its k and some adjusted for inflation. Few firms interviewed used multiple hurdle rates although for different projects most U.S. and most European firms used multiple hurdle rates. For projects in different countries, most U.S. firms used multiple hurdle rates while a majority of European firms used single hurdle rates. See Table 7–6 for survey results concerning single vs. multiple hurdle rates used by the firms in the study.

The conclusions drawn from this study suggested that most firms have difficulty measuring their capital costs although the finance literature suggests that WACC is the appropriate hurdle rate and that it should be the marginal cost at the source. The literature suggests the use of an adjusted present value so that consideration may be given to taxes, risk, inflation, and other factors and, on occasion, a continuous discount factor has been suggested as more efficient because of its convenient mathematical properties. This study found few firms that had incorporated such sophisticated techniques. Finally, the study found that strategic fit of the project may be the key factor in most MNCs' capital budgeting procedures. Thus, subjective factors concerning a foreign investment project may be quite important.

TABLE 7–5.   How Firms Adjust for Risk (percentage of N)

	U.S. Firms	European Firms
Shorten payback period	34	55
Increase discount rate	38	45
Decrease estimated future cash flows	19	36
Increase accepted accounting rate of return	16	18
Other	57	24

$N = 68$ for U.S. firms study; 56 for European firms study.

Source: James C. Baker, "Capital Budgeting in American and European Companies," *The Mid-Atlantic Journal of Business* 22 (Summer 1984):21.

---

[23] James C. Baker, "The Cost of Capital of Multinational Companies: Facts and Fallacies," *Managerial Finance* 13, No. 1(1987): 12–7; and Alan C. Shapiro, "Financial Structure and Cost of Capital in the Multinational Corporation," *Journal of Financial and Quantitative Analysis* 13 (June 1978): 221–6.

TABLE 7–6. Firms Using Multiple Cut-Off Rates (percentage of *N*)

For Different Projects	U.S. Firms (N = 64)	European Firms (N = 55)
Yes	58	53
No	42	47

For Different Countries	U.S. Firms (N = 64)	European Firms (N = 54)
Yes	52	41
No	48	59

Source: James C. Baker, ''Capital Budgeting in American and Europrean Companies,'' *The Mid-Atlantic Journal of Business* 22 (Summer 1984):23.

Although NPV, IRR, or APV calculations of a project may produce very significant numbers, which far exceed the risk threshold of financial managers, the subjective factors stemming from the project may offset quantitative analysis. For example, projects with high NPV or IRR may not be accepted because top management just does not like them. Or those with negative NPV or IRR less than the cost of capital may be accepted because top management does like the projects.

Summary and Conclusions

The MNC will encounter broad differences in performing capital budgeting for international projects compared with domestic projects. Early pioneers in the development of capital budgeting methodology for international companies included Bugnion, Stonehill and Nathanson, and Shapiro. These scholars introduced concepts such as uncertainty absorption for adjusting for risk in the formulation of capital budgeting for international projects as well as how to treat overseas earnings and the discount rate for discounted cash flow methodologies. This author and others have surveyed MNCs and found that, although the trend is toward discounted cash flow methods, they often use pay-back periods and other simple methods to decide whether to invest in a foreign project.

The cost of capital is important in serving as either a discount factor in the net present value method or as a benchmark against which to compare the internal rate of return for a foreign project. Many firms do not know their cost of capital or use an inappropriate number for their calculations. Many firms practice subjective management judgement when deciding whether to invest in foreign projects. Some scholars

---

STUDY AID

The financial structure of a MNC is a key determinant of the cost of capital of this firm. The cost of capital is a key ingredient of the discounted cash flow methods that this firm may use to make its capital budgeting decisions. It is essentially the rate of return required on an investment project. But strategic management decisions rather than some mathematical formula may determine whether a firm invests in a particular project. Form a small group and query some local international companies to see whether they use sophisticated capital budgeting methodologies or whether they resort to strategic management judgment based on qualitative factors.

have found that an optimal financial structure is present and that it is culture-bound from one country to another. Firms should use this figure when organizing their capital budgeting methodology. The adjusted present value should be the appropriate capital budgeting method for MNCs because of the ability to incorporate tax benefits, government subsidies, and other factors that affect the cash flows. Risk adjustments should be made by reductions to the estimated cash flows. Finally, the cost of capital used in the calculations should be the weighted average cost of capital, based on marginal capital for a project at the source of the capital.

Additional Readings

Baker, James C. "Capital Budgeting in American and European Companies." *The Mid-Atlantic Journal of Business* 22 (Summer 1984): 15–28.

Baker, James C. "The Cost of Capital of Multinational Companies: Facts and Fallacies." *Managerial Finance* 13 (1987, No. 1): 12–7.

Bierman, Harold, Jr., and Seymour Smidt. *The Capital Budgeting Decision.* New York: Macmillan, 1988.

Bugnion, J. R. "Capital Budgeting and International Corporations." *Quarterly Journal of AIESEC International* 1 (November 1965): 30–54.

Dean, Joel. *Capital Budgeting.* New York: Columbia University Press, 1951.

Kim, Suk H. and Seung H. Kim. *Global Corporate Finance: Text and Cases.* Miami: Kolb Publishing Co., 1993.

Lessard, Donald R., ed. *International Financial Management: Theory and Application.* New York: John Wiley, 1985.

Shapiro, Alan C. "Capital Budgeting for the Multinational Corporation." *Financial Management* 7 (Spring 1978): 7–16.

Shapiro, Alan C. "Financial Structure and Cost of Capital in the Multinational Corporation." *Journal of Financial and Quantitative Analysis* 13 (June 1978): 221–6.

Stonehill, Arthur, Theo Beekhuisen, Richard Wright, Lee Remmers, et al. "Financial Goals and Debt Ratio Determinants: A Survey of Practice in Five Countries." *Financial Management* 4 (Autumn 1975): 27–41.

Stonehill, Arthur, and Leonard Nathanson, "Capital Budgeting in the Multinational Company." *California Management Review* 11 (Summer 1968): 39–54.

Stonehill, Arthur, and Thomas Stitzel, "Financial Structure and Multinational Corporations." *California Management Review* 12 (Fall 1969): 91–6.

Discussion Questions

1. What did Bugnion contribute to the discussion of capital budgeting for international companies?
2. What was the contribution of Stonehill and Nathanson to this discussion?
3. Discuss the differences between capital budgeting for an international project and capital budgeting for a domestic project.
4. What are the advantages and disadvantages of the pay-back period for foreign project analysis? What is the discounted pay-back period?
5. How does the adjusted present value method differ from the ordinary net present value method? Is it better for foreign investment projects?
6. From whose perspective—parent firm or foreign firm—should cash flows be analyzed in a capital budgeting problem?
7. Discuss the factors that affect a foreign affiliate's financial structure.

8. What is an optimal financial structure for a multinational corporation and for its foreign affiliate(s)?
9. What issues arise in the modern day MNC concerning cost of capital?
10. What causes the differences in the cost of capital from one country to another?
11. Why might the discount rate applied to the foreign project cash flows be different from the discount rate applied to parent cash flows?

Problems

1. Assume that a firm has a before-tax cost of debt of 8 percent, a before-tax cost of equity of 15 percent, a marginal tax rate of 34 percent, and an optimal capital structure calling for 50 percent debt. What is the firm's cost of capital?

2. Assume that the weighted average cost of capital for a MNC, appropriate for its foreign project to install a punch press whose estimated life will be 5 years, is 12 percent, that the following cash flows from using the press are estimated to be remitted, after foreign taxes paid and the current foreign exchange rate is considered, for the 5 years as follows: $1 million, $1.2 million, $1.3 million, $1.3 million, and $1 million. The initial investment in the press is $6.5 million. Straight-line depreciation is allowed for the initial investment. A local government cash subsidy of $500,000 will be paid in each of the first 3 years of the project. An investment tax credit of 10 percent is allowed for the first year of the investment. Calculate the net present value using the adjusted present value method. Is the project acceptable according to your calculation?

3. Starter Athletic Company invests in a new factory in Taiwan to manufacture major athletic team uniforms and jackets for U.S. consumption. The factory project costs $2.5 million in total project costs. It will have an unlimited life and the annual cash flows after taxes, available for remittance to the parent firm, will be $300,000. What is the pay-back period for this project?

4. A U.S. MNC has total long-term capital of $100 million. Of this total, $50 million is equity capital whose dividend is currently $5 million, $40 million of long-term debt, half with a coupon rate of 5 percent and half with a coupon rate of 7 percent, and 1 million shares of preferred stock issued for $10 per share and a dividend of $0.60 per share. What is the weighted average cost of capital for this MNC?

5. A U.S. publishing company has purchased a British technical publishing company for $5 million. The U.S. company figures to hold this company for 5 years and expects foreign after-tax remittable earnings to be $1.5 million per year. The company's weighted average cost of capital is 10 percent. What is the internal rate of return for this investment project? Is the investment acceptable?

6. Air Canada plans to invest in a new freight warehouse at the Orly Airport outside Paris, France. The initial investment required is Can$ 100 million, or Ffr 400 million at the current exchange rate of Ffr 4/Can$. The project will result in annual savings from ground transportation, which amount to Ffr 100 million. At the end of 3 years, Air Canada plans to move its air freight operations to Frankfurt, Germany, and will sell the French facility at an estimated price of Ffr 200 million. The proceeds will be reinvested in other French facilities. The exchange rate is projected to be as much as Ffr 5/Can$ at the time of the sale but could remain unchanged.
   a. Calculate the NPV in Canadian dollars, assuming the present exchange rate is correct, and that Air Canada uses a discount rate of 12 percent. Assume no salvage value.
   b. Assume that the proceeds will be repatriated back to parent headquarters after the French apply a 10 percent withholding tax. Use alternative exchange rates of Ffr 4, 4.5, and 5 per Canadian dollar in your analysis.

7. A company is evaluating an investment project in Madrid, Spain. This project will have a useful life of 10 years and will need an initial investment of $20 million. Annual cash flows remitted to the parent are after all foreign taxes have been paid and, because of the foreign tax credit, will incur no additional U.S. tax liability. The parent company discount rate for such projects in Spain is 20 percent. Assume no liquidation value at the end of 10 years and depreciation allowances and investment tax credits are not available in Spain. What is the net present value of this project?

8. In the previous problem, what is the pay-back period? What is the internal rate of return?

CHAPTER 8

Planning and Organizing of the International Finance Function

---

Major Objective of Chapter 8

(1) Examine financial policy, planning, strategy, and organization of the international finance function in the MNC.

Key terms to be learned in chapter 8:

- international division structure
- product structure
- remittance of earnings

- geographical structure
- global matrix structure

Introduction

Planning and organizing the finance function in an international company must take into consideration the cultural, economic, legal, political, and social differences encountered in global operations. These environmental differences from one country to another distinguish foreign operations from domestic operations. MNCs must operate in a number of foreign currency regimes. Thus, the firm faces foreign currency risk. It encounters political risk caused by a variety of government regulations and national responses, which may affect the firm's ability to transfer earnings and capital to the parent firm, or its ability to operate overseas, or its ownership interests in foreign operations.

The finance function in the MNC can be conceptualized in various ways. In Figure 8–1, the financial management of international operations is modeled by showing the input of financial resources—in the form of an inventory of internal, institutional, money, and capital markets, and miscellaneous funds—into the financial planning and strategy phases of financial management. These aspects are couched within an envi-

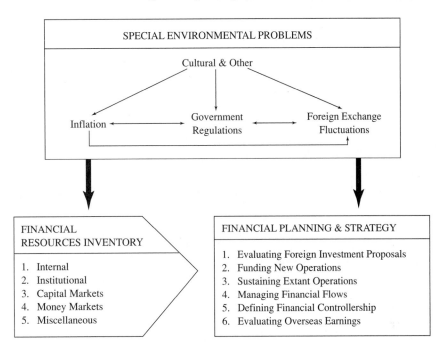

FIGURE 8–1 Financial Management International Operations

ronment of special problems unique to the international firm, including government regulations, cultural differences, inflation, and foreign exchange fluctuations in a floating rate international monetary system, all of which impact upon the type of financial resources used by the firm as well as how the firm formulates international financial planning and strategy.

The international company can be viewed according to the way its financial functions and subfunctions are organized according to the financial management cycle. One simple model, shown in Figure 8–2, merely assumes that the company must maintain its own balance of payments with the rest of the world. This is a general model of the firm, which presents a model of the firm's environment on the left side of the diagram, and firm objectives and a model of the organizational system and the firm's operation policies as inputs to the financial decision model. It is presumed that a firm would also have production, marketing, and personnel decision models.

The financial decision model is comprised of three submodels: planning and control, management of funds, and management of capital. The planning and control submodel is comprised further of several operating models including the international subfunction of planning and reporting for the balance of payments model. The balance of payments subfunction, thus, is the only international aspect of financial management in this model. All other functions are generic financial activities that might be found in ordinary domestic operations. In this model, performance standards can be compared with primary objectives so that anticipated and unanticipated deviations can be analyzed and, to adjust to these deviations, the firm can change either original objectives or performance standards or both.

Another conceptualization of the financial management function is shown in Figure 8–3, in which the financial management cycle is shown as two major steps, operations or treasury functions and reporting and control or controllership. Treasury functions include planning and forecasting operations and funds needs, budgeting for

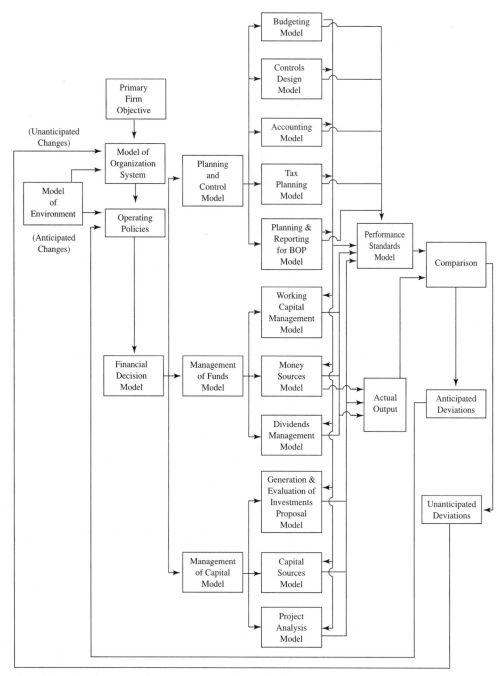

FIGURE 8–2 Finance Model Financial Functions in the Firm

short- and long-term capital, and funding of operations. In other words, these functions are designed to determine the financial needs of the firm and to acquire the necessary funds. The reporting and control function of the firm includes the accounting methodologies for recording the results of operations, reporting these results to top management and other users, and review and analysis of the results, i.e., evaluation, in order to compare the results with management objectives to determine whether company goals have been achieved.

Source: Adapted from William L. Campfield, "Selected International Trends in Financial Planning and Control in the Public Sector," *The International Journal of Accounting Education and Research* 5 (Fall 1969):128.

FIGURE 8–3 Financial Management Cycle

Financial Planning and Policy

DOMESTIC VS. INTERNATIONAL PLANNING

Top management of the MNC should distinguish between planning for domestic operations and planning for international operations before deciding on a financial strategy for operating in a foreign environment. A number of external elements affect plans and planning. These elements may also differ between domestic and international operations, as shown in Figure 8–4. The corporate planner can use Figure 8–4, to recognize the major differences between domestic and international business. An understanding of what to expect in foreign operations is imperative to successful international financial management.

FINANCIAL STRATEGY

The first priority of the chief financial officer (CFO) of any firm, domestic or international, is to make available adequate funds to finance an acceptable level of assets. To do this, he must often mismatch the maturities of his firm's assets and liabilities because costs and revenues seldom coincide. Thus risk is incurred, in the form of interest rate fluctuations for all firms that need to borrow, and in the form of foreign exchange fluctuations at any time for an international firm. The functions of the CFO in coping with the interplay of this objective with the inherent risks incurred in day-to-day international financial management are

1. to determine the magnitude, duration, and timing of the company's external financing needs in relation to the certainty of the need and the financial condition of the firm at that time;

Domestic Planning	*International Planning*
1. Single language and nationality	1. Multilingual/multinational/multicultural factors
2. Relatively homogeneous market	2. Fragmented and diverse markets
3. Data available, usually accurate and collection easy	3. Data collection: new technology requiring computer hardware and software and better trained personnel
4. Political factors relatively unimportant	4. Political factors frequently vital
5. Relative freedom from government interference	5. Involvement in national economic plans; government influences business decisions
6. Individual corporation has little effect on environment	6. "Gravitational" distortion by large companies
7. Chauvinsim helps	7. Chauvinism hinders
8. Relatively stable business environment	8. Multiple environments, many of which are highly unstable (but may be highly profitable)
9. Uniform financial climate	9. Variety of financial climates ranging from overconservative to wildly inflationary
10. Single currency	10. Currencies differing in stability and real value
11. Business "rules of the game" mature and understood	11. Rules diverse, changeable, unclear
12. Management generally accustomed to sharing responsibilities and using financial controls	12. Budgets and controls: management given new computer technology to deal with budgets, controls, and risk management

Source: Based on the model found in William W. Cain, "International Planning: Mission Impossible?" *Columbia Journal of World Business* 5 (July–August 1970):50.

FIGURE 8-4 Domestic vs. International Planning

    2. to design a financing program that
        a. guarantees the availability of funds at all times,
        b. minimizes the long-run cost of financing,
        c. incorporates forecasts of interest and foreign exchange rates and stock prices, and
        d. places the company in a sound financial position at the end of the period;
    3. to assure for financial compatibility among the individual financial demands, thus assuring that individual financing needs do not overwhelm the firm's financing ability or place the firm in an overly risky position.

Issues to Consider

To operationalize these functions of financial management in the international firm, several major issues must be decided by the financial management of MNCs. A major issue found in many areas of international financial management is whether to centralize or decentralize international finance functions. This issue will be discussed in several places in this book. The degree to which an international firm centralizes its financial operations depends on its management philosophy as well as on the way in which it has organized its global operations.

Another issue concerns whether to establish a foreign subsidiary or a branch. This issue has tax considerations since the profits or losses made by a branch automatically become part of the profits or losses of the parent firm. The profits of a subsidiary are usually not taxed by the parent's country until they have been remitted back to the parent. The company has a tax liability but it is deferred until the profits are remitted.

In many cases, a foreign tax credit can be taken by the parent firm against the foreign taxes paid when its domestic liability is calculated. These issues will be discussed in chapter 17.

The issue of equity participation by the parent in its foreign operations represents another issue for the financial planning and policy area. Should the firm's ownership objective be 100 percent ownership of foreign affiliates, as practiced by most auto manufacturers, IBM, and other companies? These firms need to exercise total control over their operations as a result of the high amounts of investment in plant and equipment. Or should the firm practice minority ownership? The now defunct Kaiser Industries companies—Kaiser Gypsum, Kaiser Aluminum, Kaiser Steel, and Kaiser Cement— held minority interests in their foreign affiliates because these companies operated in LDCs as extractive companies that faced high degrees of political risk. The minority ownership policy reduced the risk of expropriation in these countries. The host country government's perception in such cases, especially where scarce natural resources are taken by foreign firms, is that a local company with minority foreign ownership will not abuse these resources.

Some companies operate joint ventures overseas. In some countries, local government regulations preclude more than 50 percent ownership interests by foreign companies. In countries such as Japan, India, and those in eastern Europe, foreign companies operate many 50–50 joint ventures.

Some firms face the issue of whether to invest directly in overseas operations or to license firms in foreign countries to manufacture and market their products. Some firms do not have the financial resources to invest overseas. They may not have the top management that is oriented to international operations. Thus, they, licensors, rent their intangible property rights—patents, formulae, copyrights, etc.—to overseas firms, licensees, which then manufacture and market products made according to these intangible property rights. The licensee remits fees in the form of royalties to the licensor.

The firm with international operations faces the issue of whether to use internal or external funds in its foreign operations. The answer depends on foreign exchange controls practiced by the host country and on interest rates and the ability to borrow more cheaply than to transfer funds from the parent firm, which must be converted at the spot rate of exchange.

Finally, the parent firm faces the issue of what financial resources to use, if it has decided on using external funds. The solution to this issue lies in the inventory of financial resources, discussed in chapters 11 and 12. The firm's financing strategy depends on an analysis of individual financial resources in the inventory including the type of investment, its objectives, cost, availability, and interest rate and foreign exchange risks involved.

Assignment of Functional Responsibilities

The assignment of functional responsibilities in financial planning of international operations depends on a number of factors. First, the extent to which the firm engages in international financial management and the degree of centralization or decentralization of the function depends on the company's international organization. MNCs organize around at least four different major types of organization or approximations of them: international division structure, geographic or area structure, product structure, and global matrix structure. Representations of these structures are shown in Figures 8–5 to 8–8. Variations on these general organizational structure types are still being used by MNCs today.

THE INTERNATIONAL DIVISION STRUCTURE

The international division structure assumes the firm has little or no internationally oriented top management. All international executives are located in the international division, which is normally on the same level as other staff operations such as production, finance, marketing, and personnel. All questions in the field that require decisions concerning international operations are made in the international division. In Figure 8–5, the top part of the diagram shows an international division structure that is domestically oriented. Only the president has international orientation. In the lower part of the diagram, this firm has an international division structure with world orientation. All corporate staff is internationally oriented and has both corporate and worldwide responsibilities. The firm in Part B has evolved over time from the firm in Part A.

This form of organizational structure is developed by firms in which formal organizational changes sometimes threaten to disrupt delicate working relationships, espe-

FIGURE 8–5 The International Division Structure

Executives with total corporate and worldwide responsibilities. Domestic oriented line and/or staff executives. Internationally oriented line and staff executives.

A. Domestic Orientation

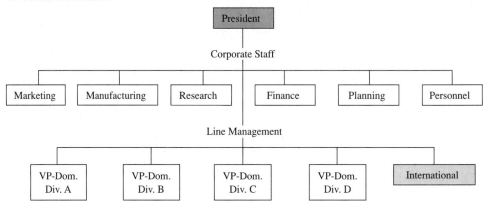

B. World Orientation

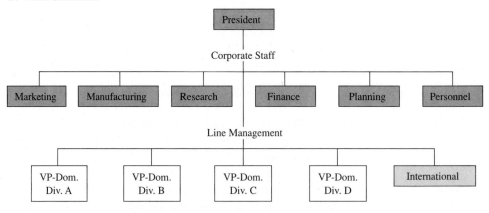

▨ Executives with total corporate and worldwide responsibilities.
▢ Domestic oriented line and/or staff executives.
▨ Internationally oriented line and staff executives.

cially in those cases of long-established foreign subsidiaries operating under strong, well-entrenched local managements accustomed to running their operations without interference. In these firms, top management believes that the foreign activities will get better direction with an international division than with a different organizational form. Overseas operations can benefit from the extra management attention that may be needed at the outset of new foreign operations. The international division is suited to companies with relatively new foreign operations and in which senior management lacks global experience.

THE GEOGRAPHIC STRUCTURE

The geographic, or area, structure assumes that geographical location of production is the key element. It is the second-most adopted organizational structure. Each division has control over a given geographical area, such as South America, Europe, Asia, etc. and responsibility for all products in a particular area is assigned to a single-line executive who reports to corporate management. All questions concerning the product are made according to the geographic area in which the operations are located. In Figure 8–6, the geographic structure is shown with the president and all corporate staff having total corporate and worldwide responsibilities. These staff functions advise the area managers about corporate staff functions such as marketing, manufacturing, R & D, finance, planning, and personnel problems.

Products that are sold globally may encounter problems because the expertise for financing and marketing the product in one area may not be available in another area. The geographic structure is used commonly by companies with closely related product lines, e.g., pharmaceuticals, farm implements, soft drinks, and packaged food products, as well as by companies with reasonably diverse product lines. The international oil companies also use geographic structures.

FIGURE 8–6 The Geographic Structure

Executives with total corporate and worldwide responsibilities. Corporate staff activities on a worldwide basis generally involve policy matters, strategic planning, basic product planning, functional guidance to line geographic units, and coordination of activities between geographic units.

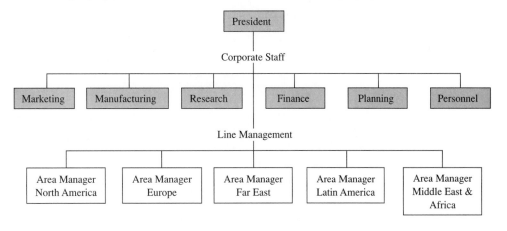

Executives with total corporate and worldwide responsibilities. Corporate staff activities on a worldwide basis generally involve policy matters, strategic planning, basic product planning, functional guidance to line geographic units, and coordination of activities between geographic units.

THE PRODUCT STRUCTURE

The product structure assumes that the end use of the product is the most important element. The company is organized around the end use of the product. Thus, all product areas will need some internationally oriented top management. The product structure involves the assignment of worldwide product responsibility to product group executives at the line management level and coordinates all product activity in a given geographical area through area specialists at the corporate staff level. It is favored by companies whose product line is widely diversified and the range of products go into a variety of end-use markets. The product structure is shown in Figure 8–7. The president and corporate staff are internationally oriented and have both corporate and worldwide responsibility. Corporate staff also advise the product group executives about corporate functions, as in the geographic structure. However, the difference between the geographic and product structures is that, in the latter, an international area specialist exists at the corporate staff level whereas in the geographic structure, each area manager is responsible for information and advice about the geographic area.

THE GLOBAL MATRIX STRUCTURE

In the global matrix structure, the firm is structured as a grid with intersecting responsibilities and a dual rather than a single chain of command. Some managers report to two superiors rather than to one and the shift is from the traditional organization to one with a balance of power and sharing of responsibility.

The global matrix structure shown in Figure 8–8 was used at one time by TRW Systems, a division of TRW, Inc., and is representative of this type structure used by

FIGURE 8–7 The Product Structure

Executives with total corporate and worldwide responsibilities. Corporate staff activities on a worldwide basis involve policy matters, overall strategic planning, coordination between product groups, and specialized advice to product groups. Executives with staff responsibilities in a particular geographic area, chiefly identifying potential investment opportunities and providing information to individual affiliates and corporate management.

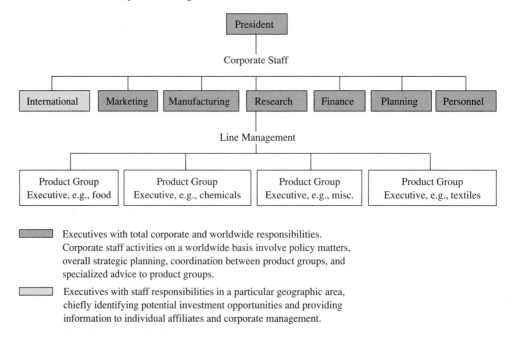

Executives with total corporate and worldwide responsibilities. Corporate staff activities on a worldwide basis involve policy matters, overall strategic planning, coordination between product groups, and specialized advice to product groups.

Executives with staff responsibilities in a particular geographic area, chiefly identifying potential investment opportunities and providing information to individual affiliates and corporate management.

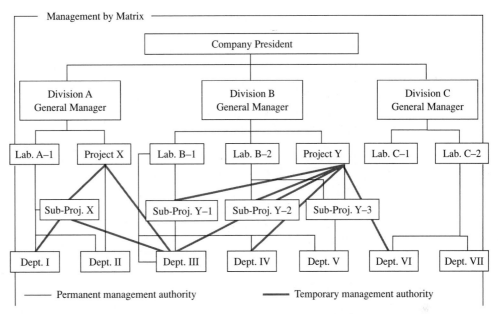

Source: "Teamwork Through Conflict," *Business Week* (March 20, 1971):44.

FIGURE 8–8 Global Matrix Structure

many firms. The division was reorganized using behavioral science techniques.[1] The motivation for this type of structure at TRW came from a layoff of 15 percent of the division's workforce. The matrix structure required managers and employees to work together on decisions in temporary teams. The matrix teams operated more efficiently with the implementation of organization development utilizing sensitivity training and confrontation sessions. Thus, the global matrix structure requires more overlap of responsibilities and more teamwork on projects. Management functions and responsibilities sometimes become blurred.

The matrix structure form has disadvantages. The high utilization of resources results in a loss of clear and permanent lines of authority. Conflicts arise between managers and employees who have different opinions about projects when several are required at the same time. Short-run goals often clash with longer run objectives.

The level of available talent determines where individual functions are located within the company and to what extent the international finance function must be staffed. Top executives in the international finance area must know the various markets in which international funding is arranged, including the foreign exchange markets, the Eurocurrency market, and the international bond markets. They should be aware of the market for derivatives including the new exotic derivatives, which are in vogue in the 1990s, for purposes of hedging cross-border interest rate, currency, and commodity price risks.

Which of these forms of organization should a firm implement? The most decisive point in the transition to a global enterprise is that top management should realize that, in order to function effectively, the ultimate control of strategic planning and policy decisions must shift from decentralized foreign affiliates or regional headquarters to corporate headquarters, where a global perspective can be focused on the interests of the total enterprise.

---

[1] Teamwork Through Conflict," *Business Week* (March 20, 1971): 44–50.

OUTSOURCING FINANCIAL FUNCTIONS

Many international companies outsource their international financial functions.[2] Companies find that they can increase efficiency and cut costs by outsourcing various financial functions. An Economist Intelligence Unit/Arthur Andersen study of 300 large international companies found that 42 percent outsource pension management, 40 percent outsource tax functions, 28 percent outsource payroll handling, 19 percent outsource leasing, and 12 percent outsource internal audit and short-term investment management. Another study by the Treasury Management Association showed that 25 percent of companies surveyed outsourced at least one financial operation with the most common being payroll, collections, check processing, and investment or risk management.

A number of reasons were given by these companies for outsourcing financial functions. The most cited reason was the need to take advantage of specialized experience. Cost reduction was a close second while the need to spend more time on company business and to keep up with technology were also frequently cited. Outsourcing of financial functions is best considered when the company is initiating international operations, when it has been spun off from another firm, or when it is in danger of losing the personnel expert in the function in question.

The International Finance Function

Some firms have located the international finance function because of historic precedent. If the firm has foreign affiliates that were originally located in a certain country for production or assembly purposes, it will most likely locate any regional staff for international financial management there. If the firm has traditionally centralized all management functions at parent headquarters, more than likely it will locate all international financial activities at headquarters. Occasionally, the communications between such centralized management and the overseas affiliates becomes quite thin. ITT Corporation, a company with extensive overseas operations, had originally located all top management in its parent headquarters. In the late 1950s when Harold Geneen took over as president, he found that overseas managers were seeking assistance from outside consultants because they did not know where to go at headquarters for company advice. Today, companies such as General Tire, a case discussed later in chapter 15, use a personal computer and specialized software to find their cash position at any given moment. Thus, some companies have management structures that inhibit close contact with headquarters while others have a desire to pinpoint their financial position at headquarters at any given moment.

The attitude of top management toward international financial matters may dictate where the company locates the international finance function. Top management should know the importance of foreign exchange in its global operations. It should know whether international money and capital markets are available and what the cost of funds is in these markets. If top management is not very knowledgeable or appreciative of international financial activities, then most or all of the foreign operation may be decentralized by default. The more top management is aware and knowledgeable of the international finance function, the more it may be willing to analyze and control it from one location.

The best location for global financial activities is at the headquarters, generally

---

[2] Carolina Esquenazi-Shaio, "Outsourcing Financial Functions," *International Business* (March 1996): 24–8.

speaking. Exceptions to this rule, however, can be found in many cases. One glaring example of decentralization of the control occurred in 1995 when a trader at the Singapore operation of Barings Bank, Great Britain's oldest bank, became overextended in trading futures contracts on the Singapore International Metals Exchange, lost more than $1 billion, and caused the demise of Barings. The trader was permitted to implement a trading system on his own with little control from parent headquarters. When the market turned against his system, he then tried to hide the losses in a special account. Eventually, the system collapsed when the losses exceeded the firm's capital position.

Centralization of the international finance function is, thus, more advantageous than its counterpart, decentralization. In practice, most companies centralize most of their global finance activities. For most MNCs, dividend remittance policies are developed and controlled at the corporate level. Long-term borrowing usually requires corporate approval. Coordination of relationships with financial institutions and markets is a major role of the international financial executive, generally located at parent headquarters. Even in the area of working capital for foreign affiliates, the issues of inflation and rising capital costs require more stringent controls over working capital and more devotion to analytical services to support the implementation of these controls. This is best achieved at the headquarters. Balance of payments planning and foreign exchange exposure management is best carried out at the corporate headquarters. However, in the latter function, participation by foreign affiliates' management will facilitate the measurement of exposure.

The day-to-day operations of the international finance function have changed drastically in the past decade. Most companies have carried out international financial planning by means of a high volume of time-consuming reports from affiliates to the parent. Actually, planning decisions were facilitated by "what-if" simulations with the aid of computer spreadsheets using high-priced mainframes and Big Six accounting firms. A cycle of multicurrency accounting often took a month or longer to complete; most of the reporting functions were manual operations, which delayed financial analysis and forecasting. Going over invoices and collecting data from remote foreign locations was difficult and tedious.

The international finance department of the 1990s has available multicurrency software for financial planning.[3] Such software and related procedures have reduced the book-closing cycle to as little as a week. A reduction in the reporting cycle of 10 days can result in annual savings of hundreds of thousands of dollars.

Inhouse financial experts can use this multicurrency, multilingual software to provide top management with valuable advice. Firms can react more quickly to currency fluctuations. Foreign currency exposures can be measured more easily. Turnaround time for financial analyses can be reduced to a day or two.

Local differences and requirements can be programmed into such software. Value-added taxes, for example, differ from country to country, as do dividend withholding taxes, charged to a subsidiary's earnings that are remitted to the parent firm. Software can be developed to accommodate these local distinctions.

A relatively small MNC can use multicurrency programs to run its international finance function like a giant firm. Some of these programs have been developed by banks to help firms keep track of their global cash position at any point in time. General Tire incorporated a multicurrency program into a spreadsheet, hired a computer analyst, and used a personal computer, all for an investment of $10,000, to give the company the capability of reporting their global cash position on a daily basis.

---

[3] John T. Hiatt, "High-tech Global Finance," *International Business* 7 (April 1994): 32–4.

The software used by the CFO of a MNC and discussed above must have a number of essential features to be able to cope with complicated international transactions.[4] The software used for the accounting systems of such a firm must be able to handle a number of currencies and languages. For example, when dealing with currencies such as the Japanese yen or the Italian lira, the software must be capable of handling 14 or more characters when dealing with billions of units of these currencies. Currency symbols and conventions for presenting numeric amounts vary from country to country. In the United States, one million dollars is presented as $1,000,000.00, while in Germany, it is presented as DM 1.000.000,00. International date formats may differ. For example, in the United States the "month/day/year" format is used, whereas in most other countries, the "day/month/year" format is used.

Some countries practice more precise decimal placement and rounding off of numbers, such as many Middle Eastern currencies that include three decimal places. Personnel at some sites may be required to work in more than one language. Frequent exchange rate changes must be automatically posted to the firm's general ledger. Many transactions require multicurrency transactions. A purchase order may be issued in U.S. dollars, the invoice may be stated in pounds, translated into German marks for accounts payable, and paid in French francs, and the transaction reported in Spanish peseta. The firm's software must handle these transactions. The various tax reporting requirements of different countries must be incorporated into the software. In addition, the software should be able to consolidate general ledgers, which use different currencies, into the parent firm's general ledger without any problems. Some countries require statutory ledgers to be remapped to an entirely different format when they are consolidated at parent headquarters.

EXTERNAL FINANCING PATTERNS

The external financing patterns between those of a U.S. domestic corporation and those of a U.S. MNC differ greatly. The international focus of the MNC is much greater. Few U.S. domestic firms resort to international money and capital markets for funds. A few totally domestic firms on occasion may fund some part of their operations with Eurocurrency funds. For example, Ohio Edison, a landlocked electric utility in northern Ohio has occasionally funded operations such as dividend payments with Eurobond flotations. Usually a U.S. domestic firm obtains financing from domestic money and capital markets and from local financial institutions. RPM, Inc., a Medina, Ohio-based firm, has a very small portion of its $1 billion in sales exported or produced abroad. However, in the 1980s, the company borrowed $90 million in three Eurobond issues. In 1992, RPM, an industrial coatings manufacturer, refinanced these issues with a LYON (liquid yield options note). This is a financial instrument marketed by Merrill Lynch, which is essentially a zero coupon bond convertible into the company's stock. Since RPM is a growth company, this issue probably will not result in a "hung" convertible, i.e., it will be converted some time in the future. In the meantime, the company is permitted to write off the interest annually as though it were actually being paid. This produces cash flow for the company in the form of tax write-offs.

The U.S. MNC obtains financing from domestic and international money and capital markets and resorts to intracompany funds flows in the form of dividends, intracompany loans, management fees, transfer pricing arrangements, and, possibly, royalties from licensing agreements to fund the company's operations. The extent to which

---

[4] International Business Information Technology Special Report, "Requirements of an International Accounting Package," *International Business* (September 1994): 3.

Typical External Financing Patterns of a U.S.
Domestic Corporation Compared with Those of an MNC

A. U.S. Domestic Corporation

B. U.S. Parent and One Foreign Subsidiary

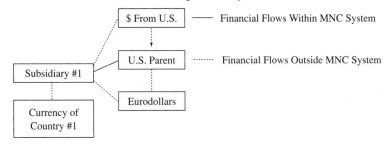

C. U.S. Parent and Two Foreign Subsidiaries

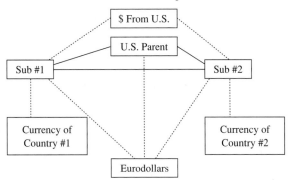

FIGURE 8–9 External Financing Patterns U.S. Domestic vs. International Operations

money and capital markets are utilized depends on the number of foreign affiliates in different foreign countries. The degree of complexity in the external financing patterns generated by international operations is demonstrated in Figure 8–9. These operations compare a domestic corporation without foreign operations with a U.S. company operating one and two foreign subsidiaries. One only needs to add a few subsidiaries in different foreign countries to see that the external financing patterns can become quite complex very quickly.

FINANCIAL STAFF RELATIONSHIPS IN MNCS

The extent of the international financial management of MNCs differs depending on the size of the MNC. This can be demonstrated by showing three relatively different sizes of MNC: the small MNC with up to $100 million in sales, the medium-sized MNC with sales of $100–500 million, and the large MNC with sales of more than $500 million.

The small MNC can be characterized as a firm that ignores the system's potential. It has a small staff that receives reports from foreign affiliates but does not interfere with an affiliate's decisions as long as operations are deemed satisfactory. The foreign

affiliate has a small staff that makes decisions without any guidelines from the parent firm. Thus, the small MNC is not fraught with the bureaucratic tendencies found in very large business organizations. It has more freedom, both at the parent headquarters and at the foreign location, to experiment with policies that may be more cost effective.

The medium-sized MNC can be characterized as one which exploits the system's potential. The parent firm has a large staff that makes decisions for the entire corporate system. The firm's foreign affiliates have small staffs that merely implement the decisions made by the parent firm. This type organization is fully centralized and the parent firm can dictate fully what the foreign managers will do.

The large MNC can be characterized as a firm that compromises with complexity. The parent firm has a large staff that issues guidelines, coordinates activity, and monitors results. The foreign affiliates have large staffs that make decisions based on the guidelines issued by the parent firm. These staff relationships are shown in Figure 8–10. This type of firm is relatively bureaucratic at both headquarters and in the field. Policy formulation and decision making becomes so unwieldy that management must compromise in order to meet minimum goals.

These financial staff relationships are important in MNC operations. To illustrate operations that utilize such relationships, the following cases covering international financing arrangements, a technique for controlling international float, and consideration of financial planning and taxes are useful.

FIGURE 8–10 Financial Staff Relationships in MNCs

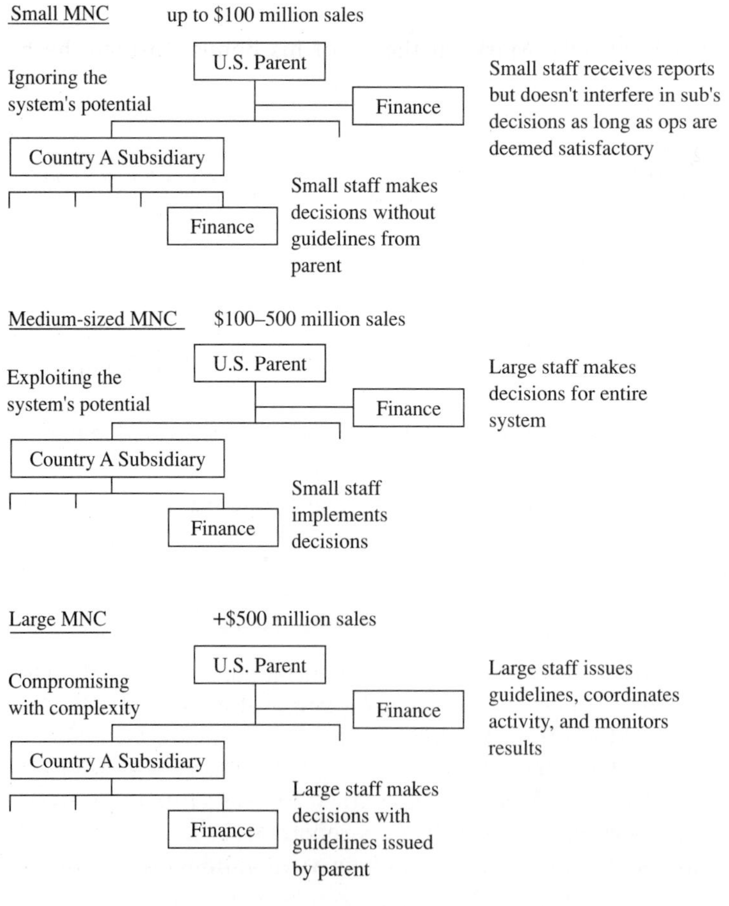

STUDY AID

By now, you have learned that MNCs organize their international operations in a number of ways. In addition, they organize their financial relationships internally in a number of ways, depending on the size of the company. Flexibility seems to dictate how they do the latter, although large MNCs tend to compromise with complexity and may not exploit the potential of their global systems. You might explore the business literature, e.g., *Fortune Magazine, Business Week, International Business*, for cases that demonstrate how specific companies organize their global operations and international finance functions.

MANAGEMENT APPLICATION NO. 10

International Financing Arrangements

This example involves the lack of flexibility caused when the parent centralizes the international finance function. An MNC formulated a policy to deter intracompany loans longer than 30 days by charging them with interest. The treasurer of the firm's German subsidiary tried to circumvent this rule. The subsidiary was short of funds and could borrow deutsche Marks at the German bank rate of 8 percent. However, he negotiated with the French affiliate of the MNC, with $2 million in sales to the German subsidiary, to forgo its payment on receivables from the German company for 9 months. The French affiliate could cover itself by borrowing francs locally at 4 percent. The French affiliate agreed to do this if the Germans paid 5 percent. When reminded by headquarters of the parent firm's rule on intracompany loans, the German treasurer balked since the arrangement was considered a 9-month intracompany loan. The interest would come out of his bonus. Instead, he borrowed $2 million from a Belgian bank at 5.5 percent. The German treasurer saved his bonus but the action cost the company $22,500 in higher interest than the original arrangement would have cost. The MNC and its affiliates had compromised with complexity.

MANAGEMENT APPLICATION NO. 11

Technique for Controlling International Float

An international oil company resorted to the following technique to control international float and reduce foreign exchange exposure. A U.S. parent firm loaned $500,000 to its North African affiliate, which produces crude oil. The North African affiliate sold the crude oil financed by the loan to a European refining affiliate for $600,000. The European refiner sold gasoline refined from the crude oil to a European marketing affiliate for $700,000. The marketing affiliate sold the gasoline to the public for $800,000. The profits were remitted to the U.S. firm. The results were: (1) none of these payments crossed a national boundary; (2) the initial loan was deposited in a New York bank; (3) the North African affiliate wrote checks on the account to pay for U.S. equipment; (4) all subsequent transactions were recorded in a New York clearing center where they were offset against each other; and (5) the final balance was credited to each affiliate but was kept in New York. This system guaranteed prompt settlement of intrasystem accounts and eliminated the risk of operating in a variety of currencies.

MANAGEMENT APPLICATION NO. 12

Financial Planning and Taxes

A British firm has subsidiaries in Switzerland, Latin America, and France. It is a highly profitable firm but is worried about its global taxes. It finds the best strategy is to get funds to its Swiss affiliate, which has a much lower tax rate. The British firm can do so by cutting its export prices to its Swiss affiliate. This means a reduction in its transfer prices. Transfer pricing will be discussed in more detail in chapters 15 and 17. The Swiss have a buoyant currency and payments from the Swiss affiliate will not only be at a lower tax rate but they will be in an appreciating currency.

This scenario is not the case where the Latin American subsidiary is located. When a devaluation of the local currency is imminent, the Latin American affiliate should send funds to the Swiss affiliate by prepaying any accounts it owes to the Swiss affiliate. It should also borrow as much as possible in the local market and send the borrowed funds out of the country—unless they are blocked by currency restrictions. Occasionally, the Swiss affiliate might give as well as receive. The parent firm has a French affiliate with high profitability but tight money conditions have been imposed by the Banque de France. The best loan in France is 8 percent but the Swiss can borrow domestically at 4 percent. The Swiss affiliate can either lend directly to the French affiliate or tell them to delay payment of all accounts owed to the Swiss affiliate—if the parent firm does not have a policy similar to the intracompany loan rule in Management Application No. 10. What matters is not that some subsidiaries gain at the expense of others but that the annual consolidated profit of the global enterprise increases.

PLANNING FOR EARNINGS REMITTANCE

Financial planning of the remittance of earnings from foreign affiliates to a U.S. parent firm involves other aspects of international financial management covered elsewhere in this book. The foreign earnings remitted to the parent is affected by foreign currency risk, covered in chapter 4. Remittance of earnings represent one of the five major intracorporate funds flows covered in chapter 15 and the dividend payout ratio affects the amount of working capital reinvested in the foreign affiliate, also covered in chapter 15. Finally, any dividends remitted to the parent firm will be subject to withholding taxes levied by the host government and will affect the amount of the foreign tax credit, if any, granted by U.S. tax authorities. This subject is discussed in chapter 17.

Zenoff and Zwick[5] held that the key to effective decision making in the remittance of profits from a foreign affiliate requires a systematic analysis. They constructed one of the earlier models of the earnings remittance procedure. Variations of this model are still being used by MNCs. This model is shown in Figure 8–11.

Planning for Risk

Business risk and its management are discussed in various sections of this book. The management of foreign exchange risk was discussed in chapter 4. Market risk in debt and equity markets will be discussed in chapter 12. The risk of using derivatives to hedge risk will be covered in chapter 13. An entire chapter is devoted to political risk and its measurement and management. In planning for international operations, the CFO of the MNC must be able to measure and manage global market risk of all of the

---

[5] David B. Zenoff and Jack Zwick, *International Financial Management* (Englewood Cliffs, NJ: Prentice-Hall, Inc., 1969), p. 438.

Stage 1	Stage 2	Stage 3	Stage 4
Should funds be remitted?	How much should be remitted?	What forms of remittance?	Synthesis
Reasons for:	Depends on:	Depends on:	
To pay for use of company-owned resources	Amount invested or loaned	Industry and company practice	
Technology	Parent company's expectations	Tax implications	
Invested capital	Parent company's objectives	Organization and structure	
Property rights	Local and U.S. tax regulations, rates, and credits	Percentage of equity possessed	Synthesis and final decision
Loans	Company and industry practice	Alternative remittance forms permitted by government	
To effect better worldwide deployment of funds	Parent company's attitude toward risk	Establishment of remittance record	
To obtain higher rate of return	Local government regulations		
To assure accessibility	U.S. government regulations		
To minimize risks	Cost and availability of funds from external sources		
	Fund requirements of affiliate and worldwide company		

Source: David B. Zenoff and Jack Zwick, *International Financial Management* (Englewood Cliffs, NJ: Prentice-Hall, Inc., 1969), p. 438.

FIGURE 8–11 Foreign Earnings Remittance Model Sequence of Analysis and Decisions

financial instruments with which the firm is operating, including the comparison of different market risks.

Summary and Conclusions

Today's MNC must plan and organize its international finance function very carefully in order to compete in a borderless world. Many differences exist between planning for domestic and international operations. Cultural variables and political risk have greater effect on foreign operations. Foreign exchange is necessary to operate in foreign countries.

Several issues must be addressed by top management of the MNC. These include whether to centralize or decentralize the international financial function or parts of it, whether to operate with subsidiaries or branches abroad, whether to finance foreign operations with equity or debt, whether to invest directly overseas or license foreign companies to manufacture and market the firm's products overseas, whether to fund operations with internal or external resources, and, finally, if external funds are used, from what money and/or capital market should the MNC obtain the funds.

The answers to many of these questions will depend on what type organization structure the MNC uses in its international operations. It can organize with an international division structure. It can organize its foreign operations by product or by geographic area. Or it can use a more complex global matrix structure.

The MNC must judiciously organize its financial staff to obtain optimal results in foreign operations. The size of the firm will dictate how the firm relates to its foreign affiliates. The question of the degree of centralization will require careful thought. Day-to-day operations will require an international financial staff that is knowledgeable of global money and capital markets, is well trained for operating in foreign cul-

tures, well motivated, and able to make key decisions about such questions as the re-mittance of earnings and repatriation of capital from foreign affiliates, including the tax implications of such decisions.

Additional Readings

Bartlett, Christopher A., and Sumantra Ghoshal. "Matrix Management: Not a Structure, A Frame of Mind." *Harvard Business Review* 68(July–August 1990): 138–45.

Clee, Gilbert H., and Wilbur M. Sachtjen. "Organizing a World-Wide Business." *Harvard Business Review* 42(November/December 1964): 55–67.

Dyment, John J. "Strategies and Management Controls for Global Corporations." *Journal of International Business Studies* 7(Spring 1987): 20–6.

Hiatt, John T. "High-Tech Global Finance." *International Business* 7(April 1994): 32–4.

Holland, J. B. *International Financial Management.* Oxford, England: Basil Blackwell, 1986, pp. 179–202.

Zenoff, David B., and Jack Zwick *International Financial Management.* Englewood Cliffs, NJ: Prentice-Hall, 1969.

Discussion Questions

1. How does financial planning differ between domestic and foreign operations?
2. Discuss the major issues to consider in the formulation of international financial strategy?
3. What are the major differences among the international, geographic, product, and global matrix organizational structures?
4. What firms might use a product structure organization? geographic structure organization?
5. What problems might arise for a firm organizing global operations according to a matrix-type structure?
6. How may the financial staff relationships differ between an international firm with $100 million in sales from one with $10 billion in sales?
7. What factors should a firm consider in planning for the remittance of foreign earnings to the parent firm?
8. How should the international finance activities of the firm be organized?

Problems

1. Draft a diagram that shows the external financing patterns possible for an international firm with operations in Europe and Asia, five wholly-owned subsidiaries, a European licensee, and sales distribution outlets in five foreign locations.
2. Find one example of a U.S. multinational company that uses the international division structure, one that uses the geographic structure, one that uses the product structure, and one that uses the matrix structure.
3. Design the international financial strategy for a firm with $800 million to $1 billion in sales in fifteen different product areas related to the single industry of coatings for industrial and consumer uses entering overseas production for the first time. The company has a very large shareownership and is considered a growth company with more than 40 years of earnings growth.

PART IV

The Role of Banks in Global Finance

The role of banks in global finance is of such significance that it deserves its own special section. Without the international banking system, international trade and investment would not be the economic phenomenon it is today. In chapter 9, the environment of global banking organizations will be examined. A major focus will be on the organizational structure of international banks. The global regulation of banks will be analyzed. Banks face a wide variety of regulations both at home and in foreign countries. Finally, the role of international banks in economic and institutional development will be discussed.

International banks offer most of the trade credits that finance the more than $5 trillion of world trade. The foreign exchange needed to finance international trade, investment, tourism, and other types of global commerce is almost all traded in the international banking system, whether at spot rates or at some forward rate of exchange. The Eurocurrency market is essentially an interbank market. The loans to sovereign nations that are not made by multilateral financial institutions are made by banks. Much of the world's investment banking transactions are carried on by intermediaries known as banks. A handful of banks worldwide create and trade the bulk of the currency and interest rate swaps and other exotic derivatives, which are used to hedge financial positions. Banks act as global custodians and facilitate the settlement of cross-border transactions for MNCs and institutional investors. These major functions will be the focus of chapter 10.

International banking is one the world's oldest financial services. Some of the oldest commercial institutions in European and

Asian countries are banks. They financed trade by the Phoenicians. They are the sole members of the German Börsen, or securities exchanges, and furnished the long-term capital for Germany's industrial companies during the Industrial Revolution there in the late 19th century by exchanging long-term loans for the equity in these companies. They finance the trading companies in Japan. They operate as holding companies of industrial companies in Belgium. They are among the most regulated of business enterprises because of their role in the formulation and implementation of monetary policy and because they act as fiduciary depositories of the savings of home country citizens.

The assumption made in chapters 9 and 10 is that international banks are also MNCs. As such, they operate in many different countries, are subject to the same cross-border and political risks that non-bank MNCs are, and must make the same kind of decisions that non-bank MNCs make with regard to foreign exchange exposure, political risk, foreign investment, organization structure, in which financial markets to operate, how to evaluate investments, what international accounting procedures to use, and how to minimize global tax liabilities.

9

The Environment and Role of International Banking

Major Objectives of Chapter 9

(1) To present an overview of the environment of international banking, and (2) to examine the role of banks in global economic and institutional development.

Key terms to be learned in chapter 9:

- foreign bank agencies
- merchant banks
- International Banking Act of 1978
- international banking facilities
- Basle Concordat
- systemic risk
- universal banks
- consortium banks

- private banks
- banques d'affairs
- Edge Act Banks
- Bank for International Settlements
- BCCI
- settlement risk
- security affiliates
- shell banks

Introduction

International banks play several important roles in the field of international business finance. The international banking system performs five major functions for international business: (1) financing international trade, (2) foreign exchange trading, (3) Eurocurrency lending, (4) sovereign or country lending, and (5) international investment banking. These functions will be discussed in more detail in chapter 10. First, it is helpful to examine the environment in which these international banks operate. This can generally be accomplished by focusing on U.S. bank operations abroad and foreign bank operations in the United States. Such analysis will be used in this chapter.

EVOLUTION OF INTERNATIONAL BANKING ACTIVITIES

The various international activities of banks have evolved fairly rapidly during the past three decades or so. In the 1960s, banks carried on traditional activities such as trade finance, foreign exchange trading, and international lending. To service these activities, banks arranged letters of credit, collected and processed drafts and other international trade documents, bought and sold foreign currencies, and made loans to foreign borrowers.

New activities were initiated by international banks in the 1970s and 1980s. These included Eurocurrency trading, syndicated Eurobond lending, and merchant banking. These banks created and dealt in Eurocurrencies, participated in Euroloan syndications, traded Eurobonds in the secondary markets, and arranged cross-border mergers and acquisitions.

In the late 1980s and early 1990s, international banks entered into a number of innovative activities including derivatives trading, global money market-making, LDC loan portfolio management, and private banking. Banks have added new operations in these innovative areas including creation of and secondary markets in currency and interest rate swaps, note issuance facilities (NIFs), 24-hour dealing room facilities, and global financial services for MNCs, including bond repurchase agreements, Euro-commercial paper, and exotic derivatives for hedging a variety of prices.

The International Banking Environment

It should be noted that international banks, like MNCs, are affected by cultural differences in the foreign countries in which they operate. They are even referred to differently in different countries. In the United States, they are commercial banks. In Great Britain, they may operate as merchant banks. In France, commercial banks are known as banques d'affairs. In Germany, they are Kreditbanken, or credit banks. In most countries, they are chartered only at the national level and, thus, are known as national banks. In the United States, they can be chartered at either the national or state level and, thus, can be either national banks or state banks. This is the basis for the dual banking system in the United States, a unique banking arrangement. They can have a nationwide branching system as in most countries, especially Canada, a country with a dozen or so banks and more than 5,000 branches nationwide. Or branching may be prohibited, as it has been in the United States where the McFadden Act of 1927 prohibited nationwide branching.[1] U.S. banks have gotten around this law by being permitted, by state laws in nearly every state, to acquire banks in other states. These have operated as wholly-owned subsidiaries and not as branches. One example of such an operation can be found in the case of Banc One of Columbus, Ohio. Banc One owns banks in states that surround Ohio as well as in Texas, and is currently acquiring other banks in states across the country. Thus, banks are able to operate nationwide in the United States.

UNIVERSAL BANKS

Banks that perform international banking functions and that are headquartered outside the United States and Japan are often characterized as universal banks because of the universal or general commercial and investment banking operations that they are

---

[1] In 1994, the Interstate Banking and Branch Act was passed by the U.S. Congress and was signed into law authorizing nationwide branching by banks in the United States in 1997.

permitted to do. Typical examples of universal banks are the Big Three banks in Germany—Deutsche Bank, Dresdner Bank, and Commerzbank.

Banks in the United States are prohibited from doing both commercial and investment banking operations by the Glass-Steagall Act, passed in 1933. In Japan, a similar law restricts Japanese banks from performing both functions. The Glass-Steagall Act became law partly because of banking abuses alleged in the 1920s. These abuses included loans to underwriting clients, easier loan terms offered to investment affiliates, and parking poorly performing stocks brought to the market by banks in the trust accounts they administered for widows, orphans, and other clients.[2]

In 1995, the Clinton administration proposed that the Glass-Steagall Act be abolished. Under this proposal, a variety of financial services could be offered from a single holding company, such as investment banking as well as traditional commercial banking services. This proposal would include insurance operations. In addition to the increase in global competition that abolition of this law could offer to U.S. multinational banks, abusive banking actions are illegal under current U.S. securities laws, thus, the Glass-Steagall Act is a superfluous law.

Competition in financial services with other industrialized countries was the reason given for this most recent attempt to abolish the Glass-Steagall Act. Proper fire walls between commercial banking business and securities and insurance operations were proposed. Under this proposal, a firm's banking operations would be supervised by the Comptroller of the Currency, the Federal Reserve System, and the Federal Deposit Insurance Corporation while the securities business would be regulated by the Securities and Exchange Commission. Other bills introduced in the U.S. Congress at that time include such a proposal coupled with the authority for such banking institutions to be involved in commercial or industrial businesses, as is the case in Belgium and other foreign countries.

Deutsche Bank, Germany's largest bank, is a near-perfect example of a universal bank. Its operations are concerned with wholesale, retail, and investment banking, as well as life insurance, while operating with a triple A rating.[3] Deutsche Bank borrows DM 8–12 billion annually and transacts most of its requirements itself. It now does its own medium-term note business, performs a lucrative derivatives trading business, and acts as lead manager on a significant number of foreign bond and Eurobond issues. In addition to these investment banking operations, it performs a large amount of wholesale and retail banking business while operating as a member of the German stock exchanges.

ORGANIZATIONAL STRUCTURE FOR INTERNATIONAL OPERATIONS

International banks also can be characterized by the way they are structured to do international banking operations. They may do a full line of banking, i.e., take deposits, make loans, do foreign exchange trading, in the form of subsidiaries or branches. They may operate agencies in foreign countries. Agencies cannot do a full line of banking because they cannot take deposits. They can, however, maintain credit balances by borrowing funds in the money and capital markets or by being funded by the parent banking firms. International banks usually have representative offices in foreign countries and some operate security affiliates, wholly-owned subsidiaries, which perform

---

[2] John R. Dorfman, "Glass-Steagall Was Born Out of View That Stock Market Is Simply Gambling," *Wall Street Journal*, 6 March 1995, p. B5B.

[3] Aline van Duyn, "A Truly Universal Bank," *Euromoney Supplement: The World's Best Credits* (September 1994): 30.

brokerage, underwriting, and other investment banking functions. These international banking structures are discussed in more detail in the following sections.

Subsidiaries, Branches, and Agencies

International banks have a number of organizational structures by which they conduct foreign operations. Subsidiaries and branches can be used to perform a full line of banking activities including taking deposits and making loans. Subsidiaries must be chartered to operate in a state or country and have their own directors, even though they may be fully owned by the parent bank. Branches are merely offices of the parent bank and do not need to be chartered or have separate directors. Many foreign banks operate agencies in other countries. Agencies—this form of organization stems from the principal-agent relationship—cannot perform a full line of banking since they cannot take deposits. They can make loans, operate in foreign exchange and Eurocurrency markets, and maintain a credit balance. They are financed by loans from the money markets and by their parent banks. Their principal business is to perform international banking operations for companies from the parent bank's home country.

Security Affiliates

Non-U.S. banks can form security affiliates that underwrite securities and offer brokerage services in the stock markets. Foreign bank securities affiliates in the United States can operate if they were established before 1978. Since the passage of the International Banking Act of 1978, the formation of new foreign bank securities affiliates has been prohibited.

Representative Offices

Most large international banks have established representative offices in foreign countries. These offices cannot perform traditional banking functions such as taking deposits, making loans, trading in Eurocurrencies or foreign exchange operations, or financing international trade. They merely represent the parent bank in the foreign location and refer business back to the parent or to its branches. Occasionally, these offices produce loans, i.e., they are loan production offices. In other words, they sell loans for the parent bank, which then services the loans.

Correspondent Banks

Many banks have correspondent relationships with other banks. Generally, this relationship consists of Bank A, e.g., a domestic bank with no foreign operations, maintaining a deposit with an unrelated foreign bank, Bank B. Bank B then performs banking business for the clients of Bank A when necessary or performs operations such as foreign exchange trading directly for Bank A. Many leading international banks have retrenched in recent years to their core domestic base of operations and have disposed of overseas branches. These banks have less scope to internalize cross-border operations through their own branches and have increasingly turned to correspondent banks to do their overseas business.

Entire systems have been developed to serve as correspondents for foreign banks.[4] These include TIPA, a system linking cooperative banks, IBOS, which links a group of EC commercial banks, Eurogiro, which links post office and giro banks, and Visa International, linking ATM networks in Europe. Barclays' BIDDS, the Bank of Scotland's TAPS service, and Midland Bank's TEMPO are individual bank initiatives that handle low value cross-border transfers as correspondents.

New electronic technologies enabled many domestic banks to expand their international correspondent relationships to include many activities normally done by in-

---

[4] Nigel Wilkins, "The Cut-throat World of the Correspondent Banker," *Euromoney* (October 1993): 88–9.

ternational banks. Some of the areas that these banks have encroached upon include asset management, custodial services for securities, and the marketing of lending and treasury services.

Consortium Banks

Expansion of international banking in the 1960s and 1970s was characterized by the rise of consortium banks.[5] These were banks that were joint ventures of several well-established parent banks. They were usually formed to accomplish banking operations that the parent banks were unable to do, either because of bank regulations or because they lacked the capital. Large banks used them to take advantage of personnel and market skills of each of the partners while smaller banks used them to venture into international financial activities.

Many of these consortium banks evolved from European banking relationships. The first such bank was Midland and International Bank, Ltd., or MAIBL, begun in 1964 by Britain's Midland Bank, the Toronto Dominion Bank, and the Commercial Bank of Australia, Ltd. Another consortium bank, the Orion Banking Group, was formed by Germany's Westdeutsche Landesbank, London's National Westminster, Mitsubishi Bank, and others. Manufacturers Hanover was able to circumvent the Glass-Steagall Act prohibition against investment banking by combining with N.M. Rothschild to form Manufacturers Hanover, Ltd. These banks operated on the reputation of the parent banks but the parents could avoid large capital inclusions for their investment banking operations. As more and more parent banks became able to operate more universally as a result of deregulation in the 1980s, consortium banks became less and less useful. Only a handful of them still have relatively active operations.

Edge Act Banks

In 1919, the U.S. Congress passed the Edge Act permitting U.S. banks to operate wholly-owned subsidiaries referred to as Edge Act Companies (EACs). This act was essentially an amendment to the Federal Reserve Act of 1913, which authorized the U.S. Federal Reserve System. After World War I, the United States became a leading international trading country. A number of U.S. banks began to finance international trade. The Federal Reserve Act did not contain provisions for supervision of such international activities, deemed to be risky by the Federal Reserve Board, thus, Congress recognized the risks of international trade financing and passed the Edge Act, giving the Federal Reserve Board regulatory and supervisory responsibility over all international activities of Federal Reserve member banks and authorizing the establishment of the bank subsidiaries known as Edge Act Companies. So-called Agreement Corporations are also supervised by the Federal Reserve Board under this legislation. They are state chartered subsidiaries that have agreed to operate functionally, as do EACs.

EACs are permitted to do only international banking operations, including international trade financing, foreign exchange operations, and Eurocurrency lending.[6] Until the International Banking Act of 1978, foreign banks in the United States could not own or operate EACs. This law permitted foreign banks to establish or buy such institutions and they now own a majority interest in 32 EACs with more than $11 billion in total assets. More than 140 EACs have been established with total assets amounting to more than $20 billion.

EACs have been active in a number of areas of international banking. They are usually located in a state other than where the head office is located in order to avoid

---

[5] Michael Moffitt, *The World's Money: International Banking from Bretton Woods to the Brink of Insolvency* (New York: Simon & Schuster, 1983), pp. 48–9.

[6] See Carole Curtis and James C. Baker, "The Evolution of the Super Edge: Regulation and Operations of Edge Act Banks," *Journal of World Trade Law* (Switz.) 21 (December 1987): 25–36.

the branching prohibition of the McFadden Act. Since the 1978 International Banking Act, EACs have become quite competitive with banks' loan production offices by giving U.S. money center banks and major regional banks access to markets from which they had been restricted before the regulation of foreign banks operating in the United States. The 1978 law, which gave U.S. bank regulators the authority to supervise foreign bank operations in the United States for the first time, will be discussed in more detail later in this chapter.

Shell Banks

A shell bank or branch is not a bank in the strict sense of the word but merely a means of getting around U.S. and other countries' bank regulations. They are generally located in the Bahamas, Grand Cayman Islands, Netherlands Antilles, or Panama, all known as tax havens, a term that will be discussed in chapter 17. Growth of shell operations in the early 1970s resulted in more than $120 billion of total assets in these "branches."

Shell banks are just that, shells, which are very sparsely furnished if at all. They usually are a "hole in the wall" with a brass plate on the front door. They do not make decisions for the bank. In the Bahamas, they are not permitted to have an office on the ground floor because they might be mistaken for a real bank. In the Caymans, only one officer must have banking experience. The only real banking asset of any value in these offices is the set of books that record off-shore banking operations. They have been referred to as "Eurocurrency market way stations.[7]

International Banking Facilities

The U.S. Federal Reserve System permitted U.S. and foreign banks operating in the United States to establish international banking facilities (IBFs).[8] These offices—actually second sets of banking books—were established to conduct a deposit and loan business with foreign residents, including foreign banks, without having to maintain reserve requirements or interest rate ceilings—the latter required by Regulation Q but abolished in 1986. IBFs did not have to pay deposit premiums for deposit insurance from the Federal Deposit Insurance Corporation. More than 400 of these institutions with more than $150 billion were formed in the first year they were permitted.

The Federal Reserve System authorized IBFs in order to maintain better control over international operations of banks operating in the United States, essentially to reduce the impact of the shell banks discussed in the preceding section. Many banks, domestic and foreign, had formed offices in the Cayman Islands, Netherlands Antilles, Bahamas, and other off-shore locations in order to handle their international operations. These offices were merely so-called "shell" banks, i.e., a small office where a separate set of books for foreign operations was located. U.S. bank regulators had difficulty in maintaining control and obtaining data concerning these operations. By permitting IBFs, regulators could monitor international operations of the parent banks to a greater extent and reduce the motivation for these banks to form off-shore or shell banks.

The advent of IBFs has had significant implications for U.S. banking.[9] After IBFs were permitted by the Federal Reserve Board, the growth of banking business in the Caribbean area declined rapidly. This result suggested that the growth of business in this area had been intended almost entirely to bypass U.S. monetary regulations.

---

[7] Moffitt, *The World's Money*, p. 50.

[8] Sydney J. Key, "International Banking Facilities," *Federal Reserve Bulletin* 68 (October 1982): 565–77.

[9] K. Alec Chrystal, "International Banking Facilities," *Federal Reserve Bank of St. Louis Review* 66 (April 1984): 10–11.

International banks operating outside the United States and particularly in Europe tend to be universal in that they perform a wide range of commercial and investment banking operations. U.S. international banks tend to be more restricted in their operations because of Federal banking laws. However, global competition is driving U.S. banks to gain permission to do a number of investment banking functions in their foreign operations. The next section will examine U.S. bank regulation concerning foreign banks in the United States as well as U.S. banks' foreign operations, in addition to the work of the Bank for International Settlements and foreign banking authorities. It might be helpful to examine the International Banking Act of 1978 as a model of the first U.S. law to regulate foreign banking in the United States.

Deregulation of U.S. banking in the 1980s had further drastic effects on the Caribbean banking business, as predicted. The regulatory changes that permitted IBFs were intended to ease the burden of domestic monetary restrictions on U.S. banks' international operations. However, this objective has been limited because IBFs play no role in financing either activities of U.S. residents or U.S. activities of nonresidents. Major U.S. banks had already found ways around restrictions on their international operations and were able to compete internationally. On the other hand, IBFs have had benefits for U.S. branch and agency operations of foreign banks. This is a result of the high proportion of their existing business that is IBF-eligible, i.e., the portion with nonresidents.

Bank Regulation

Banks are among the most regulated and supervised business firms. Asymmetric information, the fact that different parties in a financial transaction do not have the same information available, causes adverse selection of banks by individuals and companies. Potential borrowers who are most likely to produce an undesirable, or adverse, outcome, i.e., bad credit risks, are the most likely to seek out a loan and the most likely to be selected by the bank. For example, in 1984, many international business firms used Continental Illinois Bank for their international business banking. Because Illinois banking law prohibited its banks to have branches, Continental had to resort to the very volatile international money markets to fund its lending operations. A rumor started by a Japanese bank led the market to believe that Continental was having problems because of some bad loans that resulted from adverse selection, causing a run on its deposits, which placed the bank in jeopardy of failing. A government bailout by the Federal Deposit Insurance Corporation and reorganization of bank management saved Continental from being closed by Federal bank regulators.

The problem of moral hazard may arise because governments insure deposits. Moral hazard is the risk in financial markets that the borrower may engage in activities that are undesirable or immoral from the lender's viewpoint because such activities reduce the likelihood that the loan will be repaid. Banks, for example, may do riskier business than they might if they were risking their own money. Much of the U.S. savings and loan debacle in the 1980s was caused by moral hazard. Liberalization of lending laws coupled with deposit insurance prompted many savings and loan managers to issue junk bonds and make risky investments that were funded by insured deposits. They apparently decided that if these risky investments were unprofitable, the losses

would be covered by deposit insurance. Many of these financial institutions were closed by Federal authorities and many of their executives have been convicted of fraud and other crimes.

Some countries insure bank deposits but do not assess deposit premiums until a bank has failed. This is the case in Turkey where only after a bank has failed are other banks asked to furnish the funds to pay depositors of the failed bank. In addition, the requirements to open a bank are very difficult, which makes it difficult for someone to enter the business of banking. Thus, Turkish banks tend to operate more safely since no fund for depositor payoffs exists until after a bank failure. The assessments made at that time may be very high, especially if a large bank were to fail.

Bank regulation differs from country to country and much of it has evolved from cultural differences. For example, the Arab countries consider all interest to be illegal because their religious documents classify interest as usery and all usery is prohibited by their religion. Some countries carry out heavy regulation because the populace has come to distrust banks. This may be the reason for heavy-handed bank regulation in the United States. In other countries, bank regulation is a more casual activity, as in Great Britain where "a wink and a nod" from the Governor of the Bank of England cues bank management on how to behave. In reality, banks do face risks that nonfinancial firms do not.

On the other hand, because of the asymmetric information problem, bank regulation is being standardized in many countries. Several nations offer deposit insurance, but of differing coverages. Required minimum capital requirements based on risk assets has been standardized globally by the Basel Accord of 1988, which became effective in 1992.[10]

The Basel Accord was formulated by a committee commissioned by the Bank for International Settlements to coordinate and standardize bank capital adequacy globally by relating the riskiness of a bank's operations to its capital needs. Assets and off-balance sheet activities of banks are allocated into four categories, each with different weights to account for the degree of riskiness of each. Category one includes reserves and government securities that have no default risk and carry a zero weight in the bank's capital ratio, usually total capital-to-assets. Category two has a weight of 20 percent and includes items that have low default risk, i.e., interbank deposits, fully backed mortgage bonds, and federal agency securities. Category three has a weight of 50 percent and includes municipal bonds and residential mortgages, securities with higher risk. Category four is the highest risk category and has a weight of 100 percent. It includes all remaining securities such as commercial paper, loans, and fixed assets. Off-balance sheet items are treated similarly by assigning them with a "credit equivalent" percentage, which converts them into on-balance sheet items.

After adjusting the bank's assets according to their riskiness, the bank must then meet two capital requirements. First, it must have Tier 1 or "core" capital, i.e., stockholders' equity capital, excluding any subordinated debentures or capital notes, equal to at least 4 percent of risk-adjusted assets. Second, the bank's total capital, including Tier 1 or "core" capital and Tier 2 capital, which includes loan loss reserves and any subordinated debt, must be equal to or greater than 8 percent of total risk-adjusted assets. Subordinated debt includes convertible debentures and capital notes, which are paid off only after depositors and other creditors have been paid. These are global requirements imposed by the Basel Accord. In the United States, the Federal Reserve Board has imposed even higher standards, which consist of a total capital requirement

---

[10] Frederic S. Mishkin, *Financial Markets, Institutions, and Money* (New York: HarperCollins, 1995), p. 314.

TABLE 9–1.   First Multibank Balance Sheet (millions U.S.$)

Assets		*Liabilities and Net Worth*	
Loan loss reserves	$ 60	Checkable deposits	$ 400
Treasury securities	200	Nontransaction deposits	1,200
Government agency securities	140	Borrowings	220
Municipal bonds	200	Loan loss reserves	40
Residential mortgages	200	Bank capital	140
Real estate loans	400		
Commercial loans	700		
Fixed assets	100		
Total assets	**2,000**	**Total liabilities and net worth**	**2,000**

of 10 percent of risk-adjusted assets and Tier 1 capital of 6 percent of risk-adjusted assets.

Tables 9–1 and 9–2 show the application of the Basel Accord capital standards to the balance sheet of a multinational bank. Table 9–1 presents the balance sheet for First Multibank. See Table 9–2 for the application of the Basel Accord capital standards to the balance sheet shown in Table 9–1.

RECENT BANKING PROBLEMS

During the 1990s, international bank regulators have been occupied with three cases of large bank operations that have affected the way in which global banking operations

TABLE 9–2.   Basel Accord Bank Capital Standards Applied to First Multibank's Balance Sheet

Risk-adjusted Assets =			*Type of Assets*
0 ×	$60 million	= $0	Reserves
+ 0 ×	$200 million	= $0	Treasury securities
+ 0.20 ×	$140 million	= $28 million	Agency securities
+ 0.50 ×	$200 million	= $100 million	Municipal bonds
+ 0.50 ×	$200 million	= $100 million	Residential mortgages
+ 1.00 ×	$400 million	= $400 million	Real estate loans
+ 1.00 ×	$700 million	= $700 million	Commercial loans
+ 1.00 ×	$100 million	= $100 million	Fixed assets
+ 1.00 ×	$400 million	= $400 million	Letters of credit

TA = $2,400 million; RAA = $1,828 million

Core Capital Requirement
   = 4% × risk-adjusted assets
   = 4% × $1,828 million = $73.12 million
   < $140 million of core capital

Total Capital Requirement
   = 8% × risk-adjusted assets
   = 8% × $1,828 million = $146.24 million
   < $200 million of total capital ($60 million of loan loss reserves + $140 million of bank, or core, capital)

may be supervised in the future. These operations involved Bank for Credit and Commerce International (BCCI), Barings Bank, a merchant bank that was headquartered in London, and Daiwa Bank, headquartered in Japan. BCCI is discussed in more detail later in this chapter, and Barings Bank is discussed in more detail in chapter 13. BCCI was managed by corrupt senior executives and, after disclosures about drug financing operations, money laundering, and military arms support, bank regulators in the United States, Great Britain, and other major countries closed the operations of BCCI and have prosecuted leaders of this bank. Barings declared bankruptcy in early 1995 after reporting losses of $1.4 billion from derivatives trading by one bank trader in Singapore. Senior officials of Barings reportedly gave this trader too much authority without proper internal controls. In the case of Daiwa Bank, losses totaling $1.1 billion were reportedly incurred by the head of U.S. government securities trading in the bank. In the case of Barings, the losses occurred over a short period of time. But in the case of Daiwa, the losses were incurred over a period of 11 years and were made in the United States. In both the Barings and Daiwa cases, weak managerial controls had been implemented. In fact, senior officials reportedly had revealed the Daiwa losses for several years.

In all three of these cases, national bank regulators were not aware of the problems until after serious losses had occurred. In the case of Daiwa, the Federal Reserve did not know about the lack of internal controls until the last three years of the cover-up. BCCI gained control of banks in the United States before bank regulators became aware of the corruption within the bank. In the case of Barings, the Bank of England became aware of the losses at about the same time that the international community became aware. The BCCI case resulted in more strict regulatory legislation, which gave the Federal Reserve more control over the domestic operations of foreign banks in the United States. This case also resulted in a better cooperative relationship among the leading central banks with regard to the operations of international banks. The Barings case demonstrated to banks around the world that they should install better internal controls over their trading rooms. The Daiwa Bank scandal is part of an overall banking problem in Japan and should result in tighter controls over Japanese banks by regulators.

BANK RISKS

Banks face several complicated and interrelated risks in the borderless and highly integrated financial world. These risks include the following[11]:

1. **credit risk:** the possibility that a counter-party may default on its position—the Mexico default on sovereign loans from banks in 1982 is an example of credit risk;

2. **market risk:** the loss that results from unexpected general market price and interest rate changes—the Japanese banking crisis in 1995 can be somewhat attributed to market risk;

3. **exchange rate risk:** the loss that results from adverse movements in foreign exchange rates—banks incur such risk as do nonfinancial corporations but more so because of their importance in the foreign exchange market;[12]

4. **operational risk:** loss resulting from human error, fraud, or lack of internal controls—the case of Nick Leeson and the Barings Bank failure is an example of operational risk;

---

[11] "Managing Risk in a New Financial Environment," *IMF Survey* 24 (September 14, 1995): 265, 272–5.

[12] Banks manage their foreign exchange exposure by hedging for their own accounts in the forward foreign exchange market, discussed in chapter 3, by implementing policies governing bank limits, discussed in chapter 10, with regard to net position limits in any one currency, maturity gap limits in the forward market, and customer limits—a trading limit with any one customer, usually a bank—and with multilateral netting limits with other banks, discussed in the settlement section of chapter 18.

5. **legal risk:** possible loss that stems from the legal status of a contract;

6. **liquidity risk:** the possibility that a position cannot be liquidated quickly without a large price concession;

7. **settlement risk:** the possibility of loss from market and credit risk exposure during the settlement period—the Herstatt case is an example of settlement risk;

8. **specific risk:** the risk of loss from a decline in value of a particular position that is not the result of a general market movement.

Bank regulatory agencies in most countries have, among their agendas, the reduction of such risks among their constituent banks.

Some banks have very tight regulation from the central government of the country in which they are headquartered while others have decentralized supervision and regulation. Most countries have one strong central bank or other federal agency that regulates and supervises banks. In Great Britain, that agency is the Bank of England. In France, it is the Banque de France. In Germany, it is the Deutsche Bundesbank. In Japan, it is the Bank of Japan, although the Ministry of Finance and the Deposit Insurance Corporation also have regulatory oversight. Some nations use a commercial bank to perform central banking functions, as in the case of Iran with Bank Melli, which has operated as a central bank in the past.

In the United States with its dual banking system, regulation and supervision is shared by several federal and state agencies and has been referred to as a hodgepodge regulatory system. The Federal Reserve System and its Federal Reserve Board regulates monetary policy, bank holding companies, and most international banking functions, and supervises Federal Reserve state-chartered member banks. The Comptroller of the Currency supervises nationally chartered banks. The Federal Deposit Insurance Corporation supervises state-chartered non-Federal Reserve member banks along with the state bank chartering agencies and offers deposit insurance to commercial banks through its Bank Insurance Fund (BIF) and to savings and loan associations through its Savings Association Insurance Fund (SAIF).

Bank regulation and deposit insurance programs differ greatly from one region to another. For example, in Great Britain, regulation has generally been rather casual, as mentioned previously. In other countries, regulation is rather tight and rigorous. The vast variety of laws and overlapping regulatory agencies in the United States makes banking very prone to much regulation. In many countries, bank deposit insurance is funded by premiums charged to banks that are members of the system, as in the United States, Japan, Germany, and Great Britain. However, in some countries, such as Turkey, no fund is available and banks are not assessed premiums. If a bank fails, the other banks are then assessed a pro rata amount to finance the payoffs of the failed bank's depositors. Of course, bank charters are extremely difficult to obtain in Turkey; bank entry is very difficult, but so is bank failure. In Japan, the Bank of Japan, the Ministry of Finance, and the Deposit Insurance Corporation all have jurisdiction over some aspect of Japanese banking. For the first time in many years, a number of large Japanese banks failed in 1994–95. A number of problems in the Japanese economy have been blamed for these failures. Ministry of Finance authorities announced an end to bank deposit guarantees by the year 2000. They believe these guarantees, through deposit insurance, were a major part of the Japanese banking problem.[13]

This 1995 banking crisis in Japan does present a prime example of the issues that face bank regulators.[14] The six largest banks in the world are Japanese. The entire Japanese banking industry was in trouble in 1995 because of an estimated $500 billion

---

[13] Gerard Baker, "Risky Removal of a Support System," *Financial Times*, 19 September 1995, p. 15.
[14] Ibid.

in bad loans on their books. No Japanese bank had failed in decades, but in 1995, five were closed. The top 21 banks in Japan had significantly reduced their exposure to bad loans by fall 1995. While Japanese banks had faced credit risk because of their low financial ratios, they had not had problems with specific industry risk because of the low risk among their borrowers. However, a recession in Japan coupled with consumers' loss of faith in the banking system resulted in runs on Japanese banks.

Japanese banking authorities at the Ministry of Finance had practiced a policy for 50 years that held that no Japanese bank would be permitted to fail. The ensuing confidence among depositors led to a steady flow of funds from savers and a relatively stable banking system. However, in 1995, these same authorities changed their policy to allow some banks to fail. They believed that a few failures would not be a threat to the entire system. This case represents an example of significant change in regulatory philosophy by banking authorities in a major industrialized nation.

Regulation of international banking is fraught with problems that stem from nationalistic tendencies. The U.S. banking system is the largest in global terms with more than 1,000 branches and some subsidiaries operating abroad. The Federal Reserve Board regulates and supervises the international operations of U.S. banks that are carried out within the United States but does not have clear supervision over foreign operations. The U.S. Comptroller of the Currency examines foreign branches of U.S. banks in countries where such examination by a foreign agency is permitted. For example, Switzerland does not permit a foreign agency to examine banks operating in that country. The Comptroller of the Currency maintains a London office for the facilitation of bank examinations of U.S. bank branches in Europe outside of Switzerland. Bank supervision of other countries seldom extends into other countries despite the pronouncements of the Bank for International Settlements.

The Bank for International Settlements

One institution does make an attempt to regulate international banking on a global basis. This is the Bank for International Settlements (BIS), located in Basle, Switzerland.[15] The BIS was established in 1930 by the central banks of Belgium, France, Germany, Italy, Japan, and the United Kingdom. It has been referred to as a central bank for central bankers. It is owned by its 32-member central banks through shares purchased by each national central bank. The U.S. Federal Reserve System was an ex officio, nonvoting member until September 1994 when it officially joined the BIS.

The BIS serves its member banks by facilitating international banking agreements. The recent Basle Agreement on capital adequacy for banks worldwide is an example of such an agreement. It also serves to protect the integrity of its members' currencies by supporting them with currency market operations. During the 1992 European monetary crisis, the BIS acted as a central clearinghouse for currency swaps, supervised general arrangements to borrow among its member nations, and loaned money along with other member banks to member countries experiencing temporary economic problems. The BIS also participates in the formulation of international banking rules to control financial market integration by providing a forum in which member central banks can negotiate agreements. In addition, its staff performs research on topics of interest to central bankers, including the risks and advantages of derivatives.

The BIS established the Committee on Banking Regulations and Supervisory Practices in 1974 as an attempt to create stability in international banking. The committee was composed of the governors of the central banks of the ten leading industrialized nations, the so-called Group of 10, plus Switzerland. It was usually referred to as

[15] See, for example, Robert Fraser, *The World Financial System* (Burnt Mill, Essex, U.K.: Longman Group, 1987).

the Cooke Committee, for its chairman, Peter Cooke, the Governor of the Bank of England.

In 1975, the Cooke Committee issued the first Basle Concordat, aimed at the formulation of rules concerning failed foreign banks and how to handle such failures. The 1975 Basle Concordat was a very short document that offered the following guidelines on international bank supervision.[16]

1. the supervision of foreign banking establishments should be the joint responsibility of host and parent authorities;
2. no foreign banking establishment should escape supervision;
3. the supervision of bank liquidity should be the primary responsibility of the host banking authorities;
4. the supervision of bank solvency is a matter for the parent authority in the case of foreign branches and primarily the responsibility of the host banking authority in the case of foreign subsidiaries;
5. practical cooperation should be provided by the exchange of information between host and parent authorities and by the authorization of bank examiners by, or on behalf of, parent bank authorities on the territory of the host authority.

The Basle Concordat of 1975 had four major weaknesses.[17] The primary responsibility for supervision of the solvency of foreign bank subsidiaries was assigned to the host authorities. The problem arose where the host authority expected the parent authority to supervise the subsidiary under the principle of consolidation, while the parent authority expected the host authority to supervise in accordance with the Concordat. Second, the 1975 Concordat also failed to address the question of differing supervisory standards. In 1979, the Federal Reserve System became concerned with the inadequate supervision by some parent authorities. The Federal Reserve had proposed tighter reporting requirements on the U.S. offices of foreign banks, but, when the foreign banks protested, the Federal Reserve watered down its proposal. Third, the dispute between the Federal Reserve System and the other supervisory authorities also revealed different interpretations of the division of responsibilities as set forth in the concordat. Finally, when the Cooke Committee intentionally excluded lender of last resort guidelines from the concordat, a problem developed when it was interpreted that the responsibility for supervision did not technically imply responsibility for rescuing a failing foreign bank affiliate.

One case of a bank failure in Europe gave credence to these weaknesses of the original concordat. When the Luxembourg subsidiary of the Italian bank, Banco Ambrosiano, failed in 1982, the weaknesses of the 1975 Concordat were emphasized. The banking authorities of both Luxembourg and Italy disclaimed responsibility for the supervision and lender of last resort functions for the Luxembourg subsidiary because it was a holding company rather than a bank. A new concordat was drafted in 1983 that gave responsibility for supervision of an intermediate holding company to the parent authority—in the case of the Luxembourg affiliate of Banco Ambrosiano, that was the Italian authorities.[18]

The new concordat said almost exactly what the old concordat required. The major difference was that the 1975 version was three paragraphs long and the 1983 version covered three columns of an $8 1/2'' \times 11''$ page. The new concordat adopted guidelines

---

[16] Charles Grant, "Can the Cooke Committee Stand the Heat?" *Euromoney* (October 1982): 42.

[17] Richard Dale, "Basle Concordat: Lessons from Ambrosiano," *The Banker* (September 1983): 55.

[18] Revised Basle Concordat on Bank Oversight Clarifies the Division of Supervisory Roles," *IMF Survey* 12 (July 11, 1983): 201–4.

that would deal with the problem of uneven supervisory standards. The new rules provide that if a host authority considers the supervision of the parent of foreign banks operating in its territory as inadequate, it should discourage or prohibit the operation of such foreign banks in its territory. Also the host authority could impose specific conditions governing the conduct of the business of such establishments. If the host authority's supervision is, indeed, inadequate, the parent authority should extend its supervision, or discourage the parent bank from continuing to operate the establishment. Thus, the 1983 Concordat does go further than the 1975 version.

The International Banking Act[19]

The major reason why foreign banks in the United States have splintered their operations into a variety of organizational structures stems from the way in which foreign banking in the United States was regulated prior to 1978, the year in which the International Banking Act was passed. This law extended Federal regulation to foreign banking in the United States for the first time.

Before this law, foreign banking in the United States was regulated and supervised by the states in which the operations were located. Foreign banks have located in only the states that have significant amounts of international business activity, e.g., New York, Illinois, California, and to a lesser extent Texas, Florida, and a few other states. Before 1978, foreign banks had to form subsidiaries in California to take deposits from a rich retail market because state law required such deposits to be covered by Federal Deposit Insurance. Federal law at that time did not define a branch as an institution that could obtain Federal Deposit Insurance. This rule was not the case in Illinois where foreign bank branches were established and did take retail deposits—from ethnic peoples from the foreign bank's home country because they trusted such banks. After all, the parent foreign banks in question had assets totaling in the billions of dollars and none had ever failed. The agencies were operated to facilitate commercial transactions with companies from the foreign bank's home country.

After the International Banking Act was signed into law in 1978, foreign bank branches could obtain deposit insurance for retail deposits, had to maintain reserves with the Federal Reserve System, could open a branch in only one state—in conformance with the McFadden Act—could continue to operate their securities affiliates operating at the time the law was passed but could open no new securities operations—keeping them in conformance with the Glass-Steagall Act—could obtain Federal charters from the U.S. Comptroller of the Currency for branches and agencies, and were required to submit more information to the Federal Reserve Board about their operations. They were also permitted to own and operate Edge Act Companies, not permitted to foreigners before the 1978 Act. These organizations were discussed earlier in this chapter.

The Foreign Bank Supervision Enhancement Act

The Foreign Bank Supervision Enhancement Act of 1991 became law in the United States as a result of the scandal created by the operations of the Bank for Credit and Commerce International (BCCI). BCCI was a bank with global operations, which had been formed by Arab businessmen in the Middle East. The bank acquired U.S. banks illegally for the purpose of operating illegal activities in a major banking market. These activities included financing drug and military equipment sales. BCCI had banking offices in most of the industrialized countries of the world.

It was discovered that no agency was responsible for the supervision and exami-

---

[19] See James C. Baker, "The International Banking Act of 1978: Is It Working?" *The Bankers Magazine* 165 (May–June 1982): 15–9.

nation of foreign branches in the United States. The new law required all branches of foreign banks operating in the United States be examined annually by the Federal Reserve Board. In addition, any foreign banks applying to operate in the United States must demonstrate that they receive adequate supervision from their home country banking authorities.

WHOLESALE VS. RETAIL BANKING

Banks carry out a wide variety of broad operations. Some concentrate on wholesale banking, i.e., offering financial services only to business firms, while others concentrate on retail banking, i.e., offering financial services to consumers. Some others concentrate on commercial banking operations, i.e., taking deposits and making consumer and business loans. Others concentrate on investment banking, i.e., financing long-term capital needs of business firms. In the United States, the Glass-Steagall Act of 1933 prohibits banks from performing both commercial and investment banking operations. This restriction puts major U.S. banks at a disadvantage to large foreign banks, especially the European banks, which can perform both commercial and investment banking functions. In fact, in Germany, banks operate as brokers and traders on the securities exchanges and buy and sell corporate securities, for their own account or for investors. In many European countries, banks may hold large interests in corporations and can operate as holding companies of industrial firms, as in Belgium with Société Générale. In Germany, large banks can perform any financial service possible.

Merchant Banks

Banks that engage in wholesale banking, investment banking, and bank services for corporations are often referred to as merchant banks. This is a term applied to many of the large banks in Europe. Many merchant banks were established by wealthy private merchants in Italy during the twelfth and thirteenth centuries. By the fourteenth century, some of these banks were financing international trade, trading foreign currencies, and financing new industrial ventures. With deposits from the church and wealthy landowners, family-owned merchant banks established foreign subsidiaries throughout Europe. The Medici family established banking houses in the fifteenth century. Merchant banks declined because of bad loans, wars, and economic problems but revived in Germany, France, and Belgium in the sixteenth century. International commerce declined in the seventeenth and eighteenth centuries because of economic nationalism, wars, and political problems. France and Great Britain became the financial centers of Europe and many merchant banks were established there during the late eighteenth and nineteenth centuries. Barings Bank, in the news because of its 1995 bankruptcy stemming from excessive and illegal futures trading losses by a rogue trader, was established in 1770 as a merchant banking house and raised loans for foreign governments and made foreign investments in the nineteenth century.[20]

Merchant banks are able to offer corporations a large number of products, including global asset management, in various foreign markets outside their home base of operations. However, their low capital base is a disadvantage. These global banks include Hambros, Rothschild, Kleinwort Benson, Lazard, Robert Fleming, and Morgan Grenfell. The latter bank was acquired by Deutsche Bank in 1989 and the two banks have merged into a combined Deutsche Morgan Grenfell (DMG). The new bank is one of the five biggest investment banks in the world and the largest in Europe.

Some merchant banks are independently or privately owned, e.g., Schroeders

---

[20] Yoon S. Park and Jack Zwick, *International Banking in Theory and Practice* (Reading, MA: Addison-Wesley, 1985), pp. 1–3.

PLC of Great Britain. Merchant banks such as Mercury Asset Management have been leaders in pension fund management. Robert Fleming is among those merchant banks that specialize in functions such as index funds, international umbrella funds, and small company funds.[21]

NON-BANK BANKING

In many countries, including the United States, non-bank banks perform some banking functions. Merrill Lynch has often been referred to as the best bank in the world. It and other brokerage/investment companies will hold funds on deposit in so-called cash management accounts (CMA), can assist in the purchase or sale of a vast variety of financial instruments, and lend money based on such CMA accounts. Their activities are very much like banks but they are not regulated as banks. Many other brokerage firms operate in a similar fashion and offer CMA accounts.

Settlement Risk

The international interbank system is fraught with a number of special risks inherent to the settlement of millions of transactions in the foreign exchange and securities markets, which are cross-border in nature. These risks arise because of the fact that banks on either side of the clearing transaction involving international trade, investment, or securities operations may be in vastly different time zones. The difference may range from a few hours to as many as 18 hours in the case of transactions between Europeans and Japanese. The initiating bank may have delivered currency but, before it receives currency in exchange, the other bank may default for some reason. The problems that arise and some of the solutions are discussed in the following sections.

The Role of Banks in Economic and Institutional Development

Half of the more than 60 countries represented by top 500 banks worldwide are considered to be LDCs, nations with relatively low per capita incomes. A significant amount of banking operations are headquartered in these nations and, in addition, a large amount of branch operations of banks domiciled in developed countries are also located in such LDCs. During the 1960–90 period, a large amount of international and national development aid has been transferred to these countries, resulting in industrial growth and encouragement of further foreign investment in the business and banking systems of these countries.

One example of this phenomenon is South Korea. The Koreans have utilized a large amount of foreign aid from the United States coupled with more than 30 years of formal economic planning—government plans published every five years. The resulting industrialization has frightened even the Japanese. Led by Korea Exchange Bank, Korea has had as many as three banks among the 200 largest in the world. Economic growth has been sufficiently successful in Korea to encourage 45 foreign banks to locate more than 500 branches in that country by 1987.[22] The direct result of the invasion of foreign banks into Korea has been the competition fostered by these banks and the subsequent privatization of most of Korea's largest banks.

---

[21] Maximo Eng, Francis A. Lees, and Laurence J. Mauer, *Global Finance* (New York: HarperCollins, 1995), p. 665.

[22] Yoon-Dae Euh and James C. Baker, *The Korean Banking System and Foreign Influence* (London: Routledge, 1990).

International financial institutions have encouraged such growth and spread of banking operations in LDCs. For example, the World Bank Group, and specifically the International Finance Corporation (IFC) (to be discussed in chapter 11) has assisted in the development of financial institutions in LDCs. In addition, banks in industrialized nations have been encouraged to participate in the development of private enterprise in such countries through the efforts of IFC.[23] The IFC has been highly instrumental, along with the World Bank, in the formation of development finance companies, or financieras, in LDCs.[24] Other financial institutions have been established with the support of worldwide banks to assist economic development in LDCs. Prime examples are ADELA (the Atlantic Development Group for Latin America), a Luxembourg-based development finance company owned by international banks, and PICA (the Private Investment Company for Asia), also owned by international banks, whose efforts are directed toward Latin America and Asia, respectively.

ANALYSIS OF INTERNATIONAL BANKING ACTIVITIES

One illustrative way to look at international banking activities is to examine how U.S. banks operate abroad and how foreign banks operate in the United States. Total assets in the U.S. banking system amounted to $3.5 trillion at mid-1992. U.S. banks prefer to operate in foreign countries by means of a branch rather than a subsidiary. The subsidiary must be chartered locally and have local directors. The branch is just an appendage of the parent bank and does not have to meet the legal requirements of a subsidiary. Both types of organizational structure can perform a full line of banking. More than 130 U.S. banks operated some 850 branches overseas with $318 billion in assets as of year-end 1988. U.S. foreign bank branches had $556.9 billion in assets in 1990, $549.0 billion in 1991, and $542.5 billion in 1992, an increase of more than 67 percent since 1988.[25] Foreign branch assets of U.S. banks in 1992 represented about 15.5 percent of all U.S. banking assets. These overseas branch deposits are not insured by the Federal Deposit Insurance Corporation. U.S. banks also operate a handful of subsidiaries. American banks have had phenomenal growth abroad since 1960 when overseas assets amounted to only $3.5 billion.

Foreign banks in the United States have operated with different organizational characteristics. These operations had $948 billion in total assets as of mid-1993, according to the Federal Reserve Board, representing 22.4 percent of the U.S. banking market.[26] As of mid-1993, foreign banks held 205 subsidiaries chartered in the states in which they operated with $254 billion in assets in the U.S. home office. They operated 577 branches and agencies with $693 billion in assets. Foreign banking assets in the United States grew from $200.6 billion in 1980, to $440.8 billion in 1985, to $791.1 billion in 1990, to $948 billion in 1993. See Table 9–3 for a country breakdown of foreign bank offices in the United States.

---

[23] James C. Baker, "The IFC and European Banks: Key Factors in Development," *Journal of World Trade Law* 14 (May/June 1980): 264–70; and "The International Finance Corporation and Banks: IFC Syndications of Its LDC Investments," in *Foreign Exchange Issues, Capital Markets, and International Banking in the 1990s,* ed. Khosrow Fatemi and Dominick Salvatore (Washington, D.C.: Taylor and Francis, 1993), pp. 249–53.

[24] James C. Baker, *International Business Expansion into Less-Developed Countries: The International Finance Corporation and its Operations* (Binghamton, NY: The Haworth Press, Inc., 1993).

[25] *Federal Reserve Bulletin* 80 (January 1994): A55.

[26] Foreign Investment in U.S. Banking Institutions," (Washington, D.C.: Federal Reserve Board, December 1, 1993); and Daniel E. Nolle, "Are Foreign Banks Out-Competing U.S. Banks in the U.S. Market," Economic & Policy Analysis Working Paper 94–5 (Washington, D.C.: Comptroller of the Currency, May 1994), p. 4.

TABLE 9–3. Foreign Bank Operations in the United States (by country)			
	No. of Banks	*No. of U.S. Offices*	*Assets*
Japan	52	149	57.3
Canada	6	51	57.3
U.K.	10	39	46.2
Italy	13	26	46.7
France	16	37	50.3
Netherlands	3	25	25.9
Total	**299**	**740**	**$832.0 billion**

Source: Statistical Abstract, 1994.

Agencies differ from branches or subsidiaries in that they cannot perform a full line of banking. They can make loans, do foreign currency operations, and operate in the Eurocurrency markets for their parent companies. Their role is to offer financial services to subsidiaries of home country companies. They cannot take deposits but can maintain credit balances. Agencies obtain their funds from the parent bank or from Eurocurrency loans.

Summary and Conclusions

Banks that operate globally are multinational corporations and their management has the same profit motives that managers of nonfinancial corporations have. However, the environment of global banking is different from nonfinancial MNCs in its organizational structure and types and in its regulation.

International banking is accomplished by many different organizational types. In addition to subsidiaries, branches, and agencies of the parent banking firms, international banks operate security affiliates, representative offices, and correspondent banks, participate in consortium banks, own Edge Act banks and shell banks, and may concentrate on wholesale or retail banking or mix the two focuses.

Banks everywhere are fraught with domestic and international regulation. They are profit-seeking firms but also act as fiduciaries for their clients and depositors. International banks are faced with a greater variety of risks than are their domestic counterparts. As such, they must act in a much safer and sound manner and take fewer risks than do nonfinancial corporations. Thus, they are faced with regulation from domestic bank regulatory agencies as well as from central banking authorities in foreign countries.

The international banking system needs special attention from national and international regulators. In the United States, the International Banking Act of 1978 and the Foreign Bank Supervision Enhancement Act of 1991 gave regulatory and supervisory responsibility over foreign banks operating in the United States to the Federal Reserve System. On a worldwide basis, the Bank for International Settlements has some regulatory responsibility concerning the promulgation of rules about bank capital adequacy on an international basis and the formulation of rules concerning failed foreign banks and how they should be handled. Some countries have as many as three regulatory agencies with responsibility over banks, the money supply, and deposit insurance programs. Some countries have very strict bank regulation while others control their banks with "a wink and nod."

Additional Readings

Baker, James C. "The International Banking Act of 1978: Is It Working?" *The Bankers Magazine* 165 (May–June 1982): 15–9.

Fraser, Robert. *The World Financial System*. Burnt Mill, Essex, U.K.: Longman Group, 1987.

Hultman, Charles W. *The Environment of International Banking*. Englewood Cliffs, NJ: Prentice-Hall, 1990.

Key, Sydney J. "International Banking Facilities." *Federal Reserve Bulletin* (October 1982): 565–77.

World Bank Staff, "Approaches to Debt Reduction." *Finance & Development* 26 (September 1989): 16.

Discussion Questions

1. Distinguish among subsidiary, branch, and agency offices of international banks.
2. What are the functions of an Edge Act bank?
3. What are international banking facilities? Why were they established by the Federal Reserve Board?
4. Discuss the role of the Bank for International Settlements.
5. What does the International Banking Act do in the United States?
6. What international banking incident was behind the passage of the Foreign Bank Supervision Enhancement Act of 1991?
7. Distinguish among merchant banks, commercial banks, investment banks, and universal banks.

Problems

1. Identify the top ten international banks by asset size, by market value, and by total deposits.
2. Compile a bibliography of 25 entries dealing with the Bank for Credit and Commerce International and its problems.
3. Find examples of specific international banks that have encountered each of the seven risks discussed in this chapter.
4. Select a developing country and show how the banking system in that country either contributed to or deleted from the country's economic development.
5. Show how foreign banks may have contributed to the economic or institutional development of a specific developing country.
6. List the top ten Edge Act banks in the United States and show their total assets.
7. A bank has the following assets by amount on its balance sheet: commercial loans of $35 million, municipal bonds of $10 million, loan loss reserves of $3 million, fixed assets of $5 million, letters of credit of $20 million, residential mortgages of $10 million, Treasury securities of $10 million, Federal agency securities of $7 million, and real estate loans of $20 million. Adjust these assets by riskiness according to the Basel Accord rules and show whether the bank meets core and total capital requirements. Does it meet Federal Reserve Board requirements?

10

Major Functions of International Banks

Major Objective of Chapter 10

To examine the major functions of international banks: foreign exchange operations, Eurocurrency operations, financing international trade, sovereign lending, investment banking, and global custody.

Key terms to be learned in chapter 10:

- letter of credit
- consortium bank
- U.S. Export-Import Bank
- PEFCO
- COFACE
- Eurocurrency
- sovereign lending
- rescheduling
- The Brady Plan
- Brady bonds

- banker's acceptance
- forfaiting
- ECGD
- shell bank
- LIBOR
- revolving underwriting facility
- jumbo loan
- The Baker Plan
- global custody

Introduction

International banks are essentially organized to provide six major functions: international trade finance, foreign exchange operations, Eurocurrency operations, lending to sovereign countries, investment banking, and global custody and settlement. To most consumers who use international banking services, selling or redeeming international travelers checks may be the only direct contact they ever make with an international bank. However, the role of the international bank in these major functions is far more significant than just what it does for the average retail customer.

FINANCING INTERNATIONAL TRADE

Every year, more than $5 trillion of merchandise goods are traded among the countries of the world. The vast bulk of this trade will have to be financed because a period of time ranging up to three months or longer may be required from the time the transaction is entered into until the goods have been shipped by the exporter and received by the importer. In the meantime, the manufacturer must have payment for these goods so that the production cycle may be maintained. The manufacturer cannot wait until the transaction has been executed. Thus, the transaction must be initially financed.

The bank or its counterpart becomes engaged at nearly every phase of trade financing. This market has become very competitive and the ability of the bank to use some type of financial engineering in structuring the form of trade finance needed by the customer is an important quality needed by all international banks. The following sections are devoted to a discussion of the various techniques used by international banks in financing trade as well as important institutions designed to complement or supplement banks' activities in this area.

Letter of Credit

The average international trade transaction requires several steps and several pieces of documentation. The buyer may have to open a letter of credit (L/C) by order of the buyer in favor of the seller. This is obtained, usually, from the buyer's bank and essentially implies that the buyer's bank will stand behind the transaction. The L/C is a guarantee of sorts and, in cases where the seller has insufficient information about the buyer, such a document will facilitate the sale because it gives the buyer credibility.

A company can have its bank issue various types of export L/Cs. The irrevocable L/C is one issued by a foreign bank—the importer's bank—and which is confirmed irrevocably by a U.S. bank—the exporter's bank. Or the irrevocable L/C can be issued by the U.S. bank at the request of a foreign bank. Also an irrevocable L/C can be issued by a foreign bank without responsibility by the U.S. bank except to advise the exporter that a L/C has been issued. A L/C can also be revocable; however, a revocable L/C is seldom issued. In fact, L/Cs are seldom exercised after being issued although they do add a semblance of integrity and safety to the trade transaction. They are seldom issued where the parties to the trade transaction are from the United States and a western European country. L/Cs can also be issued that are ordered by the importer.

The Draft

A draft, denominated either in the exporter's or importer's currency, will then be drawn by the seller on the buyer. This is essentially a checklike document that will be paid by the importer's bank. An example of a draft is shown in Figure 10–1. This draft is completed by Padova International and drawn on Bank One, Columbus, Ohio, for $100,000 to finance imported inventory from Italy.

The Banker's Acceptance

The draft can be converted into a negotiable or marketable financial instrument when it is accepted by the exporter's bank—done when the exporter's bank stamps "Accepted" on the face of the draft. The draft can then be sold by the bank to a banker's acceptance dealer who then sells it into a special banker's acceptance market dealing with minimum amounts of $1 million or more. The investor who purchases it will hold the draft until it matures, usually up to 90 days, then it is redeemed at the exporter's bank. By this time, the exporter's bank will have collected on the draft from the importer's bank and the final accounting for the transaction will be between the importer and its bank. See Figure 10–2 for a flow chart of the creation and life of a banker's acceptance. This money market financial instrument facilitates international

Draft

BANK ONE.

• • • • • • • • • • • 90 Days • • • • • • • • • • •

April 26 ____ 19 82

Pay to the Order of **BANK ONE OF** COLUMBUS, NA

$ 100,000.00

One Hundred Thousand and no/100———————————————————————— Dollars

To BANK ONE OF COLUMBUS, NA

100 East Broad Street

Columbus, Ohio

Value received and charge to account of
Padova International

authorized Signature

FIGURE 10-1 Example of a Sight Draft International Trade Transaction

trade by moving the initial risk of the international trade transaction financing from the exporter and its bank to a dealers' market. In other words, the creation of the banker's acceptance has securitized the original draft, thus turning it into a negotiable security.

For another example of a bankers acceptance, see Figure 10–3 for the procedure practiced by Bank One of Columbus, Ohio, in creating this type of instrument. Bank One accepts the draft shown in Figure 10–1 and creates a bankers acceptance that will

FIGURE 10-2 Creation of a Banker's Acceptance

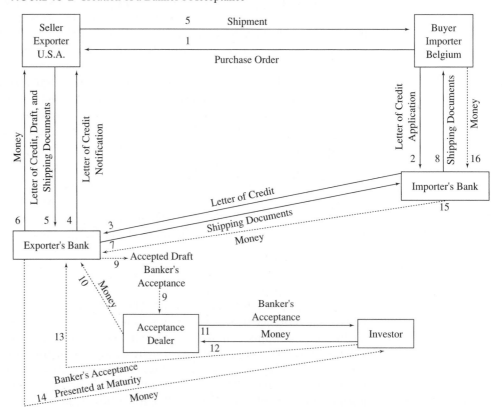

Source: Northern Trust Company, Chicago, Illinois.

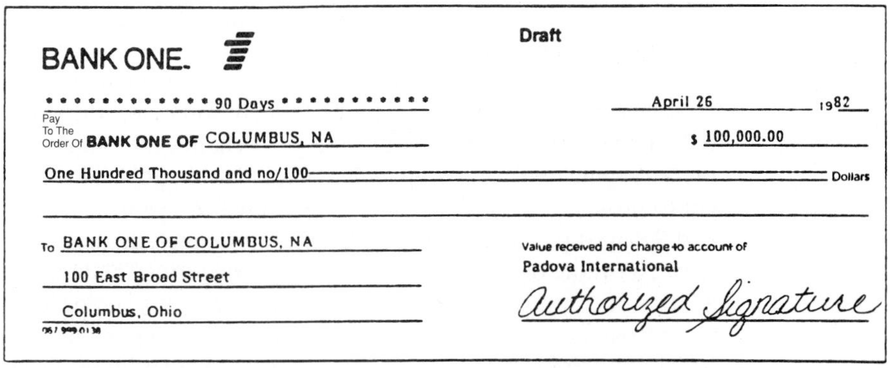

In this example, Padova International completes a draft for $100.00 drawn on BANK ONE to finance imported inventory from Italy. BANK ONE accepts the draft and creates a Bankers Acceptance which will mature 90 days after the acceptance date, on July 24, 1982.

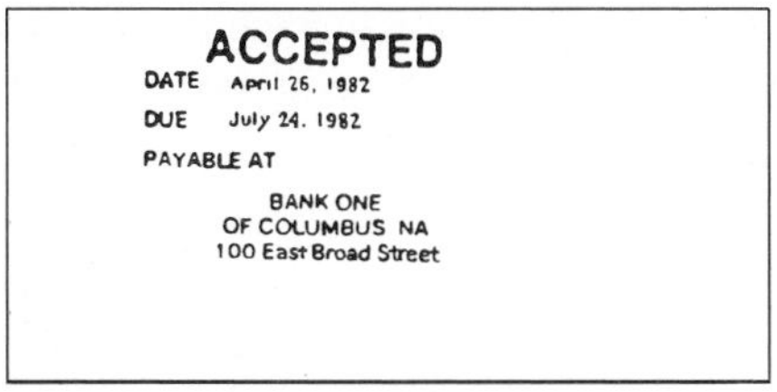

To create a Bankers Acceptance. BANK ONE affixes an acceptance stamp to the draft, indicates the acceptance and maturity dates, and adds an authorized signature.

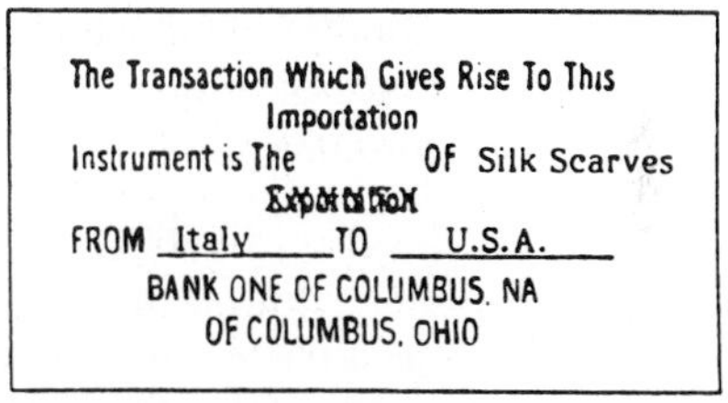

An eligibility stamp is used to describe the type of transaction, the merchandise and the countries of the importer and exporter.

FIGURE 10–3 Bank One Banker's Acceptance

mature 90 days after the acceptance date, or July 24, 1982, by affixing an acceptance stamp to the draft, shown in the top part of Figure 10–3, indicating the acceptance and maturity dates and the authorized signature. In the bottom part of Figure 10–3, the eligibility stamp is shown, which is used to describe the type of transaction, the merchandise, and the countries of the importer and exporter.

NONTRADITIONAL TRADE FINANCE

The types of international trade finance discussed in the preceding sections are generally considered to be traditional means of financing international trade. As companies demand longer dated and more structured transactions, the means of financing such business is becoming less traditional. The following trade finance methods are examples of this trend. The examples discussed are (1) a longer dated structured transaction, and (2) forfaiting.

Longer Dated Structured Transaction

The example discussed in this section is a mixture of project finance, trade finance, structured trade finance, and export finance.[1] Banks are becoming more unwilling to increase risk on their balance sheets, a result of the recently imposed risk-based capital adequacy rules, and, thus, they place trade finance paper and project-related

---

[1] Jonathan Bell and Matthew Ball, "Deals That Spell the Demise of Trade Finance," *Corporate Finance* (April 1996): 14.

notes with institutional investors by securitizing the loans. Trade finance deals are being more and more financed with medium- and long-term funding.

One such deal concerned $310 million in financing for the Angolan oil industry. A 3-year contract was negotiated between Sonangol, the Angolan oil producer, and BP, the multinational petroleum and petrochemicals company. UBS, the Swiss bank, is the arranging bank of a prepayment deal with Angola. The agreement calls for Sonangol to produce 30,000 barrels of oil per day for 3 years. The Angolans must lift the oil and BP must pay for it. The project, therefore, includes both delivery risk and payment risk. The value of the oil is in excess of $310 million. The oil shipments are covered by a letter of credit issued by UBS and a syndicate of a senior lead management group in the prepayment facility. These banks each take 10 percent of the total letter amount, which is 1.4 times the prepayment amount, or $434 million. The contract contains a provision that places a floor on the oil price. The transaction was launched as a $250 million deal but was oversubscribed and increased to $310 million. This amount is to be repaid over 29 equal monthly installments but can be completely repaid within 12 months. Thus, the financing of an international trade transaction takes on the appearance of project financing but with a letter of credit and syndicate arrangement for the funding.

Forfaiting

Forfaiting, a type of nonrecourse financing, originated in Switzerland in the 1950s as a more effective means of financing trade to the Eastern bloc countries.[2] The term comes from the French *á forfait*, meaning "without recourse." Forfaiting consists of a purchase of claims due at some clearly stated future date, which arise from merchandise exports, i.e., series of promissory notes, and without recourse to the seller of the claims, i.e., the exporter. The term "forfaiting" means lack of recourse, i.e., the buyer of the promissory notes forfeits the right of recourse. The seller of the claim is called the forfaitiste and the purchaser of such claims is the forfaiteur. In essence, short- and medium-term financing is shifted to long-term financing and the transaction risk is shifted to a third party.

The banking centers for forfaiting are Zurich and Vienna, although a handful of British, German, and U.S. banks also offer forfaiting services. Credit Suisse and Union Banque Suisse in Switzerland have pioneered in forfaiting transactions. Forfaiting is most appropriate for transactions between $1 million and $5 million involving capital goods such as aircraft, cranes, road construction equipment, or electric generating equipment, which are ordinarily financed over a period 3–5 years or longer.

The annual global forfaiting market is estimated to be $10–15 billion, with $6 billion of new forfaiting paper coming to the market each year. European banks do the vast bulk of forfaiting, handling 8–10 times as much business as do U.S. banks.[3] Capital goods exporters have found forfaiting to be a lower cost alternative than government-backed export credit. In fact, nearly all types of goods and services can now be financed by forfaiting.

To demonstrate a forfait transaction, the diagram in Figure 10–4 showing a basic example of forfaiting is useful. After the exporter (X) and the importer (M) agree on payment, delivery, and other terms, the importer's bank avalizes the importer's note(s), i.e., the bank guarantees payment of the note(s), and sends it (them) to the exporter's bank. Assuming the transaction calls for one delivery and one payment, after delivery

[2] See, for example, James C. Baker and Richard J. Wayman, "Forfaiting: A Little-Known Method of Financing International Trade," *Journal of Commercial Bank Lending* 66 (December 1983: 41–51. Reprinted with revisions in *Classics in Banking II* ed. William H. Sihler (Philadelphia: Robert Morris Associates, 1985).

[3] Nilly Ostro-Landau, "Pushing Forfaiting Forward," *International Business* (September 1995): 12.

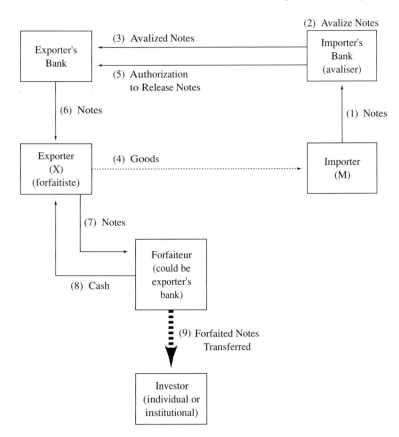

FIGURE 10–4 A Basic Forfait Transaction

is made, the importer's bank authorizes the exporter's bank to release the note(s) to the exporter. If the transaction involves a series of deliveries, the importer's bank will allow notes to be released to the exporter at previously agreed upon intervals, usually every 6 months. Or the exporter can hold the notes to maturity or sell them to a forfaiteur for immediate cash. If the latter occurs, the notes are then transferred into the *á forfait* market and may be held subsequently by more than one investor.

If the exporter does not hold the note(s) to maturity—thus bearing the risk of nonpayment by the importer—the note(s) may be sold to a forfaiteur, the exporter's bank or a third bank. The forfaiteur may then accept the note(s) without recourse to the supplier. This means that currency and credit risks shift to the forfaiteur. If payment is not made by the importer's bank/importer, the forfaiteur cannot go to the exporter for its money. Its only recourse is to the importer. The forfaiteur discounts the note(s) at a rate that is a function of (1) currency denomination of the note, (2) country risk, (3) importer risk, and (4) length of the discount period. The exporter is still responsible for the quality of the goods.

The discount rate used in forfaiting agreements may utilize the "merchants rule" whereby interest is computed on the total amount of the loan represented by the underlying document from date of acquisition to date of maturity and is deducted in advance.[4] The forfaitiste receives the net proceeds at the time the note(s) is (are) sold. The interest discount on each note is based on the following formula:

---

[4] O.E. Judar, "Exploring a European Trade Instrument," *Burroughs Clearing House* 60 (April 1976): 24.

thinking of the eight-year-old hulk in the parking lot. "For the new import-fighting economy Belchfire Six. I want it with turbo, Macpherson struts, quad stereo, electronic quartz brakes and muse fur upholstery on the orthopedic seats. It costs $27,000." His palms grew moist as he spoke.

Whipsaw frowned. "Sorry, babe," he said. "We're tapped out. We loaned $6 billion to the Republic of Tankenibia and they just told us they can't pay zip on it."

Preble was astounded. "How could you be stupid enough to lend that much to one poor country?" he said.

Whipsaw eyed him with a mixture of pity and contempt. "Where have you been living, on Pluto? Places like Tankenibia are the fast track now. Nobody gets promoted by *not* making loans, and nobody gets the office with oriental rugs, live plants and a British secretary by making teeny ones to guys like you. Gotta make country loans to get the big numbers."

But why Tankenibia? Preble insisted. Why not someplace safer? "We did it for the jollies," Whipsaw cackled. "Sure, you can loan to developed countries but they're no fun because they always repay. With the LDCs, the less developed ones, you get some kicks. But if you really want to roll dem bones, you find a BP and stuff money down its throat."

"A BP?"

"Bottomless Pit. A country with no resources, no infrastructure, an incompetent leadership, and poverty that makes you weep. Like Tankenibia. I made that loan," Whipsaw said proudly.

"Is that why you're here? Why you got, uh . . . ."

"Demoted?" said Whipsaw. "I got promoted for that, ace. I got demoted for not shoveling enough into Mexico, and for a prank a buddy and I pulled on Chase. We got a little blitzed one night and telexed them a request for $3.5 billion from the Union of Lilliput. They had a check in the mail before we could tell them Lilliput didn't exist. Lots of hoo-haw over that. But I'll come back if I throw a bif number on the board again."

This made Preble suspicious. "If you can't give me a little loan how can you make a big one to someone else?" he demanded.

"Oh, we can always find dough for a country loan," Whipsaw said airily, "Provided we don't let guys like you peck us to death with petty requests. Right now all our new deposits are going out the back door for our second Tankenibian loan, a $2 billion bailout. We're rolling over the first loan—sort of forgetting about it, really—and giving them the extra so they can develop an economic base and pay off the whole wad someday. Maybe."

Preble recalled that Tankenibia was one enormous swamp. "What kind of economic base could they possibly build?" he asked.

"Egret plumes," Whipsaw replied. "They got egrets coming out their ears. We're helping them create an industry for making women's hats with plumes on them."

Preble was aghast. "Women stopped wearing those in the '30s." He said, "Look around you, man. There's no market."

"Really?" said Whipsaw, only mildly interested. "Well, I guess we'll roll over the bailout too. No skin off my nose. By the time somebody finally pulls the plug I'll be sipping piña coladas in a half-mil retirement condo in Boca Raton. Look, it's lunchtime and I've got to get in front of a sole veronique and an interesting Chardonnay with some biddy who wants to put a pile into our Killer Jumbo CD. Sorry about the car; if you were a country we might have done a deal." And he left.

Dispirited, Preble drove home in the clunker, its valves clicking ominously. It wasn't until the next day that the idea hit him.

* * *

Mrs. Preble returned from a month's visit with her mother to find a new Belchfire in the drive, a crew putting in a swimming pool and carpenters knocking together a wing on the house. "Have you gone nuts?" she said, "We can't afford this."

Preble gave her a broad, smug smile. "Welcome home," he said. "Or, more accurately, welcome to a self-governing province of the New Confederation of Exurban States, duly chartered. Everyone on the block is in, and Citibank coughed up a $1.6 billion infrastructure loan right off. It's not much but it's a start. Our slice was $120 million."

"You lunatic," she cried. "We'll never pay it off. We can't even pay the interest."

"Exactly," said Preble. "Come on inside. We'll crack a magnum of Dom Perignon and I'll tell you about rollovers and bailouts."

Source: William E. Blundell, ". . . How Mr. Preble Got a Piece of the Action," *Wall Street Journal*, 9 February 1983, p. 24. Reprinted with permission of *Wall Street Journal*.

INTERNATIONAL INVESTMENT BANKING

One of the most significant functions of international banks in the last few decades has been international investment banking. Most of the money center banks headquartered outside the United States have no restrictions imposed by their home governments on their ability to operate in the investment banking industry. The Japanese banks, like U.S. banks, are restricted in their ability to underwrite securities because of a law similar to the U.S. Glass-Steagall Act, which prohibits U.S. banks from engaging in the securities business. Japan also has a law similar to this restriction. However, some U.S. banks have underwriting operations outside the United States and some have recently been granted underwriting powers by U.S. bank regulatory agencies. In this section, investment banks' operations in debt, equity, and derivatives will be discussed.

In 1995, U.S. investment banks, despite these restrictions, owned 70 percent of the international debt and equity underwriting business. This business was obtained by gaining the business of U.S. MNCs. The advantage slowly began moving to the European banks. As mentioned in chapter 9, Deutsche Bank, Germany's largest bank, has merged with Morgan Grenfell, Great Britain's 152-year-old merchant bank, to form Deutsche Morgan Grenfell. This investment bank will be Europe's largest. Dresdner Bank, Germany's second largest bank, acquired the British Kleinwort Benson. Swiss Bank Corporation bought the British S.G. Warburg, and the Dutch ING took over the defunct Barings Bank, 300-year-old British merchant bank by actually paying only £1 for the remaining assets of Barings.

European banks, operating as universal banks, can underwrite securities and invest in capital market issues for their own account. For example, German banks, such as Deutsche Bank, Dresdner Bank, and Commerzbank, can underwrite securities of industrial companies, trade for their own accounts on the stock markets, and actually act as trading members of the German *Börsen*. They operate investment management companies, which sell mutual funds, as well as perform a full-line of commercial banking activities.

Several international banks can be cited for their investment banking prowess. Eurobonds, for example, discussed in chapter 12, are underwritten and distributed by international banking syndicates, with lead management banks heading the syndicate. Morgan Stanley earned a Euromoney excellence award in 1994 for its underwriting of the Republic of Italy's debt buyback, an exchangeable offer for a potential $9.15 billion of outstanding debt. J.P. Morgan was cited in 1994 for its excellence as a swaps house, a government bond trading house, and an emerging market debt trading house. This bank has $680 billion of notional principal value of interest rate and currency swaps on its books, having undertaken 17,000 interest rate and currency derivative transactions for 1,300 clients in 1993. J.P. Morgan had 1993 trading volume of $227 billion in debt and Eurobonds.

The investment banking operations of other international banks can be cited. Swiss Bank Corporation has been cited for excellence as a derivatives house, especially in complex long-dated structured products. Chemical Bank arranged $113.5 billion in

syndicated loans during 1993 and early 1994, with 100 more deals than its nearest competitor. Citibank is the leading underwriter of asset-backed debt with $22 billion of assets under management in 12 countries. Some international banks perform custodial functions as investment bankers. Chase Manhattan Bank holds $1.2 trillion in assets for 1,100 customers with a network that covers 58 countries. CS First Boston is the most active broker on the Prague Stock Exchange. Deutsche Bank led a World Bank global bond issue, a 30-year jumbo issue by Austria, and large deutsche Mark denominated Eurobond issues by Crédit Foncier and Volkswagen.

Many of these international banks are permitted to trade in capital market securities for their own accounts. The Big Three commercial banks in Germany hold significant amounts of large German companies. In the 19th century when these companies were formed, German banks loaned them their original capital in return for equity positions in the companies. Thus, an annual report published by Commerzbank entitled *Wer Gehört zu Wem?* is must reading in order to determine what companies are owned by which banks. Société Générale and other banks in Belgium are permitted to own significant shares of industrial companies and are actually large holding companies.

Eurobonds and other foreign bonds, as well as the new global bonds, are underwritten by large international banks. These banks own and operate the two bond clearing houses, Cedel and Euroclear, also discussed in chapter 12. From mid-1993 to mid-1994, the three largest underwriters of deutsche Mark denominated Eurobonds and global bonds were German commercial banks.

The growing market in derivatives is dominated by international banks. These include J.P. Morgan, Chase Manhattan, Chemical Bank, Bank of America, Citicorp, and Bankers Trust. These banks account for 90 percent of the derivatives business, according to the Federal Reserve Board.[36] The market for international derivatives will be discussed in more detail in chapters 13 and 14.

International investment bankers perform all of the usual functions that domestic investment bankers offer their clients. However, in the international market, some functions need to be emphasized. Investors require better research. Global research is becoming more and more important because portfolio managers have been increasingly investing directly in local markets instead of in U.S. dollar denominated American depositary receipts (ADRs) or global depositary receipts (GDRs). The successful international investment bankers rely on local brokers for such research and analysis, especially of initial public offerings (IPO). The international investment banker must be more careful in the service of pricing offered to capital market instrument issuers. In foreign markets, it is normal to wait until the after-market to buy shares because of the emphasis placed by the lead manager on some investment bankers to get the highest possible proceeds from an IPO. European investors often are also reluctant to buy IPOs priced at a lower level than they expected.

The distribution function in the Eurobond market is also an important role of the international investment banker. In the early phase of distribution, the lead bank in a Eurobond issue parcels out some of the issue to a group of underwriter banks and some to a group of selling banks. Some banks may be members of both the selling group and the underwriting group. Many European banks have not made a best efforts basis to sell or underwrite their share of Eurobond issues. Thus, the bonds sometimes are returned to the syndicate lead or colead managers and may have to be sold at a discount. The work of Cedel and Euroclear as market-makers significantly alleviated this problem.

[36] "The Six Men Who Rule World Derivatives," *Euromoney* (August 1993): 45–9.

International banks have significant operations in the mergers and acquisition (M & A) business. Large international banks advise companies and other banks about M & A possibilities and assist in the negotiation of those that come to fruition. These banks bring the parties together, negotiate the terms of the merger or acquisition, assist in the transfer of securities and other payments, and smooth the transition to the post-merger operation. Table 10–8 shows the M & A activity in 1995 for both announced and complete deals by the leading global advising banks.

Finally, international banks are significant parties in the swaps market, both in interest rate swaps and currency swaps. Swaps are entered into by parties that exchange, in the case of interest rate swaps, one pattern of interest rate obligation for another that is preferred over the first obligation—usually the interest rate obligation of a floating rate debt instrument for that of a fixed rate instrument. The principal is not exchanged and the interest obligations are in a single currency. In a currency swap, both the interest obligation and the principal of a debt instrument in one currency are swapped for the interest and principal of a debt instrument in another currency. Currency swaps are discussed in chapter 14 and may be considered packages of forward currency contracts. However, investment banks are quite significant in promoting swaps and some not only facilitate the construction of a swap agreement but actually bring parties together acting as a broker for some swaps where a counter-party has withdrawn from the agreement or initiating a swap agreement with a company that was not originally in the market for a swap.

GLOBAL CUSTODY OPERATIONS OF BANKS

Given all of the significant functions of international banks examined in the preceding sections, these banks act as custodians for a large amount of funds owned by a large number of international business firms and individuals. The management of these banks remembers very well the case of Herstatt Bank, the relatively small German private bank which failed in 1974 and, in the process, drained the currency market of liquidity for a short time and drastically reduced the profits of many international banks

TABLE 10–8.   Leading M & A Global Adviser Banks (for the year ending 1995)

Lead Adviser	Dollars (millions U.S. $)	No. of Deals
Morgan Stanley	154,161.0	153
Goldman Sachs	123,049.5	183
CS First Boston/Credit Suisse	91,877.8	151
Lazard Houses	85,252.8	115
Lehman Brothers	66,597.6	141
Salomon Brothers	64,751.3	118
J.P. Morgan	59,750.4	94
Merrill Lynch	48,789.7	178
Bear Stearns	48,329.5	60
Baring Brothers	38,620.7	45
SBC Warburg	37,504.6	140

Source: Ellen Leander, ''Targeting Investment to Spain,'' *Global Finance* 10 (February 1996): 22.

MANAGEMENT APPLICATION NO. 15

(Caution to the reader: the following case study is included for comic relief and it is not intended to imply that all international business professionals are Michael Milkens or Ivan Boeskys.)

Diary of an Investment Banker
Jean-Claude Komarovsky Leaves Himself in an Open Position . . .

I am discovered. I had crept in quietly from Trumpers when the Boss summoned me. "You bring this house into disrepute," he said. He ground his teeth and waited. A siren howled outside.

I kept a tremor from my voice. "Are you still talking about the Finnish issue? I still think we were right." His spectacles gleamed. "I'm talking about you and your personal behaviour. You spent Christmas in Marrakech with your mistress. In the same hotel was your wife, with *her* lover. And—even I cannot believe this—there was also your mistress's husband—with *his* mistress. Do you want everyone to laugh at us?"

It was true. Imagine my shock when we walked into the restaurant to order Bollinger 1985, and saw all of them there. How could fate have left me with an open position like that, as our chief fixed-income trader might have said when his wife walked into the office party?

I escaped to Paris that afternoon. Patrick Stephenson was on the same flight, but then how can you fly to Paris or return without Stephenson being on the same flight? He is clearly warming up Air France for privatization. "Did you have an interesting Christmas?" he asked innocently. I did not stand for this: Christmas ended 10 weeks before. I checked my hair was straight: "Are you on your way to Ciments Français?" He glared at me. "*Pouf!*" he said, and turned to his papers.

I spent an amusing evening in Paris, and managed my 10 am meeting at the Trésor next morning. I presented my proposal for a $2 billion OAT[1] exchangeable into Saint Gobain shares from 2015, without making an obvious impression. Can I have brought the wrong proposal? No, the World's Greatest Investment Banker does not make mistakes like that.

I barely caught the evening flight to Singapore, hoping the Boss had not left a message waiting for my arrival, appointing me head of African frequent borrowers. But there was nothing waiting for me at the Shangri-la when I checked in at the Garden Wing. I even had time for three sets with the pro before a pleasant massage and dinner. My meeting with government people was not until 11 am next morning, so I set myself up with a hair-do and manicure after breakfast.

I was chasing the privatization prize of the year: Singapore Telecom. There are five firms on the short-list: Goldmans, CSFB, Lehmans, Warburgs and us. Even when the Singaporeans have played us off, there will be left $35 million in fees. That's a lot of issues for Staffan, Veiko and that strange outfit SBAB, whose constitution I find difficult explaining to our syndicate people. I remarked at this at a party in London to Rainer Stefan, and he puzzled me when he said: "Have you ever done an issue for LKB?" He looked at me strangely, muttered, and turned away.

The Singaporeans grilled me but, modesty aside, I was magnificent. I looked tanned and fit, even if my knees trembled. Towards the end, a chubby man in spectacles—I believe he is the finance minister—asked: "Why should we give your firm the global co-ordination role, Count Komarovsky?" I stood up to show him two metres of pure European aristocracy, and replied: "Because we didn't do China Steel, your excellency."

Yesterday I received the answer. They have given the deal to Goldman. When I got back to the hotel, there were three messages to call the boss instantly. My only hope is that he gets called home to become head of global co-ordination.

---

[1] *Obligations Assimilable du Trésor,* a long-term debt issue of the French government with maturities of 7 to 30 years. Most OATs carry fixed-rate coupons and have bullet maturities. Some are convertible into floating-rate bonds. Some have warrants attached enabling the holder to buy further bonds. The 10-year OAT is the benchmark and a new 10-year bond is issued each year. See Euromoney, The 1992 Guide to European Domestic Bond Markets, *Euromoney* (September 1992): 22.

Source: "Caught in the Act," *Euromoney* (March 1993): 22. Reprinted with permission of *Euromoney*.

that had correspondent relationships with Herstatt. At that time, the daily volume in the foreign exchange market was only $1 billion. It is now $1 trillion. Institutional investors represent a large factor in this market. The global custody function is introduced at this point but this subject will be treated more intensively in chapter 18.

Given the fact that international banks with their custodial function hold a large amount of funds sloshing around the world, the exposure to systemic, credit, interest rate, and exchange risks can be very high. One means of coping with these risks and to avoid the Herstatt risk, i.e., systemic risk that one bank's failure will be contagious and lead to other bank failures, is the use of netting agreements.[37] Bilateral and multilateral netting arrangements used by nonfinancial corporations to hedge currency exposure were discussed in chapter 4.

Netting is a rather simple concept. If Banker A owes Banker B $10 million and Banker B owes Banker A $15 million and if the liabilities are netted between the parties, Banker B will owe Banker A only $5 million. Instead of clearing, settling, and converting a total of $25 million, only $5 million has to be cleared, settled, and converted. This represents a large savings in cable and other transfer charges. The highest potential loss if one of the parties defaulted is only $5 million if a netting agreement is in place.

Computer software packages are available to facilitate netting arrangements between companies. The best of these is FX Net, Accord from S.W.I.F.T., and FX Match, available from a Citicorp subsidiary, CrossMar. Of course, netting can be sufficiently simple to be accomplished with nothing more than a bank's calculator.

One simple method to protect the parties if one of them fails to execute the agreement is closeout netting. The agreement between the parties to a forward foreign exchange contract states that all forward contracts between the parties that come due on the same settlement day will offset each other should the transactions fail. Closeout netting keeps a party less vulnerable to the failure of a custodian bank.

Multilateral netting can be accomplished among more than two parties. For example, eight U.S. and Canadian banks recently formed a clearinghouse for their forex transactions.[38] Although forex trades are typically between only two parties, this clearinghouse, called Multinet International Bank, will allow forex dealers to settle all of their trades with other dealers with one payment per currency each day, i.e., a form of multilateral netting. Multinet will initially handle the dollar, mark, yen, British pound, Canadian dollar, French franc, and Swiss franc, and will also clear trading among the members in derivatives as well as foreign exchange.

Summary and Conclusions

Banks play a major role in six areas of international finance. More than 90 percent of foreign exchange trading is transacted within the international banking system. Most of international trade financing is carried out by the banking system. The vast stateless vat of international funds known as the Eurocurrency market is an interbank system. A significant amount of sovereign loans are made by banks. Investment banking, especially outside the United States and Japan, is comprised of international commercial banks that make markets in international bonds, facilitate the issuance of American depositary receipts in the equity markets, and arrange international mergers and acquisitions.

---

[37] Greg Joslyn, "Protective Netting," *Institutional Investor* 28 (May 1994): 151–3.

[38] Steven Lipin, "Eight Banks Form Clearinghouse to Cut Cost of Foreign-Exchange Transactions," *Wall Street Journal*, 1 August 1994, p. A2.

More than 90 percent of derivatives, especially in currency and interest rate swaps and exotic derivatives, are marketed by banks. Finally, large international banks act as global custodians for multinational companies and financial institutions in the settlement and clearance of cross-border financial transactions.

Additional Readings

Baker, James C., and Richard Wayman. "Forfaiting: A Little-Known Method of Financing International Trade." *Journal of Commercial Bank Lending.* 66 (December 1983). 41–51.

Einzig, Paul. *The Euro-Dollar System.* New York: Macmillan, 1970.

Fisher, F. G., III. *Eurobonds.* London: Euromoney Publications, 1987.

Khoury, Sarkis J. "Sovereign Debt: A Critical Look at the Causes and the Nature of the Problem." *Essays in International Business.* 5 (July 1985).

Krieger, Andrew (with Edward Claflin). *The Money Bazaar.* New York: Times Books, 1992.

Miller, Steven. "Coping With the LDC Debt Crisis." *The Bankers Magazine.* 171 (May–June 1988): 29–33.

Smith, Roy C. *The Global Bankers.* New York: Truman Talley Books, 1989.

"Stateless Money: A New Force on World Economies." *Business Week.* 21 August 1978, pp. 77–85.

Discussion Questions

1. Discuss the major functions of international banks.
2. How does forfaiting differ from letter of credit trade financing?
3. What are the differences between the U.S. Export-Import Bank and the Foreign Credit Insurance Association?
4. How does PEFCO finance foreign trade?
5. What are Eurocurrencies? Discuss the market.
6. How do banks affect foreign exchange rates?
7. What is the difference between rescheduling and default in sovereign lending?
8. What are the major differences between the Baker Plan and the Brady Plan for alleviating the LDC debt problem?
9. Discuss the lesson Mr. Preble is making in Management Application No. 14.
10. Discuss the lesson Jean-Claude Komarovsky is making in Management Application No. 15.

Problems

1. Consult the *Wall Street Journal* and *The Financial Times* and compile a list of Eurocurrency 90-day lending rates for five or more major international financial centers.
2. Consult *Euromoney* and find out which are the top banks worldwide in underwriting Eurobonds, in handling Eurocurrency lending, in underwriting foreign bonds, underwriting global bonds, in forfaiting operations, in international trade financing, and in sovereign lending.
3. Consult *Euromoney*, Grabbe's *International Financial Markets*, Solnik's *International Investments*, or other sources and construct a mandate for a sovereign loan by a leading international bank to a less-developed country. Include all relevant terms in the mandate.
4. Compare and contrast the Baker, Brady, and Miyazawa Plans for alleviating the sovereign debt problem.

5. Compile a list of the top 10 global custodian banks and compare their services.
6. List the top 3 international banks shown in the last two annual reports in *Euromoney* to be the leading banks for specific investment banking functions.
7. Assume that a company ships $5 million worth of machine tools to a company located in Poland. The exporter wishes to finance the transaction with a forfaiting agreement. The $5 million liability is payable in five years. The original note is forfaited into a series of 6-month notes each with a discount rate of 20 percent. Using the merchants rule explained earlier in the chapter, calculate the amount of proceeds from each note and the amount of the discount.

PART

V

Inventory of International Financial Resources

Multinational business enterprises have large global needs for funds for both day-to-day operations as well as for long-term projects. These funds may be obtained from a wide variety of financial institutions—both public and private—and markets, which are found in a variety of national, regional, and global settings. The chief financial officer (CFO) of an MNC should be aware of the many financial institutions and markets that may be available to fund company operations. The CFO should develop an "inventory of financial resources" whose funds or market instruments are available and appropriate to fund company operations and projects. Thus, not only should the inventory of financial resources be developed but the costs and benefits of each type of funding should be analyzed.

The inventory of financial resources should include global institutions and markets that are specific to multinational corporate operations. Some of the institutions in the inventory are global enterprises, i.e., those that have global reach in the extent of their financial operations. Some of these global financial institutions will be public, i.e., government controlled, and some will be privately owned and operated. Some institutions are regional in their focus

and operations. Again some of these regional organizations may be publicly owned and operated and some may be private enterprises. Finally, some institutions whose funding operations are available to the MNC are national organizations, which again can be delineated between public and private enterprises.

In addition to these international financial institutions and markets from which firms may obtain funds, MNCs need institutions and markets that furnish tools for hedging the various risks that MNCs face and that have been discussed throughout this textbook. Thus, currency futures and options contracts, swaps, and other forms of derivatives, and the institutions and markets that facilitate their availability are included in the discussion.

Part V contains four chapters that focus on the financial institutions and markets comprising the inventory of financial resources for the MNC. Major public agencies and major private financial institutions—both global, regional, and national—are discussed in chapter 11. Financial markets relevant to funding the operations of multinational corporate enterprise are examined in chapter 12. These markets include Eurocurrency markets, international bond markets, and international equity markets. Markets for exchange-traded derivatives such as currency options and futures contracts are discussed in chapter 13 and markets for so-called plain vanilla derivatives such as ordinary currency and interest rate swaps and new exotic derivatives—all instruments for hedging some type of international risk—are covered in chapter 14.

Non-Bank Financial Institutions in Global Finance

Major Objective of Chapter 11

To examine public and private non-bank financial institutions in global finance relevant to MNC operations.

Key terms to be learned in chapter 11:

- World Bank
- International Development Association
- Asian Development Bank
- European Bank for Reconstruction and Development
- Agency for International Development
- ADELA
- development finance companies
- International Finance Corporation
- Inter-American Development Bank
- African Development Bank
- European Investment Bank
- North American Development Bank
- PICA
- merchant banks

Introduction

The primary functions of the chief financial officer (CFO) of an MNC are to raise funds for corporate operations and to raise these funds at minimum cost. International financial institutions that are not involved in commercial or investment banking operations can assist the CFO in the fulfillment of the first of these objectives, either directly with the transfer of funds to the firm, or indirectly by the transfer of funds to some government agency that in turn funds a project in which the MNC participates. Some financing by these agencies may also facilitate the second objective with relative low cost funds. Institutions representative of such international financial organizations will be discussed in this chapter.

The financial institutions and agencies discussed in the first major section of this chapter are publicly owned and/or operated. Specifically, they are organizations that are owned collectively by their member countries or they are agencies of a specific national government. Their financial resources are available to the firm on either a direct or an indirect basis. For example, if the agency's funds are generally transfer payments from the public agency to a national government and then made available to a company through a contractual arrangement, the funds are, thus, obtained by the firm(s) indirectly. If funds are obtained by the firm from the public agency, the funds are said to have been obtained directly. Those institutions discussed in the second major section of this chapter are privately-owned, by shareholders, partners, individuals, or other firms. They may operate in a manner similar to many of the public institutions.

Three categories of public and private agencies are discussed in this chapter—global, regional, and national agencies—depending on their focus and ownership basis. The organizations discussed in this chapter are not all inclusive but are considered the most important public and private financial institutions whose funds can be obtained, directly or indirectly, by MNCs.

As mentioned previously, it may be possible for the CFO to raise funds directly or indirectly from these institutions in a cost effective way. However, no attempt will be made in this chapter to furnish a comparative analysis of the costs of funds from these agencies. Many of these agencies make floating rate loans. The funds are made available in many forms and their cost may be based on specific projects. Thus, the CFO will have to determine the cost of funds from a given international financial institution based on the specific facts of the project. Negotiations between the firm's managers and the institution's officials may affect the final cost of funds.

Public International Financial Institutions

PUBLIC GLOBAL FINANCIAL INSTITUTIONS

In this section, the discussion is focussed on financial institutions whose funds are available for MNC projects and which are publicly owned and/or operated with a global outreach in their operations. The most significant of such agencies are those that are considered part of the World Bank Group: the World Bank, the International Finance Corporation (IFC), and the International Development Association (IDA).

The World Bank

The World Bank Group is headquartered in Washington, D.C. Its lead organization, the World Bank—The Bank—was established along with the International Monetary Fund at the Bretton Woods, New Hampshire, conference held in 1944 by United Nations members for the purpose of forming the lead financial agencies of the United Nations. The World Bank, also known as the International Bank for Reconstruction and Development, was originally established to make loans to member governments for the purpose of post-World War II reconstruction and for development of poor member countries. Its current activities are limited to economic development loans and related programs for developing member countries.

The World Bank has 176 members that have subscribed mandated amounts of capital. Its original capital amounted to $10 billion. The Bank has other sources of funds including return on its loans, spinoffs of its loans to other financial institutions, and borrowing in the international bond markets. Its subscribed capital in fiscal year 1993 totaled $165.6 billion, an increase from $115.7 billion in 1989. It uses these funds to make variable-rate loans whose maturities generally range from 15 to 20 years, at

rates that are relatively high for developing countries. Such terms are characterized as hard-term loans, although the World Bank loans do have grace periods of 3 to 5 years. The loans are made only for social overhead capital or infrastructure projects, e.g., dams, ports, airports, and other public structures, and the principal and interest must be guaranteed by the recipient government. The proposed projects are analyzed by a team of specialists who examine their economic, financial, and social feasibility.

The Bank has been quite successful during its nearly 50 years of operations.[1] For example, the World Bank made $16.9 billion in loans to such projects in 1993. Its loan portfolio, which has been disbursed and is outstanding, amounts to $104.5 billion and consists of loans made to more than 91 different countries.

An MNC can obtain World Bank funds indirectly by participating in construction projects in countries that have received loan proceeds for such projects. The funds are usually loaned to national government agencies, which then award contracts to domestic and foreign companies to build the project.

It is important to note the World Bank's international financial market activities. The Bank spins off some of its loans to private financial institutions with good global reputations. This encourages the private sector to participate in the development process. In addition, the World Bank floats issues in the international capital markets, which are denominated in several different currencies, have different maturities, and may be global bonds, Eurobonds, or foreign bonds. These bonds are highly rated and are well-traded in international financial markets as a result of the Bank's excellent operational history, its conservative lending policies, and because it loses no money on its investments as a result of the guarantee by the recipient government. In fiscal year 1993, the Bank borrowed a total of $12.7 billion in medium- and long-term capital markets, including four global bond issues amounting to $6.3 billion.

From a geographic viewpoint, the Bank has dispensed most of its loans to Asian and Latin American countries in recent years. In fiscal year 1990, 31 percent of its loans were to Asia, while Latin American and Caribbean nations received nearly 29 percent, European, Middle East, and North African nations received 21 percent, and the rest of Africa received 19 percent. However, during its history, 36 percent of the Bank's loans have gone to Latin American and Caribbean countries.

During fiscal year 1993, the World Bank implemented one of its fundamental objectives, i.e., sustainable poverty reduction. This program was proposed in the *World Development Report 1990*. The Bank completed nine country-specific poverty assessments, providing the basis for a collaborative approach to poverty reduction by country officials and the World Bank. The World Bank had completed twenty-seven such assessments by the end of fiscal year 1993. These assessments assist the Bank in the formulation of poverty-reduction strategies.

An examination of selected cases of World Bank loans in fiscal year 1993 can demonstrate the broad variety in its lending activity.[2] For example, of the 45 loan commitments made by the Bank to the agriculture sector, one was a $325 million commitment to China for 6-year support for the introduction of a bulk grain-handling logistical system in four grain-transport corridors and the development of two national grain markets and a grain-marketing information network. This project also received a commitment of $165 million from the International Development Association, an agency that will be discussed in a following section. In the education sector, the Bank made a $212 million commitment to Brazil for improvements in schooling quality for the first four grades in four northeast states for 3 million children. In the energy sector, a World

---

[1] World Bank, *The World Bank: A Financial Summary* (Washington, D.C.: World Bank, 1990).

[2] The World Bank, *Annual Report 1993*.

Bank commitment for $610 million was made to Russia to support existing oil-production facilities in western Siberia. In the industry sector, the World Bank made a commitment of $250 million to Peru to support the government's privatization program. In telecommunications, the Bank committed $134 million to the Philippines to assist an extension and improvement program for the Philippine Long Distance Telephone Company. In Mexico, the Bank approved a $480 million loan for rehabilitation and resurfacing of paved highways.

The World Bank also sponsors two other agencies that, although they do not make loans, are very important institutions for MNCs operating in LDCs. These are ICSID, the International Centre for Settlement of Investment Disputes, and MIGA, the Multilateral Investment Guaranty Agency. ICSID, discussed in more detail in chapter 5, was established in 1966 and is headquartered in Washington, D.C. It facilitates the arbitration of contract disputes when one party is a foreign investor from a country that is a member of ICSID and the other party is the host state government, also a member of ICSID.[3] This agency also compiles country investment laws, drafts model clauses for companies to use in their contracts that will trigger ICSID arbitration facilities if a dispute arises, and works to encourage member countries to liberalize their foreign investment laws through treaties and other laws.

MIGA is a relatively young organization, which began operations in 1988.[4] This agency insures foreign investment in member LDCs against the political risks of violence such as war or revolution, expropriation of property, interference with contractual obligations, and restrictions on the use of local currency. One of the major objectives of each of these agencies is to encourage the flow of foreign private investment into LDCs. Both institutions were discussed in more detail in chapter 5.

The International Finance Corporation

The International Finance Corporation (IFC)[5] was established in 1957 as an affiliate of the World Bank. Its 147 country members must be members of the World Bank. It is a unique financial institution in that it makes loans and takes equity positions in private enterprise projects in developing countries *without* government guarantee, as must be obtained for World Bank loans. The IFC desires that no governmental interference be present at any stage of these private enterprise projects, although it is usually necessary to obtain government approval of such investments, especially when they are located in developing countries.

The IFC has available some $5.4 billion of capital, including more than $1 billion of paid-in capital and $3.6 billion in borrowings. It can also obtain funds from return on its investments and by spinning off its investments to other financial institutions.

In its first 35 years of operations, the IFC assisted more than 1,000 private enterprises with more than $15 billion of loans or equity in projects whose total book value is nearly $60 billion. These projects range from assisting expansions of existing firms to financing new start-ups in the steel, cement, petrochemical, financial services, tourist, chemical, and agricultural industries. In recent years, IFC has concentrated on investment banking activities, including the formation of investment companies that invest in

---

[3] See, for example, James C. Baker and Lois J. Yoder, "ICSID Arbitration and the U.S. Multinational Corporation: An Alternative Dispute Resolution Method for International Business," *Journal of International Arbitration* 5 (December 1988): 81–95.

[4] James C. Baker, "Global Foreign Investment Insurance: The Case of MIGA with Comparisons to OPIC and Private Insurance," *Managerial Finance* (U.K.) 21 (June 1995): 23–39.

[5] See Bronislaw Matecki, *Establishment of the International Finance Corporation and United States Policy: A Case Study in International Organization* (New York: Praeger Publishers, 1957) and James C. Baker, *Business Expansion in Less-Developed Countries: The International Finance Corporation and Its Operations* (Binghamton, NY: Haworth, 1993).

the equity of companies in a specific country, promotion of foreign investment in LDCs, tracking the stock markets of the emerging nations, and encouragement of private international banks to participate in the development process.

According to the investment policy of the IFC, the agency's goal is to finance no more than the final 25 percent of an acceptable project. Projects are selected after a rigorous analysis of the financial, economic, marketing, and legal feasibility of the project. The IFC ideally divides its investment 50–50 between debt and equity. Projects are usually easier to complete and finance when the IFC considers them for investment. Thus, other private and public investors are easier to attract if the IFC is involved in a project. The IFC prefers that local investors will be dominant in the project but also facilitates foreign investment, especially for the technical expertise needed. MNCs can enter the project at this stage, furnishing technical as well as financial support and, thus, receiving some of the benefits from the project.

The investment application and approval process used by IFC is very complex.[6] The application for an IFC investment must contain preliminary information that any other financial institution would require including a brief description of the project, market and potential sales, technical feasibility, manpower needed, raw material resources available, investment requirements, project financing, government support and regulations and the time scale envisaged for project preparation and completion. An IFC investment officer then decides whether IFC should accept the project and whether further study is necessary. After further project analysis, the investment officer reports to the executive officers of IFC with his recommendation.

The project sponsors must demonstrate to IFC at this stage that the project is economically, technically, and financially feasible. To be economically feasible, a project must meet minimum capacity standards. For example, an ammonia plant, a paper mill, or a cement plant must meet minimum daily capacity standards, although some projects are approved that do not meet established standards. For example, a steel mill in Malaysia was financed by IFC that produced only 200,000 tons annual capacity when 1 million tons was the global standard. The Malaysian plant could produce at a much lower cost because charcoal was used as a reducing agent rather than the more expensive coke. To be technically feasible, a project must have available the necessary labor skills and raw materials. The labor skills can be imported as they were in the case of the Arewa Textile Mill in Nigeria, which was supported by a consortium of Japanese textile mills and their technical support. Financial feasibility is shown when the sponsors demonstrate that the financial plan is realistic in terms of the funds available. To then obtain IFC support, the sponsors must show that the final portion of financing is unavailable at reasonable terms from private sources.

After these procedures have been implemented, the IFC Board of Directors then vote to commit funds to the project. For every project approved by the IFC Board, four or five are declined. Most of those not approved do not meet IFC policies or its charter requirements. Some may be located in nonmember countries. Some may be applications for funds in an amount below that IFC operating standards require. Some projects are at a stage too early to be approved. Finally, others do not meet the IFC criteria for economic, technical, and financial feasibility.

In recent years, IFC has made investments in a wide variety of economic sectors in LDCs.[7] For example, a $60 million commitment in the form of quasi-equity and syndicated loans was made to Pecten Cameroon in Cameroon to develop the Rio del Rey and Lokele off-shore oil concessions. This project cost $123 million. A $305 million pro-

---

[6] Baker, *Business Expansion*, Ibid., 56–63.

[7] IFC, *1992 Annual Report*.

ject to mechanize the technology used by Ashanti Goldfields in Ghana was assisted with a $40 million loan from IFC as well as syndicated loans totaling $100 million and a hedging arrangement for $25 million. IFC made a $30 million loan coupled with $8 million of loan syndications to Panafrican Paper Mills Ltd. in Kenya for an integrated pulp and paper mill. The total project cost will be $161.9 million. IFC also made a $20 million loan to Sierra Rutile Ltd. in Sierra Leone to rehabilitate a plant and infrastructure and to develop a titanium mineral sands mine whose total cost will be $71 million.

The International Development Association

The International Development Association (IDA) was established as an affiliate of the World Bank in 1962.[8] This agency makes infrastructure loans to the lowest income developing countries—some 50 countries with an annual per capita income of $970—on the same basis as the World Bank, only with government guarantee. IDA remains the largest source of low-cost funding to low-income LDCs, accounting for nearly 50 percent of such commitments to these countries. Its loans are made on what is called soft loan terms, that is, no interest is charged, the loans are made for 50 years, and a grace period of 10 years is granted before principal has to be repaid. Only a small service fee is charged on the unpaid balance. IDA made loan commitments totaling $6.75 billion in fiscal year 1993.[9]

IDA has 152 members, all members of the World Bank, and has commitment authority of more than $250 million. Since its repayments are spread over a 50-year period with no payments for 10 years, its funds have been quickly dissipated. Member countries have had to authorize ten replenishments of IDA's funds. The latest replenishment will cover the 1994–96 period and amount to $18 billion in new funds available for IDA loans. Again, as in the case of the World Bank, an MNC can indirectly acquire IDA's funds, by participating in a nation's infrastructure construction after IDA has made a loan to that country.

REGIONAL PUBLIC FINANCIAL INSTITUTIONS

The MNC can obtain funds, directly or indirectly, from public financial institutions whose focus is regional. The most important of these organizations are the Inter-American Development Bank, the Asian Development Bank, the African Development Bank, and the European Bank for Reconstruction and Development. These institutions should all be analyzed and considered for a company's inventory of financial resources.

Inter-American Development Bank

The Inter-American Development (IDB) was established in 1959 as part of the Alliance for Progress, a development scheme to develop Latin American countries with prime support from the industrialized countries of the world and supported by the Organization of American States. Its major objective is to promote the investment of public and private capital in Latin America for development purposes. It is headquartered in Washington, D.C., and was initially capitalized at $1 billion. Its 46 members include Latin American nations as well as industrialized countries of the world but its loans are made only to Latin American members.

---

[8] For a good history of the evolution of IDA, see James H. Weaver, *The International Development Association* (New York: Praeger Publishers, 1965).

[9] The World Bank, *Annual Report 1993*.

The IDB usually finances no more than 50 percent of total project cost. It finances three different areas as follows:

1. development loans to public and private institutions for projects that promote economic development in Latin America;
2. loans to finance projects with high social value;
3. loans that have easier terms than those from the normal money and capital markets.

Defaults on loans made by IDB have been virtually nonexistent and the rate of arrearages is very low. IDB's bonds enjoy a triple-A rating.

Its cumulative lending approvals at year-end 1989 amounted to $41.6 billion for 1,801 loans.[10] Total value of these projects was estimated to be $122 billion. In 1995, the IDB disbursed a total of $4.6 billion to projects and approved a record $7.2 billion for new projects.[11]

Most of its loans have gone to the energy sector, with agriculture and fisheries second, transportation/communications and industry/mining third most important. An MNC can be a successful bidder in a project and receive funds directly from the IDB, as it finances private as well as public sector projects. An IDB project has a cycle of 6 to 8 years during which IDB staff reviews the country's development plans, identifies potential projects for foreign investment, and reviews, analyzes, and approves the projects. The paperwork alone sometimes takes a year or more, especially if costs increase drastically, as they often do in Latin American countries prone to inflation.

IDB's loans to Latin American projects have been made to a wide variety of programs. For example, IDB loaned $154 million to Argentina during 1994 for its ministries of labor and economy to develop a national job training program.[12] This program helped 170,000 unemployed Argentinians acquire skills to enter the job market and its total cost was $221 million. In addition, IDB loaned $50 million in 1994 from its Fund for Special Operations to Colombia for social, institutional, and economic development in Colombia's Pacific Coast.[13] This project's total cost was $71.4 million. Also in 1994, IDB loaned $30 million to Ecuador to reduce urban and rural poverty.[14] The total cost of this project was $33.3 million. A $70 million loan was also made in 1994 by IDB to Venezuela to strengthen and modernize transportation systems in five Venezuelan cities.[15] The total cost of this program, carried out by the National Urban Transportation Fund in that country, was $140 million.

Asian Development Bank

The Asian Development Bank (ADB) began operations in 1966 from its headquarters in Manila, the Philippines. Its major purpose is to foster economic development of Asian nations by making loans to projects in the least developed Asian nations that are members of the ADB. These loans can be to private sector projects without government guarantee. Some of ADB loans are made to national banks in Asia, which are reloaned to private enterprise projects.

Operational data concerning ADB at year-end 1995 reveal that this development bank has contributed greatly to the development of the Asian region during the past 30 years. ADB's authorized capital amounted to more than $23.2 billion. Disbursements by ADB in 1995 rose to $13.4 billion from $12.1 billion in 1994, primarily for invest-

[10] Inter-American Development Bank, *Annual Report 1993.*
[11] Adrienne Fox, "Global Capitalists," *International Business* (March 1996): 52.
[12] "New Projects," *The IDB Inter-American Development Bank* 21 (August 1994): 14.
[13] Ibid.
[14] "New Projects," *The IDB Inter-American Development Bank* 21 (September–October 1994): 12.
[15] Ibid.

ments in the energy sector. Cumulative ADB lending at year-end 1993 amounted to $47.7 billion for 1,255 projects in developing member countries. The five largest borrowing nations have been People's Republic of China, India, Indonesia, Pakistan, and the Philippines.

The ADB practices four major functions, as follows: (1) to make loans and equity investments for the economic and social advancement of developing member countries; (2) to provide technical assistance for the preparation and execution of development projects and programs and advisory services; (3) to promote investment of public and private capital for development purposes; and (4) to respond to requests for assistance in coordinating development policies and plans of member countries. Again, as with the IDB, MNCs can obtain direct or indirect funds from the ADB for participation in accepted projects.[16]

ADB has invested funds in a wide variety of projects in Asian countries. Its 53 member countries, for example, have commited $1 billion for projects in China beginning in 1993.[17] These projects include $200 million for a pumped-storage facility in Guangzhou, $25 million to restructure several fertilizer plants, and $190 million to assist the completion of expressways in Hunan and Jilin. ADB approved a $76.5 million loan for an irrigation and flood control project near Hanoi, the first ADB loan to Vietnam in two decades.[18] Finally, ADB has loaned $7.9 billion of its funds to Indonesia, about 21 percent of all of its funding, for projects in that country.[19]

African Development Bank[20]

The African Development Bank (AfDB), established in 1964 by the Organization of African Unity, is headquartered in Abidjan, Ivory Coast. As of the end of 1993, 76 countries were members of AfDB and 51 of these were African nations. In 1995, AfDB's disbursements fell to $4.8 billion from $5.2 billion in 1994. The average loan made by AfDB amounts to more $41.95 million. The geographic breakdown of AfDB loans was: 64.6 percent to North African nations, 18.4 percent to West African nations, 10.7 percent to Central African nations, and 6.3 percent to southern Africa. Loans made by AfDB in 1993 were broken down by economic sectors as follows: 33.2 percent to industry, 25.5 percent to public utilities, 15.2 percent to agriculture, 15 percent to transport, 8.5 percent to multisectors, and 2.6 percent to the social sector. Cumulative AfDB loan approvals by economic sector through year-end 1993 were: 25.7 percent to public utilities, 22 percent to industry, 21.6 percent to agriculture, 14.6 percent to transport, 10.4 percent to multisectors, and 5.7 percent to the social sector.

Its investments have been primarily in the form of loans but it has focused on equity participation in national and regional development banks and other financial institutions and in telecommunications in recent years. Its loans are made only to governments or their agencies with interest rates comparable to commercial market rates.[21]

A wide variety of loans were made by AfDB in 1993. It made 20 loans to public sector projects and 8 loans to the private sector. Five projects are representative of loans, all for 20-year maturities with 5–7 year grace periods, made to the public sector, and are as follows:

---

[16] Asian Development Bank, *Annual Report 1993.*

[17] VLW, "ADB to Spend $1 Billion in China," *The China Business Review* 20 (July–August 1993): 4.

[18] "World Watch," *Los Angeles Times*, 27 October 1993, p.n.a.

[19] Anthony Rowley, "Nice to be Needed," *Far Eastern Economic Review* 155 (May 7, 1992): 41–2.

[20] Much of the data in this section is from African Development Bank, *1993 Annual Report.*

[21] African Development Bank, *Annual Report 1993.*

1. AfDB loaned $59.3 million to Tunisia for the Sidi El Barrak Dam construction whose total cost will be $191.6 million;

2. AfDB loaned $79.4 million to Gabon for road rehabilitation and improvement whose total cost will be $111 million;

3. AfDB loaned $116.5 million to Algeria for the Koudiat Acerdoune Dam project whose total cost will be $190.8 million;

4. AfDB loaned $46.8 million to Morocco for telecommunications development whose total cost will be $552.5 million;

5. AfDB loaned $109.5 million to Morocco for consolidation of the structural adjustment program whose total cost will be $396.9 million.

AfDB made 8 loans to the private sector, 2 of which are representative loans. They are for maturities of 6 years and have 1- or 2-year grace periods and are as follows:

1. AfDB made a loan amounting to $11.2 million to a car assembly plant with technical assistance from the Citroen S.A. of France and the total cost of this project will be $41.5 million;

2. AfDB made a loan of $8.0 million to a food complex whose total cost will be $57.4 million and will be comprised of an ice cream manufacturing line, a bread bakery, and a biscuit factory.

AfDB made three borrowings in 1993 in two major currency markets. The total amount borrowed was $693.3 million. Of this amount, 56.49 percent was senior debt and the balance was subordinated debt. A 30-year Eurodollar loan raised $500 million while other funds were raised in the Japanese samurai bond market and in the Euro-medium term note market, as well as in the U.S. domestic medium-term note market.

The AfDB has been criticized for the narrow focus of its lending.[22] It has made about 50 percent of its $28 billion in loans to only seven countries—Egypt, Nigeria, Morocco, Zaire, Tunisia, Algeria, and the Ivory Coast. The bank has 46 other borrowing members. It has also encountered loan losses, now amounting to $700 million, and does not have a good record of loan monitoring.

European Bank for Reconstruction and Development

The European Bank for Reconstruction and Development (EBRD) is one of the newest of the international financial institutions, having been established in 1990. Its mission is the development of central and eastern Europe, after most of the countries in this region have disavowed socialist or communist governments and begun to reconstruct their economies based on private enterprise. The agreement to create the EBRD was signed by representatives of 42 nations, as well as the European Investment Bank and the European Community.

The largest shareholder in the EBRD is the United States with 10 percent of subscribed capital. However, European countries as a whole hold the major portion of capital. Capital can be subscribed in U.S. dollars, Japanese yen, or European currency units. The EBRD was established on the principle that at least 60 percent of its loans would be made to the private sector in the recipient countries.

The EBRD focus includes Europe and Central Asia. In 1995, EBRD financing of development projects rose to $6.2 billion from $5.7 billion in 1994. Its funding for 1997 is projected to be nearly $8 billion, mostly for energy projects. Its approved financing

---

[22] "Development Banking: Double Trouble," *The Economist* 331 (May 14, 1994): 81–2.

by country in 1995 was, as follows: Russian Federation Ecu 398.3 million, Hungary Ecu 275.3 million, Czech Republic Ecu 174.8 million, Croatia Ecu 168.1 million, Romania Ecu 161.9, and Ukraine Ecu 119.3 million.[23]

The EBRD has made some controversial loans since the advent of its operations. For example, one questionable loan was for 22.4 million Ecu to Czechoslovakia's state-owned airline, CSA.[24] Air France was a partner in this venture. Air France is headed by Bernard Attali, brother of Jacques Attali, the EBRD's president. Another controversial loan of $72 million was made to a joint venture by General Motors with Hungarian partners.[25] Some questioned why a large U.S. company needed such a loan. Finally, EBRD commited $90 million to a $350 million project to fund development of Ardalin oil field in the Timan-Pechora region, a Russian joint venture, Polar Lights.[26] The IFC agreed to provide $60 million while the Overseas Private Investment Corporation has commited another $50 million. Polar Lights is a 50–50 joint venture of Conoco and the state-owned GP Arkhangelskgeologia.

European Investment Bank

The European Investment Bank (EIB) was established in 1958 by members of the European Community. It makes investments in EC member countries for socioeconomic infrastructure or basic industries. Its loans have maturities of 12 to 20 years. It has three areas of responsibilities as follows:

1. projects involving two or more member governments;
2. promotion of the results of economies of scale by expanding operations of plants or firms in countries with a comparative advantage in certain lines of business;
3. achievement of uniform and high levels of economic maturity within the EC.

North American Development Bank

The North American Development Bank (NADB) began operations in October 1994.[27] This new financial institution was fostered by NAFTA, the North American Free Trade Agreement, with $105 million paid-in and $560 million callable capital. Over time, these amounts will be increased with U.S. and Mexican funds to $450 million paid-in and $2.25 billion callable capital. The NADB could attract $3 billion in funds from other lenders with 1–1 leverage or $15–20 billion with IFC-like 6–1 leverage. The major emphasis of the NADB will be on environmental projects.

Middle East Development Bank

Finally, the Middle East Development Bank (MeDB) will be the latest regional development bank to finance projects in a geographical area. The MeDB is expected to begin operations by 1998 and will be headquartered in Cairo. Its initial capitalization will be $5 billion, with funds from the European Union, United States, the Gulf countries, Israel, and other Middle Eastern countries. Its primary objectives will be to act as a catalyst to mobilize other investment and as a force for change. Thus, its own funds will be rationed in the formative years.[28]

---

[23] Iain Jenkins, "How the EBRD Pushes Money Out the Door Faster," *Global Finance*, 10 (March 1996): 36.

[24] "Growing Pains at the Eurobank," *The Economist* 322 (March 28, 1992): 81–2.

[25] Jane Perlez, "Development Bank Shifts on Hungary," *The New York Times* 142, 30 August 1994: n.a.

[26] *Oil and Gas Journal* 91 (September 27, 1993): n.a.

[27] *Institutional Investor* 28 (March 1994): 67–72.

[28] Carolina Esquenazi-Shaio, "Middle East Soon to be Covered," *International Business* (March 1966): 54.

NATIONAL PUBLIC FINANCIAL INSTITUTIONS

The MNC can obtain investment, trade, or operating funds from a variety of public financial institutions that are agencies of governments, in home, host, or third countries. Among these are so-called export/import banks, foreign aid agencies, and national development banks. MNCs, including firms not headquartered in the institution's home country, can use such agencies or institutions as sources of funds. However, most of these financial institutions concentrate their funding activities on firms headquartered in their home country.

Export/Import Banks

More than 30 countries have an agency whose function is to finance international trade, whether exports and/or imports. Most industrial nations have such an agency and a few developing nations have such an institution. For example, the U.S. Export-Import Bank (Ex-Im Bank) is the sole American agency that finances trade. Contrary to its name, it does not finance imports. It functions by guaranteeing the trade credits granted by U.S. banks for, primarily, short- and medium-term exports by U.S. companies. The Ex-Im Bank finances only transactions that result in U.S. exports. Some long-term loans can be obtained from the Ex-Im Bank for development purposes, e.g., for LDCs to purchase commercial jet aircraft. The exporter obtains Ex-Im Bank guarantees by purchasing a policy for a premium that guarantees the trade credits against a variety of commercial and/or political risks. The cost of the policy is passed along in the price of the exported goods. Such guarantees are usually made because of some risk on the part of the importer.

In other countries, similar agencies can finance trade in a similar method. In Japan, the Japan Import-Export Bank finances imports as well as exports because without imports of key production factors, Japan could not survive economically. In Great Britain, the ECGD—not commonly known as the Export Credits Guaranty Department—has one of the longest histories of international trade financing. In France, CO-FACE, a government agency, does this function. In Germany, Hermes, a private insurance company, performs the government's international trade financing function. Korea is one of the few developing countries that has an active trade financing agency, the Korea Export-Import Bank. Companies from industrialized countries have, in fact, used its facilities over their own government's agency to facilitate import financing needed in joint ventures with Korean companies.

Multinational companies contemplating foreign direct investment in a developing country can, for example, draw on the resources of its home country's export financing agency for guarantees of exports of raw materials or machinery to the foreign site, for guarantee of working capital funds denominated in the local currency, and for guarantee against certain political risks such as expropriation of some types of long-term capital investments in the project. The company can also use the auspices of any local agency that performs this function, since some developing countries have such an

agency. Or the company might use the facilities of an export-import bank from another industrialized country. For example, a U.S. MNC might obtain the credit guarantees from ECGD, the British agency, to finance trade or investment in a project in Egypt, as a result of the expertise of ECGD in that part of the world.

Foreign Aid Agencies

Most industrialized nations have a government agency that makes loans or grants to LDCs for development purposes. This aid is characterized as bilateral aid—aid from one nation to another, as compared with development loans from the World Bank and its affiliates—multilateral aid, or aid from an agency consisting of several member nations being made to one recipient nation. In the United States, the Agency for International Development (AID), a U.S. State Department agency, performs this purpose. In the European community, the Tactical Assistance Committee and the Development Assistance Committee disseminate aid to LDCs. Much of this aid is to former colonies of EC countries.

Foreign economic assistance is generally politically motivated. Much of this aid is given, in the form of grants or loans, by industrialized nations to LDCs to gain their political favor. For example, the United States gave away billions of dollars to European nations, including Greece and Turkey, after World War II for the purpose of reconstruction and to make them strong against the threat of communism. U.S. military aid has been given to Israel to keep it strong and independent against its Arab neighbors. European nations, such as France, the Netherlands, and Portugal, have given economic aid to former colonies in Africa and Asia to keep them friendly and to insure the flow of trade between the former colonial power and its colony. Many U.S. chemical and agriculture companies benefited from the foreign aid given by the U.S. Agency for International Development to support the so-called "Green Revolution" in LDCs, so that these countries could increase their food output. Again MNCs may indirectly receive funds for projects initiated in LDCs as a result of foreign aid.

National Development Banks

Most nations, industrialized or developing, have one or more agencies or development banks that lend or make grants to one or more economic sectors. Most LDCs have such an institution that lends to small projects, some of which may have foreign investment participation. Even in the United States, institutions such as the Farmers Home Bank make loans to sectors where some economic assistance may be necessary. Some of these development banks are public-private joint ventures. Such an example is the Nacional Financiera, a Mexican agency, which has equal ownership from both the public and private sectors.

Although national development banks may be catalysts for economic growth in their home countries as a result of their investments in private enterprise projects, they have not been without criticism. Some of these institutions have perpetuated economic stagnation by financing governmental operations rather than free market projects. Development banks that operate in countries with socialist governments have a tendency to support state enterprise. Thus, they assist in a build-up of the public sector to the disadvantage of the private sector. Their borrowing activities may crowd out private sector firms that seek capital funds. The World Bank has, in fact, been criticized for its investments in these agencies, especially in those countries in which the central government plays a large role.[29]

---

[29] Melanie Tammen, "Privatize the World Bank," *Wall Street Journal*, 17 May 1991, p. A14.

CONCLUSIONS

The publicly-owned and operated agencies discussed in this chapter represent the major global, regional, and national agencies from which an international company can obtain funding directly or indirectly. These representative institutions can form the basic foundation of an inventory of financial resources available to the firm needing funding for foreign operations.

In each case, as the chief financial officer of the international company becomes familiar with these institutions, a cost and benefit analysis should be done with regard to the financial resources the company might obtain from the agency. In some cases, the company may have to cope with too many regulations to make the funds cost effective. At any rate, each institution should be carefully analyzed before the firm uses its facilities.

Private International Financial Institutions

INTRODUCTION

The CFO of the MNC must also include in the firm's inventory of financial resources private financial institutions from which funding may be available. Again, the private financial institutions to be considered in the inventory of financial resources can be distinguished by their focus of operations: global, regional, and national. The key difference between the institutions discussed earlier in this chapter and those covered in this section is that these institutions are predominately privately owned and operated. Major examples of these private financial institutions are discussed in the following sections of this chapter.

GLOBAL PRIVATE FINANCIAL INSTITUTIONS

Some international banking operations can be classified as global private financial institutions. These banks are not owned globally, as are the World Bank Group institutions discussed earlier as global public financial institutions, but their operations are global in nature. They finance business operations and perform international banking functions[30] on a global basis without regard to national borders. However, their stock ownership is generally concentrated among shareholders who reside in the bank's home country. Examples of these banks include Salomon Brothers (U.S), Deutsche Bank (Germany), J.P. Morgan (U.S.), and Goldman Sachs (U.S.). These are mostly American and European banks that engage in a broad variety of international banking functions very well, including both commercial and investment bank operations. Fewer than 50 banks have such global operations.

According to the 1993 Annual Global Financing Guide survey for *Euromoney*,[31] the banks previously mentioned were highly rated in terms of raising capital in international markets for corporate borrowers. Goldman Sachs was ranked second, J.P. Morgan third, and Deutsche Bank sixth. In terms of structuring, pricing, and distributing public Eurobond issues, Deutsche Bank was ranked second, J.P. Morgan seventh, and Goldman Sachs with Daiwa Securities tied for eighth. When considering what banks have served lead managers of a debt issue best as comanagers, J.P. Morgan, Deutsche Bank, and Salomon were among the top 10 banks in this category. J.P. Mor-

---

[30] International banking functions were discussed in detail in chapter 10.

[31] Aline van Duyn and Rosemary Bennett, "Global Financing Guide 1993," *Euromoney* (September 1993): 150–92.

gan ranked second in the arrangement of syndicated loans. In raising capital through private placements, Goldman Sachs ranked best and J.P. Morgan tied for third. Goldman Sachs ranked first and Deutsche Bank with Credit Suisse First Boston tied for third in the structuring, pricing, and distributing of an international offering of equity. J.P. Morgan was ranked best by companies in the provision of financial instruments such as swaps, options, and futures for liability management purposes.

Among other banks with widespread global operations in foreign exchange, money, capital, and derivative markets are Chase Manhattan, Citicorp, Morgan Stanley, and Lehman Brothers, all of the United States, Credit Suisse and Swiss National Bank of Switzerland, Banque Nationale de Paris and Credit Agricole of France, ABN Amro of the Netherlands, and Barclays of the United Kingdom. These banks all operate within the top 25 in each of several international financial functions that service MNCs.

REGIONAL PRIVATE FINANCIAL INSTITUTIONS

Some private financial institutions may be owned globally but focus their financial services in a regional area of the world. Two major institutions that fit this description are ADELA and PICA.

ADELA

ADELA, the Atlantic Development Group for Latin America, was established in 1964 and has more than 200 shareholder banks or companies around the world, each subscribing to a $500,000 equity position in ADELA.[32] Thus, it is a joint venture in which all shareowners have equal shares and its objectives include socioeconomic development of Latin America. It strengthens private enterprise in this region by providing capital as well as entrepreneurial and technical services. Its headquarters is located in Luxembourg.

PICA

PICA, the Private Investment Company for Asia, is a private investment company, which is similar to ADELA in that its ownership is composed of equal shares of $500,000 subscribed by international banks and financial institutions. Its emphasis is on loans to private enterprise projects in Asian developing countries whose objectives are economic development.[33]

NATIONAL PRIVATE FINANCIAL INSTITUTIONS

Several financial institutions operate on a national basis, i.e., they are predominately owned by the citizens of the home country, and offer financial services to international companies, both from the home country and from foreign countries. Among these, the most important are commercial banks, or their equivalent, investment banks, development finance companies (DFCs), Edge Act companies (EACs), and quasi-private agencies, those which are privately owned and operated but which have strong ties to the government. The major international functions of these institutions will be discussed in this section.

Commercial Banks

All countries have private institutions that perform international banking functions but which may be called something else. In the United States and Canada, they are referred to as commercial banks. In Great Britain, they may be called merchant

---

[32] Baker, *International Business Expansion*, 17.
[33] Ibid.

banks, although merchant banks usually are restricted to financial activities aimed at business firms. In France, they are banques d'affaires. In Germany, they are Kredit-banken, or credit banks. In fact, in some countries, these organizations are still government-owned, as in Korea and India. However, where they are government-owned, the trend is toward privatization since privately owned banks seem to function more efficiently. International banks and their environment were discussed in detail in chapter 9.

Banks may be chartered by the national government in which they operate. This is the most common method for chartering banks. Or they may be chartered by the state government subdivision. This is done only in the United States and the result is the dual banking system with some banks chartered by the U.S. Comptroller of the Currency and other banks—the vast majority—chartered by a state government agency. U.S. banks can be chartered by one agency or the other but not by both. Thus, the United States is unique in that some banks are supervised by a federal agency and others by a state agency. For those banks whose deposits are insured by the Federal Deposit Insurance Corporation, such banks are supervised by two federal agencies.

International banking firms may organize in a variety of ways. They can perform a full-line of banking activities including making loans and taking deposits with branches or subsidiaries. Some international banks form agencies that cannot take deposits but can make loans, trade foreign exchange, and make Eurocurrency loans. Some foreign banks have formed wholly-owned securities affiliates, especially in the United States, which can perform some investment banking functions such as stock market trading and underwriting securities. Most international banks maintain representative offices in foreign countries. These offices cannot perform a full-line of banking. They mostly operate as promotional offices for the parent bank's services, although some of them do operate as loan production offices. Some international banking firms operate solely in the wholesale banking field, offering their services to international companies. Some operate in the retail banking area, offering loan and deposit services primarily to consumers, as the Japanese banks do in California.

Merchant Banks

Some international banking is performed by merchant banks. This type bank was discussed in chapter 9. The merchant bank is a form of banking that evolved in Europe and has spread to other regions of the world including Asia. Merchant banks undertake a wide range of financial activities including literally all banking activities except demand deposits and the insurance business.

Several merchant banks are British in origin. Among them was the now defunct Baring Brothers Bank, or Barings Bank, one of the oldest merchant banks. It failed early in 1995 when a bank employee caused the bankruptcy of Baring by alleged unauthorized trading in futures contracts. Other British merchant banks include Kleinwort Benson, Robert Fleming, and Morgan Grenfell, the latter recently merged into Deutsche Bank to form Deutsche Morgan Grenfell.

Privately Held and Private Banks

In some countries, particularly Germany, privately held banks carry out significant banking operations for companies. Nearly one-third of banking assets in Germany are held by these private banks. These are relatively small privately held banks that perform a full-line of banking. Each was established by a coterie of wealthy German businessmen and, in some cases, as long ago as the 16th century.

Private banking has been practiced in Switzerland for more than 200 years, offering money management to very wealthy people around the world. These institutions now provide portfolio management products for high net worth private clients as well as retail investors and institutions. They now offer internationally competitive financial

services. Swiss private banks established *fonds internes* to serve their smaller clients. These are larger funds comprised of pools of client assets that can be managed more actively and at a lower cost to small retail investors.

Investment Banks

Investment banks are financial institutions that operate in the money and capital markets, primarily in the latter. They facilitate the issuance of debt and equity issues with their services of consulting on the proper financial instrument to use, pricing of the issue, underwriting it, and distribution of the stock or bond.

In most countries, banks perform both commercial and investment banking functions. In the United States, as previously mentioned, these functions have been separated between commercial banks and investment banks by the Glass-Steagall Act. Japan has a similar law separating commercial and investment banking. In the United States, companies such as Merrill Lynch, Goldman Sachs, Morgan Stanley, Smith Barney Upham, and Salomon Brothers perform a wide variety of investment banking operations ranging from facilitating the issue of commercial paper, a short-term money market instrument issued by major corporations, to underwriting and distributing global, foreign, and Eurobond issues, to initial public offerings of stock or the marketing of American depository receipts (ADRs) or American shares, two different methods for issuing and marketing stock of foreign companies in the United States.

The difference between ADRs and American shares depends on their introduction to the U.S. stock market. Most ADRs are issued by international banks that hold the original shares in their vaults for safekeeping. An ADR is then issued and represents some specific amount of the original shares. Glaxo Holdings PLC, listed on the New York Stock Exchange, is an example of an ADR. American shares are registered by the foreign firm directly into the American market and are usually sold in the NASDAQ National Market or over-the-counter (OTC). Philips Lamp, the large Dutch company, has issued American shares into the U.S. market. ADRs are discussed in more detail in chapter 12.

In Europe, banks such as Deutsche Bank, Barclays, Credit Suisse, ABN-Amro, Société Générale, and Banque Nacional de Paris carry out major investment banking operations. They operate as lead managers of international syndicates of banks that underwrite and distribute Eurocurrency issues, short- and long-term, for major companies as well as for sovereign governments. They coordinate issues, arrange them, and provide funds for company operations. Most of the exotic derivatives market is composed of fewer than ten of these banks.

Development Finance Companies

Development finance companies (DFCs) are predominately privately owned finance companies located in LDCs. These companies acquire funds in the money and capital markets and make investments in small business enterprise in LDCs, much like the International Finance Corporation (IFC), discussed earlier in this chapter, but on a much smaller basis. In fact, the IFC was instrumental in the formation of most of these companies, through the work of its Development Bank Services Department, beginning in 1961.[34] DFCs promote economic development in their home countries by investing in private enterprise projects.

The activities of DFCs include[35]:

1. arrangement of general industrial surveys and feasibility studies for special projects;
2. formulation of specific proposals for new enterprises;

---

[34] Ibid., 71–87.

[35] Ibid., 74.

3. assistance in finding technical and entrepreneurial partners for local clients or for foreign investors;

4. investment in share capital and underwriting securities, in order to attract other investors;

5. arrangement of mergers in order to create more economic industrial units;

6. development of a capital market by working to broaden ownership and by other devices;

7. encouragement of the acceptance of new ideas in the economic sector.

Summary and Conclusions

The CFO of the MNC is responsible for funding the company's day-to-day and long-range operations. To facilitate this function, it is wise to develop an inventory of financial resources. This inventory will make available information to the firm concerning the relevant financial institutions that can furnish financial resources. These institutions are comprised of those owned and operated by global public organizations and national governments. These are the public international financial institutions and can be analyzed according to their global, regional, or national emphasis of operations. Private international financial institutions are also available to furnish funds for the MNC or to offer other financial services such as the arrangement of mergers and acquisitions or evaluation of foreign investment projects. These also can be analyzed according to their global, regional, or national scope of operations.

The CFO should be aware of such public global financial institutions as the World Bank, the International Finance Corporation, and the International Development Association. Regional development banks are among the public agencies that offer financing to investments in regional areas and include the Inter-American Development Bank, the African Development Bank, and the Asian Development Bank. Private institutions such as ADELA and PICA finance investments in regional areas. Many national government-owned agencies can facilitate investment or financing funds and include export-import banks, foreign aid agencies, and development banks. Private financial institutions such as commercial and investment banks, Edge Act companies, and development finance companies may offer MNCs funds for investment or working capital needs.

These institutions can make available financial resources on a direct or an indirect basis. The World Bank makes loans to countries to fund social overhead capital projects. The funds can be made indirectly available to firms that successfully bid on construction contracts to develop and complete the projects. Other agencies such as the International Finance Corporation make loan or equity funds available directly to companies to develop private enterprise projects in LDCs.

Additional Readings

Baker, James C. *Business Expansion in Less-Developed Countries: The International Finance Corporation and Its Operations*. Binghamton, NY: Haworth, 1993.

DeWitt, R. Peter, Jr. *The Inter-American Development Bank and Political Influence*. New York: Praeger, 1977.

IFC. *Annual Report*. Any year.

Morris, James. *The Road to Huddersfield: A Journey to Five Continents*. New York: Pantheon Books, 1963.

Weaver, James H. *The International Development Association*. New York: Praeger, 1965.

World Bank. *Annual Report*. Any year.

Discussion Questions

1. What is the difference between the World Bank and the International Development Association in their economic assistance?
2. What is unique about the International Finance Corporation?
3. Discuss the effectiveness of the regional public financial institutions.
4. Discuss and analyze a national development bank from the United States, Korea, Germany, and Kenya.
5. What specific roles do ADELA and PICA play? How are they owned?
6. Discuss the distinguishing characteristics of commercial banks, merchant banks, and private banks.
7. What do Edge Act companies do?
8. What is the difference between national development banks and development finance companies?

Problems

1. After consulting annual reports of the World Bank and the International Development Association, make a list of 10 countries in which both institutions have made project loans during the past 10 years and include the project financed and the amount of the loans.
2. Compile a list of ten specific projects by industry, country, amount, and type of investment, i.e., loan or equity, that the International Finance Corporation has made during the past 10 years.
3. Compile a list of financial services offered by five leading British merchant banks.
4. Compile a list of export-import financing institutions that operate around the world.

International Financial Markets

Key terms to be learned in chapter 12:

- Eurocurrency
- Eurobank
- bearer security
- Pfandbrief
- syndication leader
- mandate
- front-end fees
- participation fees
- residual pool
- floating rate notes
- Eurobonds
- Euroclear
- underwriter bank
- Cedel
- American depository receipts
- World Stock Index

- LIBOR
- Ecu bond
- registered security
- lead manager bank
- managing bank
- best-effort syndicate
- management fees
- override/praecipium
- agency fee
- global bonds
- foreign bonds
- selling bank
- bond repurchases
- global depository receipts
- SEAQ
- Tapstock technique

Introduction

The multinational corporation (MNC) needs to include international financial markets in its inventory of international financial resources. The major markets are (1) the Eurocurrency markets, (2) international and foreign bond markets, (3) foreign equity markets, (4) currency futures and options markets, (5) currency and interest rate swaps,

and (6) the market for so-called international exotic derivatives. The MNC can finance its short- and long-term funds needs and hedge currency, commodities, and other prices from these markets. The focus will be on Eurocurrency, debt, and equity markets in this chapter. Derivatives markets for exchange-traded currency futures and options will be covered in chapter 13, while derivatives not traded on exchanges, such as interest rate and currency swaps, some options, and so-called "exotic" derivatives will be treated in chapter 14.

Eurocurrency Markets

The interbank operations of the Eurocurrency markets was discussed in chapter 10 as a major function of international banks. The Eurocurrency market has several important characteristics. It is primarily an interbank market, centered in London, but it has submarkets in other major financial centers such as Singapore, Bahrain, Hong Kong, and Luxembourg. The new issue Eurobond or long-term portion of this market is centered in London and Luxembourg. However, marketing of Eurobonds is a multicountry function. The major portion of the Eurocurrency market is in short-term 90-day loans used for working capital or trade financing purposes. It is a rather impersonal market facilitated by electronic funds transfer systems. The interest rates charged are those offered by major banks to each other in the interbank market. If that market is centered in London, the rate is known as the London Interbank Offer Rate (LIBOR).

EUROCURRENCY CENTERS

In addition to the London center in western Europe, Bahrain in the Middle East, and Singapore in Asia, other Eurocurrency centers are available for business firms. Eurobanks operate in the Caribbean and Central American region from the Cayman Islands and Curaçao, in the Netherlands Antilles. In the United States, international banking facilities (IBFs), a special function permitted U.S. banks, discussed in detail in chapter 9, can do some Eurocurrency operations but cannot issue certificates of deposits (CDs), or get FDIC insurance, although as stated earlier, Eurocurrency deposits are not insured.

International Debt Markets Long-Term

International bond markets furnish long-term debt capital with which MNCs finance direct investments in plant and equipment. Companies have available four different types of long-term debt issues to finance such investments. One of these, the domestic bond, is not an international bond. It is, of course, available for portfolio investment by foreign investors. The domestic bond is issued locally by a domestic borrower and is usually denominated in the local currency. The other three bonds are relevant to the discussion of international bonds. They are the global bond, the foreign bond, and the Eurobond. These bonds will be discussed in more detail in subsequent sections.

New issues in the international bond market amounted to $481 billion in 1993, 40 percent higher than in 1992 and a new record.[1] After redemptions and repurchases, net issues in 1993 amounted to $184 billion, also a record. These issues were well divided between liquid issues and custom-made debt instruments, including a large amount of

---

[1] Bank for International Settlements, *64th Annual Report*, p. 105.

TABLE 12–1.   International Bond Issues Type and Currency Structure (1990–1993) (billions U.S. $)

Sectors/Currencies	Announced Issues*				Net Issues*				Stocks at
	1990	1991	1992	1993	1990	1991	1992	1993	End 1993
Total issues	241.7	317.6	343.8	481.1	132.1	170.5	119.3	183.8	1,849.8
Straight fixed rate issues	166.2	256.2	276.7	373.1	80.8	142.0	115.3	193.7	1,389.9
of which: U.S. dollar	52.2	75.0	90.9	113.1	16.0	27.9	41.2	63.8	455.1
Japanese yen	30.2	39.1	39.6	49.2	24.8	20.7	3.6	14.3	233.6
German mark	7.3	12.2	29.2	50.2	1.3	4.8	17.1	27.0	142.0
Floating rate notes	42.5	19.0	42.9	68.5	28.2	3.5	23.7	44.7	263.3
of which: U.S. dollar	15.0	4.4	25.1	43.0	7.6	−5.1	14.8	31.7	157.1
Pound sterling	10.8	7.6	5.4	8.6	6.9	4.6	3.0	3.5	44.3
German mark	8.2	2.8	3.5	3.9	7.3	2.7	1.9	2.7	25.2
Equity-related issues	33.1	42.4	24.2	39.6	23.1	25.0	−19.8	−54.6	196.7
of which: U.S. dollar	19.5	24.9	12.9	19.5	15.9	15.1	−20.0	−54.8	110.0
Swiss franc	8.2	7.0	5.3	9.8	4.1	2.3	−2.8	−3.6	43.8
German mark	1.9	4.7	2.1	2.3	0.7	3.7	1.5	−2.0	16.9

* Flow data at current exchange rates.

Source: Bank for International Settlements, *64th Annual Report,* p. 107.

global bond issues. Among the custom-made issues were a number of FRNs, floating rate notes, with caps, which fix maximum coupons, and collars, which set minimum and maximum coupons. Euroconvertible issues by non-Japanese Asian borrowers were popular because of the strong local equity markets.

Several measures to deregulate markets for international bonds were put into effect in 1993 and affected activity in these markets.[2] The Japanese government permitted Japanese banks' overseas subsidiaries to underwrite Euro-yen bonds, eased rating requirements for issuance on the domestic market, shortened the notification requirements for Euro-yen issues by Japanese companies and abolished the 90-day waiting period for the purchase by domestic investors of Euro-yen bonds issued by foreign governments and international agencies. The Swiss government relaxed regulations for foreign Swiss franc issues that had required the lead manager to be located in Switzerland or Liechtenstein. The Swiss stamp duty on debt issues was abolished. The Italian government authorized foreign banks to be lead managers and to trade in Euro-lira securities on the same footing as Italian banks. The French abolished the VAT, value added tax, on issuance fees in the French bond market.

This wave of deregulation has resulted in more homogeneous national debt markets and the increasing integration of global securities markets. More and more borrowing, investment, and trading have been across borders. The type and currency structure of international bond issues for the 1990–93 period is shown in Table 12–1, and the issuing activity in the international bond markets is shown in Table 12–2.

International bonds, whether global bonds, Eurobonds, or foreign bonds, have their own terminology and processes. They are distributed by syndications of banks. Each syndication has a lead bank or banks that fulfills three tasks: the negotiation of the terms of the loan with the borrower such as maturity, rates, price, etc., placement of the bonds with that group of lenders that forms the optimum syndicate for the borrower, and service of the debt by ensuring that the required provisions of the debt agreement and other documentation are implemented.

[2] Ibid., 106.

TABLE 12-2. Issuing Activity International Bond Markets (billions U.S.$)

Currencies	Net Issues* 1990	1991	1992	1993	Amounts Outstanding at End-1993
All issues	132.1	170.5	119.3	183.8	1,849.8
U.S. dollar	39.5	37.9	36.0	40.7	722.2
Japanese yen	26.8	20.6	5.9	20.5	252.0
German mark	9.2	11.2	20.5	27.6	184.1
Italian lire	6.0	9.3	6.2	9.6	29.5
French franc	7.8	15.9	21.8	34.1	92.4
Pound sterling	16.1	20.6	11.2	27.2	146.3
Canadian dollar	1.6	14.1	7.4	20.4	80.5
Swiss franc	7.4	5.4	−6.7	−2.8	149.9
Dutch guilder	−0.3	0.9	4.7	6.0	32.9
Spanish peseta	1.6	3.0	1.6	3.9	10.6
Ecu	11.2	26.2	10.3	−4.2	90.0
Other	5.1	5.4	0.4	0.7	59.5

* Flow data at current exchange rates.

Source: Bank for International Settlements, *64th Annual Report,* p.108.

The syndicate leader may invite one or more other banks to be managers or co-managers of the issue. The managing bank(s) takes a substantial position in the particular bond issue and assists in the marketing strategy and implementation. It(they) participates in the fee structure of the deal.

The mandate is the grant given to the syndicate leader by the borrower to provide funds on the agreed terms. The terms in the mandate dictate what the spread will be and spell out the fee structure in which the syndicate banks will participate.

A best-effort syndicate is one in which the syndicate leader has received the mandate from the borrower but has agreed to underwrite only a portion of the issue or none of it at all. The bonds are offered to the general public at specified terms, and if the issue is not successfully sold on the market, the offer may be withdrawn. The borrower must then seek some other alternative for funds.

RISK IN DEBT MARKETS

A number of different types of risk may be encountered by investors in the long-term debt markets. Interest rate risk affects the value of the principal of debt securities. If interest rates rise, the value of the bond declines. Reinvestment risk may affect the investor. If interest rates decline, the bond may be called by the issuer in order to refinance at a lower coupon rate. The investor will then have principal to reinvest at lower returns. Many bonds will have a call provision in the terms of the bond, or indenture, which precludes the issuer from calling the bond within some fixed time period, e.g., 5 years. Bonds with a call provision will require a higher required rate of return by the creditor because of the reinvestment risk, thus increasing the cost of capital to the borrower. Sovereign borrowers, i.e., governments or government agencies, may default on the terms of an issue or an issue may need to be rescheduled, i.e., more liberal terms will be written. The creditor may lose some or all of the interest income or the value of the bonds may decline because the market for these bonds demands a

higher return to offset the risk of a collapsing issue. Liquidity risk may affect some bondholders, particularly U.S. money managers, if the secondary market is thin and bonds cannot be sold readily without taking a hit to the price. In addition, currency risk may affect the value of interest or principal payments.

GLOBAL BONDS[3]

Global bonds were first issued in 1989 and 1990 when the World Bank borrowed in the international capital markets by floating global bonds denominated in U.S. dollars. Following are the key features of global bonds[4]:

1. they are large in size, usually $1 billion or more;
2. they are generally given the highest grades by bond rating services, e.g., Aaa or AAA;
3. they are noncallable with intermediate maturities of 5, 7, or 10 years and longer maturities to 40 years;
4. they are offered for simultaneous placement in the United States, Europe, and the Far East by an international syndicate of banks active in the worldwide trading of U.S. dollar bonds;
5. they are traded on a "home market" basis in each region;
6. their interest is non-U.S. source income exempt from witholding tax but they are, otherwise, not tax exempt generally.

Global bonds are traded by the sponsoring investment dealers from their Eurobond desks in London, their government agency desks in New York and their most active U.S. dollar desk in Tokyo. Recently, global bonds have also been floated by large MNCs, including the Japanese electronics manufacturer Matsushita, which floated a $1 billion, 10-year issue on July 15, 1992, the first global bond by a corporate borrower.[5] In 1993, a total of $42 billion of global bonds were brought to market, compared with a total of $37 billion issued at the end of 1992.[6] Of this amount, corporations issued $5.3 billion.

Legal differences from one country to another present many problems to issuers of global bonds.[7] Global issuers must be aware of the extraterritorial reach of U.S. securities laws. When a global issue is made in the United States, the issuer becomes subject to several restrictions including insider trading rules and improper payments to government officials, the latter a result of the 1977 Foreign Corrupt Practices Act. This act will be discussed in detail in chapter 16. Non-U.S. issuers seldom encounter such regulations.

One such problem hampering the development of the global bond market was resolved by the World Bank's October 20, 1993, DM 3 billion global bond issue listed simultaneously in London and Frankfurt.[8] Bonds issued in Europe are bearer bonds whereas those brought by U.S. investors have had to be registered bonds. Bearer bonds or shares are those that do not have anyone's name registered on the certificate—the usual practice in Europe. Thus, from a legal standpoint, bearer bonds or shares are es-

---

[3] Information on global bonds found in this section is from *Euromoney's* publication, *The Capital Markets Yearbook* (March 1994) p. 10.

[4] World Bank, *Global Bonds* (Washington, D.C.: World Bank) p.n.a.

[5] Brad Asher, "Matsushita Issues First Global Bond by Corporate Borrower," *FM Collection* 7 (Fall 1992): 17.

[6] "Global Bonds," *The Euromoney Capital Markets Yearbook* (March 1994) p. 10.

[7] George B. Adams and Katherine Ashton, "A Global Issuer's Guide to the US Minefield," *Euromoney* (August 1994): 23.

[8] "Eurobond Lawyers Ride the Bull Market . . .," *International Financial Law Review* 13 (February 1994): 12.

sentially legal tender in the hands of the holder or bearer. Registered bonds or shares do have the owner's name registered on the certificate—the usual practice in the United States. A ruling by the U.S. Internal Revenue System in November 1993 approved a structure for the sale and transfer of bearer bonds held by non-U.S. investors to U.S. investors, by enabling bearer bonds to be converted into registered bonds.

The transaction is facilitated by the issuance of two global certificates, one of which is in registered form and the other is in bearer form. Each time a trade takes place across the two systems in the United States and Europe, the face value of the two

TABLE 12-3. Data on Global Bond Issues By Lead Managers (through year-end 1993)

	Millions U.S.$	Issues
Top 10 Lead Managers		
Goldman Sachs	10298.63	12
Salomon Brothers	8691.20	11
Merrill Lynch	6696.65	17
Lehman Brothers	5836.34	10
ScotiaMcLeod	2617.64	8
J.P. Morgan	2424.65	3
Industrial Bank of Japan	2305.59	5
Daiwa Securities	2048.87	2
Morgan Stanley	1830.93	3
Nomura Securities	1501.61	4
Top 10 Colead Managers		
Merrill Lynch	4176.05	23
J.P. Morgan	4065.27	20
Goldman Sachs	3433.59	22
Credit Suisse First Boston/Credit Suisse	3315.87	21
Industrial Bank of Japan	2996.40	17
Morgan Stanley	2840.96	18
Nomura Securities	2758.88	19
Union Bank of Switzerland	2566.38	16
Deutsche Bank	2334.46	15
WoodGundy	1845.29	9
Top 10 Issuers		
Province of Ontario	10125.84	6
Republic of Italy	8182.64	3
World Bank	8119.99	5
Kingdom of Sweden	3500.00	2
Republic of Portugal	1839.21	2
Province of Quebec	1770.42	2
Ford Motor Credit	1500.00	1
Korea Electric Power Corp.	1350.00	1
Ontario Hydro	1204.14	1
PDV America	1000.00	1

Source: "Global Bonds," *The Euromoney Capital Markets Yearbook.* (March 1994): 10.

global bond certificates will be amended according to the style of registration or non-registration use.

Global bonds have been issued denominated in seven currencies in addition to the dollar. These include the Canadian dollar, the Australian dollar, yen, deutsche Mark, Finnish markka, Swedish krona, and the Ecu. Most global bonds are issued as fixed rate instruments with only 5 percent using floating rate structures. The four top lead managers of investment banking syndicates for global bond issues include Goldman Sachs, Salomon Brothers, Merrill Lynch, and Lehman Brothers, with a total of 50 issues since the advent of global bonds. These large jumbo bonds will become popular in the future when the dollar, yen, and mark become the most important currencies of denomination and where trading in simultaneous markets in the Triad areas will be more and more important. Currently, some companies—Matsushita Electric and Ford Motor Credit—have been dissatisfied with the global distribution of these bonds. Recent global bond issues by these companies were distributed mostly in the United States because of liquidity problems in Europe and Japan. See Table 12–3 for data on global bond issues by lead manager banks.

FOREIGN BONDS

Foreign bonds are issued in a local market by a foreign borrower, with the assistance of a large investment banker, and are denominated in the local currency. For example, General Motors might issue a debenture in Switzerland denominated in Swiss francs to obtain long-term funds for financing European operations. Foreign bonds have been given nicknames depending on where they are issued. The Yankee bond market designates issues by foreign companies in the United States. Samurai bonds are bonds issued in Japan by foreign companies or institutions. Rembrandt bonds are foreign bonds issued in Amsterdam. Bulldog bonds are issued in London. Some bonds issued in Tokyo and denominated in foreign currencies are referred to as Shogun bonds. In Spain, foreign bonds denominated in pesetas are referred to as Matador bonds. The leading foreign bond markets are located in Zurich, New York, Tokyo, Frankfurt, and Amsterdam.

The French foreign bond market is a good example of a market in which several types of bonds can be marketed. For example, index-linked bonds are issued where the coupons of these bonds are indexed to the price of gold, stock prices, or other assets. Straight debt bonds with call options are issued as are straight bonds renewable at maturity into the same straight bond terms. Straight bonds are issued that are exchangeable into floating rate notes at the option of the holder or issuer. Companies have issued floating rate notes exchangeable for bonds, as well as zero coupon bonds. In addition, the French bond market has entertained issues of floating rate notes with coupons linked to the average market long-term interest rate, floating rate notes with coupons indexed to a variety of short-term interest rates, straight bonds with warrants to purchase similar bonds, straight bonds with warrants to purchase equity or other assets, and convertible bonds.

EUROBONDS

Eurobonds are financed by long-term funds in the Eurocurrency markets. They are underwritten by a multinational syndicate of banks and placed in countries other than the one in whose currency they are denominated. The first Eurobond issue was a 5.5 percent bond floated by Autostrade, an Italian company, and denominated in U.S. dollars. The market was developed as a reaction to the U.S. Interest Equalization Tax, discussed in chapter 2, which caused the international bond market to shift from New

TABLE 12-4. Composition of the European Currency Unit by Country	
Country Currency	*Percentage Weight*
German mark	30.4
French franc	19.3
British pound	12.6
Italian lira	9.9
Dutch guilder	9.5
Belgian franc	8.1
Spanish peseta	5.2
Danish krone	2.5
Irish pound	1.1
Portuguese escudo	0.8
Greek drachma	0.7

Source: "The ECU and Its Role in the Process Towards Monetary Union," *European Economy* 48 (September 1991): 125.

York to London.[9] Eurobonds are not traded on a specific national bond market although the market centers seem to be located in Brussels and Luxembourg. This will be explained subsequently when Euroclear and Cedel, the Eurobond clearing houses, and their role are discussed.

Eurobonds can be denominated in a number of major currencies. The major currency of denomination is the U.S. dollar, followed by the Swiss franc and the Japanese yen. The latter currency was restricted by Japan in 1964 as a currency for Eurobond issues except those by foreign governments and the World Bank. This restriction, however, has been relaxed recently and the yen is becoming a popular currency of denomination. The Ecu is also used, especially in recent years.

Ecu Bonds

Ecu bonds are Eurobonds that are denominated in the Ecu. The Ecu, created in 1979 when the EC established the European Monetary System, is a hybrid currency comprised of a basket of the 12 EC currencies. The amount of each currency in the Ecu is revised every 5 years according to each country's GNP and trade volume. The deutsche Mark is currently the largest component currency. The composition of the Ecu by currency is shown in Table 12–4.

A number of large international companies have issued Ecu bonds, including General Motors, General Electric, IBM, Johnson & Johnson, Toyota, Nippon Telegraph and Telephone, and British Gas PLC. See Table 12–5 for information on the top 10 issuers of Eurobonds maturing in 1996.

The first Ecu bond was issued in 1981 by SOFTE, the Italian telecommunications company. Nearly two-thirds of all Ecu bonds are triple-A rated, much higher than the average Eurobond issue. These bonds have traditionally been viewed as an alternative to holding deutsche Mark-denominated bonds. After the voter rejection of the Treaty of Maastricht referendum in 1992, prices of 10-year Ecu bonds declined dramatically

---

[9] Edmond Israel, "International Clearing and Central Safekeeping in the Global Capital Market," *The World of Banking* 8(4) (1989): 25.

TABLE 12–5.	Issuers of Eurobonds that Mature in 1996		
Rank	Issuer or Group	Amount (millions U.S.$)	Issues
1	European Investment Bank	8,700.50	59
2	World Bank	5,741.58	28
3	Kingdom of Sweden	5,573.57	14
4	Deutsche Bank	4,354.77	29
5	General Electric	4,141.64	30
6	United Kingdom	4,000.00	1
7	Abbey National	3,387.94	18
8	Kingdom of Denmark	3,347.30	14
9	Standard Credit Card Trust 1990–95	3,091.00	4
10	Citicorp	3,003.17	15

Source: Joanna Wrighton, "The Hunt for Value," *Global Investor* (March 1996): 24.

and the value of outstanding Ecu bonds plummeted. Since then the $100 billion Ecu bond market has been slowly recovering.

Several types of instruments are issued as Eurobonds. Most are fixed rate bonds but the floating rate note (FRN) has become a sizable part of the market. The Japanese rely on convertible bonds and bonds with warrants attached. Convertible bonds, used by U.S. companies in the early years of Eurobond issues when straight-debt issues had high coupon rates, are convertible into the stock of the issuing company. Warrants attached to bonds give the holder a right to purchase stock in the parent company. Most borrowers in this market are industrial companies and supranational organizations. U.S. and Japanese corporations are heavy borrowers in the Eurobond market.

Euroconvertibles

Another source of funding available to international companies is the Euroconvertible, a convertible Eurobond. This type bond, a Eurobond convertible into the stock of the issuer, has been used by companies since the 1970s. However, Euroconvertibles became popular in the fall of 1993, especially in Asia, when coupon rates were at historical lows and stock valuations were at historical highs. At least 16 Asian companies announced or launched Euroconvertibles during that period. Overall, 43 Asian companies had outstanding Euroconvertible bond issues totaling $5.11 billion at the end of 1993.[10] Wharf Holdings, a large Hong Kong company, issued a US$402.5 million Euroconvertible bond in mid-1993. One of the largest foreign property investors in China, New World Development, raised US$300 million from a Euroconvertible issue.

Reasons given by companies for Euroconvertible issues included low-cost financing, long-term maturities, which were compatible with the long-term nature of their projects, and a method of financing that will not result in immediate dilution of earnings. These securities also appeal to investors who look for a higher yield and the chance to convert into equity shares in a bullish market. They appeal as well to convertible fund managers and to equity substitute players who are more concerned about the downside price risk.

A convertible bond because of its intrinsic value as a bond provides a floor for an investment when the stock price declines. When the stock rises, the bond should also

[10] "The Ups and Downs of Euroconvertibles," *Euromoney* (Supplement) (December 1993): 3–9.

In Theory

When the stock price declines, the intrinsic value of bond provides a floor for the investment. But when the stock price rises, the bond should also trade up because it offers the option to convert into the unlying equity.

In Practice

Wharf Holdings' 5% seven-year convertible has been performing like a text book example. It held its value when the underlying stock price dropped in July, then gained when the stock price shot up from September.

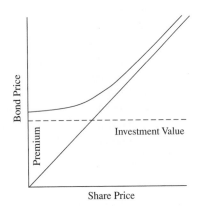

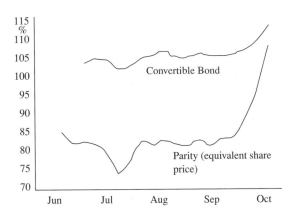

Source: Jefferies Pacific.

FIGURE 12–1 How a Convertible Bond Should Work

trade up because it offers the option to convert into the underlying equity. The theory about a convertible is shown in Figure 12–1, which also shows how, in practice, the Wharf Holdings' 5 percent 7-year Euroconvertible has performed. It held its value when the underlying stock price dropped in July 1993 and then gained when the stock price shot up from September, performing as the theory holds.

HOW FOREIGN BONDS AND EUROBONDS ARE ISSUED

Whereas a syndicate of national banks underwrites domestic bonds in any country, it is an international syndicate of financial institutions that underwrites Eurobonds. The Association of International Bond Dealers (AIBD) was formed in 1968 to increase the professional status of the foreign bond and Eurobond markets and to promulgate rules for market-makers. The AIBD was reorganized into the International Securities Markets Association (ISMA) in 1991 whose 660 members make markets in Eurobonds. However, only a handful, perhaps twelve, are market-makers that provide continuous two-way price quotations. This fact may stem from the lack of profitability in the Eurobond market. Spreads on Eurobonds are usually quite thin, averaging about 0.50 percent.

The method for calculating accrued interest also differs between the American and European bond markets. The American method for accrued interest, i.e., 360 days—where a month is 30 days—is used to price bonds. The United Kingdom, Japan, and Canada use 365 actual days for accrued interest. Eurobonds use the American convention. For example, a U.S. bond issued at par with a 12 percent coupon will pay $6 interest per $100 face value semiannually and is reported to have a semiannual yield-to-maturity of 12 percent. Europeans quote this bond as having 12.36 percent annual yield-to-maturity because of the compounding of two semiannual coupons.

Legal aspects of ownership are different depending on whether a bond is a domestic U.S. bond or a foreign bond, especially one floated in Europe. Europeans issue bearer bonds whereas registered bonds are floated in the United States. A bearer bond

does not have the name of the owner printed on its face. It is, in effect, legal tender and is owned by whomever possesses it. Bearer bonds are usually bought by individuals or companies but kept in banks' vaults, these institutions acting as depositories, and periodical statements of ownership are sent to the bond holders. Registered bonds have the name of the owner imprinted on the face of the bond and, therefore, must be delivered when the bond is sold. A new certificate is issued to the new bond holder. The 1993 ruling by the U.S. Internal Revenue System resolved this problem in the global bond market, as mentioned previously.

Some fiscal considerations concerning Eurobonds are important. Withholding taxes are generally levied on interest when bond coupons of foreign bonds are redeemed at financial institutions that accept them. These taxes may range from 0 to 45 percent. In 1984, the United States and Germany eliminated withholding taxes on foreign bonds issued in their domestic markets in order to make the market more open and competitive. Eurobonds are exempt from withholding taxes because the official borrower is a subsidiary of the borrower located off shore usually in a so-called tax haven country, i.e., a country with a very low or no tax rate.

Bond indexes are published by various sources that serve as informational services to bond investors. Salomon Brothers publishes a monthly index on all major markets in *Euromoney*. Lombard Odier & Cie., French investment banker, publishes its bond index in the *Wall Street Journal Europe*. Intersec publishes an index monthly in *Institutional Investor*. The ISMA makes available a weekly index that covers total return and price only. Chase Manhattan Bank also compiles a bond index. Most of these indexes are only available on a monthly basis. Thus, a company, institution, or individual investor desiring bond prices will have to contact a major bank member of ISMA for an up-to-date quotation.

Organization of the Eurobond Market

The organization of the Eurobond market consists of a syndicate of international investment bankers. The syndicate includes a lead manager or comanagers, a managing group of banks—a small number of assisting banks, underwriter banks, and a selling group. The managing group sells directly to the underwriters or the selling group or it sells to the underwriters, which in turn sell to the selling group.

The offering schedule for Eurobonds is accomplished in four steps. First, a decision is made by a firm to make a Eurobond issue. This is followed by a period of 2 weeks or more in which discussions are held between the borrower and the lead manager. Second, the announcement of the Eurobond issue is made to the public. This is followed by 1–2 weeks of preplacement of the issue. Preplacement is a "gray market" during which the lead manager surveys the potential underwriting and selling banks to determine the market for the issue. Third, final terms are formulated and announced on offering day. This announcement is followed by a two week public placement of the issue during which underwriters and the selling group banks essentially market the issue to their clients. Finally, on closing day, the selling group banks pay for the bonds that they have agreed to sell.

Some Eurobond issues are made in tranches, i.e., not all of the bonds are issued at first. Some proportion of the bonds is issued in subsequent tranches, or batches. This technique was introduced in 1977 when Orion Royal Company introduced it as the tap-stock concept. Under this technique, only part, about one-third, of the issue is made at the beginning in an initial tranche. Subsequent tranches of identical and interchangeable bonds are issued at later dates at the option of the issuer. These tranches are placed through the lead manager on a best efforts basis. No commissions are paid on the subsequent tranches and they are sold at the market price.

Interest Rate Calculations on Eurobonds

Interest rates on international bonds are quoted at an annual rate that is the interest payment per currency unit per year. The basis in the U.S. money markets and the Eurodollar, including the Eurobond, market is Actual/360, meaning that interest is calculated using the actual number of days between any two dates, divided by 360. In the United Kingdom, Australian, Eurosterling money, and capital markets, Actual/365 is used. Actual number of days between any two dates divided by actual number of days to maturity is used in the U.S. and Australian government security markets. In the Eurodollar market, a month has a maximum of 30 days.

Suppose that an investor buys 100 Eurobonds with a face or par value of $1,000 each. They have a coupon interest rate of 10 percent. The bonds are purchased at par value. The bonds are bought 150 days after the last interest payment. Accrued interest on the bonds, which the investor will have to pay in addition to the price of the bonds, is

$$100 \times [\$1,000 \times .10 \times (150/360)] = \$4,166.66$$

The payment net of accrued interest is

$$100 \times \$1,000 \times 1.00 = \$100,000$$

thus, the total payment is

$$\$100,000.00 + \$4,166.66 = \$104,166.66$$

Eurobond Clearing System

In the early years of Eurobond issues, no viable market-making mechanism existed. Any good secondary market for financial instruments must have both an efficient clearing as well as a good market-making mechanism. The holders of primary issues must have market liquidity so that they can sell their holdings without severe penalty when sales of such securities are needed. In the late 1960s when convertible Eurobonds were issued by U.S. MNCs, they were quite attractive at first to European investors. But when the U.S. stock market declined during that period, bondholders suffered large paper losses because the price of the bonds tracked the price of the issuing companies' underlying equities. The inability to sell these bonds without a further loss, because of the lack of a viable market-making mechanism, angered these investors and caused these bonds to become quite unpopular. Without an effective administrative and operational infrastructure in place at that time, the Eurobond market grew at a slow rate.

A Eurobond clearing system was established to correct this problem. Two institutions were developed, Euroclear and Cedel. The latter organization was established by some the world's largest banks in 1970 in Luxembourg to settle trades.[11] It settles some 25,000 transactions per day for its members and other banks and brokers. It has more than 2,600 clients and, in December 1990, it held $454 billion in securities. It held 39 percent of the market at the end of 1990. Cedel offers several services including: (1) central safekeeping of securities, (2) trade matching and confirmation, (3) securities lending, and (4) same day settlement.

Euroclear was established by J.P. Morgan in 1968 to alleviate the clearing and settlement problems that threatened the Eurobond market. After Cedel, Euroclear controls the remainder of the Eurobond market.[12] Euroclear offers several services for its more than 2,800 users including clearance and settlement, securities lending and bor-

---

[11] Erik Guyot "Cedel Aims to Double Asian Clients," *Asian Finance* 17 (15 March 1991): 10.

[12] "Global Custody: Baby Bites Back," *The Banker* 142 (May 1992): 38, 40.

rowing, money transfers, and custody. Euroclear also handles derivatives, domestic debt instruments, and equity securities. It covers more than 20 markets including Malaysia and Singapore, and added Portugal, Greece, and Turkey in 1992. Both clearing houses have bond and cash inventories in each of the Eurobond currencies; they are characterized by no physical moving of securities. The bonds are kept in bank vaults and statements of ownership are issued to bond holders. More than 7,000 securities are covered and member banks charge custody and clearing fees.

J.P. Morgan spun off Euroclear to public ownership in 1972 but retained managing control. It remains the banker to Euroclear's users. Essentially Euroclear remains a J.P. Morgan fiefdom. Some 124 financial institutions own 87.6 percent of Euroclear while 2,125 of its users own 12.4 percent under the guise of Euroclear Clearance System, Société Coopérative. However, the operating agreement behind this arrangement gives J.P. Morgan management control of accounts and operations.[13]

Cedel and Euroclear remain the major clearing houses for Eurobond issues although new clearing systems have been established. These clearing houses offer a number of risk-reducing services. Among these are nonfungibility, global safekeeping of securities, delivery against payment, trade matching and confirmation, and other market-making functions. As the functions and operations of Cedel and Euroclear have grown, Eurobond secondary volume has grown commensurately, rising to annual volume of more than $1 trillion and, thus, so too have the primary issues of Eurobonds.

Most Eurobonds are cleared through either Euroclear or Cedel. However, bonds denominated in German marks are the exception.[14] German banks, such as Deutsche Bank, are large market-makers in Eurobonds denominated in marks. They prefer to store these bonds in domestic depository banks, so-called *Kassenvereine*, which hold stocks and bonds in bearer style. The bonds are then cleared through the Effektengiro system, the German clearinghouse.

Eurobond Fee Structure

The typical spread on a Eurobond is 2–2 1/2 percent, meaning that the issuer receives 97 1/2–98 percent of the proceeds and the remainder goes to the underwriting syndicate. Of this spread, approximately 60 percent is a selling concession, 20 percent is for underwriting, and 20 percent is a management fee. The hierarchy of the syndicate is pyramidal in nature with the lead manager or comanager banks at the top. The lead bank distributes bonds to underwriters, privileged sellers that obtain the bonds at a lower price than ordinary sellers. Underwriters that are also sellers get both a selling fee and an underwriter fee. Manager banks that do both selling and underwriting get all three fees. The typical 2–2 1/2 percent Eurobond spread can be compared with foreign bond spreads, e.g., Yankee bonds 1/2–1 percent, Samurai and deutsche Mark bonds 2 percent, Rembrandts 2 1/2 percent, and Swiss franc bonds at 4 percent.

Various other fees may be imposed in syndicated loans. In addition to the front-end fees such as the management and participation fees, these may include override/praecipium fees, residual pool fees, and agency fees. The override/praecipium fee is a special fee allowed the lead manager or comanagers that gives recognition to the fact that the lead manager(s) did indeed render substantial services beyond those that might normally be expected. It is, essentially, an additional bonus. The residual pool fee is that portion of the total front-end fee remaining after all participation fees have been paid. It is usually divided among the lead managers on an agreed upon formula. The agency fee is paid to the agent bank, usually on an annual basis, by the borrower. The

---

[13] Ben Edwards, "Morgan's Magic Circle," *Euromoney* (August 1994): 35–8.

[14] J. Orlin Grabbe, *International Financial Markets* (New York: Elsevier, 1991), p.333.

agent represents all lending banks and acts on their behalf. This bank is responsible for assuring that the terms and conditions of the loan agreement are fulfilled properly.

Example of a Eurobond Syndicate

Let us presume that the Gilbert and Sullivan Steel Company (G&S), headquartered in the United States, with multinational operations including production facilities in more than 10 countries, decides to expand its European operations in stainless steel and will finance the expansion with, among other resources, a $100 million Eurobond issue. Company officials meet with the international bond department officials of Volksbank Bank, a large German bank. After discussions about the proposed debt issue, G&S gave a mandate to Volksbank to be lead manager of a banking syndicate to underwrite and sell this issue. Volksbank invited three other large European banks to be members of a managing group to assist the borrower, negotiate the debt covenants, maturity, and other terms of the issue, assess the market, and organize and manage the new issue. Another 20 large international banks were invited to be underwriting banks, or part of the underwriting group, to help underwrite the new issue. Finally, 30 additional regional banks in Europe were invited to be part of the selling group, i.e., that is to assist in selling the bonds to final investors.

G&S, the borrower, sold the bonds to the managing group. Volksbank and the managing group either sold the bonds, in turn, to the underwriting group and the selling group or the managing group sold the bonds to the underwriting group, which then took some of the bonds for its own account and then sold the remainder to the selling group banks. Selling group banks then sold the bonds to final investors. The bonds kept by the underwriting banks were also sold to final investors. Underwriting banks purchased the bonds from the managing group at a preset price. However, the bonds were sold to the selling group at a price different from the underwriters' price. Managing banks both underwrote and sold the bonds and underwriting banks also both underwrote and sold the bonds.

The fee structure of this Eurobond issue was negotiated by the lead manager bank, Volksbank, and agreed to by Volksbank and G&S, the borrower. Volksbank took one-half of the management fee and the three comanager banks equally split the remainder of the management fee. The issue was underwritten by the four managing banks (which underwrote 50 percent of the issue and shared equally in 50 percent of the underwriting fee) and by the 20 underwriting banks (which underwrote the remaining 50 percent of the issue and shared equally in 50 percent of the underwriting fee). The issue was sold as follows: the four managing banks sold $30 million, the 20 underwriting banks sold $30 million, and the 30 selling banks sold $40 million of the issue. It was assumed that each bank in each of the three groups sold an equal proportion of the total amount sold by each group. The negotiated fees were: management fee 0.4 percent, underwriting allowance 0.3 percent, and selling concession 1.3 percent, for a total of 2 percent. The lead manager did render substantial services beyond those normally expected and charged a praecipium fee of 0.1 percent. No residual pool fee was available since the front-end fees were exhausted. An agency fee for assuring that terms and conditions of the loan agreement would be fulfilled properly was waived by the managing group. Given the fee structure, the fees earned by each group and by each bank are shown in Table 12–6 and amounted to 2.1 percent, or $2,100,000 of the total issue. The syndicate, thus, returned $97,900,000 to G&S to be used to fund the company's expansion.

Selected Eurobond Issues

One of the large corporations that has recently raised capital in the Eurobond market has been Toyota Motor. In 1993, Toyota made a $1.5 billion issue in the Euro-

TABLE 12-6. **Allocation of Syndicate Fees**
Gilbert & Sullivan Company Eurobond Issue

I. *Management Fee (0.4 percent)*
   Total fee: $100,000,000 × .004 — $ 400,000.00
   Lead manager bank 50% × $400,000 — $ 200,000.00
   Comanager banks 50% × $400,000 — 200,000.00
   Each comanager bank $200,000/3 — 66,666.66

II. *Underwriting Allowance (0.3 percent)*
   Total allowance: $100,000,000 × .003 — $ 300,000.00
   Managing group 50% × $300,000 — 150,000.00
   Each bank 150,000/4 — 37,500.00
   Underwriting banks 50% × 300,000 — 150,000.00
   Each bank 150,000/20 — 7,500.00

III. *Selling Concession (1.3 percent)*
   Total concession: $100,000,000 × .013 — $1,300,000.00
   Managing group 30% × $1,300,000 — 390,000.00
   Each bank 390,000/4 — 97,500.00
   Underwriting group 30% × $1,300,000 — 390,000.00
   Each bank 390,000/20 — 19,500.00
   Selling group 40% × $1,300,000 — 520,000.00
   Each bank 520,000/30 — 17,333.33

IV. *Praecipium Fee (0.1 percent)*
   Praecipium fee to lead manager bank — $ 100,000.00
   $100,000,000 × .001
   Total Fees — **$2,100,000.00**

V. *Summary of Fees for Each Bank*
   Lead manager
       Praecipium fee — $ 100,000.00
       Management fee — 200,000.00
       Underwriting allowance — 37,500.00
       Selling concession — 97,500.00
       — $ 435,000.00

   Comanager bank (each)
       Management fee — $ 66,666.66
       Underwriting allowance — 37,500.00
       Selling concession — 97,500.00
       — $ 201,666.66

   Underwriting banks (each)
       Underwriting allowance — $ 7,500.00
       Selling concession — 19,500.00
       — $ 27,000.00

   Selling banks (each)
       Selling concession — $ 17,333.33

bond market, the largest such corporate issue to date. This issue was in the form of 5-year, noncallable notes at a dollar price of 99.78, with a 5.625 percent coupon to yield 5.24 percent. Toyota used this form to obtain European and Asian investors it desired rather than a global bond because global bonds issued previously had not delivered the worldwide placement that had been expected. In fact, Toyota also made a $1 billion Eurobond issue in 1992.[15] Most issues of this size have been structured as global bonds in

---

[15] Katherine Wells, "Why Toyota Chose a Mammoth Euro Issue Instead of Predictable Global Bonds," *Global Finance* 7 (March 1993): 17.

By now, you should be aware of the differences among global bonds, Eurobonds, and foreign bonds and how they are issued. Remember that when you calculate the price of a Eurobond that a 360-day year and not a 365-day year, as is the American custom, is used to calculate accrued interest. The fee structure for a Eurobond international syndicate is complex but remember that the lead manager bank(s) may also participate in underwriting and selling fees in addition to management fees, if it or they perform these functions. An understanding of these concepts will facilitate answering some of the problems at the end of this chapter.

order to facilitate worldwide sale of the bonds. However, previous global bond issues by Matsushita Electric and Ford Motor Credit had been distributed mostly in the United States because of liquidity problems in Europe and Japan.

The U.S. breakfast cereal company, Kellogg, issued a large Canadian dollar Eurobond in 1993 amounting to Can $265 million with a 5-year maturity and a 6.25 percent coupon. This issue was so well-subscribed that the issue price was only nine basis points over the Canadian treasury yield curve. These bonds were distributed very well across Europe with Swiss retail investors being the most dominant buyer.[16] This issue was part of $3 billion of Eurobond issues in September 1993.

Another recent Eurobond issue was made on October 11, 1994, when SmithKline Beecham marketed a $200 million Eurobond issue denominated in dollars. The coupon was 7.375 percent and the bond was priced at 99.85. Some of the proceeds were used as part of a financing program for a series of acquisitions and some were swapped into floating rate bonds to refinance bank debt.[17]

SPECIAL TYPES OF BONDS

Special types of bonds are offered in some countries. These may be available as sources of funds for foreign affiliates or as portfolio investments. Municipal bonds are issued in many countries. The mortgage-backed securities, such as collateralized mortgage obligations, are prevalent in the United States. In Germany, the Pfandbrief has a market that amounts to more than $800 billion. It is a cross between a municipal bond and a mortgage-backed security and offers a means to invest in German marks when the mark appreciates against most other currencies. It is a bond issued by a German mortgage bank secured by mortgages or loans to public borrowers but they remain obligations of the bank. If the mortgage fails, Pfandbrief owners get first claim to the assets that secure the instrument.

This security has been marketed in Germany since the 18th century but has become extremely popular in the 1990s, especially since reunification of East and West Germany. Many municipalities have used them to finance rebuilding in East Germany but they have some drawbacks. Although the primary market is large, the secondary market is thin. In addition, the retail market, especially in the United States, is restricted because, under Rule 144a of the U.S. securities law, they have been sold only to qualified institutional investors in the U.S. market. In addition to the instrument's

---

[16] Richard Phillips, "Kellogg's Canadian Dollar Eurobond Deal Sets the Pace in a Sizzling Market," *Global Finance* 7 (October 1993): 39.

[17] Richard Lapper, "Multinational Companies Find Success in Eurodollar Sector," *Financial Times*, 12 October 1994, p. 23.

relative higher yield, another advantage of the Pfandbrief is that German homeowners are not permitted to refinance their mortgages. Thus, the yield on a Pfandbrief will not decline because of refinancing.

Short- and Medium-Term Debt Markets

EURO-COMMERCIAL PAPER
AND EURO—MEDIUM-TERM NOTES

Two other Euro-debt markets were developed in the 1980s. These are the markets for Euro-commercial paper (ECP) and Euro–medium-term notes (EMTN). These markets fulfill needs for companies in the short- and medium-term areas of financing. The ECP market has been active during periods of high demand for working capital. In the early 1990s, the ECP market has slowed because of the global recession in industrialized nations. Only $19 billion of new ECP was issued in 1992 and the market stagnated.[18] The amounts of ECP outstanding at year-end amounted to $70.3 billion in 1990, $79.6 billion in 1991, and $78.7 billion in 1992.

On the other hand, EMTN issues set new highs in 1992 as this market broadened financing techniques and options for issuers, giving the market a competitive edge over commercial paper and bonds. EMTN outstanding amounted to only $9.6 billion at the end of 1989, but rose to $21.9 billion in 1990, $38.5 billion in 1991, and $61.1 billion in 1992.

The deutsch Mark is becoming more important in the EMTN market. Before 1992, only 2 percent of this market was denominated in marks. Since then, marks account for 6 percent of the $200 billion EMTN market, a three-fold increase in less than 2 years. Table 12–7 contains data about domestic and international markets for short- and medium-term notes issued during 1992 and 1993.

FLOATING RATE EURO-NOTES

Floating rate notes (FRN) represent an early innovation in the Eurobond market. In 1970, the Italian electric power utility company, ENEL, introduced the first publicly offered FRN in the Euromarket. The issue was guaranteed by the Italian government. The FRN is a short-term note with an automatic rollover. Such an instrument has the advantage of no rollover costs. The cost of advertising the new coupon rate may be the only cost of the issue. Interest is usually paid semiannually and they trade at a spread of the reference rate, e.g., LIBOR. Margin above LIBOR may amount to 25–100 basis points or more. After 6 months, the rate is reset with the same margin. A floor is usually set on the interest on FRN. Such instruments also have the advantage of a high degree of liquidity since they are usually accessible to individual investors and the transaction size is fairly large.

INTERNATIONAL REPO MARKET

Repurchase agreements, or repos, represent one of the fastest growth areas of the international capital markets since 1989.[19] Securities houses have created a market that is worth $50–125 billion dollars in daily outstandings. Repos consist of borrowing money against a pledge of securities as collateral, and then buying back the securities

---

[18] Bank for International Settlements, *63rd Annual Report*, p. 111.

[19] Julian Lewis, "Repos: The $50 Billion Secret," *Euromoney* (June 1991): 38–44.

TABLE 12–7. Domestic and International Markets Short- and Medium-Term Notes (billions U.S.$, 1992 and 1993)

| | Net Issues* | | | | Amounts Outstanding At End-1993 | |
| | *Domestic*§ | | *International*** | | | |
Sectors and Currencies	*1992*	*1993*	*1992*	*1993*	*Domestic*§	*International***
Short-term notes‡	18.8	−11.4	12.1	−5.4	782.6	109.2
U.S. dollar	17.0	8.6	14.6	−7.3	553.8	86.8
Japanese yen	−1.6	−10.3	−0.2	−0.4	98.8	0.2
French franc	−3.5	−7.6	0.2	−0.3	38.5	0.0
Spanish peseta	5.4	−4.7	0.2	−0.3	18.9	0.0
Canadian dollar	−2.4	1.2	0.1	0.4	17.3	0.5
Pound sterling	0.2	2.3	0.0	2.5	8.0	4.2
German mark	5.1	−2.7	2.5	−0.7	6.8	2.8
Other§	−1.4	1.7	−5.4	0.6	40.6	14.7
Medium-term notes	93.7	62.9	28.3	78.1	296.7	146.6
U.S. dollar	34.4	33.6	11.2	31.1	210.4	63.9
French franc	55.9	22.3	0.5	2.4	74.5	3.0
Pound sterling	3.4	7.0	2.8	6.2	11.8	10.2
Other§	0.0	0.0	13.8	38.4	0.0	69.6

* Changes in amounts outstanding at constant exchange rates.
§ Issues by residents and non-residence in local currency in the local market; OECD countries only, excluding Iceland and Turkey.
** Issues by residents and non-residents in foreign currency.
‡ Data on domestic issues relate to commercial paper only; data on international issues relate to Eurocommercial paper and other short-term Euro-notes.
§ Including the Ecu.
Source: Bank for International Settlements, *64th Annual Report,* p. 104.

at some time in the future. Bond traders engage in repos to finance their long positions in bonds. The trading firm is able to reduce its financing costs by 1/8–3/4 percent. Until the advent of the repo market, clearing houses such as Euroclear and Cedel charged 2.5–3.75 percent for borrowing bonds. The international repo market has drastically reduced this cost.

The volume in repos was originally an interdealer market with, at first, 80 percent of volume among dealers. The market is now evenly divided between dealers and customers and occasionally amounts to 70–30 in the favor of the customer.

Risks are relatively low in this market. A dealer can over-collateralize a deal by delivering securities with a market value of 102 percent or so of the amount borrowed. In addition, the collateral behind a repo is marked-to-market and the dealer can be required to furnish more collateral if security values decline.

The repo market is actually a money market. Dealers pledge top quality sovereign securities against the loan and figure the interest into the price at which the securities are repurchased. Dealers can also pay competitors to borrow securities needed to cover short positions. The primary participating borrowers in the repo market are security dealers, while the primary lenders are commercial banks and nonfinancial corporations.

TRI-PARTY REPOS

A recent alternative to deposit accounts for excess short-term cash in Europe is the use of the tri-part repurchase agreement within the Euro-repo market. Tri-part Euro-repos involve an investor, the seller, and a custodian such as Euroclear or Cedel, or some

other primary clearing organization.[20] The yield on these very short-term instruments is determined by the quality of the collateral, the currency involved, and the maturity, but generally the rate on Euro-repos is 1/16 to 3/8 of a percentage point above the London Interbank Bid Rate (LIBID), the rate at which European banks pay on deposits. Although this rate may be less than the bank deposit rate, Euro-repos may be more flexible because most bank deposits do not mature for at least 1 week. These securities can be used by U.S. MNCs operating in Europe because of their yield, safety, and liquidity.

International Equities

Firms engaged in foreign operations can use foreign stock markets for two principal reasons: to obtain equity funds for operations, or to float stock issues whose major objective is not the acquisition of equity funds but to increase public awareness of the company and its products. Foreign firms, for example, have floated more than 1,500 American depository receipts, to be discussed in a subsequent section, in order to tap the rich equity market in the United States. General Motors listed a small percentage of its shares on the Frankfurt Stock Exchange to make Germans more aware of the fact that Opel, the German auto manufacturer, was a General Motors affiliate.

On the other hand, U.S. companies have issued BDRs, bearer depository receipts, certificates that represent the U.S. parent firms' shares, in foreign countries. U.S. company shares are deposited with foreign investment banks that essentially treat the shares as initial offerings, pay the firm for them, and issue the BDRs, which are then traded on local securities exchanges.

Organized securities exchanges have been thriving around the world, especially in the LDCs, where emerging equity markets have recently outperformed markets in the industrialized countries. Some of the European markets were established in the late 15th century. For example, the Amsterdam Stock Exchange and the Hamburg Börse vie for the honor of being the first stock market. An early view of the Amsterdam Stock Exchange without its present roof is shown in Figure 12–2. Although MNCs have not tapped the emerging markets for equity funds to any degree, as these markets develop, they should offer opportunities for foreign MNCs to make new stock issues, just as local firms do.

These stock markets can be characterized in many ways. Some are very old buildings but, like the Amsterdam, Frankfurt, and Madrid Stock Exchanges, have had their trading floors completely modernized with the latest electronic equipment. Other markets are anything but modern. At the San José, Costa Rica, market, stock issues are sold in the streets in a manner similar to the sale of lottery tickets. At the Stuttgart Börse in Germany, all securities including government and corporate bonds and equities are called out for bids from floor traders—the a la crié method, which was last used at the New York Stock Exchange in the 1870s—all in less than 2 hours. At the Nairobi Stock Exchange in Kenya, Africa's most active market, five or six members of the market meet on Mondays in a hotel room to set all stock prices for the week. At the London Stock Exchange and the Tokyo Stock Exchange, thousands of companies have their equities traded. The Tokyo floor is almost a carbon copy of the New York Stock Exchange and vies for New York as the world's largest.[21] At London, trading was com-

---

[20] Theodore Justin Gage, "Tri-party Repos Take Root in Europe," *Corporate Cashflow* 14 (August 1993): 16–7.

[21] Richard I. Kirkland, Jr., "The Stock Market Upheaval in Europe," *Fortune* 112 (October 14, 1985): 158–62.

FIGURE 12-2 The Amsterdam Stock Exchange

TABLE 12-8. European Stock Exchanges (value of equity trading, in millions of Ecus)

Rank	Exchange	1995	1994	Percent Change
1	London	878,044	854,698	2.7
2	Paris	712,518	680,326	4.7
3	Germany	465,654	524,240	−11.0
4	Switzerland	245,604	207,135	18.6
5	Madrid	165,161	n.a.	n.a.
6	Amsterdam	96,433	73,346	31.5
7	Stockholm	78,031	77,356	1.0
8	Italy	66,885	121,887	−45.1
9	Copenhagen	21,756	24,570	−11.0
10	Oslo	19,145	14,900	28.5

Source: Sara Calian, ''Exchanges In Europe Vie For Business,'' *Wall Street Journal,* 18 April 1996, p. C1.

puterized by the so-called "Big Bang" in 1986 whereas at the New York Stock Exchange, all trading is executed between floor traders and specialists who hold inventories of stocks and make markets in them. Most of Europe's exchanges are relatively small. See Table 12–8 for the value of equity trading on the European stock exchanges for 1994 and 1995. The value of all shares on the Paris Bourse, for example, is about equal to the market value of IBM shares on the New York Stock Exchange.

In any case, CFOs of MNCs should become familiar with the equity markets around the world. As deregulation of financial markets advances and the privatization movement becomes even more pervasive, not only in the former socialist countries of eastern Europe but in industrialized nations such as Great Britain and France, equity will become more valuable as a financing mode for MNCs. Stock will be sold globally, thus turning these companies into the transnational enterprises mentioned in chapter 1. These markets will become more valuable to the managers in charge of long-term funding of international companies.

New global systems have facilitated cross-border equity trading.[22] New global networks comprised of leading stock exchanges such as in New York and the flotation of foreign stocks in the United States are at the heart of such systems. SEAQ International is a network of 47 market-makers that quotes prices in 587 international stocks on computer screens. SEAQ, Stock Exchange Automated Quotations, is a quote-driven automatic system for trading stocks at the London Stock Exchange. Its nearest competitor in foreign stock volume is the New York Stock Exchange with half the volume. SEAQ claims to be the dealing center for 90 percent of all cross-border equities trading in Europe. Instinet is a private system that allows anonymous electronic matching of orders between the largest intermediaries and institutional investors. Several large U.S., British, European, and Asian brokers operate 24 hours a day in trading the leading stocks. The Federation of European Stock Exchanges formed a system of cross-listing on European exchanges that will, for example, enable a Spanish investor to trade big Italian or French stocks on the Madrid Stock Exchange. The system will be implemented when the EC amends a directive to permit such listings without the need for a

[22] Peter Lee, "The Fight to Gain Control of World Equities," *Euromoney* (July 1993): 42–8.

Country	Securities Exchange	Market Capitalization (billions U.S.$) end-1993
1. Argentina	Bolsa de Comercia de Buenos Aires	44.0
2. Brazil	Sao Paulo Bolsa de Valores	99.4
3. Chile	Bolsa de Comercio de Santiago	44.6
4. Colombia	Bolsa de Bogotá	9.2
5. Greece	Athens Stock Exchange	12.3
6. Jordan	Amman Financial Market	4.9
7. Korea	Korea Stock Exchange	139.4
8. Malaysia	Kuala Lumpur Stock Exchange	220.3
9. Mexico	Bolsa Mexicana de Valores	200.7
10. Nigeria	Nigerian Stock Market	1.0
11. Pakistan	Karachi Stock Exchange Ltd.	11.6
12. Philippines	Manila Stock Exchange	40.3
13. Portugal	Bolsa de Lisboa	12.4
14. Thailand	Securities Exchange of Thailand	130.5
15. Turkey	Istanbul Stock Exchange	37.5
16. Venezuela	Bolsa de Valores de Caracas	8.0
17. Zimbabwe	Zimbabwe Stock Exchange	1.4

Source: Emerging Stock Markets Factbook 1990 (Washington, D.C.: International Finance Corporation, 1990), pp. 67–143, and Bruno Solnik, *International Investments* (Reading, MA: Addison-Wesley Publishing Co., 1996), p. 255.

FIGURE 12–3 Emerging Stock Markets

company to make a separate application or publish a prospectus in the official language of the exchange.[23]

During the 1990s, international equity markets have been extremely active. Much of this activity stems from the economic situation worldwide in which interest rates on debt instruments have been quite low and inflation remained relatively low, making equities attractive to investors. New stock markets have been developed in the emerging nations of the developing world and in eastern Europe, where economies are being privatized. See Figure 12–3 for a listing of stock markets in the emerging countries.

A global revolution has occurred during the past decade in the LDCs and other economies in transition, such as the eastern European countries. This revolution is represented by the burgeoning equity markets emerging in these countries. During the year ending June 1993, the world's best performing equity markets were Turkey (up 111 percent), Brazil (up 83 percent), and Indonesia (up 29 percent). Markets in Hong Kong, Singapore, and the Philippines also performed quite well.[24] The performance of these and several other emerging markets are followed by the International Finance Corporation and its Emerging Markets Department.[25]

Other reasons can be cited for the large demand for global equity issues. Although the Mexican peso crisis in late 1994 may slow down global equity sourcing in the

---

[23] Glenn Whitney, "Europe's Cross-Listing System For Big Stocks Nears Completion," *Wall Street Journal*, 15 September 1993, p. C1.

[24] Michael G. Papaioannou and Lawrence K. Duke, "The Internationalization of Emerging Equity Markets," *Finance & Development* 30 (September 1993): 36.

[25] *Emerging Stock Markets Factbook* (Washington, D.C.: International Finance Corporation, various years).

TABLE 12–9. Volume International Equity Issues (billions U.S.$)*

Region	1990	1991	1992	1993	1994
Europe	58.1	7.16	6.71	13.1	30.3
Latin America	98.3 mn	3.95	3.96	6.06	3.64
Asia	1.74	781.7 mn	2.33	3.99	12.03
Total**	**9.99**	**20.26**	**22.44**	**38.73**	**53.60**

* Excludes funds and preference shares.
** Includes North American and rest of world.
Source: Richard Lapper, "Spreading the World's Wealth," *Financial Times,* 23 January 1995, p. 13.

short-run, over the longer term period, global demand for equities should continue.[26] Institutional investors, especially U.S.-based firms, believe overseas investments can increase returns and, because of diversification, can reduce risk. In addition, improvements in communications facilitates the marketing of shares by international banks and securities firms to investors in diverse national markets. Such improvements also reduce the cost of equity capital. Finally, the trend toward liberalization of securities markets in other countries has removed many of the restrictions facing foreign investors in global markets. See Table 12–9 for the volume of international equity issues in major regions of the world.

MARKET INFORMATION ABOUT FOREIGN STOCKS

A number of good sources are available on a frequent basis that offer information about the price of foreign equities and market index levels. Daily newspapers such as the *Wall Street Journal*, *Financial Times*, and *Investor's Business Daily* report the major stock market indexes including the DAX 30-stock index of Frankfurt-listed shares, the Nikkei 225-stock index of Tokyo Stock Exchange shares, and the *Financial Times* stock exchange 100-share index of London Stock Exchange equities. This index is known in the trade as the "Footsie 100." The *Wall Street Journal* with Dow Jones & Company established the Dow Jones World Stock Index, reported every day in the *Wall Street Journal*. This index contains stocks in 28 industrialized countries around the world. An index for the stocks from each country is tabulated daily and these indexes make up the final Dow Jones World Stock Index for each day. See Table 12–10 for this index reported for May 7, 1996.

Finally, the *Wall Street Journal* also reports daily prices of selected major company stocks traded in several stock exchanges in its "Foreign Markets" column. These include Tokyo, London, Hong Kong, Sydney, Frankfurt, Mexico, Paris, Stockholm, Amsterdam, Brussels, Milan, and Switzerland. The prices shown are in the currency of the home country. See Figure 12–4 for the "Foreign Markets" prices for May 7, 1996.

RISK IN THE EQUITY MARKETS

In addition to interest rate fluctuations that affect the earnings of individual companies and the political risk, discussed earlier, which in turn may affect the operations of companies in emerging markets, international equity issues may be adversely affected by

[26] Richard Lapper, "Spreading the World's Wealth," *Financial Times*, 23 January 1995, p. 13.

FOREIGN MARKETS

Tuesday, May 7, 1996

TOKYO
(in yen)

	Close	Net Chg.
Aiwa	2350	+ 20
Ajinomoto	1240	....
Alps Elec	1210	+ 10
Amada Co	1150	– 30
ANA	1140	....
Ando Elec	1970	....
Anritsu	1520	– 30
Asahi Chem	770	– 16
Asahi Glass	1230	– 10
AT&T Global	1120	+ 10
Banyu Pharm	1460	– 40
Bk of Yokohama	879	– 29
Bridgestone	1960	+ 40
Brother Ind	698	+ 10
Canon Inc	2030	– 10
Canon Sales	2990	....
Casio Computer	1070	– 20
Chichibu Onoda	629	+ 13
Chubu Pwr	2610	– 20
Chugai Pharm	999	– 1
Citizen Watch	879	– 15
CSK	3320	+ 10
Dai Nippon Print	1930	....
Dai-Ichi Kangyo	2080	– 20
Daiei	1380	+ 20
Daiichi Seiyaku	1730	....
Dainippon Ink	539	– 10
Dainippon Pharm	1080	– 30
Daiwa House	1640	....
Daiwa Securities	1560	– 20
Eisai	2010	....
Ezaki Glico	1040	– 40
Fanuc	4340	– 80
Fuji Bank	2240	– 30
Fuji HI	473	– 9
Fuji Photo Film	3120	+ 10
Fujisawa Pharm	1110	– 20
Fujitsu	1060	– 20
Furukawa Elec	606	– 22
Green Cross	605	– 9
Haseko	470	– 9
Hirose Elec	6340	+ 40
Hitachi Cable	870	– 5
Hitachi Credit	1910	– 40
Hitachi Ltd	1100	– 20
Hitachi Maxell	2260	....
Hitachi Metals	1330	+ 20
Honda Motor	2330	– 10
Hoya	3490	– 80
IHI	498	+ 2
Ind Bank Japan	2720	– 10
Intec	1800	....
Isetan	1500	– 20
Isuzu	576	– 12
Ito-yokado	6130	....
Itochu Corp	770	– 5
Iwatsu Elec	640	– 10
JAL	812	+ 9
Japan Aviat El	828	– 2
Japan Energy	409	– 8
Japan Radio	1530	– 50
JEOL	880	– 18
JUSCO	3100	– 70
Kajima	1160	– 10
Kandenko	1380	– 20
Kansai Elec	2530	....
Kao Corp	1380	+ 10
Kawasaki HI	532	– 12
Kawasaki Steel	383	+ 6
KDD	10200	+ 200
Kinden	1640	– 40
Kirin	1300	– 30
Kobe Steel	327	– 6
Kokusai Elec	2160	....
Kokuyo	2800	– 20
Komatsu Ltd	1000	....
Konica	780	– 15
Kubota	713	– 3
Kumagai Gumi	433	– 6
Kuraray	1180	– 10
Kureha Chem	636	– 3
Kyocera	7830	+ 60
Kyowa Hakko	1000	– 20
Kyushu Matsushit	2240	+ 20
Lion	654	– 5
Makino Milling	1120	....
Makita Elec	1680	– 40
Marudai Food	777	– 28
Marui	2250	+ 10
Mats' Elec Ind	1810	– 20
Mats' Elec Wrks	1170	– 20
Matsushita Com	2780	+ 10
Mazda	488	– 7
Meiji Seika	647	– 9
Minolta	620	– 5
Misawa Homes	944	+ 5
Mitsubishi Chem	545	– 1
Mitsubishi Corp	1450	– 20
Mitsubishi Elec	809	+ 6
Mitsubishi HI	922	– 7
Mitsubishi Matl	605	– 14
Mitsubishi Real	1420	– 30
Mitsubishi Trust	1730	– 50

	Close	Prev. Close
Mitsubishi Whse	1750	– 20
Mitsui & Co	985	+ 7
Mitsui Fudosan	1350	– 20
Mitsui Mar&Fire	860	– 7
Mitsui Trust	1160	– 60
Mitsukoshi	1270	....
Mochida Pharm	1500	+ 10
NEC	1310	– 10
New Oji Paper	948	– 6
NGK Spark	1290	– 10
NIFCO	1410	– 20
Nihon Unisys Ltd	1240	– 20
Nikko Securities	1260	– 30
Nikon Corp	1350	– 30
Nintendo	8300	+ 200
Nippon Chemi-con	720	– 9
Nippon Columbia	732	....
Nippon El Glass	1920	+ 30
Nippon Express	1010	– 30
Nippon Hodo	1810	....
Nippon Meat	1580	– 10
Nippon Oil	693	– 2
Nippon Paper	718	– 22
Nippon Sanso	562	– 3
Nippon Shinpan	777	+ 5
Nippon Steel	370	+ 1
Nissan Motor	852	– 1
Nissin Food	2850	+ 30
Nitsuko	1130	– 20
NKK	323	– 5
Nomura Securitie	2180	– 60
NSK	826	– 14
NTN	768	+ 9
NTT	798000	– 4000
Obayashi Corp	942	– 3
Odakyu Railway	725	– 1
Oki Elec Ind	811	– 15
OKK	592	+ 12
Okuma Corp	1120	– 20
Olympus Optical	1120	....
Omron	2300	– 100
Ono Pharm	3860	– 90
Onward	1770	– 10
Orient Corp	626	– 20
Pioneer Electron	2240	....
Renown	428	– 7
Ricoh Co	1200	+ 20
Royal Co	1990	– 10
Ryobi	555	– 2
Sakura Bank	1180	– 20
Sankyo Co	2510	....
Sanrio	1320	– 10
Sanwa Bank	2030	– 50
Sanyo Elec	646	– 3
Sapporo Brewery	980	– 12
Secom	7310	+ 10
Sekisui House	1280	– 20
Seven-eleven	7350	+ 30
Sharp	1790	....
Shimizu Corp	1160	– 20
Shin-etsu Chem	2190	– 40
Shionogi	920	– 19
Shiseido	1320	– 20
Showa Denko	331	– 9
Skylark	2230	– 20
SMK	775	+ 40
Sony	6720	– 50
Sumitomo Bank	2140	– 30
Sumitomo Chem	548	+ 2
Sumitomo Corp	1200	+ 10
Sumitomo Elec	1460	– 40
Sumitomo Marine	961	– 9
Sumitomo Metal	331	+ 5
Sumitomo Realty	820	– 29
Sumitomo Trust	1450	– 30
Suzuki Motor	1290	– 10
Taisei	779	– 8
Taisho Pharm	2170	– 50
Taiyo Yuden	1190	– 30
Takeda Chem	1760	– 10
Tanabe Seiyaku	857	– 33
TDK	6010	– 20
Teijin	577	– 1
Toho Co	18800	+ 300
Tokio Mar&Fire	1370	– 30
Tokyo Denki Kom	1160	– 20
Tokyo Elec Pwr	2790	– 30
Tokyo Electron	3710	– 60
Tokyo Gas	401	– 3
Tokyo Style	1900	....
Tokyo-Mitsbs Bnk	2340	– 50
Tokyu Corp	800	– 15
Tonen Corp	1510	....
Toppan Print	1490	– 10
Toray	706	+ 1
Toshiba	800	– 3
Toto	1530	– 20
Toyo Seikan	3670	+ 100
Toyobo	404	– 8
Toyoda Mach	1130	+ 20
Toyota Motor	2340	– 30
Tsugami	632	– 4
Uny	1950	+ 10
Ushio	1270	+ 10
Wacoal	1370	– 50

	Close	Prev. Close
Yamaha	1830	....
Yamaichi Sec	806	– 2
Yamanouchi Phm	2450	+ 10
Yamatake-Hnywl	1940	– 10
Yamato Trnsprt	1260	....
Yamazaki Baking	2100	– 20
Yasuda Fire	811	+ 1
Yokogawa Elec	1170	....

LONDON
(in pound/pence)

	Close	Net Chg.
Abbey National	5.48	– 0.03
Allied-Domecq	4.98	+ 0.07
Argyll Group	3.28	+ 0.05
Arjo Wiggins	1.83	+ 0.01
Assoc Brit Fds	3.82	– 0.06
BAA PLC	5.36	+ 0.01
Barclays	7.45	+ 0.02
Bass	7.66	– 0.01
BAT Indus	4.95	– 0.11
Blue Circle	3.71	+ 0.01
BOC Group	8.94	– 0.04
Body Shop	1.78	– 0.02
Boots	6.21	– 0.01
Borland	10.50	– 0.75
BPB Indus	3.27	....
British Aero	8.63	– 0.11
British Airwys	5.27	+ 0.06
British Gas	x2.18	– 0.12
British Pete	5.69	– 0.13
British Steel	1.93	– 0.02
British Telcom	3.36	– 0.03
BTR	3.13	– 0.02
Burmah Castrol	10.43	– 0.05
Cable&Wireless	4.70	– 0.09
Cadbury Schwp	5.06	– 0.03
Caradon	2.30	+ 0.03
Charter plc	9.57	+ 0.05
Coats Viyella	1.80	....
Commercial Un	6.05	– 0.10
Cookson Group	3.07	– 0.04
Courtaulds	4.13	– 0.08
Eng Ch Clay	2.88	– 0.01
Enterprise Oil	4.32	– 0.02
Euro Tunnel	0.75	+ 0.01
GEC	3.52	+ 0.01
Genrl Accidnt	6.34	– 0.13
GKN	9.76	+ 0.06
Glaxo	7.79	– 0.21
Granada	8.16	+ 0.11
Grand Metrop	4.26	– 0.03
Great Universl	6.88	– 0.08
Guardian Royal	2.68	– 0.03
Guinness	4.72	+ 0.02
Hanson PLC	1.98	+ 0.01
Hillsdown	1.82	+ 0.03
Imp Chem Ind	8.84	– 0.09
Inchcape PLC	2.89	– 0.01
Jefferson Smurf	1.80	+ 0.02
Johnson Mathy	6.08	– 0.07
Kingfisher	5.70	– 0.05
Ladbroke Grp	1.92	– 0.01
Land Securs	6.52	+ 0.06
LASMO	1.88	– 0.01
Legal & Genl	7.28	– 0.01
Lloyds TSB Grp	3.09	....
Lonrho	1.92	– 0.02
Lucas	2.34	+ 0.26
Marks&Spencer	4.26	+ 0.01
MEPC	4.23	+ 0.04
Nat Power PLC	5.39	– 0.04
Nat Wstmn Bk	6.29	– 0.02
NFC	1.65	– 0.02
P & O	5.30	+ 0.03
Pearson	6.88	+ 0.11
Pilkgtn Bros	2.09	– 0.01
PowerGen PLC	5.49	– 0.08
Prudential	4.44	– 0.03
Rank Org	5.32	– 0.01
Reckit&Colman	7.11	+ 0.05
Redland	x4.09	– 0.03
Reed Intl	11.28	+ 0.04
Rentokil	3.97	+ 0.02
Reuters	7.45	+ 0.02
Rexam Plc	3.80	+ 0.01
RMC	10.63	– 0.10
Rolls Royce	2.24	– 0.03
Royal Insur	4.24	– 0.13
RTZ Corp	10.74	+ 0.13
Sainsbury J	3.57	– 0.05
Scottish Pwr	3.66	– 0.01
Sears	0.98	....
Sedgwick Grp	1.48	– 0.01
Severn Trent	5.78	+ 0.02
Shell	8.55	– 0.09
Siebe PLC	8.43	– 0.10
Smith&Nephew	x1.96	– 0.01
Std Chartrd	6.03	– 0.11
Sun Alliance	4.02	– 0.12
Tarmac	1.29	– 0.01

	Close	Prev. Close
Tate & Lyle	4.76	– 0.08
Tesco	2.67	– 0.01
Thorn EMI	17.88	+ 0.02
TI Group	5.50	....
Tomkins	2.62	– 0.04
Trafalgar Hse	0.51	....
Unilever	12.15	+ 0.12
Utd Biscuits	2.32	....
Vodafone	2.55	– 0.05
Williams Hldgs	x3.25	– 0.12
WPP Group	2.01	– 0.03

South African Mines
(in U.S. dollars)

	Close	Net Chg.
Bracken	0.25	....
Deelkraal	1.05	+ 0.05
Durban Deep	9.50	+ 0.25
E. Rand Gold	x2.62	– 0.10
E. Rand Prop	0.69	....
Elandsrand	6.78	....
Grootvlei	3.13	....
Harmony	11.52	– 0.05
Hartebstftn	3.46	– 0.10
Impala Pltm	17.63	– 0.19
Kinross	10.31	....
Leslie	1.35	....
Loraine	4.22	+ 0.20
Randfontein	7.38	– 0.06
Rustenburg	19.88	– 0.13
Southvaal	43.75	+ 0.25
Stilfontein	1.00	....
Unisel	4.37	+ 0.07
Winkelhaak	9.56	....

HONG KONG
(in Hong Kong dollars)

	Close	Net Chg.
Bank E Asia	25.55	– 0.15
Cathay Pacific	13.50	– 0.05
Cheung Kong	52.75	– 0.25
China L & P	36.20	+ 0.40
Hang Seng Bk	76.00	+ 0.25
HK Electric	24.50	+ 0.10
HK Telecom	15.60	+ 0.40
HSBC Hldgs	112.00	....
Hutchsn Whmp	x46.70	+ 0.05
Hysan Develop	23.35	+ 0.05
New World Dev	32.80	+ 0.10
Sun Hung Kai	72.25	....
Swire Pacific	62.75	....
Tsingtao Brew	2.58	+ 0.08
Wharf Holdings	28.25	+ 0.20

SYDNEY
(in Australian dollars)

	Close	Net Chg.
Amcor	8.68	+ 0.01
ANZ Group	6.00	+ 0.01
Ashton	2.15	....
Boral	3.24	– 0.02
Bougainville	0.65	....
Brambles Inds	17.60	+ 0.10
Brokn Hill Prp	19.93	+ 0.15
Burns Philp	2.64	– 0.01
Centrl Norsemn	1.15	....
Coles Myer	4.66	– 0.02
Comalco	7.50	+ 0.15
CRA	21.20	+ 0.33
CSR	4.50	....
Foster's	2.31	– 0.01
Gld Mns Kalgo	1.45	....
Goodman	1.27	....
Leighton	3.98	+ 0.06
Mayne Nickless	7.56	+ 0.03
MIM Holdings	1.92	+ 0.04
Nat Aust Bnk	11.32	+ 0.10
News Corp	7.20	....
Normdy Poseldn	2.18	– 0.02
North Ltd	4.01	+ 0.01
Orbital Engine	0.87	+ 0.01
Pacific Dunlop	3.10	+ 0.03
Renison Gldflds	6.56	+ 0.01
S Pac Pete	1.22	+ 0.02
Santos	4.50	....
Syd Har Casino	1.92	– 0.01
TNT Ltd	1.71	– 0.02
Western Mining	9.82	+ 0.24
Westpac	5.98	+ 0.03
Woodside	7.54	+ 0.07

a-New Zealand quote; in New Zealand dollars.

FRANKFURT
(in marks)

	Close	Net Chg.
AEG	166.20	+ 0.20
Allianz	2590.00	+ 17.00
Asko	920.00	+ 8.00
BASF	419.30	+ 4.40
Bayer	491.00	+ 2.70
BMW	813.50	....
Byr Vereinsbk	42.67	+ 0.15
Commerzbank	330.50	– 0.20
Continental	25.70	– 0.30
Daimler Benz	825.00	+ 1.50
Degussa	543.50	+ 0.50
Deutsche Bank	73.00	+ 0.38
Dresdner Bank	38.41	+ 0.01
Heidlbg Zemnt	953.00	– 5.00
Henkel	615.50	+ 8.50
Hochtief	578.00	– 2.00
Hoechst	481.00	+ 0.50
Karstadt	568.50	+ 1.20
Kaufhof	476.00	– 3.00
Linde	937.00	+ 4.00
Lufthansa	247.00	+ 1.20
MAN	395.50	– 3.00
Mannesmnn	526.50	+ 4.00
Metallges	29.87	+ 0.82
Munchen Rck	2787.00	+ 19.00
Porsche	850.00	....
RWE	57.65	– 0.20
SAP	201.00	+ 1.50
SAP Pfd	205.00	+ 1.00
Schering	110.60	– 0.40
Siemens	83.10	+ 0.60
Thyssen	278.30	+ 3.30
Veba	74.93	+ 0.89
VEW	444.00	+ 0.50
Volkswagen	516.50	– 1.50

MEXICO
(in pesos)

	Close	Net Chg.
Alfa A	108.60	+ 0.70
Apasco A	42.40	+ 0.90
Banacci B	16.94	+ 0.04
Bimbo A	33.00	– 0.80
Cemex B	30.10	+ 0.25
Cifra B	9.80	+ 0.08
Cifra C	9.66	+ 0.10
Femsa B	21.05	– 0.55
Gcarso A1	55.20	– 0.30
Kimber A	135.00	+ 0.70
Maseca B	7.00	....
Tamsa	63.90	– 0.70
Televisa	117.60	– 1.40
Tolmex B2	38.50	....
Vitro	17.00	+ 0.36

PARIS
(in French francs)

	Close	Net Chg.
Accor	697.00	– 3.00
Air Liquide	891.00	– 11.00
Alcatel Alstm	483.60	– 0.20
AXA Group	297.00	– 3.40
Bic	571.00	– 5.00
BNP	204.60	– 2.20
Carrefour	2642.00	– 5.00
Club Med	496.00	+ 1.00
Danone	789.00	– 7.00
Dassault Avitn	485.20	– 21.80
Elf Aquitaine	379.00	– 5.00
Euro Disneyld	15.15	+ 0.05
Generale Eaux	544.00	– 6.00
Havas	422.30	+ 0.10
Imetal	785.00	– 5.00
L'Oreal	1529.00	– 11.00
Lafarge	314.50	– 1.60
Lagardere Grp	134.90	+ 1.10
LVMH	1241.00	– 16.00
Michelin	246.00	+ 1.10
Paribas	313.30	+ 9.30
Pernod Ricard	333.80	+ 3.50
Peugeot	715.00	– 3.00
Renault	148.80	– 1.80
Saint Gobain	619.00	+ 11.00
Sanofi	390.00	– 10.10
Schnd Ex Sple	233.00	– 0.70
Soc Generale	579.00	– 2.00
Suez	204.50	+ 0.90
Thomson CSF	131.30	– 1.00
Total Francais	346.00	– 1.70
Usinor	80.50	+ 0.50

STOCKHOLM
(in krona)

	Close	Net Chg.
AGA	109.00	....
Asea	705.00	+ 12.00
Astra	300.50	– 7.00
Atlas Copco	129.50	– 0.50
Electrolux	342.50	– 4.00

	Close	Prev. Close
Ericsson	142.50	– 1.50
SE Bank	49.80	– 0.20
Skanska	216.50	– 1.00
SKF	156.50	– 1.00
Volvo	162.50	+ 1.00

AMSTERDAM
(in guilders)

	Close	Net Chg.
ABN Amro	89.90	– 1.30
Aegon	84.80	+ 0.60
Ahold	86.30	– 0.60
Akzo Nobel	198.60	+ 0.90
AMEV	128.00	+ 2.90
Bols Wessanen	33.50	+ 0.20
DSM	177.80	+ 0.30
Elsevier	25.80	+ 0.10
Fokker	0.75	+ 0.02
Gist-Brocades	x53.40	+ 0.10
Heineken	360.50	+ 0.30
Hoogovens	67.10	– 0.50
Hunter Dgls	x113.20	+ 4.15
ING Groep	133.90	– 1.00
KLM	62.90	– 0.10
KNP BT	43.30	+ 0.10
Nedlloyd	37.70	– 0.10
Oce-van Grntn	155.40	+ 1.00
Pakhoed Hldg	43.30	+ 0.60
Philips	60.80	– 0.80
Robeco	124.40	– 0.90
Rodamco	49.00	+ 0.50
Rolinco	135.60	– 1.40
Rorento	95.60	– 0.20
Royal Dutch	239.40	– 0.20
Royal PTT	65.20	+ 0.30
Unilever	234.90	+ 2.60
VNU	28.00	– 0.20
VOC	63.60	– 0.30
Wolters Kluwer	184.90	+ 1.20

BRUSSELS
(in Belgian francs)

	Close	Net Chg.
Arbed	3400	+ 40
BBL	5970	– 30
Bekaert	24000	+ 25
CBR	12375	....
Delhaize	1575	....
Electrabel	7040	....
Gen de Bnque	11200	....
Gevaert	2035	– 15
GIB	1402	+ 8
Petrofina	8950	– 70
Soc Gen Belg	2455	+ 5
Solvay	18250	– 25

MILAN
(in lire)

	Close	Net Chg.
Banca Com	3515	+ 31
Benetton	18985	+ 92
CIGA	729	– 11
CIR	995	– 2
FIAT Com	5378	+ 76
FIAT Pref	2957	+ 34
Generali	39165	+ 498
Mediobanca	11383	+ 157
Montedison	926	+ 7
Olivetti Com	988	+ 21
Olivetti NC	780	– 2
Pirelli Co	2076	– 9
Pirelli SpA	2363	....
RAS	17410	– 49
Rinascente	10257	+ 27
Saipem	5951	+ 103
Snia	1830	+ 54
Stet	5328	+ 3
Telecom Ital	3243	+ 4

SWITZERLAND
(in Swiss francs)

	Close	Net Chg.
Alusuisse br	1007	+ 7
Brown Bov reg	x298	+ 8
Brown Boveri	x1508	+ 43
Ciba-Geigy br	1362	– 8
Ciba-Geigy reg	1368	– 8
CS Holding	111	– 1
Hof LaRoch br	16300	– 50
Nestle reg	1418	+ 1
Roche div rt	9540	– 40
Sandoz br	1276	– 10
Sandoz reg	1285	– 5
Sulzer br	787	+ 2
Swiss Bnk Cp	463	....
Swiss Reins reg	1275	– 24
Swissair	1232	+ 22
UBS	1228	+ 15
Winterthur br	765	+ 9
Winterthur reg	765	+ 9
Zurich Ins	332	– 2

Source: *Wall Street Journal*, 8 May 1996, p. C16. Reprinted by permission.

FIGURE 12–4 Foreign Markets

MANAGEMENT APPLICATION NO. 16

An Emerging Stock Market

The International Finance Corporation tracks more than 1,450 companies listed on 26 emerging markets with its Emerging Markets Data Base, discussed earlier in chapter 11. One example of an emerging and successsful stock exchange is the Bursa Efek Jakarta (Jakarta Stock Exchange) in Indonesia. Before 1989, this stock exchange had been a low-key, government owned, highly regulated market. The market came alive after financial deregulation and privatization in 1992.

The Jakarta Stock Exchange expanded rapidly in 1994. By May 1995, its capitalization had increased by 318.5 percent in 1 year to the equivalent of $46.4 billion. The number of listed companies increased by 42 percent in this period to 217 firms. Share volume in 1995 is three times that of 1992. The exchange was computerized in May 1995 and transactions on a daily basis have increased from 1,500–2,000 trades to more than 3,000. Of the total free float of about $10 billion (the amount of securities available for trading and not closely-held), local investors account for 20 percent, while foreign investors trade more than two-thirds. All but one of the top brokerage firms trading at the Jakarta Stock Exchange are foreign and these account for 60–70 percent of daily trading. Foreign investors account for 30 percent of all listed shares.

The Jakarta Stock Exchange is faced with a number of problems, all inherent in emerging stock markets. The Indonesian government regulates securities market activities through Bapepam, the Capital Market Supervisory Agency. The head of the exchange is a former head of the transaction bureau at Bapepam and the exchange board members are mostly former civil servants. Thus, they are distrusted by private sector trading firms. Competition in trading comes from foreign stock exchanges, especially Singapore. Two other domestic Indonesian exchanges have agreed to merge to create a large competitive market. One of these, Surabaya, is the first private Indonesian stock exchange and has become a conduit through which botched trades on the Jakarta Stock Exchange are corrected and Surabaya also offers lower trading costs. Some Jakarta member firms have executed large transactions on the Surabaya Exchange. In addition, Bursa Paralel Indonesia, a second domestic exchange, has nearly tripled the number of its member firms during the 1994–95 period and has captured 60 percent of bond listings in Indonesia through lower listing fees.

Source: Daniel Yu, "And Now for the Hard Part," *Euromoney Supplement*, August 1995, p. 1.

---

market risk. Market risk occurs in different ways. Some country markets may be favored by international investors over other markets. With mutual funds and pension funds increasing their interest in foreign markets, especially the emerging markets, in recent years, the stocks in some countries will increase dramatically because of the added market demand. However, some of these markets may lose the favor of international institutional investors. This occurred after the December 1994 Mexican peso cri-

---

STUDY AID

You are advised to examine the market pages of the *Wall Street Journal, Investor's Business Daily*, and the *Financial Times* to familiarize yourself with the types of information available about international equity markets. These daily periodicals contain a wealth of market information concerning global markets for financial instruments.

TABLE 12–10 Dow Jones World Stock Index (May 7, 1996)

Region/Country	DJ Equity Market Index Local Currency	Pct. Chg.	Closing Index	Chg.	Pct. Chg.	12-mo High	12-mo Low	12-mo Chg.	Pct. Chg.	From 12/31	Pct. Chg.
Americas			149.49	− 0.60	− 0.40	153.90	121.78	+ 26.99	+ 22.03	+ 5.88	+ 4.09
Canada	137.59	+ 0.53	116.40	+ 0.55	+ 0.48	116.49	98.83	+ 17.49	+ 17.69	+ 8.16	+ 7.54
Mexico	224.37	+ 0.02	91.83	+ 0.15	+ 0.16	97.59	61.72	+ 14.21	+ 18.31	+ 13.86	+ 17.78
U.S.	603.64	− 0.44	603.64	− 2.69	− 0.44	623.15	490.31	+ 109.92	+ 22.27	+ 22.22	+ 3.82
Europe/Africa			140.72	− 0.11	− 0.08	143.90	124.01	+ 12.83	+ 10.04	+ 3.71	+ 2.71
Austria	108.93	+ 0.55	108.58	+ 0.47	+ 0.44	113.71	96.56	+ 1.58	+ 1.43	+ 7.29	+ 7.20
Belgium	143.43	− 0.10	143.76	+ 0.33	+ 0.23	148.48	127.30	+ 7.98	+ 5.88	+ 1.20	+ 0.84
Denmark	115.41	+ 0.04	116.35	+ 0.40	+ 0.35	118.94	105.76	+ 6.87	+ 6.28	+ 3.93	+ 3.50
Finland	238.66	− 1.63	206.5	− 2.88	− 1.38	303.04	186.32	− 22.56	− 9.87	+ 3.17	+ 1.56
France	129.03	− 0.28	129.74	− 0.29	− 0.22	132.63	111.60	+ 2.80	+ 2.21	+ 9.72	+ 8.10
Germany	141.75	+ 0.48	140.76	+ 0.75	+ 0.54	147.79	126.99	+ 8.95	+ 6.79	+ 2.52	+ 1.83
Ireland	204.58	+ 0.31	165.35	+ 0.73	+ 0.44	166.46	131.51	+ 30.72	+ 22.82	+ 12.52	+ 8.20
Italy	145.65	+ 0.71	115.52	+ 0.93	+ 0.81	121.02	94.98	+ 2.16	+ 1.90	+ 12.02	+ 11.61
Netherlands	180.95	+ 0.03	178.74	+ 0.02	+ 0.01	179.33	145.56	+ 25.59	+ 16.71	+ 11.44	+ 6.84
Norway	149.82	− 0.05	137.13	+ 0.50	+ 0.37	142.01	123.57	+ 5.41	+ 4.11	+ 7.92	+ 6.13
South Africa	211.86	+ 0.18	132.59	+ 0.77	+ 0.58	160.95	125.20	+ 1.97	+ 1.51	− 10.12	− 7.09
Spain	159.51	− 0.69	122.30	− 0.24	− 0.20	125.00	97.02	+ 19.06	+ 18.47	+ 7.99	+ 6.99
Sweden	220.85	− 0.71	179.74	− 0.73	− 0.40	183.93	130.02	+ 46.17	+ 34.57	+ 16.59	+ 10.17
Switzerland	214.43	− 0.22	233.57	− 0.45	− 0.19	249.58	182.28	+ 44.58	+ 23.59	+ 0.94	+ 0.41

In US. Dollars (columns from Closing Index onward)

Region/Country											
United Kingdom	153.92	– 0.59	124.41	– 0.56	– 0.45	129.26	+ 113.95	+ 9.35	+ 8.12	– 0.08	– 0.06
Europe/Africa (ex. South Africa)			140.99	– 0.15	– 0.11	143.87	+ 124.01	+ 13.10	+ 10.24	+ 4.45	+ 3.26
Europe/Africa (ex. U.K. & S. Africa)			153.56	+ 0.09	+ 0.06	155.91	+ 132.26	+ 15.63	+ 11.33	+ 7.34	+ 5.02
Asia/Pacific			124.83	– 1.07	– 0.85	128.31	+ 109.12	+ 1.54	+ 1.25	+ 5.03	+ 4.20
Australia	136.51	+ 0.59	143.66	+ 1.46	+ 1.03	143.85	+ 110.46	+ 25.58	+ 21.66	+ 15.75	+ 12.32
Hong Kong	238.04	+ 0.00	239.09	– 0.01	– 0.00	260.15	+ 193.58	+ 45.51	+ 23.51	+ 15.41	+ 6.89
Indonesia	223.61	+ 1.65	191.56	+ 3.16	+ 1.68	201.11	+ 157.34	+ 34.22	+ 21.75	+ 19.08	+ 11.06
Japan	98.67	– 0.89	117.11	– 1.39	– 1.17	121.16	– 102.27	– 3.07	– 2.56	+ 3.03	+ 2.66
Malaysia	235.99	– 0.21	257.44	– 0.63	– 0.24	264.21	+ 198.20	+ 36.92	+ 16.74	+ 34.36	+ 15.41
New Zealand	140.26	+ 0.14	178.62	+ 0.81	+ 0.46	189.29	– 168.79	– 6.16	– 3.34	+ 2.46	+ 1.40
Philippines	338.25	+ 1.94	335.85	+ 6.40	+ 1.94	335.85	+ 239.18	+ 50.72	+ 17.79	+ 54.36	+ 19.31
Singapore	178.38	+ 0.31	205.85	+ 0.54	+ 0.26	224.73	+ 171.93	+ 25.10	+ 13.89	+ 9.94	+ 5.07
South Korea	160.32	+ 1.46	156.23	+ 2.24	+ 1.46	167.89	+ 135.98	+ 5.62	+ 3.73	+ 10.66	+ 7.32
Taiwan	152.39	– 0.94	144.81	– 1.40	– 0.96	148.01	+ 105.15	+ 3.33	+ 2.35	+ 25.36	+ 21.23
Thailand	222.48	– 0.09	207.95	– 0.03	– 0.01	227.64	+ 179.94	+ 7.84	+ 3.92	+ 11.19	+ 5.69
Asia/Pacific (ex. Japan)			191.06	+ 0.57	+ 0.30	193.26	+ 161.44	+ 29.59	+ 18.32	+ 17.61	+ 10.15
World (ex. U.S.)			129.81	– 0.62	– 0.48	132.46	+ 116.28	+ 6.57	+ 5.33	+ 4.69	+ 3.75
DJ WORLD STOCK INDEX			138.51	– 0.64	– 0.46	141.61	+ 120.11	+ 14.59	+ 11.78	+ 5.05	+ 3.78

Indexes based on 6/30/82 = 100 for U.S., 12/31/91 = 100 for World.

Source: Wall Street Journal, 8 May 1996, p. C16. Reprinted by permission. All rights reserved.

sis when foreign mutual funds that were heavily invested in Mexico withdrew their funds in large amounts from the Mexico City Stock Exchange and from investments in Mexican companies. This event caused portfolio managers of many global and country funds to rethink their asset allocation strategies with regard to foreign markets, especially those in emerging markets. As a result, many foreign market indexes declined during 1995.

Another risk that faces international investors may stem from the globalization of markets. Some analysts believe that major stock markets around the world are integrated to some extent and a crash in one market may be contagious and result in drastic declines in other markets. This contagion theory seemed to hold in the October 1987 crash of the U.S. stock market. Other markets worldwide fell drastically. However, other severe downturns of markets such as Tokyo, Mexico, and some in Europe since the 1987 crash have not had the same result. Empirical tests by finance scholars have had mixed results with regard to the correlation between and among international equities markets.

TRANSACTIONS DIRECTLY ON THE FOREIGN MARKET

Investors have several alternatives available for participation in international equities. Studies have shown that diversification by countries as well as by industries will enhance return and reduce risk. For investments in individual securities, an investor can invest in a company's stock by purchasing it directly from the foreign stock market. This can be costly because two brokerage fees might be charged, one by the investor's domestic broker and one by the foreign broker. In addition, a foreign tax might be charged on the transaction, such as in Germany where each state in which a stock exchange is located charges a turnover tax on the transaction. Another risk of buying equities directly in the foreign market is manifest in the inability to get information about activities in the stock such as stock splits, cash and stock dividends, or other important news. The registration service in many foreign countries is not as well developed as it is in the United States.

ADRS, AMERICAN SHARES, AND GDRS

Special stock certificates have been developed to reduce some of the risks incurred from holding shares in foreign companies. These are American depository receipts (ADRs), American shares, and global depository receipts (GDRs). The use of such financial vehicles has become significant in recent years, especially in the United States with ADRs and India with GDRs. These financial instruments are discussed in the following sections.

American Shares and American Depository Receipts

To avoid these risks, the U.S. investor can purchase American shares or ADRs, American depository receipts, issued and traded in the United States. American shares are shares registered in the United States and listed on the major stock exchanges or traded over-the-counter in the NASDAQ market. Philips Lamp, the Dutch MNC, is an example of a company that has floated American shares in the U.S. market.

ADRs were invented by J.P. Morgan in 1927 and are receipts that represent the underlying stock held by a major bank in its vault. ADRs were designed to alleviate the information risks just mentioned. The bank keeps track of all information disseminated by the issuing corporation and notifies shareholders of ADRs about dividends, annual meetings, proxies, etc. ADRs trade at a small premium in return for this service and may represent a fraction of the original share or some multiple of it.

More than 1,100 ADRs were traded in the United States in 1993 and many of

these are listed on the New York and American Stock Exchanges or traded in the NAS-DAQ National Market. The value of ADRs traded on U.S. stock exchanges in 1993 amounted to $200 billion.[27] Most ADRs are traded over-the-counter on the NASDAQ National Market, and many have their prices quoted only on the so-called "pink sheets," the sheets showing daily bid/ask prices for very thinly traded securities. Those traded on the NASDAQ National Market can be identified by a five-letter stock symbol ending in the letter "Y". For example, the symbol for Volvo, the Swedish auto manufacturer, is VOLVY. ADRs can be sponsored, i.e., brought to market by banks that hold the original shares and that promote such equities, or they may be unsponsored, i.e., not held by any particular bank but issued directly by the corporation into the market.

Trading of ADRs on the New York Stock Exchange has been extensive during the past few years. ADR turnover accounted for about 4.6 percent of all NYSE trading in 1992. In fact, the most active stock listed on the NYSE in 1992 was the ADR for Glaxo Holdings, a British company.[28] In 1993, the Argentinian state-owned oil company, Yacimientos Petroliferos Fiscales (YPF), sold one-third of the company for $3 billion and much of this was issued in the form of ADRs in the United States. In fact, foreign companies have used ADRs to obtain record amounts of equity funds in the United States in recent years. Non-U.S. companies raised $9.1 billion with ADRs in 1992, versus $6.8 billion in 1991, and only $2.6 billion in 1990.[29] The global distribution of ADRs traded in the United States shows that 34 percent are from Asian companies, 32 percent are from European companies, 21 percent are from Australian companies, 11 percent are from African companies, and the remainder from Central and South American companies.[30]

Other ADRs have been issued in the United States by several well-known foreign companies. These include Porsche of Germany, Jardine Matheson of Hong Kong, Sony of Japan, and Novo Industri of Denmark. In addition to the advantages and uses of ADRs mentioned previously, they do have certain disadvantages.[31] Some of the companies that have issued them have lower reporting standards and may disclose less financial and company information than is required for U.S. companies. The number of ADRs and shares traded are limited and, thus, they may be less liquid than their domestic counterparts. ADRs usually represent more conservative foreign companies and, thus, may not meet growth requirements of some investors. However, the number of ADRs has increased rapidly in recent years and they are presenting the ability to better diversification of investment objectives.

Global Depository Receipts

Global depository receipts, GDRs, have also gained an increasing share of the market in the past few years. These are similar to ADRs but can be simultaneously introduced in the United States, Europe, and Asia. They were first issued in 1993.

Both ADRs and GDRs can be issued in the United States under Rule 144A, a Securities and Exchange Commission regulation that permits foreign equities to be issued without the lengthy SEC regulation procedure. The first five GDRs were issued by companies headquartered in emerging markets and were the Mexican companies Vitro, FEMSA, and Grupo Gigante, and the Korean companies, Samsung and Samsung Electronics. Citibank has become a major player in the 144A and GDR markets.

---

[27] John Goff, "ADRs: Decline and Fall Was Never This Good," *Global Finance* 8 (January 1994): 31.

[28] Ellen Memmelaar, "Why Momentum's Building for ADRs," *Global Finance* 7 (June 1993): 62.

[29] "International Corporate Trust: A Global Commitment to Relationships," *Global Finance* 7 (June 1993): 42.

[30] Ibid.

[31] Alan L. Tucker, Jeff Madura, and Thomas C. Chiang, *International Financial Markets* (St. Paul, MN: West Publishing Co., 1991), p. 171.

Bank of New York is a leader in trading ADRs over-the-counter. The first issues of GDRs were made in 1990 and totaled $40 million. By late 1994, GDR issues had amounted to $5.5 billion.[32]

GDRs have recently become quite popular in the emerging markets of Latin America, Asia, and eastern Europe. For example, many Indian companies plan to use GDRs because of the ability to use inexpensive foreign currencies to issue their stock globally.[33] Foreign institutional investors in these securities will have a simpler qualifying process to complete with simplified paperwork. These GDRs will not be subject to the Indian capital gains tax and, since the GDRs will be traded in Luxembourg, the required 45-day settlement and custody problems encountered in the Bombay market will be alleviated. A GDR issue will cost about 4 percent, much lower than the typical 8–10 percent cost of stock issues in India.

Other GDR issues have been highly publicized.[34] In addition, Kleinwort Benson, a U.K. merchant bank, planned a multibillion dollar GDR issue of Gasprom of Russia, the world's largest gas company. Jardine Fleming, the U.K.-based investment company, orchestrated a $250 million GDR issue for Benpres, the largest broadcasting group in the Philippines, which will permit foreigners to own GDRs but not the underlying shares. Foreigners are prohibited by Philippines law from owning shares in media companies.

COUNTRY FUNDS

A large number of open-end (mutual funds) and closed-end investment companies have been established for the purpose of investing only in the equities of a specific country. Closed-end investment companies can be traded on stock exchanges, whereas mutual funds, open-end investment companies, cannot. Examples of these funds are Germany Fund, Japan Fund, Spain Fund, and Korea Fund from the industrialized nations, and Mexico Fund and Hungary Fund from LDCs or former socialist nations. A list of closed-end country funds is shown in Table 12–11. Most of these funds trade at a discount from net asset value. This is typical of closed-end investment companies. Several of these country funds were established with the assistance of the International Finance Corporation, a global development finance agency discussed in chapter 11.

Many mutual funds, not traded on stock exchanges, also invest in the equities of a specific country, of a regional area, or globally. The Janus Worldwide Fund is an example of the latter. These global equity mutual funds include families of funds including those of Templeton, Fidelity, Janus, and Lexington companies. A listing of global equity funds is shown in Table 12–12. These mutual funds can be classified by the proportion of their portfolio devoted to specific country or foreign market securities. A country fund has 100 percent of its portfolio in investments in a specific country. A global fund has at least 25 percent of its portfolio invested in foreign market securities. An international fund has at least 50 percent of its portfolio invested in the securities of foreign markets.

---

[32] Martin Brice, "Four Years of Explosive Growth for GDRs," *Financial Times*, 10 November 1994, p. 24.

[33] The GDR Issue Queue Lengthens," *Euromoney Supplement: India Steps into the Big League*, (September 1994): 15–6, and "Issuers Prepare to Enter the GDR Fray," 18–20.

[34] Brice, *Financial Times*, 24.

TABLE 12-11. Selected Closed-End Country Funds

Fund	Price	NAV*
Brazil Fund	$ 8.62	$ 8.76
First Australia	7.63	8.61
Germany Fund	11.50	11.16
Italy Fund	10.00	11.37
Korea Fund	12.25	10.04
Malaysia Fund	12.37	12.42
Mexico Fund	14.00	15.37
Spain Fund	10.87	11.20
Taiwan Fund	21.37	15.63
Thai Fund	15.88	14.74
U.K. Fund	9.25	11.04

* NAV = net asset value of shares in the portfolio.
Source: Ian H. Giddy, *Global Financial Markets* (Lexington, MA: D.C. Heath, 1994), p. 442.

TABLE 12-12. Global Equity Funds

Funds	Total Assets (millions U.S. $)
Templeton World	$3,667.0
Templeton Growth	2,329.9
Freedom Global Fund	1.567.0
Oppenheimer Global	790.7
Putnam Global Growth	574.2
Scudder Global Fund	245.8
Pru-Bache Global Fund	244.1
Merrill Lynch Int'l Holdings	174.9
Lexington Global	51.3
Van Eck World Trends	49.1
Transamerica Global Growth	6.8

Source: Ian H. Giddy, *Global Financial Markets* (Lexington, MA: D.C. Heath, 1994), p. 440.

Summary and Conclusions

The CFO of a MNC needs to include the major international financial markets in the inventory of financial resources. International financial markets include the Eurocurrency market and the international debt and equity markets. From these markets, the MNC can obtain short-, medium-, and long-term funds.

Eurocurrencies represent currencies that are deposited outside of their country of origin. The market is essentially a stateless vat of funds that favors no particular country and that is minimally, if at all, regulated by any government. A variety of short-, medium-, and long-term financial instruments can be denominated in Eurocurrencies including commercial paper, CDs, medium-term notes, equities, and Eurobonds.

Three major types of international bonds, global bonds, foreign bonds, and Eurobonds, can be issued and traded in the international debt market. Eurobonds have no withholding taxes. Global bonds are very large denomination bonds that can be traded simultaneously in the United States, Europe, and Tokyo. Each major foreign capital market makes a market in particular foreign bonds, e.g., Yankee bonds in the United States, Samurai bonds in Japan, Rembrandt bonds in Amsterdam, and Bulldog bonds in London. Euroclear and Cedel were established by major banking interests to facilitate a secondary market in international bonds by holding inventories of currencies and Eurobonds and standing ready to buy or sell Eurobonds.

International equity markets available to MNCs include the major stock markets in New York, London, Paris, and Tokyo, as well as those in the emerging markets of the LDCs. In addition to having their stocks traded on organized securities exchanges, companies can issue American depository receipts or global depository receipts, which represent underlying stock certificates. These instruments facilitate trading of foreign companies' stocks because the banks that issue them are able to keep the stockholder informed about valuable information concerning the issuing company.

In recent years, stocks from particular countries or regions have been included in country funds. These funds are investment companies and can be either open-end—mutual funds—or closed-end types. The closed-end country funds are traded on secu-

rities exchanges. Both furnish an outlet for new stock issues of foreign companies and a means of reducing the risk to the investor by diversification of portfolios.

Additional Readings

Bank for International Settlements. *Annual Report*. Any year.

Callaghan, Joseph H., Robert T. Kleiman, and Anandi P. Sahu. "The Investment Characteristics of American Depository Receipts." *Multinational Business Review* 4 (Spring 1996):29–39.

Dufey, Gunter, and Ian Giddy. *The International Money Market*. Englewood Cliffs, NJ: Prentice-Hall, 1994.

Emerging Markets Data Base. Washington, D.C.: International Finance Corporation, 1994.

Evans, John S. *International Finance: A Markets Approach*. Orlando, FL: Dryden Press, 1992.

Giddy, Ian H. *Global Financial Markets*. Lexington, MA: D.C. Health, 1994.

Goff, John. "ADRs: Decline and Fall Was Never This Good." *Global Finance* 8 (January 1994): 31–32.

Grabbe, J. Orlin. *International Financial Markets*. Englewood Cliffs, NJ: Prentice-Hall, 1996.

Harr, J., K. Dandapani, and S. Harr. "The American Depositary Receipt (ADR): A Creative Financial Tool for Multinational Companies." *Global Finance Journal*. 2 (1990): 163–171.

Maxwell, Charles E. *Financial Markets and Institutions: The Global View*. St. Paul, MN: West Publishing Co., 1994.

Solnik, Bruno. *International Investments*. Reading, MA. Addison-Wesley Publishing Co., 1996.

Tucker, Alan L., Jeff Madura, and Thomas C. Chiang. *International Financial Markets*. St. Paul, MN: West Publishing Co., 1991.

Discussion Questions

1. Discuss the characteristics of the Eurocurrency market.
2. What are the major Eurocurrency centers?
3. Distinguish among global bonds, foreign bonds, and Eurobonds.
4. What entities issue global bonds?
5. Describe the organization of the Eurobond market.
6. What roles do Euroclear and Cedel play in this market? Why are such institutions necessary?
7. What are ADRs? Why have they become so popular in the past few years?
8. What is the difference between so-called country funds and mutual funds that specialize in foreign stocks?

Problems

1. Find and list 25 companies that are traded on the NASDAQ National Market list found in the *Wall Street Journal*.
2. Discuss how a long-term bond denominated in a foreign currency is equivalent to a domestic currency bond with a series of forward exchange contracts attached to it. How then can this bond be fully hedged against foreign currency risk?
3. An investment banking syndicate issues and underwrites a $100 million, 10-year Eurobond issue. The syndicate has 1 lead manager, which takes half of the management fee, and 6 comanagers that split the remainder equally. The issue is underwritten by these 7 banks, which underwrite 40 percent of the issue, 50 major underwriters, and 50 minor underwriters, which underwrite the remainder. The underwriting allowance

is split up according to the amount underwritten. The issue is sold by the 7 managers, $40 million total, divided equally; 50 major underwriters, $30 million total; 50 minor underwriters, $15 million total; and 100 additional selling banks, $15 million total. The selling concession is split according to the amount sold. Given the following table of flotation costs, or fees, calculate the dollar amount of total fees going to: (1) the lead manager, (2) each of the comanagers, (3) each of the major underwriters, (4) each of the minor underwriters, (5) each of the selling banks, and (6) the company. Assume that all bonds are sold at the issue price of 100, or par.

Maturity	Management Fee(%)	Underwriting Allowance (%)	Selling Concession (%)	Total(%)
5 years	0.25	0.25	1.25	1.75
5–8 years	0.25	0.25	1.25	1.75
>8 years	0.375	0.375	1.25	2.00

4. An investor buys 100 Eurobonds in the secondary market at a price of 92. The par value of each bond is $1,000. Each bears an annual coupon of 10 percent. As of the value date for the trade, 220 days have passed since the last coupon. What is the investor's total dollar payment for the bonds?

5. Compare recent interest rates quoted in the *Financial Times* and *Wall Street Journal* on Euro-repurchase agreements overnight, London Interbank Bid Rate (LIBID) on Eurodollar deposits, and U.S. Federal Funds. Show bid and ask rates where possible.

6. You are a Janus Worldwide Fund manager and wish to buy 1,000 shares of Telefonica de Espana, the Spanish telephone company. Your Spanish broker at the Madrid Stock Exchange quotes a bid and ask price of 41–41$^1/_4$, with a commission of 0.5% of the transaction value. Your bank quotes the Spanish peseta at Spta 110/$ net. What would be your total costs in dollars?

7. Select one ADR traded on the New York Stock Exchange, one from the American Stock Exchange, and one from the NASDAQ Stock Market and show the following information:
   a. the high and low prices quoted during 1995;
   b. the price of the stock traded on the home stock exchange, translated into U.S. dollars;
   c. show whether arbitrage opportunities exist between ADRs and the underlying foreign stock for each ADR selected.

8. Select three closed-end country funds traded on the New York Stock Exchange and show whether they trade at a premium or discount to their book value and how they compare in market value for 1995.

9. Select three mutual funds, which have global portfolios, and show their performance for the current year-to-date and the past 3- or 5-year period, whichever is available.

10. Select a sample of emerging countries. For each of them collect monthly stock market indexes, consumer price indexes, and exchange rates. Calculate the following:
    a. their mean return measured in local currency, in real terms (after local inflation adjustment), and in dollar terms;
    b. their standard deviation of return measured in local currency, in real terms (after local inflation adjustment), and in dollar terms;
    c. the correlation across the various markets, using, successively, returns measured in local currency terms, in real terms (after local inflation adjustment), and in dollar terms.

11. Determine, from the *Wall Street Journal*, the total annual yield for five leading mutual funds that invest entirely in foreign stocks.

13

International Derivatives Exchange-Traded

Major Objectives of Chapter 13

(1) An examination of derivative financial instruments traded on organized exchanges that are of value to the CFO of MNCs for hedging purposes, (2) to introduce how these instruments are traded, and (3) to analyze the problems inherent in these markets, including the various risks incurred and regulation of the markets.

Key terms to be learned in chapter 13:

- notional value
- margin
- SIMEX
- LIFFE
- Finex
- Deutsche Terminbörse
- credit risk
- legal risk
- systemic risk
- efficient markets hypothesis
- expiration
- in the money
- basis risk
- strike price
- call option
- Philadelphia Stock Exchange
- time value
- CFTC

- currency futures
- mark-to-market
- MATIF
- Chicago Mercantile Exchange
- Chicago Board of Trade
- market risk
- operational risk
- settlement risk
- agency theory
- asymmetric information
- at the money
- out of the money
- currency options
- volatility
- put option
- intrinsic value
- synthetic currency futures
- clearing house

Introduction

During the past 15 years, derivative financial instruments have drastically changed the way financial managers have coped with various financial risks. According to the *Financial Times*, the 1990s has been referred to as the decade of derivatives.[1] This has been especially so in international financial operations. The growth of derivatives trading to manage commodity price, exchange rate, and interest rate risks has caused great concern among regulators, bankers, and shareholders. According to the *New York Times*, Spring 1995, approximately two-thirds of U.S. corporate treasurers were using derivatives, but many of those treasurers either had not been trained in their use or had been trained as long as 10 years earlier, when they took their MBA course work.

A derivatives transaction is represented by a contract whose value depends on the value of some underlying, or derivative, asset, reference rate, or index. Derivatives may be (1) standard futures or options contracts traded on organized exchanges, (2) over-the-counter instruments that are privately negotiated contracts provided directly by dealers such as banks to end-users and that consist of swaps based on interest rates, currencies, equities, and commodities, or (3) exotic derivatives custom-designed and issued by banks and other financial institutions, based on some underlying financial instrument but whose terms are arranged in some very esoteric way to hedge a very specific event.[2] The second and third categories of derivatives will be discussed in chapter 14.

The phenomenal growth of derivatives trading can be demonstrated by an examination of the trend in derivatives trading between organized exchange trading and trading executed over-the-counter (OTC), from 1986 through 1991. The value of derivatives instruments is measured by notional principal. In 1986, the notional principal—the market value of the assets that underlay derivatives—of futures and options traded on exchanges amounted to $583 billion while the notional principal of swaps and other interest rate and currency derivatives traded OTC amounted to $500 billion. By 1991, exchange volume had risen to $3,518 billion but had been surpassed by OTC volume of $4,449 billion.[3]

The notional value of all derivatives contracts outstanding in March 1994 was estimated to be $16 trillion, or more than twice the gross domestic product of the United States. The estimated notional value of derivatives traded by the 20 financial institutions that are most active in the derivatives markets is shown in Table 13–1. The growth of the notional principal outstanding for the markets for selected derivative instruments for the 1988–93 period is shown in Table 13–2. The notional principal outstanding at the end of 1993 for derivative financial instruments traded on organized exchanges is shown in Table 13–3, as well as the annual trading volume, by notional value, of these instruments for the period 1989–93. Finally, the notional principal for selected derivative instruments marketed over-the-counter for 1990–93 is shown in Table 13–4.

Current concern over the growth of derivatives overlooks the fact that commerce has used instruments similar to derivatives in order to spread risk and reward so that trade and investment are not inhibited by uncertainty. This practice can be traced back for centuries. Aristotle discussed an options contract in Book I of *Politics*.[4] Aristotle

---

[1] "*Financial Times* Survey: Derivatives," *Financial Times*, 20 October 1993, p. I.

[2] Global Derivatives Study Group, *Derivatives: Practices and Principles* (Washington, D.C.: Group of Thirty, July 1993), p. 2.

[3] Peter Lee, "American Exchanges Plan to Fight Back," *Euromoney* (January 1993): 46.

[4] Aristotle, *Politics*, Book 1, Chapter 11 (Norwalk, CT: The Easton Press, 1979), pp. 24–6.

TABLE 13–1.	Notional Value Held by Top 20 Financial Firms Derivatives Markets (Billions of 1993 U.S.$)
1. Chemical Bank	$2,416
2. Bankers Trust	1,982
3. Citicorp	1,981
4. J.P. Morgan	1,660
5. Union Banque Suisse	1,452
6. Banque Suisse	1,352
7. Société Générale	1,209
8. Mitsubishi Bank	1,182
9. Crédit Lyonnais	1,110
10. Chase Manhattan	1,042
11. Crédit Suisse	1,017
12. Salomon	967
13. BankAmerica	964
14. Banque Indosuez	945
15. Merrill Lynch	918
16. Goldman Sachs	752
17. Barclays	751
18. Paribas	742
19. National Westminster	577
20. Royal Bank of Canada	554

Source: Carol J. Loomis, "The Risk That Won't Go Away," *Fortune* 129 (March 7, 1994): 44.

TABLE 13–2. Selected Derivative Instruments (notional principal outstanding in billions of U.S.$ (1988–1993)

Instruments	1988	1989	1990	1991	1992	1993
Exchange-traded instruments	1,306.0	1,768.3	2,291.7	3,523.4	4,640.5	7,839.3
Interest rate futures	895.4	1,200.6	1,454.1	2,157.1	2,902.2	4,960.4
Interest rate options*	279.2	387.9	599.5	1,072.6	1,385.4	2,362.4
Currency futures	11.6	15.6	16.3	17.8	24.5	29.8
Currency options*	48.0	50.1	56.1	61.2	80.1	81.1
Stock market index futures	27.8	41.8	69.7	77.3	80.7	119.2
Stock market index options*	44.0	72.2	96.0	137.4	167.6	286.4
Over-the-counter instruments†	—	—	3,450.3	4,449.4	5,345.7	—
Interest rate swaps	1,010.2	1,502.6	2,311.5	3,065.1	3,850.8	—
Currency swaps**	319.6	449.1	577.5	807.2	860.4	—
Other swap-related derivatives‡	—	—	561.3	577.2	634.5	—

*Calls and puts

†Data collected by the International Swaps and Derivatives Association only; the two sides of contracts between ISDA members are reported once only; excluding instruments such as forward rate agreements, currency options, forward foreign exchange contracts and equity and commodity-related derivatives.

**Adjusted for reporting of both currencies; including cross-currency interest rate swaps.

‡Caps, collars, floors, and swaptions.

Source: Bank for International Settlements, *64th Annual Report*, p. 112.

TABLE 13–3.   Derivative Financial Instruments Trading Volume on Organized Exchanges and Amount Outstanding, Year End 1994 (notional principal outstanding in billions U.S.$) (1989–1993)

Instruments	*Annual Turnover of Contracts*					*Notional Principal Outstanding*
	1989	*1990*	*1991*	*1992*	*1993*	*End-1994*
Interest rate futures	201.0	219.0	230.9	330.1	427.0	5,757.4
On short-term instruments	70.2	76.0	84.8	130.8	166.8	5,401.8
of which: 3-mon Euro$ rates[1]	46.8	39.4	41.7	66.9	70.2	2,468.6
3-mon Euro¥ rates[2]	4.7	15.2	16.2	17.4	26.9	1,467.4
3-mon EuroDM rates[3]	1.6	3.1	4.8	12.2	21.3	425.7
On long-term instruments	130.8	143.1	146.1	199.3	260.2	355.6
of which: U.S. Treasury bonds[4]	72.8	78.2	69.9	71.7	80.7	36.1
French govt bonds[5]	15.0	16.0	21.1	31.1	36.8	12.7
Japanese govt bonds[6]	19.1	16.4	12.9	12.1	15.6	164.3
German govt bonds[7]	5.3	9.6	12.4	18.9	28.1	41.7
Interest rate options[8]	39.5	52.0	50.8	64.8	82.9	2,622.7
Currency futures	27.5	29.1	29.2	30.7	38.0	33.0
Currency options[8]	20.7	18.9	22.9	23.4	23.8	54.5
Stock market index futures	30.1	39.4	54.6	52.0	60.7	127.7
Stock market index options[8]	101.7	119.1	121.4	133.9	141.8	242.4
Total	**420.4**	**477.7**	**509.8**	**634.9**	**774.2**	**8,837.8**
of which: In the United States	286.2	310.3	300.7	339.4	379.0	4,754.9
In Europe	64.4	83.0	110.5	185.0	255.9	1,832.0
In Japan	45.7	60.6	66.2	51.7	57.8	1,498.2

[1] Traded on the Chicago Mercantile Exchange—International Monetary Market (CME-IMM), Singapore Mercantile Exchange (SIMEX), London International Financial Futures Exchange (LIFFE), Tokyo International Financial Futures Exchange (TIFFE), and Sydney Futures Exchange (SFE).

[2] Traded on the TIFFE and SIMEX.

[3] Traded on the Marché à Terme International de France (MATIF) and LIFFE.

[4] Traded on the Chicago Board of Trade (CBOT), LIFFE, Mid-America Commodity Exchange (MIDAM), New York Futures Exchange (NYSE), and Tokyo Stock Exchange (TSE).

[5] Traded on the MATIF.

[6] Traded on the TSE, LIFFE, and CBOT.

[7] Traded on the LIFFE and Deutsche Terminbörse (DTB).

[8] Calls and puts.

Source: Bank for International Settlements, *64th Annual Report*, p. 113, and *IMF Survey* 24 (September 14, 1995): p 272.

tells of the development of "a financial device which involves a principle of universal application" by the philosopher Thales. Thales had been able to forecast the quality of the following season's olive harvest. He made agreements with owners of olive presses in the area by placing small deposits with each to guarantee he would be the first to use their presses during the coming harvest. When harvest time came, he leased out the presses at high rates and became a wealthy man.

USERS OF DERIVATIVES

Two groups are active in the derivatives markets, end-users and dealers. End-users consist of corporations, government agencies, institutional investors, and financial in-

TABLE 13–4. Selected Derivative Instruments Traded Over-the-Counter* (notional principal outstanding in billions of U.S.$) (1990–1993)

	New Contracts Arranged					Amounts Outstanding End-1992
Instruments	*1990*	*1991*	*1992 HI*	*1992 HII*	*1993 HI*	
Total	1,769.3	2,332.9	1,768.0	1,949.0	2,605.0	5,345.7
Interest rate swaps	1,264.3	1,621.8	1,318.3	1,504.3	1,938.5	3,850.8
Currency swaps†	212.8	328.4	156.1	145.8	156.8	860.4
Other swap-related derivatives**	292.3	382.7	293.6	298.8	509.7	634.5

*Data collected by ISDA only; the two sides of contracts between ISDA members are reported once only; excluding instruments such as forward rate agreements, currency options, forward foreign exchange contracts and equity and commodity-related derivatives.

†Adjusted for reporting of both currencies; including cross-currency interest rate swaps.

** Caps, collars, floors, and swaptions.

Source: Bank for International Settlements, *64th Annual Report*, p. 115.

stitutions. Dealers include banks, securities firms, insurance companies, and some highly rated corporations. An individual, on occasion, may even be a derivatives dealer, especially in the writing of options. End-users utilize derivatives to lower funding costs, increase yields, diversify sources of funding, and hedge commodity price, interest rate, and foreign exchange risk of underlying financial instruments. Dealers create derivatives and trade for their own accounts, speculating on the price of derivatives.

RISKS OF DERIVATIVES

Derivative instruments are subject to a number of risks.[5] These include market risk, credit risk, settlement risk, operating risk, legal risk, and systemic risk. *Market risk*, stemming from price behavior of the underlying instruments, refers to any market-related factor that changes the value of a derivatives position. It can be further divided into liquidity risk, in which a large transaction in a particular instrument might have a large effect on the price of the instrument. Basis risk may be incurred where the difference between the price of the underlying instrument and the derivative change correlation. Investing and funding risk each stem from the inability of dealers and other participants who manage derivatives portfolios to be able to meet the investing and funding requirements stemming from cash flow mismatches. In fact, concentration of derivatives business among a small number of institutions may lead to liquidity risk, or some of the other risks discussed in this section. One Federal Reserve Board report found that 90 percent of the derivatives business was being done by 6 U.S. commercial banks.[6] Such concentration certainly may lead to a lessening of competition and less market efficiency. *Credit risk* stems from the loss that occurs when one counterparty to a derivatives contract defaults. *Operational risk* arises when losses occur because of inadequate systems and control, human error, or management problems. Lack of involvement or understanding by a firm's top management or board of directors creates

[5] For a good analysis of the various risks of derivatives, see Peter A. Abken, "Over-the-Counter Financial Derivatives: Risky Business?" *Economic Review of the Federal Reserve Bank of Atlanta*, 79 (March/April 1994): 5–11.

[6] Rosemary Bennett, "The Six Men Who Rule World Derivatives," *Euromoney* (August 1993): 45–9.

an operating risk. The demise of Barings Bank, the British merchant bank, was caused by the lack of managerial controls over one trader in the Singapore office. This case will be discussed in detail in subsequent section. *Legal risk* may occur when a contract cannot be enforced and losses happen. Participation in derivatives markets crosses national borders. Each nation has different securities and bankruptcy laws. Derivatives counterparties risk losses caused by legal actions that render their agreements unenforceable. A notorious case occurred when the U.K. House of Lords ruled null and void swaps contracts established by the borough of Hammersmith and Fulham during the 1980s on the grounds that the municipality did not have legal authority to enter into derivatives transactions. *Settlement risk* is the risk of default during the first day or two when one counterparty has fulfilled its obligation under a contract and awaits settlement by payment or delivery of securities from the other counterparty. *Systemic risk* is the contagion from the failure of one institution or firm that causes disruption or failure in other market segments or to the financial system as a whole. Although defaults have been rare in derivatives trading and no systemic crisis has occurred, the global scope of such trading in these unregulated instruments has increased the concerns of government regulators and national legislators. This risk may also be referred to as contagion risk.

These risks can be alleviated by better controls exercised by the firms and banks that trade or create derivatives, by the formulation of accounting standards aimed at accounting and reporting of derivatives trading, and by tighter supervision and regulation by federal regulatory authorities. For example, in 1994, the Financial Accounting Standards Board (FASB) issued an exposure draft designed to tighten disclosure standards.[7] The new standard will require more detailed explanation of derivatives positions whose objective is to hedge anticipated transactions such as unbooked but certain foreign currency cash flows. This and other moves by regulatory authorities to tighten derivatives reporting rules came in the light of adverse stock market reaction to the disclosure by Dell Computer and Banc One in the United States and Metallgesellschaft in Germany that these companies had engaged in derivatives trading. In addition, Piper Capital Management Inc., the subsidiary of Piper Jaffray Companies, a Minneapolis-based regional brokerage firm, lost nearly 50 percent of its stock value during 1994. The company held derivatives in its bond fund and failed to disclose this fact to investors. Investors attributed the losses to the derivatives held in the fund and to being misled by Piper.[8] Other major losses stemming from derivatives trading have been suffered by, among other firms, Procter & Gamble and Gibson Greeting Cards. In a number of these and other cases, the firm that suffered losses had dealt in derivatives with Bankers Trust, one of the leading firms globally dealing in derivatives. Procter & Gamble, in fact, is pursuing legal relief in a suit against Bankers Trust.

Metallgesellschaft

The losses by Metallgesellschaft represent one of the most serious cases of a problem in this area of risk management.[9] The company nearly went out of business at the end of 1993 because of a liquidity crisis. The crisis was brought on by a failed hedging strategy on the part of MG Corporation, the U.S. subsidiary of Metallgesellschaft, leading to losses in excess of $1.5 billion. MG used futures contracts to hedge long-term fixed price contracts to supply oil products to small independent service stations around

---

[7] Bill Millar, "Hedging Unveiled," *International Business* 7 (May 1994): 32–4.

[8] Suzanne Wooley, "Piper Jaffray: A Steal or a Sinking Star?" *Business Week*, 7 November 1994, p. 128.

[9] Richard Waters, "Academics Open Wounds of MG Corp's Oil Crisis," *Financial Times*, 6 October 1994, p. 27.

the United States. These futures contracts were traded on the New York Mercantile Exchange. The hedging strategy was designed to protect MG from a rise in oil prices.

MG's problems were exacerbated by the drop in oil prices. As oil prices declined, the value of the futures contracts held by the company also fell, requiring the company to put up additional margin payments with the New York Mercantile Exchange. For every decline of $1 in the price of oil, extra margin of $160 million had to be paid by MG. New management was forced on Metallgesellschaft by one of its major shareholders, Deutsche Bank. One of these new managers liquidated many of the positions instead of rolling them forward, thus causing additional losses. Some analysts say that profits could have been made in 1994 because of higher oil prices in addition to higher futures prices. Thus, paper losses were converted into real losses.

Finally, academic research published during 1994 has placed the blame on the supervisory board of the parent company rather than the derivatives group that had formulated the hedging strategy.[10] This study held that the supervisory board, as well as the company's banks, did not understand the derivatives market or the hedging strategy and, because the strategy was quite complex, premature liquidation of MG's hedge positions was forced, resulting in the company's losses. One of the lessons stemming from this case is that a firm should only acquire derivatives positions that they can afford to margin. The cost of funds is a major consideration.

Barings Bank PLC

In February 1995, the Barings PLC, a merchant bank headquartered in London and founded in 1762 by the Baring family, declared the British equivalence of bankruptcy. The event occurred when the bank lost more than $1 billion from derivatives trading by a general manager of a Singapore subsidiary. The loss exceeded the capital of the parent bank, one of the most venerable banks in the world, ranked 15th largest in Great Britain and 489th in the world by *The Banker*.[11] The manager bought stock futures contracts in Tokyo and Osaka and sold them in Singapore. These contracts were derived from the Nikkei 225 stock index and the trader's objectives were of an arbitrage nature—to profit on small price differences between two markets. The trader then stopped selling Singapore contracts, expecting the Japanese market and the Osaka contracts to increase in price. Instead, Japanese stocks continued to decline and the trader continued to buy contracts. Barings notional exposure was more than $27 billion. The trades were highly leveraged and, when Barings' liabilities exceeded its capital, the bank was closed.

Bank regulation of such a situation is very complex. This problem was discussed in chapter 9 when the implications of Banco Ambrosiano and the Basle Concordat were examined. Barings was a European banking company operating in the Far East and trading in a third country. Singapore had a thriving financial services sector with excellent communications and the Singapore International Monetary Exchange (SIMEX) had become a leading futures exchange and a center for derivatives products, but with a regulatory system that had not kept up with changes in derivatives trading. Thus, international bank regulation was relatively ineffective in such a situation. Internal controls in Barings apparently broke down. A young manager operating in a foreign affiliate apparently had few if any managerial controls imposed on his operations, although it was believed that he had approval from other top managers at Barings. In the United States, the Comptroller of the Currency, the supervisor of national banks, has imposed continuous auditing by separate bank departments on all derivatives deal-

---

[10] Ibid.

[11] Janet L. Fix, "For 233 Years, It Survived War, Disasters," *USA Today*, 28 February 1995, p. 2B.

ing. However, global trading in these instruments places a burden on such internal controls.

Bank regulatory authorities, especially in the United States, have suggested proposals for regulation of derivatives trading that approach moral hazard status. These include regulations that interfere with the normal workings of the market, e.g., deposit insurance or creation of an atmosphere that over-the-counter derivatives trading is less risky than exchange trading. The Federal Deposit Insurance Corporation inferred in 1988 that it would stand behind swaps contracts held by U.S. banks.[12] Regulatory accounting rules in the United States permit banks to carry loss positions at cost or at marked-to-market values. No margin calls are required for over-the-counter derivatives as is the practice for exchange trading. An exchange trader who cannot meet margin calls generally will have his or her position sold.

With regard to the Barings holdings of Nikkei futures contracts, it has been said that losses for the exchange clearing house were limited because of a 9 percent maintenance margin, although some have said that 5 percent was more common for a large customer such as Barings, and the actual requirement might have been closer to 3 percent.[13] At any rate, the market in exchange-traded derivatives does have standard practices that regulate derivatives risk in a manner that is more efficient than bank regulatory authorities.

Many large banks have imposed their own controls on derivatives business. At Citicorp, internal surveillance has been increased, new manuals on derivatives trading have been written, and employee training in this area has been increased. Trading limits in derivatives have been tightened. However, the Barings case is evidence that such controls may not be sufficient. Further recommendations to reduce risk in derivatives trading will be discussed later in this chapter.

This case also has implications for one of the key issues discussed in various parts of this book, that of centralization versus decentralization. Barings' operation in Singapore was highly decentralized, which may have been the case with the Bankers Trust/Procter & Gamble case. In the case of Barings, the casual regulatory behavior of the Bank of England, supervising financial institutions with a "wink and a nod" as discussed in chapter 9, may have permitted the environment that led to the demise of this bank.

Relating Financial Theories to the Use of Derivatives

A number of financial theories have been advanced by various writers and analysts in financial management textbooks. Such theories have not been examined except by inference in this book because of the assumption that students of international financial management have such background. However, some of these theories can be applied in the use of derivatives to hedge financial risks. They include agency theory, the efficient markets hypothesis (EMH), and the asymmetric information problem.

Agency theory states that, in the principal and agent relationship, a conflict of interest exists. The shareholder is the principal and management is the agent. Management is presumed to act in the best interests of the shareholders. But shareholders select the board of directors who, in turn, hire management. Derivatives can be used to hedge financial decisions made by management with regard to financial assets, interest rates, and foreign exchange rates. The conflict of interest still exists because management, the agents of the shareholders, selects the derivatives with which to hedge. Procter & Gamble and Metallgesellschaft shareholders were left with such a problem.

---

[12] Martin Mayer, "How the Market Regulates Derivatives Risk," *Wall Street Journal*, 2 March 1995, p. A14.

[13] Ibid.

The EMH holds that the market price of securities quickly incorporates new information. The question remains, however, whether the stock market accurately reflects aggregate information about agency conflicts? Incentive contracts can be designed that may eliminate agency conflicts. To what extent does the stock market reflect these changes? The agency conflicts are still not wholly alleviated so accounting variables such as profit margins or earnings per share are used as minimum variables to measure results. Incentives are then given for better performance, as rated by these variables.

Some shareholders, however, may benefit over others. This is the basis for the asymmetric information problem. Some shareholders have better information than others may have. Derivatives can be used to hedge the risk of asymmetric information and, thus, EMH and the agency cost problem as well.

Proposed Regulatory Legislation

In the United States, a number of bills have been introduced in Congress to regulate the use of financial derivatives.[14] One bill would create a Federal Derivatives Commission whose objective would be to prevent unexpected large losses by firms trading in derivatives. Another bill would regulate bank derivatives activities. A third bill is designed to protect the federal deposit insurance program and control financial market risk by increasing oversight of the derivatives markets. This legislation establishes appropriate standards for the supervision of derivatives trading and gives bank regulators more ability to gather information regarding the use of derivatives by financial institutions. Finally, a U.S. Senate bill would require proprietary trading of derivatives to be done by separately capitalized subsidiaries of banks.

Near the end of 1994, U.S. regulatory agencies, including the Federal Reserve, the Securities and Exchange Commission, and the Commodity Futures Trading Commission, had singled out Bankers Trust, the most high-profile bank in derivatives, for punitive action. An agreement in December 1994 between the agencies and the bank required Bankers Trust to: (1) set out in writing investor safeguards, (2) use clear pricing policies when selling derivatives, and (3) improve management control and supervision of its derivatives business. Bankers Trust had been involved in the two most highly publicized American losses from derivatives trading—Procter & Gamble and Gibson Greetings. Both companies sued Bankers Trust and the latter settled out of court for compensation while not admitting fraud.[15]

Although the risks are high, the return from derivatives, particularly the so-called exotics to be discussed in the next chapter, can be quite high. The return on equity (ROE) from some exotics can be as high as 35–50 percent. These derivatives are custom-designed and may be expensive to construct. They can be very complex and spreads can narrow very quickly after they are issued. The life cycle of some new exotic derivatives can be as short as a few hours to a few weeks.[16]

In the following sections, the most important derivatives relevant to global financial management will be discussed. Risks and regulatory implications will be discussed as well as the reasons for their use. Cases involving their use are included. Major derivatives markets are included in the analysis.

Derivatives Exchanges

During the 1980s, the number of different exchange-traded derivatives products traded cross-border quadrupled from 25 to more than 100. New exchanges were estab-

---

[14] Thomas F. Siems, "Financial Derivatives: Are New Regulations Warranted?" *Financial Industry Studies of the Federal Reserve Bank of Dallas* (August 1994): 6–8.

[15] "Hands off Bankers Trust," *Euromoney* (December 1994): 5.

[16] K. Michael Fraser, "What It Takes To Excel In Exotics," *Global Finance* 7 (March 1993): 48.

lished in several countries emulating the U.S. trading in currency, interest rate, and stock index options.[17]

In 1980, only one foreign and four U.S. exchanges traded financial derivatives. The Chicago Board of Trade (CBOT) now trades the most active product, the T bond futures contract. The Chicago Board Options Exchange trades the most active option contract, the S&P 100 index option. Three very active futures contracts, the 3-month Eurodollar, S&P 500 stock index, and the deutsche Mark currency futures, are traded on the Chicago Mercantile Exchange (CME or Merc). For example, the Merc began trading a Eurodollar futures contract in 1981 and, currently, the notional value of outstanding contracts in this future is $2.8 trillion, making it the largest futures contract being traded anywhere. According to John Damgard, President of the Futures Industry Association, the Merc could challenge for the lead among the world's derivatives exchanges with its Eurodollar contract.[18] The Merc had a slight edge in contract volume trade in 1994, through December 19, with 221.5 million contracts traded compared with 216.5 million traded at the Chicago Board of Trade.

Markets have been established and have flourished in other countries. While the Merc's volume increased in 1994 over 1993 by 35 percent and that of the CBOT grew by 28 percent, foreign exchanges grew even faster. The Tokyo International Financial Futures Exchange (TIFFE) opened in 1989 and now trades 13 percent of global volume. The most actively traded stock index futures contract, the Nikkei 225 stock index futures contract, is offered by the Osaka Stock Exchange. The Singapore International Monetary Exchange (SIMEX) has offered a number of products in conjunction with the Chicago Mercantile Exchange since 1984. The Marché à Terme International de France (MATIF) began trading in 1986 and, in 1994, its trading increased by 96 percent over 1993. Germany's first financial derivative exchange, the Deutsche Terminbörse (DTB), was opened in 1990 after that country amended its gambling law to permit retail trading in derivatives. The London International Financial Futures Exchange (LIFFE) is the oldest and largest European financial futures exchange and its volume increased 152 percent for 1994 over 1993. European company stock options are traded on the European Options Exchange in Amsterdam. Other markets have been established in Belgium, Spain, Switzerland, and other countries, mostly the result of deregulation of European financial markets.

Currency Futures and Options

Foreign exchange markets have been discussed, including both markets for spot prices and those for forward prices. The latter markets are used for hedging positions in currencies in which settlement is in the future. Currency exposure risk can also be hedged in the currency futures and options markets. The liquidity in these markets is produced by speculators who trade for their own accounts and whose objectives are profit-driven. These markets will be examined in the following sections.

FOREIGN CURRENCY FUTURES

Foreign currency futures contracts are traded in organized markets. A futures contract is a commitment to purchase or deliver a specified quantity of goods, i.e., a foreign cur-

---

[17] Janet A. Napoli, "Derivative Markets and Competitiveness," *Economic Perspectives (Federal Reserve Bank of Chicago)* 16 (July/August 1992): 13–24.

[18] Steven F. Levingston, "Chicago Exchanges Boast They're Both No. 1," *Wall Street Journal*, 28 December 1994, p. C1.

rency, on a designated date in the future for a price determined competitively in an auction market when the contract is transacted. The forward market also consists of trading currencies for future delivery at a future price determined by the foreign exchange market.

However, these markets are different in several ways and it is useful to examine these differences. In the forward market, no money is exchanged at the time the contract is made. In the futures markets—and this is true of all futures markets whether currencies, commodities, or securities—margin is charged at the time the party buys or sells a contract. Most contracts for financial instruments involve both initial margin and maintenance margin—both set by the exchange on which the contract is traded. In the futures markets, settlements are made daily via the Exchange's Clearing House while in the forward market, settlement of spot transactions takes place two days after the spot transaction and for forward transactions, gains or losses are realized on settlement date.

The two types of markets also have differences in administrative characteristics. In the futures markets, trading takes place on the floor of an organized futures exchange, whereas forward market trading takes place in the global banking system of unorganized contacts between traders by means of telephone and other electronic means. Standardized contracts are traded in the futures markets while forward market contracts are customized as to amount. For example, the size of a Japanese yen contract on the International Monetary Market (IMM) at the Chicago Mercantile Exchange is ¥12.5 million. A deutsche Mark contract is 125,000 marks, the Canadian dollar contract is Can$100,000, the British pound contract is £62,500, and the Swiss franc contract is Sfr 125,000. Figure 13–1 shows a day's market in currency futures.

A number of other differences are practiced in the two markets. Prices in the futures markets are quoted in U.S. terms, i.e., dollar units per one foreign currency unit; whereas in the forward market, prices are quoted in European terms, i.e., units of local currency to the dollar, as well as some Commonwealth currencies. In futures markets, the market participants are unknown to one another, except when a firm is trading its own account through its own brokers on the trading floor. In the forward market, participants in each transaction always know the other trading party. In futures markets, the participants include banks, corporations, financial institutions, individual investors, and speculators. In the forward market, participants are banks that deal with each other, as well as other major commercial entities. Access for individuals and smaller firms is quite limited.

Figure 13–1 contains several points of information. It shows prices for six foreign currency futures contracts traded at the CME. Let's examine one particular contract, the Japanese yen. See the following data from Figure 13–1.

	Open	High	Low	Settle	Change	Lifetime High	Low	Open Interest
Japan Yen (CME)—12.5 million yen; $ per yen (.00)								
June	.9553	.9638	.9518	.9633	+ .0082	1.3130	.9259	63,326
Sept	.9640	.9750	.9640	.9749	+ .0084	1.2085	.9390	2,610
Dec	.9845	.9865	.9833	.9864	+ .0086	1.0500	.9520	1,095
	Est vol 29,252; vol Wed 14,883; open int 67,122, − 1,368							

This strip gives the standard amount of Japanese yen in a contract: 12.5 million yen for a contract traded at the CME (Chicago Mercantile Exchange). The opening, high, low, and closing prices are given, in hundredths of a dollar per yen along with the daily

CURRENCY

	Open	High	Low	Settle	Change	Lifetime High	Low	Open Interest
JAPAN YEN (CME)-12.5 million yen; $ per yen (.00)								
June	.9553	.9638	.9518	.9633 + .0082		1.3130	.9259	63,326
Sept	.9640	.9750	.9640	.9749 + .0084		1.2085	.9390	2,610
Dec	.9845	.9865	.9833	.9864 + .0086		1.0500	.9520	1,095
Est vol 29,252; vol Wd 14,883; open int 67,122, − 1,368.								
DEUTSCHEMARK (CME)-125,000 marks; $ per mark								
June	.6525	.6560	.6513	.6555 + .0028		.7315	.6513	85,490
Sept	.6560	.6592	.6553	.6593 + .0028		.7312	.6553	3,627
Dec	.6612	.6625	.6600	.6635 + .0028		.7070	.6600	582
Est vol 28,691; vol Wd 17,417; open int 89,720, − 1,001.								
CANADIAN DOLLAR (CME)-100,000 dirs.; $ per Can $								
June	.7356	.7366	.7340	.7343 − .0010		.7500	.6930	34,801
Sept	.7372	.7374	.7353	.7353 − .0010		.7490	.7170	2,389
Dec	.7381	.7381	.7365	.7361 − .0010		.7460	.7130	2,388
Mr97	....	....	....	.7367 − .0010		.7395	.7117	453
June	....	....	....	.7368 − .0010		.7395	.7185	197
Est vol 5,261; vol Wd 4,063; open int 40,251, + 1,578.								
BRITISH POUND (CME)-62,500 pds.; $ per pound								
June	1.4910	1.5036	1.4890	1.5014 + .0112		1.5870	1.4880	59,706
Sept	1.4926	1.5020	1.4920	1.5000 + .0114		1.5840	1.4860	254
Est vol 18,294; vol Wd 22,053; open int 59,998, − 1,155.								
SWISS FRANC (CME)-125,000 francs; $ per franc								
June	.8033	.8078	.7999	.8064 + .0034		.9120	.8013	42,996
Sept	.8087	.8140	.8075	.8137 + .0034		.9188	.8090	1,891
Dec	....	....	....	.8213 + .0035		.8999	.8180	681
Est vol 19,798; vol Wd 14,349; open int 45,571, − 276.								
AUSTRALIAN DOLLAR (CME)-100,000 dirs.; $ per A.$								
June	.7890	.7957	.7890	.7952 + .0072		.7957	.7260	11,744
Est vol 1,515; vol Wd 1,258; open int 11,776, + 259.								
MEXICAN PESO (CME)-500,000 new Mex. peso, $ per MP								
June	.13100	.13100	.12930	.12930 − .0125		.13400	.09020	9,505
Sept	.12200	.12200	.12040	.12050 − .0140		.12700	.08600	4,973
Dec	.11400	.11400	.11270	.11300 − .0175		.11530	.09900	1,508
Mr97	.10710	.10710	.10650	.10620 − .0195		.10800	.10070	253
Est vol 2,646; vol Wd 301; open int 16,239, + 7.								
Est vol ; vol ; open int , .								
EUROYEN (CME)-Yen 100,000,000, pts. of 100%								
June	99.10	99.10	99.10	99.10		99.34	99.10	1,971
Sept	98.77	98.78	98.76	98.76 − .01		99.20	98.76	2,978
Dec	98.44	98.45	98.41	98.42 − .01		98.99	98.43	4,088
Mr97	98.13	98.13	98.11	98.11 − .01		98.72	98.12	1,860
June	....	....	....	97.84		98.38	97.83	283
Sept	97.57	97.57	97.56	97.57 − .01		98.10	97.58	324
Dec	97.33	97.33	97.33	97.32 − .02		97.81	97.34	204
Mr98	....	....	....	97.11		97.56	97.11	310
Est vol 3,511; vol Wd 2,903; open int 12,130, − 301.								

Source: Wall Street Journal, 18 May 1996, p. C12. Reprinted with permission. All rights reserved.

FIGURE 13–1 The Currency Futures Market (for May 2, 1996)

change, high and low closing prices and open interest for contracts to be delivered in June, September, and December 1996, and which currently are being traded. The open interest shows the number of contracts that are outstanding and have not yet been offset by a trade in the opposite direction and that are still in effect. For example, on May 2, 1996, the ¥ futures contract for delivery in June closed at $120,412.50 ($0.009633 × ¥12.5 million—remember the quotation is .9633 which means .009693). That price closed up $0.000082/¥ from the close on May 1, 1996. The contract for September delivery closed at $121,850.00 ($0.009748 × ¥12.5 million). The open interest reported for a June contract was 63,326, meaning that traders were long 63,326 contracts for June 1996 delivery with the CME, i.e., the number of contracts still in effect at the end of the previous day's trading session. Each unit represents a buyer and a seller who still have a contract position. The high and low prices for the lifetime of this contract are shown. On the last line, volume for contracts for all delivery dates on May 2, 1996, was reported as 29,252 contracts with comparison to the prior day's volume of 14,883 contracts, and total open interest of 67,122, the sum of the four contracts' open interest: (63,326 + 2,610 + 1,051). The discrepancy of 135 from the addition of the volume for these three contracts may mean that 135 contracts were traded for delivery in 1997 and were not reported in *Wall Street Journal*. The last two figures on the bottom line represent the total of the right column, and the change from the prior trading day. Thus, these five lines of data for each futures contract reveal much information about a specific currency futures contract.

Some information is not given in this newspaper report but is information that all traders are presumed to know. Such information includes initial and maintenance margin, minimum fluctuations per contract, and daily contract limits—the change up or down in a contract that will trigger an end to trading for the rest of that period.

Delivery

The process of delivery is different between the two markets. Delivery is always made on forward contracts unless the contract is swapped for some other currency or date of maturity. Futures contracts are seldom delivered at expiration date. Instead a futures contract bought long will be offset on or before expiration date, generally four times a year, by selling that contract, offsetting the long position, so that the trader or hedger has no net open position in that contract. If the contract was originally short, or sold, the trader expects the market to decline and, thus, the contract can be bought at a lower price and a profit can be made, the trader then buys an offsetting contract on or before contract expiration date. It is extremely rare when a futures contract is delivered, usually an occurrence when the trader forgets to purchase or sell an offsetting contract before expiration date.

Marking-to-Market

Finally, futures contracts are marked-to-market on a daily basis. That is, the value of the futures contract traded is calculated daily so that the required margin can be maintained. For example, the Canadian dollar contract on the IMM has a face value of Can$100,000. Let's say that this contract closed after Day 2 at U.S.$ 0.8577 (all U.S. currency futures are quoted in U.S. dollars unless they are futures on cross rates). Thus, this contract is worth $85,770 (Can$100,000 × $0.8577) if marked-to-market. The IMM sets initial margin at $1,080 and maintenance margin is $800. This means that only $1,080 per contract must be put down to control one contract worth $85,770. This is the entry fee for playing the game. Thus, leverage is extremely high, nearly 99:1 in this case. However, once a position has been established in one contract, the account only has to show a positive balance of $800 each day it is marked-to-market. This is the margin that has to be maintained, or the maintenance margin. If the trader had bought at $0.8677 on

Day 1, or $86,770 for a contract, a decline to $85,770 would mean that the original contract is down $1,000. All but $80 of the initial margin is wiped out and the trader must remit $720 to bring the account back to a maintenance margin level of $800 from the −$80 balance. This is the proverbial margin call that the trader will receive. The trader either remits the $720 or the IMM will sell the position, leaving the trader with a loss. At the close of trading on Day 3, the contract closes at $0.8677, or $86,770, for a gain of $1,000. The margin account is credited for $1,000 and increases to $1,800 (the original $800 plus the $1,000 gain). At the end of trading on Day 4, the contract closes at $0.8477, or $84,770, for a loss of $2,000. The margin account is debited for $2,000, maintenance margin falls to −$200 and a margin call is sent to the trader for $1,000 (−$200 plus $1,000) to raise the account to the required maintenance margin of $800 on this contract. Thus, each day the contract is valued, or marked-to-market. Figure 13–2 shows the process with regard to this example. On forward contracts, margin is not required. The counterpart of margin is set at the initial transaction and is represented by the interbank spread on the difference between the spot and forward prices. The contract specifications required at the IMM are summarized for foreign currency futures contracts in Figure 13–3.

Trading Mechanics on Futures Exchanges

Traders should be aware of the most important trading mechanics of the currency futures markets. For example, margin is required to be deposited at the time of the initial transaction, as shown in Figure 13–2. At the IMM, initial margin for the pound is $4,050 while maintenance margin is $3,000; for the deutsche Mark, initial margin is $2,700, maintenance margin is $2,000; for the Japanese yen, initial margin is $1,890, maintenance margin is $1,400; for the Mexican peso, which is a more volatile and speculative currency, initial margin is $4,000, while maintenance margin is $3,000. Trading

FIGURE 13–2 Marking-to-Market

A Currency Futures Transaction

Contract Face Value	
Canadian dollar contract	C$100,000
Initial Margin	1,080
Maintenance Margin	800
Day One	
Trader buys 1 contract@$0.8677/C$	86,770
Contract closes on day one@$0.8677	86,770
Day Two	
Closing price@$0.8577	85,770
Trader marked-to-market after day two	
Loss after day two	1,000
Margin account declines to ($1,080−1,000)	80
Margin call	720
Maintenance margin restored to	800
Day Three	
Closing price@$0.8677	86,770
Gain after day three	1,000
Margin account increases to ($800 + $1,000)	1,800
Day Four	
Closing price@$0.8477	84,770
Loss on day four	2,000
Margin account declines	2,000
Maintenance margin after day four	− 200
Margin call ($1,000 + [−$200] = $800)	1,000

	Australian Dollar	British Pound	Canadian Dollar	Deutsche Mark	Japanese Yen	Swiss Franc	Mexican Peso
Contract size	A$100,000	£62,500	C$100,000	DM 125,000	¥12,500,00	Sfr 125,000	Mp new 500,00
Symbol	AD	BP	CD	DM	JY	SF	MP
Margin requirements							
Initial	$1,215	$4,050	$1,080	$2,700	$1,890	$4,050	$4,000
Maintenance	900	3,000	800	2,000	1,400	3,000	3,000
Minimum price change	0.0001 (1 pt.)	0.0002 (2 pts.)	0.0001 (1 pt.)	0.0001 (1 pt.)	0.000001 (1 pt.)	0.0001 (1 pt.)	— —
Value of 1 pt.	$10.00	$6.25	$10.00	$12.50	$12.50	$12.50	—
Months traded	January, March, April, June, July, September, October, December, and spot month						
Regular trading hours	7:20 A.M.–2:00 P.M. (Central Time)						
Last day of trading	Second business day before third Wednesday of the delivery month						

Source: Minimum Performance Bond Requirements and Contract Specifications, Chicago Mercantile Exchange, 1992.

FIGURE 13–3 Foreign Currency Futures
Contract Specifications
(Chicago Mercantile Exchange)

is executed in standard contracts as to quality and quantity of each currency traded. Trading is in minimum fluctuations or ticks of 1 basis point, or .01 of a cent, and some exchanges have daily limits of increases or declines for the day. However, the IMM does not impose daily limits on currency futures contracts. Contract values are marked-to-market each day.

Transactions in the Currency Futures Markets

Assume that an American MNC needs to hedge a transaction. The company has a plant in Switzerland. This plant is short of funds to meet operating expenses. The peak farm machinery buying season is six months away. The Swiss plant will then be liquid again. The U.S. firm can transfer funds to the Swiss plant for six months. At the end of that period, the Swiss plant will return the funds to the U.S. plant. The U.S. firm expects the Swiss franc to appreciate in value and will want to hedge the transaction in the currency futures market, e.g., the International Monetary Market at the Chicago Mercantile Exchange, by selling Swiss francs for delivery in six months. In six months, the currency futures position will be reversed by the purchase of Swiss franc futures. The spot rate for Swiss francs on December 1, when the U.S. firm transfers funds to the Swiss plant, is $0.25600/Sfr. Swiss franc currency futures for June delivery are selling for $0.25500. The spot rate for Swiss francs in six months turns out to be $0.26100/Sfr and Swiss franc currency futures are selling for $0.26090/Sfr. The transaction is presented in Figure 13–4.

This transaction is called a selling hedge because currency is bought in the spot market and sold in the futures market. It anticipates that the foreign currency will rise in price. The MNC incurred a profit of $2,500 in the cash market. This profit was made when the MNC purchased spot Swiss francs with excess dollars on December 1 and swapped the currencies back in the spot market when the Swiss plant repaid the parent firm. Since the basis changed during the 6-month period, the firm incurred a loss of $2,950 in the futures market. The net loss between the two markets was $450.00, only 1/3 of 1 percent of the entire transaction. Had the market gone in the opposite direction, the firm could have made a profit. However, the objective of this transaction was

Cash Market		Futures Market
	December 1	
Buy Sfr 500,000 @$0.25600/Sfr = $128,000		Sell 4 Sfr contracts for June delivery @$0.25500/Sfr (4 × Sfr 125,000 = Sfr 500,000) = $127,500
	June 1	
Sell Sfr 500,000 @$0.26100/Sfr = $130,500 Gain $ 2,500		Buy Sfr 500,000 @$0.26090/Sfr = $130,450 Loss $ 2,950
	Net Loss = $450.00	

FIGURE 13–4 Swiss Franc Currency Futures Transaction (a selling hedge)

to reduce or eliminate any potential loss by hedging in the futures market. The MNC could have lost in the spot market had the spot Swiss francs gone down in price.

When a buying hedge is transacted, foreign currency is anticipated to decline in value. Currency is sold in the cash market and bought in the futures market. For example, the Swiss plant described previously is doing well and has excess funds in the form of Swiss francs. It does not need these funds for six months. The parent MNC has a domestic assembly plant that needs working capital funds. The Swiss plant transfers funds to the U.S. assembly plant for 6 months. Thus, it converts the excess Swiss francs into dollars and transfers them to the U.S. plant. The Swiss plant sells the spot Swiss francs and buys Swiss franc contracts on, for example, the London International Financial Futures Exchange for future delivery in a buying hedge. The transaction is shown in Figure 13–5.

The prices moved in this example the same as they did in the selling hedge example. The MNC incurred a loss of $2,500 in the spot market and, since the basis changed during the period, a gain of $2,950 was made in the futures market, resulting in a net profit of $450. Transactions costs and tax on the capital must be taken into effect and then the net gain should be compared with the risk free return on the beginning cash amount invested in T bills for six months. The residual is the actual after-tax gain. At

FIGURE 13–5 Swiss Franc Currency Futures Transaction (a buying hedge)

Cash Market		Futures Market
	March 1	
Sell Sfr 500,000 @$0.25600/Sfr = $128,000		Buy 4 Sfr contracts for September delivery @$0.25500/Sfr (4 × Sfr125,000 = Sfr500,000) = $127,500
	September 1	
Buy Sfr 500,000 @$0.26100/Sfr =$130,500 Loss $2,500		Sell Sfr 500,000 @$0.26090 = $130,450 Gain $2,950
	Net Gain = $450.00	

any rate, had the MNC not hedged in the futures market, it would have lost the entire amount of $2,500 in the spot market.

Finally, currency futures contracts can be used to guarantee foreign interest payments. Suppose that an individual investor borrows $1.5 million at 8 percent and converts the dollars into £1 million by buying pounds for $1.50 each. The investor buys a British security maturing in one year that pays 10 percent interest. The investor then sells British pounds for delivery in one year by selling 44 contracts (at £25,000/contract) at $1.5180/£ in the futures markets. One year later the market price of the pound might fall to $1.35/£. If so, when the individual converts his £1.1 million (principal and interest) back to dollars, he would receive only $1,485,000, or less than he borrowed. Without hedging, he could not repay the $1.5 million debt, much less the 8 percent interest due. However, if the market price of pound sterling were $1.35/£, the futures price might be $1.3550/£. Thus, a gain of $0.1630/£ would be made on the short-sale in the futures market. The total gain in the futures market, then, would be $179,300. The total gain on the transaction would be:

$1,485,000	Value of $ received by converting £1.1 million
+179,300	Gain on futures transactions
−1,500,000	Repayment of principal borrowed
−120,000	Repayment of interest due on $1.5 million at 8 percent
$44,300	**Net gain**

Thus, instead of taking a loss because of the decline in the value of the pound, the futures market transaction allowed the individual investor to borrow cheaply at home and guarantee a positive rate of return by investing the borrowed funds abroad.

Other Currency Derivatives Markets

The MidAmerica Commodity Exchange in Chicago also offers currency futures contracts in the British pound, the Canadian dollar, deutsche Mark, Japanese yen, and Swiss franc. These currency futures are somewhat different from other markets. Their size is one-fifth to one-half that of contracts traded at other futures exchanges. For example, the pound contract is £12,500, the mark is DM 62,500, the Canadian dollar is Can$50,000, the yen is ¥6,250,000, and the Swiss franc is Sfr 62,500. The advantages of these smaller contracts is that traders can trade more than one currency at a time with a small amount of capital and the smaller contract size gives them more staying power during periods of adverse price change. In addition, exchange margin requirements will be comparatively smaller. The trading floor at the MidAmerica is open longer than at most other exchanges.

USDX Futures Contracts

One rather unique contract is available to international business firms to hedge foreign exchange risk, especially in multicurrency transactions. This is the U.S. dollar

index contract (USDX), traded at the Finex, short for Financial Exchange, which is a division of the old New York Cotton Exchange.

The Finex uses a currency management philosophy to promote its USDX contract, which differs from the traditional theory whereby currency trading is viewed as a passive hedging program in which 100 percent of a firm's foreign exchange exposure should be hedged. The critics of such a program believe that long-run returns can be negatively affected with a 100 percent passive currency hedging program if currencies embody a non-zero risk premium. In other words, if currencies move by a significantly and systematically different amount than implied by forward premiums/discounts, then a 100 percent hedged program may result in substantial costs and portfolio or project performance will be diminished. Thus, advocates of a different policy believe that foreign currency movements can enhance portfolio or project returns, but full hedging of currency exposures will reduce these returns. Thus, the Finex contract has twin objectives of reduction of overall risk as well as enhanced portfolio or project performance. This philosophy may be gaining strength among global firms whose managements may advocate more than just risk reduction from hedging instruments in their attempt to increase profits.

The USDX contract is based on the U.S. dollar index compiled by the Federal Reserve Board, an index that is comprised of a market basket of ten trade-weighted major currencies vis-à-vis the U.S. dollar with a weighted-average exchange value of the U.S. dollar against currencies of ten industrial countries. The weight for each of the ten countries is the 1972–76 average world trade of that country divided by the average world trade of all ten countries combined. The USDX futures contract at Finex has a face value of 1,000 times the U.S. dollar index, compiled by the Federal Reserve Board. The base of this index is 100 and the prices quoted are deviations from this base. Thus, the closing price, for example, of the December contract, 90.08, would be multiplied by the face value of the contract to determine its market value. The USDX option contract will be discussed in the subsequent section covering foreign currency options.

Traders and hedgers can use a number of strategies with USDX contracts. If they expect the dollar to rally, they can purchase USDX futures, call options, or call option spreads. These contracts have relatively low risk but returns during a dollar rally are also smaller. If a dollar rally is forecast, the USDX will rise as the dollar's value increases. For example, assume the value of a USDX futures contract is 97.48. If a long position is taken in USDX futures having a value of $97,480 (97.48 × $1,000), the value of this contract will rise in value by $10 for every tick increase in the USDX price. On the other hand, it will also decline by this amount if the USDX falls. The trader or hedger is exposed to currency loss if the dollar moves in an unanticipated direction. Downside risk can be limited with the USDX option contract.

The U.S. Dollar Composite Index Futures Contract

In 1993, the Chicago Board of Trade (CBOT) launched a contract, the U.S. Dollar Composite Index Futures, designed to compete against the FINEX USDX contract. This contract differs from the USDX in that it is based on the U.S. dollar's value relative to only the five major world currencies, fewer than the ten currencies in the U.S. dollar index. They are the German mark, Japanese yen, British pound, Canadian dollar, and Swiss franc. The CBOT contract is aimed at: (1) institutional investors seeking to hedge a currency basket or portfolio with multiple currency exposure, (2) corporations that desire to reduce cross-border borrowing and lending costs, and (3) traders speculating on overall dollar moves. Contract highlights for the CBOT U.S. Dollar Composite Index Futures contract include: contract months of March, June, September, and December; the face value of the contract is $1,250 times the CBOT's U.S. Dollar Composite Index and price quotations in increments of 0.01 of one index point, each

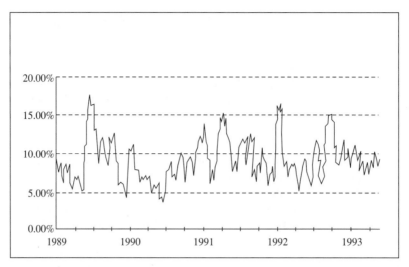

FIGURE 13–6 CBOT U.S. Dollar Composite Index
(20-day moving average of cash historical volatility)

point worth $1,250; and the contract has no daily price limits. This contract was introduced as a result of the volatility in the U.S. dollar composite index during the 1989–93 period, as shown in Figure 13–6.

Advantages of Currency Futures

Currency futures have several advantages over forward market operations. A trader can transact in small amounts at reasonable transaction costs. The market is extremely liquid. Margins are generally lower than in the interbank market where the amount is the bank spread between the spot and the forward price. Most hedging of future currency prices is done in the forward market while the futures market is used primarily for speculation. Finally, futures markets act as middlemen through their clearing facilities and thus, can guarantee each contract. This guarantee eliminates the risk that a trade will default.

Risks of Currency Futures

The major risks from trading any futures contract are basis risk and credit risk. Basis is the difference between the spot price and the futures price. If this difference changes between the time a contract position is established and the time it is closed out, the trader is subject to a loss of value. Basis reflects (1) the interest rate differential among countries and (2) expectations. If stable conditions exist and no restrictions are presently imposed on trade and capital flows, futures rates will vary inversely with the interest rate differential between two countries. This, of course, is interest rate parity, a condition explained in chapter 3. Credit risk stems from the inability of the trader to maintain the required amount of margin and, thus, the position will be liquidated at a loss.

Basis risk is eliminated if the contract, whether to buy or to sell, results in a perfect hedge. This situation occurs when the basis does not change between the time the contract position is established and the time it is offset and eliminated. Perfect hedges seldom can be created because of basis risk—resulting from unexpected fluctuations in the basis, and from cross-hedge risk—the imperfect correlation between the asset and the contract.

Finally, futures prices converge to the spot price of the currency at expiration.

MANAGEMENT APPLICATION NO. 17

Basis Risk

A trader is long £62,500 in the cash market and sells short one futures contract to hedge the cash position; spot is $1.1545/£ and one futures short is priced at $1.1620/£; 1 month later, spot is $1.1350 and the £ contract is $1.1460; the basis has changed and the hedge is not perfect.

	Spot	Basis	Futures
		(Spot–Future)	
Beginning	$1.1545	−0.0075	$1.1620
T + 30 Days	$1.1350	−0.0110	$1.1460

Loss in cash market → $1,218.75
  ($1.1545 − 1.1350)(£62,500)
Gain in futures market → $1,000.00
  ($1.1620 − 1.1460)(£62,500)
Net loss is → $218.75

or $-0.0110 - (-0.0075) = -0.0035$
$-\$.0035 \times £62,500 = \$218.75$
  Could have lost $1,218.75 without hedging in the futures market.

Thus, basis usually does not stay the same throughout the life of a futures contract. Losses can occur when this happens, as in the preceding example. Change in basis can be attributed to a number of economic phenomena. For example, interest rates may change over a period of time and these changes may affect the level of foreign exchange rates. Basis can change over time because, as mentioned previously, future prices will converge to the spot rate at expiration.

This is not necessarily a risk but those who trade or hedge using futures contracts should be aware of this characteristic of the futures market. Futures prices and forward rates also will be virtually identical for some future date.

Cross Rate Futures Contracts

Cross rate futures contract prices are determined by cross rates in spot foreign exchange rates. Cross rates and their determination were discussed in chapter 3. Currency futures contracts usually express the exchange rate of the U.S. dollar relative to another currency. Suppose a Swiss investor wants to hedge the currency risk of British assets. Until recently, this investor had to take two positions in the futures markets: one in British £/$ and the other in Sfr/$. For example, to hedge British assets against the risk of a £ depreciation against the Swiss franc, an investor would have to sell £ futures and buy Swiss franc futures. It is now possible to hedge in both cross rate futures and options since such contracts have been made available on the Chicago Mercantile Exchange and the Philadelphia Stock Exchange.

Regulation of Currency Futures Trading

In the United States, all futures trading is regulated by the Commodities Futures Trading Commission (CFTC). This agency was established in 1975 and has regulatory and supervisory responsibility over all U.S. futures and options trading. In Great Britain, LIFFE is regulated by the International Commodities Clearing House, a trade group owned by British banks. Other countries in which futures contracts are traded, such as Singapore, Japan, Germany, and Spain, have similar government agencies or trade associations that regulate the trading on these markets.

FOREIGN CURRENCY OPTIONS

Options give one the right, but not the obligation, to do something. On the other hand, delivery must be executed for a forward market transaction whereas a futures contract must be closed out and offset on or before expiration date. In other words, forward and

Nick Leeson and Barings PLC[1]

Nick Leeson was a 28-year old "rogue" trader[2] in the Singapore office of Barings PLC, a 233-year-old merchant bank headquartered in London. In late February 1995, his trading in Nikkei 225 index contracts, a derivative traded on the Singapore International Monetary Exchange (Simex), resulted in the collapse of Barings.

For several months, Leeson had traded these contracts and regular bond futures contracts based on the Nikkei 225 index—the Tokyo Stock Exchange counterpart of the Dow-Jones Industrial Index—betting that Japanese stock prices would go up. Instead Japanese stocks continued to go down in price and Leeson bought even more puts on the Nikkei 225 index, highly leveraging his position. This action resulted in margin calls by SIMEX and these margin calls exceeded the capital held by Barings. The bank had to declare bankruptcy in order to limit the losses, which were estimated to be more than $1.25 billion.

Mr. Leeson fled Singapore and was arrested in Frankfurt, Germany, to be held there until a decision could be made as to whether to send him on to London, his destination, or extradite him back to Singapore where authorities accused him of fraud. The financial world accused Barings top executives of condoning Leeson's trading and a Dutch bank, ING, bought Barings for the sum total of £1, therefore assuming the liabilities of the bankrupt bank.

In this case, derivatives were used. Derivatives are a valuable means of hedging against unavoidable risks, as has been discussed previously in this chapter. Farmers hedge the price of soybeans between the time they plant their crops and the time they harvest them and sell them to the markets. Derivatives are more the tools of the risk averse than of risk takers. A major problem in the Barings case can be generalized to many other similar cases: this company's internal controls collapsed. In other cases, such as Procter & Gamble, Gibson Greetings, and Metallgesellschaft, corporate treasurers had little knowledge of the complexities of the financial instruments they used to hedge asset positions.

---

[1]George Melloan, "Leeson's Law: Too Much Leverage Can Wreck a Bank, *Wall Street Journal,* 6 March 1995, p. A15.

[2]A rogue trader is one who trades according to his/her own objectives and is not controlled by top management.

futures market transactions create obligations that the party must fulfill even if the market has changed adversely. No margin is required for options contracts and they are not marked-to-market, except in the case of futures style options such as those traded at the IMM, a division of the CME. The principal customers for these instruments are leading institutional investors and multinational corporations having payments and receivables in different currencies.

Currency options are used by a significant number of MNC corporate treasurers to hedge foreign currency exposure despite the corporate losses that have been reported from the use of derivatives during the early 1990s. A *Euromoney* survey of corporations and non-bank financial companies found that treasurers had regained confidence in derivatives by 1995, especially in the use of short-dated currency options[19]. They have become a central part of the risk and liability programs for many international companies.

Options Characteristics

The characteristics of options are the same no matter what is the underlying commodity. However, in the following sections, the discussion is focused on the currency option. Options may be either calls or puts. A call is an option to buy a stated number

---

[19] Mark Parsley, "Playing It Safe with Currency Options," *Euromoney* (December 1995): 104–6.

PHILADELPHIA OPTIONS

Thursday, May 2, 1996

		Calls Vol.	Calls Last	Puts Vol.	Puts Last
JYEN					95.76
6,250,000 Japanese Yen-100ths of a cent per unit.					
96	Jun	10	1.48	...	...
97	Jun	2	0.80	40	1.86
101	Sep	3	1.30	...	...
Australian Dollar					79.59
50,000 Australian Dollars-Eurpoean Style.					
73	Jun	10	6.00	...	...
50,000 Australian Dollars-cents per units.					
76	Sep	...	...	6	0.43
77	Jun	1	2.60	...	...
78	Sep	...	...	1	1.00
79	May	2	0.64	...	...
80	May	40	0.18	...	...
British Pound					150.25
31,250 British Pound EOM-cents per unit.					
150	May	...	...	500	1.30
31,250 British Pounds-European Style.					
148	Jun	...	...	16	0.65
31,250 British Pounds-cents per unit.					
137½	Jun	19	2.10	...	...
158	Jun	...	...	8	8.20
Canadian Dollar					73.42
50,000 Canadian Dollars-cents per unit.					
73½	May	...	...	33	0.18
77	Jun	...	...	13	3.50
French Franc					193.48
250,000 French Francs-10ths of a cent per unit.					
19	Jun	...	...	4	0.84
250,000 French Francs-European Style.					
19¼	Jun	6	2.50	6	1.74
German Mark					65.36
62,500 German Marks-European Style.					
66	May	10	0.14	...	...
62,500 German Marks-cents per unit.					
60	Sep	...	...	350	0.17
62	Sep	...	...	150	0.40
63½	Jun	...	...	125	0.21
64	Jun	...	...	12	0.33
65	May	615	0.53	10	0.25
65½	May	50	0.24	...	...
66	May	...	...	35	0.82
66	Jun	10	0.55	...	...
67	Jun	127	0.29	10	1.98
67	Sep	9	1.15	...	...
68	Jun	7	0.15	...	...
68	Sep	6	0.81	...	...
Japanese Yen					95.76
95½	May	200	0.47	...	...
6,250,000 Japanese Yen EOM-100ths of a cent per unit.					
95	May	7	1.67	...	...
97	May	200	0.60	...	...
6,250,000 Japanese Yen-European Style.					
94	May	...	...	320	0.11
95	May	...	...	160	0.35
96	Jun	10	1.36	...	...
98	Jun	10	0.63	...	...
Swiss Franc					80.24
62,500 Swiss Franc EOM-cents per unit.					
80	May	...	...	5	0.93
62,500 Swiss Francs EOM.					
79½	May	3	0.99	...	...
62,500 Swiss Francs-European Style.					
78	Sep	...	...	140	0.94
83	Jun	...	...	30	2.76
85	May	...	...	10	4.72
86	Jun	...	...	10	5.49
62,500 Swiss Francs-cents per unit.					
78	Jun	...	...	1	0.30
79	Jun	1	1.77	10	0.59
79½	Jun	13	1.68	...	...
80	May	6	0.63	49	0.35
80	Jun	36	1.38	10	0.90
80½	May	...	...	35	0.66
80½	Jun	150	1.18	...	...
81	Jun	230	0.95	1	1.63
81½	May	20	0.10	...	...
82	Jun	60	0.47	3	2.37
82	Sep	...	...	4	2.95
83	Jun	...	...	50	3.40
83½	May	...	...	5	3.26
Call Vol.......13,306			Open Int.......162,732		
Put Vol........ 5,265			Open Int.......177,907		

FIGURE 13–7 Currency Options Prices
Philadelphia Stock Exchange (May 2, 1996)

342 PART V *Inventory of International Financial Resources*

of units of the underlying instrument at a specified price per unit during a specified period. A put is an option to sell—by the buyer of the option—a stated number of units of the underlying instrument at a specified price per unit during a specified period. If the option is American-style, it can be exercised anytime prior to the expiration date. If it is European-style, it can be exercised only on the expiration date. The option buyer or holder is the party that obtains the rights, by paying a premium, that are conveyed by an option, i.e., the right, but not an obligation, to buy the underlying commodity if the option is a call or to sell it if the option is a put. The option seller or writer is the party that is obligated to perform if an option is exercised, i.e., to sell the underlying commodity at a stated price if a call is exercised or to buy it if a put is exercised. The option writer may be an exchange, such as the Philadelphia Stock Exchange (PHLX), or an individual, bank, or non-bank corporation.

Currency Options Exchanges

Currency options in some form are traded on several organized exchanges. Options on spot prices are traded at the Philadelphia Stock Exchange (PHLX), as shown in Figure 13–7, and on the London Stock Exchange (LSE). PHLX, once only a coffee trading house and then a small regional stock exchange, is now the world's leading currency options exchange in volume and number of contracts.

The chart from the *Wall Street Journal* shown in Figure 13–7 shows: (1) the size of each contract, e.g., 62,500 German marks or 6,250,000 Japanese yen; (2) whether the option is American- or European-style; (3) the trading volume of each put or call contract; (4) the exercise price—the first column on the left in cents per unit, except for the Japanese, for which it is 100ths of a cent per unit; (5) the delivery month; and (6) the premium, or market price of the contract. For example, looking at Figure 13–7, the premium for a September German mark American-style call with an exercise price of 67 ($0.67 per mark) is 1.15, or $0.0115/unit. The premium cost is $718.75 ($0.0115 × 62,500 marks). The premium quotation for a Japanese 101 call whose expiration month is September is 1.30 or $0.000130 per unit for a total premium of $812.50 ($0.000130 × ¥6,250,000).

Currency options are traded in a number of forms. Options on currency futures contracts are traded on the CME's IMM. See Figure 13–8 for examples of these contracts. Note that they have a strike or exercise price and, thus, are similar to currency options on spot. These contracts will be discussed in more detail in the section on options later in this chapter. Futures-style option contracts on currency spot are traded at the LIFFE. Futures-style options contracts on futures, such as those traded on bonds, are not yet traded on currency prices.

Options may be exercised at some exercise or strike price—the price at which the call option buyer has the right to purchase or the put option holder has the right to sell the underlying commodity and which is established by the marketplace. Expiration months for options on the Philadelphia Exchange, where most of the world's listed currency options are traded, are March, June, September, December, or more often. At any given time, trading is conducted in the nearest three of these months. See Figure 13–7 for an illustration of one day's trading of options at the PHLX. The expiration date is the last date on which an option can be exercised. For foreign currencies, it is the Saturday before the third Wednesday of the expiration month.

Currency options may have two kinds of value, intrinsic value and time value. If and to the extent that an option would currently be profitable to exercise, it is said to have intrinsic value. In the case of a call, if the spot price is higher than the option exercise price, the option has intrinsic value. In the case of a put, if the spot price is less than the option exercise price, the option has intrinsic value. Such options are said to be "in the money." If the opposite is true of either calls or puts, they have no intrinsic

JAPANESE YEN (CME)
12,500,000 yen; cents per 100 yen

Strike Price	Calls-Settle			Puts-Settle		
	May	Jun	Jly	May	Jun	Jly
9550	.92	1.72	2.89	.09	.89	.92
9600	.54	1.45	2.59	.21	1.12	1.11
9650	.28	1.21	2.29	.45	1.38	1.31
9700	.14	1.01	2.04	.81	1.68	1.55
9750	.06	.84	1.79	. . . .	. . . .	. . . .
9800	.03	.69	1.57	1.70	2.35	2.08

Est vol 11,295 Wd 4,691 calls 3,281 puts
Op int Wed 58,045 calls 51,357 puts

DEUTSCHEMARK (CME)
125,000 marks; cents per mark

Strike Price	Calls-Settle			Puts-Settle		
	May	Jun	Jly	May	Jun	Jly
6450	1.07	. . . .	. . . .	.02	.33	.47
6500	.60	1.04	1.55	.05	.49	.63
6550	.23	.75	. . . .	.18	.70	1.07
6600	.07	.53	1.00	.52	.98	1.66
6650	.01	.36	.78	.96	1.30	. . . .
6700	0.00	.25	.60	1.45	. . . .	. . . .

Est vol 6,210 Wd 3,820 calls 5,157 puts
Op int Wed 59,822 calls 67,538 puts

CANADIAN DOLLAR (CME)
100,000 Can.$, cents per Can.$

Strike Price	Calls-Settle			Puts-Settle		
	May	Jun	Jly	May	Jun	Jly
7250	.93	1.01	. . . .	0.00	.09	.18
7300	.44	.62	. . . .	.01	.19	.30
7350	.06	.31	. . . .	.13	.38	.07
7400	.01	.14	.30	.58	.71	. . . .
7450	0.00	.06	. . . .	1.07	1.12	. . . .
7500	. . .	.02	. . . .	. . . .	1.58	. . . .

Est vol 189 Wd 140 calls 122 puts
Op int Wed 8,218 calls 5,668 puts

BRITISH POUND (CME)
62,500 pounds; cents per pound

Strike Price	Calls-Settle			Puts-Settle		
	May	Jun	Jly	May	Jun	Jly
14800	. . . .	. . . .	. . . .	.04	.52	.90
14900	1.24	1.94	. . . .	.10	.80	1.24
15000	.42	1.30	1.68	.28	1.18	1.68
15100	.10	.86	1.24	.96	1.72	2.22
15200	.04	.54	.88	1.90	2.38	. . . .
15300	.02	.32	.62	2.88	3.16	. . . .

Est vol 37,782 Wd 11,881 calls 8,902 puts
Op int Wed 57,901 calls 76,199 puts

FIGURE 13–8 Options on Currency Futures (for May 2, 1996)

SWISS FRANC (CME)
125,000 francs; cents per franc

Strike Price	Calls-Settle			Puts-Settle		
	May	Jun	Jly	May	Jun	Jly
7950	. . . .	. . . .	. . . .	. . . .	.54	.67
8000	.69	1.36	. . . .	.05	.72	.84
8050	.33	1.08	. . . .	.19	.94	. . . .
8100	.12	.84	. . . .	.48	1.20	1.23
8150	.04	.65	. . . .	.90	1.51	. . . .
8200	.01	.49	. . . .	1.37	1.84	. . . .

Est vol 3,543 Wd 1,614 calls 2,549 puts
Op int Wed 21,660 calls 19,454 puts

Source: *Wall Street Journal*, 3 May 1996, p. C13. Reprinted with permission.

FIGURE 13–8 *Continued*

value and are said to be "out of the money." For example, if the spot price for the deutsche Mark is $0.43, a DM 40 call—the strike price—has intrinsic value of $0.03/DM, whereas a DM 40 put has no intrinsic value. Time value is what traders are willing to pay above the intrinsic value. Time value evaporates as the maturity date nears and is zero at expiration date. Figure 13–9 demonstrates the decay of time value.

A buyer of an option pays a premium for the option—paid in advance by the buyer of an option. In the over-the-counter market, premiums are quoted as a percentage of the transaction amount. For listed options, they are quoted in currency units. The total premium is the amount of the option in units times the premium.

Dealers in currency options express the prices of these options as implied volatilities.[20] Implied volatility is usually an estimate of the degree of uncertainty in the currency options market about future exchange rates. For example, a 1-year call on a dollar denominated in Swiss francs might be quoted as costing 10 percent in implied volatility terms. An implied volatility of 10 percent indicates that the market is twice as uncertain about the future spot exchange rate one year from now than an implied volatility of 5 percent would indicate.

A New Option at the Philadelphia Stock Exchange (PHLX)

When an option with a new expiration month is introduced at PHLX, the exercise price established by the exchange reflects the current spot prices of the underlying currency. Two options are usually introduced, one with an exercise price above the current spot price and one with an exercise price below spot. As spot changes over time, other options may be introduced with exercise prices above or below the spot price. Exercise price intervals are $0.01 for German marks, Swiss francs, and Canadian dollars, $0.05 for British pounds, $0.005 for French francs, and $0.0001 for Japanese yen.

The option premiums—the prices for foreign currency options—are set by open competition between buyers and sellers on the trading floor. The premium quoted at any given time represents a consensus opinion among traders of the option's current value and includes either intrinsic value and time value, or both. For example, if the spot price of German marks is $0.42 per mark, a DM 40 call with 3 months until expiration might command a premium of $1,700, including $1,250 intrinsic value ($0.02 × DM 62,500) and the remainder, $450, representing time value. Time value will com-

---

[20] Allan M. Malz, "Currency Option Markets and Exchange Rates: A Case Study of the U.S. Dollar in March 1995," *Current Issues in Economics and Finance* (A publication of the Federal Reserve Bank of New York) 1 (July 1995): 2.

Decay of Time Value

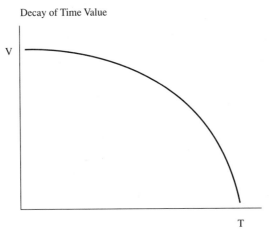

FIGURE 13–9 Decay of Time Value of Options

pletely evaporate at expiration. If the option has no intrinsic value at expiration, it will expire worthless.

Synthetic Currency Futures and Options Contracts

Traders or hedgers can create synthetic currency options. For example, selling a forward contract and a call option is the same as buying a put. Buying a put option and a forward contract is the same as buying a call. Several strategies can be implemented in the currency options market and these will be discussed in a subsequent section.

In addition, options can be held in certain combinations to create synthetic currency futures contracts. The combination of a written currency call and a purchased currency put, with the same strike price and expiration, behaves in a manner similar to a short position in a currency futures contract. A long position in a synthetic currency futures contract can be created by buying a currency call option and writing a corresponding put.[21] One would think that the use of options to create synthetic futures contracts makes currency futures redundant financial instruments. However, empirical research has shown that the transactions costs of option combinations are higher than those for actual currency futures and have less hedging effectiveness than actual futures. Thus, this research implies that actual currency futures contracts are not redundant instruments.[22]

Pricing Currency Options

Several option pricing models have been developed. The first and best-known of these is the Black-Scholes option pricing model developed in 1973 to explain the determination of options prices.[23] Since then, several other models have been developed. Highlights of the Black-Scholes model are found in Appendix 1 at the end of this chapter.

Option prices, in general, are determined by the mix of several key factors. These are: (1) time to maturity, (2) today's spot or cash market exchange rate minus the exercise price, (3) the forward or future spot rate expected in the cash market at maturity,

---

[21] See Allan I. Tucker, Jeff Madura, and Thomas C. Chiang, *International Financial Markets* (St. Paul, MN: West Publishing Co., 1991), chapter 14, appendix 14A, for good examples of synthetic currency futures contracts.

[22] J. Chang and L. Shanker, "Hedging Effectiveness of Currency Options and Currency Futures," *Journal of Futures Markets* (April 1986): 289–306.

[23] Fischer Black and Myron Scholes, "The Pricing of Options and Corporate Liabilities," *Journal of Political Economy* 81 (May–June): 637–54.

(4) the strike price, (5) the exercise feature—whether American- or European-style, (6) the expected future volatility of the underlying asset, and (7) the cost of borrowing or investing in the home currency compared with the cost of borrowing or investing in the foreign currency. Factors 1, 2, 3, and 7 position the option against the forward cash markets while factors 4 and 6 allow a hedged trader to determine the probability of exercise of the option and to construct what is referred to as a delta neutralized hedge. A delta neutral hedge is the weighted hedge required to protect the trader against changes in the option value on a one for one basis versus the underlying asset. For more detailed coverage of the pricing of options, see Appendix 2 at the end of this chapter.

Options thrive on volatility of the underlying commodity. Volatility is the expected average change, up or down, in the price or yield of the underlying instrument. For example, after Denmark initially rejected the Maastricht treaty and the ERM was nearly abandoned in 1992, the currency markets became extremely volatile. As a result, currency options trading volume was extremely heavy.

Risks in Foreign Currency Options

Traders and hedgers in foreign currency options may encounter two major risks in this market—market inefficiency and price volatility. Premiums established by the market may be too high or too low. Generally speaking, when a market for a particular financial instrument is relatively new, premiums will be too high, sometimes the result of weak volume.[24] This was true of the early trading in most foreign currency options at the PHLX. Options markets thrive on volatility in the underlying instrument. Markets for some foreign currency options can become quite thin when volatility declines. For example, premiums on European currency options tend to be higher than normal because of the volatility in the underlying market, thus presenting banks with more risk when they write currency options.

How risk is handled in a futures or option transaction determines the difference between hedging and speculating. The speculator begins with no risk and buys or sells options or futures contracts, assuming risk in order to make profits. The hedger begins with a preexisting currency risk generated from normal business operations. Options or futures are used by the hedger to reduce or eliminate that preexisting risk.

The Markets

Currency options can be traded on organized exchanges or they may be traded over-the-counter. The latter type of currency option is discussed in the next chapter and is generally accomplished in the interbank market in New York and London. True currency options are traded at the PHLX. Contract sizes at that exchange are £31,250, DM 62,500, Sfr 62,500, ¥6,250,000, Can$50,000, and Ffr 250,000. Options on spot foreign exchange are traded at the Chicago Board Options Exchange and the London International Financial Futures Exchange (LIFFE) and contract face values are equal to the International Monetary Market (IMM) contract size and twice the Philadelphia contract size. The IMM, at the Chicago Mercantile Exchange, offers options currency futures contracts, which are the same size as IMM currency futures contracts. In the OTC market, currency options can be customized as to amount, maturity date, and strike price. As with foreign currency futures contracts, exchanges trading foreign currency options contracts have established specifications for these contracts. An example of such specifications for the Philadelphia Stock Exchange is shown in Figure 13–10.

Recently, futures exchanges have attempted to adapt products from the OTC

---

[24] See Andrea L. DeMaskey and James C. Baker, "The Efficiency of Options Markets in Foreign Currencies: An Empirical Analysis," *The International Journal of Finance* 3 (Autumn 1990): 1–39.

	Australian Dollar	British Pound	Canadian Dollar	Deutsche Mark	Swiss Franc	French Franc	Japanese Yen
Symbol							
American style	XAD	XBP	XCD	XDM	XSF	XFF	XJY
European style	CAD	CBP	CCD	CDM	CSF	CFF	CJY
Contract size	A$50,000	£31,250	C$50,000	DM 62,500	SFr 62,500	Ffr 250,000	¥6,250,000
Exercise price intervals*	$0.01	$0.025	$0.005	$0.01	$0.01	$0.0025	$0.01
Premium quotations	Cents per unit	Cents per unit	Cents per unit	Cents per unit	Cents per unit	Tenths of a cent per unit	Hundredths of a cent per unit
Minimum contract price change	$5.00	$3.125	$5.00	$6.25	$6.25	$5.00	$6.25
Expiration months & cycles	March, June, September, and December + 2 near-term months						
Exercise notice	No automatic exercise of in-the-money options						
Expiration date	Friday before third Wednesday of the month						
Expiration settlement date	Third Wednesday of expiring month						
Position and exercise limits	100,000 contracts						

* Half-point strike prices for DM ($0.005), Sfr ($0.005), and ¥ ($0.00005) in the 2 near-term months only.

Source: Philadelphia Stock Exchange, 1994.

FIGURE 13–10 Foreign Currency Options Contract Specifications (Philadelphia Stock Exchange)

market. Some standardized contracts offered by futures exchanges have the flexibility of the OTC market. One example is the flex option traded at the Chicago Board Options Exchange. These options allow standard contracts to be adjusted to meet individual needs by permitting customization of some of the terms of the contract, including the expiration date, strike price, and whether the options can be exercised at any time, as with American-style options, or only at expiration date, as with European-style options. Such contracts are slowly blurring the differences between standard contracts and highly customized contracts. Table 13–5 shows the contract volume on futures and options exchanges for 1991 and 1992. This data shows that the Chicago Board of Trade and the Chicago Mercantile Exchange are much more active than all of the other derivatives exchanges around the world. The data also show, however, that the vast majority of these exchanges have experienced significant increases in their trading volume.

Another attempt by the futures exchanges to take business away from the privately traded derivatives market was made by the Chicago Mercantile Exchange when it listed a currency "forward" contract in September 1994.[25] As mentioned in chapters 3 and 10, the forward market in currencies is one of the world's largest financial markets. The value of outstanding contracts was estimated to be $9 trillion at the end of 1993. These new contracts are quoted in European terms, by the amount of foreign currency equal to one dollar. For example, just as in the forward market for foreign exchange, a quote for the mark would be, say 1.5430, meaning 1.5430 marks buys 1 dollar. In the traditional futures market, the mark would be quoted at 64.80 cents, its value in

---

[25] Steven E. Levingston, "Chicago Merc Begins Trade Of Currency 'Forwards,'" *Wall Street Journal*, 15 September 1994, p. C1.

TABLE 13-5. Volume on International Futures and Options Exchanges (number of contracts traded)

	1991	1992
Chicago Board of Trade	139,437,140	150,030,460
Chicago Mercantile Exchange	108,128,604	134,238,555
LIFFE, U.K.	38,583,877	71,977,025
MATIF, France	36,978,966	55,474,238
New York Mercantile Exchange	40,786,714	47,212,417
BM&F, Brazil	18,768,564	35,072,146
DTB, Germany	15,369,730	34,842,778
London Metal Exchange	16,937,909	24,736,920
Osaka Securities Exchange	33,478,949	21,184,310
Sydney Futures Exchange	12,496,018	17,557,685
Stockholm Options Exchange	13,442,850	17,147,096
Tokyo Intl Financial Futures Exchange	15,149,104	15,540,487
Tokyo Stock Exchange	16,601,899	14,538,717
Tokyo Comm Exchange Industry	14,949,199	13,585,379
Commodity Exchange, Inc.	15,123,655	12,673,179
Tokyo Grain Exchange	9,699,883	12,416,671
SIMEX, Singapore	6,068,044	12,180,174
Intl Petroleum Exchange, U.K.	8,412,689	10,674,803
Coffee, Sugar & Cocoa Exhange	9,494,734	9,275,708
Soffex, Switzerland	6,971,740	9,258,859
Osaka Grain Exchange	4,123,743	5,441,392
European Options Exch, Amsterdam	3,469,945	3,856,247

Source: Tracy Corrigan, "Quirky Offshoots Gain Respect," *The Financial Times*, 20 October 1993, p. VI.

dollars. The contracts will involve a larger amount, $250,000, and will offer monthly settlements in addition to traditional quarterly settlements. This contract was initially established in marks, with contracts following in yen, British pounds, Swiss francs, and Canadian dollars. The advantages of size of market and 24-hour global trading still make the forward foreign exchange market more advantageous to most multinational companies.

Reasons for Currency Options

Currency options, being rights, but not obligations, to buy or sell currency at a future date at a future price, in addition to the profits they may offer speculators, are useful for hedging future contingencies. Suppose, for example, that a U.S. construction company plans to offer a bid on a large construction project in Germany and will need deutsche Marks at the outset of the project—providing the company wins the bid. Bids are not to be opened for three months, at which time the winning bidder will have to present a construction bond for DM 5 million. The company can hedge the DM 5 million in the forward market but is obligated to deliver dollars for marks in three months. Futures contracts in marks can be used to hedge this position but in three months, these contracts will have to be offset to avoid delivery of the marks. In either of these cases, the U.S. company has an obligation to do something, no matter what happens in the spot currency markets or whether the company fails to win the bid. Foreign currency

---

MANAGEMENT APPLICATION NO. 19

A Currency Options Scenario

John Smith expects to be short, i.e., will need foreign currency amounting to DM 312,500 by the third Wednesday in June. This coincides with the June expiration date for foreign currency options on the Philadelphia Exchange. Mr. Smith can buy 5 DM calls (contract size = DM 62,500) for June delivery and decides on a call with a strike price of 63, which expires in June. This would give him the right to buy DM 312,500 at $0.63/DM, or $196,875 on the third Wednesday in June. The price, or premium, of these options is $500 per contract, for a total premium of $2,500.

If spot DM is $0.65 on expiration date, the marks would cost Mr. Smith $203,125 in the spot market ($0.65 × DM 312,500). Had he bought the 5 calls, he could exercise them and get DM 312,500 for $196,875 ($0.63 × DM 312,500) + the $2,500 premium, or $199,375, for a savings of $3,750 over a spot transaction. Mr. Smith should analyze the opportunity cost of investing the call premium of $2,500 at the risk-free Treasury bill rate and deduct income on such an investment from the $3,750 to determine his net savings. Mr. Smith could also sell the 5 calls at the value quoted on the Philadelphia Exchange up to the expiration date, provided they are American-style options. Or he could do nothing and let the calls expire. He would lose his premium but he would do this only if the calls were out of the money, i.e., the spot rate at expiration date is less than the strike price of the calls by an amount totaling more than the total premium. For example, if the DM falls to $0.61, Mr. Smith can buy DM 312,500 on the spot market for $190,625 ($0.61 × DM 312,500), or less than the $196,875 for the 63 calls purchased.

MANAGEMENT APPLICATION NO. 20

Buying a Jaguar and Currency Options[1]

During Spring 1988, when the pound was selling very high against the dollar, Mrs. S. Montague Smith of New York City ordered a Jaguar sedan. Her banker forecast that the exchange rate for fall 1988, when she had to take delivery of the car, would be $1.90/£ and, thus, Mrs. Smith planned to pay £25,000, or $47,500, for the car.

However, she worried that pound sterling might rise sharply from the current rate. Mrs. Smith's broker advised her to buy a 6-month pound call (contract size = £31,250) with a strike price of $1.90 for a premium of 4.75 cents/£, or $1,484.38. If the pound were to fall, she will let the calls expire without exercising them, thus losing only the premium of $1,484.38. If spot sterling rises to $1.95, she can sell the calls to cover the increase. The commission would add $18–30 per contract.

Questions: How much did Mrs. Smith make if the £ rose to $1.95? If she was interested in a pure hedge, what did the exchange rate have to be for her to break even, assuming away taxes?

Answers: (1) [$0.05(£31,250) = $1,562.50 Gross Profit less Option Premium of $1,484.38 = $78.12]
(2) [$1,484.38/£31,250 = $0.0475 + $1.90 = $1.9475/£]

---

[1] Joe Weber, "Seeking Foreign Intrigue? Try Currency Options," *Business Week*, 16 May 1988, p. 140.

Foreign Currency Call Options: An Example[1,2]

Consider a hypothetical example of a U.S. importer buying machinery from Germany. The importer knows the bill will come due in three months, when he must pay the German producer of the machinery DM 31 million, or $10 million, say, at a spot exchange rate of DM 3.10 per US dollar. To hedge against an adverse movement in the exchange rate, the importer pays a $200,000 premium to buy a European call option that gives him the right to buy in three months DM 31 million at a strike price of DM 3.10 per US dollar. (For simplicity, it is assumed that the strike price and the spot exchange rate when the option is purchased are the same, and the option can only be exercised on the maturity date of the contract.) Three of the possible outcomes after three months are:

(1) *The DM appreciates from DM 3.10/$ to DM 3.00/$.* Without the option, the U.S. importer would have to pay $10.3 million, that is the DM 31 million owed to the German producer converted into dollars at the new spot rate of DM 3.00/$. By exercising the option, the U.S. importer instead pays $10 million for the DM 31 million. Hedging with the option cost $200,000 for the premium but saved $300,000. (Figures are rounded to the nearest $100,000. For simplicity, the interest foregone on the $200,000 premium does not appear in the calculations.)

(2) *The DM depreciates from DM 3.10/$ to DM 3.20/$.* The U.S. importer pays $9.7 million (DM 31 million converted into dollars at the new spot rate of DM 3.20/$, or approximately $300,000 less than the amount calculated on the basis of the initial spot rate. The option is not exercised because doing so would mean paying $10 million rather than $9.7 million for the needed deutsche Marks. Hedging with the option thus cost $200,000 for the premium, but because exercising the option required no obligation, the importer was able to benefit from the $300,000 decline in the cost of the machinery as a result of the depreciation of the deutsche Mark.

(3) *The DM remains unchanged at DM 3.10/$.* The U.S. importer is indifferent between exercising and not exercising the option, because in either case the machinery will cost him $10 million. No gains nor losses on account of exchange rate movement are incurred, but the premium cost $200,000.

The decision to exercise the option depends on whether the foreign currency in question appreciates or depreciates relative to the striking, or exercise, price. If the deutsche Mark appreciates in the above illustration, the call option would be exercised because the option allows its holder to buy the needed foreign currency at a more favorable exchange rate. The option would not be exercised if the deutsche Mark depreciates because it would then be cheaper to buy the currency at the new spot rate than at the striking price. Unlike a forward or futures contract, the option allows the importer to take advantage of the depreciating foreign currency by simply not exercising the option, although he incurs the "insurance" cost of the option's premium. By using the foreign currency option to hedge, the importer cannot, however, lose more than the premium; options thus limit the downside risk from exchange rate movements while allowing the contract holder to profit from any favorable exchange rate changes.

Clearly the importer could have chosen not to cover his foreign currency exposure at all. Had he done so and had the deutsche Mark depreciated or remained unchanged, he would have been better off—in an *ex-post* sense—since the option he might have purchased would not have been exercised but would have cost him the premium. Had the deutsche Mark appreciated substantially, however, he could have been far worse off for not hedging. In either case, moreover, by not covering his position, he incurs an *ex-ante* exchange rate risk, something he presumably would prefer to avoid if he is risk averse.

Alternatively, the U.S. importer could have hedged his foreign currency exposure by purchasing marks in the forward market. For example, suppose that the forward mark exchange rate against the U.S. dollar was DM 3.06 per dollar. Had the importer covered his position through a forward purchase, he would have locked in the cost of $10.1 million (DM 31 million divided by DM 3.06/$) for the machinery, and subsequent exchange rate movements would have no bearing on this cost. Subsequent spot rate movements would, however, influence the cost when an option contract is used. So at different future spot

rates, either the option or the forward contract would prove to be more advantageous than the other. In the example, at an exchange rate of DM 3.10/$ or below (an appreciation of the mark from its initial level), the cost (including the premium) would be $10.2 million with an option contract—higher than with outright forward cover. At an exchange rate of DM 3.14/$, the option and the forward contract would yield the same cost of $10.1 million (DM 31 million divided by DM 3.14/$ plus $200,000 for the premium). And for an exchange rate above DM 3.14/$ (a depreciation of the mark from its initial level), the cost would be lower under an option contract. Whether using the forward market is a less costly alternative than the option market depends, *ex-post*, on the realized value of the spot exchange rate. (It also depends, of course, on the size of the premium as well as on the striking price of the option contract and on the forward rate at the time that the transaction is undertaken.) In an *ex-ante* sense, whether an option is preferable to a forward contract as a means of hedging foreign currency exposure will likely depend on judgments regarding the future movements of the exchange rate. The added flexibility associated with an option contract can make it a preferred way of hedging, as it allows its holder to benefit from favorable exchange rate changes.

> In the options market it is the premium that is determined by market forces and there is generally a choice of different striking prices, each striking price associated with a different premium, while in the forward (or futures) market the exchange rate is market determined.

---

[1]This case is reprinted with permission from Robert A. Feldman, "Foreign Currency Options," *Finance & Development* 22 (December 1985): 40.

[2]This case uses the foreign exchange rates in effect at the time of the case and are not up-to-date.

options can be used by the company for a small premium. If the company fails to win the bid, it can merely allow the options to expire worthless, that is, without exercising them. The cost to the company is the insurance premium paid up front. If the company loses the bid and the options have not yet expired, they can be sold in the market, thus reducing the premium cost, or they might be exercised—depending on the movement of the $/DM rate—and the marks received could be sold in the spot market for a possible profit.

Currency options contracts can be written by companies for the purpose of gaining premium income. Suppose a U.S. company has a German subsidiary which requires a long deutsche Mark position in liquid, short-term assets in order to cover operating expenses. This is a position that will be maintained. Thus, the parent firm can write covered call options, selling the right for the buyer of the call to purchase deutsche Marks from them. Should the option be exercised, the parent has deutsche Marks in reserve to cover the option. If the option is not exercised, the parent gains the premium.

More Examples of Currency Puts and Calls

Example No. 1   The buyer of a call option will gain a profit, or will be "in the money" if the value of the option at expiration or when exercised is greater than the premium paid to buy the option, i.e., spot > option exercise price, plus the initial option premium. Suppose that an investor paid a premium of $1,062.50 ($0.017 × DM 62,500) to buy one DM December 63 call at the PHLX and by expiration date, the DM spot price had risen to $0.66. The call gave the investor (or hedger) the right to purchase DM 62,500 at $0.03/DM less than spot. By exercising the option, the investor realizes $1,875 ($0.03 × 62,500), less the $1,062.50 premium, or a net $812.50. This is an investment return of 80 percent in 3 months. Had spot at expiration been $0.63 or below, the option would have expired worthless and the investor would have lost the $1,062.50 premium. Table 13–6 shows the effect on profits at various forex rates.

TABLE 13-6. Buying a Call Option

DM Spot Price at Expiration	Loss	Profit
$0.63	$1,062.50*	
0.64	437.50†	
0.65		187.50**
0.66		812.50‡
0.67		1,437.50
0.68		2,062.50
0.69		2,687.50

*Premium × Contract amount, or $0.017 × (DM 62,500) = $1,062.50.

†Buy at strike = $0.63; Pay $0.63 (DM 62,500) = $39,375; Sell at spot = $0.64; Receive $0.64 (DM 62,500) = $40,000; Loss = Difference; $40,000 − (39,375 + 1,062.50) = −$437.50.

**Buy at strike = $0.63; Pay $0.63 (DM 62,500) = $39,375; Sell at spot = $0.65; Receive $0.65 (DM 62,500) = $40,625; Profit = Difference; $40,625 − (39,375 + 1,062.50) = $187.50.

‡Buy at strike = $0.63; Pay $0.63 (DM 62,500) = $39,375; Sell at spot = $0.66; Receive $0.66 (DM 62,500) = $41,250; Profit = Difference; $41,250 − (39,375 + 1,062.50) = $812.50.

Example No. 2   If the foreign currency is expected to decline relative to the U.S. dollar or the dollar is forecast to strengthen against that currency, a put option will give the investor or hedger the right to sell the underlying currency at a strike price anticipated to be higher than spot for the foreign currency when the option expires. Suppose, for example, that an investor could have purchased a Swiss franc December 73 put in August, giving the investor the right to sell 62,500 Swiss francs at a price higher than the spot market price of the currency at expiration date. The investor paid a premium for this put of $800 ($0.0128 × Sfr 62,500). By expiration date, the Swiss franc had declined to $0.69/Sfr. The investor exercised the option to sell the contract at $0.73/Sfr. The intrinsic value was $0.04/Sfr, or $2,500. The investor's net profit was $1,700 ($2,500 less the $800 premium), assuming away transactions costs and taxes. Table 13–7 shows the effect on profits of spot Swiss franc falling to various levels.

Example No. 3   Assume that it is currently June. September deutsche Mark futures are trading at $0.3400. September DM put options with a $0.35 strike price are trading at $0.0135 ($0.0135 × DM125,000 = $1,687.50, the premium set by the market). In this example, the intrinsic value is $0.01, found by deducting the $0.34 futures price from the $0.35 strike price. This is the option's value if it were exercised today. The time value of the option is $0.35 and this represents the current risk associated with possible price changes between June and September. If the outlook for the market in marks is uncertain, buyers are willing to pay higher premiums for price protection and sellers will require higher premiums to accept the risk associated with writing the option contract. The higher the market volatility is and the longer the time until the option expires, the higher the option premium will be. The lower the probability of price change and the fewer days until the option's expiration, the lower will be the option's premium. An option will be in the money, at the money, or out of the money. If the call option is in the money, the underlying futures or spot price will be above the strike price of the option. If the call option is at the money, the underlying futures or spot price will be

TABLE 13–7. Buying a Put Option		
Sfr Spot Price at Expiration	*Loss*	*Profit*
$0.73	$800*	
0.72	175†	
0.71		$ 450**
0.70		1,075‡
0.69		1,700§
0.68		2,325
0.67		2,950
0.66		3,575

*Premium $\times$ Contract amount, or $0.0128 $\times$ (Sfr 62,500) = $800.00.

†Sell at strike price: $0.73; Receive $0.73; (Sfr 62,500) = $45,625; Buy at spot: Pay $0.72 (Sfr 62,500) = $45,000; Loss: $45,625 − ($45,000 + 800) = −$175.00.

**Sell at strike price: $0.73; Receive $0.73; (Sfr 62,500) = $45,625; Buy at spot: Pay $0.71 (Sfr 62,500) = $44,375; Profit: $45,625 − ($44,375 + 800) = $450.00.

**Sell at strike price: $0.73; Receive $0.73; (Sfr 62,500) = $45,625; Buy at spot: Pay $0.70 (Sfr 62,500) = $43,750; Profit: $45,625 − ($43,750 + 800) = $1,075.00.

§Sell at strike price: $0.73; Receive $0.73; (Sfr 62,500) = $45,625; Buy at spot: Pay $0.69 (Sfr 62,500) = $43,125; Profit: $45,625 − ($43,125 + 800) = $1,700.

equal to the strike price. If the call option is out of the money, the strike price will be above the option strike price. These relationships will be just the opposite for a put option. The profit and loss possibilities are shown in Figure 13–11 for a currency call option and in Figure 13–12 for a currency put option. These examples use premiums and strike prices for DM options on May 2, 1996 shown in Figure 13–7. The option used in Figure 13–11 is the June 67 call, i.e., a call option contract expiring in June with a strike price of $0.67 per DM. The option used in Figure 13–12 is the June put, i.e., a put option contract expiring in June with a strike price of $0.67 per DM. Figure 13–11 shows that profits are made when the spot price is above $0.6729/DM ($0.67 strike price + the premium of $0.0029/DM = $0.6729/DM). The holder of the call option would not exercise it at spot rates below $0.6729. Figure 13–12 shows that profits are made when the mark falls below $0.6502 ($0.67 strike price − the premium of $0.0198/DM = $0.6502).

Example No. 4   An investor paid a $900 premium for a 6-month DM 40 call. Three months later, the DM spot price rises to $0.42 and the option is quoted at $1,700—an intrinsic value of $1,250 and time value of $450. The investor, fearing that a further increase in the DM spot price may not be sufficient to offset the option's eroding time value, may take a profit of $800 by selling the option for $1,700, rather than exercise it. Suppose the same circumstances, but with three months until expiration, the DM spot price falls to $0.39 and the DM 40 call purchased for $900 is now quoted at $400. In order to limit his loss to $500, the investor may sell an offsetting option for $400.[26]

---

[26]For a better understanding of currency options traded at the Philadelphia Stock Exchange, see "Understanding Foreign Currency Options: The Third Dimension to Foreign Exchange," published by the Philadelphia Stock Exchange, 1900 Market Street, Philadelphia, PA 19103.

Currency:	German Mark
Contract Size:	DM 62,500
Exercise (strike) Price:	$0.67 per DM for June Call
Premium (price):	0.29 U.S. cents per DM ($181.25 per contract)

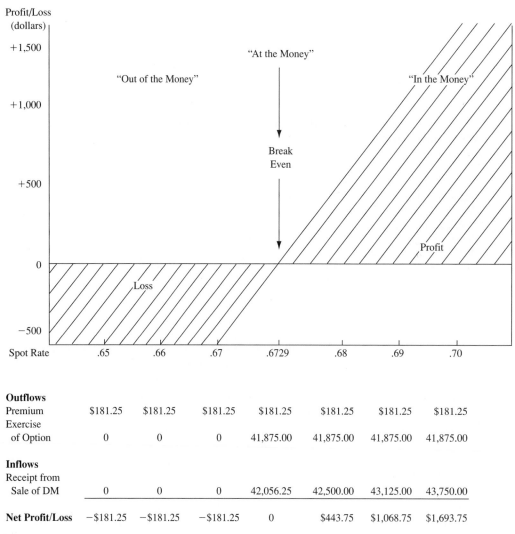

Outflows							
Premium	$181.25	$181.25	$181.25	$181.25	$181.25	$181.25	$181.25
Exercise of Option	0	0	0	41,875.00	41,875.00	41,875.00	41,875.00
Inflows							
Receipt from Sale of DM	0	0	0	42,056.25	42,500.00	43,125.00	43,750.00
Net Profit/Loss	−$181.25	−$181.25	−$181.25	0	$443.75	$1,068.75	$1,693.75

FIGURE 13–11 Currency Call Option
Profit and Loss at Selected Spot Prices

Options on Currency Futures

In addition, options on currency futures are traded on the IMM at the CME. Prices for these contracts are shown in Figure 13–8. These contracts give the hedger or trader the right but not the obligation to purchase or sell a currency futures contract at a strike or exercise price per unit of currency. They are similar to currency options but the trader does not buy or sell the actual currency. Instead futures contracts to buy or sell currency will be bought or sold when the option is exercised.

For example, a call on a futures contract is a contract between a buyer and a writer in which the buyer pays a premium, the price of the option, to the writer for the right, but not the obligation, to go long an exchange-traded foreign currency futures

Currency:	German Mark
Contract Size:	DM 62,500
Exercise (strike) Price:	$0.67 per DM for June put
Premium (price):	1.98 U.S. cents per DM ($1,237.50 per contract)

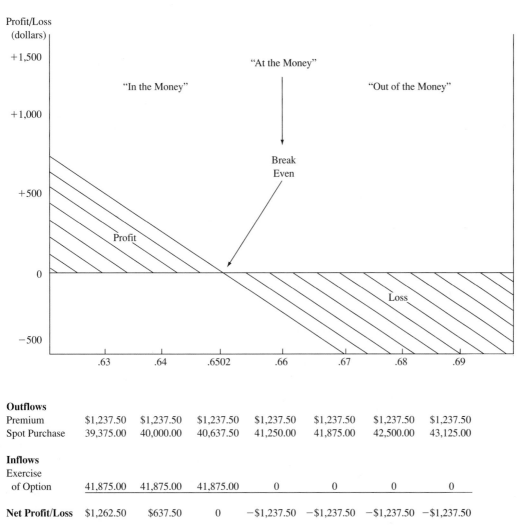

Outflows							
Premium	$1,237.50	$1,237.50	$1,237.50	$1,237.50	$1,237.50	$1,237.50	$1,237.50
Spot Purchase	39,375.00	40,000.00	40,637.50	41,250.00	41,875.00	42,500.00	43,125.00
Inflows							
Exercise of Option	41,875.00	41,875.00	41,875.00	0	0	0	0
Net Profit/Loss	$1,262.50	$637.50	0	−$1,237.50	−$1,237.50	−$1,237.50	−$1,237.50

FIGURE 13–12 Currency Put Option
Profit and Loss at Selected Spot Prices

contract at the strike, or exercise, price, i.e., an opening price in terms of a second currency. If the buyer exercises this option, the writer must go short the futures contract. In a put on a currency futures contract, the buyer obtains, for the premium, the right, but not the obligation, to go short in a foreign currency futures contract. If the buyer exercises at the strike price, the writer must go long the futures contract. All such options on currency futures are American-style and can be exercised at any time prior to expiration.

Suppose that an American-style call on June deutsche Mark futures has a strike price of $0.65 and the current futures price is $0.67. This call has a premium quoted at the Chicago Mercantile Exchange of 1.70 or $0.0170 per mark. If this call is exercised,

the buyer will have a long position of one June deutsche Mark futures contract at an opening futures price of $0.65 per mark. Since the current futures price is $0.67/mark, the value of this futures position is

$$\$0.67 - [\$0.65 \text{ (the strike price)} + \$0.0170 \text{ (the premium)}] = \$0.0030/\text{mark}$$

This profit can be taken immediately by closing out the futures position, i.e., going short one contract to offset, or by withdrawing cash from the account, provided all futures margin requirements have been met.

Options on Options

An option on an option is an option that pays off the value of another option if it is exercised. For example, a cacall, or call option on a call option has a value at maturity of the $\max(0, x - y)$, where x is the value of the underlying call, and y is the cacall strike price. On the contrary, a caput, or call option on a put option, has a payoff of the $\max(0, z - y)$, where z is the underlying put price and y is the caput strike price. The holder of a cacall, for example, has the right, but not the obligation, to buy a call option, further giving him, if he exercises it, the right, but not the obligation, to purchase foreign currency at the strike price.

Such options can be used by a company that will bid on a contract involving a large foreign exchange exposure. An option on an option will have a premium smaller than that on the option. The company can save money if the contract is not won. If the company wins the bid, the total cost to the company will be a little higher if it holds an option on an option rather than the underlying option.

USDX Currency Options

In the section on currency futures contracts, the USDX contract traded on the Finex in New York was discussed. Finex has also developed a currency option contract based on the U.S. dollar index, compiled by the Federal Reserve Board. The principles underlying the USDX option contract are the same as with PHLX-traded options. Downside risk can be limited with the USDX option contract in the same way that a PHLX contract may be used.

For example, if the avoidance of downside loss is the objective when a dollar rally is forecast, a USDX call option can be bought. The holder of the USDX call option has the right to purchase a USDX futures contract at a price equal to the strike price of the option up to a specified date, the maturity date, for a premium. Options are discussed in more detail later in this chapter. For example, if the March USDX futures contract is trading at 97.48, a March call option having a strike price of 98 might be priced at 1.23 USDX points or $1,230 (1.23 × $1,000). The buyer of this option would have the right to purchase a March USDX futures at 98.00 on or before the expiration in early March—USDX options expire two Fridays before the third Wednesday of the expiring contract month at 5:00 P.M., though trading stops at 3:00 P.M.—thus limiting the loss to a maximum of $1,230, if the March futures price is at or below 98.00 at the time of the option's expiration. On the other hand, the option will increase in value if the dollar rallies above this point.

USDX call option spreads can also be used in a dollar rally. A call option spread consists of buying a call option of a particular maturity and strike price while, at the same time, selling another call option of the same maturity but at a higher strike price. Suppose that a March 98 call can be bought for 1.23 USDX points and a March 100 call can be sold for 0.56 USDX points. The sale of the second option provides some revenue to offset the premium cost of the purchased option. Thus, the net premium of the spread is reduced, in this case, to 0.67 USDX points, or $670, or [(1.23 − 0.56) × 1,000]. In return for the premium reduction, the short option position limits the maximum

---

STUDY AID

The market for options contracts thrives on volatility in prices of the underlying asset. Track premiums quoted at the Philadelphia Stock Exchange during periods of relative calm in currency markets and during periods of turmoil and specu-lative activity in these markets. Notice the difference in the premiums. They should be higher during the latter periods and lower during the calm periods.

---

profit attainable during any dollar rally. The spread is profitable if the dollar rises and is then referred to as a bull call spread. The maximum profit attainable is equal to the difference between the strike prices of the two options less the net premium paid $[(100 - 98) - 0.67] \times 1,000$. In this example, this is \$1,330 ($2.00 - 0.67 = 1.33$ USDX points, or \$1,330). The break-even point for this spread, if hedging is the objective, is 98.67, at the time the spread was entered. Reverse strategies can be used if the dollar is expected to decline.

Conclusion

In conclusion, an option is "in the money" if the strike price is less than the spot price for a call or if the strike price exceeds the spot price for a put. Options can be bought directly from banks, which write them for any contract size or maturity date. The OTC options have greater flexibility. Some companies write their own options for income purposes. OTC options are discussed in more detail in the next chapter.

Interest Rate Futures and Options

MNCs and their financial management face another variety of increased volatility, the fluctuations in interest rates, or the price of money. International companies resort to a variety of debt instruments to fund various operations of the firm. Since the end of fixed exchange rates in the early 1970s and relatively fixed interest rates in the 1950s, firms have had to hedge their debt positions or manage their asset/liability balance sheet positions. The exchange-traded interest rate futures contract has been a solution to these needs.

The first interest rate futures contract traded on an exchange was the Government National Mortgage Association (Ginnie Mae) collateralized depository receipts contract, which opened on the Chicago Board of Trade in 1975. By 1991, more than \$2 trillion of notional value of short-term and long-term bonds was covered by interest rate futures contracts.[27]

Among the most active single interest rate futures contracts are the U.S. Treasury bond futures contract traded on the Chicago Board of Trade and the Eurodollar contract traded on the Chicago Mercantile Exchange. In fact, Eurocurrency futures contracts are traded on exchanges all around the world.[28] A DIBOR contract, Dublin Interbank Offer Rate, is traded on the Irish Futures and Options Exchange in Dublin, a PIBOR contract, Paris Interbank Offer Rate, is traded on the MATIF in Paris, a Euromark contract is traded on the MATIF in Paris and on LIFFE in London, a HIBOR

---

[27]Anant Sundaram, International Financial Markets, in *The WG&L Handbook of International Finance* ed. Dennis E. Logue. (Cincinnati, OH: South-Western, 1995), p. 77.

[28]J. Orlin Grabbe, *International Financial Markets* (New York: Elsevier, 1991), p. 271.

contract, Hong Kong Interbank Offer Rate, is traded on the Hong Kong Futures Exchange, a Euro-yen contract is traded on the Tokyo International Financial Futures Exchange (TIFFE) and SIMEX (the Singapore International Metals Exchange), a Eurosterling contract is traded on the LIFFE, and Eurodollar contracts are traded on the LIFFE, SIMEX, TIFFE, and, as mentioned, the Chicago Mercantile Exchange.

Eurodollar futures contracts are based on 3-month LIBOR, the interest rate for 3-month Eurodollar deposits for forward delivery. The face value of a contract is $1 million. The price quoted is 100 less the interest rate, in percentage terms, of the Eurodollar 3-month deposit for forward delivery. For example, on September 15, 1994, the Chicago Mercantile Exchange quoted a closing price for its Eurodollar futures contract for September delivery at 94.95, meaning the Eurodollar deposit offer rate for September delivery was 5.05 percent. Thus, if interest rates go up, the price of this contract will decline. If interest rates go down, the contract price will increase. The minimum price movement is one basis point, or 0.01 percent. The value of a one basis point change in price on a Eurodollar futures contract whose face value is $1 million is $100 for a 360-day deposit and, thus, for a 90-day deposit, the usual maturity of Eurodollar deposits, it is $25. If the September 1994 delivery contract for Eurodollars falls from 94.95 to 93.95, the long side of a contract will lose $2,500 (100 basis points × $25) and the short side of the contract, i.e., a trader who expects prices to fall, that is, interest rates to rise, and who sells the contract, will gain $2,500. These contracts are traded for delivery in March, June, September, and December. Generally, the contract price will converge to the spot price on the last day of maturity because the exchange, after sampling major trading banks, will force them to use the spot price as a final settlement price for the contract that expires.

The most actively traded futures contract on the LIFFE is the German Bund future. The Bund, short for Bundesanleihen, is the German Federal Government long-term bond. It is a benchmark for other sectors of the bond market and its market is highly liquid. Nearly two-thirds of the Bund futures turnover is traded on LIFFE.

Finally, the first European exchange to trade flexible options on government bonds was the European Options Exchange (EOE), located in Amsterdam. Flexible options, or flex options as they are referred to in the market, permit institutional investors to set their own option style, i.e., European or American, expiration dates, and strike price. The EOE is one of the most liquid exchanges in Europe and offers bond options American-style as well as many other derivatives.

HEDGING WITH INTEREST RATE FUTURES

Interest rate futures contracts can be used to hedge exposure to the risk that future interest rates will change and adversely affect the return on deposited or invested funds. Several different futures contracts can be utilized. Those with the highest liquidity and deepest markets are the Treasury bill contract and the Eurodollar contract traded at the International Monetary Market on the Chicago Mercantile Exchange. Since we are interested in global finance, we are more interested in the Eurodollar futures contract, perhaps the most actively traded financial futures contract. This contract is priced to yield the London Interbank Offer Rate (LIBOR). Eurodollar contracts can be used to hedge short-term deposits. A 6-month Eurodollar deposit beginning in December could be hedged by two December 1994 contracts, called a stack hedge. Or a strip hedge could be used whereby the Eurodollar deposit beginning in December could be hedged by one December 1994 contract and one March 1995 contract. These contracts can be used to hedge other interest rate assets and liabilities, including T bills, commercial paper, and banker's acceptances. On September 15, 1994, Eurodollar futures contracts for December delivery closed at a price of 94.30, meaning that a contract was

worth \$943,000 (\$1 million × 0.9430). Thus, one contract could hedge a \$943,000 Eurodollar deposit maturing in December, thus locking in a yield of 5.7 percent (100 − 94.30).

OPTIONS ON INTEREST RATE FUTURES

Options on interest rate futures are contracts to buy (call) or sell (put) futures contracts in which the underlying or derivative instrument is a money market instrument of some kind. Several options contracts on interest rate futures are traded on the floors of a number of exchanges. An option on Treasury bond futures is traded at the Chicago Board of Trade, as are options on 5-year Treasury note futures. At the Chicago Mercantile Exchange, trading is offered in options on Eurodollar futures, LIBOR futures, and 2- and 5-year mid-curve Eurodollar futures. Options on Euromark futures, Long Gilt futures, and German Government Bond futures are traded at LIFFE.

Summary and Conclusions

A variety of derivative financial instruments can be traded on relatively liquid exchanges in several industrialized countries. These instruments can be used to hedge asset, commodity, and financial instrument prices such as interest rates, foreign exchange

FIGURE 13–13 Derivatives Contracts and Securities

Privately Negotiated (OTC) Forwards	*Privately Negotiated (OTC) Options*	*Exchange Traded Futures*	*Exchange Traded Options*
Derivatives Contracts			
Forward commodity contracts	Commodity options	Eurodollar (CME)	S&P futures options (Merc)
Forward foreign exchange contracts	Currency options	U.S. T bond (CBOT)	Bond futures options (LIFFE)
Forward rate agreements (FRAs)	Equity options	9% Brit. Gilt (LIFFE)	Corn futures options (CBOT)
Currency swaps	FRA options	CAC-40 (MATIF)	¥/\$ futures options (IMM)
Interest rate swaps	Caps, floors, collars	DM/\$ (IMM)	
Commodity swaps	Swap options	German Bund (DTB)	
Equity swaps	Bond options	Gold (COMEX)	

Structured Securities and Deposits	*Stripped Securities*	*Securities with Option Characteristics*
Derivative Securities		
Dual-currency bonds	Treasury strips	Callable bonds
Commodity-linked bonds	IOs and POs	Putable bonds
Yield curve notes		Convertible securities
Equity-linked bank deposits		Warrants

Source: Global Derivatives Study Group, *Derivatives: Practices and Principles* (Washington, D.C.: Group of Thirty, July 1993), p. 29.

rates, and securities such as equities and bonds. The major amount of liquidity in these markets is derived from the trading by speculators whose primary objective is to profit from their transactions.

Several different types of financial derivative instruments are traded on a variety of organized exchanges. These include currency and interest rate futures and options, options on currency and interest rate futures, futures and options on financial price indexes, and options on options to buy or sell interest rate futures.

Several exchanges have been established for organized trading of these standardized derivatives. The most active of these include the Chicago Mercantile Exchange, Chicago Board of Trade, London International Financial Futures Exchange (LIFFE), Philadelphia Stock Exchange, European Options Exchange, Chicago Board Options Exchange, MATIF in France, Tokyo International Financial Futures Exchange, and the Deutsche Terminbörse in Germany. These markets are regulated by a variety of government agencies or trade association groups. The Commodities Futures Trading Commission regulates and supervises all exchange trading of derivatives in the United States. Trade groups usually supervise organized exchanges in Europe.

Among the most active contracts traded in these markets are currency futures on the Chicago Mercantile Exchange and LIFFE, Eurodollar futures contracts at Chicago Mercantile Exchange, currency option contracts at the Philadelphia Stock Exchange, and the USDX futures and options contracts traded at Finex in New York. See Figure 13-13 for a listing of selected derivatives and the exchange where they are traded.

APPENDIX 1

Options Pricing Concepts

The Black-Scholes option pricing model made a number of contributions to financial economics. It improved the understanding by students of finance of a wide range of contracts with optionlike features, such as the call feature in corporate and municipal bonds. This feature is clearly an option as is the refinancing privilege in mortgages. Black-Scholes also improved our understanding with regard to traditional financial instruments. When, for example, shareholders can turn a company over to creditors, the company has negative net worth. Corporate debt can then be considered a put option bought by shareholders from creditors.

Black-Scholes explains the prices of European options that can only be exercised at the expiration date. Another feature of the model is that the call option is equivalent to a portfolio constructed from the underlying assets. Furthermore, the model is derived by identifying an option replicating portfolio and, then, equating the option's premium with the value of that portfolio. One essential assumption of Black-Scholes is that investors arbitrage away any profits created by gaps in asset pricing. For example, if a call is trading high "in the money," investors will write calls and buy the replicating portfolio, thereby causing prices to fall back in line. If the option is trading low in the money, investors will buy the option and short the option-replicating portfolio, i.e., sell stocks and buy bonds in the correct proportions. By incorporating such trading strategies, traders can make profits from risk-less opportunities and, thus, force option and underlying asset prices into an equilibrium relationship.

The following represents the Black-Scholes model developed in 1973.[29] The model considers a share of common stock, although it is applicable to other financial

---

[29]This discussion is adapted from Peter Fortune, "Anomalies in Option Pricing: The Black-Scholes Model Revisited," *New England Economic Review* (March/April 1996): 19.

assets such as foreign currency, that pays a continuous dividend at a constant yield of q at each moment, and a call option that expires at time T. The current price of a share, at time t, is denoted as S_t. This price can be interpreted as the sum of two components: (1) the present value of the dividends to be paid over the period up to time T, which is the expiration date of a call option on the stock, and (2) the value that is "at risk." Because payment of dividends reduces the value of the stock at the rate q, the price of the stock at time T is reduced by the factor $e^{-q(T-t)}$, so the present value "at risk" is $S_t e^{-q(T-t)}$.

Denoting the "at risk" component as S^*, Black-Scholes assumes that S^* evolves over time as a diffusion process and this can be written as

$$dS^*/S^* = \mu dt + \sigma dz$$

in which μ, called the "rift," is the expected instantaneous rate of change in S^4, and σ, called the "volatility," is the standard deviation of the instaneous rate of change in S^4. The term dz, called a Wiener variable, is a normally distributed random variable with a mean of zero and a standard deviation of $\sqrt{dt}$. Thus, the rate of change in S^* vibrates randomly around the drift. If this is converted to a statement about the value of S^*, then S^* will be found to be log-normally distributed, i.e., the logarithm of S* will be normally distributed.

Now assume a European call option on this stock which expires in $(T-t)$ days. Black-Scholes describes the equilibrium price, or premium, on an option as a function of the risky component of the stock price $(S_t e^{-q(T-t)}$, the present value of the option's strike price $(Xe^{-r(T-t)}$, the risk-less rate of interest (r), the dividend yield on the stock (q), the time remaining until the option expires $(T-t)$, and the "volatility" of the return on the underlying security (σ). The volatility is defined as the standard deviation of the rate of change in the stock's price.

Recalling that $S_t^4 = S_t e^{-q(T-t)}$, the Black-Scholes relationship is

$$C_t = S_t^* N(d_1 - Xe^{-r(T-t)} N(d_2)$$

where

$$d_1 = [1n(S/X) + (r - q + \tfrac{1}{2}\sigma 2)(T-t)]/\sigma\sqrt{(T-t)}$$
$$d_2 = d_1 - \sigma\sqrt{(T-t)}$$

In this formula, $N(d)$ is the probability that a standard normal random variable is less than d. $N(d_1)$ and $N(d_2)$, both positive but less than 1, represent the number of shares and the amount of debt in a portfolio that exactly replicate the price of the option. Therefore, a call option on one share is exactly equivalent to buying $N(d_1)$ shares of the stock and selling $N(d_2)$ units of a bond with present value $Xe^{-r(T-t)}$. For example, if $N(d_1) = 0.5$ and $N(d_2) = 0.4$, the call option is exactly equivalent to one-half share of the stock plus borrowing 40 percent of the present value of the strike price; thus the option's "replicating portfolio" and a position of one call option, shorting $N(d_1)$ shares, and purchasing $Xe^{-r(T-t)} N(d_2)$ of bonds, create a perfect hedge, exposing the holder to no price risk.

APPENDIX 2

Pricing Options with Simultaneous Equations

Prices of currency options can be determined by solving a series of simultaneous equations that involve several market characteristics.[30] For example, the **delta** of the option

[30]Information for this section was taken from J. Orlin Grabbe, "Foreign Currency Options: A Survey" (paper presented at International Banking and Finance Symposium, University of California, Berkeley, CA,

must be considered. Delta is the amount the option premium changes vis-à-vis a small increase in the spot or futures price. If delta is −0.479, then if the spot price goes up 0.1 cent, say from $0.3482 to $0.3492, then the option value will change by ($0.001)(−0.479) or −$0.0479, or from $0.915 to $0.8671. The **gamma** is the amount the option delta changes vis-à-vis a change in the spot or futures price of the currency. It is the measure of risk inherent in a delta neutral hedge. For example, if delta is 0.540 and gamma is 0.160, then if spot increases 1 cent, from $0.3482 to $0.3582, a gamma of 0.160 indicates that the delta will increase from 0.540 to 0.700 (0.540 + 0.160). **Theta** is the measure of change in the option value with the passage of time. **Elasticity** is the percentage change in the option premium for a 1 percent change in the underlying price. **Rho** is the rate at which the price of an option changes in response to a given move in interest rates. **Lambda** is the change in the option value for a unit increase in volatility. The unit is in increments of 0.01 to volatility. If lambda is 0.069, for example, then if volatility—the yearly standard deviation rate—goes from 0.14 to 0.15 (0.14 + 0.01), then the option premium will increase 0.069, or, for example, from $0.869 to $0.938. Computer programs can be obtained in the marketplace and all of these pricing factors can be input to determine the price and hedging characteristics of the option.

This section has included a discussion of the concepts that are relevant to the pricing of options and stem from the partial derivatives of the price of an option when the underlying determinant variables are considered. For example, delta is a partial derivative of an option price in relation to the spot rate of the underlying foreign currency. Gamma is a second partial derivative of an option price in relation to the spot rate, i.e., it is the partial derivative of the delta with regard to that same spot rate. Theta is the partial derivative of an option price in relation to time. Lambda is the partial derivative of an option price in relation to its volatility. And elasticity is the delta multiplied by the spot rate-to-option value for options on futures contracts.

Additional Readings

DeMaskey, Andrea, and James C. Baker. "The Efficiency of Options Markets in Foreign Currencies: An Empirical Analysis." *The International Journal of Finance* 3 (Autumn 1990): 1–39.

Global Derivatives Study Group. *Derivatives: Practices and Principles.* Washington, D.C.: Group of Thirty, July 1993.

Hull, J. C. *Options, Futures and Other Derivatives.* Englewood Cliffs, NJ: Prentice-Hall, 1993.

Jarrow, R., and A. Rudd. *Option Pricing.* Englewood Cliffs, NJ: Prentice-Hall, 1993.

McDonough, William J. "The Global Derivatives Market." *Quarterly Review of the Federal Reserve Bank of New York* 18 (Autumn 1993): 1–5.

Shastri, Kuldeep, and K. Tandon. "Valuation of Foreign Currency Options: Some Empirical Tests." *Journal of Financial and Quantitative Analysis* 21 (1986): 145–60.

Stoll, Hans R., and Robert E. Whaley. *Futures and Options: Theory and Applications.* Cincinnati, OH: South-Western Publishing Co., 1993.

Discussion Questions

1. What is a derivative financial instrument? Why is it traded?
2. What is notional value and why is it important?
3. How are prices quoted in foreign currency futures contracts?
4. What major international contracts are traded on the Chicago Mercantile Exchange? the Chicago Board of Trade? Finex? Philadelphia Stock Exchange? LIFFE in London?
5. Why have so many futures exchange markets been established throughout the world?

6. Discuss the differences between forward and futures markets in foreign currency.

7. What advantages do foreign currency futures have over foreign currency options? Discuss.

8. What is meant if an option is "in the money," "out of the money," or "at the money"?

9. What are the disadvantages of a passive hedging program that covers 100 percent of the foreign currency exposure?

10. What is the difference between the USDX Futures and the U.S. Dollar Composite Index Futures contracts?

11. What are the risks of foreign currency futures contracts? of foreign currency options?

12. Discuss the regulation of currency futures and options trading.

13. Discuss the major foreign counterparts to the U.S. Commodities Futures Trading Commission.

14. What are the characteristics of foreign currency options?

15. Discuss the pricing determinants of foreign currency options.

16. What transactions are most appropriate for hedging with foreign currency options?

17. What are the alternatives available to a hedger, trader, or investor in the use of foreign currency options? Discuss.

18. Discuss the significance of volatility in the currency options markets.

19. Suppose the average premium on foreign currency calls has decreased. On the other hand, the average premium on foreign currency puts has increased. How would you explain this?

20. A British exporter will be paid $1 million in three months. He hesitates to sell $1 million forward or to buy currency options for that amount. What are the differences between the two strategies?

Problems

1. From Table 1 in chapter 3, the spot rate on May 2, 1996, for the Swiss franc was $0.8039. The premium quoted, from Figure 7 in this chapter, on a Swiss franc call option with a June expiration date and an exercise price of $0.82—American–style—at the Philadelphia Stock Exchange was $0.0047. What is the intrinsic value of one Sfr 62,500 call option?

2. Calculate the time value, if any, in the preceding problem.

3. In Figure 7 of this chapter, find the total premium cost of 5 British pound 158 puts trading American style.

4. In early May 1996, multinational company needs a selling hedge. Suppose a U.S. truck manufacturer has a plant in Germany. The German plant is short of funds to meet payroll expenses in the amount of DM 500,000. In 6 months, it expects to be in a sound financial position because peak purchases of trucks will take place at that time. The U.S. parent can transfer the necessary funds to the German plant for 6 months. In 6 months, the German plant will return the funds to the U.S. parent. Assume the facts are as in Table 1, chapter 3, and Figure 1, chapter 13, i.e., the spot rate for marks is $0.6542, the 180-day forward rate is $0.6620, and the futures contract with a delivery date nearest to 6 months from now is the September contract that closed at $0.6593. What should the truck manufacturer do to hedge this transaction? Which market, forward or futures, would be best? Assuming away taxes and transactions costs, calculate the hedge in each market and discuss which would be best.

5. How many Canadian dollars could a company hedge if 10 December futures contracts had been bought at the closing price on May 2, 1996, assuming no taxes or transactions costs?

6. According to Figure 1, chapter 13, a trader could have purchased long one British pound September contract at the opening price of $1.4926 on the IMM at the Chicago

International Communications Networks

Finally, the international cash management environment includes international communications networks devoted to facilitating the global flow of funds or instructions underlying such funds flows. These include both bank and commercial non-bank networks. Bank networks include systems that transfer funds and those that only transfer instructions behind funds flows. The former include Fedwire in the United States, CHIPS (Clearing House Interbank Payment System) in the United States, IFTS (Interbank Funds Transfer System) in the European Community, CHAPS (Clearing House Automated Payment System) in Great Britain, CHATS (Clearing House Automated Transfer System) operated by Hong Kong & Shanghai Bank, CB Express System in Germany, FX Net, centered in London, and the Zengin System in Japan.

Fedwire   Most of these systems have become active in the 1980s. Fedwire is an electronic network that connects Federal Reserve Banks, depository institutions, the U.S. Treasury Department, and other government agencies. Remnants of Fedwire date back to 1913 when the Federal Reserve System was established, but it was not fully automated until 1973.

CHIPS   CHIPS, the Clearing House Interbank Payments System, was established in 1970 for the purpose of replacing paper checks stemming from international transactions between foreign and U.S. banks with electronic check images. It is operated by the New York Clearing House Association whose members represent the core of the system, although 150 banks worldwide have access. Transfers handled by CHIPS are nearly evenly divided among those related to the settlement of foreign exchange transactions, the settlement of Eurocurrency trades, and the settlement of export/import transactions. CHIPS annually settles an average of $865.8 billion via 150,000 messages. It has settled as much as $1.59 trillion via 300,000 messages in a year's time.

CHAPS   CHAPS, the Clearing House Automated Payments System, is owned by the Association for Payment Clearing Services, a consortium of U.K. banks. It was established in 1984 and settles an average 34,000 payments totalling £76 billion on a daily basis.

FX Net   FX Net is a London-based foreign exchange bilateral netting settlement system whose principal business is directed at foreign exchange traders. At least 19 financial institutions are linked to FX Net, some of which are located in New York.

Some of these electronic funds transfer systems have widespread membership while others cater to a relatively few members. In 1990, the German CB Express System, with 14,696 members, had the largest number of bank participants, Fedwire had 11,435 participants, the Japanese Zengin System had 4,917 bank participants, while CHAPS had 317 and CHIPS had 139 participants[1].

SWIFT   SWIFT, the Society for Worldwide Interbank Financial Telecommunications, is a private cooperative-type organization that transmits financial messages to benefit member banks and other financial institutions.[2] SWIFT was created in Belgium

---

[1] C.E.V. Borio and P. Van den Bergh, *The Nature and Management of Payment System Risks: An International Perspective* (Basle: Bank for International Settlements, 1993), pp. 14–7.

[2] For comprehensive coverage of SWIFT, see James C. Baker and Raj Aggarwal, Evaluation of Global Electronic Funds Flow System: The Society for Worldwide Interbank Financial Telecommunications (SWIFT), in *Global Information Systems and Technology: Focus on the Organization and Its Functional Areas* ed. P. Candace Deans and Kirk R. Karwan, (Harrisburg, PA: Idea Group Publishing, 1994), pp. 107–31, and "Global Interbank Communication Systems: the Role of S.W.I.F.T.," in *Payment Systems in the Group of Ten Countries* (Basle: Bank for International Settlements, 1993), pp. 482–5.

6. Discuss the differences between forward and futures markets in foreign currency.

7. What advantages do foreign currency futures have over foreign currency options? Discuss.

8. What is meant if an option is "in the money," "out of the money," or "at the money"?

9. What are the disadvantages of a passive hedging program that covers 100 percent of the foreign currency exposure?

10. What is the difference between the USDX Futures and the U.S. Dollar Composite Index Futures contracts?

11. What are the risks of foreign currency futures contracts? of foreign currency options?

12. Discuss the regulation of currency futures and options trading.

13. Discuss the major foreign counterparts to the U.S. Commodities Futures Trading Commission.

14. What are the characteristics of foreign currency options?

15. Discuss the pricing determinants of foreign currency options.

16. What transactions are most appropriate for hedging with foreign currency options?

17. What are the alternatives available to a hedger, trader, or investor in the use of foreign currency options? Discuss.

18. Discuss the significance of volatility in the currency options markets.

19. Suppose the average premium on foreign currency calls has decreased. On the other hand, the average premium on foreign currency puts has increased. How would you explain this?

20. A British exporter will be paid $1 million in three months. He hesitates to sell $1 million forward or to buy currency options for that amount. What are the differences between the two strategies?

Problems

1. From Table 1 in chapter 3, the spot rate on May 2, 1996, for the Swiss franc was $0.8039. The premium quoted, from Figure 7 in this chapter, on a Swiss franc call option with a June expiration date and an exercise price of $0.82—American–style—at the Philadelphia Stock Exchange was $0.0047. What is the intrinsic value of one Sfr 62,500 call option?

2. Calculate the time value, if any, in the preceding problem.

3. In Figure 7 of this chapter, find the total premium cost of 5 British pound 158 puts trading American style.

4. In early May 1996, multinational company needs a selling hedge. Suppose a U.S. truck manufacturer has a plant in Germany. The German plant is short of funds to meet payroll expenses in the amount of DM 500,000. In 6 months, it expects to be in a sound financial position because peak purchases of trucks will take place at that time. The U.S. parent can transfer the necessary funds to the German plant for 6 months. In 6 months, the German plant will return the funds to the U.S. parent. Assume the facts are as in Table 1, chapter 3, and Figure 1, chapter 13, i.e., the spot rate for marks is $0.6542, the 180-day forward rate is $0.6620, and the futures contract with a delivery date nearest to 6 months from now is the September contract that closed at $0.6593. What should the truck manufacturer do to hedge this transaction? Which market, forward or futures, would be best? Assuming away taxes and transactions costs, calculate the hedge in each market and discuss which would be best.

5. How many Canadian dollars could a company hedge if 10 December futures contracts had been bought at the closing price on May 2, 1996, assuming no taxes or transactions costs?

6. According to Figure 1, chapter 13, a trader could have purchased long one British pound September contract at the opening price of $1.4926 on the IMM at the Chicago

Mercantile Exchange. He held the contract at the end of the day and was marked-to-market. The trader held this contract at the close of business on the next 3 trading days. The contract closed at $1.50 on the first day, $1.51 on the second day, and $1.49 on the third day. Assume that initial margin is $4,050 and maintenance margin is $3,000. Make the proper daily entries for this account and calculate the trader's profit or (loss).

7. Assume that Citibank in New York quotes a 30-day forward rate on the German mark of $0.6330 while the IMM German mark futures for delivery in 30 days is being quoted at $0.6322. Calculate the arbitrage profit that could be earned per contract on each mark futures contract.

8. You buy a Swiss franc December futures contract on the IMM for $0.7460. If the spot rate for Swiss francs at the date of settlement is $0.7511, what is the gain or loss on this contract?

9. You buy five German mark call options on the Philadelphia Stock Exchange at a premium of $0.017. If the exercise price is $0.63 and the spot price of the mark at the time of expiration is $0.61, what is the total profit or (loss) on these five call options?

10. Check the *Wall Street Journal* for the most recent closing price for the USDX contract traded at the Finex in New York. Calculate the total value of this contract.

11. Obtain the contract specifications for any three foreign currency contracts traded at the Chicago Mercantile Exchange.

12. At the Philadelphia Stock Exchange, the 68 May call for German marks is trading at a premium of 0.62. The spot price for German marks on this day is $0.6892. Is this contract "in the money"? If it is "in the money," what is the profit if the holder of this option exercises at the strike price?

13. Determine whether any German mark call contracts traded most recently at the Philadelphia Stock Exchange have time value in addition to intrinsic value.

14. It is April and John Brown, an international currency trader, is considering a June call option contract on the British pound traded at the Philadelphia Stock Exchange. The strike price for this call is $1.52. The premium quoted at the Exchange is $0.0194 per British pound. Diagram the profit and loss potential for this call option. What is the break-even price for this call? What would Brown expect to make as profit or loss on this call option if by June the spot exchange rate for British pounds is $1.5450?

15. A U.S. investor believes that the dollar will depreciate against the German mark and buys a call option on the mark at the Philadelphia Stock Exchange with a strike price of $0.65/mark. The option premium is $0.01/mark, or $625 per contract of DM 62,500.
    a. For what range of exchange rates should the investor exercise the call option at expiration?
    b. For what range of exchange rates will the investor realize a net profit, taking the original cost into account?
    c. If the investor had purchased a put with the same strike price and premium, instead of a call, how would you answer the previous two questions?

14

International Nonexchange Traded Derivatives

Major Objectives of Chapter 14:

(1) To introduce derivatives that are not traded on organized exchanges, including currency options written by banks or non-financial corporations, currency and interest rate swaps, and so-called "exotic" derivatives; (2) to discuss and analyze the risks associated with these derivatives.

Key terms to be learned in chapter 14:

- interest rate futures
- currency swap
- diff swaps
- LEPO
- notional value
- hedge funds
- cap
- interest-only strip
- range structure
- dual currency floater
- callable step-up note
- FX range floater

- options on interest rate futures
- interest rate swaps
- exotic derivatives
- convertible reset bond
- knock-out option
- swaption
- floor
- principle-only strip
- knock-in swaption
- one-way floater
- boost structure
- dynamite warrant

Introduction

A large part of the international derivatives markets is not transacted on organized exchange trading floors. Many derivatives instruments are bought and sold over-the-counter or constructed by banks or dealers for the benefit of specialized customers. These include some currency options, written by companies, banks, institutions, or in-

dividuals, and sold to business customers who generally have some risk to hedge. In addition, interest rate and currency swaps are arranged by banks and dealers for customers that need currency or debt risks hedged or asset liability positions to manage. Finally, exotic derivatives have been constructed by a number of large international banks for customers needing a very customized hedge. These derivatives will be discussed in the following sections of this chapter. The discussion will begin with swaps instruments, one of the most heavily used nonexchange traded derivatives.

Currency and Interest Rate Swaps

Swaps represent one of the fastest growing derivatives markets, both in swaps for interest rate contracts and those for currencies. Whereas currency options and futures are traded on exchanges—some options are written over-the-counter by banks, companies, or individuals—swaps are instruments created and traded over-the-counter primarily by financial institutions. Swaps, in general, represent exchanges of periodic cash flows between two parties. They evolved from parallel or back-to-back loans popular in the 1970s. In a back-to-back loan for example, a French company loaned French francs for five years to a U.S. company at a rate of 10 percent. In return, the U.S. company loaned an equivalent amount of U.S. dollars to the French company at a rate of 8 percent with the same schedule. Both the interest obligation and the principal were exchanged under this arrangement. This swap was actually a long-term forward currency contract. Examples of these loans will be described in more detail in chapter 15 on working capital management.

Parallel or back-to-back loans had problems. First, they appeared on the balance sheet for accounting and regulatory purposes, although the two sides to the swap offset each other. Second, a default by one party did not release the other party from making its contractual payments. The swap, introduced about 1981, was designed to alleviate these problems.

CURRENCY SWAPS

The currency swap is an exchange of liabilities in two different currencies, but it is packaged as a single transaction rather than as two separate loans. For example, a French company wants to borrow dollars, say $20 million at an annual interest rate of 7 percent, to finance a foreign investment but this company is little known outside France. The data for this example is shown in Figure 14–1. The swap is diagrammed in Figure

French franc principal = Ffr 140 million
U.S. principal = $20 million
Ffr interest rate = 8% (Ffr 11.2 million annual interest)
U.S.$ interest rate = 7% ($1.4 million annual interest)
Beginning swap exchange rate = Ffr/$ (Ffr 140 million/$20 million) = 7.00
Year 1 forward commitment = $1.4 million and Ffr 11.2 million (the interest commitments)
  or Ffr/$ = 8.00 (Ffr 11.2 million/$1.4 million)
5th year forward commitment, i.e., end of five years:
  $21.4 million
  Ffr 151.2 million
  or Ffr/$ = 7.06 (Ffr 151.2 million/$21.4 million)

FIGURE 14–1 A Currency Swap and the Data Involved

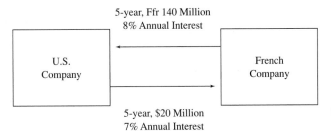

5-year, Ffr 140 Million
8% Annual Interest

U.S. Company

French Company

5-year, $20 Million
7% Annual Interest

FIGURE 14–2 A Currency Swap (based on data in Figure 14–1)

14–2. A U.S. company needs French francs, say Ffr 140 million, for its French subsidiary but it has easier access to the U.S. bond market. The French company contracts to pay the U.S. company principal and interest on its U.S. debt, while the U.S. company pays the French company principal and interest of 8 percent on its French debt. The contracts are conditional so that if one party defaults, the other party is released. After a period of time, e.g., 5 years, the principals will be swapped back. This is effectively a package of forward currency contracts.

In Figure 14–1, the swap given as an example nearly locked in the beginning exchange rate of Ffr 7/$, because the exchange rate at the end of 5 years from this swap was Ffr 7.06/$, even though the first year interest obligation swaps were made at an exchange rate of Ffr 8/$.

Many companies operating in international markets use currency swaps to hedge currency risk. For example, when it opens stores in developing countries, McDonald Company will use currency swaps. One example that can be cited is its operation in Thailand where it uses currency swaps to hedge the risk in Thai bahts. This enables the company to protect more dividends for stockholders. In some of these cases, the leverage may be as high as 99 : 1 and adds risk to the investment.

MANAGEMENT APPLICATION NO. 22

Currency Swap Example

Suppose that a U.S. company, HiTech Inc. enters into a swap transaction with a British bank, Brokely Bank. A U.S. swap dealer acts as intermediary because it has the relevant credit information about the swap counterparties, which they do not have on their own. HiTech is establishing a British subsidiary and has issued dollar denominated floating rate bonds tied to LIBOR to finance the project. HiTech wants to hedge in two areas: (1) against foreign exchange fluctuations because the affiliate's sales revenue will be in sterling but will be needed to service the dollar denominated floating rate debt, and (2) the company prefers to make fixed rate payments. By entering into a currency swap, the firm could make sterling denominated fixed rate payments while receiving dollar denominated LIBOR, which it could pass along to its floating rate bondholders.

Meanwhile, Brokely Bank would like sterling denominated fixed rate cash flows instead of dollar denominated LIBOR payments from floating rate notes that it holds in a portfolio within its trust department. The fixed rate sterling cash flows will extend the duration of its portfolio. This swap involves an exchange of principal at the beginning and end of the swap. The exchange rates for both the fixed rate and floating rate swaps are established at the beginning of the arrangement. The gross amount of the cash flows is paid at each of the settlement dates. This swap is shown in Figure 14–3.

Fixed Rate Pound Sterling

Floating Rate
U.S. Dollar LIBOR

FIGURE 14–3 A Currency Swap

Source: Based on Peter A. Abken, "Beyond Plain Vanilla: A Taxonomy of Swaps," *Federal Reserve Bank of Atlanta Economic Review* 76 (March/April 1991):23–4.

INTEREST RATE SWAPS

Interest rate swaps are exchanges of liabilities in the same currency but are based on two different interest rates. Essentially, an interest rate swap is a transaction involving two parties that exchange their interest payment obligations (no principal is exchanged) on two different kinds of debt instruments, one bearing a fixed interest rate and the other a floating interest rate. This swap allows each party to borrow with its preferred type of interest obligation usually at a lower overall cost of financing than either party could obtain on its own. An example of a modern day interest rate swap is shown in Figure 14–4.

The example shown in Figure 14–4 shows the swap arrangement whereby Company A needs to borrow $250 million at a fixed rate for 5 years and Company B needs a variable rate loan of Ecu 200 million for 5 years. The relevant exchange rate is 1 Ecu = $1.2549. Company A borrows $250 million at a variable rate because of a favorable interest rate and Company B borrows Ecu 200 million at a fixed rate because of a favorable interest rate. Blank Global Inc. is an investment bank that then arranges a swap. In 5 years, Blank Global reverses the swap.

Interest rate swaps usually involve one party that is an established, highly rated issuer preferring floating rate obligations but can sell fixed rate debt at a relatively low rate while the other party is usually a lower rated issuer preferring fixed rate obligations. The exchange is for the interest obligations only and involves an exchange of a fixed rate obligation for a floating rate obligation, such as a Eurocurrency loan based on LIBOR. The swap can also involve two floating rates in which interest obligations involving basis points are swapped. Interest rate swaps involving currency swaps can be arranged so that liabilities in two different currencies, one a fixed rate instrument and the other a floating rate instrument, are swapped.

At first, interest rate swaps were arranged by the counterparties themselves. However, in the 1980s, international banks entered the swaps market as intermediaries. The intermediary bank or swap dealer arranges the swap and transfers the interest rate payments. A counterparty may not know who is the other counterparty. The intermediary bank actually incurs some of the financial risk of the swap. In addition, banks themselves may enter an interest rate swap for asset/liability management purposes, as in Management Application No. 23.

Default Risk in Interest Rate Swaps

The swap dealer in a matched interest rate swap is exposed to default risk of the counterparties. If either counterparty defaults, the swap dealer is liable to the nondefaulting counterparty. The swap dealer essentially guarantees the swap agreement. This risk can be quite high because the swap dealer is committed for the duration of the swap. Thus, the swap dealer is compensated for bearing default risk by the bid-ask spread in the swap. The swap dealer may also default, but the risk is quite low because most swap dealers are large international banks.

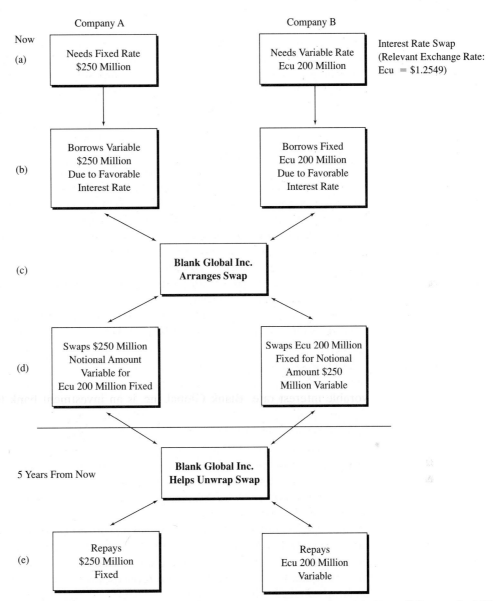

Source: Charles E. Maxwell, *Financial Markets and Institutions: The Global View* (Minneapolis, MN: West Publishing Company, 1994) p. 641. Reprinted with permission from South-Western Publishing Company.

FIGURE 14–4 An Interest Rate Swap

The market for swaps involve all the major currencies although $/interest rate swaps have the largest share of the market. A sizable portion of Eurobond issues are swapped. Swaps cut across borders and often involve swaps for interest obligations of U.S. domestic bond issues and Eurobond issues.

Various parties enter into swaps for a number of reasons. Borrowers and investors may desire to structure their cash flows and take on credit risks in a manner that is not more conveniently arranged with existing financial instruments. Companies use swaps to manage their long-term exposure to currency and interest rate risks. For example, if a corporation borrowed in Swiss francs 2 years ago and thinks this currency

will appreciate markedly, a U.S.$/Sfr swap can transform the Swiss franc liability into a U.S.$ liability. Interest rate swaps are also used by banks as a form of asset/liability management and they enable the expansion of securities markets into minor currency areas of trading. Swaps have become an attractive source of off-balance sheet earnings for commercial and investment banks, although some banks have had their common stock penalized in the market because of extensive interest rate swap transactions. Early in 1994, Banc One, a leading U.S. regional banking firm headquartered in Columbus, Ohio, lost more than 20 percent of its value in the stock market because of rumors about its trading in these instruments. The loss caused cancellation of an important acquisition by Banc One of another bank because the value of Banc One's stock, which it planned to use for the acquisition, had declined so drastically.

Other reasons can be advanced for interest rate and currency swaps. They facilitate other types of business, such as Eurobond underwriting. Investment banks consider them to be negotiable securities and, in the process, they can be used to remove default risk and standardize the contract. Commercial banks consider swaps an extension of their traditional credit activities in stressing their expertise in the assessment of credit risk and the ability to carry long-term market and credit risks.

The secondary market for swaps is undeveloped because of the customized nature of swaps. However, investment banks can standardize swaps and eliminate credit risk, an operation that could make them attractive to investors. Otherwise their minimum size and lack of a viable secondary market make them valuable primarily to companies and banks.

Results of Swaps Markets

Despite some of the shortcomings of the swaps markets, a number of benefits have been attributed to the market for these instruments. Markets are more closely linked than before the advent of swaps. The distinction between domestic and international markets is slowly eroding, as a result of global deregulation and liberalization of financial markets. For example, the popularity of yen swaps stems from the use of the swaps market by Japanese banks to manage assets and liabilities in order to circumvent regulations that have limited their access to direct domestic longer term borrowing.

Swaps market volume increased dramatically during the 1980s. A study by the Bank for International Settlements, collected from members of the International Swap Dealers Association, shows that swap volume rose from virtually nothing at the beginning of the 1980s to $1,327 billion by the end of 1988. This swap volume represented 43 percent of total outstanding bank credit and bond financing of $3,200 billion at the end of 1989. Volume in interest rate swaps totaled $1,012.2 billion, or 76 percent of the total swap volume.

Diff Swaps

The differential swap, or diff swap, is currently one of the hottest products in the swaps markets. The diff swap is a correlation product, i.e., a product defined by two characteristics of its cash flow: the cash flow must be a function of at least two risk factors and at least two of these risk factors must be combined in a nonadditive way. A change in one risk factor will affect the price of another risk factor. The correlation between the various risk factors determines the pricing of these instruments rather than an analysis and aggregation of the variables of the individual financial instruments. A discussion of the pricing of diff swaps, the most popular of the correlation products, and related risk management issues is found in the Appendix 1 to this chapter.

This swap permits investors to earn on foreign currency interest rates without currency risk. U.S. money market investors enhance their returns with diff swaps by receiving LIBOR rates associated with other currencies at a time when low returns on

---

MANAGEMENT APPLICATION NO. 23

Interest Rate Swap Example

Morgan National Bank, a U.S. bank with multinational operations, enters into an interest rate swap with Home Savings and Loan Association, a small Ohio thrift institution. Morgan has a large long-term mortgage loan portfolio but has a tendency to borrow short-term funds in the money market. Morgan has $1 million more of rate sensitive assets than it has rate sensitive liabilities. Morgan management believes that interest rates will rise in the near future and, thus, as rates rise, the cost of funds will be greater than the increase in interest payments the bank receives on its assets, which are primarily long-term. Morgan desires to convert $1 million of its fixed rate assets into $1 million of rate sensitive assets. Such a move will eliminate its income gap, leaving its net interest margin and bank profitability unchanged when interest rates rise.

At the same time, Home Savings and Loan issues long-term bonds to raise funds and uses them to make short-term loans. It has $1 million more of rate sensitive assets than it has rate sensitive liabilities. If interest rates were to decline, as Home management worries, the larger drop in income from its assets would offset the decline in the cost of Home's funds and, thus, profits would decline.

In the swap, Morgan National Bank agrees to pay Home Savings and Loan a fixed rate of 6 percent on $1 million of notional principal for the next 10 years and Home will pay the 1-year Treasury bill rate plus 100 basis points on $1 million of notional principal for 1 year. The interest obligations are swapped each year of the agreement. The principal is not swapped. This interest rate swap is shown in Figure 14–5.

U.S. LIBOR investments prevail. For example, an investor might receive an interest rate equal to DM LIBOR but he receives payments in U.S. dollars. The swap dealer takes on all of the currency risk, because he can make a profit. Part of this profit stems from the fact that the dealer hedges 95 percent of the risk and, thus, must be willing to forecast the direction of interest rates. This should encourage investors to enter the foreign exchange markets because of the large spreads between domestic and LIBOR instruments. Forex risk is avoided because payments are in dollars. The bet in the market is that U.S. rates will remain low or go lower while DM LIBOR will remain high or go higher.

Suppose the following scenario: the sterling LIBOR yield curve is relatively flat, implying that future short-term interest rates will remain at about the same level. Furthermore, the U.S. dollar LIBOR curve is fairly steep, implying that short-term U.S. dollar LIBOR will rise significantly over time. However, the CFO of an MNC believes interest rates in the two countries will move differently from the direction their yield curves imply. In fact, he believes that the U.S. dollar LIBOR curve is too steep and that short-term interest rates will not rise as quickly or to a level implied by the yield curve.

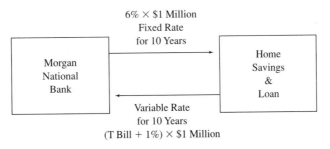

FIGURE 14–5 An Interest Rate Swap

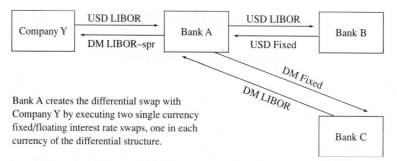

Bank A creates the differential swap with Company Y by executing two single currency fixed/floating interest rate swaps, one in each currency of the differential structure.

Source: Erik Banks, *Complex Derivatives* (Chicago, IL: Probus Publishing Co., 1994), p. 176.

FIGURE 14–6 A Differential Swap

He also does not believe, given his assessment of Great Britain, that the sterling LIBOR yield curve reflects the proper level of British future short-term interest rates. He believes that sterling LIBOR will rise moderately over the next few years.

The CFO decides to take a position on the two yield curves by using a diff swap. He enters into a diff swap with an investment banking firm whereby he will pay the firm 3-month dollar LIBOR and receive 3-month sterling LIBOR—the amount of notional principal is not important in this example. A small profit margin in basis points will be added to each leg of the swap by the investment banker. All interest is paid in dollars. The CFO makes a play on the expected difference in short-term rates between the two countries, i.e., the diff swap. The CFO speculates in a way that the spread between the two rates will narrow over time. If the CFO is correct, U.S. dollar LIBOR will not rise as quickly as forecast and sterling LIBOR will rise instead of remaining flat. The CFO will then pay a lower overall rate of interest than will be received from the investment bank, i.e., a positive net cash flow, without currency risk.

A diff swap may be referred to as a correlation product because its pay-out is modified by the correlation between the relevant foreign exchange and interest rates in the transaction.[1] As in the pricing of options where volatility is an important ingredient of the price, correlation between two markets in which the diff swap indexes are traded also affects the price of the diff swap. Thus, correlation risk must be taken into consideration.

Figure 14–6 shows the construction of a differential swap. Bank A is an investment bank that creates the diff with Company Y, a hedge counterparty, by executing two single currency fixed/floating interest rate swaps, one in each currency of the differential structure, in this case, the deutsche Mark and the U.S. dollar. Bank B is a hedge counterparty and Bank C is a diff swap counterparty.

The investment banker is exposed to both interest rate and currency risk. These risks are hedged by the execution of offsetting rate swaps. The investment banker must execute two offsetting swaps simultaneously to offset the risk of two different currency legs.[2] The investment bank offsets its interest rate risk by arranging simultaneous interest rate swaps with two hedge counterparties. Each hedge counterparty swap offsets the interest rate risk of one of the legs of the original diff swap.

The interest payments offset each. They merely flow through the investment banker from the diff swap counterparty to one of the two hedge counterparties, or vice versa, thus offsetting the floating interest rate risk of the investment bank.

---

[1] Erik Banks, *Complex Derivatives* (Chicago, IL: Probus Publishing Company, 1994), p. 176.
[2] P. Doust, "User Strategies: Pricing & Hedging Diff Swaps," *Financial Products Group Newsletter*, (London: Barclay de Zoete Wedd, April 1993).

STUDY AID

Select two short-term interest obligations from the market pages of the *Financial Times*, e.g., the obligation for U.S.$ LIBOR for 6 months and the domestic U.S. 6-month Treasury bill. Construct a diff swap based on this information. Try it for DM LIBOR and Treasury bill rates for the same maturities. Remember that foreign exchange risk is avoided because payments are in dollars.

The currency risk is encompassed by the difference between the fixed dollar rate and the fixed deutsche Mark. A comprehensive hedge will cover both interest rate and currency risk but investment banks have had difficulty in adequately hedging such a transaction. This is part of the cause for regulatory concern over the rising volume of derivatives business practiced by commercial banks.

Summary

Interest rate and currency swaps have certain advantages and disadvantages. They can be used to reduce risk with no change in the balance sheet. And they can be used for a longer term than futures or options can offer. However, swaps lack liquidity, although brokers are now beginning to act as market-makers in swaps. And they are subject to default risk, although the evolution of market-makers in swaps has alleviated this risk to some extent by furnishing counterparties that can take over the swap in the event of a default by one of the parties.

Interbank Currency Futures and Options

A large market has developed in recent years for currency options written by banks and traded on an interbank basis.[3] Currency forward contracts are customized within the interbank market and markets are made in them by commodities brokers and other

MANAGEMENT APPLICATION NO. 24

A Sallie Mae Currency Swap

An example of a swap involving Sallie Mae, the Student Loan Marketing group, is illustrative of the currency swap. Sallie Mae privately placed two $100 million deals in 1991, one maturing in 5 years and the other in 3 years, carrying DM LIBOR rates minus some spread—from 170 to 270 basis points. The U.S. investor received dollar interest payments regardless of the fact he received DM rates. Sallie Mae has DM exposure but swapped out of that risk by paying the swap dealer U.S. LIBOR and receiving DM LIBOR to pass on to its investors. Sallie Mae achieved rates of LIBOR less 50 basis points, less than its funding target of LIBOR − 45 basis points—much more than could be received from the issue of fixed rate bonds and then swapping for a floating rate interest obligation—a simple interest rate swap.

---

[3] Alan L. Tucker, Jeff Madura, and Thomas C. Chiang, *International Financial Markets* (St. Paul, MN: West Publishing Co., 1991), pp. 271–3.

banks. These markets have been discussed previously in chapters 3, 4, and 10. Over-the-counter currency options are European-style, i.e., they can be exercised only at maturity. The markets are centered in London and New York and the open interest is about 20 times that of Philadelphia Stock Exchange options, discussed in chapter 13.

Many exchange-traded derivatives products do meet the needs of large currency traders such as dealers, investment funds, and corporations. Trading in foreign exchange typically amounts to more than $1 trillion per day and individual trades are in multimillion dollar amounts. In comparison, the typical contract on the Chicago Mercantile Exchange has an underlying value of $125,000 or less and the largest contract amounts to no more than $250,000. On a given day, trading on the Chicago Mercantile Exchange amounts to about $12 billion in currency contracts. The Philadelphia market for options is even smaller. The average contract there trades for $45,000 of underlying value and daily volume amounts to $1.5 billion. In addition, the Philadelphia market prohibits traders from holding more than 100,000 contracts—limiting their position to $4.5 million—and, even though the Chicago Mercantile Exchange does not limit traders' positions, it requires them to justify their trading strategies and imposes difficult reporting requirements. For big currency traders, these markets are too small. Thus, they turn to the much larger and more liquid interbank markets and other private over-the-counter markets where they can trade large amounts 24 hours a day and cause little distortion to foreign exchange market prices.

Over-the-counter options differ in a number of ways from exchange-traded currency options. They are usually much larger, being $1 million or more of foreign currency. Most listed options are American-style, i.e., they can be exercised anytime before or at maturity, whereas most over-the-counter options are European-style. Interbank options can be obtained in a greater variety of foreign currencies including those of the LDCs. They are customized to the needs of the customer and, thus, are rarely traded in a secondary market. Banks that write these options for MNC clients and others usually hedge their positions in foreign currency options traded at the Philadelphia Stock Exchange.

In addition to the writing of options by banks, they can be written by non-bank firms and by individuals. A company or individual can write options that are covered by foreign exchange in the amount of the option being held by the firm or individual. These covered options are generally written to produce premium income. For example, a company that has excess short-term funds, which are needed infrequently to pay some recurring cost, can write a call giving the buyer the right to buy some part of the excess funds held by the company. If the option is exercised, the firm has the foreign exchange to deliver to the call holder. If the call expires unexercised, the writer pockets the premium income.

MARKET EFFICIENCY TESTS OF OTC OPTIONS

Several studies have been done to test the efficiency of exchange-traded options. Early studies found currency options for most currencies to be inefficient.[4] These findings were at a time when volume was relatively low and options prices were higher than warranted. As volume increased, markets for exchange-traded options became more efficient.

One study of the OTC currency options market found large and statistically significant profits for options markets in deutsche Marks, Japanese yen, British pounds,

---

[4] Andrea DeMaskey and James C. Baker, "The Efficiency of Options Markets in Foreign Currencies: An Empirical Analysis," *The International Journal of Finance* 3 (Autumn 1990): 1–39.

and Swiss francs.[5] Thus, abnormal profits in OTC markets for some foreign currency options may dictate a strategy of arbitraging options prices against absolute price movements rather than the usual practice of arbitraging them against volatility. More research in this area is required to arrive at conclusive results.

SWAPTIONS

Swaptions are options that are associated with swaps. Swaption contracts give the right to enter into a swap agreement, or to exit from a swap, under some prearranged terms and conditions. The International Swap Dealers Association has published estimates that the notional value of swaptions outstanding is more than $109 billion.

A swaption call gives the buyer the right, but not the obligation, to receive fixed payments on a fixed interest rate obligation, which is the call strike price, and to pay a floating rate. In other words, the buyer has the right to go short a swap. The short side or seller receives fixed interest payments. The writer of the swaption call has the obligation to go long the swap if the call buyer exercises. Swaptions that can be exercised at any time prior to expiration are American-style and those that can be exercised only at expiration date are European-style. A swaption put gives the put buyer the right, but not the obligation, to pay a fixed rate and receive floating, i.e., the right to go long a swap. The premium on a swaption is paid upfront and, therefore, an interest opportunity cost is incurred.

One type of swaption gives the holder the right to terminate a swap.[6] This is associated with callable bonds. If a company issues a bond with a call feature and if interest rates fall and the price of the bond rises above the prearranged ceiling level, then the issuer can recall the bonds and the principal at an early date. The company might have sold a swap when it issued the bond. With this swap, the issuer receives fixed payments, passing them along to bondholders, and pays a floating rate. Thus, the company, with this swap, has floating rate debt. If rates fall sufficiently low to cause the company to recall the bond issue, it will also want to terminate the fixed payments it receives from the swap. The issuer would then sell the long side or buyer an option to terminate the swap. An exercise of this swaption by the buyer would terminate fixed payments to the company, which would then recall the bonds, and terminate fixed payments to the bondholders. Thus, such a swaption is equivalent to the call feature on a coupon bond issue.

Exotic Derivatives

WHAT ARE EXOTIC DERIVATIVES

We have discussed foreign currency futures and options and interest rate and currency swaps. Futures and options are instruments traded in the burgeoning derivatives markets. Other derivatives exist that can be classified as ordinary derivatives.[7] These include interest rate and currency swaps, discussed in the previous sections. Such derivatives are often referred to as "plain vanilla" derivatives.

Other more complex derivatives are custom-designed by financial institutions to

---

[5] William C. Clyde and James Gislason, "Foreign Exchange Options Markets Inefficiency: The Abnormal Profits Generated By An Implied Volatility Based Rule," *Global Finance Journal* 6 (Spring 1995): 9–24.

[6] J. Orlin Grabbe, *International Financial Markets* (Englewood Cliffs, NJ: Prentice-Hall, 1996), pp. 329–30.

[7] For a comprehensive look at the banks that make markets in derivatives, see "*Global Finance*'s Derivatives Superstars," *Global Finance* 8 (February 1994): 44–58.

hedge against a very specific event that may be unique to the purchaser of such a derivative. These exotic derivatives, referred to as "exotics" in the trade, are designed to meet the specific hedging needs of companies and banks. They include specific options and future contracts and, in addition to being custom-designed, are traded over-the-counter, if traded at all. A secondary market for these derivatives is generally not possible because of the customized nature of the instruments.

These derivatives are not basic forwards, swaps, futures, or even options on exotic currencies, such as the Thai baht or the Mexican peso. They are complex options, hybrid swaps, or combinations, which are often embedded in securities. One example is the convertible reset bond. This instrument permits the investor to choose between a bond's nominal yield and the return on another underlying asset, such as the performance of a stock market index. Reset periods can be established to allow the investor a periodical change of mind. This could include a money-back guarantee. Exotic derivatives are one-of-a-kind solutions to a client's problems, something no one else may offer to solve the client's problem.

Exotics have been used since the early 1980s. Convertible bonds with several options were early pioneers of exotic derivatives. The market as practiced today began about 1988 when a few U.S. and Japanese banks sold bonds with embedded puts on the Nikkei 225 index. These instruments limited the risk that bond buyers and Japanese institutional investors had incurred in the event the Nikkei fell.

The Marketplace for Exotic Derivatives

The exotic derivatives market is very concentrated. It has been estimated that nine investment banking firms control 80 percent of the market. These derivatives represent only 5–10 percent of the entire derivatives market but their notional value, the theoretical value of the underlying securities, could amount to trillions of dollars, based on the value of ordinary derivatives. For example, the notional value of interest rate and currency swaps is estimated to be $5 trillion. The notional value of equity derivatives is estimated to be $300–500 billion, whereas notional value of currency derivatives may amount to $25–35 billion/day. See Table 14–1 for the top 20 banks and the notional value of their derivatives business.

Bankers Trust is one of the most active of the top nine firms that control most of the exotic derivatives market.[8] It was the first bank to be involved in derivatives. Since U.S. banks could not underwrite, trade, or distribute corporate stocks or bonds in the United States, Bankers Trust built its business in the mid-1980s on interest rate and currency swaps. With the liberalization of banking regulations, it is no longer true that these investment restrictions hinder such banks. Other leading firms include Chemical Bank, Citicorp, Credit Suisse Financial Products, Merrill Lynch, and J.P. Morgan.

A highly structured derivatives deal may involve a number of financial service firms. The deal may involve a swap, an equity investment, and a foreign exchange derivatives contract. The parties may include an investor who buys the instrument, a U.S. corporation or Eurobank that issues the instrument, and an insurance company in another part of the world that implicitly provides the hedge. A firm that does not have all of these legs has to buy exotic derivatives from another firm. The largest banking firms dealing in these instruments sell them through intermediaries and the return on equity may run as high as 35–50 percent.

If an exotic is very innovative, the price charged for it may be high but, since competition is fierce, the spread may narrow quickly. The life cycle on a new product may run from a few hours to a few weeks. In order to model riskiness in exotics, they must be priced correctly. In order to price exotics, the historical volatilities of the underlying

---

[8] Michelle Celarier, "The Biggest Banks in Derivatives," *Global Finance* 7 (August 1993): 27–34.

TABLE 14–1.	Dealers and Their Derivatives Notional Value (Billions of 1993 U.S.$)
1. Chemical Bank	$2,416
2. Bankers Trust	1,982
3. Citicorp	1,981
4. J.P. Morgan	1,660
5. Union Bank of Switzerland	1,452
6. Swiss Bank	1,352
7. Société Générale	1,209
8. Mitsubishi Bank	1,182
9. Crédit Lyonnais	1,110
10. Chase Manhattan	1,042
11. Crédit Suisse	1,017
12. Salomon	967
13. BankAmerica	964
14. Banque Indosuez	945
15. Merrill Lynch	918
16. Goldman Sachs	752
17. Barclays	751
18. Paribas	742
19. National Westminster	577
20. Royal Bank of Canada	554

Source: Carol J. Loomis, ''The Risk That Won't Go Away,'' *Fortune* 129 (March 7, 1994): 44.

assets are used. If more than one asset is involved, their price movements must be correlated. In order to do this, investment banks need good, expensive research. Historical volatilities and correlations furnish guidelines and to use them to predict prices of exotics, knowledge of the capital markets is necessary. So these firms must hire expensive "rocket scientists" and systems programmers who understand the product.

Exotic derivatives were originally developed to hedge risk in rising markets in which volatility is high. However, in the environment of a number of bear markets in 1993–94, some exotic derivatives were developed for such declining markets. These are shown in Figure 14–7.

An Exotic Derivative in Foreign Exchange Markets: The Knock-Out Option

During the U.S. dollar/foreign exchange crisis in early 1995, one type of exotic derivative in foreign exchange trading resulted in driving the dollar lower. Because of technical selling pressures compounded by options and other derivatives, the dollar not only declined in value but liquidity nearly evaporated and spreads between bid and ask prices widened to three times their normal amount. In an environment of $1 trillion trading days, this was a strange phenomenon. The problem may have been attributed to an exotic derivative called a "knock-out" call option on the dollar.[9] Hedge funds that bought these options had the right, but not the obligation, to buy dollars at a present price. However, if the dollar fell below a specified trigger level, the knock-out options expired worthless, i.e., they were "knocked out." This specified trigger level is agreed

---

[9] Laura Jereski, "Currency Speculators Post Huge Gains Amid Turmoil," *Wall Street Journal*, 10 March 1995, p. C1.

Range structure: a derivatives structure with a payoff that depends on how long the value of the underlying asset, often an interest rate, is within a predetermined range.

Dual currency floater: a floating rate note that allows an investor to play the expectation that interest rates in one country will rise and those in another country will fall.

Knock-in swaption: a swaption is an option on a swap. When the option is structured as a knock-in option, the whole thing becomes a knock-in swaption, which comes into existence when the value of the underlying asset reaches the option's trigger.

Index-amortizing swap: an interest rate swap with a notional principal amount—the hypothetical value of its underlying asset—that declines at the rate of a short-term money rate such as LIBOR or the yield on constant maturity treasuries.

One-way floater: a floating rate note whose coupon can rise but never fall.

Callable step-up note: a callable note with a coupon that increases, or steps up, over time if interest rates move according to a predetermined pattern. Usually, the issuer can call the note only after a certain period of time.

Boost structure: a range instrument in the form of a floating rate note, swap, or option with a payoff that is pushed up, or boosted, by virtue of the fact that the underlying asset can never leave the pre-established price band; otherwise the note becomes worthless.

FX range floater: a floating rate note that pays off for every day that the exchange rate between two currencies stays within a certain exchange rate band.

Dynamite warrant: a warrant that pays off only if the rate at which two currencies can be exchanged remains within a band for the entire lifetime of the warrant.

Source: K. Michael Fraser, "Refitting Exotics For a Bear Market," *Global Finance* 8 (July 1994):70.

FIGURE 14–7 Exotic Derivatives for a Bear Market

to in the beginning and is known as the outstrike. When this level is reached, the holder cannot exercise the option if it remains or, subsequently, goes in-the-money.

During the 1994–95 period of U.S. dollar weakness, two types of knock-out currency options were used.[10] These were down-and-out calls and down-and-out puts. The down-and-out call on the dollar had a positive payoff to the option holder if the dollar strengthened but could be canceled if the dollar fell. The down-and-out put had a positive payoff to the option holder if the dollar weakened but could be canceled if the dollar weakened beyond the agreed upon point because the outstrike was in-the-money.

Dealers selling these derivatives were on the hook if the dollar did not fall to below the mid-¥90 to the dollar. In order to hedge that risk, these dealers accumulated large dollar positions. They were forced to sell these as the dollar fell. Or they resorted to a technique known as dynamic hedging, the buying or selling of currencies incrementally as exchange rates change. For example, a dealer who sold dollar puts also sold dollars to hedge the puts against losses in case the dollar depreciated and the puts expired in-the-money. In doing this, they sold, at more favorable exchange rates, at least some of the dollars delivered to them by option holders.

This action is a dynamic hedging strategy, one whereby dealers sell the underlying asset into a falling market and buy into rallies. Regulators and other investors worry about such strategies because they exacerbate the drop in prices. Knock-out options appeal to hedge funds because their cost is lower than regular currency options. Speculators can take large market positions at relatively lower costs. Dealers have to engage in heavy trading of these options and this heavier trading encourages speculators because of the market moves. A more detailed discussion of the currency market behavior in March 1995 is found in Appendix 2 at the end of this chapter.

---

[10] Allan M. Malz, "Currency Option Markets and Exchange Rates: A Case Study of the U.S. Dollar in March 1995," *Current Issues in Economics and Finance* (A publication of the Federal Reserve Bank of New York) 1 (July 1995): 3.

MANAGEMENT APPLICATION NO. 25

Euro-Yen Bond with Warrants

During Fall 1994, the Swiss pharmaceutical company Roche issued notes in Europe with warrants attached exercisable in June 1998. This was the third such debt issue in this form made by Roche since 1991 and these issues raised $1 billion. The most recent issue was a 7 1/2-year issue denominated in yen with warrants attached that enable investors who exercise the warrants to acquire shares of Roche Genußscheine, Roche's publicly traded nonvoting stock. Investors forfeit their dividends when they exercise the warrants and their upside is capped at Sfr 7,100 per share (about $5,599), a price 20.7 percent above the price of Roche Genußscheine at the time of the issue. This issue was the first Euro-yen equity linked transaction by a European company.[1] The equity content of this issue is only 25–30 percent of the issue. Such deals usually contain 100 percent equity. Thus, a $1 billion debt issue is usually linked to $1 billion of equity. Investors purchased the issue at a yield to maturity of only 5.19 percent.

---

[1]John Hintze, "A $1 Billion Euroyen Issue Gives Roche Low-Coupon Debt with a Small Equity Outlay," *Global Finance* 8 (November 1994): 23.

DERIVATIVES FOR EMERGING MARKETS

An example of a derivative concerned with hedging investments in emerging markets is the LEPO, a low-exercise price option. Swiss Bank issued two LEPOs in September 1993 on stocks from Malaysia and Singapore and a third in January 1994 on a basket of 24 stocks listed in Singapore, Malaysia, and Thailand.[11] In the case of a LEPO, the strike price is set so far below the value of the underlying stocks so little doubt exists that the option will be exercised. In the case of the Singapore-Malaysia-Thailand basket, the strike price is $1 vs. an underlying value of $1,409. The price of a LEPO behaves more like an index than an option and, thus, gives investors full upside and downside risk. A LEPO's value is the value of the basket of securities minus dividends. They perform much like a passive open-end investment fund but take much less time to set up than do country funds and are much less costly. Some 25,000 European-style, 2-year LEPOs with face value of $37 million can be settled in cash or with delivery of the stock. Individuals and institutional investors trade in this market.

Variations of these derivatives enable investors to bet on securities of countries without stock exchanges. S.G. Warburg, for example, issued 50 million 1-year call warrants on a basket of seven companies doing business in Vietnam that were based in Australia, Hong Kong, Singapore, and Japan.

REGULATION OF DERIVATIVES

Market risk in the derivatives business, especially in the exotics market, has become the subject of regulators' attention. Market risk stems from the possibility of losses because of movements in interest rates, exchange rates, or equity values. It is difficult to quantify and can lead to credit risk. Regulators worry that one large firm might fail because of the pervasiveness of derivatives trading and this event could lead to a systemic risk in the international banking system, i.e., other large banks could fail.

---

[11] K. Michael Fraser, "A Hot Combination," *Global Finance* 8 (February 1994): 78.

In order to avert the possibility of a systemic collapse, the Bank for International Settlements (BIS) in Basel, Switzerland, published a study, the Promisel Report, which analyzed the derivatives market and made several recommendations. Later, the BIS Committee on Banking Supervision recommended higher capital levels to cover market risk in derivatives for banks that trade these instruments. These new capital standards were scheduled to become effective in 1996.[12] Some analysts of these markets believe that higher capital standards and tighter regulation may reduce liquidity in the marketplace but do recognize that liquidity might be disrupted by adverse consequences in the market, such as a war in Russia. Others believe that markets might not all move together and that systemic risk exposure may be lower than some estimate.

Another problem from the increased use of derivative instruments, which faces financial institutions and market regulators, stems from inadequate accounting concepts and principles in this area.[13] This has reduced the transparency of a company's exposures to derivatives risk specifically and of the financial system more generally. This accounting weakness coupled with advances in technology and telecommunications has made the global financial system more susceptible to market risk. Solutions to this problem may be found in international harmonization of accounting and reporting standards regarding the market for derivatives.

During the mid-1990s, derivatives were singled out as the cause of several corporate and government incidents involving poor investment performance. As mentioned previously, regulation of the derivatives business has been strengthened. In fact, regulators may have overreacted to the problems involving Procter & Gamble, Gibson Greetings, Metallgesellschaft, Orange County, California, Barings Bank, and others. Several experts have addressed a number of so-called myths about derivatives. These are discussed in the following section.

Dealing with Myths About Derivatives[14]

Myth #1: Derivatives are Always Dangerous and Cause Only Losses for Customers
According to Alan Greenspan, Chairman, Board of Governors of the Federal Reserve System, derivatives transfer risk from one market participant to another and someone inevitably loses. However, the use of derivatives may be more efficient and less costly than other substitutes when used for hedging financial risks.

Myth #2: Most Institutional Investors Take Huge Gambles with Derivatives   The Committee on Investment of Employee Benefit Assets (CIEBA) of the Financial Executives Institute reported that the majority of its members use derivatives but their use was limited to a very small part of their assets (less than 5 percent of their portfolios were allocated to derivatives). CIEBA members manage more than $702 billion in corporate pension assets.

Myth #3: All Instances Where the Media has Cited Derivatives Losses Do In Fact Involve Derivatives   Actually a number of the incidents reported in the media have involved financial instruments other than derivatives. One of the most widely publicized incidents involved Orange County, California. This local government actually in-

---

[12] Michelle Celarier, "New Catastrophe Scenarios Bedevil Derivatives," *Global Finance* 7 (October 1993): 60–5.

[13] William J. McDonough, "The Global Derivatives Market," *Federal Reserve Bank of New York Quarterly Review* 18 (Autumn 1993): 1–5.

[14] Chicago Mercantile Exchange, "Dealing with Myths about Derivatives," (Summer 1995): 1–4.

CHAPTER 14 *International Nonexchange Traded Derivatives* **381**

curred most of their losses from the purchase of long-term securities with short-term loans, according to Frank N. Newman, acting U.S. Treasury Secretary, and Mary L. Schapiro, Chairman of the Commodity Futures Trading Commission. Such a strategy increased their exposure to increases in short-term interest rates.

Myth #4: Derivatives Have No Economic Value   According to the Bank for International Settlements, derivatives improve the efficiency of financial markets and by permitting more risk to be hedged, they also may allow some borrowers greater access to funding sources. According to Chairman Greenspan of the Federal Reserve Board, they enable pension funds and other institutional investors to hedge and adjust positions quickly and without large transactions and administrative costs.

Myth #5: More Government Regulation and Micromanagement Would Protect Investors From Any Mistakes   The periodical *Pensions & Investments* editorialized in its December 12, 1994, issue that government regulation did not protect savings and loan investors or taxpayers. Government regulatory legislation in some states has also cost public pension funds opportunity costs because of bans on investment in equities.

Myth #6: No Guidelines Can be Found for the Prudent use of Derivatives   The Federal Reserve Board gives banks that use sophisticated financial instruments risk management guidance for several years. The Group of Thirty has formulated and published a number of recommendations for dealers and end-users of derivatives.[15] These include: (1) determination at the highest level of policy and decision making the scope of the organization's use of derivatives; (2) value derivatives positions at market; (3) quantify the organization's market risk under adverse market conditions against limits, perform stress simulations, and forecast cash investing and funding needs; and (4) establish market and credit risk management functions with clear authority, independent of the dealing function.

The use of derivatives, as with any other financial management function in the firm, should be controlled. Control functions were absent or below minimum standards in the cases of Barings Bank, Procter & Gamble, Metallgesellschaft, Gibson Greetings, and other firms. Individuals were permitted to use these sophisticated financial instruments who, in some cases, were unfamiliar with the instruments. Top management in some of these cases were unaware of the magnitude of the use of derivatives. The agency cost problem, discussed earlier in chapter 13, was evident in some or all of these cases. Two results of the most publicized losses attributed to the use of derivatives is

---

STUDY AID

Query a sample of local international companies and ask whether they use derivatives for hedging foreign currency transactions and whether these are plain vanilla or exotic derivatives and, if so, what kinds of derivatives. Ask them what internal controls they have implemented if they use derivatives.

---

[15] Global Derivatives Study Group, *Derivatives: Practices and Principles* (Washington, D.C.: The Group of Thirty (G30), 1993).

the civil suit brought by Procter & Gamble and Gibson Greetings against Bankers Trust and the decline in derivatives business during 1994–95 by Bankers Trust and other leading banks in this area of business.

Summary and Conclusions

Derivatives are financial instruments arranged between two parties whose payments are based on, or derived from, the performance of some underlying currency, commodity, government or corporate debt, home mortgage, stocks, interest rates, or any combination. The most common forms are option-type contracts and forward-type contracts. Options and futures contracts can only be traded on exchanges. Options, forwards, and swaps can be privately traded in the over-the-counter market. Contracts traded on exchanges are standard instruments whereas OTC instruments are generally custom-designed.

Exotic derivatives have been the fastest growing segment of this market. These instruments add features that permit the management of only those risks that are of interest to the user. Designing such instruments requires financial "rocket scientists," highly trained in finance and mathematics, in order to competitively price them. Risks can be quite high for such narrowly designed instruments.[16] But the return to the creator can be as high as 35–50 percent and the hedger can save equally as much.

Different types of risks must be assessed and managed in the derivatives markets. These include market risk, credit risk, settlement risk, operational risk, and legal risk. Some financial institutions regulators believe these risks can lead to systemic risk in the financial system. Others believe derivatives are designed to hedge these risks and do not introduce risks fundamentally different from those already present in the financial markets. Thus, this argument holds that systemic risks are not increased by derivatives. However, top management of firms and banks that use derivatives should understand what these instruments are and have controls implemented in the firm so that any risks stemming from derivatives can be managed.

Many of the risks in exchange-traded derivatives are alleviated or eliminated by the trading procedures of the exchange. For example, marking-to-market of the position on a daily basis is a very good disciplinary tool. Margin maintenance requirements imposed by the exchanges reduce risk. The clearing house mechanism operated by the exchange acts as a middleman to guarantee that all trades will be made good if one counterparty fails to perform. However, firms and banks using such derivatives can still incur losses. The Barings fiasco involved listed derivatives. Such was the case with Metallgesellschaft, which traded oil futures listed at the New York Mercantile Exchange and Codelco, the Chilean state-owned copper producer that lost half of its 1993 profits trading in copper futures on the London Metal Exchange. In all of these cases, proper oversight and control mechanisms were not in place within the top management of the firms. These firms simply did not understand the financial instruments with which they were involved.[17]

---

[16] Kosrow Dehnad, Marc S. James, and James C. F. MeVay, "Mundane Problems, Exotic Solutions," *Euromoney* (August 1992): 42–6.

[17] Suzanne McGee, "'Plain Vanilla' Derivatives Can Also Be Poison," *Wall Street Journal*, 20 March 1995, pp. C1, C14.

APPENDIX 1

Correlation Products: The Diff Swap[1]

Correlation products represent one growing class of financial derivatives that have become popular in recent years. Although the market is small compared with that of the "plain vanilla" market, the market for these products has grown rapidly in over-the-counter trading. These products do not appeal to hedgers because the exposure found in correlation products is not found in existing cash or derivative instruments. Correlation products are generally used to outperform an index or some other return measure.

These instruments have created problems for traditional measurements of price risk. Price risk is the risk that the value of a portfolio will change as a result of shifts in market conditions. These market conditions include a host of risk factors including foreign exchange rates, equity and commodity prices, and interest rates. Traditional products, known as plain vanilla financial derivatives, have price risk that is separable, i.e., the sensitivity of the traditional portfolio's value to one risk factor is independent of the level of any other risk factor. One can estimate the price risk of such portfolios by measuring their sensitivity to individual risk factors and then aggregating these sensitivities to calculate an overall risk factor profile. With a correlation product, price risk is nonseparable. A change in one risk factor will affect the price sensitivity of another risk factor. Pricing, hedging, and risk management of such products are all determined by the correlations between the various risk factors. Separable risk of plain vanilla derivatives can be expressed as

$$CF(x^1, x^2) = CF(x^1) + CF(x^2)$$

whereas nonseparable risk of correlation products is expressed as

$$CF(x^1, x^2) = CF(x^1) \times CF(x^2)$$

The diff swap, discussed in this chapter, represents a large portion of the exotic derivatives market. The notional value of diff swaps has been estimated to be $40–50 billion. Diff swaps can be used to enhance returns by swapping into currencies with higher yields. A wide range of currency pairs can be used in diff swaps including U.S. dollar LIBOR against LIBOR of the deutsche Mark, British pound, Swiss franc, and Australian dollar, as well as LIBOR of the deutshe Mark and Swiss franc against LIBOR of the Italian lira, Spanish peseta, and other currencies of the European Rate Mechanism. Risk managers account for nonseparable risks by making assumptions about the future correlations between various risk factors inherent in these instruments.

HEDGING AND PRICING A DIFF SWAP

Assume the following problem: valuing the cash flows of a diff swap.

Suppose a dealer enters into a diff swap for 1 year. The dealer receives 6-month U.S. dollar LIBOR in U.S. dollars while it pays 6-month DM LIBOR in U.S. dollars to the end user. The semi-annual interest payments are based on a $100 million notional principal and are settled in arrears. This diff swap with its generic cash flows is shown in Figure 14–8.

---

[1]The material for this appendix is based on James M. Mahoney, "Correlation Products and Risk Management Issues," *FRBNY Economic Policy Review* 1 (October 1995): 7–20.

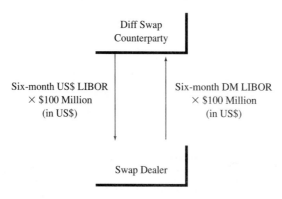

FIGURE 14–8 A Diff Swap Generic Cash Flows

Source: James M. Mahoney, "Correlation Products and Risk Management Issues," *FRBNY Economic Policy Review* 1 (October 1995):11.

In order to value the cash flows in this diff swap, the dealer should determine the level of the cash flows that will take place in the future, i.e., in 6 months and in 1 year. These flows should be discounted to the present. The present value of the diff swap, therefore, can be stated as

$$PV_{6\text{-mon}} [\$100 \text{ m} \times (r_{\text{U.S.\$ LIBOR}}^{@t = today} - r_{\text{DM LIBOR}}^{@t = today})]$$
$$+ PV_{12\text{-mon}} [\$100 \text{ m} \times (r'^{@t = 6 \text{ mon}}_{\text{U.S.\$ LIBOR}} - r'^{@t = 6 \text{ mon}}_{\text{DM LIBOR}})]$$

where $PV_t(CF)$ is the present value of a cash flow, CF, occurring at time t, and r is the prevailing interest rate in market x at time t.

The value of the cash flow in six months is relatively simple to determine. The parties swap the difference between the current value of U.S.\$ LIBOR and DM LIBOR paid in U.S. dollars on a notional amount of \$100 million. The cash flow does not change as interest rates change and the cash flows can be discounted at the risk-free U.S. dollar 6-month interest rate.

The problem arises with the cash flows that will be received in 12 months. These are more difficult to determine. The dealer cannot convert the DM liability embedded in the swap into a U.S. dollar liability, because the level of DM exposure faced when the swap was started will be determined by the level of DM LIBOR and the DM/\$ exchange rate in 6 months' time. Typical hedging instruments protect against exposure by converting a fixed principal amount from one currency to another. But the exposure faced by a dealer in a diff swap involves a floating DM principal. The lack of a static hedge causes the dealer to make assumptions concerning the future correlation between the DM/\$ exchange rate and DM LIBOR and to update the hedging position dynamically, i.e., buying or selling the underlying financial instrument itself.

Once the cash flows of the diff swap have been determined, the cost of hedging the floating interest rate exposures is estimated by observing the costs of entering into two plain vanilla interest rate swaps: one in U.S. dollars and the other in deutsche Marks. These swaps, based on the notional principal amount of the diff swap in U.S. dollars or its dollar equivalent of deutsche Marks, will have the same maturity and payment dates as the diff swap. The diff swap hedged with interest rate swaps is shown in Figure 14–9.

The market for interest rate swaps is very competitive. Thus, it can be assumed that these two hedging swaps will be entered into at a present value of zero. Therefore, the diff swap's overall value will be the same before and after hedging. The combination of the diff swap and the two hedging swaps will not eliminate all price risk. Some

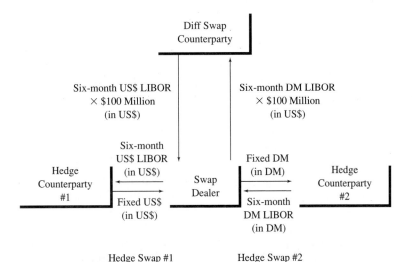

Source: James M. Mahoney, "Correlation Products and Risk Management Issues," *FRBNY Economic Policy Review* 1 (October 1995):11.

FIGURE 14–9 Diff Swap Hedged with Interest Rate Swaps

residual risk suggests that the market prices of existing securities cannot be used by themselves to determine the value of the diff swap. This residual risk is unseparable and may go unmeasured.

In conclusion, the primary problem with correlation products such as diff swaps is that their risk profile cannot be determined by evaluating individual risk factors of the instruments to individual financial institutions and then aggregating their estimates. For diff swaps, this technique is not totally effective because the sensitivity of one risk factor is always a function of the level of another risk factor.

APPENDIX 2

Effect of Knock-Out Options on the Currency Market[1]

As discussed earlier in this chapter, the U.S. dollar weakened sharply during four trading sessions between March 2 and March 7, 1995, after having strengthened during the preceding several months. During the March 1995 period, the dollar fell 7 percent against both the German mark and the Japanese yen. This was the sharpest move in the price of the dollar in several years during such a short period of time. The knock-out option market, as discussed in the chapter, was found to be a significant cause of the fall in the price of the dollar.

To better appreciate what occurred then, it helps to examine what the seller of the down-and-out put might have done as the dollar began its slide toward DM 1.45. At this point, the down-and-out put plus its hedge would no longer be protected against exchange rate fluctuations. If the dealer thought the dollar might weaken to, say DM 1.42, he might have bought back the large standard DM 1.44 put and sold a large standard DM 1.41 put. This move would have established a new protected range above DM 1.42. Or if the forecast called for the dollar to weaken even further to, say DM 1.40 or lower, the dealer could have canceled the down-and-out put and bought back the large standard DM 1.44 put.

---

[1]This discussion is based on Allan M. Malz, "Currency Option Markets and Exchange Rates: A Case Study of the U.S. Dollar in March 1995," *Current Issues in Economics and Finance* 1 (July 1995): 4.

However, the dealer would have had to buy back the DM 1.44 put before the dollar fell below DM 1.45 for the strategy to work. This would have made the DM 1.44 put quite expensive. If the dollar were to drop suddenly and sharply, the dealer could buy back the DM 1.44 put, but he would have had a significant loss. The worst case scenario would have been a sharp drop in the dollar occurring simultaneously with an increase in implied volatility. This would have increased the cost of the option to be bought back even more. The loss from doing this would have offset the gains from the cancellation of the down-and-out put.

This scenario is what happened in March 1995. Sellers of down-and-out puts hedge their risks by selling large numbers of standard puts. These standard puts are exercised only when the dollar depreciates sharply. If we examine the position of the dealers in February 1995, some had large quantities of down-and-out dollar puts and some down-and-out dollar calls with outstrikes between DM 1.45 and DM 1.35 or ¥95 and ¥85. When the dollar dropped sharply in March, knock-out options were canceled and others were thought to be likely candidates for cancellation, thus resulting in gains for dealers. But the standard options sold by the dealers to hedge the knock-outs went "in the money," becoming more valuable, and exposing the dealers to losses that were greater than the gains from cancellation of the knock-outs. The vicious circle resulted when dealers tried to buy large quantities of standard puts to minimize their losses. This drove the prices of standard puts even higher. Even though the down-and-out puts represented a small portion of outstanding options, they were hedged by a large amount of standard options. Thus they posed a disproportionate amount of pressure on option prices during that period, further exacerbating the downward move in the price of the dollar in the foreign exchange market. Dealers had bought a large volume of standard options for hedging purposes at the same time as other market participants. These participants also sold dollars outright when cancellation of the down-and-out puts left them exposed against the declining dollar, thus causing the dollar to fall even further.

Additional Readings

Antl, Boris, ed. *Swap Financing Techniques*. London: Euromoney Publications, 1983.

Banks, Erik. *Complex Derivatives*. Chicago, IL: Probus Publishing Company, 1994.

Beidleman, C. *Financial Swaps*. Homewood, IL: Dow Jones-Irwin, 1985.

Brown, Keith C., and Donald J. Smith. "Default Risk and Innovations in the Design of Interest Rate Swaps." *Financial Management* 22 (Summer 1993): 94–105.

Dehnad, Kosrow, Marc S. James, and James C. F. MeVay. "Mundane Problems, Exotic Solutions." *Euromoney* (August 1992): 42–6.

"Dictionary of Derivatives." *Euromoney Supplement*. London: Euromoney Publications, June 1992.

Fernald, Julia D. "The Pricing and Hedging of Index Amortizing Rate Swaps." *Quarterly Review of the New York Federal Reserve Bank* 18 (Winter 1993–94): 71–4.

French, Martin, Virginia Gidley-Kitchen, Linda Keslar, Sarah Priestley, and Ian Verchere. "*The Global Swaps Market.*" *Corporate Finance/Euromoney* (June 1986, Suppl):1–60.

The Globecon Group, Ltd. *Derivatives Engineering: A Guide to Structuring, Pricing and Marketing Derivatives*. Homewood, IL: Irwin, 1995.

Hunter, William C., and David W. Stowe. "Path Dependent Options." *Economic Review of the Atlanta Federal Reserve Bank* 77 (March/April 1992): 29–34.

Marki, Susan Ross. *Derivative Financial Products*. New York: Harper Business, 1991.

Orlando, Deborah K. "Swaptions Offer New Keys to Better Protection." *Corporate Cashflow* 11 (July 1990): 33–6.

Overdahl, James. "Derivatives Regulation and Financial Management: Lessons From Gibson Greetings." *Financial Management* 24 (Spring 1995): 68–78.

Smith, Clifford W., Jr., Charles W. Smithson, and Lee MacDonald Wakeman. "The Market for Interest Rate Swaps." *Financial Management* 17 (Winter 1988): 34–44.

Solnik, Bruno. "Swap Pricing and Default Risk: A Note." *Journal of International Financial Management and Accounting* 2 (Spring 1990): 79–91.

Stone, D. "Knock-Out Options: When and How to Use Them." *Corporate Finance* (June 1993): 11–3.

"Swaps: Versatility at Controlled Risk." *World Financial Markets* (April 1991, No. 2): 1–22.

Turnbull, S. "Valuing and Hedging Path Dependent Options." *Proceedings of Advanced Exotic Options Course.* London: Euromoney Publications, 1993.

Discussion Questions

1. Distinguish between an interest rate swap and a currency swap.
2. From what early financial transactions did today's interest rate swaps evolve? Why?
3. For what underlying, nonspeculative, reason might a commercial company choose to use a differential swap?
4. What risks are encountered in the swaps markets?
5. Why are swaps used? What is swapped in an interest rate swap? a currency swap?
6. Compare and contrast options traded over-the-counter with those traded on an organized exchange.
7. Name the traditional "plain-vanilla" derivatives.
8. Discuss one or two specific examples of exotic derivatives and their use.
9. What are the risks of exotic derivatives? Are these risks higher for exotic derivatives than for any other financial derivative or financial market instrument?
10. How are exotic derivatives priced? How are they regulated?
11. What is the Promisel Report? Who sponsored it? What are its provisions?
12. Discuss the myths that have been advocated about derivatives.

Problems

1. Your company is a small, obscure firm with a relatively low rating. Its management would like a fixed rate, long-term loan. However, the company presently has access to floating interest rate funds at LIBOR +1.6 percent. It can borrow directly in the fixed rate bond market at 12 percent. Another company is a much larger, more highly rated company that prefers a floating rate loan but has access to the Eurobond market for fixed rate funds at 10 percent and floating rate funds at LIBOR +3/8 percent. Can these companies use a swap to their mutual advantage and, if so, how? If they split the cost savings by negotiation, how much could your company pay for its fixed-rate loan? How much would the other company pay for floating rate funds?
2. Construct a currency swap between a large British bank, e.g., Standard Bank, and Falls Savings Bank of Cuyahoga Falls, Ohio.
3. Construct the diagram for a differential swap using the example in this chapter in which 3-month U.S. dollar LIBOR is paid, 3-month sterling LIBOR is received, a fixed rate U.S. dollar obligation is received, and a fixed rate sterling obligation is paid.
4. Construct a knock-out swap for a company desiring to hedge U.S. dollars in the current global economic environment.
5. Compile a list of equivalent investments to swaptions.

PART VI

Short-Term Capital Management of International Operations

MNCs have short-term day-to-day international financial operations that must be managed in a different way from domestic operations. Among those areas that are most important are foreign exchange exposure management, inflation risk coverage, and international cash management, including international cash receipts and disbursements and the use of electronic funds flows systems, accounting and reporting foreign operations, and international tax management. The principal differences between domestic and international operations lies in the treatment of foreign currencies and exchange controls practiced by foreign countries, international accounting, and the various tax treatments of foreign source income.

With the exception of foreign exchange risk management, these topics will be the center of discussion in Part VI. Forex risk management was covered in chapter 4 because of its relation to foreign exchange in general. The discussion of international cash management assumes that accounts receivables and inventory will be converted at some time into cash. Thus, cash is the most important commodity, its management will be discussed in chapter 15. The

conversion of accounts receivables into cash by methods such as factoring will be discussed. The focus in chapter 16 is on international accounting, including consolidation of foreign accounts, accounting for these operations, reporting foreign operations to parent headquarters, the role and formulation of international accounting standards, and the need for a set of international generally accepted accounting standards, principles, and practices. In addition, chapter 16 contains a discussion of evaluation, control, and auditing in international operations. Foreign operations must be evaluated and control systems should be implemented. These functions are much more important than for domestic operations because of the distance and cultural variables involved. This section concludes with an analysis of the taxation of international operations in chapter 17, including international differences in tax methods, the use of tax deferrals and tax credits, fiscal incentives for foreign operations, and various other tax rules, with emphasis on those tax provisions that affect U.S. MNCs.

International Cash Management

Major Objectives of Chapter 15

(1) To examine the day-to-day financial operations of the MNC, (2) to examine the international cash management function and, (3) to introduce the student to the major types of funds flows in the MNC.

Key terms to be learned in chapter 12:

- CHIPS
- FX Net
- transfer pricing
- management fees
- intracorporate loans
- CHAPS
- SWIFT
- Section 482
- royalties

Introduction

The primary subject of this chapter is international cash management in the MNC. It is assumed that accounts receivables and inventories will ultimately be converted to cash, either domestic or foreign currency. Thus, the focus will be on international cash management, receipts and disbursements of cash, and the international cash manager and his/her requirements. The funds flows that facilitate this function will also be discussed. These include transfer pricing, dividend payments, loan payments, management fees, and licensing royalties.

The management of working capital and day-to-day international financial operations has been affected by three significant changes during the past 25 years or so. These have been the advent of a global floating exchange rate system, the introduction in the 1970s of FASB-8, which treated foreign currency translation for U.S. companies, and the surge in new technologies and telecommunications systems used by the global financial system. The floating rate system brought volatility into the currency equation and required firms to manage their exposure to foreign exchange rate fluctuations more carefully. FASB-8, because of the problems analyzed in chapter 4,

forced U.S. MNCs to put into effect hedging operations whose cost would not have been justified previously. Some of these operations have been quite elaborate and expensive, as pointed out in chapter 4. Finally, the electronic means to transfer funds and to facilitate markets for a broad variety of trading instruments has resulted in the interrelationship of global markets by means of hundreds of thousands of computer screens, so much so that the systemic risk from one large bank failure could trigger a meltdown in the global financial system. Thus, it is important for international financial managers to consider the implementation of an optimal international funds and cash management system.

The ultimate objective for an international funds management system is that the company should be able to go about its business of making as much profit as it normally would if it faced no currency problems. The implication of this objective is that the corporation's fundamental priority is to alleviate the financial effect of any foreign currency exposure. The ideal situation for the company would be for it to buy from countries with a weak currency and sell to those with strong currencies. The economic rationale for decision making in international funds management is to compare the possible cost of remaining unhedged with the cost of hedging, as discussed more fully in chapter 4. This cost/benefit analysis presumes some prowess in forecasting foreign exchange rates by evaluating the factors that affect the national current accounts, such as the trade balance, price movements, fiscal and monetary policies, and the volume and diversification of exports, and to evaluate the factors that affect capital markets in key foreign countries, such as trends in economic aid, the foreign investment climate, and whether the government will intervene to support the local economy.

Two areas of important consideration for international funds management techniques are the information reporting system and management strategies. For example, information reporting suggests that a systematic procedure be implemented that includes short-term forecasts of currency rates, longer term balance sheet forecasts, and measurement of foreign currency exposure, as well as more frequent reports such as monthly management reports on investment, banking, and borrowings. Strategies concerning the management of international funds must take into consideration the risk preference of the firm's top executives as well as the expected value of foreign exchange to the company.

Finally, a key element of international funds management that must be considered is how the exposure management process is controlled. Effective control must incorporate an effective information reporting system. Good forecasts of future spot exchange rates must be made, and effective hedging and financial strategies must be developed.

The remainder of this chapter is devoted to a discussion of two important areas of working capital management: international cash management and intracorporate funds flows. Sources of funds for an international company include both intracorporate funds and those obtained from external sources. The subject of external sources of funds was discussed in chapters 11 and 12, which covered international financial institutions and markets. Thus, only internal or intracorporate funds flows will be covered in this chapter. The analysis of international cash management presumes that accounts receivables and inventories will be converted to cash. The management of international accounts receivables and inventories is not very different from the management of their domestic counterparts. Thus, the focus will be concentrated on international cash management.

International Cash Management

THE INTERNATIONAL CASH MANAGEMENT ENVIRONMENT

International cash management is more complex than the practice of cash management in any single country. It is not intrinsically different from domestic cash management, however, the scope of international cash management is much broader and the applications are highly specific. The nature of cross-border financial transactions adds complexity to the equation.

The environment facing the international cash manager is quite different from that facing a domestic manager. This environment, first, includes a variety of subscription services made available mostly by financial institutions that facilitate international currency and cash management. Second, the environment consists of a broad variety of reporting services. Third, the environment includes international communications networks established to facilitate the flow of funds or instructions underlying financial transactions. Fourth, international trade and investment necessitates dealing in foreign exchange, as has been pointed out in the discussion of foreign exchange. Various conflicting national regulations regarding foreign exchange must be recognized. Cost comparisons from one country to another are difficult because bank compensation practices and services are different from one country to another. Finally, the most important difference is that international cash management involves more than one currency. In fact, the international treasurer usually must cope with multiple currencies and interest rates.

International Money Management Subscription Services

First, the MNC has available several subscription services available for facilitating international money management. During the past 25 years, several international banks have designed services incorporating foreign exchange and cash management systems. Computer technology has facilitated the formulation of these systems. These subscription services available can be distinguished by a variety of service delivery relationships as follows: (1) the bank offers a proprietary service and owns or leases the delivery network, (2) the offering bank has a proprietary service and utilizes a commercial network for delivery, (3) the offering bank is aligned with a third party processor, which owns or brokers a delivery network, and (4) the company receiving the service may subscribe directly with a third party processor. One example of the first type of service may be found in the Chemsphere system offered by Chemical Bank for currency exposure management.

Reporting Services

Several types of reporting services are available to the firm to enable it to manage its international cash position more effectively. These include some systems similar to domestic reporting facilities: single bank balances, lock box reporting, multibank balances, money transfers, cash flow accounting and cash budgeting models, and money and capital markets systems. Lock-box services comparable to those found throughout the United States are not used as prevalently in foreign locations. The reason for the lack of use of lock-box systems seems to be attributed to the higher efficiency and relatively short time associated with local postal banking services. Other systems that are unique to international cash management are available including foreign exchange reporting and multilateral netting, a facility discussed in chapter 4.

International Communications Networks

Finally, the international cash management environment includes international communications networks devoted to facilitating the global flow of funds or instructions underlying such funds flows. These include both bank and commercial non-bank networks. Bank networks include systems that transfer funds and those that only transfer instructions behind funds flows. The former include Fedwire in the United States, CHIPS (Clearing House Interbank Payment System) in the United States, IFTS (Interbank Funds Transfer System) in the European Community, CHAPS (Clearing House Automated Payment System) in Great Britain, CHATS (Clearing House Automated Transfer System) operated by Hong Kong & Shanghai Bank, CB Express System in Germany, FX Net, centered in London, and the Zengin System in Japan.

Fedwire   Most of these systems have become active in the 1980s. Fedwire is an electronic network that connects Federal Reserve Banks, depository institutions, the U.S. Treasury Department, and other government agencies. Remnants of Fedwire date back to 1913 when the Federal Reserve System was established, but it was not fully automated until 1973.

CHIPS   CHIPS, the Clearing House Interbank Payments System, was established in 1970 for the purpose of replacing paper checks stemming from international transactions between foreign and U.S. banks with electronic check images. It is operated by the New York Clearing House Association whose members represent the core of the system, although 150 banks worldwide have access. Transfers handled by CHIPS are nearly evenly divided among those related to the settlement of foreign exchange transactions, the settlement of Eurocurrency trades, and the settlement of export/import transactions. CHIPS annually settles an average of $865.8 billion via 150,000 messages. It has settled as much as $1.59 trillion via 300,000 messages in a year's time.

CHAPS   CHAPS, the Clearing House Automated Payments System, is owned by the Association for Payment Clearing Services, a consortium of U.K. banks. It was established in 1984 and settles an average 34,000 payments totalling £76 billion on a daily basis.

FX Net   FX Net is a London-based foreign exchange bilateral netting settlement system whose principal business is directed at foreign exchange traders. At least 19 financial institutions are linked to FX Net, some of which are located in New York.

Some of these electronic funds transfer systems have widespread membership while others cater to a relatively few members. In 1990, the German CB Express System, with 14,696 members, had the largest number of bank participants, Fedwire had 11,435 participants, the Japanese Zengin System had 4,917 bank participants, while CHAPS had 317 and CHIPS had 139 participants[1].

SWIFT   SWIFT, the Society for Worldwide Interbank Financial Telecommunications, is a private cooperative-type organization that transmits financial messages to benefit member banks and other financial institutions.[2] SWIFT was created in Belgium

---

[1] C.E.V. Borio and P. Van den Bergh, *The Nature and Management of Payment System Risks: An International Perspective* (Basle: Bank for International Settlements, 1993), pp. 14–7.

[2] For comprehensive coverage of SWIFT, see James C. Baker and Raj Aggarwal, Evaluation of Global Electronic Funds Flow System: The Society for Worldwide Interbank Financial Telecommunications (SWIFT), in *Global Information Systems and Technology: Focus on the Organization and Its Functional Areas* ed. P. Candace Deans and Kirk R. Karwan, (Harrisburg, PA: Idea Group Publishing, 1994), pp. 107–31, and "Global Interbank Communication Systems: the Role of S.W.I.F.T.," in *Payment Systems in the Group of Ten Countries* (Basle: Bank for International Settlements, 1993), pp. 482–5.

MT 100 Customer Transfer

MT 200 Bank Transfer for its Own Account

MT 202 Bank Transfer in Favor of a Third Bank

MT 205 Bank Transfer Execution

MT 400 Advice of Payment

MT 500 Order to Buy

MT 501 Order to Sell

MT 580 Cedel Message

MT 740 Authorization to Reimburse

MT 950 Statement Messages

MT n91 Request for Payment of Charges, Interest

MT n95 Queries

MT n99 Free Format Message

Source: James C. Baker and Raj Aggarwal, "Evaluation of Global Electronic Funds Flow System: The Society for Worldwide Interbank Financial Telecommunications (SWIFT)," in *Global Information Systems and Technology: Focus on the Organization and Its Functional Areas* eds. P. Candace Deans and Kirk R. Karwan (Harrisburg, PA: Idea Group Publishing, 1994), p. 112.

FIGURE 15–1 Selected SWIFT Message Types

in 1973 and is owned by more than 2,000 banks worldwide while serving more than 3,500 financial institutions in 88 countries through its network. Although its shareholders are all banks, since 1987, its users have included securities brokers and dealers, investment management institutions as well as clearing institutions such as Euroclear and Cedel, discussed in chapter 12. SWIFT also develops and markets specific network applications and does research, development, marketing, and sales of terminals and related software.

SWIFT's principal service includes the exchange of financial messages over its computer network through which messages are accepted, validated, stored, and delivered. Its network is operable 24 hours a day, 7 days a week, and in 1992, a total of 405 million messages were transmitted by SWIFT, an average of 1.6 million per day. The messages are highly structured and standardized and cover a wide range of financial orders.

A typical SWIFT message transmission begins when a customer presents a payment order to its bank. This order is not like the electronic message that is sent through a domestic large-value funds transfer system such as CHIPS or Fedwire since it does not create an irrevocable obligation on the part of the sending bank. It is an instruction behind the funds flow that is encoded and initiated through a member bank's computer made secure by a codeword or key.

SWIFT messages can be both domestic and international and include such orders as customer transfers, foreign exchange confirmations, bank transfers, and letters of credit. The standardized message formats are in a common language, which is computer readable. Selected message formats are shown in Figure 15–1.

The message travels through a regional processing unit (RPU), where it is encoded, on through a central processing unit (CPU) by satellite, through another RPU where the message is decoded, and then received by a user bank in the foreign country. The message is transmitted, encoded, decoded, validated, and received all in about 1 minute or less. Thus, the system is secure, fast, and, because of the low per message cost, has a much lower total cost than other forms of transmission such as cables. The financial institutions that exchange SWIFT messages have arranged for clearing and settlement of incoming payment orders by relying on their own bilateral correspondent relationships or by forwarding such orders to the domestic interbank funds transfer sys-

tems, such as those mentioned earlier. SWIFT has become one of the most successful global systems for transmitting financial transaction messages to the point of being emulated by other country and single bank systems.

Commercial networks also offer similar services to MNCs. These include telex and cable transmissions as well as proprietary systems such as GTE Telenet. These services tend to be much more expensive than systems such as SWIFT. Cables are relatively expensive when compared with most other transmission services.

OBJECTIVES OF INTERNATIONAL CASH MANAGEMENT

The MNC should derive certain objectives from its international cash management program. Management of the international cash position alleviates the financial pressures that are bound to appear in one or another operation at various times. International cash management should reduce the need for external borrowing. Thus, it should also reduce the cost of borrowing. The MNC should place emphasis on these objectives when formulating and implementing an international cash management system.

INTERNATIONAL CASH MANAGEMENT REQUIREMENTS

To be successful, any international cash management system has essential requirements. First, a good reporting system is necessary. The average MNC has many reporting requirements including monthly cash flow statements and forecasts, foreign exchange exposure reports, and other financial statements whose frequency may be biweekly, weekly, or even daily. James S. Howard, chairman of Asset Growth Partners Inc., a New York City financial boutique that specializes in management consulting for medium-sized companies, believes that many CEOs and CFOs concentrate on short-term sales and earnings growth and overlook the importance of daily monitoring of their net asset positions.[3] Some firms have begun to examine their cash positions on a more frequent basis. General Tire in Akron, Ohio, installed a system that reported its daily international cash position all with a small investment in a personal computer, spreadsheet and specialized software, and personnel training.

Second, an international cash management system must be operated by personnel who recognize the major problems encountered in international business. These problems include differences in foreign operations, currencies, language, training of executives, and accounting practices. Once these problems have been recognized, management can adjust by implementing strategies that alleviate the risks that stem from these problems.

Finally, cash generated by the foreign subsidiary must be converted to the parent's currency when it is remitted back to the parent firm. This operation is best accomplished at headquarters by a centralized organization. This point was stressed in chapter 8 in the discussion of organizing the international finance function.

---

[3] Lori Ioannou, "Managing Assets to Grow," *International Business* (September 1994): 26.

KEY QUESTIONS FOR INTERNATIONAL CASH MANAGEMENT

Top management must identify and answer a number of essential questions in formulating and implementing international cash management policy. The following questions are representative:

1. **policy:** has the cost of cash increased so much that basic relationships should be changed, i.e., is liquidity maintained?

2. **implementation:** who is responsible for what—headquarters or subsidiary?

3. **accounting:** how can you keep track of cash in the system? Regular reporting shows only how things stand at some cutoff date; for cash management, one needs to keep a constant finger on the pulse.

4. **forecasting:** the essence of good cash management lies not so much in where cash has been but in predicting where it will be.

5. **banking:** one of the biggest cash blotters overseas is the commercial bank transmission belt—checks can float for 2–3 weeks from one subsidiary to another (in the banking system, this problem has been alleviated by CHIPS, and SWIFT, as well as some of the clearing systems discussed in chapter 18).

6. **borrowing:** whether to use supplier credits and shifting sourcing to take advantage of export credit packages.

7. **contingency planning:** what should companies do now to prepare—at headquarters and in the field—for the likelihood of more flexible exchange rates?

Once these and related questions have been sufficiently answered, top management should address the organization of the international cash management function. This function and its basic components, the international cash receipts system and the international cash disbursements system, will be addressed in the following sections. The discussion will also analyze the company's policy toward bank deposits and loans. A discussion of the specific form of management of this function will conclude the coverage.

International Cash Receipts System

A key to any successful international cash management system lies in the speedy settlement and collection of claims held by the company against other parties. Conversion of inventory and claims on a timely basis is a necessary ingredient of the process. Management of this function must focus on several principles in order to fulfill these objectives.

PRINCIPLES OF INTERNATIONAL CASH RECEIPTS

Invoice dates and payment terms may be more important for international sales than they are for domestic sales. They must be checked more closely because of cultural differences in their usage. Computers may not be maintained as well in foreign subsidiaries as they are in the home office, especially in LDCs. One company had a computer breakdown, backdated invoices, and saved $10,000 in one year by doing so. A French-based company found that sales would not suffer if the firm granted a 2 percent discount for prompt payment instead of 3 percent. The firm saved $24,000/year. One firm granted wholesale credit terms of 60 days but found that the definition of these terms, especially starting dates, differed from country to country. The firm established a policy to start counting from the end of a fortnight—a concept universally understood—and saved $40,000/year.

Payment terms from one country to another may be different. Often such differences stem from cultural diversity. Where U.S. companies typically pay in 30 days, for example, European firms are more accustomed to 90–120 day terms.

The currency of sales may result in speedier and more secure collections of payments. Under a floating rate system, a company can change to other than the customer's currency in order to avoid some foreign exchange risk. A French manufacturer used a new sales company registered in Germany. It invoiced the sales company, which then reinvoiced the customer. The clerical work was all done in Paris. The sales company then borrowed an amount equal to its invoices in deutsche Marks, converted to French francs, and paid the manufacturer. Interest rates at that time were 8 percent in Germany and 12 percent in France. The risk of loss from forex changes was eliminated because the company's debt was in marks, which equaled customers' receivables, also in marks.

Leads and Lags

One useful technique for either cash receipts or disbursements is known as "leads and lags." (Refer to a more detailed discussion of leading and lagging in chapter 4, especially the discussion of Figure 4–9.) Leading and lagging are means of shifting liquidity between corporate subsidiaries by accelerating or delaying the payment of intersubsidiary accounts with different credit terms extended by one unit to another. This is useful when currency changes are forecast, which might possibly have an adverse impact on the firm. The MNC will want to speed up payments in a stronger currency and delay payments in the currency forecast to depreciate in value.

The Role of Central Banks

Central banks play a role in funds flow management. Some of the operations of central banks relevant to this topic have been discussed previously. Central banks occasionally intervene in foreign exchange markets in order to move the home currency in one direction or the other. The largest central banks have a reciprocal currency arrangement with the Bank for International Settlements, which provides for a pool of foreign exchange reserves totaling more than $30 billion to be held for the purpose of currency intervention. Intervention was discussed in chapter 3 and the Bank for International Settlements and its functions were discussed in chapter 9.

These monetary authorities operate in international commerce in other ways. They invest their foreign currency resources in a variety of market securities that possess a high degree of safety, quality, and liquidity. Thus, they compete as investors in the short-term money markets with other investors. Some of them operate funds transfer systems, which facilitate the funds flow operations of MNCs. Fedwire, discussed earlier in this chapter, is an electronic network system, operated by the U.S. Federal Reserve System, which makes more than 250,000 daily transfers whose daily average value is more than $750 billion. The Bank of England, Deutsche Bundesbank, and Bank of Japan are among the central banks having such capabilities.

Use of Banks

The firm should use its banks in a manner resulting in an acceleration of settlement and collection of its receivables and other claims. Concentration banks can be used in each country of sale to collect, clear, convert, and transfer receipts locally. Companies sometimes fail to realize that a check must clear in the country on whose currency it is drawn. A French manufacturer had Belgian customers mail Belgian franc checks to Paris but this procedure took 13 days to receive usable funds. The firm opened a Belgian account and reduced the average delay to 9 days. This action also re-

duced transfer costs from $250/week to $2.50/week and freed cash that represented 4 days' sales.

Other policies with regard to a company's banks can be implemented. Concentration banks can be used to accumulate funds in hard currency countries from sales to customers in soft currency countries, such as Latin America through the United States to Europe. The firm should negotiate with its banks to reduce the clearing time to same day debits. The subject of clearance and settlement will be discussed in more detail in chapter 18. Finally, the firm can use post office transfers offered by the postal and telegraph systems, so popular in many foreign countries. The public has widely accepted these institutions and may place more confidence in them and, thus, utilize them to a greater degree than they do local banks.

International Factoring

International companies can also obtain short-term funds by factoring accounts receivable.[4] Companies and some banks offer a service for factoring international accounts. These companies and banks can discount receivables for as much as 80 percent of the accounts receivable and usually without recourse to the company whose accounts are factored. Factoring may represent a quicker means of obtaining funds since it is a short-term function involving the discounting of an ongoing stream of paper on a continuous basis from preagreed clients, who have had their credit checked by the factor. However, factoring is not inexpensive money. The factor's fees to cover the nature of the financing, the credit risk, other charges, and the factor's profit may amount to 6–7 percent over prime lending rates.

Challenge Inflexible Thinking

Finally, top management of the international firm must challenge inflexible and intransigent banks. Banking service is slow in many countries, despite a national branch banking system.[5] Only a few banks may dominate business and they often lack competition. In addition, national banking laws and regulations may control currency movements. This generally results in excessive delays in clearing transactions, which are in the process of collection. The geographic spread of customers may be large and, thus, mail times for receipt of payments by check may be quite long. Many corporations have instructed customers to wire transfer large payments. If such payments are not controlled carefully, wire transfers can be quite expensive. Such transfers also commonly go astray and funds are often lost. Again institutions such as SWIFT can facilitate the transfer of cross-border funds. Competition in international banking is forcing banks to give same day value for transfers. This problem will be discussed in more detail in chapter 18.

The firm can challenge these impediments by negotiating between or among banks. For example, a European company doing business in West Africa had a situation where the host country had slowed money transfers to 5 months. The firm introduced a policy of using a letter of credit for these transfers and reduced the transfer time to 6 weeks. Even though the firm dealt with its own branch, it adopted a letter of credit policy for all imports and realized a $26,000 annual interest savings, while significantly reducing its devaluation exposure. The fact that this company's transactions were backed by letters of credit gave confidence to companies with which they did business, thus speeding up the execution and payment of these transactions.

---

[4] "Factoring: Going Abroad," *The Banker* 136 (June 1986): 54.

[5] Kenneth L. Parkinson, "Dealing with the Problems of International Cash Management," *Journal of Cash Management* 3 (February/March 1983): 16–25.

Examples of Short-Term Bank Financing

The international financial manager should be aware of the facilities offered by commercial banks for funding working capital needs. A number of considerations need to be recognized. Among these are the maturity of the loan, interest rates, any bank fees charged, whether the bank requires a compensating balance, and foreign exchange rates if the loan is denominated in a foreign currency.

Suppose, for example, that the Crawford Tool Company can borrow £1 million at 10 percent, payable in 1 year, with a compensating balance of 20 percent. What is the effective percentage cost of the loan? The solution is the annual interest paid divided by the amount of funds received, or £100,000—the interest cost of the loan—divided by £800,000, the proceeds from the loan after the bank has required 20 percent of the loan to be set aside in a compensating balance deposit

$$£100,000 \div £800,000 = 12.5\%$$

Assume that Peachtree Software Corporation needs Lira (L)90 million to buy inventory for its Milan, Italy, operations. The Banca di Roma offers the company either an 11 percent loan payable at maturity or a 10 percent loan on a discount basis. Which is the best loan for the company? The first alternative has an effective cost of 11 percent, equal to the interest rate offered on the loan. The discount loan costs L10 million but the company must pay it from proceeds at the beginning of the loan and, thus, receives proceeds of L90 million from the loan. The loan costs 11.1 percent

$$L10 \text{ million} \div L90 \text{ million} = 11.1\%$$

Thus, banks offer several alternatives in lending to companies. The international cash manager must work through these alternatives to insure that the lowest cost loan is obtained. In addition to the bank terms, if the loan obtained is denominated in a foreign currency, the exchange rate must be factored into the question in addition to any tax relief from deductibility of the interest.

FLOAT TIME

From the early 1970s until the present, the conclusions of a number of studies have resulted in the means to reduce the average float time, which was often found in western European countries to be about 7 days. Some major banks now offer same day value for global money transfers. Even a reduction of one day in float time can result in significant savings for MNCs. The following formula can be used to estimate the capital that is tied up by float and the resulting cost[6]:

$$(\text{Float time} \div 365) \times \text{interest rate} \times \text{annual cash receipts}$$

Suppose that average float is 7 days and a medium-size MNC has annual sales in one area amounting to $500 million. If the local interest rate, i.e., overdraft rate, is 8 per-

---

STUDY AID

Suppose that a company does business in a foreign region where the float time has customarily been 8 days and this firm has annual sales of $250 million in this region. If local interest rates are 10 percent, what will this company save on an annual basis if a more efficient banking system in the area results in a reduction of float time to 5 days?

---

[6] Karl Wündisch, "Centralized Cash Management Systems for the Multinational Enterprise," *Management International Review* 13 (June 1973): p. 46.

cent, the interest cost is approximately $767,000. A reduction in float time of only one day will increase the cash flow to the company by more than $1.3 million and save more than $100,000.

CLEARING AND SETTLEMENT

In addition, the world's leading central banking systems have initiated studies to develop more efficient clearing and settlement systems. A number of proposals aimed at such an objective were reported at the International Symposium on Banking and Payment Services held in Washington, D.C., in May 1994. The conference covered international financial markets and the major clearing and settlement systems. Specifically, the meeting focused on global changes in payment systems and financial markets, on risks and risk management in banking, on developments in banking and payment systems in key currencies, on cross-border and multicurrency settlement, and on clearing house arrangements in the OTC derivatives markets. Most of these topics will be discussed in chapter 18.

International Cash Disbursement System

OBJECTIVES OF THE CASH DISBURSEMENT SYSTEM

Strategies used in a company's management of its international cash disbursement function are usually the opposite of some of the international cash receipts function. While with the latter function, the objective is to accelerate collection and settlement of cash, the objective of a cash disbursements system should be to slow down payments or reduce their size. Thus, a company should pay by check since international float may be slow. Although a check may take only a few days by mail to reach the creditor, another 7–10 days or longer may be required to clear the check through the banking systems of two or more countries. One company changed from bank transfers by electronic means to checks and increased the time for clearance of the payment from 2 days to 12 days. This practice saved the company $46,000. Company management must be careful so they do not get the reputation of being "fast operators."

Purchase Discounts

Companies may reduce their payments by taking discounts for prompt payment. Some companies do not evaluate purchase discounts and, thus, do not measure the annual savings from such a practice. For example, if discounts are always taken by a firm when terms are 2/10, net 30, i.e., a 2 percent discount if the bill is paid within 10 days, or the net bill if paid within 30 days, the savings can amount to more than 36 percent of the cumulative charges.

Netting

Finally, a netting system can be implemented by the firm. Netting, as discussed in chapter 4, reduces foreign exchange exposure. However, one of the firm's international suppliers may be a customer. Management must be careful. Implementation, for example, of a leads and lag system where the firm tries to accelerate its collections while slowing its payments to creditors may present a problem if the firm slows payments to a major supplier that also might be owned by the local government agency. A foreign subsidiary does not need political problems of this nature.

Control of Bank Accounts

The international firm must implement processes that extend control to the company's bank deposits and loans. The processes should have two major objectives: to re-

duce cash to a bare minimum and to eliminate unrestricted cash. The firm should eliminate inactive accounts and the cost of all but the most active should be justified. Banks should be precisely compensated for their services and loan agreements. Too often firms are overcharged by banks. However, firms should fairly compensate their banks for foreign exchange operations, international cash management, and other global services since these services are generally more complex than domestic financial services. Firms should make transfers to special accounts on a more timely basis or eliminate such transfers entirely. The key question is: *why should the firm have any uninvested cash at all?*

Banks as Global Custodians

Banks play an important global role for other banks, non-bank financial corporations, and institutional investors in their role as global custodians. Global custodians are usually international banks. They offer a number of services to firms involved in cross-border transactions. They facilitate foreign exchange transactions, portfolio valuation and analysis, assist in reporting and accounting functions, securities lending, gain information for clients and facilitate business contacts within foreign markets, maintain large telecommunications infrastructure, and provide execution and settlement of financial market transactions as well as security asset management services. Global custodians are discussed more fully in chapter 18.

Restrictions on Global Cash

Restrictions on global cash usage should be eliminated. The firm should forecast daily bank balances worldwide and, even though the rate of return on short-term investments is less than for short-term loans, if the latter is invested for less length to maturity than the former, they still may be profitable. Top management should also be careful with regard to different definitions of interest rates. A computer simulation program based on different definitions of interest rate terms may be needed. For example, if a company lends for 27 days, does it charge interest for 30 days? If it lends for 31 days, should it charge for 30 days? Should it use 360 days or 365 days for accrued interest?

The International Cash Manager

Organization of the international cash management function is highly important.[7] The time of the specialist in international cash management has arrived at most large money management banks in western Europe and, for many years, such a specialist has been the norm in the United States.[8] The management should be assigned to one person, even in large companies, because control can be more precisely defined and the value of the position can be continually and objectively evaluated. Chief responsibilities of this position should include: negotiation and selection of bank services, clearance of intercompany transfers, and monitoring of foreign exchange fluctuation exposures. Tax implications are important because profits created in a high tax country and losses made in a low tax country may result in a net global tax increase. The international cash manager may be able to monitor such situations.

This position should also be responsible for netting or matching intercompany balances, for local borrowing and currency conversion in order to offset net asset positions or for the anticipation of receipts, the purchase and deposit of local currency to

---

[7] For excellent coverage of cases of the international cash management function, see *Journal of Cash Management* and *Journal of Cash Flow*.

[8] Jean Hardy Robinson and Miriam Ben-Yoseph, "International Cash Management: Problems and Opportunities," *Journal of Cash Management* 10 (September/October 1990): 35.

MANAGEMENT APPLICATION NO. 26

Cash Flow Management in Germany

Even in Germany with its strong currency, free and well-developed financial markets, and liberal cross-border regulations, treasury management practices, especially cash flow management, are important. The environment in which corporate treasurers operate includes the Deutsche Bundesbank, Germany's central bank, which supervises 6,000 individual banks with 40,000 branches. The big three banks—Deutsche Bank, Dresdner Bank, and Commerzbank—handle 40 percent of all commercial bank payments and foreign banks account for another 10 percent. Commercial banks clear through the regional central banks while cooperative banks, saving institutions, and the postal girobank all have their own clearing houses. The German banking system is very instrumental to the success of treasury management by German companies.

The domestic cash flow management of companies in Germany results in commercial transactions being settled by direct debits and credits that are instructed by writing, phone, or magnetic tape, or by paper-based intruments such as checks or discountable drafts. Each instrument includes value-dating practices depending on whether a payment is intraregional or interregional as well as whether the beneficiary maintains an account with the same bank. Value dating is a European practice involving the recalculation of book balances into available, interest bearing balances. It has also been referred to as institutionalized float and is prevalent in many European systems, particularly France. The value date may be 1 day prior to the debit of the payor's account and 1 to 4 days after the beneficiary's account has been credited. The number of days taken by a bank to credit an account will vary by country—northern European countries take fewer days than Mediterranian countries, by payment instrument, and by the size of the paid amount. German banks charge a fee for each item although the German postal girobank executes all payments free of charge and does not value-date payments so they are available balances.

International cash flows are usually executed through SWIFT. German banks charge a transfer commission on these flows. Value dating is fairly straightforward in that same day value is given for debits if no currency conversion is necessary and two days for everything else. One day is taken if the payment is incoming, unless currency must be converted, if so, value is for two days.

Companies can meet liquidity needs with various financial instruments. A company can use its overdraft facility and can accept either company or bank drafts for payment. These drafts can be discounted. Bank drafts are used for large amounts, usually for international trade transactions. Call money can be obtained in the money market in minimum amounts of DM 1 million at the local interbank rate plus a small mark-up. Fixed loans of DM 1 million or more can be obtained for maturities up to 3 months at the interbank rate plus 0.5–1.0 percent. Eurocurrency financing can be obtained from Luxembourg subsidiaries of German banks, which are maintained to avoid reserve requirements imposed by the Deutsche Bundesbank.

[1]Willem N. Oosthoek, "A Blueprint For Treasury Management in West Germany," *Journal of Cash Management* 6 (July/August 1986): 39–42.

---

offset net borrowed positions or the anticipation of disbursements, the purchase or sale of foreign exchange forward contracts for later delivery of the currency owed or owned, and changes in the currency of invoicing. A company project to improve the international cash management function should begin with the determination of the time delays experienced in international transfers. Whenever delays occur, they should always be challenged.

Finally, the international cash manager should have working knowledge of the foreign language of the country in which his operations are most significant. Treasury

professionals in MNCs should be able to converse in the language of other international treasurers and bankers. Certainly this official may not be fluent in the foreign language but he should be familiar with the cultural differences of the foreign settings in which he operates and the nuances of financial terms in the foreign language.

Although the international cash management function should be assigned to one person rather than to a committee or group, primarily for control purposes, a team approach may be the preferable method in the modern MNC for facilitating better communication of the international cash management process to the entire company. In fact, many large companies are now organizing cross-functional teams to implement management decisions. These teams consist of management personnel responsible for various but interrelated decision areas. For example, the international finance area might consist of two cross-function teams, one for short-term finance and the other for long-term finance. The short-term finance team might consist of someone from the foreign exchange risk management area, someone from the international cash management area, and someone from the short-term funding area. The long-term team might consist of experts in foreign investment decisions, capital budgeting, and long-term funding. More general cross-functional teams might be comprised of managers from international marketing, international management staffing, and international financial management.

Principles for MNC Money Managers

MNC money managers should practice certain principles given the requirements of the international cash management function.[9] Financial management should be anticipatory and based on the money manager's perception of future risks and opportunities. To permit such a response, the money manager should review and strengthen the firm's reporting systems and, especially, forecasting capabilities. Control over exposure risk and liquidity utilization should be centralized as much as possible. Economic and transaction exposure should be covered generally and translation exposure should be covered when the maximum potential losses are considered to be unacceptable by defined corporate criteria. Financial decisions should be analyzed and made on an after-tax basis, including foreign taxes. The availability of credit in uncertain markets should be guaranteed on an individual subsidiary basis, even when additional costs are incurred. The money manager should be skeptical of exchange rate forecasting that provides one basis point or very narrow band estimates of future spot rates. Exchange risk management should be coordinated closely with liquidity management since both have common goals and are equally affected by environmental and structural constraints. Finally, the money manager should be aware of nonfinancial implications of financial strategy, including the effects on personnel from centralization and the necessity for dealing with an array of governmental and institutional contacts.

SELECTED EXAMPLES OF INTERNATIONAL CASH MANAGEMENT

This section contains selected examples of international cash management in MNCs. Many of these companies use full function, multibank treasury workstations to diver-

---

[9] Andreas R. Prindl, "Guidelines for MNC Money Managers," *Harvard Business Review* 54 (January–February 1976): 73–80.

sify their international banking needs. The following cases are representative of this move to rationalize global cash management.[10]

Eli Lilly, the U.S. drug manufacturer, uses the services of ADS Associates, a California-based provider of a treasury workstation software, ResourceIQ. The new workstation replaced six different systems the company had used, including one that was Excel, a simple spreadsheet. Lilly's international cash management policy is set at headquarters and its inhouse banking for overseas operations is coordinated through a Belgian regional center. The system does not use pan-European electronic integration. Funding requirements are decided locally and funding requests are phoned or faxed to Belgium. The ADS system will enable Lilly to integrate its international cash management.

Peugeot UK, a car dealer in Great Britain, uses Barclays Trading Master, a payment system that facilitates electronic payments to 1,000 domestic suppliers and 350 non-U.K. suppliers. The system automatically generates remittance advice, which is sent electronically to suppliers that have a receiving facility. The company saves £200,000 a year over the cost of a paper-based system.

Some companies use another alternative: an electronic banking delivery platform. Such a system includes the functions of multibank products. Companies that use this system purchase the core treasury management software from independent vendors. The European treasury manager at Merck in London uses such a system and functions as the inhouse bank for all of the company's European subsidiaries. Each subsidiary deals with one local bank. Every Monday the European treasury manager uses Citibank's platform and determines from each local Merck company whether it has an excess or deficit of cash. If a subsidiary has excess cash, it is transferred to Merck's Citibank branch in that country. The cash is then moved from country to country through the Citibank network to remove excess cash from one subsidiary to fund another's deficit. The cash-rich subsidiary is paid interest and the cash-deficit subsidiary is charged interest. The software product used is MCM Global Treasury Management System, developed by a New Jersey company, into which a company enters its foreign exchange deals, including amounts, rates, dates, and counterparties. The system then monitors all currency positions and produces the correct payments and confirmation letters. A file is created that is uploaded directly into Citibank's system for authorization of payments instructions and appropriate transfers.

SELECTED GENERALIZATIONS ABOUT WORKING CAPITAL MANAGEMENT

Top management of the international company, particularly the MNC money manager, should be aware of some of the generalizations about global working capital management. Working capital, especially international cash, should be protected from two problems encountered in the international environment: losses from foreign exchange fluctuations and from inflation, especially hyperinflation. Forex risk management was discussed in detail in chapter 4.

Minimizing Forex Losses

A number of situations involving currency fluctuations and possible losses from these changes face the international cash manager.[11] Techniques for hedging foreign

---

[10] Joan Ogden, "How Cash Managers Play the Banks Against One Another," *Global Finance* 9 (October 1995): 50–2.

[11] Jeff Madura and E. Theodore Veit, "Use of Currency Options in International Cash Management," *Journal of Cash Management* 6 (January/February 1986): 42.

exchange exposure were discussed in more detail in chapter 4. However, some problems facing the cash manager are directly related to foreign exchange risk management. These problems include:

1. the foreign exchange rate may increase before the future date when a U.S. importer must pay for foreign goods in the exporter's currency;
2. the foreign exchange rate may decline before payment is received by the U.S. exporter who agrees to accept foreign payment for its goods, which will be shipped in the future;
3. the foreign exchange rate declines before securities mature that are owned by a U.S. firm or its affiliate and denominated in a foreign currency;
4. remitted profits from a foreign affiliate will be lower if the foreign exchange rate declines.

The firm can minimize forex losses from possible local currency devaluation by adopting any or all of the following strategies:

1. minimize cash balances;
2. accelerate remittances to parent company;
3. accelerate repayment of debt to parent or to an external source;
4. borrow locally as much as possible, when possible;
5. place excess funds into less vulnerable assets;
6. reduce receivables;
7. reduce inventory or make sure it is of a type that is less susceptible to inflation;
8. make little or no prepayments of expenses;
9. hedge in the forward forex market.

In an environment where the local currency is forecast to revalue, the opposite strategies would be put into effect.

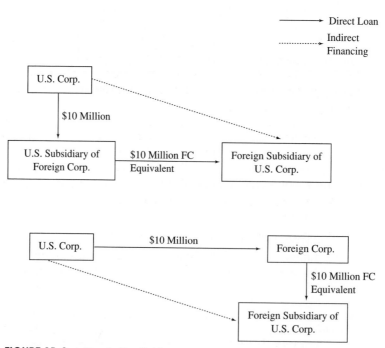

FIGURE 15–2 A Simple Parallel Loan

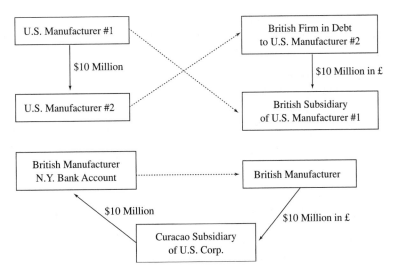

FIGURE 15–3 A Variation of a Simple Parallel Loan

Parallel Loans   A company can use parallel or back-to-back loans as a means of international funds management. These types of loans were the forerunners of currency and interest rate swaps, which were introduced in chapter 4 as techniques for hedging foreign exchange risk, and also discussed in more detail in chapter 14 in their role as financial derivatives. Examples of these parallel loans are shown in Figures 15–2, 15–3, and 15–4.

In Figure 15–2, a simple arrangement is shown in which a U.S. corporation makes a direct loan to the U.S. subsidiary of a foreign corporation, which then transfers foreign currency to the foreign subsidiary of the U.S. company. The result is indirect financing by the U.S. company of its foreign affiliate without transferring funds across national borders. In the bottom part of Figure 15–2, the same goal is accomplished by a loan from the U.S. company to a foreign company, which in turn makes a loan in foreign currency to the foreign affiliate of the U.S. company.

A variation of the simple swap, in Figure 15–3, shows indirect financing by a U.S. manufacturer of its British subsidiary and the payment of a loan owed by a British firm to a U.S. manufacturer. No funds cross national borders because a Curaçao affiliate of one of the U.S. manufacturers is used. This is an off-shore financing unit in a tax haven country.

In Figure 15–4, a version of the parallel or back-to-back loan is used to avoid the foreign transfer of capital. Again the dashed lines represent indirect financing and the solid lines represent direct financing.

These loans were replaced by the modern versions of currency and interest rate swaps in order to avoid the legal problems that arose when one of the parties defaulted. These legal problems were discussed in chapter 14.

FIGURE 15–4 A Parallel Loan to Avoid a Capital Transfer

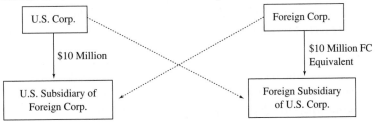

Financing Under Inflation

The following strategies should be implemented to protect foreign operations from the impact of inflation, especially in hyperinflation economies:

1. stay in debt;
2. establish overdraft lines;
3. keep accounts receivables down by speedy collections;
4. discount accounts receivables and customers' debts;
5. maintain tight financial control over inventories;
6. stretch out suppliers credits as much as possible;
7. issue promissory notes;
8. borrow from a firm with excess cash or funds in the same country and place the funds in short-term investments;
9. delay payments of taxes, social security, etc.;
10. increase prices—may result in local political problems;
11. make no price guarantees on delivery;
12. invest in property that is prone to increase in value along with the rate of inflation.

SHORT-TERM FINANCING PRINCIPLES

Short-term financing has certain principles that are related to international cash management and working capital issues. Some of these key factors that top management should consider include the interrelationships of the economic factors that facilitate foreign exchange rate forecasts. These include the Fisher effect, international Fisher effect, interest rate parity, purchasing power parity, and the forward exchange rate as the unbiased predictor of future spot rates, all topics discussed in detail in chapter 3. International operations risks including forex risk and political risks are important, as are tax differences, to be discussed in chapter 17. The implication here is that if forward contracts exist to hedge foreign exchange exposure, then the only valid objective of short-term financing is to minimize after-tax interest costs. In the absence of forward exchange markets—some currencies are not traded or, as in Brazil, some countries prohibit forward market operations—firms can either attempt to minimize expected costs or establish trade-offs between reduction of expected costs and reduction of the degree of cash flow exposure.

International financial management should have certain objectives for short-term financing operations. These include minimization of expected costs, minimization of risk regardless of cost, trade-off between expected cost and systematic risk, and trade-off between expected cost and total risk. Financing options for short-term finance include intercompany financing and local currency financing.

INTRACOMPANY FINANCING

Short-term financing can flow from parent firm to subsidiaries, from subsidiaries to parent firm, or from one subsidiary to another. Such funds flows can take the form of intracorporate loans or the flow of income from one affiliate to another. This flow of funds, when in the form of dividends, is generally done for tax management reasons and will be discussed in chapter 17. The principal on intracorporate loans in a U.S. MNC may never be paid back but some interest should always be paid because of the implications for the firm from aggressive enforcement of Section 482 regulations by the Internal Revenue Service. Section 482 ensures that transactions between affiliates, e.g.,

intracorporate loans, are done at an arm's length basis. Section 482 issues will be discussed in chapter 17.

Local Currency Financing

The international firm may obtain short-term financing in local currency from bank loans, commercial paper, and Euro-notes and Euro-commercial paper. Bank loans can be obtained in several forms. These include: (1) term loans—loans made for a medium-term period to maturity; (2) a line of credit granted by the bank against which funds can be drawn; (3) overdrafts—a popular form of borrowing, especially in Great Britain, in which checks can be written against a demand deposit with insufficient funds; (4) a revolving credit agreement; and (5) discounting notes. Short-term financing can be obtained by flotation of commercial paper. Commercial paper is an unsecured promissory note issued with a maturity of up to 6 months. Since commercial paper is usually issued by large, well-known companies, such funding will probably be secured by the parent firm. This may be done in the domestic market or by an issue in the Eurocurrency markets, in which the issue is denominated in a foreign currency and the paper is marketed in Eurocurrency banking centers. Euro-notes, notes issued for medium-term maturities in the Eurocurrency markets, also have become popular in recent years as a source of relatively short-term finance.

Manuevering Liquid Assets

Short-term intracompany financing can be achieved by maneuvering liquid assets from parent firm to subsidiary, from subsidiary to subsidiary, or from subsidiary to parent firm. This financial operation will be discussed in this section and will include an analysis of the organizational patterns used by firms to handle their liquid assets and a discussion of the major methods for transferring funds.

The major forms of intracompany liquid funds flows that MNCs use include transfer pricing, managerial fees, royalties, dividends, and intracorporate loans. These funds flow methods will be discussed in the following sections.

Transfer Prices   Transfer prices are the prices charged by one unit of a MNC to another unit for goods. In certain well-defined cases, these prices may be changed so that funds can be moved from one unit to another and taxable income can be allocated between the two countries in which the units operate. Transfer prices can be used to move funds and to reduce taxes. Such transfer prices should be set so that allocation of income is to low tax rate countries from high tax rate countries. Because of this strategy, local governments normally have the attitude that MNCs' use of transfer prices is disadvantageous to the country and, thus, is often classified as tax evasion. The tax aspects of transfer pricing will be discussed in chapter 17 on tax management.

Transfer pricing is fraught with two major problems. First, prices may be set in such a manner that a local manager may be penalized for his relatively efficient and income producing operation. If transfer prices result in moving his income to a unit in another country, morale may suffer and the company may encounter a human resources problem. Second, transfer pricing may result in a conflict with either local or U.S. tax authorities, an issue to be discussed in chapter 17.

A study by Robbins and Stobaugh found that transfer pricing can also be used to reduce the effect of foreign exchange controls.[12] A MNC may increase the intercompany price for sales to its affiliate that has funds blocked by local foreign exchange controls. The parent may very well increase overall corporate taxes in order to gain the

---

[12]Alan C. Shapiro, *International Corporate Finance: Survey & Synthesis* (Tampa, FL: Financial Management Association, 1986), p. 44.

affiliate's funds. The parent needs to analyze several factors before deciding to implement such a strategy, including the effective tax rates of the selling and purchasing affiliates, the duration of foreign exchange controls, and any investment alternatives available to the subsidiary with blocked funds.

Management Fees   Management fees are charges by headquarters for managerial advice and allocated headquarters overhead made to subsidiaries. These fees may be compensation for technical assistance or unique managerial skills rendered by the parent firm to the affiliate. Of the various funds flows discussed here, management fees are the easiest flows to hide from tax authorities. Such fees may actually be charged for little or no concrete service rendered by headquarters. On the other hand, management fees are most difficult to measure and regulate by tax authorities.

Royalties and Licensing Fees   Royalties and licensing fees are payments received by firms that license or give to unrelated firms permission to use intangible property rights such as patents, copyrights, formulae, and trademarks. These intangible properties can be used by the licensee, or unrelated firm, to manufacture and market products in a foreign country, which are usually produced by the licensor, or owner of the intangible properties. The licensee compensates the licensor with royalties or other licensing fees, usually a percentage of the sales of the products made from these intangible properties. Licensing usually requires formal agreements between the parties and can be suitable conduits through which to move funds. However, exchange control agencies of host countries exercise a great deal of supervision over licensing arrangements. In addition, the licensor must maintain tight control over the licensee because of the potential infringement of intangible property rights. Thus, the company should have a tightly written contract with the licensee as well as good international legal advice.

Intracorporate Loans   Intracorporate loans are quite prevalent in MNC organizations. Affiliates may lend to other affiliates or to the parent firm. The latter may lend to the affiliates. Such loans can be affected by a speed-up or delay in invoicing shipments between a pair of subsidiaries, i.e., technically, a lead or lag situation. Leads and lags can be accomplished because normal terms of payment may exist between two nations, because of tax savings in some cases, or to bypass restriction on remittances. Again, Section 482 of the U.S. Internal Revenue Code affects U.S. MNCs in the area of intracorporate loans because, although principal may never be paid by one company affiliate to another, the borrowing firm should be careful to pay interest on the loan. Otherwise, the transaction may be considered not at arms-length by tax authorities and income may be reallocated, resulting in higher tax liabilities.

Another problem often encountered by intracompany loans is the tax treatment by the host country.[13] For example, companies operating foreign affiliates in Mexico must choose among borrowing locally in pesos or with a parental guarantee in dollars or borrowing at the parent level. Any of these choices has a different tax and risk management consequence. An intracompany loan subjects the interest payments to a high withholding tax. Borrowing dollars may create a mismatch between revenues and liabilities for the parent firm.

Dividends   Dividends represent the fifth and final type of intracorporate funds flows. As discussed in chapter 17 on taxation of international corporate operations, the flow of dividends from the affiliate to the U.S. parent firm is affected by the Revenue

---

[13] Nilly Landau, "Competitive Finance," *International Business* 7 (August 1994); 24.

Acts of 1962 and 1976, and is also considered under Subpart F income rules, as well as planning for foreign base company operations in a tax haven country. The flow of funds from affiliates to the parent firm in the form of dividends is frequently restricted, especially in developing countries, as a form of foreign exchange control. Thus, MNCs are subject to both tax and foreign exchange controls when they use dividends as a form of intracorporate funds flows.

Firms can use three organizational patterns or philosophies when maneuvering liquid assets. These are ethnocentric, polycentric, and geocentric patterns. The firm that incorporates an ethnocentric pattern is essentially centralized in nature and its management at headquarters does not want subsidiary managers to hold liquid assets from year to year. These firms will insist that overseas affiliates declare frequent dividends to headquarters. Polycentric corporations view each subsidiary as totally independent and have little involvement in the management of liquid assets. This pattern has the fewest negative behavioral consequences because of its essential decentralization, but the system results in a high level of total short-term assets needed for operations. The geocentric corporation moves liquidity to subsidiaries when necessary by manipulating transfer prices, managerial fees, royalties, dividends, and intersubsidiary loans. The firm maximizes interest received on liquid assets minus total taxes paid on a worldwide basis. The objective, thus, of maneuvering liquid assets is to enable the MNC to react to anticipated changes in exchange rates, currency controls, and related risks and opportunities.

EXAMPLES OF INTERNATIONAL LIQUIDITY MANAGEMENT

International liquidity management may depend on the extent of a company's international operations. The company may be: (1) a single currency/single entity firm, (2) a single currency/multiple entity firm, or (3) a multiple currency/multiple entity firm. A number of techniques are available to firms in each of these categories.[14]

Single Currency/Single Entity Firm

A firm may have sales subsidiaries in several foreign countries, each of which operates with only its own country's currency. The firm receives cash flows at the central headquarters in a number of currencies and each subsidiary runs its own idle balances or deficits. Thus, this company will desire to reduce interest rate spreads by minimizing opposite balances denominated in different currencies. This firm should also reduce its cross-border movement of funds because differences in correspondent banking and clearing will increase the cost of these cross-border flows.

This firm might, therefore, resort to cross-border cash concentration. A central account for concentration of each currency is created at central headquarters. All cash

─────────────

[14] Christine D. O'Brien and Leonard H. Stolk, "International Liquidity Management: Solutions for the 21st Century," *TMA Journal* (March/April 1995).

flows from foreign countries are channeled through this account. Surpluses in one country can be used to fund deficits in other countries while reducing cross-border transfers.

Single Currency/Multiple Entity Company

A firm may have more than one subsidiary operating in each foreign country. The country, for example, might have three German subsidiaries all operating in German marks. One might have a surplus operating account while the others have deficits. If adequate liquidity management techniques are not used, interest rates for deficit balances—through overdrafts—may be much higher than interest on credit balances. The combined interest charge can be quite high. This firm might request its deficit subsidiaries to borrow in the money markets where rates are more attractive. Or this firm might save on interest charges by utilizing intercompany lending. The surplus affiliate can lend at more favorable rates to the deficit affiliates. A third alternative is the use of cash pooling administered by the company's bank. A master account is established in each country and the company's bank administers this cash pool over a group of affiliated accounts.

Multiple Currency/Multiple Entity Company

This company has more than one subsidiary in each country and these affiliates operate in more than one currency. This firm faces the problems of management of nonfunctional currencies or currencies that are not indigenous to each country.

The firm may establish a single currency/cross-border cash pooling arrangement. Local cash pools are formed in each country for a specific nonfunctional currency, e.g., Belgian francs in France. These pools are combined at central headquarters and deficits are funded from the money markets. A managed cross-currency cash pooling arrangement can also be established. Single currency cash pools can be linked and one currency can be converted into another in the foreign exchange market. Again deficits in one currency can be filled with surpluses in another. This technique uses corporate funds in an optimal manner, improves the company's financial ratios, reduces consolidated leverage, and lowers the overall treasury workload by centralization of balance management. Transfers become intercompany loans, which require administration. However, the currency accounts may be kept within the countries in which they are indigenous so that better pricing is achieved. Finally, taxes on the gains from these techniques need to be considered. Depending on the country in which the currency management technique is used, capital gains and income tax liabilities may be generated. These topics will be discussed in chapter 17.

Organizing Foreign Currency Accounts

Given the principles and practices considered in the preceding sections, the international company needs to organize the foreign currency accounts of the firm in an optimal manner. The firm should consider the establishment of foreign currency accounts to collect foreign currency receipts. The factors that need to be considered are the volume and value of foreign exchange receipts, the currency of disbursements, and the availability of electronic banking services. Knowledge of the first two factors and the presence of the third will facilitate the optimum organization of such a system.

BENEFITS FROM AN OPTIMAL ORGANIZATION

Several benefits stem from the optimum organization of foreign currency accounts. Among these are: improved value from these accounts, reduced foreign exchange-re-

lated costs from the conversion of larger amounts, and the netting of payables and receivables. Better organization of foreign accounts makes them easier to manage and noninterest bearing accounts may be converted into interest bearing accounts. One drawback of such a system may be increased account charges.

ORGANIZATIONAL DESIGN

The options available to the firm in the design of the organization of foreign currency accounts are incountry accounts, i.e., a decentralized system, a centralized or regional account structure, or a hybrid structure, which has characteristics of both centralization and decentralization. The factors that have to be considered in the determination of which structure to use include: the legal structure of the affiliates, i.e., whether branches or subsidiaries, or whether they receive exports from the parent firm; management/personnel issues including morale factors and the possibility of bonus payments to expatriate managers; the nature of subsidiary sales, i.e., domestic or cross-border; the presence of foreign exchange controls; foreign exchange exposure management; and liquidity management practices.

DECENTRALIZED FOREIGN CURRENCY ACCOUNTS

The adoption of incountry or decentralized foreign currency accounts may be indicated by certain environmental factors. These include subsidiaries with domestic, local currency sales, which only make their own disbursements and investments. Billings are made only in a few currencies. Foreign exchange controls face the firm in its foreign locations. Sales revenues are generated on the basis of credit card receipts. The benefits from an incountry system of foreign currency accounts include the presence of a domestic clearing system, the possibility of using a lock-box system in a few countries, and lower charges to the remitter or beneficiary. However, decentralization has its drawbacks. The firm may have to deal with too many banks. Bank services will vary in quality. Problem resolution may be more difficult from a decentralized position.

CENTRALIZED FOREIGN CURRENCY ACCOUNTS

The use of centralized accounts may be indicated by a number of factors. Billings may be necessary in several major currencies. The management of accounts has been traditionally carried out from the United States or from a centralized location. Receipts are not made by check or credit card. The company does not have treasury personnel in the field. The benefits of centralization of foreign accounts include the ease of management, better terms and conditions, and easier problem resolution. The drawbacks of centralization include increased charges to the remitters, possible loss of value from translation, settlement, and banking fees, and earlier cutoff times for payments.

HYBRID SYSTEM

Finally, the firm might consider a hybrid foreign accounts system, i.e., one that has some characteristics of centralization and some of decentralization. Indications for such a system include a company with local offices that do not control cash, several subsidiaries, which bill in both local and foreign currency, and the use of regional treasury centers for centralized foreign exchange management and centralized liquidity management. Multilateral netting of accounts can be accomplished in these regional centers. The benefits of a hybrid system are ease of management and control and the maximization of investments while minimizing borrowings. The drawbacks include a potential increase in bank charges, although these should be offset by some savings from such a system.

Summary and Conclusions

The day-to-day financial operations are quite important to the successful MNC. They are simply not as glamorous as longer term financial management. The advent of the personal computer and financial spreadsheet software has enabled companies to more effectively manage and control the international finance function. International cash has to be managed. Accounts receivable and inventories are quickly converted into cash. Thus, the management of international cash receipts and disbursements is a highly significant part of international cash management.

International cash management is facilitated by international communications networks such as CHIPS, CHAPS, and SWIFT. Computer systems have been developed by banks such as Chemical Bank and Citicorp to assist companies in the management of global cash. The problems of differences in foreign operations, currencies, language, training of executives, and accounting practices all contribute to the complexity of international cash management. Thus, such systems require a speedy reporting system operated by personnel who recognize the major problems encountered in international business.

The international cash management system incorporated by the MNC should be capable of minimizing foreign exchange losses. In addition, it should be capable of reducing interest costs of money as well as tax liabilities incurred in international business operations. Operations must be protected from the impact of inflation, particularly hyperinflation, prevalent in many LDCs.

Finally, the company should maneuver its liquid funds so that the cost of funds is reduced as much as possible. The major funds flows—transfer prices, management fees, intracorporate loans, dividends, and licensing royalties—must be structured in such a way that the firm can be financed internally or externally with the lowest cost funds possible. At the same time, the CFO should be able to explain the use of all funds in the company as well as any idle funds.

Additional Readings

Baker, James C., and Raj Aggarwal. "Evaluation of Global Electronic Funds Flow System: The Society for Worldwide Interbank Financial Telecommunications (SWIFT)." In *Global Information Systems and Technology: Focus on the Organization and Its Functional Areas* ed. Deans, P. Candace and Kirk R. Karwan. Harrisburg, PA: Idea Group Publishing, 1994.

Bokos, W. J., and A. P. Clinkard. "Multilateral Netting." *Journal of Cash Management* 3 (June/July 1983): 24–34.

Gentry, James A., Dilep R. Mehta, S.K. Bhattacharya, Robert Cobbaut, and Jean-Louis Scaringella. "An International Study of Management Perceptions of the Working Capital Process." *Journal of International Business Studies* 5 (Spring–Summer 1979): 28–38.

Masson, Dubos J. "Planning and Forecasting of Cash Flows for the Multinational Firm: International Cash Management." *Advances in Financial Planning and Forecasting* 4, Part B (1990): 195–228.

Mirus, Rolf, and Bernard Yeoung. "The Relevance of the Invoicing Currency in Intra-Firm Trade Transaction." *Journal of International Money and Finance* 6 (December 1987): 449–64.

Robinson, Jean Hardy, and Miriam Ben Yoseph. "International Cash Management Problems and Opportunities." *Journal of Cash Management* 10 (September/October 1990): 35–40.

Shapiro, Alan C. *International Corporate Finance: Survey & Synthesis*. Tampa, FL: Financial Management Association, 1986.

Shapiro, Alan C. "Payments Netting in International Cash Management." *Journal of International Business Studies* 4 (Fall 1978): 51–8.

Soenen, Luc A., and Raj Aggarwal. "Corporate Foreign Exchange and Cash Management Practices." *Journal of Cash Management* 7 (March–April 1987): 62–4.

Srinivasan, VenKat, and Yong H. Kim. "Payments Netting in International Cash Management: A Network Optimization Approach." *Journal of International Business Studies* 12 (Summer 1986): 1–20.

Discussion Questions

1. Discuss the major international money management subscription services.
2. Compare and contrast Fedwire, CHIPS, CHAPS, and FX Net.
3. Describe the organizational structure of SWIFT.
4. What are the advantages of SWIFT?
5. What are the key questions that top management must answer when establishing an international cash management system?
6. Why is float time sometimes longer in countries that have national banking systems and nationwide branching?
7. Show how netting of accounts can make an international cash disbursements system more efficient.
8. What attributes should the international cash manager have? What responsibilities?
9. Discuss the five major means for maneuvering liquid assets within the multinational corporation.
10. Should the organization of foreign currency accounts be centralized, decentralized, or a hybrid of both types? What are the benefits of an optimal organization of these accounts?

Problems

1. Assume that Tootsie Roll Company needs to finance working capital for an affiliate in Australia. The bank in Melbourne offers a 1-year loan of A$1.25 million at 10 percent payable at maturity with a 10 percent compensating balance. What is the effective percentage cost of this loan?
2. If the compensating balance of this loan is 20 percent, what is the effective percentage cost?
3. If the compensating balance of this loan is 10 percent and it is a discount loan, what is the effective percentage cost?
4. If Tootsie Roll Company requires A$1.25 million, how much must it borrow if the compensating balance is 10 percent and it is a discount loan? Hint: Let X be the size of Tootsie Roll's loan.
5. Suppose that average float time is 10 days for the Benneton Company. European operations and sales volume of these operations amounts to $1 billion. The average interest rate for the company's bank loans is 7 percent.
   a. What is the interest cost attributed to this float time?
   b. If float time is reduced to 9 days, how much will cash flow be increased?
6. Suppose Conrack International borrows from a German bank DM 1 million for 1 year. The bank imposes a 10 percent compensating balance on this loan. Interest of 8 percent is charged at an annual rate. What is the effective cost of the loan?
7. Venerable PLC, a British widget maker, needs £2 million to pay for machinery. The company can borrow for 1 year in either of the following methods:
   a. a loan whose principal and interest are payable at maturity with an annual interest rate of 9 percent;
   b. a loan on a discount basis with an 8 percent interest rate charged. Which is the best loan for Venerable PLC?

CHAPTER 16

Accounting, Control, and Auditing for International Operations

Major Objectives of Chapter 16

(1) To introduce the differences in accounting from one country to another, (2) to compare and contrast FASB-8 and FASB-52, foreign currency translations methods in the United States, (3) to examine the process for setting international accounting standards, (4) to examine the control process of the international finance function and evaluation of foreign subsidiary performance, and (5) to introduce the function of international auditing and the establishment of international auditing standards.

Key terms to be learned in chapter 16:

- hidden reserves
- temporal method
- FASB-8
- functional currency
- International Federation of Accountants

- International Accounting Standards Committee
- current rate method
- FASB-52
- cumulative translation

416

Introduction

MNCs must periodically report their foreign operations back to the parent firm, at least annually if not more often. Overseas operations must be consolidated for this purpose and the accounts of the foreign operations, usually denominated in the local currency, must be translated into the parent company's currency. Many of these foreign operations are located in countries with high inflation rates. If the parent firm is a U.S. firm, historical cost accounting rules may dictate whether replacement values of the foreign assets are taken into consideration. Accounting rules may be different from one country to another creating problems because the definitions of creditable items, expenses, base values of assets, and what is a capital gain may differ from nation to nation. Accounting for international operations, thus, is a very complex and expensive function that needs special attention.

These differences from one country to another can be attributed to the effects of culture.[1] Culture has a large influence on the accounting system in a particular country. Culture, for example, will determine whether a country's accounting system is based on professionalism or on statutory control. In the United States and Great Britain, professional societies such as the American Institute of Certified Public Accountants and the British Accounting Society have been primarily instrumental in the development of accounting standards, practices, and principles. On the other hand, company laws have dictated the form by which accounting is practiced in Germany. Culture determines whether accounting is practiced on a uniform basis rather than on a flexible basis according to an industry-by-industry approach. Culture may impact the accounting system by creating a conservative approach to measurement of financial operations rather than an optimistic approach in which companies take more risks and operate as though the system is based on laissez-faire. Finally, culture may dictate whether companies keep their financial operations more confidential, as in Germany where companies maintain hidden reserves, or more open and transparent, as in the United States, where federal agencies such as the Securities and Exchange Commission and the Federal Trade Commission require firms to disclose a relatively high amount of information for investors and customers.

Since the 1950s, the global environment in which MNCs have operated has grown tremendously. Total world trade now amounts to more than $5 trillion annually. More than $150 billion of net capital is imported into the United States annually. Global volume in foreign exchange trading exceeds $250 trillion annually. International money and capital markets in stocks, bonds, foreign exchange futures, options, and Eurocurrencies approach 24 hours a day operational status. Because of this growth in international commercial transactions, cross-border investments, funds flows, and financial operations in general have to be considered when international firms plan, formulate, and implement optimal organizational structures for their international operations. These international operations must be consolidated, translated into the parent country currency, reported back to parent firms, accounted for, and attested to, so that international top management may properly manage their respective companies.

The first part of this chapter will focus on the major functions of international accounting in the MNC. These are consolidation of foreign operations, accounting for foreign operations including translation of foreign accounts and accounting for price level changes, and reporting worldwide operations. First, however, one of the major problems of international accounting, which touches on all of the major subjects of this

---

[1] Lee H. Radebaugh, "International Accounting," in *The WG&L Handbook of International Finance* ed. Dennis E. Logue (Cincinnati, OH: South-Western, 1995), p. 157.

chapter, will be analyzed. This problem is the insufficiency of a set of international generally accepted accounting principles and the work now being done to correct this problem. The second part of the chapter will deal with control of the international finance function, evaluation of foreign subsidiaries, the international auditing function, and the establishment of international auditing rules and standards.

Lack of Uniform International GAAP

Each industrialized nation and some LDCs have formulated a set of generally accepted accounting principles (GAAP) under which their accountants and financial analysts operate. The principal assumption for a viable system of international accounting is that accounting standards, principles, and practices are uniform and generally accepted on a global basis. Many of the problems that arise in multinational accounting in the major areas covered in this chapter—consolidation, accounting for foreign operations, and reporting those accounts back to the parent firm—stem from the lack of an international GAAP.

European company annual reports demonstrate the need for international GAAP. For example, in early 1994, the large German auto manufacturer, Daimler Benz, applied for listing of its shares on the New York Stock Exchange (NYSE). After great cost in adapting its accounts to the requirements of U.S. stock exchanges, Daimler Benz' application was approved, making it the first German company to list its shares on any organized securities exchange in the United States. (See Management Application No. 27 for a detailed discussion of this case.) Companies from many foreign countries have their shares listed on the NYSE.[2] Among these countries are Spain, Japan, the Netherlands, Belgium, the United Kingdom, and Mexico. German companies did not conform to the accounting rules required by the U.S. Securities and Exchange Commission or the NYSE. German law dictates how German firms formulate their financial statements. For example, the *Aktiengesetz* (Company Law) does not require, among other accounts, the cost of goods sold to be reported. German firms have traditionally held hidden reserves without reporting them, although this practice is prohibited by German law.

A.B. Volvo, the Swedish auto manufacturer, is another example of the use of reserves to camouflage earnings. Volvo publishes a high quality annual report that shows detailed product line data as well as comparative sales by geographic area. Volvo had shifted much of its profits into reserve accounts because of high Swedish tax rates. Most Swedish companies do this in order to announce low profits for tax purposes, in contrast to U.S. companies, which generally try to report as much profit as possible. However, Volvo needs capital from worldwide equity markets and has, thus, reconciled its net income report according to Swedish law with net income according to U.S. accounting standards.[3]

The problems discussed here can be alleviated by the development of accounting objectives, standards, and practices that are universally accepted on a global basis. Several major domestic and worldwide factors influence the development of these objec-

---

[1] For a discussion of this issue, see, for example, G. K. Meek and S. J. Gray, "Globalization of Stock Markets and Foreign Listing Requirements: Voluntary Disclosures by Continental European Companies Listed on the London Stock Exchange," *Journal of International Business Studies* 20 (Summer 1989): 315–36.

[3] John N. Slipkowsky, "The Bottom Line in European Accounting," *Wall Street Journal*, 24 August 1987, p. 12.

tives, standards, and practices.[4] The nature of the enterprise including the form of business organization and its operating characteristics plays a role in accounting standard development. The accounting profession itself makes an impact in terms of the nature and extent of the profession in a given country as does the importance of professional associations.

Academic influence on accounting standards and practices is manifest through the educational infrastructure, basic and applied research, and academic associations. Government plays a role in formulating financial and accounting regulations and as a user of financial and accounting information, i.e., tax planning. Enterprise users, including management, employees, supervisory councils, and boards of directors all demand uniform accounting standards and practices. Financial institutions, investors, and organized markets are external users that need universal accounting standards and practices.

Local environmental characteristics have an impact. These include the rate of economic growth, inflation, public vs. private ownership and control of the economy, and cultural attitudes. Finally, a number of international influences have an impact on the standard-setting process. These include any colonial history of the country involved, foreign investors, international committees, regional cooperation, and regional capital markets.

ADVANTAGES OF UNIVERSAL INTERNATIONAL GAAP

International GAAP present several advantages to the MNC. Among these are: the facilitation of comparability of international financial information, the savings of time and money currently spent to consolidate divergent financial information when more than one set of reports is required to comply with different national laws or practice, and the tendency for accounting standards throughout the world to be raised to the highest possible level consistent with local economic, legal, and social conditions.

BARRIERS TO UNIVERSAL INTERNATIONAL GAAP

A number of barriers confront attempts to harmonize national accounting rules into generally acceptable international accounting standards. First, widespread cultural differences affect language, law, governments' priorities, and societal concepts.[5] Nationalism is, thus, fostered leading to compromises of international accounting standards and their enforcement. Second, intergovernmental organizations have muddied the waters with their interest in the GAAP setting process. Overlapping analysis of this area by the United Nations, the European Community, the Organization for Economic Cooperation and Development, African Accounting Council, and other groups has added confusion to the formulation and implementation of international accounting standards. Third, few countries have formal procedures for enforcement of international accounting standards. Fourth, these standards are generally Anglo-Saxon or American in their orientation while many European nations practice code law. The adoption of international accounting standards is made more difficult by these legal differences.

Because of the need for international accounting standards and the barriers to their formulation and acceptance, several organizations have been active in pursuing

---

[4] Lee H. Radebaugh, "Environmental Factors Influencing the Development of Accounting Objectives, Standards, and Practices—The Peruvian Case," *The International Journal of Accounting* 11 (Fall 1975): 41.

[5] James F. Gaertner and Norlin Rueschhoff, "Cultural Barriers to International Accounting Standards," *CA Magazine* 113 (1980): 36–9.

Daimler Benz Lists on the New York Stock Exchange

In 1993, Daimler Benz, the large German auto manufacturer, became the first German company to list its shares on any organized securities exchange in the United States when it became listed on the New York Stock Exchange (NYSE). The company agreed with requirements of the U.S. Securities Exchange Commission (SEC) to change its accounting practices in order to obtain the listing. The U.S. market has 10,000 institutional investors and 51 million individual shareholders. The amount of funds raised in the U.S. securities markets equals or exceeds the capital raised in all other international markets combined. The broad market was attractive to Daimler Benz at the time that the company had decided to manufacture cars in the United States.

A number of reasons have kept German companies from being listed on U.S. stock markets. Germany does not have a regulatory agency comparable to the SEC. German companies have been able to hide reserves in their subsidiaries even though the 1967 *Aktiensgesetz* (Company Law) prohibited such a practice. German law does not distinguish between published accounts and tax accounts. A nonaccounting reason why Daimler Benz had not listed on the NYSE was that many U.S. institutional and individual investors had already invested in the company by means of U.S.-traded American depositary receipts (ADRs)—discussed earlier in chapter 12—or by purchasing the company's stock directly on the Frankfurt Stock Exchange.[1]

One of the foundations of German corporate mythology is the maintenance of hidden reserves or *stille Reserven*, which include unrealized gains on real estate and securities holdings, undervalued inventories, excessive provisions for pensions, bad loans, and costs of potential lawsuits.[2] Germany's oldest companies have the largest hidden reserves. Daimler Benz disclosed $4.5 billion in reserves, mostly provisions for pensions, in order to list the company's shares on the NYSE.

Hidden reserves have been used by German companies to avoid paying tax rates that are among the world's highest. These reserves can accumulate in four areas: fixed assets, depreciation allowances, inventory accounting, and provisions. German companies keep fixed assets, for example, on the books at cost. The difference between cost and market value is a hidden reserve. Reserves hidden in provisions, such as pensions, creates the largest question and lowers earnings and taxes. Reserves hidden in real estate do not furnish much liquidity because companies cannot revalue the real estate unless it is sold. A sale of real estate, however, would create a large tax liability.

German companies also create hidden reserves by their practice of owning large interests in one another. Banks such as Deutsche Bank are among the worst practitioners of hidden reserves. The largest German bank owns 28 percent of Daimler Benz, as well as significant interests in Karstadt, Allianz, Phillipp Holzman, Klöckner-Humboldt-Deutz, and others. German company law requires any holding of 25 percent or higher to be disclosed.

One severe problem stemming from hidden reserves is the inability to properly evaluate a company's stock. Some investment analysts ignore these reserves without further information. Unions seeking higher wages and competitors are frustrated by the lack of information on hidden reserves.

In order to list on the NYSE, Daimler Benz had to publish financial information in accordance with U.S. generally accepted accounting principles (GAAP) for its entire corporate group, including a breakdown of cash flow in the operating, investing, and financing areas. One question that will remain for U.S. accounting regulators to watch will be the length of time the company is permitted to depreciate goodwill against equity in various areas of the company. In any event, Daimler Benz and other German companies that desire an American stock market listing, e.g., Deutsche Bank, will have to conform to the disclosure rules of the world's largest capital market.

---

[1] David Duffy and Lachlan Murray, "The Wooing of American Investors," *Wall Street Journal*, 25 February 1994, p. A14.
[2] Michelle Celarier, "Germany's Phantom Reserves," *Global Finance* 7 (May 1993): 60–3.

standards that lead to an international GAAP. These include the United Nations, the European Community, the International Federation of Accountants (IFAC), the African Accounting Council, the Inter-American Accounting Association, and the International Accounting Standards Committee (IASC). The latter and most significant of these organizations in the formulation of international accounting standards will be examined in more detail in the following sections.

THE INTERNATIONAL ACCOUNTING STANDARDS COMMITTEE

The move to a universally accepted international GAAP has been facilitated during the past two decades by the International Accounting Standards Committee (IASC).[6] At the 10th International Congress of Accountants meeting in Sydney, Australia, in 1972, the IASC was established to formulate international accounting standards (IAS) and reduce international accounting diversity. The IASC began deliberations in 1973 with representatives of nine charter countries and now has representatives of 89 accounting bodies from 60 different countries representing more than one million accountants.

The IASC methodology includes three steps: (1) the preparation of exposure drafts of proposed standards developed by a due process procedure used in the study of accounting issues; (2) analysis of written input from interested parties; and (3) the issuance of IAS. IASC had set 31 international accounting standards as of January 1, 1993. Figure 16–1 contains a list of IAS issued or proposed.

IASC Problems

The IASC selectively identifies the problem areas most in need of harmonization and then deals with them on as technical a level as is reasonably possible. A primary goal of IASC is that IAS will be enforced by the majority of nations with subsequent acceptance and enforcement to be implemented by individual nations on a voluntary basis. This enforcement object is fraught with problems. The leading industrial nations must recognize and enforce IAS if the adoption strategy is to be successful. Some nations have already agreed to adopt IAS as national standards, among these are Italy, Malaysia, Singapore, and Kenya. The French will also give IAS the same status as they give to domestically formulated standards. Regional accounting action groups, such as the Union Europeene des Experts Comptables, Economiques et Financiers, the Asociacion Interamericana de Contabilidad, and the Confederation of Asian and Pacific Accountants, operate around the world but have insufficient influence over international standards because of their regional orientation.[7]

The IASC would be successful if only the United States, United Kingdom, France, Germany, the Netherlands, and Japan were to recognize and enforce IAS. The global standard of quality in financial reporting and accounting has been set by the practice of the United States, United Kingdom, and the Netherlands alone. Adoption of IAS by only these three nations would be a giant step toward fulfillment of the objectives of IASC.

In the United States, the American Institute of Certified Public Accountants (AICPA) and the Financial Accounting Standards Board (FASB) play major roles in getting U.S. firms to accept IAS, although the latter organization has downplayed the importance of global standards.[8] Dennis Beresford, Chairman of FASB, has stated that globalization of financial markets is important because of capital mobility and the

---

[6] See Stephen L. Taylor, "International Accounting Standards: An Alternative Rationale," *Abacus* 23 (1987): 157–71.

[7] Slipkowsky, "The Bottom Line in European Accounting," 12.

[8] Dennis R. Beresford, "What's the FASB Doing About International Accounting Standards," *Financial Executive* 6 (May/June 1990): 17–23.

IAS No. 1   Disclosure of Accounting Policies (1975)

IAS No. 2   Valuation and Presentation of Inventories in the Context of the Historical Cost System (1975)

IAS No. 3   Consolidated Financial Statements (1976)

IAS No. 4   Depreciation Accounting (1976)

IAS No. 5   Information to Be Disclosed in Financial Statements (1976)

IAS No. 6   Accounting Responses to Changing Prices (1977)

IAS No. 7   Statement of Changes in Financial Position (1977)

IAS No. 8   Unusual and Prior Period Items and Changes in Accounting Policies (1978)

IAS No. 9   Accounting for Research and Development Activities (1978)

IAS No. 10   Contingencies and Events Occurring After the Balance Sheet Date (1978)

IAS No. 11   Accounting for Construction Contracts (1979)

IAS No. 12   Accounting for Taxes on Income (1979)

IAS No. 13   Presentation of Current Assets and Current Liabilities (1979)

IAS No. 14   Reporting Financial Information by Segment (1981)

IAS No. 15   Information Reflecting the Effects of Changing Prices (1981)

IAS No. 16   Accounting for Property, Plant, and Equipment (1982)

IAS No. 17   Accounting for Leases (1982)

IAS No. 18   Revenue Recognition (1982)

IAS No. 19   Accounting for Retirement Benefits in the Financial Statements of Employers (1983)

IAS No. 20   Accounting for Government Grants and Disclosure of Government Assistance (1983)

IAS No. 21   Accounting for the Effects of Changes in Foreign Exchange Rates (1983)

IAS No. 22   Accounting for Business Combinations (1983)

IAS No. 23   Capitalization of Borrowing Costs (1984)

IAS No. 24   Related Parties Disclosures (1984)

IAS No. 25   Accounting for Investments (1986)

IAS No. 26   Accounting and Reporting by Retirement Benefit Plans (complements IAS No. 19)

IAS No. 27   Consolidated Financial Statements and Accounting for Investments in Subsidiaries (amends IAS No. 3)

IAS No. 28   Accounting for Investments in Associates (amends IAS No. 3)

IAS No. 29   Framework for the Preparation and Presentation of Financial Statements

IAS No. 30   Disclosures in the Financial Statements of Banks and Similar Financial Institutions (1991)

IAS No. 31   Financial Reporting of Interests in Joint Ventures (1992)

Source: International Accounting Standards Board.

FIGURE 16–1 International Accounting Standards

speed of telecommunications but he believes that domestic markets are insulated from the impact of foreign market forces by national monetary policies and, since domestic accounting standards have been adopted in most countries, harmonization of global standards is not a short-run problem but is rather a long-term issue.

A major problem of acceptance of IAS can be demonstrated by the issue of which rules to use. This is an issue in many countries, particularly in the United States. For example, American firms can amortize goodwill over 40 years according to U.S. account-

ing standards, whereas proposed international standards would reduce this allowance to 5 years. U.S. firms are reluctant to accept such international standards. The same problem can be found for other national differences in accounting for mergers, inventory, and research and development costs.[9]

One significant problem that is an obstacle to IAS acceptance stems from the objectives of the major accounting standards setter in any given country.[10] For example, the FASB sets domestic standards in the United States. FASB is undecided whether to promote domestic or international standards. Three major differences can be cited between U.S. and IASC requirements. FASB standards cover more topics. The IASC has issued some 30 standards while the FASB has issued many more. FASB standards cover topics in greater depth while IASC standards are typically statements of broad principles. Finally, FASB standards are accompanied with a large body of common practice, which is an integral part of U.S. GAAP but which is not covered by formal pronouncements of standard setting bodies. No such body of international common practice is available.

MAJOR AREAS IN WHICH IAS ARE NEEDED

Research covering 1,000 companies in 24 countries found that financial reporting practices differ from one country to another.[11] Major differences were found in (1) consolidation practices, and (2) accounting for such miscellaneous areas as goodwill, deferred taxes, long-term leases, discretionary reserves, inflation, and foreign currency translation.

It is in these areas of accounting that a global framework for formulating and implementing accounting and financial reporting standards is needed. At least two reasons can be cited for such a system.[12] All MNCs require international accounting standards to insure that the results of each of their activities are recorded on a comparable basis. In other words, IAS insure that financial analysts do not compare apples with oranges. Second, financial statement users require IAS to insure that such statements are comparable and reflect the economic facts about the company regardless of its national origin.

STUDY AID

Consult the accounting faculty at your university or college for materials published by the IASC on international accounting standards. Familiarize yourself with the more than 30 standards promulgated by IASC and determine how many have been accepted in the United States.

---

[9] Roula Khalaf, "Esperanto for Accountants," *Forbes* 149 (March 2, 1992): 50.

[10] Dennis Beresford, "Internationalization of Accounting Standards," *Accounting Horizons* (March 1990): 99–107.

[11] Frederick D. S. Choi and Vinod B. Bavishi, "International Accounting Standards: Issues Needing Attention," *Journal of Accountancy* 155 (March 1983): 62–8.

[12] Thérèse Tremblay, "Toward Accounting Without National Boundaries," *CA Magazine* 119 (October 1986), 54.

Consolidation of Foreign Operations

OWNERSHIP OF VOTING STOCK IN A FOREIGN CORPORATION

The ownership of voting stock in a foreign corporation is generally handled in three different ways. The operation is valued on the parent's books at some cost, using the cost method, if the parent firm owns less than 10 percent of the foreign firm. If the parent firm owns between 10 and 50 percent of the foreign firm, the equity method is used, whereby the foreign operation is treated as equity owned by the parent firm and dividends are remitted based on this ownership interest. If the parent firm owns more than 50 percent of the foreign operation, the entire foreign operation is consolidated into the parent firm's books. The affiliate's income statement and balance sheet are translated into the parent firm's currency and reported as part of the parent firm. In some cases, firms will consolidate operations, domestic or foreign, with ownership interests of less than 50 percent.

Advantages of Consolidation

Foreign operations are consolidated because of a number of advantages to the MNC. Consolidation presents a more complete picture of the global firm and enables company analysts to better evaluate and plan operations. Hidden reserves can be more readily disclosed. Consolidation reduces secrecy, especially for tax authorities. Consolidated operations facilitate the implementation of companywide employee incentive programs. In summary, consolidation offers the MNC a more concise view of the firm's internal operations.

However, consolidation of foreign operations may be disadvantageous to the MNC. This function is a high cost operation that creates time pressures for top management. Deadlines for consolidation and subsequent reporting must be met. A more speedy reporting system is necessary but can be very costly. Differing accounting definitions from one country to another present problems. The severity of this problem has been reduced in recent years with the publication of booklets by Price Waterhouse, Ernst & Whinney, and other accounting firms that discuss and define various accounting terminology differences by country. Another problem of consolidation arises when the foreign operations must be translated into the parent firm's unit of account. Finally, the lack of international accounting standards hinders the process of consolidation.

The consolidation of foreign operations begs the questions of what, when, and why: *What operations should be consolidated? When should these operations be consolidated? Why should they be consolidated?* The issue key to the MNC in answering these questions may be the degree of centralization vs. decentralization practiced by the MNC and the type of international organization it uses.

Accounting for International Operations

Two areas of accounting for international operations are sufficiently different to merit discussion in depth. These involve accounting for price level changes and translation of foreign currency accounts.

PRICE LEVEL CHANGES

American firms operate under an accounting system that recognizes the concept of historical cost accounting. Thus, assets such as plant and equipment and inventory are val-

ued by the use of historical cost principles. The economic environment of many countries is fraught with high rates of inflation—hyperinflation in some countries. Replacement value accounting, or current cost accounting, is practiced in many countries to overcome the effects of creeping inflation as well as hyperinflation. FASB in the United States has only recently dealt with replacement value and still does not require firms to adjust their accounts according to their replacement or current value.

Next In, First Out

Some U.S. firms with operations in hyperinflationary economies have had to resort to internal managerial accounting practices, which may not be universally accepted or even legal. For example, Caterpillar has foreign investments in Brazil. Brazil has had periods of severe inflation. Caterpillar has used a NIFO—next in, first out—accounting method to value the inventory held by its foreign operation in Brazil. This method is not legal for tax reporting purposes but can be used in an advisory sense by management to control internal operations.

Replacement Value Theory

No country requires replacement value, or current cost, accounting but some firms in the Netherlands have been permitted to use such a system in the valuation of their capital assets. This practice stems from replacement value theory advanced by Professor Theodore Limperg.[13] Dutch firms using replacement value accounting include the electronics giant, Philips Lamp. The underlying principle of the Dutch form of replacement value accounting is that income cannot be earned unless the source of the income of the business, as a going concern, has been maintained.[14]

Replacement value accounting in the Netherlands involves an index composed of prices of a market basket of capital goods items. At the end of an accounting period, accountants calculate the new index of capital goods prices, apply the index to the company's capital assets, make the appropriate adjustments to account for the changes in the price level, and report the new capital asset values. Thus, the capital at the beginning of the accounting period has been maintained at the end of the period, regardless of the price level change. The rationale behind the practice of this accounting method in the Netherlands stems from the creeping inflation, which has been present in that country for several years.

N.V. Philips, the Dutch multinational, has fine-tuned replacement value accounting with adjustments to the methodology.[15] Under its system, balance sheet and income statements are justified. For example, standard costs of inventory are determined at the beginning of each year. An index is formulated by the purchasing department as prices change during the year and it is applied to the standard cost to yield the current cost. If price levels change more rapidly, the index may be prepared monthly or quarterly. The purchasing department also prepares indexes for fixed assets while the engineering department prepares them for specially designed items of equipment and the building design and plant engineering department prepares them for buildings.

TRANSLATION OF FOREIGN ACCOUNTS

When foreign accounts are consolidated, they must be translated into the parent firm's currency before they can be reported back to the parent. Accounts can be translated

---

[13] Jeffrey S. Arpan and Lee H. Radebaugh, *International Accounting and Multinational Enterprises* (New York: John Wiley, 1985), p. 63.

[14] A. Goudeket, "An Application of Replacement Value Theory," *Journal of Accountancy* 110 (July 1960): 37–47.

[15] See Adolf J. H. Enthoven, *Current Value Accounting: Its Concepts and Practice at N.V. Philips Industries, The Netherlands* (Richardson, TX: Center for International Accounting Development, 1982).

with either of two foreign exchange rates: the current rate, i.e., the rate in effect at the time the books are closed, and the historical rate, i.e., the rate in effect at the time the asset, liability, revenue, or expense was incurred or obtained.

The firms of most industrialized nations generally have not had a problem with translation of foreign accounts. They have translated all accounts at the current rate. However, U.S. firms, operating under an accounting system that recognizes historical cost accounting principles, have encountered problems because of the fact that some accounts were translated at the current rate while others were translated at the historical rate.

Before 1975, U.S. firms translated foreign currency accounts in the balance sheet with a number of different methods. Some used the current/noncurrent method in which all current assets and liabilities were translated at the current rate and all noncurrent assets and liabilities were translated at the historical rate. Some used the monetary/nonmonetary approach in which all monetary assets and liabilities were translated at the current rate and all nonmonetary assets and liabilities were translated at the historical rate. Some firms used the temporal approach, similar to the monetary/

FIGURE 16–2 Translation Methods Balance Sheet Items

| | *Translation Methods* | | | |
	Current/ Noncurrent	*Monetary/ Nonmonetary*	*Temporal/ FASB-8*	*Current/ FASB-52*
Assets				
Cash	C	C	C	C
Marketable securities:				
Carried at cost	C	C	H	C
Carried at current market price	C	C	C	C
Current receivables	C	C	C	C
Long-term receivables	H	C	C	C
Inventory				
Carried at cost	C	H	H	C
Carried at current replacement or selling prices	C	H	C	C
Carried at net realizable value	C	H	C	C
Carried at contract price	C	H	C	C
Prepaid expenses	C	H	H	C
Fixed assets	H	H	H	C
Permanent investments	H	H	H	C
Patents and intangibles	H	H	H	C
Liabilities and Capital				
Current liabilities and accruals	C	C	C	C
Other current liabilities	C	C	C	C
Long-term liabilities	H	C	C	C
Deferred income	C	H	H	C
Capital stock	H	H	H	H
Paid-in surplus	H	H	H	H

C = Closing rate of exchange.

H = Historical rate of exchange.

Source: Raj Aggarwal, "Analyzing Multinational Company Financial Statements: Role of the New Accounts Translation Standard," *Southern Business Review* 4 (Spring 1978):1–10.

nonmonetary approach except for inventory and appropriated earnings, which were both translated at the current rate. These methods are shown in Figure 16–2.

The temporal method had been formulated in an accounting research study commissioned by the Accounting Principles Board and was advocated as an approach that could be used to translate foreign accounts without changing the financial relationships of accounts.[16] Some firms used the "all current except plant" method in which all balance sheet items other than plant are translated at current rates and historical rates are used to value fixed assets. This was also known as the modified monetary/nonmonetary approach.[17] In addition, many European firms used the British method, also known as the current rate method, in which all balance sheet items were translated at the current rate.

The Current Rate Method

Analysts of the problem of foreign currency translation held that the current rate method was the better method. Most European companies used this method to translate their financial statements. Thus, they had few, if any, problems with translation exposure. However, in the United States, the concept of historical cost accounting seemed to mandate that some items such as inventories purchased some time ago and plant and equipment had to be translated at the historical rate.

The current rate method has three objectives.[18] They are: (1) to produce amounts that all conform with generally accepted accounting principles, e.g., inventories should be stated at the lower of acquisition cost or market after translation; (2) to retain in the consolidated financial statements the results and relationships in the domestic money financial statements of the foreign operation; (3) to produce information on the foreign operation that is compatible with the expected effects on the parent company's cash flows and equity of the changes in the foreign exchange rate between the money the foreign operation uses and the money in which the consolidated financial statements are stated. Only the third objective is helpful in accounting for foreign operations. The first two objectives are not helpful because they incorporate accounting for domestic operations in the presentation of foreign operations.

The current rate method has a basic advantage over other methods, particularly the temporal, or monetary/nonmonetary, method.[19] It recognizes the effects of a change in a foreign exchange rate on both monetary and nonmonetary items in the same reporting period. It does not, however, present all the effects in the income statement of the period, but rather directly into equity.

FASB-8

The use of different methods to translate foreign currency accounts by U.S. firms caused difficulty for financial analysts in their comparative analyses of companies, especially those in the same industry that used different translation approaches. In 1974, FASB issued an exposure draft of a new translation method for company comments. The new rule, FASB-8, was put into effect in 1975 and required corporations to translate all foreign denominated assets and liabilities into the dollar to reflect any gains or losses for each income quarter. These gains or losses were to be recorded in a firm's income statement. The temporal method, similar to the monetary/nonmonetary approach, was to be used. The translation rate used for each particular asset or liability should be the exchange rate in effect at the time to which the measurement basis of the

[16] Leonard Lorensen, *Reporting Foreign Operations of U.S. Companies in U.S. Dollars*, Accounting Research Study No. 12 (New York: American Institute of Certified Public Accountants, 1972).

[17] "FASB Statement 8." *International Currency Review* 9 (1977): 57.

[18] Paul Rosenfield, "Accounting for Foreign Operations," *Journal of Accountancy* 164 (August 1987): 109.

[19] Ibid.

asset or liability related. Assuming historical cost accounting, the temporal method is the same as the monetary/nonmonetary method. Monetary assets—cash, marketable securities, accounts receivable, long-term receivables—were translated at the current rate. All other assets and liabilities were translated at the historical rate.

The approach used by FASB-8 created several problems. Large volatility was injected into quarterly earnings reports. Companies were required to manage their foreign currency exposure more than they needed in the past. Much of the foreign exchange exposure management methodology discussed in chapter 4 was incurred at a high cost for expertise and organizational changes. Banks became involved with the formulation of foreign exchange exposure management schemes that they offered to U.S. MNCs, especially medium-sized firms most susceptible to credit rating reduction and loss of prestige from foreign exchange translation losses. In short, FASB-8 resulted in yo-yo effects on earnings reports, especially in the short-run.[20]

The key problem with FASB-8 was caused by the requirement that inventories and fixed assets had to be translated at historical rates, while all debt was translated at current rates.[21] Unrealized exchange adjustments were recognized in the determination of income, on a quarterly basis. A highly leveraged foreign affiliate might report a significant translation loss during a period when the dollar was depreciating, thus resulting in an accounting risk exposure. Little, if any, economic risk exposure might be generated if the debt, fixed in amount, was payable in foreign currency and from revenues generated by the foreign affiliate.

Furthermore, many companies changed their corporate policies in order to minimize translation risk.[22] These firms added to their debt costs by borrowing strong currency debt to replace foreign debt in cases where the foreign currency was expected to depreciate or to replace U.S. debt with foreign debt in cases where the foreign currency was expected to appreciate. Market rates of interest usually rise when currency devaluations are anticipated, thus resulting in higher debt service costs for these companies.

FASB-52

By 1980, FASB-8 had become the most controversial accounting rule promulgated in any country. The FASB introduced a new exposure draft for comment and hearings. FASB-8 hearings required one day for 13 presentations. FASB-52 hearings required four days to hear the 43 papers presented. The demands for a new translation method were so complex that a revised exposure draft was published for further written comments. Finally, in 1981, FASB-52 was issued, replacing FASB-8.

The new standard required that, in most cases, all assets and liabilities in foreign currency financial statements were to be translated at the current rate. With few ex-

---

STUDY AID

FASB-8, Foreign Currency Translation, became one of the most controversial accounting standards ever promulgated in the United States. Develop a bibliography of articles written during the 1975–80 period that discussed some of the problems encountered by firms when using FASB-8.

---

[20] Gaffney Feskoe, "Reducing Currency Risks in a Volatile Foreign Exchange Market," *Management Accounting* 62 (September 1980): 19–24.

[21] Donald T. Anderson, Robert B. Welker, and Donna Lynn Welker, "Foreign Currency Translation—Sweeping Changes," *The Ohio CPA Journal* 61 (Spring 1982): 91.

[22] Ibid., 92.

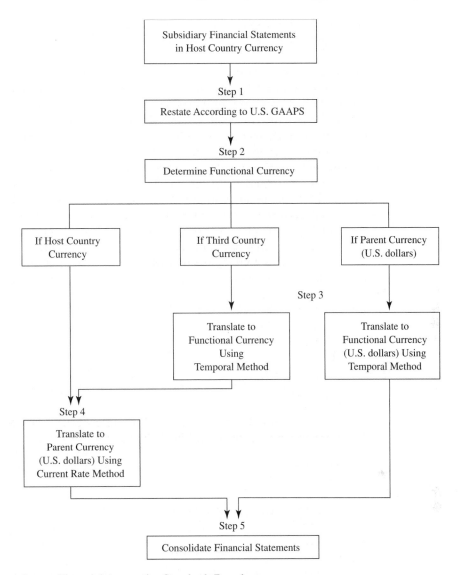

Source: Financial Accounting Standards Board.

FIGURE 16–3 A Flowchart Summary of FASB-52

ceptions, the adjustments resulting from such translations would be taken directly into a separate cumulative translation adjustment account in stockholders' equity rather than be reflected in income. The objective of the new standard was a reduction in large earnings fluctuations, which some companies had reported, and a reduction in hedging operations for some companies, which had been done in order to stabilize earnings. FASB-52 went into effect for all companies in 1982. Figure 16–3 contains a summary of FASB-52 in flow-chart form.

Under FASB-8, all assets, liabilities, revenues, and expenses denominated in a foreign currency were to be translated into the dollar. Under FASB-52, the financial results in effect before translation are preserved by using a foreign entity's *functional currency* to translate foreign currency accounts. Thus, a 3:1 current ratio in foreign currency will remain 3:1 in the home currency. Compatibility of exchange adjustments with the expected economic effect, not required under FASB-8, was an objective of

FASB-52. Under FASB-8, such compatibility could not be achieved without major changes in the basic historical cost accounting model.

The Functional Currency   As mentioned, FASB-52 requires foreign currency accounts to be translated using a functional currency. This may be the dollar, it may be the foreign affiliate's currency, or it may be a third country currency. Certain tests are available to facilitate the choice of functional currency. It presumably is the currency most used by the foreign affiliate in funding its operations and selling its goods or services.

If a foreign affiliate is merely an extension of the parent firm's domestic operations, the functional currency would be the reporting currency of the parent. FASB-8 rules would govern and any resulting gain or loss from the translation would be shown on the income statement. Normally, the functional currency is the currency of the economic environment in which cash flows are generated or expended by the foreign affiliate. It may be difficult to determine the functional currency in complex operations where the affiliate operates in many economic environments or with many currencies.

According to FASB-52, the following factors will support the use of a foreign currency as the functional currency[23]:

1. cash flows related to the foreign entity's individual assets and liabilities are primarily in the foreign currency and do not directly affect the parent company's cash flows;

2. sales prices for the foreign entity's products are not primarily responsive on a short-term basis to changes in exchange rates but are determined more by local competition or local government regulation;

3. an active local sales market exists for the foreign entity's products, although significant amounts of product are exported;

4. labor, materials, and other costs for the foreign entity's products or services are primarily local costs, even though imports are made from other countries;

5. financing is primarily denominated in foreign currency, and funds generated by the foreign entity's operations are sufficient to service existing and normally expected debt obligations;

MANAGEMENT APPLICATION NO. 28

Rouse Company

Many companies complained that FASB-8 misstated profit margins and inventory costs. Rouse Company, a developer of major shopping centers, had built two large shopping centers in Canada. More than 90 percent of their $60 million cost was financed with a loan from Canadian lenders with no recourse to Rouse. Under FASB-8 rules, Rouse had to translate its Canadian assets each quarter at their historical cost and translate the full amount of the loan at the current rate for the Canadian dollar. This caused large translation gains that boosted one bottom line quarterly report by ten times. Rouse believed the combination of nonrecourse Canadian debt and rental payments in Canadian dollars was a "natural hedge" against currency fluctuations. FASB did not permit Rouse to limit its exposure to only the company's equity investment so Rouse sold the properties. The company blamed FASB-8 requirements for the sale.

Source: "A Major Audit for FASB-8," *Business Week* (January 29, 1979): 102, 106.

---

[23] Richard Kochanek and Corine Norgaard, "Foreign Currency Translation SFAS No. 52 Requirements and Implications," *Akron Business and Economic Review* 16 (Summer 1985): 9.

6. the firm has a low volume of intercompany transactions, and no extensive interrelationship is present between the operations of the foreign entity and the parent firm; however, the foreign entity's operations may rely on the parent's or affiliate's competitive advantages, such as patents and trademarks.

Once the functional currency is determined, it is to be applied consistently unless changes in company operations dictate that it should be changed. The ability to decide on the functional currency gives management a choice, which FASB-8 did not do.[24]

Once the functional currency is chosen, all foreign assets and liabilities should be translated using the current rate as of the balance sheet date. Revenues, expenses, gains, and losses are translated at the current rate in effect on the dates these elements are recognized, essentially the weighted average exchange rate for the year.

In those cases where the functional currency is the dollar and records are maintained in foreign currency, the translation principles of FASB-8 are retained. FASB-52 contains a treatment of translation of foreign accounts in a hyperinflationary economy. If the cumulative inflation over the last 3-year period is more than 100 percent, the functional currency will be the dollar and the firm will revert to the FASB-8 rules.

Cumulative Translation Account   The gains and losses from translation will be carried to a special shareholders' equity account, the cumulative translation account (CTA), and will remain in this account until the company is sold, merged, or liquidated. Presumably, over the long-run, these translation fluctuations will not accumulate as all gains or all losses, otherwise, the equity value of the firm might change drastically over time. The current rate assumed is $1.835/£. An application of FASB-8 rules in translating the balance sheet of a firm is shown in Figure 16–4. Figure 16–4 shows that monetary assets and liabilities have been translated at the current rate whereas nonmonetary

	Balance Sheet Accounts (£ Sterling)	Exchange Rate	Balance Sheet Accounts (U.S.$)
Assets			
Cash	£ 1,000	$1.835	$ 1,835
Accounts receivable	2,000	1.835	3,670
Inventory	3,000	1.967	5,901
Land	1,300	1.784	2,319
Building-net	8,000	1.784	14,272
Equipment-net	7,000	1.784	12,488
Total assets	**£22,300**		**$40,485**
Liabilities and Stockholders' Equity			
Note payable/current	£ 1,000	$1.835	$ 1,835
Accounts payable	4,000	1.835	7,340
Notes payable–long-term	4,000	1.835	7,340
Deferred income taxes	2,000	1.835	3,670
Capital stock	4,000	1.784	7,136
Retained earnings	7,300	*	13,164
Total liabilities and stockholders' equity	**£22,300**		**$40,485**

* Retained earnings has been translated at various historical rates in each of the years it was acquired.

The average exchange rate for retained earnings amounts to $1.8033/£.

FIGURE 16–4 Modern Widgets PLC (temporal method—FASB-8)

---

[24] Ibid.

	Balance Sheet Accounts (£ Sterling)	Translation Currency Rate	Balance Sheet Accounts (U.S.$)
Assets			
Cash	£ 1,000	$1.835	$ 1,835
A/R—net	2,000	1.835	3,670
Inventories	3,000	1.835	5,505
Land	1,300	1.835	2,386
Buildings—net	8,000	1.835	14,680
Machinery & Equipment	7,000	1.835	12,845
Total assets	**£22,300**		**$40,921**
Liabilities and Stockholders' Equity			
Notes payable	£ 1,000	$1.835	$ 1,835
Accounts payable	4,000	1.835	7,340
Note payable—LT	4,000	1.835	7,340
Deferred income taxes	2,000	1.835	3,670
Capital stock	4,000	H	7,136
Retained earnings	7,300	H	15,599
Cumulative translation account			(1,999)
Total liabilities and stockholders' equity	**£22,300**		**$40,921**

H = historical exchange rate.

FIGURE 16–5 Modern Widgets PLC July 31, 1981 (current rate—FASB-52)

assets and liabilities have been translated at the historical rate, i.e., the rate in effect at the time these assets and liabilities were first entered in the balance sheet. See Figure 16–5 for an application of FASB-52 rules to the translation of a company's balance sheet. The current rate assumed is $1.835/£ and the historical rates for inventory, land, buildings, and capital stock vary according to the rate in effect at the time the assets were entered in the books. In Figure 16–5, only capital stock and retained earnings have been translated at the historical rate, according to FASB-52 rules, while all other assets and liabilities have been translated at the current rate. In addition, the gains and losses, in this case losses, have been included in the cumulative translation account introduced by FASB-52. Figures 16–6 and 16–7 contain examples comparing FASB-8 with FASB-52 translation, in this case the balance sheet and income statement of a German affiliate of a U.S. company. The loss from translation of these accounts is entered in the income statement under FASB-8, shown in Figure 16–7, and in the cumulative translation account under FASB-52, shown in Figure 16–6.

FASB-52 has resulted in a number of improvements in foreign currency translation for U.S. MNCs. The reporting requirements of FASB-52 are less than for FASB-8. Detailed aging records of plant and equipment are not needed. Also the recomputation of depreciation allowances over years based on historical rates is unnecessary. Financial managers have had the erratic effect on the income statement alleviated and have been released from some of the hedging requirements needed for floating exchange rates.[25] At each subsequent balance sheet date, balances denominated in any currency other than the functional currency should be adjusted to reflect

---

[25] Laurence J. Mauer, "MNCs Gain New Freedom Under FAS 52 Flexibility," *Management Accounting* 65 (December 1983): 30–3.

	In Foreign Currency	Statement No. 8		Statement No. 52	
		Translation Rate[1]	*In U.S. Dollars*	*Translation Rate*[1]	*In U.S. Dollars*
Current Assets					
Cash	DM 330,000	.5575	$ 190,575	.5775	$ 190,575
Accounts receivable	1,225,000	.5775	707,438	.5775	707,438
Inventories	1,500,000	.5676	851,400	.5775	866,250
Prepaid expenses	25,000	.5472	13,680	.5775	14,437
	3,080,000		1,763,093		1,778,700
Property, P&E					
Land	250,000	.4500	112,500	.5775	144,375
Buildings	1,200,000	.4500	540,000	.5775	693,000
Equipment	1,000,000	[2]	469,440	.5775	577,500
	2,450,000		1,121,940		1,414,875
Less accumulated depreciation	410,000	[2]	186,444	.5775	236,775
	2,040,000		935,496		1,178,100
Other Assets					
Notes receivable	125,000	.5775	72,187	.5775	72,187
Deferred charges	50,000	.4500	22,500	.5775	28,875
	175,000		94,687		101,062
	DM 5,295,000		$2,793,276		$3,057,862
Current Liabilities					
Accounts payable	DM 970,000	.5775	$ 560,175	.5775	$ 560,175
Income taxes pay	200,000	.5775	115,500	.5775	115,500
Current portion of long-term debt	400,000	.5775	231,000	.5775	231,000
Long-Term Debt—Less Current Portion	1,600,000	.5775	924,000	.5775	924,000
Deferred Income Taxes	60,000	[2]	31,349	.5775	34,650
Stockholders' Equity					
Capital stock	600,000	.4500	270,000	.4500	270,000
Paid-in capital	200,000	.4500	90,000	.4500	90,000
Retained earnings	1,265,000		571,252		551,370
Cumulative translation account					281,167
	2,065,000		931,252		1,192,537
	DM 5,295,000		$2,793,276		$3,057,862

[1] The current exchange rate at December 31, 1981, is .5775. All other rates used are historical rates.

[2] These balances are based on historical exchange rates.

Source: Ernst & Whinney, "Foreign Currency Translation," *Financial Reporting Developments* (October 1980):4.

FIGURE 16–6 Translation FASB-8 vs. FASB-52 Balance Sheet (overseas company—West Germany) (year ended December 31, 1981)

the current exchange rate. Figure 16–8 shows the journal entries that demonstrate these periodical adjustments. Assume the exchange rates for pound sterling for spot, 30-days, and 90-days are as reported in chapter 3, Table 3–1. Assume that on June 1, the American Gasket Company has purchased a new machine from a British exporter for £1 million, with payment to be made on September 1. The U.S. company's fiscal year ends on June 30.

	In Foreign Currency	Statement No. 8		Statement No. 52	
		Translation Rate[1]	In U.S. Dollars	Translation Rate[1]	In U.S. Dollars
Sales	DM 7,800,000	.5530	$4,313,400	.5530	$4,313,400
Other income	31,250	.5530	17,281	.5530	17,281
	7,831,250		4,330,681		4,330,681
Costs and Expenses:					
Cost of goods sold	6,200,000	[4]	3,376,140	.5530	3,428,600
General and adm.	65,000	[4]	354,656	.5530	359,450
Depreciation	150,000	[4]	69,444	.5530	82,950
Interest	220,000	.5530	121,660	.5530	121,660
	7,220,000		3,921,900		3,992,660
	611,250		408,781		338,021
Translation Loss			(50,878)		
Income b/income taxes	611,250		357,903		338,021
Income Taxes					
Current	290,625	.5530	160,716	.5530	160,716
Deferred	15,000	.5530	8,295	.5530	8,295
	305,625		188,892		169,010
Net income	305,625		188,892		169,010
Retained Earnings at January 1, 1981	1,259,375		546,520		546,520[2]
	1,565,000		735,412		715,530
Less Dividend Paid	300,000	.5472[3]	164,160	.5472[3]	164,160
Retained Earnings at December 31, 1981	**DM 1,265,000**		**$ 571,252**		**$ 551,370**

[1] The average exchange rate for 1981 is .5530.

[2] Assumes the current rate method was adopted as of January 1, 1981, and prior years' financial statements were not restated.

[3] Exchange rate on date dividend was declared.

[4] These balances are based, in part, on historical exchange rates.

Source: Ernst & Whinney, "Foreign Currency Translation," *Financial Reporting Developments* (October 1980):5.

FIGURE 16–7 Translation FASB-8 vs. FASB-52 Income Statement (overseas company—West Germany) (year ended December 31, 1981)

Although the international dimension of MNCs is better reflected by FASB-52, the new standard may, however, have created some problems.[26] The translation at current exchange rates of items that are local currency denominated and that entered the books at historical cost may cause results that are not meaningful descriptions of past cash flows or of future cash flows. Furthermore, the interpretation of the effects of translation may be confounded because these meaningless balances are consolidated with the parent firm's accounts. Finally, FASB-52 will necessitate increased centralization of the treasury management process, especially in three areas involving the functional currency.[27] These areas are: (1) the development of financial policies that are consistent with the selection of a functional currency, (2) the development of hedging strategies consistent with such a selection, and (3) the development of information sys-

[26] Thomas I. Selling and George H. Sorter, "FASB Statement No. 52 and Its Implications for Financial Statement Analysis," *Financial Analysts Journal* 39 (May–June 1983): 64–9.

[27] Frederick C. Militello, Jr., "Statement No. 52: Changes in Financial Management Practices," *Financial Executive*, 51 (August 1983): 51.

Assume the following exchange rates from chapter 3, Table 1, and that the forward rate becomes the future spot rate, according to the theories discussed in chapter 3:

$1.5424 = $1: spot rate on June 1
$1.5413 = $1: forward rate for July 1
$1.5392 = $1: forward rate for September 1

In June, the American Gasket Company purchased a special machine from a British manufacturer for £1 million, with payment to be made on September 1.

June	Equipment	$1,542,500	
	Accounts payable		$1,542,500
June 30	Accounts payable	1,200	
	Gain		1,200
September 1	Accounts payable	1,539,200	
	Cash		1,541,300
	Gain		2,100

FIGURE 16–8 Foreign Currency Transaction (journal entries under FASB-52)

tems and software compatible with the functional currency selection. The standard itself did not address the centralization issue adequately.

Problems with Translation

As the boxed discussion points out, problems are encountered in translating foreign currency accounts. These problems can be alleviated by accounting for foreign operations with one of the acceptable methods. Among the problems are[28]:

1. starting with domestic money financial statements that do not reflect the peculiarity of foreign operations;
2. accounting in one reporting period for only the beneficial or only the detrimental effect on the reporting entity of a change in a foreign exchange rate;
3. violating a rule of arithmetic;
4. incorporating more than one perspective in the information;
5. recognizing relevant effects of rate changes too late for the information to affect decision making;
6. dealing with accounting for foreign operations as merely a measurement conversion process.

Reporting Worldwide Operations

Once the foreign operations are consolidated into the parent's books and translated into the parent's currency of denomination according to some accounting rule, these accounts are reported to the parent firm. Firms report their global operations for several reasons. First, company objectives can be formulated on the basis of foreign operations that have been reported to the parent firm. Second, the parent firm can better control operations so that these objectives can be implemented. Third, the parent firm can spot departures from the objectives. Fourth, the parent firm can compare performances of foreign affiliates so that corporate resources will be economically allocated.

---

[28] Rosenfield, "Accounting for Foreign Operations," p. 110.

Fifth, reporting foreign operations enables the parent firm to acquire timely data so that long-range planning can be implemented.

The parent firm should analyze the characteristics of the data reported. The complexity of the data reported depends on the operations, organization, and management

---

MANAGEMENT APPLICATION NO. 29

ITT Corporation

ITT Corporation praised the FASB for replacing FASB-8 with FASB-52. At the time FASB-8 was in effect, ITT had 230 financial reporting units representing more than 950 legal entities, including over 600 operating locations in 80 different national environments on 7 continents. Its global sales were $23 billion, 53 percent in the United States and 42 percent in western Europe. It had $29 billion in assets, 61 percent in the United States and 33 percent in western Europe. Under FASB-8, ITT had a net exposed liability position amounting to $1.2 billion.[1]

The company included a footnote on foreign exchange in its 1980 annual report, which was virtually unchanged since the adoption of FASB-8. The footnote is as follows:

Foreign Currency Translation: Net assets are translated from foreign currencies into United States dollars at the rates of exchange in effect at year-end, except for inventories and certain other investments, deferred business development and policy acquisition costs, fixed assets and certain deferred taxes which are translated at historic rates.

Income accounts are translated at the average rates of exchange prevailing during the year, except for those accounts related to assets and liabilities translated at historic rates of exchange, which are translated at historic rates.

Including insurance and finance subsidiaries, net foreign exchange gains (losses) arising from the conversion of foreign currencies and the translation of balance sheet items are included in income as shown below (in thousands of dollars):

	1980	1979
Before minority interest and income taxes	$190,254	$(94,806)
After minority interest and income taxes	145,778	(81,850)
Per share	$1.00	($0.59)

In addition, translation of the 1980 income statement at average rates of exchange differing from those applicable to the prior year affected earnings adversely by $151,092,000 or $1.05 per share. Economic and operating consequences of the changing dollar relative to foreign currencies cannot be effectively quantified. If they could be, they might significantly alter these results.

Realized gains and losses and balance sheet translation caused a positive comparison of $1.59 per share over the 2 years, 1979 and 1980. When the effects of rate change is factored into the comparison of the two years, the differential is reduced to $0.55 per share. ITT reported net income of $6.12 per share in 1980 so foreign currency translation introduced a significant change into the final results.[2] ITT top management believed that the income fluctuations caused by FASB-8 were not understood very well by the financial community and were very confusing to company management.

The second quarter of the 1980 fiscal year caused much of the problem for ITT. Second quarter results "were severely affected by foreign exchange computations required by the Financial Accounting Standards Board. These, in effect, reduced reported earnings by $1.05 per share as compared with a reduction of $0.31 per share in the second quarter of 1979."[3]

---

[1]Raymond H. Alleman, "Why ITT Likes FAS 52," *Management Accounting* 64 (July 1982): 23–9.
[2]Ibid., 25.
[3]ITT, Second Quarter 1980 Report to Shareholders, August 6, 1980.

STUDY AID

Determination and use of a functional currency is one of the major differences between FASB-8 and FASB-52. Examine annual reports of leading U.S. MNCs to see whether any of these report what the functional currency is for translating their foreign currency operations and whether they report the factors they use to determine this functional currency.

---

philosophy of the company. A company with global operations in several countries that include direct investment in manufacturing facilities as well as sales and service outlets, joint ventures, a regional netting center, and licensing operations, will have to report more complex information to headquarters than will a firm that merely exports to sales representatives abroad. A firm that has organized its overseas operations on a product-by-product basis or a geographical basis will generally report more foreign operations information to headquarters than will a firm with an international division structure. A firm with a high threshold of risk in terms of political, interest rate, and foreign exchange risks, will probably report less information back to the parent than will a firm with a low threshold of risk.

The amount of foreign operations data reported will vary from firm to firm. How much data depends on the answer to the following question: *What are the critical data needs that must be met to implement with relative speed the policy decision to operate a business on a worldwide basis?* The key questions to be answered by top management in terms of what is reported from abroad are: *How much, when, to whom, and what kind of information is to be reported to the parent firm?*

The answers to these questions may encounter problems inherent in the local country in which the MNC is operating. Laws may dictate what data can be transmitted to the parent firm. Timing is an important characteristic of the reporting function.

Control, Evaluation, and Auditing

Evaluation and control are among the most important phases of any business function—marketing, production, finance, and administration. Successful operations will be very difficult for any firm that does not practice evaluation and control at each step of operations. In this and the following sections, the two phases of evaluation and control of financial management of the MNC will be examined. International auditing, its problems, and attempts to develop international auditing standards will be included in the discussion.

Foreign subsidiaries inherently have agency problems. Agency theory states that a firm's financial managers should serve the best interests of the shareholders. They are agents for the shareholders in the process of achieving the major objective of the firm—to maximize shareholder wealth. Agency problems are caused by the potential conflict between the goals of the managers and the shareholders. Thus, agency costs are incurred in the steps taken to assure that the managers make decisions that are in the best interests of the shareholders. Foreign subsidiaries operate far away from the managers at headquarters and in a different cultural and political system.

These agency problems inherent in the operations of foreign subsidiaries point out the importance of the implementation of a well-developed evaluation and control system. Top management must implement a control system capable of managing price

fluctuations in an inflationary environment and currency fluctuations in a volatile foreign exchange environment. The managerial aspects of organization and control of the international finance function are discussed in chapter 8 and in chapter 17 in organizing foreign operations to minimize corporate taxation. Thus, the emphasis in this chapter will be on control concerning inflation and foreign exchange fluctuations, although some aspects of the former were discussed in chapter 15 on working capital management and some aspects of the latter were discussed in chapter 4 on foreign exchange. In addition, evaluation of foreign affiliates and their operating profits will be examined. Finally, the chapter will conclude with a discussion of the problems and issues of international auditing, both external and internal.

CONTROL OF THE INTERNATIONAL FINANCE FUNCTION

MNCs must implement a viable control system in order to be successful in international operations. The two most distinct areas that a MNC must control in the international environment are: (1) operations in an inflationary environment, particularly when hyperinflation is rampant in the foreign location, and (2) operations in a volatile foreign exchange market.

The degree of control exercised by a MNC over its foreign subsidiaries has prompted questions for managerial analysis. First, when will a firm need to exercise more control, i.e., when do lower control outcomes become less desirable, and second, when will the benefits of increased control more than outweigh the costs of resource commitment and the inherent risk?[29]

Foreign operations can be controlled with expatriate managers sent from parent headquarters to implement appropriate controls at the foreign subsidiary. Such operations can also be controlled by accessing and analyzing information from the foreign subsidiary obtained from a lot of financial statements and other managerial reports. Generally speaking, firms will structure their control function so that it will promote asset utilization while minimizing risk. It has been hypothesized that a firm will exercise more control over proprietary products or processes. In fact, some firms do exert more control as proprietary content increases. For example, as research and development increases, the firm will license more of its processes and this will lead to more direct investment.[30]

Often this direct investment abroad is in the form of joint ventures. But as MNCs increase their experience with foreign investment, they tend to prefer wholly-owned subsidiaries, witness the U.S. auto manufacturers that eventually controlled 100 percent of their European subsidiaries. It is believed that the body of information about how a firm should operate foreign projects is difficult to transmit and, thus, the firm needs to learn by actually operating abroad.

Information

A vital ingredient of any control system is data, or information. In general, three phases of information systems dealing with data are necessary to implement financial control over international operations. These are collection of data, analysis of data, and storage of data. This data is needed for dissemination to government and government agencies, to shareholders and creditors, to labor, to other publics, and, primarily, to

---

[29] Hubert Gatignon and Erin Anderson, "The Multinational Corporation's Degree of Control over Foreign Subsidiaries: An Empirical Test of a Transaction Cost Explanation," *Journal of Law, Economics, and Organization* 4 (Fall 1988): 305–36.

[30] Ibid., 307.

management. Management needs information in the form of business projections, company budgets, expenditures, variances from the objectives, and the effects from inflation.

The acquisition of information for control purposes is fraught with many problems. Many users demand company information, as just mentioned. Distance between one operation and another may be large. Culture in the foreign location may impose serious hindrances for expatriate managers unaccustomed to practices quite different from their self-reference criterion (SRC). Statistical data gathered in many foreign countries may have inherent validity and reliability problems.

Finally, design of the reporting system may be a complex problem. The design will depend on the organizational structure of the corporation and the requirements of that structure. For example, a company with an international division structure often has personnel in the foreign field who make end runs around the international division and go directly to some other aspect of top management, e.g., finance, marketing, production, or personnel, instead of making inquiries of internationally oriented executives in the international division. Companies with a product structure of organization may have product experts in the field who need international advice but who do not communicate with the area specialists at company headquarters.[31] These organizational types for international companies were discussed in chapter 8.

Types of Reports

To facilitate an efficient information reporting system in a MNC, several reports will have to be transmitted from affiliates to parent headquarters. The corporate controller and treasurer combine to manage the finance function and each has reporting demands to be satisfied by foreign affiliates. For example, management reports will be sent to the corporate controller. These include reports on aging of accounts receivable, consolidated income and sales, consolidations, and numerous government reports. The latter may include foreign currency forms for the Department of Treasury and reports on foreign units for the Department of Commerce. The corporate treasurer will need reports on corporate finance including a cash forecast for the month ahead, a debt calendar, calculation of cash excess (deficit) for the month ahead, as well as reports on tax payments, pension payments, payroll, risk management, and shareholder records.

In addition, other units in the company may require reports from various foreign affiliates. Among these are pension plan history cards for new work entrants and employee stock purchase plan reports for the industrial relations area, dividend reinvestment plan and investor relations reports for the investor relations area, legal department reports, and other miscellaneous systems and data processing reports. The number of monthly reports needed to be filed by foreign affiliates to headquarters has been estimated to be in excess of 100 items, excluding reports at the subsidiary level only.[32]

The magnitude of reporting depends on a number of corporate factors. The determinants include the types of reports, e.g., several may be necessary on foreign exchange exposure only, how well the company controls the finance function, on changes in the corporation over time, and the design of the planning and control functions within the company's overall organizational structure.

---

[31] For a good discussion of these organizational problems, see the Coca-Cola Company case in Jeffrey S. Arpan and Lee H. Radebaugh, *International Accounting and Multinational Enterprises* (Boston: Warren, Gorham & Lamont, 1981), chapter on control and evaluation, pp. 291–322, especially pp. 298–302.

[32] Richard M. Hammer and Marianne Burge, *Accounting for the Multinational Firm* (New York: Financial Executives Institute, 1977), p. 244.

The Effects of Inflation and Currency Fluctuations and Their Control[33]

When a period of rising prices is encountered by foreign operations, assets valued at their original cost will generally understate the value of a foreign affiliate's investment base. Such undervaluation can cause a company's ROI (discussed in the next major section) to be overstated. Such overstatement could induce foreign managers to, for example, delay replacement of old equipment. New investments that reflect higher current replacement costs would typically reduce what would otherwise constitute a satisfactory return.

Using historical costs during inflationary periods may lead to overstatement of reported earnings because sales and depreciation charges are based on lower original asset valuations. Artificially high reported earnings can lead to unrealistic dividend policies, demands for higher wages, and unfavorable reactions by host governments.

Thus, accounting for inflation must be performed, for both internal and external reporting, as discussed earlier in this chapter. Historical revenues and costs for the operation should be converted to their purchasing power equivalents, per the Dutch method discussed earlier in this chapter. These costs can be multiplied by the ratio of the general price level index at the beginning of the period to the ending price index.

Finally, accounting for specific price changes can be implemented. The firm's original position can be adjusted, using appropriate and specific price indexes. For example, if the firm's inventory prices increase by 40 percent during the accounting period, this increase should be multiplied by the cost of goods sold in order to adjust this cost. The adjusted cost can then be subtracted from the current period's revenues in order to produce an inflation adjusted net income.

A Special Issue: The Foreign Corrupt Practices Act

During the 1970s, large U.S. companies including Lockheed, Northrop, and Gulf Oil paid large sums of money to high government officials in foreign countries such as Korea and Iran in order to close important deals including shipments of military equipment. These payments are common place in many countries and are an accepted form of business. In some countries, they are known as bribes and have their own nomenclature, e.g., *baksheesh* in the Middle East, "greasing the skids" in Mexico, and in Nigeria these payments are known as *dash*.

During the Carter administration, the U.S. Congress passed the Foreign Corrupt Practices Act (FCPA), a law passed in 1977. The hearings, during which this bill was considered, determined that more than 400 companies had made questionable or illegal payments amounting to more than $300 million during the preceding three years. Many of these payments were falsely recorded by U.S. companies involved. False record keeping was prohibited by the FCPA.

The FCPA contains accounting provisions that mandate a company to have internal controls that guard against[34]:

1. transactions that are not executed in accordance with general authorizations of management;

2. transactions that are not recorded as necessary to permit the preparation of financial statements in conformity with generally accepted accounting principles;

---

[33] For an elaboration of this topic, see Wendy L. Henry, "Foreign Subsidiary Evaluation: Methods and Considerations," (paper written for the International Financial Management course, Kent State University, Kent, OH, December 10, 1991) pp. 10–2.

[34] Thomas G. Evans, Martin E. Taylor, and Oscar J. Holzmann, *International Accounting and Reporting* (Cincinnati, OH: South-Western, 1994), p. 404.

3. access to assets permitted without general authorization of management;

4. lack of recorded accountability for assets that are compared with the listing assets at reasonable intervals and without appropriate action being taken with respect to any differences.

The law has become quite controversial. Criminal penalties are fairly severe for violations of the FCPA. Some payments are legal while others are illegal and companies have had legal costs increased to determine what payments are correct and within the FCPA. U.S. companies must compete against foreign companies headquartered in countries that permit questionable payments and bribes. During the April 1994–May 1995 period, the U.S. government has documented 100 cases in which U.S. firms lost contracts valued at $45 billion to foreign companies that pay bribes.[35] In December 1995, the U.S. government filed a request with the World Trade Organization to place the topic on the organization's agenda. Asian nations such as Indonesia denounced the idea. The Bank for Credit and Commerce International (BCCI), referred to earlier, was able to circumvent the laws of several countries in acquiring foreign banks and operating illegally by bribing government and banking officials.

EVALUATION OF FOREIGN SUBSIDIARY PERFORMANCE[36]

One of the major financial goals of any corporation is profit maximization. If such is the goal of a multinational corporation, then the company must have clear, measurable procedures for evaluating the profitability of overseas subsidiaries. In order to insure that parent company objectives are being met, periodic surveillance of foreign affiliates is necessary. Some type of internal performance evaluation system must be implemented to judge the profitability of foreign operations. Such a system will facilitate resource allocation decisions, the signalling of potential operating problems, and the evaluation of subsidiary managers.

Multinational corporations usually have many interrelated affiliates, which form an interconnected network. The parent can incorporate a number of measures to assess the performance of these foreign affiliates. When multiple criteria are used for this purpose, top management may pressure affiliate managers to improve one aspect of performance at the expense of some other objective. The two most common financial performance criteria available for assessment of overseas subsidiaries are return on investment (ROI) and budget comparisons. Some other criteria may include income or profit contribution, residual income, and cash flow analysis, but ROI and budgets are the best criteria.

Return on Investment (ROI)

ROI measurement offers a number of benefits to the parent firm. ROI relates company income with some specific investment base. The emphasis on ROI can keep managers aware of the need to use assets economically. In other words, it keeps them on their toes. Second, the ROI ratios for related and unrelated segments of the company can be compared with the company's cost of capital to insure that profitability exceeds the company's minimum required rate of return. Third, ROI is a rather simple, straightforward computation.

ROI does have its disadvantages. Its major problem is that it can be manipulated, i.e., the income or investment base can be manipulated by managers who want to look good. The future performance of the subsidiary can be jeopardized by the manipula-

[35] "Is Corruption an Asian Value?" *Wall Street Journal*, 6 May 1996, p. A14.
[36] Ibid., 1–9.

tion of ROI inputs in order to look good for the moment. Second, a number of questions also arise with regard to what items should be included in the calculation of ROI, which is the numerator of the ratio, and what items should be considered the investment base, or the denominator. Should the investment base be total assets, stockholders' equity, invested capital, or some other combination? Third, an argument has arisen with regard to whether net book value should be used for asset measurement purposes or whether gross book value should be used. If net book value is used, ROI may increase with just the passage of time, as depreciation reduces the investment base. If gross book value is used, managers may be motivated to scrap useful assets in order to increase their ROIs. Fourth, inflation levels may present problems for ROI. Managers must decide whether to restate asset values to reflect rising prices. Earnings as well as the investment base may be affected by these restatements. Failure to account for inflation may lead to an overstated ROI. Fifth, if ROI is used for internal comparisons, vastly different operations may have very different earning potentials and wide disparities in risk. Such factors are not often built into the ROI model. Sixth, if the parent company establishes one required ROI for all subsidiaries, this figure may have no relationship to the cost of capital in a particular country. The discussion of optimal financial structures and their effect on cost of capital in chapter 7 should be consulted. Finally, ROI may not be the most appropriate measure for some operations, especially if they were put in place for strategic reasons.

Budget Comparisons

Budget comparisons have been a popular means of foreign subsidiary evaluation. Budgets are estimates of the company's expectations of operating results. Actual results are then compared with the budgeted amounts and resulting variances are analyzed. These deviations may result in company changes in either the objectives or the operating factors.

Budgeting has become a significant input in both profit and strategic planning. Budgeting as an evaluative tool has its shortcomings. One of the most serious problems with budgets is that a realistic budget that is neither too ambitious nor too conservative is difficult to formulate.

MANAGEMENT APPLICATION NO. 30

Return on Investment

Assume the following financial statement information for a foreign subsidiary:

Assets		Liabilities & Net Worth	
Cash	FC 2,000	Current liabilities	FC 1,200
Accounts receivable	800	Long-term debt	3,200
Inventory	1,200	Net worth	3,600
Plant & equipment	4,000		
Total Assets	**FC 8,000**	**Total Liabilities & Net Worth**	**FC 8,000**

Assume that earnings before interest and taxes (EBIT) are FC 800. Interest rates in the local environment average 10 percent. Many companies compute return on investment (ROI) by computing the ratio of EBIT to plant and equipment, i.e., fixed assets, plus net working capital. Net working capital in this case is FC 2,800. Thus, if we calculate ROI in this manner, the result is 11.76 percent = ROI (FC 800 ÷ [FC 4,000 + FC 2,800]). To place this result in its proper perspective, it should be compared with similar ROIs of companies in that foreign environment. These figures may be available in publications from investment analyst firms.

Other Methods

Parent companies can use other methods to evaluate the performance of overseas subsidiaries. These methods include income or profit contribution, residual income, cash flow analysis, and nonfinancial analysis. These methods have their pros and cons. Income or profit contribution includes accounting information that may be misleading, because of the common practice of allocating corporate headquarters costs to subsidiaries. These allocations appear on the subsidiary's income statement and can reduce the level of net income for the subsidiary. Such information is useful if it is a supplement to other forms of evaluation, such as ROI or budget comparisons.

Residual income is equal to a foreign subsidiary's net income less an investment carrying charge equal to the affiliate's investment base multiplied by the company's cost of capital. It offers the advantages of ROI but has fewer disadvantages. It overcomes the limitations of net income or profit contribution analysis because it relates income to the investment costs of generating that income.

Financial Statement Analysis   Subsidiaries can be compared with other affiliates or with unrelated companies by means of financial statement analysis. Accounting firms and investment analysis in various countries have compiled average ratios that can be applied to the financial statements of companies in order to perform financial statement analyses.

Cash Flow Analysis   Cash flow analysis requires that a distinction be made between cash flows to the foreign operation and those to the parent. The former are determined much like those to the parent, except that additional elements of return should be included. Such returns to the rest of the company are made possible by the operations of the foreign affiliate. Cash flows to the parent are appropriate to use when evaluating the performance of a foreign operation.

Nonfinancial Analysis   Foreign subsidiaries can be evaluated by nonfinancial criteria. Examples of nonfinancial analytical tools are market share, personnel development, employee morale, and productivity measurements. These are usually combined with financial criteria to evaluate subsidiary operations. They reinforce financial criteria and can account for actions that may not contribute directly to profits in the short-run. The major disadvantage of nonfinancial criteria is that they may be subjective in character and difficult to quantify.

Foreign Exchange Considerations

These evaluations can be done in terms of local currency, home country currency, or both. Home country currency is generally used when the company's management is accustomed to thinking in terms of domestic currency. These managers place emphasis on profit in terms of domestic, and not local, currency terms. Home country currency also facilitates comparison of all subsidiary results. Steps in financial statement consolidation can also be saved, because the parent must translate foreign operation results before reporting to shareholders.

Foreign currency also has its usefulness in foreign subsidiary evaluation. Foreign subsidiary operations take place in the foreign environment and, thus, should be evaluated in terms of the currency of operations. If two or more currencies are used in performance evaluation, the budgeting process may become complicated. Foreign exchange rates must be used at two points in the operation when operating budgets are drafted, at the beginning of the period and at the end of the period. Actually, because of the time lag between the beginning of the budget period and the end, three exchange

rates have to be used. These are the spot rate at the beginning of the period, a projected future rate, and the spot rate at the end of the period. The use of each exchange rate has important implications that must be considered.

Some Conclusions

A number of control and evaluation systems have been used by MNCs to analyze the operations of their foreign subsidiaries. A number of studies have compared the methods discussed in the preceding sections. One study of 188 foreign affiliates of U.S.-based MNCs showed that budgetary comparisons and return on sales were the most important financial measures used to evaluate foreign subsidiary performance.[37] This study also examined the most preferred nonfinancial measurements used by foreign managers to analyze foreign subsidiary performance. The most important of these were customer satisfaction, growth in market share, and quality concerns.

AUDITING

Auditors perform the attest function in financial reporting by reviewing the financial information reported by the company and attesting to its reliability, fairness, and truthfulness. Without the audit function, financial information produced by any firm would lack credibility.

Users

Many users rely on company audits to verify financial information. These include investors who are considering capital investments in the company. They include tax authorities at local, state, and federal levels of government who require such information to be truthful for the purpose of levying the proper taxes. Various levels of management in the company use audited financial information in order to evaluate performance and efficiently allocate scarce resources. Such information is a necessary ingredient in conceptual areas such as agency theory, information economics, the demand for and the supply of audits, and for the measurement and management of various risks in the company.[38]

Each country has its own auditing standards. These standards are determined by a number of factors, including the growth and development of accounting practices in each country, the number of accountants—especially those who specialize in auditing—and the amount of commercial transactions carried out in the country. These factors are all predicated on the stage of economic development as well as accounting development present in the country.[39] For example, Japan is a highly industrialized country. However, because of the inadequacy of professional auditors, government agencies may use company auditors to perform audits needed by the agencies. Thus, an apparent conflict of interest may be involved in obtaining useful company information for various public uses.

Audit standards may differ from country to country but in the United States, Canada, Germany, the Netherlands, the United Kingdom, Japan, Norway, and Sweden, they are quite similar. These countries require audits to be performed by independent public accountants. However, in some countries such as Japan, the company

---

[37] Lawrence Peter Shao, "Comparative Analysis of Foreign Performance Measures Employed by U.S. Subsidiaries," *Journal of Global Business* 5 (Spring 1994): 37–45.

[38] See W.A. Wallace, *The Economic Role of the Audit in Free and Regulated Markets* (New York: Touche Ross & Co., Aid to Education Program, 1980).

[39] For a good analysis of the international auditing environment, see Frederick D.S. Choi and Gerhard G. Mueller, *International Accounting* (Englewood Cliffs, NJ: Prentice-Hall, 1984), pp. 329–38.

auditors may also perform audits of the same company for the government, as just mentioned. In some developing countries, auditors from the parent company's home country who perform audits of the parent company may perform audits of the foreign subsidiary.

Auditing procedures may differ from country to country. Trade accounts receivable are confirmed and physical inventory counts are taken by auditors in the United States but, in Europe, these procedures are generally not performed. In some Latin American and European countries, some companies have problems in verifying their disbursements because canceled checks become the property of banks and may not be returned to the companies that issued them.

The internal auditor of foreign accounts incurs other problems in general. These include adaptation to very different local business practices and customs, restrictions incurred from working in a foreign currency and foreign language, and geographic distance between the parent company and the foreign affiliate.

Certification of auditors differs from country to country. Even in countries where high auditing standards have been promulgated, they are worthless if they are not implemented. In some countries, such as Peru, a college degree in accounting qualifies a person to be an auditor. This standard is also true in Indonesia except that the individual must have worked for the government for at least three years. In the United States, each state has its own certification procedures with regard to education and experience coupled with a common licensing examination administered by the American Institute of Certified Public Accountants. An auditor in Germany must have a background similar to that in the United States and usually has a degree in commerce, law, engineering, or economics. Almost anyone, regardless of qualification, may become an auditor in Switzerland whereas a fairly rigorous examination must be passed in France. In the United Kingdom, an auditor must have worked for a chartered accountant and passed a series of examinations. Many countries do not permit an auditor to practice locally if they are not licensed in that country. Foreign auditors sometimes have trouble qualifying to audit local companies. Reciprocity is still a problem in international auditing in some countries.

Audit Opinions

Audit opinions found in company annual reports and other financial statements may differ from country to country. In the United States, the audit opinion is usually rather long and states that the opinion is based on generally accepted accounting principles. These principles may even be defined in detail. In contrast, in some countries, the audit opinion is quite brief, perhaps only a paragraph, as in German companies' annual reports, and refers to the opinion being based on the auditor's professional standards. In other countries, the opinion may state that the audit has been performed in accordance with relevant laws and regulations, as well as generally accepted accounting principles. For example, the 1995 Annual Report of Fokus Bank in Norway states that the opinion was prepared in accordance with the Joint Stock Companies' Act.

International Auditing Standards

IFAC Attempts have been made for at least two decades to harmonize auditing standards. As with international accounting standards and the International Accounting Standards Committee, an international organization comprised of practicing representatives is charged with harmonization in the area of international auditing. This is the International Federation of Accountants (IFAC), which is empowered to formulate and issue so-called guidelines regarding international auditing issues. These guidelines do not override local regulations but they apply whenever an independent audit is carried out.

UEC   In addition, the Union Européenne des Experts Comptables Economiques et Financiers (UEC), a European organization, formed in 1951 and located in Paris, has also been instrumental in the trend toward international auditing standards. UEC, through its Auditing Statements Board, issues auditing statements, not standards or guidelines, and its work is recognized as a relatively strong international accounting body by the European Community and IFAC. The work of IFAC and UEC in the harmonization and formulation of international auditing standards has produced quite similar rules and has strengthened the field of auditing on a global basis as well.

The Audit Function

Two types of audits are practiced. Internal audits are performed by company accountants for the purpose of attesting to the financial information and other performance data reported by various divisions of the firm. These can deal with foreign environmental problems, foreign exchange restrictions, and a whole host of operations of foreign affiliates, including payments made that might be subject to the Foreign Corrupt Practices Act of 1977, which prohibits bribes, political contributions, or even extortion. External audits are those made by an independent accounting or auditing firm for some of the same purposes covered by internal audits or to facilitate conformance by the company with local or national legal requirements.

Foreign Audit Fees

Fees charged for foreign subsidiary audits have risen sharply during the past 20 years. Audit fees are like any other cost, they delete from the profitability of the firm and should be minimized wherever possible. Audit fees have risen because of inflation, expanded foreign operations, and the increasing complexity of operating in the international business environment. As professional fees, their amount is not questioned in many countries. Thus, the parent company must take the initiative to encourage local subsidiary management to control audit fees.

Management should examine the five distinct areas in which it can control the costs of audits. First, the parent company should review the corporate structure. For example, if a company has more than one subsidiary in a single country, these affiliates could be combined into one company for reporting purposes. It should not matter if the affiliates are in different lines. Thus, internal accounting control and materiality limits can be increased. The larger the company is, the greater will be adequate internal accounting control. Materiality benefits stem from the fact that various accounts of the combined enterprise will contain larger amounts. Such combination will result in a larger universe from which the auditor can select transactions for testing. For example, one company might have 3,000 accounts receivable that require only 80 to be selected for audit in order to get the same assurance as if the company had three subsidiaries with 1,000 accounts receivable in each and some 200 overall audits.

A second area in which the firm can control foreign audit fees is to conform the subsidiary's accounting principles with those of the parent. The accounting system used by the subsidiary must be consolidated with the parent's accounts. Although local statutory accounts may have to be followed, the subsidiary can follow U.S. GAAP in preparing them. Extra audit time may be required if, for example, the foreign affiliate records fixed assets at appraised values, or fails to provide a tax allocation by the deferred method, or other rules according to U.S. GAAP are not followed. More time will be required for the auditor to rearrange the accounts.

A third method that can result in lower foreign audit costs might be for the parent to encourage foreign affiliates to prepare the reports, using the same forms year after year. The auditor might then be limited to performing only the review and approval. Thus, report preparation costs can be accomplished at a lower cost using the local staff rather than the cost charged by professional auditors.

Another method that can result in lower audit fees is to coordinate the foreign audit function with parent company auditors. The issue is whether to use parent company auditors or a foreign auditor in the foreign country. The parent company auditor will probably use a U.S. format of a formal set of audited accounts. This is a luxury. However, the foreign auditor is not in a position to determine materiality vis-á-vis consolidated accounts and, thus, may do more than is necessary during the audit. The parent company can issue instructions to the foreign affiliates on how to handle this issue. Many firms have combined parent auditors with foreign country auditors. The parent auditors will know company policy to a greater extent than will local auditors but the latter will have the advantage of working in their native language.

Finally, the company can better control foreign audit fees by becoming very familiar with their foreign auditors. This can be accomplished by more face-to-face contact with the foreign auditor. Internal control memoranda and management reports on each foreign affiliate can be distributed to all the others. Auditors can be required to attend regional controllers meetings or visit corporate headquarters more often. When dealing with auditors in LDCs, the parent firm can often take advantage of foreign exchange controls by using national airlines of the local country.

One case history of international auditing in a company showed the adoption of specific company policies developed by the internal audit department for audits of international operations.[40] For example, English-language auditors were used in English-speaking countries while the company's Latin American operations were audited by bilingual employees. The company found it necessary to sell the foreign managers on the benefits of audits. Foreign plant managers and accountants had to be informed that internal auditors were the specialists in this area and that their recommendations had to be followed. The company developed an internal audit plan for foreign operations, which contained the following:

1. a study of the culture and customs of countries visited by internal auditors;
2. employment of people who are able to work completely and competently on an independent basis because of the unstructured atmosphere of the audit staff outside North America;
3. use of auditors who are good businesspersons so that they are able to cope with flexible business situations;
4. added status for international auditors by giving them calling cards, first-class air travel, first-class hotels, etc.;
5. having auditors who are well informed about home office operations;
6. sending a top accounting official from the home office to attend the audit review with local management;
7. mandatory written answer to the audit report from the foreign affiliate's management;
8. complete flexibility in the foreign operation in order to be able to perform a quick re-review of the operation.

Again it is important to determine whether the audit should be done by a home-based auditor, a foreign national resident auditor, or an expatriated resident auditor. An efficient international audit may demand a mix of these alternatives.

---

[40] John W. Parker, "International Auditing: A Case History," *The Internal Auditor* (November/December 1975): 63–6.

Summary and Conclusions

Accounting systems differ from country to country. A global GAAP is not yet fully practiced on a global basis. Some attempts have been made to standardize international accounting principles and practices. The work of the International Accounting Standards Committee as well as the major professional accounting societies in the United States, Europe, and Japan have contributed to the attempt to formulate a set of international GAAP.

The most important differences in accounting are found in the areas of consolidation, accounting for foreign operations, and reporting foreign operations. Translation of foreign currency accounts has been especially important in the United States where FASB-8 became the most controversial accounting standard ever promulgated. It was replaced by FASB-52 in the early 1980s. Replacement value accounting has caused some controversy in its practice in other countries, especially the Netherlands. A major obstacle to replacement cost accounting in the United States is the adherence to historical cost accounting principles practiced in this country.

Reporting foreign operations is a costly function but must be done in order for users of financial and accounting data to analyze the entire company including its global operations. Reporting of foreign operations requires a speedy and costly system. The amount of data reported varies from firm to firm but top management must answer the questions of how much to report, when to report, to whom to report, and what kind of information to report in order for the reporting system to be successful.

Finally, the function of international auditing must be taken seriously by MNCs. The financial information reported by foreign affiliates to the parent firm must be reviewed and attested for its reliability, fairness, and truthfulness. The auditor adds credibility to the financial information produced by the firm for the many users of such data.

Thus, international auditing standards and practices are necessary. Organizations such as the International Federation of Accountants and the Union Européenne des Experts Comptables Economiques et Financiers issue guidelines or statements that harmonize international auditing standards.

Additional Readings

Al-Hashim, Dhia D., and Jeffrey S. Arpan. *International Dimensions of Accounting*. Boston: Kent Publishing Co., 1992.

Arpan, Jeffrey S., and Lee H. Radebaugh. *International Accounting and Multinational Enterprises*. New York: John Wiley, 1985.

Choi, Frederick D. S., and Gerhard G. Mueller. *International Accounting*. Englewood Cliffs, NJ: Prentice-Hall, 1992.

Enthoven, Adolf J. H. *Current Value Accounting: Its Concepts and Practice at N. V. Philips Industries, The Netherlands*. Richardson, TX: Center for International Accounting Development, 1982.

Lorensen, Leonard. *Reporting Foreign Operations of U.S. Companies in U.S. Dollars, Accounting Research Study No. 12*. New York: American Institute of Certified Public Accountants, 1972.

Nobes, Christopher W., and Sidney J. Gray. *Comparative International Accounting*. Deddington, UK: Philip Alan Publishers, 1991.

Radebaugh, Lee H. "International Accounting." In *The WG&L Handbook of International Finance*. Ed. Dennis E. Logue, Cincinnati, OH: South-Western, 1995.

Selling, Thomas I., and George H. Sorter. "FASB Statement No. 52 and Its Implications for Financial Statement Analysis." *Financial Analysts Journal* 39 (May–June 1983): 64–9.

Taylor, Stephen L. "International Accounting Standards: An Alternative Rationale." *Abacus* 23 (No. 2, 1987): 157–71.

Walker, R. G. "International Accounting Compromises: The Case of Consolidation Accounting." *Abacus* 14 (December 1978): 97–111.

Discussion Questions

1. Discuss the state of uniform international generally accepted accounting principles.
2. Why, until the recent listing of Daimler Benz, have German companies never listed their shares on organized securities exchanges in the United States?
3. How will the listing of Daimler Benz on the New York Stock Exchange affect other German companies that elect to list their shares on U.S. exchanges?
4. Discuss the barriers to uniform international generally accepted accounting principles.
5. What is the International Accounting Standards Committee? How does it formulate international accounting standards? How are these standards enforced?
6. What are the advantages to consolidation of foreign operations by a multinational corporation?
7. What is replacement value theory? Discuss how it is implemented. Why is its practice not very feasible in the United States?
8. Compare and contrast FASB-8 and FASB-52.
9. What is the temporal approach to foreign currency translation? Discuss in detail.
10. How is the functional currency selected in FASB-52?
11. Why was FASB-8 such a controversial accounting standard?
12. What problems confront an international company in reporting worldwide operations?
13. What are the three phases of an optimal information system?
14. Discuss the problems with regard to information needs of the firm.
15. What are some of the differences between internal and external audits?
16. Discuss the methods for evaluating foreign affiliates.
17. How should the comparative performance of domestic and foreign subsidiaries be measured and evaluated?
18. Compare and contrast the return on investment method with comparative budgeting as means to evaluate foreign operations.
19. What can be done to reduce the relative high cost of audits of foreign affiliates? Why are these costs high?
20. What is the role of the International Federation of Accountants in international auditing?
21. Compare and contrast the international standards set by the IASC with the guidelines drafted by IFAC with the statements formulated by UEC.
22. Why do financial statements differ that are issued by companies based in different countries?

Problems

1. Compare and contrast international auditing guidelines formulated by the International Federation of Accountants with similar standards promulgated by American accounting organizations.

2. Compare and contrast international accounting standards approved by the International Accounting Standards Committee with standards set by the Financial Accounting Standards Board in the United States.

3. Choose any one of the U.S. top 100 companies worldwide, as measured by some standard such as *Fortune Magazine*, determine which are its two leading foreign subsidiaries, located in two different countries, and determine what the parent firm uses as functional currency under FASB-52.

4. The Schmidt Stahlwerke AG is a wholly-owned subsidiary of a U.S. firm. Its balance sheet is as follows

Assets		Liabilities & Net Worth	
Cash	DM 12,000	Accounts payable	DM 36,000
Accounts receivable	24,000	Long-term debt	48,000
Inventories	36,000		
Fixed assets, net	72,000	Stockholders' equity	60,000
Total assets	**DM 144,000**	**Total liabilities**	**DM 144,000**

According to Table 1 in chapter 3, the spot exchange rate is $0.6333 to DM 1.

a. Translate the deutsche Mark balance sheet of Schmidt Stahlwerke AG into dollars at the current exchange rate of $0.6333 = DM 1. All monetary accounts in Schmidt's balance sheet are denominated in deutsche Marks.

b. Assume the deutsch Mark revalues from $0.6333 = DM 1 to $0.6733 = DM 1. What would be the translation effect if Schmidt's balance sheet were translated by the current/noncurrent method? By the monetary/nonmonetary method?

c. Assume that the mark devalues to $0.60. What would be the translation effect under each of the two methods?

d. Assume the abovementioned information. What would be the translation effect if Schmidt's balance sheet were translated by the temporal method under FASB-8 assuming a mark revaluation of 25 percent? What would be the translation effect if translated by the current rate method? Show the effects if translated by the rules of FASB-52.

e. Assume that the mark depreciates by 20 percent. What would the translation effects be under both the temporal method and the current rate method?

5. Smith Industries S.A. is a U.S. subsidiary located in Mexico City and uses FIFO to account for its inventories. The parent company translates its inventories at the current rate. Year-end inventories are recorded at Mpeso 172,100. During the year, the replacement cost of inventories increases by 30 percent. Inflation and exchange rate information were as follows

$$\text{January 1:}\quad \text{Commodity price index} = 100$$
$$\$1 = \text{Mpeso } 2.77$$
$$\text{December 31:}\quad \text{Commodity price index} = 130$$
$$\$1 = \text{Mpeso } 3.37$$

On the basis of this information, calculate the dollar current cost adjustment for cost of sales while avoiding a "double charge" for inflation.

6. Assume that Company X has a foreign subsidiary with the following balance sheet data

Assets		Liabilities & Net Worth	
Cash	FC 1,000	Current liabilities	FC 600
Accounts receivable	FC 400	Long-term debt	1,600
Inventory	600		
Plant/equipment	2,000	Net worth	1,800
Total assets	**FC 4,000**	**Total liabilities & net worth**	**FC 4,000**

Calculate the return on investment for this subsidiary. If this is a Spanish affiliate, compare and evaluate the result, using published data.

7. Choose one of the international accounting standards formulated and approved by the International Accounting Standards Committee. By consulting accounting publications, especially those issued by the Financial Accounting Standards Board or IASC, prepare a flow chart showing how a specific accounting issue reached the IASC agenda and eventually became an IAS. How long did it take for this issue to be selected by IASC and for an IAS to be issued?

8. The balance sheet for a German subsidiary of a U.S. firm and its translation into U.S. dollars at the current exchange rate of $0.60 per German mark is shown below.

German Subsidiary Balance Sheet and Translation

	DM	*DM = US$0.60*
Cash	3,000	$ 1,800
Accounts receivable	7,000	4,200
Inventory	30,000	18,000
Fixed assets	70,000	42,000
Total assets	**110,000**	**$66,000**
Accounts payable	10,000	$ 6,000
Long-term debt	50,000	30,000
Equity	50,000	30,000
Total debt and net worth	**110,000**	**$66,000**

a. What is the U.S. firm's exposure under three alternative translation methods: the current/noncurrent method, the monetary/nonmonetary method, and the current method?

b. The U.S. firm anticipates that the mark will depreciate to $0.50. Construct pro forma U.S. dollar translations of the balance sheet at this new exchange rate for the mark under each of the three alternative translation methods.

c. Relate the change in the equity account found in part (b) for each of the three methods to the exposure calculations in part (a).

9. Assume a French subsidiary of a U.S. company has the following: (1) cash = Ffr 2,000, (2) accounts receivable = Ffr 3,000, (3) inventory = Ffr 4,000, (4) fixed assets = Ffr 5,000, (5) current liabilities = Ffr 2,000, (6) long-term debt = Ffr 6,000, (7) net worth = Ffr 6,000, and (8) net income before translation gain or loss = Ffr 800. Further assume that the historical exchange rate is $0.25 per French franc, the current exchange rate is $0.20 per French franc, the average exchange rate is $0.225 per French franc and inventory is carried at cost.

a. prepare the balance sheet of the U.S. subsidiary in France;

b. determine the dollar net income without the translation gain or loss;

    c. determine the translation gain or loss under both FASB-8 and FASB-52;

    d. if the functional currency is determined to be the U.S. dollar, which translation method should be used? And what would be the impact on the parent company's net income?

    e. compute the French franc current ratio, return on investment, and long-term debt-to-equity ratio. Compare these ratios with the ratios in dollars under both FASB-8 and FASB-52.

10. The following is the current year-end balance sheet of a foreign subsidiary of the Toasted Oats Cereal Company, a U.S.-based MNC, stated in local currency

Toasted Oats Cereal Company Balance Sheet
Fiscal Year June 30, 1996
(in thousands of LC)

Cash	LC 400	Current liabilities	LC 300
Current receivables	400	Long-term debt	2,400
Merchandise inventory	500	Common stock	1,050
Long-term receivables	450	Retained earnings	0
Net fixed assets	2,000		
Total assets	**LC 3,750**	**Total liabilities and net worth**	**LC 3,750**

This foreign affiliate has operated at breakeven ever since it was acquired by Toasted Oats Cereal Company. The LC has been a stable currency since then, at the rate of LC 1 = $1.00. Suppose, however, foreign currency traders forecast that the exchange rate will decline to LC 1 = $0.90.

Calculate, in dollars, the expected translation gain or loss (or adjustment), using the following translation methods

    a. the current/noncurrent method;

    b. FASB-8;

    c. the current rate method, i.e., FASB-52 (assume the LC is the functional currency).

Taxation of International Operations

Major Objectives of Chapter 17

(1) To introduce the differences in taxation from one country to another, (2) to examine the foreign tax credit as a tool for tax reduction, (3) to analyze the various tax benefits available to the MNC, and (4) to demonstrate how companies can organize and manage international taxation as just another cost of operations.

Key terms to be learned in chapter 17:

- separate system
- territorial assertion
- foreign tax credit
- foreign sales corporation
- foreign base company
- Subpart F

- partial integration system
- worldwide assertion
- foreign tax deferral
- possessions corporation
- tax haven
- unitary taxation

Introduction

Taxation of multinational corporate operations is a very complex element and, to many MNCs, a very troublesome cost of doing business internationally. Taxes represent just another type of expense or cost of operations. However, the taxation of business operations can have a great deal of influence on how and where the firm does business. The tax laws of a nation can influence where the firm decides to invest. The type of organization—joint venture, holding company, highly decentralized, highly centralized—can be influenced by national tax laws. The firm can be influenced in how it finances for-

453

eign investments. Domestic and foreign tax laws can dictate the form taken in setting transfer prices. Viewing the international tax problem from the other side of the coin, most nations are extremely sensitive about their sovereignty when the subject is about taxation, particularly in the global environment in which most nations are under pressure to reduce budget deficits and taxation of their citizens.

The primary company objective with taxes, as with any other expense, is to minimize their payment. Tax laws from one country to another, or from one subdivision of a country to another, are often vague in their interpretation. The tax authority may have one opinion about a certain tax and the company executive may have another opinion. Tax laws may change quite frequently, even though new tax laws or revisions of the existing tax code may take long periods of legislative debate before they are passed into law. International tax attorneys are few in supply but they are constantly in demand by MNCs.

It, therefore, is a major objective of the MNC to coordinate and manage both domestic and foreign tax burdens. The more globally spread out the company, the more complicated are the issues. The bottom line for MNCs is to reduce foreign taxes as much as possible while avoiding controversy abroad as much as possible.

Overview of International Taxation

HOW MULTINATIONAL BUSINESS IS TAXED

MNCs are taxed differently from one country to another. Tax rates may be different from one country to another, and variations in the entire corporate tax system may exist from one country to another. The definition of taxable profits, deductible expenses, and creditable items may be different from one country to another. As corporate funds crisscross national borders, withholding taxes and relief from double taxation may differ from one country to another. Table 17–1 includes a list of income and withholding tax rates in effect in several foreign countries. These are statutory tax rates in each of the countries and may not be similar to tax rates imposed by these same countries against U.S. firms operating in their countries. Bilateral tax treaties have been enacted between the United States and several other countries. These treaties will be discussed in a subsequent section. Such tax rates are shown in Table 17–2 and are significantly lower than the statutory rates in many cases.

NATIONAL TAX SYSTEMS

A variety of tax systems are practiced around the world. These systems govern the extent to which distributed or retained earnings are taxed and how extensive is a nation's tax jurisdiction. Some countries make no distinction between retained and distributed profits when levying taxes. They practice a *separate system* and levy a corporate income tax on all profits, whether retained or distributed. The United States uses this system and also taxes dividends received by the investor. Thus, these earnings are double taxed. This is also referred to as the classical system for integrating company and personal taxes.

Other countries make some distinction between retained and distributed earnings, but the degree may differ from country to country. Germany practices a form of the *partial integration system*, the split rate system or company two rate system, by levying a lower tax rate on distributed profits than on retained earnings. Another form of the partial integration system, the *shareholder imputation system*, is practiced in Austria, Canada, France, and Korea, among others. Under this system, the same tax rate is

	Domestic Income	Foreign Income	Dividends	Interest	Royalties
Country					
Europe					
Belgium	39	19	25	25	10
Denmark	40	40	30	0	0
France	34	34	25	45	33
Germany	35	35	35	35	35
Greece	34	34	30	30	30
Ireland	43	43	0	30	30
Italy	36	36	32	12	21
Netherlands	35	35	25	0	0
Norway	51	51	25	25	0
Spain	35	35	20	20	20
Sweden	30	30	30	0	0
Switzerland	27	27	35	0	0
United Kingdom	35	35	0	25	25
The Americas					
Argentina	20	36	20	14	29
Brazil	30	30	25	25	25
Bahamas	0	0	0	0	0
Canada	29	25	20	30	38
Columbia	30	30	30	38	38
Mexico	25	25	55	42	42
U.S.A.	34	34	30	30	30
Venezuela	50	50	20	20	20
Others					
Australia	39	39	30	10	39
Hong Kong	16	16	0	0	0
Japan	37	37	20	20	20
Korea	34	34	0	10	0
Singapore	31	31	0	31	31
South Africa	50	50	15	0	15

TABLE 17-1   Foreign Income and Withholding Tax Rates (as a percent on January 1, 1992)

Source: Worldwide Corporate Tax Guide and Directory (New York: Ernst & Young, January 1992).

levied on retained and distributed earnings but the shareholder receives a credit for part of the corporate income tax paid on retained earnings. He can use this credit to off-set his personal income taxes. Other countries may fully assimilate the corporate income tax to the individual income tax. For example, distributed profits may not be taxed at all at the company levels in Greece. Other countries have proposed a variety of this system in which the shareholder would get a credit for all of the tax paid by the corporation. The shareholder exempt system imposes no taxes on dividend income received by shareholders. Companies pay ordinary income taxes.

Personal and company income may be calculated by one of two methods.[1] These are: (1) the profit and loss statement method where gross income is offset by allowable

[1] Ray August, *International Business Law: Text, Cases, and Readings* (Englewood Cliffs, NJ: Prentice-Hall, 1993), p. 699.

TABLE 17–2 Foreign Withholding Rates Enacted in U.S. Income Tax Treaties (as a percent)

Country	Dividends	Interest	Patent and Know-How Royalties
Australia	15	10	10
Austria	15	0	0
Belgium	15	15	0
Canada	15	15	10
Denmark	15	0	0
France	15	0	5
Germany	15	0	0
Italy	15	15	10
Japan	15	10	10
Korea	15	12	15
Netherlands	15	0	0
Norway	15	0	0
Russia	30	0	0
Sweden	15	0	0
Switzerland	15	5	0
United Kingdom	15	0	0

Source: Worldwide Corporate Tax Guide and Directory (New York: Ernst & Young, January 1992).

losses and deductions, and (2) the balance sheet method where income is the difference between net worth at the beginning and end of an accounting period. The former is practiced in the United States, United Kingdom, Canada, Mexico, and the Philippines. The latter method is practiced in France, Germany, Italy, and the Netherlands.

Finally, the jurisdiction or extension of the tax laws, referred to as the source principle, in a particular country may have a global reach, referred to as the nationality principal,[2] or the taxing country may have only a *territorial assertion*. Countries with territorial assertion of their tax laws include Hong Kong, Panama, and Switzerland. Territorial assertion means that the tax jurisdiction extends only to profits made inside the company's country of domicile. Only domestic income, that originating from within a particular country, is taxed. For example, Nestlé is headquartered in Switzerland but has 95 percent of its operations outside Switzerland. The Swiss corporate income tax extends only to the 5 percent of operations in Switzerland. The United States, on the other hand, practices *worldwide assertion*, or the nationality principle of the personal and corporate income tax laws. In other words, no matter where in the world a natural person or company makes its income, the United States may tax this income. The U.S. income tax laws have global jurisdiction. In other words, the tax is levied on worldwide income from whatever source.

Worldwide Tax Issues

MNCs face many tax issues in their global operations. The most important of these will be discussed in the following sections. For given MNCs, many of these issues will be in a state of flux—as legislative bodies make changes in national tax codes.

---

[2] Ibid., 688

AGGREGATE LEVEL

The aggregate level of national taxation, the ratio of income tax revenues to gross national product or gross domestic product, has a wide range. It is very high in the Scandinavian countries, running as much as 50 percent in Denmark, while in the United States, it is 30 percent, and in Turkey, it is less than 20 percent.

BURDEN ON THE FIRM

Corporate taxation as a burden on the firm also has a wide range. The corporate income tax rate is an appropriate measure of taxes as a burden on the firm and runs from 50 percent or more in some European countries to 34 percent in the United States to about 30 percent in some LDCs, and to less than 10 percent in Switzerland. When the U.S. Congress reduced the corporate income tax from 46 percent to 34 percent with the U.S. Tax Reform Act of 1986, many countries around the world also reduced their corporate income tax rates. Thus, the average tax burden is currently between 33 and 45 percent. Bilateral double taxation treaties between developing and emerging market countries have also reduced withholding tax rates.

One must be careful in comparing national corporate tax rates since, as just discussed, what profits are taxed may differ from country to country. Distributed profits may be taxed at a lower rate than are retained earnings in many European countries. In some cases, the shareholder can take a credit against his tax liability for his pro rata share of corporate income taxes paid on his dividends. In Mexico, reinvested corporate earnings are not taxed at all.

In addition, tax rates do not always indicate whether a country is "tax friendly." For example, the corporate tax rate in Malaysia and Thailand is 30 percent, the same as in Indonesia and Argentina. However, Malaysia and Thailand are ranked first and second most "tax friendly" among the emerging market countries while Indonesia is ranked ninth and Argentina is ranked 15th.[3] Other factors may offset the effect of relatively high tax rates. These factors include the availability of tax holidays and other tax incentives, the number of tax treaties in force, and the availability of enhanced deductions, allowances, export incentives, and tax-free zones.

TAXATION OF CAPITAL GAINS

Capital gains are taxed in some countries and not taxed in others. In some, the individual is taxed for long- and short-term capital gains, as currently practiced by the United States where the individual is taxed at a 28 percent rate on such gains. Some 55 nations do not tax individuals for long-term capital gains on corporate stock.[4] In addition, the definitions for what constitutes the basis valuation of an investment or a capital gain may differ from one country to another.

TYPE OF TAX

Several types of taxes are levied by governments. Among the various taxes in effect around the world in addition to income taxes are wealth or property taxes, consumption or sales taxes, transaction or use taxes, value added taxes, capital gains taxes, dividend taxes, withholding taxes, import taxes, and export taxes. It seems that if it moves, it should be taxed.

---

[3] "Choose Your Poison...Er, Tax," *Global Finance* 9 (October 1995): 96.

[4] Bruce Bartlett, "Slaying a Pair of CapGains Villains," *Wall Street Journal*, 10 June 1993, p. A12.

PROGRESSIVENESS OF THE INCOME TAX

Personal and corporate income tax rates tend to be progressive. Examples of the progressivity of income taxes include the three-tiered system in the United States—although the 1993 tax change may have added a fourth tier for high-income individuals—to the schedular system in Latin America, which moves taxpayers into a new bracket when only a small increase in income is received.

DUALITY OF CORPORATE TAXATION

This issue was previously discussed with regard to the taxation of retained and distributed earnings and whether credits are granted to shareholders for taxes paid by the company.

PURPOSE

Several purposes can be cited for various taxes. The purpose of a tax may be to raise revenue, to control economic activity, to stimulate economic growth, or to direct economic activity into a specific area.

OBSERVANCE

Taxpayers observe the payment of taxes differently from country to country. In some, noncompliance seems to be the practice, e.g., Spain and Italy. In others, voluntary observance is practiced by most citizenry, as in the United States.

BASIS FOR JURISDICTION

The tax laws of a nation may have jurisdiction over a taxpayer by different means. For example, the taxpayer may be liable for taxes depending on his domicile or legal situs, permanent establishment, nationality, seat of control, the conduct of an active trade or business, or by treaty.

JURISDICTION CLAIMED

This issue is concerned with the worldwide or territorial assertion of the tax laws practiced by each nation. This was previously discussed.

IN RECOGNIZING COSTS

A variety of differences are practiced in recognizing costs or defining taxable income from one country to another. Tax incentives may have been granted by a nation's tax code. These may include depreciation allowances, investment tax credits, credits for foreign taxes paid, and tax abatements. They may also include different definitions for transfer prices or for the allocation of overhead expenses from headquarters to the subsidiary in the form of management fees.

IN THE TIMING OF TAXES

Tax liabilities may be subject to the timing of income remittances from the subsidiary to the parent. For example, the U.S. tax code permits a foreign tax deferral. The tax liability on foreign source income is deferred until the earnings are remitted to the parent firm. Foreign base companies located in tax haven countries—countries with small or no corporate income tax—may be set up to change the timing of remittances to the parent firm. Foreign base companies will be discussed further in a subsequent section.

TAX SPARING

Some countries grant tax holidays to foreign investors, i.e., tax sparing. These are exemptions for some period of time from income taxes or other types of levies in return for locating in some specified region of the country. The purpose of the tax holiday is to stimulate foreign direct investment. Ireland grants such an exemption from corporate income taxes for as much as 10 years or more.

TAX NEUTRALITY

A tax system should adhere to the principle of tax neutrality. From an international viewpoint, taxation should not affect the location of the investment or the nationality of the investor. Domestic tax methods should give equal treatment to a country's citizens whether they invest at home or abroad, whereas foreign country tax methods should not place a higher burden on foreign investors than is placed on domestic citizens. In real practice, many nations discriminate in favor of their own citizens. Thus, the average national tax system may not be neutral.

RECOGNITION OF TAX EXEMPTIONS

Some countries grant special exemptions from tax liability to certain types of income. Ireland grants an exemption for profits derived from exports. Japan grants an exemption for income generated from the exportation of technology and skills. Singapore grants an exemption to income having its origin in neighboring Southeast Asian nations.

FLEXIBILITY

Some companies have the capacity to adjust depreciation allowances to pace inflation or to adopt an appropriate inventory accounting practice such as LIFO or FIFO. The ensuing flexibility is the result of accounting rules permitted by the parent's home government.

TAX INCENTIVES

Most countries grant some type of tax incentive to domestic and foreign investors. These include tax abatement or holidays as well as low-cost loans.

JURISDICTIONS CLAIMING TAXES

Most countries have several political units that claim tax revenues in a variety of means. For example, an American company may be subject to as many as 50 state governments with regard to income, franchise, property, license, network, sales, and use taxes plus Federal and local taxes. Some companies may have to file more than 1,000 tax returns and reports annually.

CONTRACTOR/COUNTRY CLAUSES

Some countries permit the inclusion in investment contracts of clauses that trigger reimbursement of corporate taxes levied from within the country in which the investor is operating. Such clauses are prevalent in Mexico but are illegal in some countries, e.g., Venezuela.

METHODS FOR TAXING FOREIGN SOURCE INCOME

Finally, several basic methods may be authorized for taxing foreign source income. These include exemption from taxation, tax reduction, crediting foreign taxes, expensing foreign taxes, and double taxation. See Table 17–3 for a comparison of the five methods. The assumptions for this material are: (1) the foreign corporate income tax in all cases is 40 percent; (2) a 100 percent after foreign tax dividend, $60, is issued to the parent; (3) no withholding tax is levied on the remitted income; (4) the tentative parent country tax rate is 10 percent in the case of tax reduction and 50 percent in the cases in which income is fully taxed.

Exemption
In this case, the parent country levies no tax on foreign source income, exempting such income from domestic taxation. Thus, the only income tax this company pays is to the foreign country.

Tax Reduction
In this case, the parent country levies a reduced tax rate, 10 percent, against the foreign source income. Thus, the company pays $40 to the foreign government and $10 to the parent's home country, for a total of $50.

Crediting Foreign Taxes
In this case, the parent's home country grants a credit for the foreign taxes paid. The full tax rate, 50 percent, is levied against the foreign source income, but a tax credit is given for the $40 paid to the foreign government. Thus, the domestic tax liability is only $10.

Expensing Foreign Taxes
In this case, the firm is permitted to deduct the foreign tax paid, $40, from the total foreign source income as a business expense. This is the method used in the United States for handling taxes paid to state and local governments. The 50 percent tax rate is applied then to the after-tax dividend and the domestic liability is $30.

Double Taxation
This method is more theory than fact. In practice, some relief from double taxation can usually be found. If no credit is given for foreign taxes against the domestic liability or if the foreign tax paid cannot be expensed, or if the foreign source income

TABLE 17–3 Methods for Taxing Foreign Source Income

	Exemption	Tax Reduction	Crediting Foreign Taxes	Expensing Foreign Taxes	Double Taxing
Taxable income abroad	$100	$100	$100	$100	$100
Foreign tax (assume 40%)	40	40	40	40	40
Dividend to parent	60	60	60	60	60
Tentative parent country tax (assumes 50% in the full case, 10% in the reduced case)	0	10	50	30	50
Tax credit	0	0	40	0	0
Tax liability to parent country	0	10	10	30	50
Total tax paid	**$ 40**	**$ 50**	**$ 50**	**$ 70**	**$ 90**

were not exempt from domestic taxation, or if no reduced tax rates were levied, the company, would have the foreign source income fully taxed in both the foreign and home countries. The company would pay the 40 percent rate on the foreign source income to the foreign country and then would pay 50 percent on the same income to the home country because of its full 50 percent tax rate. The company would have only 10 percent of the foreign source income remaining for reinvestment after the total taxes were paid. Table 17–3 also shows the comparative effect of expensing foreign taxes paid, i.e., treating them as tax deductions instead of receiving a tax credit. Under this method, the total tax liability is much higher than for those systems granting a foreign tax credit, offering a lower tax rate on the domestic tax liability, or exempting the foreign source income from domestic taxation.

U.S. Income Tax Treaties

The United States has entered into tax treaties with a number of other nations to reduce the burden of taxation of overseas operation of U.S. companies. These treaties have three specific objectives: to enable U.S. companies to avoid double taxation on foreign source income, to reduce tax harassment, which many U.S. companies encounter in foreign operations, and to prevent tax avoidance by these companies of legitimate taxes owed the U.S. government. Double taxation is avoided by foreign tax credits and deductions for some expenses encountered in international business. Tax harassment is reduced by including clauses in the tax code designed to eliminate discrimination by foreign governments, which favor domestic business firms over foreign firms, by the establishment of rules regarding sources of income, and by rules governing foreign tax rules that deal with commercial travelers, who sometimes are discriminated against by the foreign government tax authorities. In addition, in many of these treaties, the statutory tax rate imposed on U.S. companies has been reduced, as can be seen in a comparison of the rates shown in Tables 17–1 and 17–2.

Remittance of Income by U.S.-Owned Foreign Corporations

The remittance of foreign source income by subsidiaries to the parent firm depends on a number of factors. The amount to be remitted is a function of the firm's dividend payout policy. This policy is set according to: (1) management's business goals and objectives within each country and worldwide, (2) requirements and opportunities for reinvestment, including the availability of funds, (3) the stability of the local currency and whether foreign exchange convertibility restrictions are in effect, (4) economic and political considerations at home and abroad, (5) the cost of conversion of foreign currency to the parent's home currency, (6) the existence of miscellaneous remittance restrictions or distribution incentives, and (7) foreign and domestic taxation of foreign source earnings.

U.S. TAXATION OF FOREIGN SOURCE BUSINESS INCOME

Taxation of foreign source business income should be based on certain tax principles. First, the tax should avoid international double taxation. In other words, such taxation should remain neutral with respect to the firm's decision to invest at home or to invest abroad. Second, the tax should not destroy the competitive position of a domestic-based MNC relative to its foreign counterparts.

Taxation of foreign source earnings by foreign subsidiaries and affiliates may significantly impact the overall worldwide earnings of the U.S. MNC.[5] The foreign earnings tax methodology involves tax concepts usually not well-known by corporate accountants and the foreign tax calculations can be complex and time consuming.

Foreign source earnings are usually subject to taxation on three levels:[6]

1. taxation of the earnings of the subsidiary by the foreign country where its operations are located;

2. withholding taxes imposed by the foreign country in which the operations are located when these earnings are remitted back to the parent firm;

3. U.S. federal and state income taxation of the earnings distributed by the foreign affiliate to the parent firm.

In fact, one or more levels of taxation may be applied to foreign source income that is maneuvered from the country of income source through one or more other countries before being remitted to the parent firm because of differences in the withholding tax rates of these countries, thus resulting in a lower overall tax on the operations. This is discussed subsequently in the section on planning and organizing international operations to minimize taxes.

THE FOREIGN TAX CREDIT

The major component in U.S. tax treaties with other nations is the foreign tax credit (FTC). No matter where an American company makes a profit, such profit incurs a domestic tax liability. The foreign tax deferral protects the U.S. firm's foreign source income from paying this liability until the income has been remitted to the parent firm. Once, however, the income has been remitted to the parent firm, a tax liability is payable. This liability can be reduced by a foreign tax credit for the amount of foreign income taxes paid.

The FTC is given for income taxes *and* withholding taxes paid to the foreign government by the affiliate. No FTC is allowed for foreign excise, sales, or value-added taxes. These can be passed on in the form of higher prices. No FTC is given for royalties or fees paid to local foreign governments. These are considered costs of doing business. Some may be illegal under the U.S. Foreign Corrupt Practices Act of 1977, which prohibits some payments to foreign companies or governments if they are deemed to be bribes.

The FTC may result in a violation of the principle that international taxation should be neutral. Under the FTC rules, a firm cannot claim a credit in excess of the tentative U.S. liability. Thus, where the combined foreign income and withholding taxes exceed the U.S. tax liability, the tax in such a case is not neutral.

The following examples demonstrate how the FTC is handled when the U.S. parent firm calculates its U.S. tax liability. The major assumption is that tax treaties have been formulated and approved between the United States and the foreign countries in which the foreign affiliates are operating. Figure 17–1 describes the FTC calculation when the foreign affiliate operates in Alpha, a country with a corporate income tax rate lower than the U.S. rate. In this example, the parent company will owe tax to the U.S. government after the FTC has been taken. In Figure 17–2, the foreign affiliate operates in a country Beta, whose corporate income tax rate is higher than the U.S. rate. In this

---

[5] Rene C. Schlag, "Accounting for Taxes of Foreign Subsidiaries—a Simplified Approach," *Management Accounting* 61 (December 1979): 15–9.

[6] Ibid., 17.

Assumed: Country Alpha's corporate income tax rate is 20%; the U.S. corporate income tax rate is 34%; the company's dividend payout ratio is 50% of after-foreign tax income.

Assumed Distribution of Foreign Earnings

$1,000	Gross foreign earnings
−200	Alpha's income tax (20% rate)
800	After-tax foreign earnings
−400	Retained earnings
400	Dividends—50% dividend
−40	Alpha's withholding tax on dividends (10% rate)
$360	Net dividends remitted to U.S. parent after all foreign taxes

Calculation of ''Grossed-up'' Dividends

$360	Net dividends remitted to U.S. parent
+100	Portion of Alpha's income tax attributable to dividends = 50% (dividend payout ratio) × $200 (total income tax paid to Alpha)
+40	Alpha's withholding tax on dividends
$500	''Grossed-up'' dividend earnings

Calculation of U.S. Tax Liability

$170	Tentative U.S. tax = 34% (U.S. corporate income tax rate) × $500 (Grossed-up dividends)
	Tentative foreign tax credits: $100 (foreign income tax paid on dividends)
−140	+$40 (Alpha's withholding tax)
$30	U.S. tax due on foreign earnings after credits

Summary of Taxes Paid

$200	Alpha's corporate income tax
10	Alpha's withholding tax
30	U.S. corporate income tax
$270	Total taxes paid on foreign earnings, or 27% effective rate

FIGURE 17–1 Foreign Tax Credit Alpha Country

case, the parent firm will owe no taxes on the foreign source income after the FTC has been calculated.

A third case is presented in Figure 17–3, which is a hypothetical example assuming no foreign tax deferral and FTCs are extended to retained earnings. The objective of this case is to show the effect of the loss of the foreign tax deferral to a MNC.

If the tax code followed this pattern, i.e., no foreign tax deferral and tax credits were extended to retained earnings, two significant differences can be seen between this case and the Alpha example in Figure 17–1. First, the U.S. company would have a tax liability after credits amounting to $100. It paid no U.S. taxes in the first example. Second, however, the effective tax rate after all taxes are paid is exactly equal to the U.S. corporate income tax. Thus, the tax would be neutral between domestic and foreign operations. Such a change might cause MNCs to change their dividend policy regarding foreign source income. The parent company would be indifferent whether it reinvested 50 percent of foreign earnings or remitted all earnings to headquarters. At any rate, the company in Figure 17–1 would pay $70 less in taxes under the existing system in which the foreign tax deferral is practiced.

The first two cases, Alpha and Beta, are predicated on a "per country" limitation. The U.S. Revenue Act of 1976 allows an "overall" limitation. Under this rule, the $105 excess FTC from the Beta operation can be applied against U.S. tax of $30 due on the Alpha operation income. Thus, no U.S. tax would be due overall. However, a MNC operating in only one country cannot take this advantage. If the parent firm were operating only in Alpha or only in Beta, an excess tax credit would only reduce the tax due

Assumed: Beta's corporate income tax rate is 50%; the U.S. corporate income tax rate is 34%; the company's dividend payout ratio is 50% of foreign source income after-tax.

Assumed Distribution of Foreign Earnings

$1,000	Gross foreign earnings
−500	Beta's income tax (50% corporate income tax rate)
500	After-tax foreign earnings
−250	Retained earnings
$ 250	Dividends—50% pay-out ratio
25	Beta's withholding tax (10% rate)
$ 225	Net dividends remitted to U.S. parent

Calculation of "Grossed-up" Dividends

$ 225	Net dividends remitted to U.S. parent
+250	Beta's income tax attributable to dividends (50% × 500)
+ 25	Beta's withholding tax on dividends
$ 500	"Grossed-up" dividends

Calculation of U.S. Tax Liability

$ 170	Tentative U.S. tax (34% corporate income tax rate × $500 grossed-up dividends)
−275	Tentative foreign tax credits ($250 foreign income tax paid +$25 withholding tax)
−$105	Excess foreign tax credit (*)

(*) No tax liability in United States, but excess foreign tax credit cannot be used because of foreign tax credit limitation

Summary of Taxes Paid

$ 500	Beta's corporate income tax
25	Beta's withholding tax
0	U.S. tax
$ 525	Total taxes paid on foreign earnings, or 52.5% effective tax rate

FIGURE 17–2 Foreign Tax Credit Beta Country

and payable from operations in that country. If the company were only operating in Alpha, no excess tax credit is available and the company would owe $30 to the U.S. government. If the company operated only in Beta from whose operations the company generated a tentative U.S. corporate income tax of $170 on the foreign source income and a $275 foreign tax credit, it would owe no corporate income tax to the U.S. gov-

FIGURE 17–3 Alpha Country No Foreign Tax Deferral; Tax Credits Extended to Retained Earnings

Taxable Foreign Earnings

$1,000	Gross foreign earnings

Calculation of U.S. Tax Liability

$ 340	Tentative U.S. tax (34% corporate income tax rate)
−240	Tentative foreign tax credits ($200 Alpha's income tax +$40 Alpha's withholding tax)
$ 100	U.S. tax due on foreign earnings after credits

Summary of Taxes Paid

$ 200	Alpha's corporate income tax
40	Alpha's withholding tax
100	U.S. corporate income tax after credits
$ 340	Total taxes paid on foreign earnings, or 34% effective tax rate

ernment. It would have excess tax credits amounting to $105 but could not apply these against, for example, profits of the parent company. But if the company had operations in both Alpha and Beta, it could apply the $105 excess foreign tax credit against the $30 owed on the Alpha operation. Thus, no U.S. corporate income tax would be due for the Alpha and Beta operations combined under the rules of the "overall" limitation.

A second provision of the tax code governing foreign operations does provide some relief, especially in situations where the company is operating in only one country. The company is permitted to shift FTCs in excess of the limitations forward 5 years or backward 2 years.

Tax Reform Act of 1986—Changes

The Tax Reform Act of 1986 (TRA), passed by the U.S. Congress, made further changes with regard to the FTC limitation.[7] Essentially, the new law resulted in the creation of excess credits for taxpayers that have not had excess credits in the past and it increased excess credits for those taxpayers already in an excess credit position. These changes were enacted for two reasons. First, the TRA lowered the top U.S. tax rate (34 percent for corporations and 28 percent for individuals—the latter was increased for high-income individuals by a 1993 law). Most foreign operations are taxed abroad at higher rates. Second, many changes were made to the provisions affecting the FTC, which further squeezed the margin of credit limitation for many U.S. MNCs.

The TRA included other amendments to provisions affecting the FTC. The Deficit Reduction Act of 1984 had been an attempt to alleviate some problems in the FTC by changing the limitation calculation shown in Figures 17–1 and 17–2. Congress, however, considered these changes insufficient since new, lower tax rates would place more corporations in an excess FTC situation. As mentioned, the TRA reduced the corporate tax rate to 34 percent and the individual maximum rate to 28 percent. These rates were relatively lower than tax rates in most other countries. TRA also initiated five new areas that affected the FTC limitation. These were the baskets of income approach, allocation of overall foreign losses, sourcing rules for gross income, allocation and apportionment of expenses to foreign income, and the credit allowed against the alternative minimum tax.

Baskets of Income   TRA retained the overall limitation of the previous law but required taxpayers to separate income into different types or baskets of income, for the purpose of calculating the FTC limitation. In addition to active income, three new baskets of income must be considered in addition to the overall limitation. These are passive income, high withholding tax interest income, and dividends from foreign corporations that are 10–50 percent owned by a U.S. company. The most significant difference in the new provisions is the distinction between active income, which tends to be taxed at higher rates abroad, and passive income, which tends to be taxed at low rates overseas. The new income types to be considered will make it more difficult for a MNC to increase excess FTCs.

A number of exceptions to passive income were included in TRA. Under this act, income will not be classified as passive income if it is related party income, active royalties or rents, qualified commodity gains or foreign currency gains, or high-taxed passive income. To show the effects of these provisions, assume that U.S. parent corporation A owns all of the stock of foreign subsidiary B. A receives from B a dividend of $500, a royalty of $200, and interest of $300. Since A is related to B, the entire

---

[7] Gerald T. Ball, Donald B. Carter, and Tom B. Wight, "New Tax Law Makes Major Changes to the Foreign Tax Credit Limitation," *The Journal of Taxation* 66 (March 1987): 140–9.

$1,000 is exempt from passive income treatment and the income is considered active income unless A's underlying income is passive.

The related party income rule offers an opportunity for U.S. companies with foreign subsidiaries to repatriate profits of a foreign subsidiary that have been subject to little or no foreign tax and average the low-taxed income with high-taxed business profits. For example, such profits may have been repatriated in the form of royalties. Let's assume that A's subsidiary B earns active business profits before royalties of $1,000. B is taxed on its profits by the foreign country at a rate of 40 percent. If B paid a tax deductible royalty of $200 to A, the foreign tax on B's profits would be only $320 ($800—after deduction × 40 percent) and A would have effectively repatriated $200 of profit, which would be characterized as active income for foreign tax credit purposes. Assuming that no withholding tax is levied on the repatriated royalties, the effective foreign tax rate on the profits has been reduced from 40 percent to 32 percent and excess tax credits may be avoided.

Allocation of Overall Foreign Losses   The TRA requires that a foreign loss in one basket be offset against foreign income in other baskets on a pro rata basis before it can be used to offset U.S. source income. For example, consider the case where a U.S. firm incurs a $500 active basket loss overseas and $100 of U.S. source income.[8] Furthermore, the firm earns $600 of foreign shipping income and $400 of passive income during the same tax year. Of the $500 active basket foreign loss, $300 could be used to offset shipping income and $200 to offset passive income. For purposes of calculating the FTC, the firm has $100 of U.S. income, $300 of shipping income, and $200 of passive income. During the following year, the firm has $1,000 of active foreign source income, $600 of shipping income, $400 of passive income, and $200 of U.S. source income. If the taxpayer corporation desires to recapture the entire prior loss in that year, $300 of the active basket income can be recharacterized as shipping income and $200 as passive income. For FTC calculation purposes, the firm has $500 of active basket income, $900 of shipping income, and $600 of passive income.

Sourcing Rules for Gross Income   Under TRA, the amount of available FTC is limited to the ratio of foreign taxable income to worldwide taxable income. Thus, the determination of foreign source income and its expenses is critical to the determination of the allowable FTC. Before TRA, companies could manipulate income and expenses to maximize foreign source income and, thus, could increase the taxpayer's FTC limitation by including income that qualified as foreign source income but that was not subject to foreign tax. The TRA tightened the source rules.

Allocation and Apportionment of Expenses to Foreign Income   TRA amended the rules for allocating and apportioning expenses to foreign and domestic gross income. Expense allocations to foreign source income of U.S. taxpayers will increase, thus reducing the taxpayer's FTC limitation. This change, thus, reduces the amount of foreign taxes that can be used to offset U.S. tax on foreign source income.

Credit Allowed Against Alternative Minimum Tax   Before TRA, individuals were permitted to calculate an alternative minimum tax (AMT). Corporations subject to the add-on minimum tax were allowed no FTCs. Under TRA, corporations are now subject to AMT and both corporations and individuals will be allowed to offset their AMT with an AMT FTC. For AMT purposes, the credit is subject to two limitations. First, a

---

[8] Ibid., 146.

formula, ([Foreign AMTI ÷ Worldwide AMTI] × AMT) before credits, is used to limit the FTC. AMTI is alternative minimum taxable income. Second, a taxpayer may use AMT FTC to offset only up to 90 percent of AMT liability.

The implications of the TRA changes concerning the FTC are that corporations can no longer fully utilize FTCs, U.S. tax liability on foreign source income will increase, and the focus for companies will be to minimize foreign taxes on a global basis. In addition, companies will incur added costs for recordkeeping but the U.S. tax authorities will incur more difficulty in auditing the tax records of MNCs.

Foreign Tax Deferral

A company with foreign operations can defer payment of the U.S. tax liability on foreign source income until the earnings are remitted to the parent firm. This is called the foreign tax deferral. However, the foreign tax deferral is allowed only when the overseas operation is a subsidiary. A branch operation does not receive the foreign tax deferral, except in special situations when the foreign operation is a possessions corporation. This form of overseas operations will be discussed later in this chapter.

In the cases shown in Figures 17–1 and 17–3, the presence of the foreign tax deferral has rather dramatic conclusions. In Figure 17–1 showing the Alpha operation, total taxes paid on the foreign source income amount to $270. However, in Figure 17–3 showing a foreign operation in a parent country tax environment, which does not permit the foreign tax deferral, the parent company would pay $340 in total taxes on the foreign source income. The foreign tax deferral offsets the advantages that may be given to domestic operations by the tax authority including loss carryovers, accelerated depreciation allowances, and investment tax credits. These benefits may not always be given to foreign subsidiaries by foreign governments.

The deferral provision of the U.S. internal revenue code offers no benefits to the MNC in cases where the foreign corporate income tax rate is greater than the U.S. corporate income tax rate. Thus, U.S. MNCs should be encouraged to retain earnings in foreign subsidiaries with relatively low corporate income tax rates. Some studies have shown that lower foreign tax rates have encouraged retention of earnings abroad while reduction in the U.S. corporate tax have encouraged remittance of foreign income to the parent firm.

Subsidiary vs. Branch Operations

A U.S. corporation engaged in continuous foreign operations may elect to perform these business operations through either a subsidiary or a branch. Income of foreign

---

STUDY AID

Foreign tax treaties, the foreign tax credit, and the foreign tax deferral are all part of a number of ways to reduce the burden of international taxation on MNCs. They offer relief against double taxation. You might familiarize yourself with some of the tax court cases that have established some of these principles or tools, including *Director General of Inland Revenue v. Rothmans of Pall Mall (Malaysia) Bhd* found in the *Malayan Law Journal (1989)*,[9] and *Johansson v. United States*, found in the *Federal Reporter (1964)*.[10]

---

[9] August, *Business Law* pp. 707–8.
[10] Ibid., 710–12.

branches is taxable currently in the United States because the U.S. parent corporation and its branches are considered one entity for tax purposes. To compute the amount of U.S. tax payable on the foreign branch operations, the branch income must be translated into U.S. dollars. The parent firm has two methods to compute such income. Under the profit and loss method, the branch net profits are stated in terms of the foreign currency. Remittances made by the foreign branch to the U.S. parent are subtracted from the net profits. The amount remitted is converted into U.S. dollars at the rate of exchange in effect on the date the remittance is made and the balance of the net profits is converted into U.S. dollars at the rate of exchange in effect at the end of the taxable year. Under this method, unrealized exchange rate gains and losses are not recognized currently.

The parent firm may also use the "net worth" or "balance sheet" method. Under this method, the current assets and current liabilities of the foreign branch at year end are converted into U.S. dollars at the current exchange rate. Noncurrent assets and noncurrent liabilities are recorded at the currency exchange rate in effect at the time such assets were acquired or such liabilities were incurred. Taxable income for the year is the amount by which the dollar value of the branch's net current assets, plus the adjusted basis of its net noncurrent assets as of the end of the year, exceed the dollar value of these items at the beginning of the year plus the dollar value of remittances during the year, when valued at the rate of exchange in effect at the time of the remittance. Under this method, some unrealized exchange gains and losses are currently recognized.

A subsidiary is a separate legal entity from its parent and its income is not taxable until remitted to the parent firm, under the foreign tax deferral rules previously mentioned. The parent firm, however, cannot currently deduct losses of its subsidiaries, including any loss resulting from the shrinkage in value of a foreign currency. The rules of the foreign tax credit are applicable when the foreign subsidiary is located in a country that has a foreign tax treaty with the United States, as discussed earlier. A company that expects an overseas project to run at a loss for several years may prefer to operate the overseas project as a branch because these losses can be consolidated in the parent's income statement for tax purposes.

To demonstrate the difference in tax treatment of a subsidiary and a branch of a U.S. parent company, assume the following information. A U.S. MNC, A, has a wholly-owned manufacturing subsidiary B and a sales outlet branch C located in Lapland. Lapland has a corporate tax rate of 20 percent and no withholding tax on remitted foreign profits. Lapland has a tax treaty with the United States. B earns net profits of $1,000 in Lapland and remits 50 percent after foreign taxes to the parent firm A. A total of $1,000 in net profits is earned in Lapland by C. These profits are taxed at the Lapland 20 percent tax rate. The U.S. corporate income tax rate is 34 percent.

We can now show the difference in U.S. taxation of foreign source income earned by a subsidiary in the case of B and by a branch in the case of C. By "grossing-up" the foreign source income of B for U.S. tax purposes according to the calculations in Figure 17–1, we add the following: $400 dividends after foreign tax $200 and the portion, $100, of Lapland's income tax attributable to dividends (20 percent × $200) for grossed-up dividends of $500. The tentative U.S. tax before credits is $170 ($500 × 34 percent). To calculate the U.S. tax liability on this foreign source income, we deduct $100, the foreign income tax attributable to dividends, as a foreign tax credit from the $170 tentative U.S. tax liability. Thus, the U.S. tax on the foreign source income made by B is $70 ($170 − $100). U.S. taxes on the $400 of profits retained by B are deferred until these profits are remitted to A, because of the foreign tax deferral provision.

In the case of C, the foreign tax deferral does not apply and an immediate U.S.

tax is owed on the entire $800 of profits after Lapland taxes because, in the case of a branch, the after-tax profits are consolidated into the parent company's income statement. The tentative U.S. tax on these profits is $272 ($800 × 34 percent). The foreign tax credit in the case of the branch is the entire $200 paid to Lapland in corporate income taxes. The U.S. tax liability after foreign tax credits in this case is $72 ($272 − $200), resulting in a tax liability of $2 more in the case of the branch. In the case of branch operations, the U.S. tax liability will always be higher because of the inability to defer U.S. taxes on the foreign source income.

Other U.S. Tax Code Changes

WESTERN HEMISPHERE TRADE CORPORATIONS

The U.S. Congress has created a number of tax breaks for international business over the years. Some of these laws are still in effect and some of them have been abolished. In the early 1940s, Congress permitted companies to establish Western Hemisphere Trade Corporations (WHTC).[11] These were intended by Congress to expand trade with Latin America by permitting U.S. companies to establish wholly-owned subsidiaries that would derive a minimum of 95 percent of their gross income from outside the United States and earn 90 percent of their gross income from active conduct of a trade or business. These subsidiaries had to be domestic corporations and all of their business had to be conducted in the Western Hemisphere. In return for keeping operations in conformance with these guidelines, the parent companies received an approximate 14 percent reduction in their corporate income tax rate covering these operations. This essentially reduced their corporate income tax rate to as low as 34 percent. However, the administrative cost to maintain operations that conformed with the statutory requirements generally consumed most of the tax break. The law has not been in effect since 1980.

DOMESTIC INTERNATIONAL SALES COMPANIES

Another law, passed in 1971, permitted U.S. companies to establish so-called Domestic International Sales Companies (DISC). The DISC permitted U.S. companies to establish wholly-owned subsidiaries that would carry on the international trade activities for the parent company. In return, the parent received an indefinite deferral for taxes due on half of a firm's exporting income. The other half was deemed distributed to shareholders and they were taxed on this income. The objective of this law was to encourage small U.S. firms to engage in exporting activities. At that time, only about 5 percent of some 300,000 potential exporting manufacturers in the United States were actually exporting their products. This objective never was well achieved and the administrative costs of record keeping were high. Thus, the DISC program was phased out in 1985 in favor of the Foreign Sales Corporation (FSC).

FOREIGN SALES CORPORATIONS

The U.S. government replaced the DISC with the Foreign Sales Corporation (FSC) in 1985. In addition to the fact that the major objective of the DISC, to encourage small firms to export, was not successful, another complaint came from foreign business. The

---

[11] James C. Baker and Thomas H. Bates, *Financing International Business Operations* (Scranton, PA: International Textbook Co., 1971), p. 53.

DISC was perceived as a way to subsidize U.S. exporters by the use of the corporate income tax. This was deemed a violation of the rules of GATT (General Agreement on Tariffs and Trade) an organization established primarily by Europeans. European exporters could be subsidized with indirect tax revenues, a policy approved by GATT.

The FSC is another benefit offered by the U.S. government to firms that establish a subsidiary for the purpose of exporting. The subsidiary must be located in a U.S. possession or in a foreign country. A company can save about one-third of the tax due on its exporting operations by setting up a FSC. Under the Tax Reform Act of 1986, a company gets a 30–32 percent tax reduction for the export business done by a FSC. Tax breaks of up to 15 percent on the export profits of manufactured goods which are at least 50 percent American-made are possible with this type organization.

Beginning in 1988, up to 25 exporters were permitted to share one FSC. This concept was authorized for the purpose of helping small- and medium-sized business firms to participate in the exporting business. A small exporter will spend, on average, about $3,000 to establish a FSC and, thus, will need $60,000 in exports to save money by joining a shared FSC.

Several other administrative requirements must be met by the parent firm in its FSC operation.[12] If it meets these requirements, some of the FSC income is permanently exempt from U.S. tax liability. Under the FSC law, the taxes deferred under the DISCs were permanently forgiven.

Example of a FSC[13]

Infocus Systems, Inc., a U.S. manufacturer of liquid crystal display projection panels and video projection systems, had generated 40 percent of its $124 million in revenues from foreign sources. In 1990, the company decided not to open sales subsidiaries in Europe and Asia. Its objectives were to avoid double taxation of overseas profits, difficulty in remittance of overseas earnings, and transfer pricing compliance and audits both in the United States and abroad.

The company decided to export all its product from its Oregon manufacturing plant to local distributors abroad through a FSC based in the U.S. Virgin Islands. It did open support centers in Italy and the Netherlands. The FSC cost only $5,000 to establish and has saved the company hundreds of thousands of dollars annually since 1990.

POSSESSIONS CORPORATION

The U.S. government has also extended tax benefits to U.S. business operations located in the U.S. possessions, e.g., U.S. Samoan Islands, U.S. Virgin Islands, Guam, and Puerto Rico, although the law treats U.S. business operations in the U.S. Virgin Islands specifically differently than it treats U.S. business in the other U.S. possessions. Any U.S. firm that operates within a U.S. possession can receive tax benefits if: (1) it is a domestic U.S. corporation, (2) 80 percent of its gross income during the last 3 years is derived from operations in the U.S. possession, and (3) at least 75 percent of the firm's gross income is from an active trade or business. Possessions corporations can exclude from U.S. gross income any income earned outside the United States and can receive FTCs for this income. Possessions corporations are treated as domestic corporations for most purposes but not as controlled foreign corporations under Subpart F.

---

[12] Suk H. Kim and Seung H. Kim, *Global Corporate Finance: Text and Cases* (Miami, FL: Kolb Publishing Co., 1993), p. 441.

[13] Lori Ioannou, "Taxing Issues," *International Business* (March 1995): 44–5.

Planning and Organizing MNC Operations to Minimize Taxes

MNC operations and funds flows can be structured in a way that will minimize tax liabilities, both at home and abroad. With regard to income flows and foreign tax credits, the MNC should structure its payments in a way that will minimize the loss of excess FTCs. For example, payments should be structured to minimize withholding taxes on remittance by flowing the funds through subsidiaries in countries with low withholding rates. If we assume that Country Y has a withholding tax of 30 percent on remittances of income to the United States, but only 10 percent on remittances of income to Country Z, and if Country Z imposes only a 5 percent withholding tax on remittances to the United States, then it will behoove the firm to transfer earnings from the subsidiary in Country Y to the subsidiary in Country Z, before transferring this income to the United States.

Research has shown that, since World War II, foreign companies operating in the United States have posted lower profits than their U.S. contemporaries. Government tax authorities believed that foreign firms routinely manipulate their books to understate their U.S. income and avoid U.S. taxation.[14] Foreign tax officials, of course, be-

---

MANAGEMENT APPLICATION NO. 31

Hitachi Corporation of Japan and Others[1]

One of the major political stories in 1994 in the United States was concerned with the alleged accounting techniques used by large MNCs operating in the United States to avoid U.S. income taxes by shifting their income into the accounts of related companies abroad. At that time, this practice was perfectly legal and is, of course, also practiced around the world by U.S. MNCs. Single audits of the books of large MNCs can take years and require the review of millions of pages of documents and financial statements by U.S. internal revenue agents.

One example involves the operations of Hitachi Corporation of Japan. Hitachi produces one model of VCR in Japan at a cost of $90 and sells them to its subsidiary in Singapore for $100. The Japanese income tax paid on each VCR is, thus, quite small. The Singapore affiliate adds value of $100 to the VCRs and sells them to Hitachi, United States, for $200. Singapore does not levy a tax on the value added because of a tax treaty

with Japan. The Hitachi affiliate in the United States sells them to American consumers for $200. No profits are reported in the United States and, thus, no U.S. taxes are levied.

Other cases are similar in nature. In 1982, the U.S. affiliate of Yamaha Motors in Japan paid so much for motorcycles and parts it imported from the Japanese factory that its books showed very little profits. It paid $123 in U.S. corporate income taxes that year. The IRS contention was that the company owed $27 million in U.S. taxes. National Semiconductor, Inc., of California, reported $300 million in paper losses for materials it sold to highly profitable Asian affiliates from 1976–81. The materials had value added, as in the Hitachi case, by Asian workers and were transferred to the United States for sale to consumers. The Asian affiliates are not subject to U.S. income taxes and no tax was owed on the U.S. operations because of the paper losses.

---

[1]Jeff Nesmith, "Firms Avoid Billions in Taxes," *The Akron Beacon Journal*, 11 September 1994, pp. C1, C3.

---

[14] *Wall Street Journal*, 2 November 1994, p. A1.

lieve that U.S. companies also resort to such practices in their international operations. Some of this difference may be attributable to the fact that foreign firms increased their U.S. operations in the 1970s and 1980s and paid too much for underperforming companies, many of which continued to underperform after the foreign acquisition.

However, the long-term political and managerial considerations should be given attention before such restructuring is implemented. The actual cost of such restructuring should be measured as well as the need for U.S.-based international companies to obtain permission from the U.S. tax authorities under the requirements of Section 367 of the Internal Revenue Code.

Section 367 was enacted in 1932 to prevent U.S. taxpayers from taking advantage of a loophole in the tax code. It precluded a U.S. taxpayer from transferring appreciated assets held in a foreign country in a manner, essentially a reorganization, which would remove any gain realized from U.S. taxation. Before 1976, Section 367 required a firm to obtain an advance ruling on any reorganization of foreign operations that might result in a tax-free situation.[15]

The Revenue Act of 1976 amended Section 367. All requirements for advance rulings on reorganization of foreign operations were removed. The Act divided tax-free organization, reorganization, and liquidation transactions into two groups, as follows: (1) transactions that involve the transfer of property from a U.S. person to a foreign corporation, and (2) other transfers, including transfers into the United States and transfers that are entirely foreign. Under these changes, appreciated property or inventory can be removed from U.S. tax jurisdiction.[16]

A MNC may also reorganize the corporation to minimize taxation.[17] A U.S. parent firm, X, owns 100 percent of subsidiaries, Y, in countries A and B. The U.S. firm is 100 percent owned by U.S. shareholders. First, the U.S. parent firm reduces ownership of the foreign subsidiaries. Two steps are necessary. In Step 1, the U.S. parent firm exchanges subsidiary stock for cash or shares in a foreign parent firm, Z, in country C. A nonrecurring tax is levied on subsidiary earnings that previously were excluded from U.S. income taxes and on any capital gains that result from the sale or exchange of stock. In Step 2, the U.S. parent firm may buy its stock from U.S. shareholders or exchange shares in the new foreign parent firm for its own stock. A nonrecurring tax is levied on any capital gains that accrue to the shareholders. The U.S. firm now holds 20 percent of the stock in its foreign subsidiaries, and the U.S. shareholders may own stock in the new foreign parent firm.

The U.S. firm then moves abroad. This is a two step process. In Step 1, the U.S. firm exchanges its stock for the stock of a foreign parent, newly formed in a tax haven country, a country with little or no corporate income tax. Nonrecurring taxes are levied on the previously excluded subsidiary income and on any capital gains that result. In Step 2, the U.S. firm exchanges the stock of the new foreign parent firm for all of its stock.

Finally, the U.S. firm establishes a new foreign parent firm and becomes wholly-owned by it. The ultimate shareholders now hold stock in the newly formed foreign parent firm. This reorganization is shown graphically in Figure 17–4.

---

[15] George C. Watt, Richard M. Hammer, and Marianne Burge, *Accounting for the Multinational Corporation* (Homewood, IL: Dow Jones-Irwin, 1977), p. 470.

[16] Ibid., 471.

[17] Kramer & Hufbauer article in *International Tax Journal* 1 (Summer 1975): 301–24.

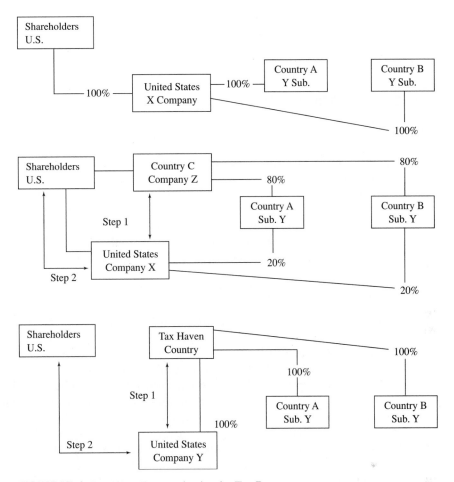

FIGURE 17-4 Corporate Reorganization for Tax Purposes

COMPANIES BEWARE

In addition to Section 367 of the Internal Revenue Code, U.S. and other countries' MNCs must be careful when they resort to treaty shopping. This is the practice that influences where and how MNCs are operated in foreign countries by locating operations in low-tax countries and organizing their financial flows across borders so that they will receive more favorable tax treatment. Many governments are cracking down on this practice. For example, new bilateral tax treaties between the United States and other nations contain provisions that prohibit treaty shopping.[18]

AN EXAMPLE OF RESTRUCTURING

One electronics company, Vishay Intertechnology Inc., integrates tax planning into the company's long-range international business strategy. The company earns 50 percent of its $1 billion in sales from Europe and the Pacific Rim. Vishay locates manufacturing plants in low-tax areas whenever possible in order to keep its global average tax burden to just above 20 percent. For example, Vishay has manufacturing facilities in Israel to produce for European and U.S. markets. Israel taxes the company's earnings at

[18] Lori Ioannou, "Taxing Issues," p. 43.

a flat 10 percent and provides employee and equipment grants. The company estimated that it had increased net profits by $30 million in the 1991–94 period because of the low Israeli tax rates.[19]

Other Tax Issues Facing MNCs

TAX HAVEN OPERATIONS

The MNC can reduce overall taxation of global operations by operating a foreign base company (FBC) in a tax haven country. A FBC is a corporation based in or registered in a country in which it does not conduct active operations, such as manufacturing. The term was adopted in the Internal Revenue Code by the Subpart F legislation introduced by the Revenue Act of 1962. A tax haven country, or tax haven, is one that levies a very small tax on corporations or none at all, i.e., they are countries that have a favorable tax structure. Such countries are, thus, able to attract overseas funds. Among the countries that may be classified as tax havens are Switzerland, Panama, the Netherlands Antilles, Liechtenstein, the Cayman Islands, and Bermuda. A FBC can be established in one of these countries to control overseas operations in general. For U.S. companies, a tax haven operation was much more valuable before the passage of the Revenue Act of 1962, which greatly reduced the benefit to be derived from a FBC in a tax haven. The pre-1962 U.S. tax haven company is shown in Figure 17–5.

Essentially, the FBC received all funds from overseas operations. The parent company shipped goods to the overseas affiliates, which sold the goods, sent all re-orders to the FBC, and remitted all sales proceeds to the latter. Only local value-added or excise taxes were generally levied against the sales affiliates. Little or no taxes were paid by the FBC to the tax haven government, and the parent paid no taxes on the foreign source income until earnings were remitted to it. Before 1962, a U.S. company

FIGURE 17–5 Tax Haven Company

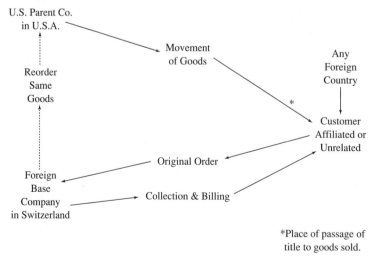

*Place of passage of title to goods sold.

Source: Andrew W. Brainard, "Impact of the Revenue Act of 1962 on U.S. Business Operations Abroad," *Export Trade* (January 14, 1963):9.

---

[19] Ibid., 45.

could reap large benefits from such an operation because of the tax savings. In short, U.S. MNCs used these tax haven FBCs to avoid taxes on royalties and other foreign source income.

The Kennedy administration characterized these tax haven companies as a form of tax evasion, although it was perfectly legal at the time. Thus, the U.S. government enacted the Revenue Act of 1962, drastically reducing the tax benefits from these operations. Subpart F was introduced by this new law as a method to preclude U.S. MNCs from using tax haven FBCs to avoid U.S. and foreign taxes.[20] Subpart F, or foreign base company income, was defined to include "payments made to 'related' parties 'in connection with the performance of technical, managerial, engineering, architectural, scientific, skilled, industrial commercial or like services' outside of the country of incorporation of the controlled foreign corporation."[21] The section applies where two or more incorporated or unincorporated organization, trades, or businesses are controlled directly or indirectly by the same interests. The control itself is considered to be decisive and not in its form or method by which it is exercised. A presumption of control arises when income or deductions have been arbitrarily shifted.[22]

The new law included a so-called "10-70" rule. If less than 10 percent of a controlled foreign corporation is FBC income, then none of the earnings will be taxed until distributed to the parent. A controlled foreign corporation is a foreign company of which more than 50 percent of the voting shares is held by U.S. shareholders. In other words, the foreign tax deferral rules apply. However, if more than 70 percent of foreign source income is FBC income, i.e., passive income, then all of the foreign source income is taxed as Subpart F income. The income is said to be attributed, or "tainted," and a tax is owed on the income, whether or not it is remitted to the parent firm. The tax law issue arises when the FBC income is between 10 and 70 percent. A good international tax attorney becomes a good investment in such cases.

Other types of foreign income may be excluded from the 1962 Revenue Act rules. Shipping profits are excluded if they are reinvested in shipping operations. Any foreign source income from a controlled foreign corporation that does not have as one of its significant purposes the substantial reduction of U.S. tax liability is excluded. Manufacturing income is excluded until it is remitted to the parent firm. In addition, income is excluded from this law if it arises from the sale of local products, from extraction operations, from agricultural operations, assembly, local services, or from any other local commercial or industrial activity.

Tax haven FBCs are still marginally attractive for U.S. companies. If the U.S. firm places majority ownership in the hands of non-U.S. nationals or holds each U.S. shareholding to less than 10 percent, the tax haven rules of the 1962 Revenue Act do not apply. Also, if Subpart F income is maintained at a level below 10 percent of the total taxable income of the controlled foreign corporation, the parent firm will receive some marginal tax benefits. A tax haven FBC will also be helpful if the parent firm needs to concentrate cash for investment in a particular subsidiary, desires to avoid foreign exchange rate fluctuations, or fears capital controls or expropriation in its foreign operations.

The U.S. parent firm must be careful in dealing with these tax issues. The spinoff of assets of an existing U.S. parent to a foreign subsidiary, a possible option in setting

---

[20] R Suk H. Kim and Seung H. Kim, *Global Corporate Finance: Text and Cases* (Miami, FL: Kolb Publishing Co., 1993), p. 439.

[21] Andrew W. Brainerd, "Impact of the Revenue Act of 1962 on U.S. Business Operations Abroad," *Export Trade*, January 14, 1963, p. 10.

[22] George C. Watt, Richard M. Hammer, and Marianne Burge, *Accounting for the Multinational Corporation* pp. 456–7.

up a FBC, requires IRS prior approval. This is difficult to obtain unless compelling business reasons can be demonstrated. Tax avoidance is not considered a valid business reason.

Examples of Tax Haven Countries

A number of countries can be characterized as tax havens, offering foreign firms and investors some favorable tax treatment to attract their funds. Among these are Cyprus, Bermuda, Singapore, Ireland, and Luxembourg.[23] Cyprus has attracted manufacturing investment in Russia and other former Soviet nations with favorable tax treaties. It levies only a 4.25 percent tax on the income of resident firms. Bermuda is a favorite location of captive insurance companies. It is regulated by the British government and has been a relatively scandal-free tax haven. Singapore attracts Pacific Rim companies that locate their regional finance companies there. Singapore offers tax holidays for foreign exchange trading. Ireland offers companies that locate in the old wharf area in Dublin, as Dublin Dock Companies, a 10 percent tax on financial gains and a lower rate on profits from manufacturing operations. The profits must be reinvested in Ireland or in the EU. Luxembourg levies virtually no tax on local holding companies. It is a major location for foreign reinsurance captive companies because of the attractive deductions granted them for such items as catastrophic losses.

TRANSFER PRICING AND SECTION 482

A recent survey by the global accounting firm of Ernst & Young of 200 MNCs operating worldwide ranked the major tax concerns that face these firms.[24] The vast majority of these firms (82 percent) ranked transfer pricing as their number one international tax concern. No other concern was ranked by more than 10 percent of these firms as very bothersome. An overwhelming 71 percent of these firms believe that transfer pricing will become an even bigger issue in the near term as a result of the growth in the percentage of foreign trade conducted by related parties and the global crackdown by government tax authorities on MNC tax evasion.

Transfer pricing practices by MNCs, especially U.S. companies, have created problems for the tax authorities of many nations that require these companies to use fair market prices, so-called arm's length prices, as their transfer pricing policy. But these tax authorities are different from country to country in how they observe and regulate transfer pricing by MNCs. Historically, international transfer pricing policies established by U.S. MNCs have been designed to take advantage of countries with differing tax rates. Essentially, the issue is to require the companies to refrain from reducing tax liabilities by shifting income from one country to another as well as to enable these tax authorities to reallocate income and deductions to reflect the proper taxable income and to prohibit tax abuses in this area by MNCs.[25] Of course, foreign tax authorities who naturally attempt to maximize tax revenues are suspicious of any practices that limit taxable income by foreign companies operating in their jurisdictions.

American tax authorities proposed new tax penalties on unreported income and new IRS code provisions, which were finalized into new regulations in 1994. The IRS believes that MNCs resort to the practice of selling products and services to their affiliates at high markups to limit their profitability and, thus, their tax liabilities to the United States. These provisions will require much more documentation for the reasons

---

[23] Paul Burnham Finney, "Searching Out Foreign Tax Havens," *International Business* (June 1995): 76–7.

[24] Nilly Ostro-Landau, "Avoiding the Global Tax Web," *International Business* (September 1995): 12.

[25] Kim and Kim, *Corporate Finance* pp. 450–1.

a given transfer pricing system is used. The Clinton administration has argued that the IRS is at a disadvantage in substantiating its rulings under Section 482 concerning the arm's length standard. For example, the IRS attempted to collect $1.5 million in back taxes and penalties against a Georgia defense contractor and manufacturer of military combat boots. When two IRS lawyers and a legal technician were sent to the Puerto Rico affiliate of the company, they found the affiliate's plant empty, abandoned, and locked up.[26] Although more documentation will be required under the new rules, the IRS argues that these rules offer MNCs more flexibility, judgment, and subjectivity in their determination of what they charge their overseas affiliates for certain services.[27] One of the new regulations requires the taxpayer to determine the best way to determine what prices it charges overseas affiliates, better known as the "best-method rule."

As a result of the U.S. Government's attack on transfer pricing, other countries have retaliated.[28] The IRS levied large claims during 1993 and 1994 on such Japanese companies as Hitachi, Yamaha, and Nissan. The latter company was accused of inflation of prices paid by its U.S. subsidiary for finished cars imported from the parent firm. The Japanese National Tax Administration Agency has levied a $145 million tax deficiency on Coca-Cola Company for 1990–92 as well as a bill for $87 million to AIU Insurance Company, the Japanese subsidiary of American International Group Inc. At the same time, the IRS has also levied back tax liabilities on PepsiCo, an American company, because of their transfer pricing systems with their subsidiaries such as Taco Bell, Pizza Hut, and Kentucky Fried Chicken.

The IRS applies Section 482 of the Internal Revenue Code to transfer pricing practices by U.S. MNCs. Section 482 gives the internal revenue agent the authority to reallocate or readjust the income of a company in order to prevent tax evasion. A number of tests can be applied to five different areas: loans and advances, performance of services, use of tangible property, use of intangible property, and the sale of intangible property. Essentially the IRS mandates a firm to charge interest on loans and advances to affiliates—the principle may never be paid off but some or all of the annual interest must be charged. Arm's length charges should be made on the performance of services that are charged management fees by the parent firm. In transactions involving the sale of tangible goods, the internal revenue agent can apply tests that include comparable uncontrolled prices, resale prices, cost-plus, or a combination of appropriate other methods. In the area of intangible transfers, such as technology, patents, formulae, etc., no comparable third party transfer is available so the internal revenue agent has a difficult test. Companies need to be careful in this area. In the use of tangible property, the test used is a formula based on a "safe haven" rate, e.g., on leasing transactions, this might include a pro rata share of depreciation on a straight-line basis, and all direct and indirect expenses of the property, plus the addition of 3 percent of the depreciable basis of the property.

A 482 reallocation may result in other effects on the company in addition to an increase in taxes. It can result in double taxation in cases where the combined U.S. and foreign tax rates are in excess of 100 percent of profits, loss of foreign tax credits against U.S. tax liabilities, loss of Subpart F exclusion—the payment of taxes on money not yet received from a subsidiary to its U.S. parent—loss of foreign base company manufacturing income exclusion under Subpart F, loss of less developed country corporation

---

[26] Jeff Nesmith, "Firms Avoid Billions in Taxes," *The Akron Beacon Journal* (September 11, 1994): C3.

[27] Lucinda Harper, "New Tax Rules Expand Multinationals' Flexibility in Dealings With U.S. Units," *Wall Street Journal*, 6 July 1994, p. A2.

[28] Stanley Reed, Larry Holyoke, and Douglas Harbrecht, "Here Comes the Great Global Tax War," *Business Week* (May 30, 1994): 55–6.

tax benefits, and other benefits from previous programs, such as the Western Hemisphere Trade Corporation, where a U.S. company's operation has been "grandfathered," i.e., permitted to remain in existence after the law was abolished.[29]

Some MNC executives do not believe that the tests used by IRS agents, to show whether arm's length standards have been used in intracompany operations, are valid tests. Section 482 is based on the premise that a subsidiary is a legally and economically separate entity from its parent company. One survey has held that less than half the corporations actually operate in this manner.[30] On the other hand, some believe such tests contain no serious deficiencies and that IRS agents need to be reeducated in their use and to be reasonable in their enforcement.[31] Such basic differences in philosophy between tax authorities and company executives is the central reason for any controversy concerning Section 482 and transfer pricing.

New 482 Regulations in 1994

The new regulations promulgated in 1994 place the emphasis on comparable transactions. The arm's length standard is applied in the determination of taxable income of a controlled taxpayer. Such taxpayers must have the same income as would have been realized if uncontrolled taxpayers were engaged in the same transactions under the same circumstances. Section 482 requires comparison of intragroup transfer prices with arm's length prices. IRS uses this procedure to monitor transfers in the following areas: (1) loans and advances, (2) performance of services, (3) use of tangible property, (4) use of intangible property, and (5) sale of intangible property. Subsidiaries are assumed to be legally and economically separate from their parent corporation.

The most significant new change in the 1994 regulations is the introduction of a new pricing method. The comparable profits method (CPM) was adopted and relies on the general principle that similarly situated taxpayers will tend to earn similar returns over a reasonable period of time. The CPM should provide an accurate result for measuring an arm's length result unless the tested party uses valuable, nonroutine intangible property that it acquired from uncontrolled taxpayers or developed itself.

Another alternative test introduced in the 1994 changes is the profit-split alternative. This method allows profit between controlled parties to be split in an arm's

---

<table>
<tr><td colspan="2" align="center">**STUDY AID**</td></tr>
<tr><td>

Transfer pricing is a problem facing the tax authorities of most major countries. This is a device used by affiliated companies to take advantage of differing tax rates in different countries. Transactions between these firms should be made according to the arm's length principle, meaning that the transactions should be carried on as if they were unrelated companies dealing at arm's length. Sec-

</td><td>

tion 482 of the U.S. Internal Revenue Code gives the IRS regulatory authority over transfer pricing systems used by U.S. firms and by foreign firms operating in the United States. A good discussion of transfer pricing can be found in Organization for Economic Cooperation and Development, *Transfer Pricing and Multinational Enterprises.*

</td></tr>
</table>

---

[29] Charles S.P. Barker and Richard L. Teberg, "Avoiding the '482' Tax Ricochet in a Multinational Situation," *Worldwide P & I Planning* 5 (March/April 1971): 60–5.

[30] Jane O. Burns, "How IRS Applies the Intercompany Pricing Rules of Section 482: A Corporate Survey," *Journal of Taxation* 59 (May 1980): 308–14.

[31] Joseph B. Mihalov, "Retaining the Section 482 Arm's-Length Standard," *Taxes* 60 (May, 1982): 331–43.

length manner. In addition, the 1994 regulations allow a company to apply the best method rule, i.e., the method that provides the most accurate measure of an arm's length result under the facts and the circumstances of the transaction under review. Under previous rules, the company had to go through a hierarchy of the tests, which were described previously.

Other Transfer Pricing Issues

As discussed in the chapter on Working Capital Management, new regulations concerning transfer pricing were issued by the U.S. Internal Revenue Service in 1994. These regulations require U.S. companies with transfer pricing systems to furnish detailed documentation that explains the company's selection and application of the transfer pricing method used. This documentation must be furnished to IRS within 30 days of a request. Thus, the regulations essentially require prior approval of the transfer pricing system used by U.S. firms.

In the area of transfer pricing, CFOs of MNCs should be familiar with all of the relevant tax codes with regard to related affiliate operations, including the laws of all of the countries in which they are operating, as well as Section 482 in the United States, and multilateral codes such as that of the OECD. More and more countries are strengthening their tax codes with regard to transfer pricing because their tax authorities believe that global firms have abused the tax system of many countries. Countries consider their tax systems to be a part of their sovereignty but, at the same time, they do not want to drive international business away because of burdensome tax rules. Thus, many nations are working with MNCs to create a less hostile tax environment.

For example, in the United States, an American company can negotiate an advanced pricing agreement (APA) with the IRS. An APA offers IRS approval of a company's transfer pricing policies. Such an agreement can also be obtained from foreign tax authorities. An APA may cost as much as $200,000 to obtain because of the time involved in negotiating the agreement with government agencies as well as the external data needed concerning comparable transactions in the marketplace. The time needed

---

MANAGEMENT APPLICATION NO. 32

A Transfer Pricing Example

Transfer pricing to reduce taxation can be demonstrated by the following example. Suppose that a U.S. clothing retailer has a foreign affiliate in Mexico, which manufactures polyester, and one in Venezuela, which manufactures men's neckties for the parent. The Mexican affiliate ships polyester for 500,000 ties to the Venezuelan affiliate for $5.00 per tie. The Mexican affiliate increases the price of the polyester to $5.50 per tie, which will increase its income by $250,000 and reduce the Venezuelan affiliate's income by the same amount. If it is assumed that the tax rate on domestic income for the Mexican affiliate is 25 percent and for domestic income for the Venezuelan affiliate is 50 percent, the transfer price change will increase the Mexican affiliate's taxes by $62,500 (0.25 × $250,000) and lower the Venezuelan affiliate's domestic tax by $125,000 (0.50 × $250,000). This reduces the overall corporate tax liability by $62,500 annually. The company has shifted profits from a higher tax jurisdiction to a lower one. If the Mexican affiliate had just begun operations and had high start-up costs, high depreciation allowances, or other investment tax credits, its marginal tax rate might be even lower and the overall tax liability might be even lower. Of course, any foreign tax credit treaty between the two countries may require further adjustment of these tax liabilities.

to negotiate one APA may be as long as 2 years. Apple Computer has negotiated three bilateral APAs with Australia, Canada, and Japan, which are considered industry models. The latter APA was negotiated between Japanese tax authorities and Apple Japan KK, an Apple marketing and distribution subsidiary. The agreement emulates similar agreements the company has with the Australian Taxation Office for Apple Computer Australia Pty. Ltd. and with Revenue Canada for Apple Canada Inc. Dow Chemical, which operates in 60 countries servicing 120 world markets, has also negotiated APAs. Most companies using APAs consider their cost worth the effort.[32]

In addition to problems with tax authorities, MNCs also run the risk of declining morale in the way their transfer prices are set. If the prices are set too high—to maneuver liquid assets for tax or financing reasons—the foreign affiliate manager may perceive that he is being penalized. His bonus may suffer if his profits decline because of transfer pricing methods. Singer Company, an early pioneer of transfer pricing, encountered this problem and found it necessary to completely revamp the company's foreign transfer pricing system. Transfer pricing will require two or more sets of accounts to avoid tax and morale problems. At the heart of this problem is the degree of centralization or decentralization practiced by the firm. This problem was discussed in more detail in chapter 8. At any rate, an international transfer pricing system should be designed in such a manner that it allows the foreign subsidiary manager to make decisions that are in the best interests of the MNC as a whole.

OECD and Transfer Pricing

In addition to individual countries strengthening their tax codes with regard to transfer pricing, multilateral organizations are also examining this issue. The Organization for Economic Cooperation and Development (OECD), comprised of European countries, Canada, United States, and Japan, is in the process of establishing a global standard for transfer pricing. In June 1995, the OECD reaffirmed its support of the principle that a company's foreign affiliates should be treated for tax purposes as if they were unrelated parties, operating at "arm's length."[33]

UNITARY TAXATION

The unitary taxation dispute has been an issue since the early 1980s. Unitary taxation is the method used by several states in the United States, which takes into consideration a corporation's worldwide earnings when assessing a subsidiary's state tax liability.[34] In 1983, some 13 states used some version of unitary taxation. The State of California was the largest state to use this method. Under the approach, income from all related affiliates of a company, foreign and domestic, is combined to determine the worldwide taxable income of the unitary business. If, for example, one-third of the firm's business activity, as measured by sales, payroll, and property, takes place in the unitary state, then one-third of the worldwide taxable income would be attributed to that state. See Figure 17–6 for an example of the unitary tax method.

Unitary taxation differs from the "arm's-length" or separate accounting method used by other states, the U.S. government, and most foreign countries. The arm's-length method taxes a MNC by allocating income among related affiliates according to arm's-length or unrelated party prices. European companies complain that unitary taxation results in an unreasonable tax burden, double taxation, and high administrative

---

[32] Ioannou, "Taxing Issues," p. 44.

[33] Ioannou, "Taxing Issues," p. 42.

[34] Jonathan Todd, "Battle Threatens Over Tax on Multinationals," *Europe* (November–December 1983): 22–3.

Formula

[(Instate sales/total sales) + (instate property/total property)

+ (instate payroll/total payroll) ÷ 3] × total net income

= apportioned net income

Example	Corp A	Corp B	Corp C	Total
Worldwide taxable income	750	200	50	1,000
California factors				
Property	—	—	36	36
Payroll	—	—	26	26
Sales	—	—	400	400
Worldwide factors				
Property	500	64	36	600
Payroll	300	74	26	400
Sales	4,000	600	400	5,000

Allocation percentages

Property	6.0%
Payroll	6.5
Sales	8.0
Total	20.5%
Average%	6.83%

Taxable income allocated to the state $68.3

FIGURE 17–6 Unitary Taxation Method

costs to measure their taxable income. Unitary taxation taxes a company not on the basis of local business but of global activities.

On June 27, 1983, the U.S. Supreme Court held, in the case of Container Corporation vs. the State of California, that states could, in the absence of legislation, resort to unitary business taxation. This ruling did not apply to foreign subsidiaries in a state, many of which threatened to pull out of the states that used unitary taxation, but this part of the finding was unclear. The Supreme Court could have ruled the tax method unconstitutional or it could have limited the definition of a unitary business. After this ruling, the Oregon Legislature voted to drop the unitary tax method after some MNCs threatened to move their operations elsewhere.[35]

In 1994, the Supreme Court ruled on two cases brought against California by Barclays Bank PLC, a British bank, and Colgate-Palmolive Company, a New York-based company that does business in California.[36] Prior to this case, California had amended its unitary tax law permitting foreign companies to sidestep the state's rules.[37] With Clinton administration support, the Supreme Court upheld the California tax law, even though the state had made it easy for MNCs to avoid the tax provisions. Some 60 large British companies with U.S. operations had threatened to ask the British government to enact a countermeasure to the unitary taxation method. The vote was unanimous as concerned with U.S. companies and 7–2 in the case of foreign-based companies.

---

[35] Scott D. Schuh, "Oregon Votes to Abandon Unitary Tax In Victory for Multinational Companies," *Wall Street Journal*, 1 August 1984, p. 10.

[36] Paul M. Barrett, "California's Multinationals Tax Is Upheld," *Wall Street Journal*, 21 June 1994, pp. A3–4.

[37] Paul M. Barrett, "High Court to Hear Challenge to Policy of California on Taxing Multinationals," *Wall Street Journal*, 2 November 1993, p. A4.

Direct vs. Indirect Taxation

The United States tax system relies for the most part for revenues on direct taxes, e.g., the personal and corporate income taxes. On the other hand, the European Community members rely on indirect taxes for the major part of their revenues. In Europe, most countries have switched from a cascaded turnover tax on sales to a value-added tax, effectively added at each level of production or sales.

The major implication stemming from this difference in tax-raising methods is concerned with the GATT rules vis-à-vis rebates to exporters. GATT rules prohibit rebating direct tax revenues, i.e., the type raised in the United States, to exporters as subsidies. Since import tariffs are indirect taxes, these revenues can be rebated to exporters. However, in the United States, revenues from DISC operations were deemed by Europeans as direct tax revenues and should not have been rebated to exporters. Some also complain that FSC revenues rebated as subsidies are wrong. The GATT organization was primarily established by European nations and, thus, its rules seem to be designed to reward European exporters. This problem has contributed to the debate that a value added tax be enacted by the U.S. government.

Taxation of the Expatriate U.S. Manager

The coverage in this chapter has concentrated on company operations and the effect of domestic and foreign taxation on these operations. This section is devoted to an examination of the taxation of U.S. expatriate managers. The overseas manager must adapt to a new currency, new language, as well as a potential new tax code. Most U.S. companies practice a form of tax equalization for their expatriate managers. The company, under this system, deducts from the expatriate's salary an amount equal to the tax that the expatriate manager would have paid at home. At year-end, the company pays the actual tax liability in the foreign jurisdiction, as well as any residual domestic taxes. The U.S. Federal income tax liability is generally zero because of an exemption of $70,000 granted on foreign individual income and any foreign tax credits allowed.

Most U.S. companies alleviate the problem of facing a new tax regime for their expatriate employees. These companies practice tax equalization for their expatriates.[38] Companies using this system deduct from the expatriate's salary an amount equal to the tax he or she would have paid at home. At the end of the tax year, these companies pay the actual tax bill in the foreign country in addition to any residual domestic taxes. See Figure 17–7 for an example of the tax equalization method used by one U.S. company headquartered in New York state.

Impact of Taxation on MNC Decisions and Policies

The discussion in this final section examines the impact of taxation on key decision and policy areas of the MNC. Taxation has many impacts on the firm and its managerial decisions. The following analysis focuses on selected impacts. First, with regard to decisions concerning the location of FDI, tax relief may be provided by the host country. If so, such relief may dictate in which of various countries the parent firm may locate foreign affiliates, including but not necessarily placing the affiliate in the country granting the most tax relief.

---

[38] Brad Asher, "Trimming the Expatriate Tax Bite," *International Business* 7 (July 1994), 48–50.

	Example No. 1[1]	Example No. 2[2]
Base salary	$270,000	$270,000
Hypothetical tax	45,884	71,707
Total base payroll	224,116	198,293
Total allowances	294,357	294,357
Total relocation cost	66,868	66,868
Net compensation	585,341	559,518
U.K. tax cost	306,463	288,586
Net U.S. tax cost	8,167	8,997
Less hypothetical tax collected	45,884	71,707
Total tax cost of assignment	**$268,746**	**$225,876**

[1] No hypothetical state tax, 14 percent hypothetical federal deduction, and hypothetical tax on personal income collected at year-end.

[2] New York state tax assessed, no federal deduction, tax on personal income collected during the year.

Source: Brad Asher, "Trimming the Expatriate Tax Bite," *International Business* 7(July 1994): 48.

FIGURE 17–7 Tax Cost of 3-Year Assignment to United Kingdom Executive with Annual Salary of $90,000

Second, when the form of organization is the decision/policy area, tax treatment may be the form of home country tax treatment for a branch as compared with a subsidiary. The MNC response may be to establish a subsidiary in the country where a high profit is expected, because of the application of the foreign tax deferral. On the other hand, a branch may be favored where losses are expected.

Third, with regard to financing decisions/policies, the host government may allow interest to be deducted as an expense. In this case, the MNC may finance the foreign affiliate with parent debt when the tax rate is higher in the host country than in the home country. An alternative response might be to treat the debt repayment as a return of capital, not subject to tax.

Finally, if the decision/policy area concerns remittance of foreign income and the tax treatment is between the home and host country tax rules, the MNC may have income remitted from the country with the smallest incremental tax liability. Or the MNC may resort to a policy of mixing the countries from which remittances will be made, based on the sources of profit and the national tax rates.

MNC MANAGEMENT POLICIES TOWARD TAXATION

It is clear that MNC management must adopt long-term strategies designed to cope with global tax issues. These strategies must include sourcing, production, and marketing based on different national and regional tax systems around the world. Some of the tax policies that MNCs have considered are[39]

1. establishment of foreign finance companies to take advantage of favorable tax legislation;
2. location of manufacturing facilities in low tax havens;
3. use of foreign sales corporations to reduce taxes on export earnings;
4. use of swaps and other derivative products to create more foreign source income in order to take advantage of U.S. foreign tax credits.

---

[39] Ioannou, "Taxing Issues," p. 43.

| MANAGEMENT APPLICATION NO. 33 |

Tax Minimization Strategies for the MNC

The following situation is illustrative of a global tax minimization strategy practiced by a U.S.-based MNC. The strategy is composed of several objectives that can be combined for the purpose of reducing the company's global tax burden.

First, the company should maximize excess foreign tax credits, as discussed previously. Such practice requires the company to have operations in two or more foreign countries in order to take advantage of the application of tax credits from a high-tax rate country against those from low-tax rate countries. Most MNCs will have no problem since their operations are usually scattered among several countries. As mentioned previously, excess foreign tax credits from an operation in one country can be applied against taxes due where a foreign operation has a lower tax rate imposed than the U.S. corporate income tax. Thus, in the absence of excess foreign tax credits, the firm would be liable for additional U.S. taxes.

Second, the company can transfer earnings from a country with a high withholding tax rate to an intermediate country that has a relatively low withholding tax rate before remitting those profits to the United States. This was demonstrated earlier in this chapter in the section on "Planning and Organizing MNC Operations to Minimize Taxes." Company management must be aware of the tax laws governing such transfers, including Section 367 of the U.S. tax code, and should adhere to these laws before implementing such cash flow reorganization plans.

Third, the company should conform to U.S. Internal Revenue Code Section 482 regulations and recent modifications when implementing its transfer pricing system. The company should investigate any advantages of an advanced pricing agreement (APA). The advance approval for a company's transfer pricing system, which an APA offers, can reduce the administrative costs normally incurred by a transfer pricing system.

Fourth, MNCs that do some exporting from the United States may draw some gains from the establishment of a foreign sales corporation (FSC). The FSC was discussed earlier and can offer the parent firm tax deferral on some profits made from export operations.

Fifth, the firm may also gain some marginal benefits from the use of a foreign base company located in a tax haven country. Although the Revenue Act of 1962 reduced the advantages from tax haven operations of U.S. companies, small tax benefits can be generated. However, if the tax gains do not offset the administrative costs of remaining within the law's guidelines, such an operation should not be used.

Finally, the MNC may be able to take advantage of the tax benefits extended to foreign investment by other countries. These include tax holidays that exempt new foreign investment from local income tax liabilities for some set period of time. The company must determine whether locating in such countries will benefit the company's other objectives, including adequate factor markets, transportation and communications facilities, and sufficient financial resources. Ireland might be considered for such tax advantages.

The U.S. MNC can derive these and other benefits from taking advantage of the variation in tax codes in other countries. The formulation of strategic operating decisions should integrate global tax planning wherever possible. Global tax minimization should always be an important ingredient of the firm's formulation of management strategy.

Summary and Conclusions

Taxes are just another cost to the MNC, however, these are costs that have to be paid as a license to operate in a foreign country, but they can be minimized. Overall, taxes come in many types and sizes. The U.S. MNC may be able to take a foreign tax credit

for income and withholding taxes paid to a foreign country. If the United States has a foreign tax treaty with the foreign country, the foreign tax credit probably can be taken. The calculation of the foreign tax credit is complicated and becomes even moreso after every tax code change made by the U.S. government. The U.S. tax liability on foreign source income can be deferred if the affiliate is a corporate subsidiary.

The CFO of the MNC must be aware of the many types of taxes in other countries that have an impact on the firm's earnings. Governments also grant reductions, or exemptions, or other tax breaks for foreign investors as incentives to encourage them to enter their countries.

U.S. MNCs can reorganize their companies to take advantage of tax breaks. Foreign base companies can still take advantage of low-tax rates in tax haven countries, despite the 1962 Revenue Act. Foreign sales corporations can be established for the purpose of reducing taxes on exporting income. Transfer pricing and other funds flows can be restructured and redesigned to reduce global taxes. However, tax authorities in every country, home and host, are watching foreign companies. A violation of one tax law may lead to the loss of benefits bestowed by other tax laws. A good international tax attorney is an important investment for the MNC.

Additional Readings

Arthur Andersen and Company, *Tax and Trade Guides*. Separate booklets, New York: Arthur Anderson and Company, 1978–91.

August, Ray. "Taxation." In *International Business Law: Text, Cases, and Readings*. Englewood Cliffs, NJ: Prentice-Hall, 1993, Chapter 13.

Barker, Charles S. P., and Richard L. Teberg. "Avoiding the '482' Tax Ricochet in a Multinational Situation." *Worldwide P&I Planning* 5 (March-April 1971): 60–6.

Commerce Clearing House. *World Tax Series*. Chicago, IL: Commerce Clearing House, various issues.

Eiteman and Stonehill. "Principles of Multinational Taxation." In *Multinational Business Finance*. Reading, MA: Addison-Wesley, 1995, Chapter 21.

Hufbauer, Gary C., assisted by Joanna M. van Rooij. *U.S. Taxation of International Income: Blueprint for Reform*. Washington, D.C.: Institute for International Economics, 1992.

Rodriguez, Rita M., and E. Eugene Carter, "International Taxation," In *International Financial Management*. Englewood Cliffs, NJ: Prentice-Hall, 1984, Chapter 13, Appendix 2.

Shapiro, Alan. "International Tax Management." In *Multinational Financial Management*. Englewood Cliffs, NJ: Prentice-Hall, 1996, pp. 640–75.

Discussion Questions

1. How do Switzerland and the United States differ in the extent of their tax jurisdiction over individuals and companies?
2. Discuss worldwide tax issues facing MNCs.
3. What is tax sparing? Give some examples.
4. Compare and contrast five methods for taxing foreign source income of companies.
5. Why does the United States give foreign tax credits for foreign source income tax payments? What established this mechanism?
6. What is the difference between a foreign tax credit and a foreign tax deduction?

7. How does the foreign tax deferral work?
8. What changes did the Tax Reform Act of 1986 make in the foreign tax credit?
9. What is the difference between the income tax treatment for subsidiaries and that for branches?
10. Discuss the foreign sales corporation and the possessions corporation.
11. What is a tax haven? What is the relation of a tax haven with a foreign base company?
12. What is Section 482? How does it affect transfer pricing?
13. How should a logical and defensible basis for transfer pricing be established?
14. Describe the unitary taxation method. Why is it used? Is it constitutional?
15. In what area does the direct vs. indirect taxation methods affect international trade? Discuss.
16. Discuss the impact of taxation on the decisions and policies of MNCs.

Problems

1. Assume a MNC has worldwide taxable income totaling $5 billion that is allocated as follows: $3 billion made by the parent operations located entirely in Ohio, $1.5 billion made by the International Subsidiaries located in several overseas locations, and $500 million by the operations located in California. Property is allocated as follows: $1 billion in Ohio, $500 million overseas, and $100 million in California. The company's payroll is allocated as follows: $500 million in Ohio, $100 million in overseas subsidiaries, and $50 million in California. California uses the unitary tax method to determine how much of the MNC's income is subject to the California corporate income tax. Calculate how much of this income is taxable by California under the unitary taxation method.

2. Assume a MNC makes $5 million foreign source income in its only foreign subsidiary. The local tax rate is 40 percent. The company has a dividend pay-out ratio of 40 percent. The local withholding tax rate on dividends is 20 percent. Assume a foreign tax credit treaty is in effect between the foreign country and the United States. Calculate by the grossing-up method what the U.S. tax liability will be after the foreign tax credit. The U.S. corporate income tax rate is 34 percent.

3. Assume that the company has operations in two foreign countries. Both have a 20 percent withholding tax on dividends and have foreign tax credit treaties with the United States. In Country A, the corporate income tax rate is 40 percent, in Country B, it is 28 percent. The U.S. corporate tax rate is 34 percent. Calculate by the grossing-up method the final U.S. tax liability on the foreign source income.

4. Kent Worldwide Products Company has affiliates in Countries A and B. The Country A manufacturing subsidiary incurs costs of $1,400,000 for goods that it manufactures and sells to a sales affiliate in Country B. The goods are then resold to final consumers for $3,600,000. Both subsidiaries have operating expenses of $200,000. Both Countries A and B levy a corporate income tax of 50 percent on taxable income in their respective countries. If Kent Worldwide raises the aggregate transfer price so that shipments from its manufacturing plant to its sales outlet increase from $2,000,000 to $2,400,000, what effect would this change have on consolidated taxes? What would the tax effects of this pricing action be if corporate income tax rates were only 30 percent in Country A, but remained the same, 50 percent, in Country B?

5. Tiger Enterprises is a MNC based in the United States and has a 100 percent-owned subsidiary operating in Chile. The Chilean affiliate has foreign earnings before taxes of $400,000. After the affiliate pays a corporate income tax of 35 percent, it remits a dividend of $100,000 to its parent in the United States. If the dividend withholding tax is 15 percent, what is the applicable U.S. tax liability? What would the tax liability be if the Chilean affiliate were a branch of the Tiger Enterprises?

6. If TRW, Inc., has $1 million in excess foreign tax credits, how might its dividend remittance decision be affected?

7. Assume the following information: a U.S. corporation remits foreign after-tax earnings of a foreign subsidiary to the U.S. parent in the form of a dividend of $120,000. The foreign corporate income tax is 40 percent. The withholding tax levied against the dividend payment is 4 percent. Excess foreign tax credits are unavailable. Find the incremental U.S. tax owed on the foreign source earnings.

Payment Systems, Custody, and Settlement of Cross-Border Transactions in Global Finance

---

Major Objectives of Chapter 18

    To introduce the problems encountered by financial managers of MNCs in the payment, clearing, custody arrangements, and settlement of transactions involving financial instruments and financial market operations of the firm, as well as the risks that arise in such operations.

Key terms to be learned in chapter 18:

- bilateral netting
- value date
- counterparty
- delivery versus payment (DVP)
- principal risk
- payment risk
- credit risk
- replacement cost risk
- systemic risk
- novation
- custody service
- Access

- multilateral netting
- Multinet International
- clearing house system
- real-time gross settlement
- FX Net
- payment system
- liquidity risk
- operational risk
- settlement risk
- Globex
- SOFFEX
- Euroquote

Introduction

A number of special issues in the field of international financial management can be identified. One major issue that has faced international management of MNCs during the past 25 years has been international monetary stability, especially in foreign exchange markets. This has been especially true when one considers the several international financial crises that have threatened global business. The fixed exchange rate crises in the early 1970s resulted in a major modification of the international monetary system when a floating rate regime was established in 1973 and led to major expenditures by U.S. MNCs for the implementation of foreign exchange exposure management systems. The market highs and lows encountered by the U.S. dollar in the 1980s threatened the floating rate system but cooperation among the major monetary authorities resulted in a more entrenched system of floating rates, which still encounters government intervention. The October 1987 stock market crash with its global spread showed that global clearing and settlement systems may have been less efficient than desired by investors as contagion risk was encountered in securities markets around the world. The 1992 crisis involving the European Rate Mechanism nearly led to a global currency meltdown as trillion dollar trading days were experienced for the first time on a regular basis. The latest test of the international monetary system occurred at the end of 1994 when the Mexican peso fell drastically against the dollar and other major currencies. An attempt by President Clinton to gain authorization from the U.S. Congress for a bailout failed because the American public did not support such a plan. The peso was shored up only after the IMF and the Bank for International Settlements joined forces with the U.S. Executive Branch to make available $52.8 billion of loan guarantees. The U.S. Congress did not become the lender-of-last-resort to the global financial system. A multilateral safety net became quite important in shoring up the Mexican government, thus saving the world from a global liquidity crisis and possible downturn in international economic growth.

As important as the issue of international monetary stability seems, from the examples just discussed, the institutional structure of the global financial markets seems even more important. Thus, this treatment of the study of managerial aspects of international finance will focus on payment systems, custody, and settlement of cross-border transactions in international business as parts of an even more important special issue. International business is driven by the satisfaction of customer demand for goods and services from international firms. Supplying these goods and services requires global finance. Funds to satisfy MNCs come more and more from international financial markets and less and less from banks. Every day more than a trillion dollars is traded in the foreign exchange markets. These funds are used to pay for the $5 trillion or so of annual international trade. They support the more than $2 trillion of foreign investment placed around the world and the trillions of dollars of stocks, bonds, mutual funds, and derivative financial instruments traded in financial markets on a cross-border basis.

The execution of the financial transactions that involve trillions of dollars and other currencies is facilitated by various payment systems established by banks, government agencies, and other private firms. International banks play an increasing role in these activities as integral to the settlement systems by which securities and other financial instruments are delivered and for which payment is made and as custodians of investment portfolios for individuals, companies, and governments. The discussion in chapter 18 will focus on these operations.

A variety of risks are encountered by international business in the payment systems, custody and clearing house arrangements, and settlement operations used in global transactions. These include credit risk, liquidity risk, replacement cost risk, op-

erational risk, and systemic risk. It is believed that such risks need to be emphasized again and, thus, these risks and their management will be discussed in more detail in this concluding chapter. The chapter will conclude with an analysis of recommendations made in a number of recent studies by international monetary groups to improve global clearing, custody, settlement, and payment systems.

This book began with the theme of a borderless world in which Europe, Japan, and the United States make up the major consumer markets of the world, and the yen, the dollar, and the deutsche Mark represent the major currencies used for commercial and financial transactions. In chapter 3, foreign exchange was introduced as the life blood of this global market. Volume of transactions in the foreign exchange market, primarily an interbank market, has expanded greatly in the past decade. In 1989, an international survey of banks showed daily foreign exchange trading volume to be $640 billion. This total was exceeded during the 1992 European monetary crisis when trillion dollar trading days were registered. Transactions currently exceed a trillion dollars on an ordinary day.

Such large trading volume is necessary to facilitate international commercial transactions in trade and investment and to furnish the liquidity, which narrows spreads. Banks, firms, and individuals participating in these markets face a variety of risks if parties to their transactions were to default on payments needed to settle the transactions. These risks can be alleviated by more efficient payment and settlement systems, more extensive netting arrangements, and more effective custodial operations. Most of these facilities are, by nature, carried out by the global banking system. Such systems form the basis of the remainder of this chapter.

Payment, settlement, netting, and global custody were once functions that were given little attention in international business transactions. These functions were taken for granted and were discussed very little or not at all in international financial management literature. Custody has now become a core business for many large international banks and a service offered by nearly every bank. It is a business which now amounts to billions of dollars and includes investment accounting, cash management and treasury services, and securities lending, all activities needed by global firms. It is a function that, because of a number of big bank mergers, will more and more be performed by a small number of large international banks by the end of the decade.

GLOBALIZATION OF FINANCIAL MARKETS

Globalization of financial markets coupled with the deregulation of financial markets around the world, integration of many major markets, 24-hour trading, and the increased use of computers and electronics to facilitate trading have all contributed to the tremendous increase in international financial transactions and the need for more foreign exchange. One result stemming from international financial globalization has been the enhanced ability of investors to diversify their risk. Another benefit has been access to broader markets for funds by firms and individuals demanding funds.

Cross-border financial transactions have increased greatly during this period of market globalization. A French citizen may purchase dollars in the foreign exchange market to invest in shares of General Electric Company listed on the New York Stock Exchange. A German insurance firm may sell deutsche Marks in the foreign exchange market for dollars to purchase Treasury bond futures contracts to hedge receipt of funds from an annuity to be marketed a year from now. Every minute some such transaction is executed. Risks arise from these transactions. Some of the risks can be alleviated by increased coordination of global financial markets. They can be hedged by dealing in any of a number of the derivatives discussed in chapters 13 and 14.

The globalization of financial markets can be measured by the increase in market

volume during the past decade as well as the increase in the number of new financial markets established and new financial instruments traded.[1] For example, foreign transactions in securities of U.S. companies increased from $75.3 billion in 1980 to $361.4 billion in 1990. U.S. transactions in securities of foreign firms increased from $17.85 billion to $253.4 billion during the 1980s. Twenty new futures exchanges were established during the late 1980s. Between 1983 and 1988, trading volume in futures and options market contracts increased nearly 200 percent. Eurodollar interest rate futures contract volume increased by 70 percent during this period.

Growth of global financial markets has continued at an even faster rate in the 1990s. As mentioned previously, foreign exchange volume has increased by more than 50 percent since 1989. The development of exotic derivatives, discussed in detail in chapter 14, and the use of other ordinary derivatives such as futures, options, and swaps is testimony to such growth of cross-border financial transactions. This growth has increased a number of the risks faced by CFOs of MNCs. These risks will be discussed in more detail in the next section.

Financial Market Risks

A number of risks that are faced by the financial management of the international firm were introduced in chapter 1 and discussed with reference to a specific operation in other places in this text. These and other risks are inherent in the clearance and settlement of cross-border financial transactions and, thus, must be reiterated in this final chapter. These risks need to be measured and managed by institutions and firms within the financial markets in which they are encountered. In the day-to-day management of these financial risks, a number of issues arise. One of these issues is whether risk management should follow the corporation's organizational structures. That is, should risk be managed on a centralized or decentralized basis? Or should risk management be carried out within one geographic center across several products or across a number of geographic centers for a given product? These issues are briefly considered in chapter 8.[2] In any case, effective risk management requires that the CFO of a MNC is aware of the various risks. It may be even more important that the company's banker is able to recognize, measure, and manage these risks, since much of the foreign exchange and securities transactions may be handled in the interbank markets. This is especially true for foreign exchange, Eurocurrencies, and some derivatives. Relevant financial risks encountered by participants in clearing systems and ordinary financial markets will be discussed in the following sections.

CREDIT RISK

Credit risk arises when one of the counterparties to a transaction does not settle in full, either when the funds are due or on some later date. A counterparty is merely one of the parties to a transaction. Credit risk may result in bankruptcy of a counterparty. A party to a transaction may conduct a credit analysis of financial data and information furnished by the other party or by credit rating agencies. Companies whose counter-

---

[1] Jodi G. Scarlata, "Institutional Developments in the Globalization of Securities and Futures Markets," *Federal Reserve Bank of St. Louis Review* 74 (January/February 1992): 17–8.

[2] A good discussion and analysis of these issues may be found in *Recent Developments in International Interbank Relations*, (Basel, Switzerland: Bank for International Settlements, October 1992), pp. 20–1. This is a report prepared by a Working Group of the Group of Ten countries and is referred to as the Promisel Report for Larry J. Promisel, at that time, a staff member of the Federal Reserve Board of Governors.

parties are major firms with whom they have a major relationship are generally monitored and evaluated inhouse. Counterparties with smaller credit lines are usually checked out by rating agencies hired by the firm. In cases where the firm operates within a clearing house system, credit risk may be minimal because the clearing house is usually well-capitalized and will stand behind the transaction.[3] In most international transactions, clearing houses do not exist. Where they do, bilateral and multilateral netting of payments is possible.

When credit risk leads to a default by one of the counterparties, the credit risk may include the risk of the loss of unrealized gains on unsettled contracts with the defaulting counterparty as well as risk of the loss of securities delivered or payments made to the defaulting counterparty prior to discovery of the default. Credit risk can be priced, especially for longer run contracts. For short-term contracts, default probability is usually low and, thus, pricing of such risk is considered a low priority. Even in longer term contracts, such pricing is difficult from both a theoretical and conceptual standpoint.

REPLACEMENT COST RISK

Credit risk that results in default by one of the counterparties may result in replacement cost risk. Replacement cost risk is the risk of loss of unrealized gains. The unrealized gain is determined by comparing the market price of a security at the time of default with the contract price. If the market price is below the contract price, the seller of the security or other financial instrument is exposed to a replacement cost loss. The buyer of the security is exposed to this loss if the market price is above the contract price. In both cases, the price of the security changes between trade and settlement. In cross-border markets, adverse changes in the exchange rate can exacerbate this risk.

PRINCIPAL RISK

Another exposure to loss that may stem from credit risk is principal risk. Principal risk is the risk of loss of the full value of securities or funds that a firm has transferred to the defaulting counterparty where settlement is made on the date or just prior to the date of default by the counterparty. Principal risk is essentially the same as cross-currency settlement risk, or Herstatt risk, and may also be referred to as settlement risk.

Banks wishing to avoid or reduce Herstatt or settlement risk have studied arrangements to achieve such objectives. One such proposal would require parties to a financial transaction to deposit funds in a third party escrow account until settlement of the different currency legs is completed. A delivery versus payment system, to be discussed in a subsequent section, can also alleviate Herstatt risk.

LIQUIDITY RISK

Liquidity risk arises when clearing, or settlement, payments are not made when due, even though one or more counterparties do have sufficient funds and net worth ultimately to make the payments. Liquidity risk may be caused by a variety of events, such as a temporary inability by a counterparty to convert assets to cash, because of various operational difficulties, or by the inability of the counterparty's banking correspondent to perform settlement functions of one kind or another.

---

[3] A clearing house system is a mechanism for calculation of mutual positions within a group of participants or counterparties in which the settlement of their mutual obligations is facilitated on a net basis.

Liquidity risk may also arise because of failure of the counterparty's bank. The failed bank holds the counterparty's funds to, for example, pay for securities or foreign exchange purchased by the counterparty. This risk can be avoided by using central banking facilities to settle the transactions. However, in many foreign countries, non-bank firms dealing in financial markets are not permitted access to central bank accounts.

OPERATIONAL RISK

Operational risk is the result of some technical failure in computer systems, telecommunications facilities, or institutionalized procedures during trading and before settlement of the transaction. New trading systems cause market participants to place heavy reliance on technology in accessing global financial markets. The CME has put into practice several safeguards in implementing its Globex system. Such safeguards include measures to prevent unauthorized individuals from accessing the system, such as the use of as many as four different identification codes, as well as termination of a computer operator's session if nonstandard instructions are entered and, in the failure of the central computer, recovery involving automatic switchover to a back-up mainframe within 60–90 seconds.[4]

SYSTEMIC RISK

Systemic risk may affect payment systems and financial markets and, thus, may have direct effects on banks and MNCs operating within such systems or markets. Systemic risk is the risk that the inability or failure of one participant in a payment system or financial market to meet obligations when they are due will cause other participants to fail to meet their obligations when due. In the banking system, systemic risk is characterized by a run from deposits to currency. In futures and options markets, systemic risk occurs when agents no longer trade through established channels such as an exchange.

Most of the risks discussed and analyzed in the preceding sections are encountered by international firms and banks in the clearance and settlement of cross-border transactions. These risks may be reduced or eliminated by the use of more efficient payment systems, by netting payments on a bilateral or multilateral basis, and by more reliance on global custodians, banking institutions. Global custodians manage clearance, settlement, tax reclamation, and other activities that are part of cross-border investments executed with agent banks in foreign countries. In subsequent sections of this chapter, the role of payments systems including settlement, netting, and clearing arrangements will be examined. The discussion will focus on the problems in these areas that face the CFOs of MNCs.

In addition to these risks, custodians face other risks mentioned in other parts of this book. Country risk, discussed in chapter 5, is a major factor, especially when dealing in developing countries. This is the risk of holding assets in a foreign country and includes the risks generated by local market practice, the local clearing system, and currency transfer risk. Foreign exchange risk, discussed in more detail in chapter 4, is incurred constantly by global custodians. In addition, custodians encounter market price risk, issuer risk, or investment risk—the amount of risk if the issuer defaults or fails to meet his legal obligation to pay interest and principal on, e.g., a bond. Finally, custodians face settlement risk, the risk that a party will default on one or more delivery or payment obligations to its counterparties or to a settlement agent. These risks were discussed in chapter 12.

---

[4] Scarlata, "Globalization of Securities and Futures Markets," p. 24.

Payment Systems: An Overview

Bank managers are faced with four key environmental factors in the assessment of the future of their payments systems.[5] These are consolidation, regulation, technology, and globalization. First, companies have consolidated their purchases while using fewer banks but buying more services from each bank. U.S. banks—because of their proliferation—have a large infrastructure cost from the transactional handoffs required to the Federal Reserve System, clearing houses, or correspondences. Second, regulation of such mundane operations as same day settlement, mandated by competition, check clearing, daylight overdrafts, coupled with the reduction of disbursement float, and increased use of electronic payments, will be an increasing threat to some banks and opportunity for others. Third, the pace of change and rate of technological innovations including increased customer demand for better, faster, more timely information has pushed banks to specialize more and more and to be more selective in what products they offer customers. Fewer banks are engaged in full service, cash management operations. Finally, globalization of financial services requires more and more banks to send payments to off-shore beneficiaries, to make more cross-currency payments to international counterparties, and to use more multicurrency payments. The advent of NAFTA, increasing growth rates in Asian nations, and economic recovery in Latin America, coupled with the privatization movement in eastern Europe, and recovery in Europe from recession in general are all factors that have increased the globalization of business and need for more improved global payments systems and more efficient financial services.

SELECTED PAYMENT SYSTEMS

Payments systems were discussed in chapter 15 as international communications networks in the coverage of working capital management in MNCs. The remainder of this section will contain an overview of selected major payment systems, both bank and commercial non-bank networks.[6] The most important of these are: (1) Fedwire connecting the 12 U.S. Federal Reserve Banks, U.S. depository institutions, U.S. Treasury Department, and other U.S. government agencies; (2) CHIPS, the Clearing House Interbank Payments System whose members include 41 U.S. banks and 98 foreign banks; (3) CHAPS, the Clearing House Automated Payments System, owned and operated by a consortium of U.K. banks; (4) FX Net, a foreign exchange bilateral netting settlement system with a membership of some 20 financial institutions; and (5) SWIFT, the Society for Worldwide Interbank Financial Telecommunications, headquartered in Brussels, Belgium, with more than 2,000 member banks.

Other Systems

Other systems have been developed in recent years to clear and settle financial transactions. The International Clearing Systems, Inc., was established in 1992 as a bilateral netting system covering eight Canadian and U.S. banks. The system may be upgraded to a multilateral netting system. A multilateral netting system known as ECHO, the European Clearing House Organisation, was established in London in 1994. ECHO is planned to include 50 OECD banks and settle transactions in as many as 24 curren-

---

[5] Donald R. Hollis, "The Payments System Evolution at the Crossroads," *Bank Management* 70 (July/August 1994): 51.

[6] For a detailed examination of these and other payment systems, see C.E.V. Borio and P. Van den Bergh, *The Nature and Management of Payment System Risk: An International Perspective* (Basel, Switzerland: Bank for International Settlements, February 1993).

cies. The International Swap Dealers Association (ISDA) plans to begin a bilateral net-ting operation for swaps. Although its primary objective will be to reduce credit risks on outstanding obligations, this scheme will also provide for netting of settlement flows connected with swap contracts.

In Hong Kong, a nation without a central bank, payment system functions are handled by private sector banks. Settlements are done by the Hongkong & Shanghai Bank, which operates a manual clearing house, a magnetic tape exchange system and CHATS (Clearing House Automated Transfer System), an on-line interbank funds transfer system. These systems are provided a credit facility by the Hongkong & Shang-hai Bank, although the system could still encounter liquidity risk if these facilities would have insufficient funds to cover a deficit.[7]

ROLE OF CENTRAL BANKS

As one can see from Figure 18–1, central banks represent one of the most important parts of the payment system.[8] They have direct relationships with clearing house and banks and indirect relationships with non-bank financial institutions. Central banks are

FIGURE 18–1 Payment System Participants, Message Flows and Funds Transferred

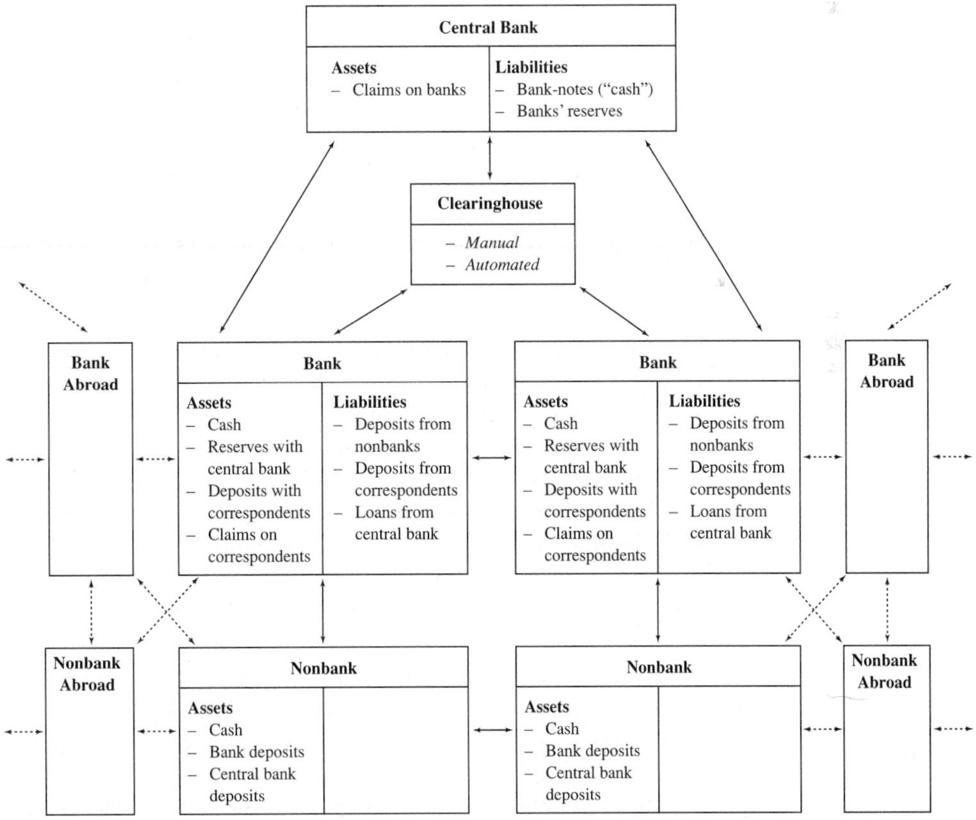

Source: C.E.V. Borio and P. Van den Bergh, *The Nature and Management of Payment System Risks: An International Perspective* (Basel, Switzerland: Bank for International Settlements, 1993), p. 9.

---

[7] Mitsuo Yamaguchi, "An Assessment of Payment System Risk in Asia," *Payment Systems Worldwide* 4 (Winter 1993–94): 22.

[8] See Ibid., 19–23, for a detailed discussion of the role of central banks in global financial systems.

responsible for the soundness and smooth functioning of the financial system. In Sweden, the central bank has statutory responsibility to safeguard the efficiency and soundness of the system. In Italy, the central bank operates the clearing house. Both the Banca d'Italia and the Banque de France work toward improvement of the domestic systems in their respective countries.

Central banks may be quite active in the various functions of the payment system. They may own, operate, audit, and set and enforce regulations. Some have expanded their role in the settlement and clearance of securities transactions. In the United States, United Kingdom, and the Netherlands, they keep the book-entry system for government or private debt instruments. The G-10 central banks are directly involved in the supervision of their respective financial systems. In Italy, Japan, the Netherlands, and the United States, the central banks conduct separate audits of banks' electronic data processing systems, and in Italy, Japan, and the United States, the central banks' supervisory powers extend to other parts of the payment system, e.g., CHIPS in the United States.

Banks' Role in Payment Systems

Banks play an important role in payment systems. As mentioned previously, they make up a large part of systems such as CHIPS, CHAPS, CHAT, and SWIFT. The foreign exchange market is dominated by banks. In foreign countries, investment banking is dominated by universal banks that facilitate clearing, settlement, and, as will be discussed subsequently, the custody function. Netting operations can be carried out by banks. Netting facilities are discussed in the next section.

NETTING ARRANGEMENTS

Netting arrangements, bilateral and multilateral, and their mechanics were discussed in chapter 4 as a method international companies can use to hedge foreign exchange risk and in chapter 15 as a tool for facilitating working capital management and funds flows within and among international companies. Netting arrangements are important facilities that can be used to net out amounts due between banks that arise from foreign exchange contracts or from the exchange of payment instructions. The primary objectives of such bank netting facilities are to increase the efficiency of financial markets and cross-border payment systems and to reduce counterparty credit and liquidity risks.[9] Most netting systems operate by a method in which one financial obligation is exchanged for a similar and offsetting obligation. Only the net difference is then settled in money. See Figures 4–6, 4–7, and 4–8 in chapter 4 for illustrations of netting centers and arrangements with and without multilateral netting. With bank netting arrangements, such facilities have monetary implications in that bank demand for both intraday and overnight balances held at central banks as well as credit from such central banks may be affected, especially if netting results in significant reductions in bank funds needed.

The demand for netting arrangements with respect to demand and supply of foreign exchange has a number of objectives.[10] First, the number of payment messages between counterparties and their correspondent banks in the country of each foreign

---

[9] Bank for International Settlements, *Report on Netting Schemes* (Basel, Switzerland: Group of Experts on Payment Systems, 1989), p. 3. This is also referred to as the Angell Report, for Wayne D. Angell, Chairman of the Group of Experts on Payment Systems and then member of the Federal Reserve Board of Governors.

[10] Ibid., 11.

currency can be reduced, thus reducing message transmission costs. Second, counter-party credit and liquidity risk can be reduced because netting reduces a bank's credit risk from a gross amount to be settled to a net amount. Third, the need for intraday liquidity or credit to bridge timing gaps between gross payments and gross receipts can be reduced. Finally, banks may be able to minimize the amount of free capital necessary to be allocated to that segment of their business. This is possible because banks can reduce their off-balance sheet assets and/or liabilities on a daily basis.

Examples of Bank Netting Arrangements[11]

In Table 18–1, several transactions are itemized that involve settlement of foreign exchange trading under gross settlement and bilateral netting. These transactions are shown in Figure 18–2 as a flow of currencies between banks under gross settlement and bilateral netting. Under gross settlement, the banks will make payments to each other in the settlement of transactions between them. As shown in Figure 18–2, to settle transaction #1, Bank A pays £100 to Bank B and receives $175 in turn. The exchange rate is $1.65 on the value date. Thus, the exchange of currencies yields a profit of $10 to Bank A. Bank A pays $85 to Bank B in settlement of transaction #2 and receives £50. This exchange yields a loss of $2.50 for Bank A on value date.

The banks can reduce the number of transactions by netting their payments as shown in the bottom of Figure 18–2. Bank A can pay £50 to Bank B and receive $90

TABLE 18–1   Payments in Settlement of Foreign Exchange Transactions under Gross Settlement and Bilateral Netting

Counterparties	Transaction Number	Gross Settlement		Bilateral Netting	
		Direction of Payment	*Units of Currencies*	*Direction of Payment*	*Units of Currencies*
Bank A and Bank B	1	Bank A to Bank B	£100	Bank A to Bank B	£50
		Bank B to Bank A	$175	Bank B to Bank A	$90
		(Profit of $10.00 for Bank A)		(Profit of $7.50 for Bank A)	
	2	Bank A to Bank B	$85		
		Bank B to Bank A	£50		
		(Profit of −$2.50 for Bank A)			
Bank A and Bank C	1	Bank A to Bank C	£100	Bank A to Bank C	$92.50
		Bank C to Bank A	$170	Bank C to Bank A	£50
		(Profit of $5.00 for Bank A)		(Profit of −$10.00 for Bank A)	
	2	Bank A to Bank C	$262.50		
		Bank C to Bank A	£150		
		(Profit of −$15.00 for Bank A)			
Bank B and Bank C	1	Bank B to Bank C	£150	Bank B to Bank C	£100
		Bank C to Bank B	$262.50	Bank C to Bank B	$177.50
		(Profit of $15.00 for Bank B)		(Profit of $12.50 for Bank B)	
	2	Bank B to Bank C	$85.00		
		Bank C to Bank B	£50		
		(Profit of −$2.50 for Bank B)			

Source: R. Alton Gilbert, ''Implications of Netting Arrangements for Bank Risk in Foreign Exchange Transactions,'' *Federal Reserve Bank of St. Louis Review* 74 (January/February 1992): 7.

---

[11] R. Alton Gilbert, "Implications of Netting Arrangements for Bank Risk in Foreign Exchange Transactions," *Federal Reserve Bank of St. Louis Review* 74 (January/February 1992): 3–16.

Gross Settlement

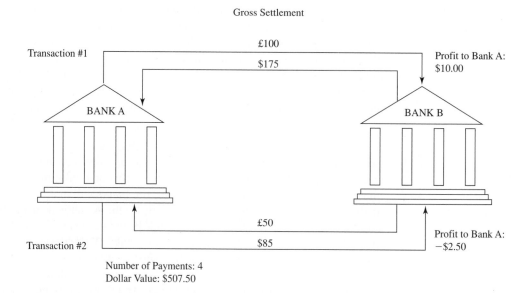

Number of Payments: 4
Dollar Value: $507.50

Bilateral Netting

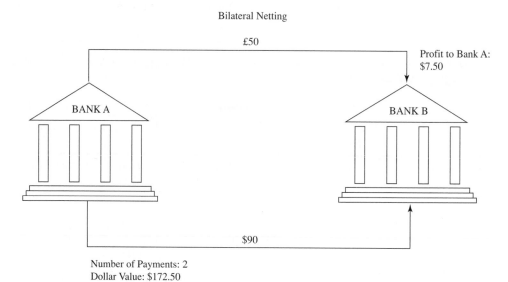

Number of Payments: 2
Dollar Value: $172.50

Source: R. Alton Gilbert, "Implications of Netting Arrangements for Bank Risk in Foreign Exchange Transactions," *Federal Reserve Bank of St. Louis Review* 74 (January/February 1992):9.

FIGURE 18–2 Flow of Currencies Between Banks Under Gross Settlement and Bilateral Netting

from Bank B. The number of payments is reduced from four to two by using bilateral netting and the value of the payments, using the exchange rate of $1.65, declines from $507.50 to $172.50.

Payments between members of a multilateral netting arrangement and the clearing house are shown in Figure 18–3. The arrangement shown in Figure 18–2 has been operational for several years. The arrangement shown in Figure 18–3 is modeled after the ECHO netting system introduced in London in 1994.

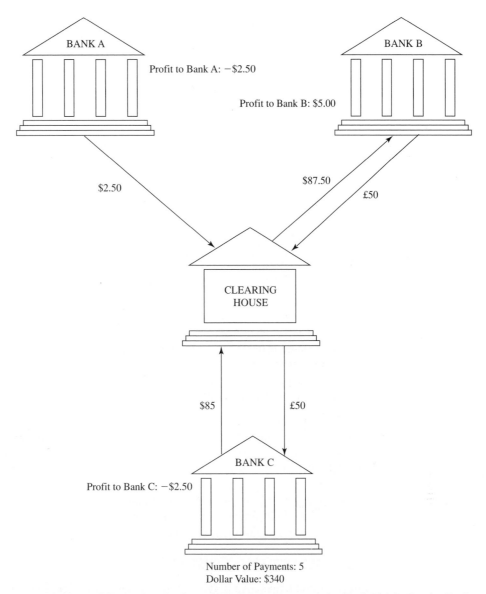

Source: R. Alton Gilbert, "Implications of Netting Arrangements for Bank Risk in Foreign Exchange Transactions," *Federal Reserve Bank of St. Louis Review* 74 (January/February 1992):13.

FIGURE 18–3 Payments Between Members of a Multilateral Netting Arrangement and the Clearing House

In Figure 18–2, the exchange rate on the value date is $1.65/£. Transactions to be settled on this date were negotiated a few days earlier when the exchange rate was higher. Some trades were at $1.70/£ and others were at $1.75/£. The transactions varied in size, thus creating imbalances in the flows of currencies between counterparties. Under gross settlement, shown at the top of Figure 18–2, banks make payments to each other to settle each transaction between them. In the bottom half of Figure 18–2, the banks economize on transactions by netting their payments flows. The number of pay-

ments is reduced from four to two and the value of the payments, converted at the exchange rate of $1.65/£ are reduced from $507.50 to $172.50. With a multilateral netting arrangement and a clearing house, shown in Figure 18–3, five payments totaling $340 will be made. In either case, netting reduces the amount of foreign exchange to be converted, thus resulting in lower transactions cost and lower settlement risk. These savings can be passed on to corporate customers.

Minimum Standards

Minimum standards should be formulated for the design and operation of international and multicurrency netting and settlement schemes. Among these are the following:[12]

1. netting schemes should have a well-founded legal basis under all relevant jurisdictions;

2. netting scheme participants should have a clear understanding of the impact of the particular scheme on each of the financial risks affected by the netting process;

3. multilateral netting systems should have clearly defined procedures for the management of credit risks and liquidity risks, which specify the respective responsibilities of the netting provider and the participants;

4. multilateral netting systems should, at a minimum, be capable of ensuring the timely completion of daily settlements in the event of an inability to settle by the participant with the largest single net debit position;

5. multilateral netting systems should have objective and publicly disclosed criteria for admission, which permit fair and open access;

6. all netting schemes should ensure the operational reliability of technical systems and the availability of backup facilities capable of completing daily processing requirements.

Finally, central banks play key roles in the formulation and implementation of netting arrangements. Central banks, in general, have common policy objectives with regard to netting systems. The large trading increases in the foreign exchange markets make it crucial that efficiency be maintained in interbank settlements and markets. Supervision of these systems by central banks can insure this efficiency. Central bank oversight should maintain stability of financial markets as well as contain and reduce systemic risk. And central banks should maintain the effectiveness of the instruments of monetary and exchange rate policy.

SECURITIES SETTLEMENT SYSTEMS

International banks also play important roles in the clearance and settlement process. The types and sources of risks incurred by companies, banks, and individuals are the

---

STUDY AID

Both bilateral and multilateral netting arrangements can be used to reduce foreign currency exposure and related costs to cross-border financial transfers. By now, you should be familiar with these techniques. Make sure you understand the superior qualities of multilateral netting. Problem No. 2 at the end of this chapter is an exercise to help you with these concepts.

---

[12] Bank for International Settlements, *Report of the Committee on Interbank Netting Schemes of the Central Banks of the Group of Ten Countries* (Basel, Switzerland: Bank for International Settlements, 1990), p. 26. This is also referred to as the Lamfalussy Report for M.A. Lamfalussy, Chairman of the Committee on Interbank Netting Schemes.

same whether they arise in the clearance and settlement of foreign exchange contracts, in the purchase and sale of securities, or in the consummation of cross-border mergers and acquisitions.

Euroclear and Cedel

In chapter 12, two important facilities for clearing and settling Eurobond trades were discussed. These were Euroclear and Cedel, institutions that are representative of clearing and settlement organizations owned and operated by international banking institutions. Cedel was established by some of the world's largest banks in 1970 in Luxembourg to settle Eurobond trades. Euroclear was formed by J.P. Morgan in 1968 to alleviate the clearing and settlement problems, which had threatened the viability of the Eurobond market. Morgan spun off ownership of Euroclear to public ownership in 1972 but has retained managing control. The vast bulk of Euroclear is owned by some 124 financial institutions. Cedel was converted by its owners into a bank in 1995.

Euroclear, Cedel, and other similar institutions offer a number of risk-reducing services. These include non-fungibility, i.e., non-substitutability, global safe-keeping of securities, delivery against payment, trade matching and confirmation, and other market-making functions, including central safekeeping of securities, securities lending, and same day settlement.

One of the challenges to Euroclear and Cedel is how to streamline the settlement of transactions between the two institutions. The processing cycles used by the two organizations are not currently in sync. Thus, settlement of some transactions between them cannot be executed.[13]

Delivery Versus Payment

One of the issues that has arisen in recent years in the clearance and settlement of cross-border financial transactions is the process of delivery versus payment (DVP), or rather the systems that facilitate this process.[14] A DVP system is a securities settlement system which provides a mechanism insuring that delivery occurs if and only if payment occurs. Such a system will reduce principal risk in financial transaction, the risk that the seller of a financial instrument could deliver the instrument but not receive payment or the risk that the buyer of a financial instrument could make payment but not receive delivery of the instrument. Principal risk can lead to systemic risk, the risk that the inability of one institution to meet its obligations when due will cause other institutions to be unable to meet their obligations, thus jeopardizing the entire system and the stability of financial markets in general.

A study of each of the national securities settlement systems in the G-10 countries, as well as Euroclear and Cedel, carried out by the Committee on Payment and Settlement Systems, facilitated by the Bank for International Settlements, identified 18 different systems.[15] The Committee identified three common structural approaches or models for achieving DVP. These include (1) gross, simultaneous settlements of securities and funds transfers, (2) gross settlements of securities transfers followed by net settlement of funds transfers, and (3) simultaneous net settlement of securities and fund transfers. The latter system eliminates principal risk by achieving DVP. The first

---

[13] Clarisse M. Persanyi, "Global Custody: Take a Journey to 1992," *ABA Banking Journal* 82 (May 1990): 96,100.

[14] For a detailed discussion of the delivery versus payment issue, see Bank for International Settlements, *Delivery versus Payment in Securities Settlement Systems* (Basel, Switzerland: Committee on Payment and Settlement Systems, 1992). This report is referred to as the Parkinson Report, for Patrick Parkinson, Chairman of the Committee on Payment and Settlement Systems and a member of the Federal Reserve Board of Governors.

[15] Ibid., Annex, 1–27.

two systems merely limit principal risk. Any system that reduces or eliminates the risk of failure of a settlement bank, guarantor, or custodian will reduce the risk from using foreign exchange and securities markets encountered by MNCs in the fulfillment of their day-to-day operations.

Global Custodians and Clearing Houses

The large amount of foreign currency transactions around the world, either to facilitate international trade or investment or some other commercial endeavor, requires institutions to serve as custodians for the parties and the financial instruments involved. In addition, these transactions require clearing house arrangements able to clear and settle these cross-border transactions in a wide variety of currencies. These functions will be discussed in this section.

The demand for global custodians for cross-border securities transactions will increase greatly in the years ahead. A number of reasons can be cited for this prognosis.[16] First, the single European market is becoming more integrated despite crises such as the 1992 ERM collapse. Cross-border transactions will increase in Europe and regulatory restrictions such as those in Germany will be abolished making it easier for investment banks in other EU countries to deal in the German securities market. Second, deregulation of capital controls around the world in the 1980s have made it easier for international investors to diversify their portfolios on a global basis. For example, pension funds will be able to invest throughout Europe because of liberalization of investment laws in that region. Third, international investors have become more and more interested in the emerging markets of Latin America, Southeast Asia, and central and eastern Europe. The risk diversification from international portfolios of securities into these areas will create more demand for global custodians.

Concomitant to the growth of global custodial business, an international settlement system will become even more necessary.[17] Investors, companies, and dealers operating in these securities markets will need a settlement system that is very fast and capable of operating in several time zones with several currencies. Custody services must be safe and reliable and the cost of settlement in these international markets must not be higher than the cost of conducting business in domestic markets. Finally, banks operating in these markets need fast and low-cost access to clearance and settlement systems in such markets as well as sufficient information to administer securities transactions in emerging markets.

SOURCES OF INFORMATION

A good source of information on global custody and international clearance and settlement systems is *Payment Systems Worldwide*, an independent international magazine which focuses on payment systems innovations and developments in financial institutions and central banks globally. This quarterly publication[18] examines such issues as payment settlement and clearing developments, evolving regulatory and legal issues on payments, prevention of fraud in electronic funds transfers, issues in large value payments, settlement systems for securities, international netting schemes, costs and benefits in payment services, electronic systems developments in retail banking, central banks and payment/clearing systems, and electronic payment system security.

---

[16] Rüdiger von Rosen, "A Global Perspective of Securities Settlement Issues," *Payment Systems Worldwide* 4 (Winter 1993–94): 8.

[17] Ibid., 9.

[18] *Payment Systems Worldwide* is published by the F.I.A. Financial Publishing Company, Lake Forest, IL.

GLOBAL CUSTODIANS

The custodial function in global finance is more significant than the term implies, that of being a sort of janitorial institution to clean up the world's global financial transactions. Investors use global custodians to move funds through international financial markets with as little risk as possible. Essentially, these financial agents are merely banks that master large amounts of detail in a variety of cross-border time zones.[19] One example of a large global custodian bank is Chase Manhattan. In 1994, Chase merged with U.S. Trust's securities processing business. Chase now holds more than $1.8 trillion in trust and custody assets.[20] The top 5 global custodian banks, ranked by total assets under custody are: Bank of New York with $2.98 billion of custody assets, State Street Bank with $1.9 billion, Chase with $1.8 billion, Bankers Trust with $1.4 billion, and Citibank with $343 million.[21] Table 18–2 shows how the five largest global custodian banks compare.

Global custodians seldom get much publicity unless their operations have had adverse effects on their clients.[22] An Australian investment manager used a New York–based global custodian that left a trade unsettled and one client's account overdrawn by $65 million for 12 days. The global custodian of one U.S.-based mutual fund manager did not ask the manager for help in resolving a settlement problem for 7 months after its occurrence. A U.K.-based custodian failed to report a corporate action for 2 1/2 years, resulting in an inaccurate valuation of a British mutual fund for the entire period. Another custodian failed to convert 56 million Spanish pesetas to U.S. dollars and then debit the amount from a dollar account. The custodian debited £56 million from a sterling account instead, resulting in a huge overdraft.

These examples, however, represent a minority of custodial operations. For the most part, corporations and investors are satisfied with the services performed by these institutions, given the results of surveys of corporations and investment managers. For those companies that are not satisfied with their global custodians, the alternative is to use the services of an agent bank in a foreign country when cross-border financial trans-

TABLE 18–2 Comparison of the Five Largest Global Custody Banks (ranked by assets under global custody)

	Assets Under Global Custody ($ billion)	Proportion From Non-U.S. Clients (%)	Total Assets Under Custody ($ billion)	Custody Division Revenue ($ million)*	Share of Total Revenue (%)
Chase Manhattan	$634	75.4	$1,800	$1,095	16.2
Bank of New York	385	48.1	2,980	967	26.7
Citibank	323	80.3	343	1,667	10.3
Bankers Trust	300	52.0	1,400	n/a	10.9
State Street	228	31.6	1,900	673	53.5

Source: John Pitt, ''Battle of the Banks,'' *Global Finance* 9 (June 1995): 33.

---

[19] Jeanne Iida, "Two Cheers for Custody," *Global Finance* 8 (December 1994): 103.
[20] "Global Custodian: Chase Manhattan," *Euromoney* (July 1995): 80.
[21] Charles Thurston, "The Big Get Bigger," *Global Finance* 9 (December 1995): 92.
[22] Jeanne Iida, "Hall of Shame," *Global Finance* 8 (December 1994): 106.

actions require clearance, settlement, tax reclamation, and other related activities for which global custodians are responsible and for which they charge global custody fees.[23] Many custodial fees may be hidden in other services. For example, many banks hide custodial fees in the foreign exchange trading operations.[24] Some of these global custodians charge only 1–2 basis points for simple custody services such as maintaining a predominately U.S. or British securities portfolio.

Services Offered by Global Custodians

Custodians, usually international banks, offer a number of services for corporations and investors involved in cross-border financial transactions. These institutions may facilitate foreign exchange transactions for customers, as well as portfolio valuation and analysis, reporting and accounting functions, securities lending, and performance measurement. Citibank has global custody services in 46 countries as well as global custody service centers in the United States, United Kingdom, Luxembourg, Dublin, Channel Islands, Hong Kong, Singapore, Australia, France, and Switzerland. Such extensive proliferation of services enables Citibank to offer custodial services on two levels, as global custodian and as subcustodian in a particular region. Some global custodians gain information for clients and facilitate introductions to business contacts within a given foreign market. Most global custodians maintain large telecommunications infrastructure. They provide execution and trading as well as asset management services in foreign countries.

The global custodial services of many U.S. banks are restricted by the Glass-Steagall Act, which prohibits commercial banks from engaging in securities-related transactions.[25] However, U.S. bank regulators have given some large U.S. banks with strong capital limited entry into the underwriting business.[26] European universal banks, not faced with this impediment have an advantage in global custody operations. As more and more U.S. wealth is invested globally, custody will become a significant part of the banking/corporate relationship.

The structure of a typical custodial arrangement involving a bank is shown in Figure 18–4. The bank in this case is an international bank with a global presence. The subcustodians are banks located in foreign countries and acting, in many cases, as agents for the global custodian. Investors acquiring the services of a global custodian may be individuals, institutions, or corporations. The investment target may be any financial instrument or a proposed merger and acquisition.

FIGURE 18–4 Structure of a Global Custodian Arrangement

Investor	$\longrightarrow$	Bank Custodian	$\longrightarrow$	Investment
—Individual		Subcustodians		Target
—Institutional		Several, e.g.,		
—Corporate		30+ located		
		in foreign		
		countries		

[23] Tom Leander, "The Perils and Possibilities of Going Direct," *Global Finance* 7 (January 1993): 68.

[24] Nick Kochan, "The Squeeze on Custody has Begun," *Euromoney* (August 1993): 100.

[25] In early 1995, the Clinton administration recommended that the Glass-Steagall Act be abolished. The proposal was supported by Alan Greenspan, Chairman, Federal Reserve Board of Governors.

[26] Amy Barrett and Dean Foust, "It's Time to Guillotine Glass-Steagall," *Business Week* (March 13, 1995): 33.

Global Custodians in Emerging Markets

The global custodian has played an important role in emerging markets. During the 1982–92 period according to the International Finance Corporation, the combined market capitalization of the stock markets in developing countries increased from $67 billion to $770 billion.[27] During the past few years, foreign direct investment in emerging markets by MNCs, mutual funds, and other investors has increased the need for institutions that have the capacity to inform clients of legal developments, regulatory changes, tax legislation, and insider information. Global custodians are able to furnish these services. One example of their usefulness is evident from their assistance in the recent electronic renovation of the Prague Stock Exchange.[28]

Many of the fastest growing areas of mutual fund investment in 1992 were in Latin America and Asia. Several large global custodians had invested heavily in services dealing with investments in these areas. Among them were Chase, Citibank, Morgan Stanley, J.P. Morgan, State Street, Boston Safe, Bankers Trust, and Brown Brothers Harriman. Barclays and Bank of New York have also increased their custodial presence in these regional areas. Global custodians have carried out the due diligence necessary in these markets as well as an analysis of the infrastructure and the state of the local banking systems in these foreign countries. They also determine the level of capitalization, reporting, and auditing capabilities, as well as the legal and regulatory framework in foreign countries. These services in emerging markets are relatively more costly for clients investing in such areas. Custody costs generally run 20–50 basis points higher than the costs of such services in mature, less risky markets.[29]

CLEARING HOUSE ARRANGEMENTS

Payment systems involving multicurrency transactions and many counterparties require some type of clearing institution. In London, more than 80 percent of the foreign exchange turnover is with other banks. More than 80 percent of the cross-border assets and liabilities in the Bank for International Settlements area is comprised of interbank assets and liabilities. With foreign exchange volume exceeding $1 trillion every day, with volume on futures and options exchanges increasing significantly, and with the burgeoning growth of the over-the-counter market in derivatives, the risks discussed above have increased greatly for the international participants in these markets. Global bank regulators are concerned about systemic risk. Bankhaus Herstatt failed more than 20 years ago, however, some other more recent problems could have resulted in the contagion that can result from Herstatt risk.[30] Ten years ago, the computer glitch at the Bank of New York could have caused a widespread problem in the financial markets but the Federal Reserve Bank of New York was able to quell the impending disruption. The Drexel bond trading problem could have had global implications but the assistance of the Federal Reserve and the Bank of England enabled Drexel to complete its securities and foreign exchange transactions. The international cooperation among central bankers to close the Bank for Credit and Commerce International (BCCI) avoided global disruption to the U.S. payments system and minimal losses in the global financial system.

---

[27] Carol Bere, "Emerging Markets Custody: Can This Marriage Be Saved?" *Global Finance* 7 (October 1993): 20.

[28] "Solving Problems in Terra Incognito," *Global Finance* 8 (October 1994): 70.

[29] Bere, "Emerging Markets Custody" 24.

[30] Eddie George, "International Banking, Payment Systems and Financial Crises," *Proceedings of the International Symposium on Banking and Payments Services* (Washington, D.C.: Federal Reserve Board of Governors, 1994), p. 75.

Clearing house arrangements coupled with payment concepts such as real-time gross settlement (RTGS)[31] have facilitated these problems while reducing settlement and other types of risk. In addition, the financial markets have been made more efficient and costs of participating in these markets have been reduced. These methods, coupled with the netting arrangements discussed earlier in this chapter, are all means by which capital losses can be eliminated in global financial markets because of uncompleted settlement of securities or foreign exchange transactions by counterparties.

The volume of transactions passing through settlement and payment systems globally has increased dramatically in recent years. This increased volume is the result of financial deregulation since 1980 and globalization of financial markets, as well as innovations in data processing and telecommunications because of computerization and electronic breakthroughs. Deregulation and innovations in hardware, for example, have permitted the implementation of such services as the German Bundesbank's Electronic Counter, a funds transfer system that utilizes RTGS of financial transactions.

The latter method of settlement facilitates 24-hour global trading of securities and foreign exchange because of the need for intraday settlement to speed up financial operations. For example, in the Bundesbank's Electronic Counter system, the amount of funds involved is immediately credited to the recipient bank. Thus, all participants have immediate certainty that the payment executed will be final and immediately at the disposal of the beneficiary. No lag in payments occurs. The payor, must, of course, cover the payment immediately. Thus, the leads and lags strategy discussed in chapter 15 could not be used with this system. The Fedwire system in the United States also operates in a similar way.

CHIPS, the system operated by the New York Clearing House and often used to settle the dollar leg of foreign exchange transactions, has been strengthened since 1974 to reduce the Herstatt risk in its settlement of foreign exchange transactions. CHIPS has implemented "same day" settlement of payments, formulated tougher risk controls, and enacted settlement support arrangements. Despite these improvements, large time gaps remain between settlement in different foreign currencies. Some of these gaps are the result of central bank operational policies. The Federal Reserve announced in 1994 that Fedwire's operating day will be expanded from 10 to 18 hours. But this change will not be implemented until 1997.[32]

Delivery Versus Payment and Herstatt Risk

Another principle, delivery versus payment (DVP) of multicurrency settlements, when implemented by payment and settlement systems, will alleviate Herstatt risk. The DVP concept, just discussed, is a mechanism in the exchange for value system, which ensures that the final transfer of an asset occurs if and only if payment occurs. Although DVP reduces liquidity and credit risks, policy issues and concerns can be created. Herstatt risk could be eliminated if the hours of operation of certain payment systems were extended or if central bank multicurrency services would create the technical ability to conduct a DVP settlement of several currencies on the same value date. Thus, central bank policies need to be changed. A major concern of a DVP system arises from the interdependencies or settlement linkages between payment systems involved in such DVP systems. A disruption in the settlement of one currency because of operational problems or liquidity shortages might disrupt the settlement of other currencies. This

---

[31] Real-time gross settlement is a system in which processing and settlement of gross balances between parties take place in real time, i.e., continuously, rather than on a net basis at some specified time.

[32] Edward J. Kelley, Jr., "Developments in the Dollar Payments System," *Proceedings of the International Symposium on Banking and Payments Services* (Washington, D.C.: Federal Reserve Board of Governors, 1994), pp. 108–9.

possibility stems from the fact that a DVP settlement requires that payments in one currency will not be made unless payments in the other currency are made.[33]

Multilateral Clearing

Futures exchange transactions are often cleared through a third-party clearing house arrangement. The clearing function is the back-office processing of traded contracts and involves a determination of the amounts due between counterparties and the subsequent settlement of these transactions with cash transfers. Since 1925, all U.S. futures exchanges, for example, have used multilateral clearing systems whereby all traded contracts are cleared through a member of an exchange-affiliated clearing house. The clearing house is interposed in each contract between a buyer and a seller, which necessitates replacement of the original contract by two contracts. The original seller, thus, obtains a contract to sell to the clearing house and the original buyer obtains a contract to buy from the clearing house. The financial standing of the counterparties is not in question in this process because the clearing house guarantees all positions created between its clearing members, the various brokers that belong to the clearing house association.[34]

Private economies can be derived from the multilateral clearing of futures contracts. Since payments are netted bilaterally between each pair of counterparties, the number of payments required is reduced. When multilateral netting is performed across many different counterparties, even more savings are possible. Since credit risk is reduced by multilateral clearing, less collateral is required for each contract. Bilateral contracts require a certain minimum amount of monitoring as part of risk management. Centralization of the monitoring activity at the clearing house can result in a significant reduction in cost.

In addition to private economies, some savings are possible from public economies as a result of multilateral clearing. These savings stem from the centralization of information gathering by the clearing house and the mutualization of risks. The members of the multilateral clearing system are exposed to defaults created by system-wide problems. Thus, each member has an incentive to monitor the system to protect its own interests.

Multinet International

Multinet International is a system designed to clear and net foreign exchange transactions on a global basis. In collaboration with International Clearing Systems, Inc. (ICSI), wholly-owned subsidiary of the Options Clearing Corporation of Chicago, several U.S. and Canadian banks established Multinet. These banks include Bank of Montreal, Bank of Nova Scotia, Canadian Imperial Bank of Commerce, Chase Manhattan, First National Bank of Chicago, National Bank of Canada, Royal Bank of Canada, and Toronto-Dominion Bank.

Gross transaction volume by Multinet consistently amounts to more than $150 billion per month. Currencies whose trading is cleared and netted by Multinet are of the seven major nations: United States, Canada, Great Britain, Germany, Switzerland, France, and Japan. Settlements of amounts more than $1 billion are often made among the members. Bilateral netting was begun in 1992 with a step-by-step process to develop a multilateral netting system. Systemic risk has been reduced by bilateral netting

---

[33] Tim E. Noël, "Report on Central Bank Payment and Settlement Services with Respect to Cross-Border and Multi-Currency Transactions," *Proceedings of the International Symposium on Banking and Payments Services* (Washington, D.C.: Federal Reserve Board of Governors, 1994), p. 126.

[34] James T. Moser, "What is Multilateral Clearing and Who Cares?" *Chicago Fed Letter* (November 1994): 1.

and simulations run by Multinet show that multilateral netting will be even more effective in risk reduction.[35] These simulations show that multilateral netting can reduce risk by 50 percent or more.

The ECHO System

The ECHO System was created by 15 major international banks from 7 countries.[36] ECHO is comprised of a clearing house that permits banks to net all of their foreign exchange contracts with other participants. Thus, a participant will need to make or receive only one payment in each currency during any one trading day by clearing through ECHO. The system will have in place a mixture of a pool of marketable securities pledged by the users as well as committed standby lines of credit also furnished by the users. Such a pool will grow as more banks joint the system. It is estimated that once a broad range of banks join ECHO, the asset pool will amount to more than $1 billion. As this pool grows, less reliance will be made on credit lines. Essentially, ECHO is an interbank trading, clearing, netting, and settlement system. It was introduced in 1994 after regulatory problems were alleviated with banking authorities.

Proposed Clearing Systems

Such clearing systems are primarily national in focus or limited to the market for one type of financial instruments, e.g., futures contracts. Because of the tremendous volume of cross-border financial transactions, so-called pipeline liquidity risk is an ever increasing problem. Pipeline liquidity risk occurs because of gaps between the time when money or securities start through the processing pipeline and the time when they are definitively transferred to owners—in other words, because of gaps or discontinuities in processing times. Much of these gaps occur in the operations of central securities depositories or domestic payment systems such as those just discussed in the U.S. futures markets or earlier with regard to systems such as CHIPS, Fedwire, or the Electronic Counter in Germany.

A study done in 1993 under the auspices of Euroclear whose objectives were to increase efficiency and reduce risks in cross-border settlements proposed five different models designed to achieve these goals.[37] These were Worldclear, a global central processing unit, bilateral links between national securities depositories, a global hub, and a multiple access model.

Worldclear   Worldclear is a model built on the assumption of a single, global clearing settlement and payment facility. This organization would take over all domestic and cross-border securities transfers and payments. Whereas Worldclear would handle cross-border transactions in the same way as domestic financial trades, the investment costs to implement such a system would be quite high as would some of its operational costs. Worldclear would have no competition and could evolve into a bureaucracy unresponsive to the market and unable to capitalize on economies of scale and scope. Figure 18–5 shows the Worldclear model.

[35] Garrett R. Glass, "Multinet's FX Netting Solution," *Proceedings of the International Symposium on Banking and Payments Services* (Washington, D.C.: Federal Reserve Board of Governors, 1994), pp. 152–67.

[36] Graham M. Duncan, "Clearing House Arrangements in the Foreign Exchange Markets," *Proceedings of the International Symposium on Banking and Payments Services* (Washington, D.C.: Federal Reserve Board of Governors, 1994), pp. 168–74.

[37] Rolf-E. Breuer, "Risk Management in Cross-Border and Multi-Currency Securities Clearance and Settlement," *Proceedings of the International Symposium on Banking and Payments Services* (Washington, D.C.: Federal Reserve Board of Governors), pp. 133–41.

Global Central Processing Unit (CPU)   The Global CPU is modeled after U.S. and German domestic systems but would be international in scope. It probably would not improve cross-border settlement and might increase operational and systemic risks. Sunk investment by existing systems would cause little enthusiasm for such a system. The Global CPU model is shown in Figure 18–6.

Bilateral Central Securities Depositories Links   Bilateral links of central securities depositories (CSDs) would permit access for investors in any domestic market to any number of foreign markets through a single system. Some degree of standardization across markets might be possible. Very few financial markets currently have sufficient volume to make such a hook-up feasible. This system would have little appeal to trading organizations or institutional investors. The bilateral links model showing CSDs is presented in Figure 18–7.

FIGURE 18–5 Worldclear Model

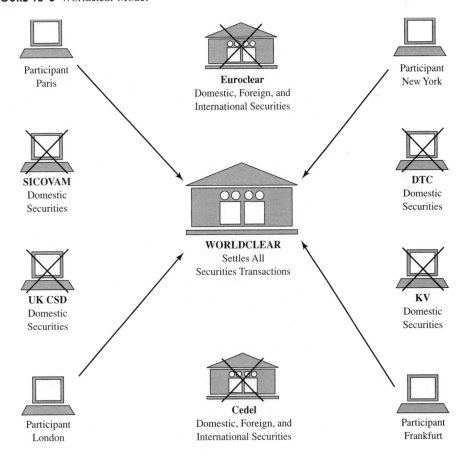

→ Each participant has a securities account with Worldclear for all securities.

Source: Cross-Border Clearance, Settlement, and Custody: Beyond the G30 Recommendations (Brussels, Belgium: Morgan Guaranty Trust Company, 1993), p. 34.

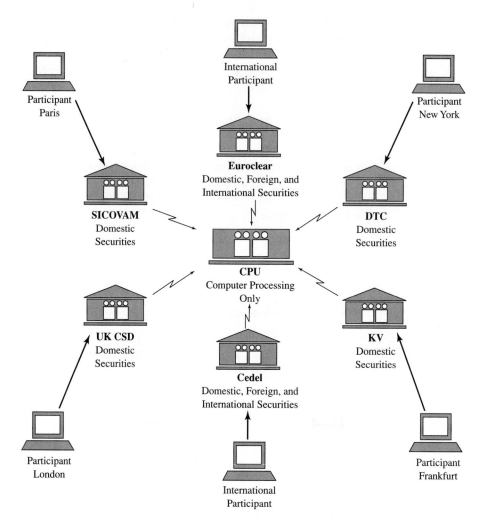

→ Each participant has a securities account with its home CSD for all home-market securities.

⇝ Data Processing Link: Each CSD transmits data to the Global CPU for processing; results of processing are relayed to CSDs, which maintain participant accounts.

Source: Cross-Border Clearance, Settlement, and Custody: Beyond the G30 Recommendations (Brussels, Belgium: Morgan Guaranty Trust Company, 1993), p. 43.

FIGURE 18–6 Global CPU Model

Global Hub   A global hub would link together some or all domestic and international securities depositories. Such a system could offer the requisite functions and economies of scale. However, the start-up costs would be high. Operational and systemic risks might be exacerbated by a global hub. Large amounts of credit would be required by central securities depositories. Cash clearing systems would have to stay open longer. The global hub model is shown in Figure 18–8.

Multiple Access Model   The multiple access model was judged the best proposal by the Euroclear Study Committee. The current system is the starting point for a multiple access model. Such a system would work today because of the interaction of local custodians, global custodians, CSDs, and international securities depositories such as Eu-

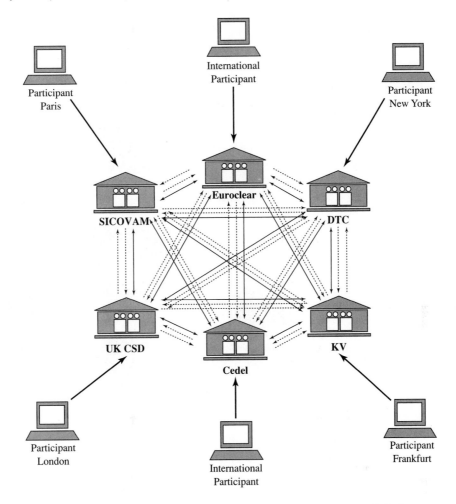

——▶ Each participant has a securities account with its home CSD for both home-market and all other securities accessible through its bilateral links.

┄┄▶ Home-market Links: each CSD has securities accounts with each other CSD reflecting its positions in the other's home-market securities. These links allow each CSD to settle transactions between participants and those of the other CSD in the home-market securities of each CSD.

◀——▶ Other-market Link: each CSD has securities accounts with each other CSD reflecting its positions in third-market securities. This allows each CSD's participants to settle transactions with those of the other CSD in third-market securities.

Source: Cross-Border Clearance, Settlement, and Custody: Beyond the G30 Recommendations (Brussels, Belgium: Morgan Guaranty Trust Company, 1993), p. 46.

FIGURE 18–7 Bilateral CSD Links Model

roclear and Cedel. Thus, global custodians will be at the center of such a model. They will continue to expand their specialized services to cover both established and emerging markets while reducing their costs. These elements of the multiple access model are instrumental in maintenance of liquidity in cross-border trading as well as the absorption of pipeline risks and costs, usually without compensation. The multiple access model is shown in Figure 18–9.

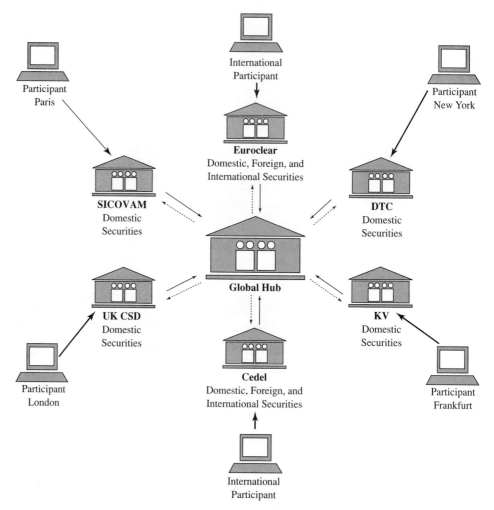

→ Each participant has a securities account with its home CSD for all home-market securities and all other-market securities accessible through the Global Hub.

┄┄► Home-market Link: Global Hub has securities accounts with the home CSD reflecting its positions in home-market securities held for other CSDs. This allows the Global Hub to settle transactions between participants of the home CSD and other CSDs.

→ Other-market Link: home CSD has securities accounts with the Global Hub reflecting its positions in other-market securities. This allows its participants to settle transactions with participants of all other CSDs.

Source: Cross-Border Clearance, Settlement, and Custody: Beyond the G30 Recommendations (Brussels, Belgium: Morgan Guaranty Trust Company, 1993), p. 39.

FIGURE 18–8 Global Hub Model

German Securities Depositories

The Germanic countries, Germany, Switzerland, and Austria, have traditionally used securities depositories, referred to as *Kassenvereine,* for the safekeeping and custody of securities such as stocks and bonds. Bearer shares and bonds are used in these countries. A bearer bond or share certificate does not bear the name of the owner as does registered share and bond certificates in countries such as the United States, which

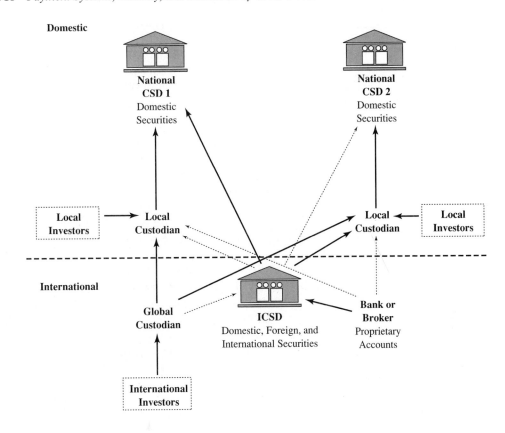

Signifies the access option selected for cost or efficiency reasons by each player (bank, broker, custodian or ICSD).

Signifies an alternative option that might be selected on the basis of competitive analysis.

Source: Cross-Border Clearance, Settlement, and Custody: Beyond the G30 Recommendations (Brussels, Belgium: Morgan Guaranty Trust Company, 1993), p. 32.

FIGURE 18–9 Multiple Access Model

use registered securities. Thus, bearer share and bond certificates are legal tender, belonging to the bearer. Since banks are the primary and, usually, sole investment broker in the stock or bond transaction with an investor, these banks have created securities depositories, which hold the certificates for safekeeping. These bearer securities, if equity, have had their proxies voted by the bank in whose depository they are held. This practice has given these banks even more economic power, because they can also hold shares in companies for their own benefit. The depository will issue monthly statements to the investor showing the current holdings. The securities depository practice is similar to holding securities in "street name" in the United States.

REGULATION OF GLOBAL CUSTODIANS

The international banks that are heavily involved in performing the functions of global custody are regulated by the banking authorities in their home countries and, to a lesser extent, by the Bank for International Settlements. However, the global custody func-

tion has not been well regulated in the past. It is an activity that has grown rapidly in the past decade concomitant with the growth in the volume of cross-border financial transactions.

Two international banking scandals have brought demands for tougher regulation of global custodians. These were the failure of Barings Bank, discussed elsewhere in this book, and the Robert Maxwell case wherein, after his death, it was discovered that he had misappropriated his employees' pension funds to support his global business operations.

The Securities & Investments Board of the United Kingdom, the equivalent of the U.S. Securities and Exchange Commission, has asked for tougher rules.[38] Among the proposed regulations are: (1) more enhanced regulatory standards for custody providers, (2) more segregation of customer investments from those of the firm, and (3) government licensing of global custodians.

The proposed regulatory changes have caused some banks to sell off their global custody operations, thus creating even more consolidation, which was discussed earlier in this chapter. Among the banks that sold their global custody operations were J.P. Morgan, Bank of America, Nations Trust, U.S. Trust, and National Westminster. Some of these operations were acquired by Bank of New York, Chase Manhattan, and Lloyds of London. It appears that some 80 percent of global custody operations could become owned by less than 20 percent of the international banks.

Such consolidation could create higher fee structures for global custody operations. However, new competition has entered this field in the form of central securities depositories (CSDs).[39] These institutions, such as Cedel—already owned by a number of banks—have begun to perform global custody services. At the time of this writing, fees had leveled off, primarily as a result of this added competition.

Clearing and Settlement in Derivatives Markets

The final subject in this chapter deals with an examination of the problems in the clearing and settlement specifically encountered in the derivatives markets. Derivatives relevant to the subject of international finance were introduced and discussed in detail in chapters 13 and 14. Although the problems encountered by many firms and banks with these financial instruments in 1994 reduced the volume in the derivatives markets, particularly the OTC markets for customized derivatives including so-called exotic derivatives, these instruments will continue to be used by MNCs and investors to hedge cross-border transactions and by traders who speculate in these markets. The trading volume in many of these instruments will continue to increase and different types of risk will continue to be encountered by derivatives market participants. As a result,

---

[38] Nick Kochan, "Shackling the Custodians," *Euromoney* (May 1996): 137.
[39] Ibid., 138.

new and better clearing and settlement systems will be needed. Global custodians will need to handle these instruments with care.

Regulatory agencies around the world have examined these markets in great detail. The U.S. Commodities and Futures Trading Commission (CFTC) published the results of its study in 1993 entitled *OTC Derivative Markets and Their Regulation*. This study recommended the establishment of an interagency council to consider, among other items, a new clearing facility for OTC derivatives. A report on financial derivatives was prepared by the minority staff of the U.S. House of Representatives Banking Committee, which examined the benefits of a clearing house system for swaps and other types of OTC derivatives.

The OTC market for derivatives consists of all privately negotiated trades in derivatives, including interest rate and currency swaps, currency options written by private parties such as MNCs and banks, and exotic derivatives. Some of the same risks discussed in previous sections of this chapter are encountered in these markets. For example, settlement and credit risk were among the causes of the 1994 losses incurred by Gibson Greetings Company, Procter & Gamble, Metallgesellschaft, and Piper Jaffray Brokerage Company. In 1992, the settlement risk exposure in swap payments amounted to about $4 billion per day, compared with $1 trillion daily volume in the foreign exchange markets. However, because of the large notional values of swap transactions, some analysts have perceived that a much larger risk exists in the swap markets and, thus, regulators have been convinced that settlement risk is sufficiently high to warrant increased attention to clearing house arrangements for these markets. This seems to be a logical extension of the requirement by the CFTC that all futures exchange contracts flow through centralized, margined clearing house arrangements.

A clearance facility has been established as a test model in the derivatives market. Delta Government Options Corporation has joined with RMJ Options Trading Corporation to form a brokerage and clearance arrangement for one specific derivative, OTC options written on U.S. Treasury securities.[40] Delta is a clearing agency registered with the U.S. Securities and Exchange Commission and operates as the counterparty to each transaction submitted to it for clearance. Margin is collected by Delta in the form of central bank funds or U.S. Treasury securities on a daily basis. Some 40 institutions have been entitled to use the RMJ/Delta system. Most of these are U.S. institutions, which comprise the U.S. primary dealer community. The average size of notional value of transactions is $40 million. The system cleared $38 billion worth of trades in 1993.

THE MAJOR ISSUE

Although a small experimental clearing house arrangement for OTC derivatives has been established, the major issue in this field is the call for innovation by market users, organized exchanges, regulators, and political leaders on a global basis. Regulators and politicians are concerned with systemic risk, as discussed comprehensively in the Promisel Report. Market practices, concentration, and structure of the market for OTC derivatives was covered in this study. The International Swap Dealers Association (ISDA) is acting as the focal trade association to foster change and improvements in OTC trading of derivatives.

Much of the discussion of derivatives trading risk stemmed from the analysis of the 1992 ERM crisis, discussed in detail in chapter 3, by the Bank for International Set-

---

[40] Stephen K. Lynner, "Prospects for an Over-the-Counter Derivatives Clearing House," *Proceedings of an International Symposium on Banking and Payments Services* (Washington, D.C.: Federal Reserve Board of Governors, 1994), pp. 188–94.

tlements.[41] This report found that trading volume increased dramatically for organized markets when liquidity dried up in the OTC market for derivatives. Such illiquidity results because: (1) OTC dealers hedge with products traded on organized markets, (2) the quasi-public sector nature of organized markets places them in the position of serving as a "market for last resort," and (3) entry and exit from organized markets is relatively easy.[42]

The solution to this problem, thus, is the establishment of a clearing house for OTC derivatives. A properly structured system should have 5 key characteristics[43]: (1) a governance structure that will provide direct oversight by market participants who provide some of the risk capital, which gives substance to the guarantee, (2) predefined admission standards should be established by the clearing house, which address operational and financial considerations, (3) the clearing house should provide for the ongoing financial and operational monitoring of its participants, (4) the clearing house must provide accurate, reliable, and timely processing capabilities with sufficient redundancy to assure uninterrupted service, and (5) the clearing house should arrange for immediate access to reasonable levels of liquidity to insure timely settlement of all obligations. The Chicago Board of Trade and the Board of Trade Clearing Corporations have entered a joint venture to establish such a clearing house arrangement for these such OTC derivatives.

Summary and Conclusions

The focus of this chapter has been on the examination and analysis of one of the major issues facing MNCs, investors, and other participants in the world of global finance. This is the issue of payment systems in general and global custodians and clearing and settlement systems specifically. The environment facing the chief financial officer of the MNC is one of a borderless world with barriers to global trade and investment falling as a result of the international cooperation stemming from such concepts as the European Union, North American Free Trade Agreement, General Agreement on Tariffs and Trade, Association of South East Asian Nations, and others. This borderless world has a major market of three broad regional groupings, Asia, Europe, and the United States (North America) with a population of more than one billion persons having per capita income in excess of $10,000. This is an environment with daily foreign exchange trading volume of more than $1 trillion, huge amounts of bond and equity investments by companies, individuals, institutional investors, and governments, and a burgeoning market for derivative financial instruments of the plain vanilla-type or of the exotic-type, designed to reduce or eliminate various types of risk from exchanging financial instruments on a cross-border basis.

Participants in these financial markets, whether they be CFOs of MNCs or domestic companies, individual or institutional investors, or government financial offi-

---

[41] *Bank for International Settlements 63rd Annual Report* (Basle, Switzerland: Bank for International Settlements, June 14, 1993), pp. 123–4.

[42] John C. Hiatt, "The Potential for Clearing House Arrangements in the OTC Derivatives Market," *Proceedings of an International Symposium of Banking and Payments Services* (Washington, D.C.: Federal Reserve Board of Governors, 1994), p. 199.

[43] Ibid., 200.

cers, must cope with the vagaries of such an environment. They must be aware of the inherent risk involved in dealing with every type of financial instrument, market, or institution, and whether the risk be credit, replacement cost, principal, liquidity, operational, or systemic. They must be aware of the various payment systems, including the restrictions, risks, and costs of such systems. Some of these systems involve netting arrangements. Netting can be operated on a bilateral or a multilateral basis and by a MNC dealing with its global payments among and between foreign affiliates or by a bank or banks in an interbank system. Any of these modes can reduce the cost of payments as well as some of the risks. Banking systems, however, may have to cope with regulatory policy formulated by banking authorities in order to move to a system that may cause drastic changes in the structure of monetary policy.

The CFOs of MNCs should be aware of funds transfer systems such as CHIPS and SWIFT and their competitor institutions. Large MNC global networks transfer large amounts of funds every day. It is necessary for the firm to transfer these funds in the lowest cost, speediest, and most secure method possible. Systems that utilize concepts such as delivery versus payment or real-time gross settlement may result in significant reduction of risk in cross-border financial transactions. MNCs may require the services of securities settlement systems such as Euroclear and Cedel when funding long-term operations with Eurobond issues.

The global custodian, whether an international bank, investment house, or proprietary firm, has facilitated the tremendous growth in cross-border financial transactions. Global custodians are paid by investors to move their funds through foreign financial markets with as little risk as possible. Surveys have shown that, for the most part, users of their services are quite satisfied with their assistance, especially in the emerging nations fraught with financial institutions and markets, which are undeveloped, poorly regulated, and in which operational risk is quite high.

Custodians perform all of the financial operations of dealing in financial instruments, institutions, and markets in foreign countries. They collect the dividends on stock issues and interest income on debt issues for investment managers and mutual funds. They must be prompt and accurate in these operations. Global custodians have moved operations into remote areas of the world such as Mongolia in order to speed up the custodial services offered companies and investors. They inform clients of legal developments, regulatory changes, tax legislation, and insider information, which is relevant to their clients' operations. It is becoming increasingly impossible for companies and individuals to enter cross-border financial transactions without the assistance of global custodians.

Finally, clearing and settlement arrangements—clearing houses—are becoming more and more important in settling the large volume of financial transactions, which are cross-border in nature. These institutions, whether domestic, bilateral, international, or completely global, may be the future solutions to alleviating the risk and cost of international financial transactions. Several different models have been proposed in studies carried out by G-10 central banks, the Bank for International Settlements, and by other clearing houses, such as Euroclear. A few international clearing houses have begun operations on a regional basis. Among these are Multinet International and the ECHO System.

The major market area in which current problems have been exacerbated in the mid-1990s is the derivatives market, especially the OTC market for negotiated derivatives instruments. A number of studies have concentrated on this industry in light of the 1994 losses suffered by banks and companies such as Banc One, Procter & Gamble,

Gibson Greetings, Metallgesellschaft, and Piper, Jaffray. These studies all point to the need for CFOs of companies and banks that use such derivatives to implement better internal control systems and to understand as much as possible about the derivatives instruments they use.

These are complex issues that face MNCs and international banks in the global finance environment of the 21st century. It is possible that electronic innovations can keep up with the burgeoning increases in trading volume of foreign exchange, securities, and derivatives. However, the people skills must grow at the same rate.

Additional Readings

Bank for International Settlements. *Central Bank Payment and Settlement Services with Respect to Cross-Border and Multi-Currency Transactions* (Basle, Switzerland: Committee on Payment and Settlement Systems, 1993).

———— *Delivery Versus Payment in Securities Settlement Systems.* Basle, Switzerland: Committee on Payment and Settlement Systems, 1992.

———— *Recent Developments in International Interbank Relations.* Basle, Switzerland: Working Group of Central Banks of Group of Ten Countries, 1992.

———— *Report of Committee on Interbank Netting Schemes of the Central Banks of the Group of Ten Countries* (Basle, Switzerland: Bank for International Settlements, 1990).

———— *Report on Netting Schemes.* Basle, Switzerland: Group of Experts on Payment Systems, 1989.

Borio, C. E. V., and P. Van den Bergh. *The Nature and Management of Payment System Risk.* Basle, Switzerland: Bank for International Settlements, 1993.

Cross-Border Clearance, Settlement, and Custody: Beyond the G30 Recommendations. Brussels, Belgium: Morgan Guaranty Trust Co., 1993.

Commodities Futures Trading Commission. *OTC Derivatives Markets and Their Regulation.* Washington, D.C.: Government Printing Office, 1993.

Federal Reserve System. *Overview of the Federal Reserve's Payments System Risk Policy.* Washington, D.C.: Federal Reserve System, 1993.

Gilbert, R. Alton. "Implications of Netting Arrangements for Bank Risk in Foreign Exchange Transactions." *Federal Reserve Bank of St. Louis Review* 74 (January/February 1992): 3–16.

von Rosen, Rüdiger. "A Global Perspective of Securities Settlement Issues." *Payment Systems Worldwide* 4(Winter 1993–94): 7–11.

Scarlata, Jodi G. "Institutional Developments in the Globalization of Securities and Futures Markets." *Federal Reserve Bank of St. Louis Review* 74 (January/February 1992): 17–30.

Symposium Proceedings: International Symposium on Banking and Payment Services. Washington, D.C.: Federal Reserve Board of Governors, 1994.

Yamaguchi, Mitsuo. "An Assessment of Payment System Risk in Asia." *Payment Systems Worldwide* 4 (Winter 1993–94): 21–4.

Discussion Questions

1. Discuss the globalization of financial markets. Why has this occurred?
2. List and discuss the major risks incurred in financial markets.
3. How does credit risk result in replacement cost risk?
4. What events can lead to liquidity risk?
5. Select and discuss the operations of any two of the following payments systems: Fedwire, CHIPS, FX Net.
6. What is SWIFT and how does it operate?

7. What are the major characteristics of SWIFT that make it one of the world's most favored institutions for facilitating the transfer of funds globally?
8. What services do Euroclear or Cedel offer for international investors?
9. What is the role of central banks in global payments systems?
10. What is the difference between a bilateral and a multilateral netting system? What minimum standards should be incorporated into a bank netting payments system?
11. What are global custodians in financial market transactions? What services do global custodians perform?
12. What is real-time gross settlement and what risk does this process alleviate?
13. What is delivery versus payment and how does it alleviate Herstatt risk?
14. What are the advantages and disadvantages of the proposed clearing systems discussed in the chapter?
15. What are Multinet International and the ECHO system designed to do?
16. What problems have arisen in the clearing and settlement of derivatives market transactions? What should be implemented in this area to protect firms and investors from losses?

Problems

1. Construct a hypothetical transaction via the SWIFT system involving a transfer of funds from the parent bank of a U.S. MNC to the French bank of its French affiliate with some of the funds to be credited to the affiliate's local account, some of the funds to be used to purchase French franc 90-day government securities, and some of the funds to be used to purchase futures contracts on the MATIF market to hedge long-term earnings from a new product to be introduced in 2 years.
2. Assume the following payments in settlement of foreign exchange transactions under gross settlement and bilateral netting.

Gross Settlement		Bilateral Netting			
Counterparties	*Transaction Number*	*Direction of Payment*	*Units of Currencies*	*Direction of Payment*	*Units of Currencies*
Bank A and Bank B	1	A to B	£200	A to B	£100
		B to A	$350	B to A	$180
		(Profit of $20.00 for A)		(Profit of $15.00 for A)	
	2	A to B	$170		
		B to A	£100		
		(Profit −$5.00 for A)			
Bank A and Bank C	1	A to C	£200	A to C	$185.00
		C to A	$340.00	C to A	£100
		(Profit of $10.00 for A)		(Profit of −$20.00 for A)	
	2	A to C	$325.00		
		C to A	£300.00		
		(Profit of −$30.00 for A)			
Bank B and Bank C	1	B to C	£300.00	B to C	£200.00
		C to B	$325.00	C to B	$355.00
		(Profit of $30.00 for B)		(Profit of $25.00 for B)	
	2	B to C	$170.00		
		C to B	£100.00		
		(Profit of −$5.00 for B)			

The exchange rate on the value date is \$1.55/£. Transactions to be settled on this date were negotiated earlier at exchange rates ranging from \$1.55–1.65/£. According to Figures 17–2 and 17–3, diagram the flow of currencies between banks under: (1) gross settlement and bilateral netting, and (2) under a system of multilateral netting and a clearing house.

3. Compare and contrast the securities clearing system in the United States with that used in Germany.

Glossary

Accounting exposure. Exposure to the potential risk of an accounting derived change in owner's equity, which results from exchange rate changes and the restatement of the financial statements of the foreign affiliate of the parent corporation according to some set of accounting rules.

Adjusted present value. A method of present value analysis in capital budgeting that incorporates the various tax shields provided by the deductibility of interest and other financial charges and the benefits of project specific concessional financing such as investment tax credits or depreciation allowances.

AIBD (Association of International Bond Dealers). A private organization founded in 1969 to formulate uniform issuing and trading rules in the international bond markets. *See* **International Securities Market Association.**

American depositary receipt (ADR). A certificate of ownership issued by a U.S. bank that represents a foreign stock for domestic trading. The U.S. bank holds the foreign shares and issues ADRs against them.

American-type option. An option that can be exercised at any time before expiration.

Appreciation. An increase in the market value of a currency with respect to some other currency.

Arbitrage. The simultaneous purchase or sale or lending or borrowing of the same or similar asset in different markets in order to profit from a price difference.

Arm's length price. The free market price for goods or services transacted between a willing buyer and a willing unrelated seller. It is the price applied by tax authorities on transactions involving transfer prices between related affiliates.

Asked price. The price at which an institution or market-maker will sell an asset or the price sought by any seller of the asset.

At the money option. The term used for a call or put option whose strike price is equal or nearly equal to the current spot price of the asset on which the option is written.

Back-to-back loan. A loan in which two companies in separate countries borrow each other's currency for a specific period of time and repay the other's currency at an agreed maturity.

Backwardation. The opposite of contango. The near months' futures contract prices are higher than those for more distant months. Such a situation may occur in commodity futures markets when the costs of storing the product until eventual delivery are effectively subtracted from the delivery price today.

Balance of payments. A statistical compilation formulated by a sovereign nation of all economic transactions between residents of that nation and residents of all other nations during a stipulated period of time, usually a calendar year.

Balance of trade. *See* **trade balance.**

Balance on current account. *See* **current account.**

Bank for International Settlements (BIS). An international bank headquartered in Basel, Switzerland, which serves as a forum for monetary cooperation among several European central banks, the Bank of Japan, and the U.S. Federal Reserve System. Founded in 1930 to handle the German payment of reparations after World War I, it now monitors and collects data on international banking activity and promulgates rules concerning international bank regulation.

Bankers' acceptance. An unconditional promise of a bank to make payment on a draft when it matures. The acceptance is in the form of the bank's

endorsement of a draft drawn against that bank in accordance with the terms of a letter of credit issued by the bank. The banker's acceptance then becomes a financial instrument that can be traded in the acceptance market made up of dealers and investors.

Barrier options. Contracts with trigger points that, when crossed, automatically generate buying or selling of other options. This type is the most traded of the exotic derivatives.

Basic balance. In a balance of payments, the basic balance is the net balance of the combination of the current account and the capital account.

Basis. The difference between the cash or spot price and the futures price.

Basis point. One one-hundredth of a percentage point (.0001).

Basis risk. The risk that the difference between the cash and futures prices will change between the time a futures contract is entered and the time the position is eliminated.

Basket options. Packages that involve the exchange of more than two currencies against a base currency at expiration. The basket option buyer purchases the right, but not the obligation, to receive designated currencies in exchange for a base currency, either at the prevailing spot market rate or at a preagreed rate of exchange. A basket option is generally used by a multinational corporation with multicurrency cash flows since it is cheaper to buy an option on a basket of, for example, Scandinavian currencies than to hedge each currency against the home currency.

Bearer bonds. Bonds on which the coupon and principal is payable to whomever has possession of the certificate, i.e., the certificate is not registered in the name of any investor.

Beta. A statistical measure of market risk on a portfolio. Beta is traditionally used to estimate the elasticity of a stock portfolio's return relative to that of the market index.

Bid-ask spread. The difference between a bid and an ask quotation.

Big Bank. The term applied to the liberalization in 1986 of the London Stock Exchange in which trading was automated with the use of computers.

Black market. An illegal foreign exchange market.

Bourse. A term of French origin used to refer to stock markets, e.g., the Paris Bourse.

Brady bonds. Bonds issued by emerging countries under a debt reduction plan named after Nicholas Brady, former U.S. Secretary of the Treasury.

Bretton Woods Agreement. An agreement signed by the original United Nations members in 1944 that established the International Monetary Fund (IMF) and the post-World War II international monetary system of fixed exchange rates.

Bulldog bonds. Foreign bonds issued in London, which are denominated in British pound sterling.

Call option. A contract giving the purchaser the right, but not the obligation, to buy an asset at a stated strike, or exercise, price on or before a stated date.

Capital account. Those items in the balance of payments that show net changes in the domestic private sector's holdings of foreign financial assets or in foreign holdings of domestic financial assets and that usually have maturities longer than the period for which the balance of payments accounts.

Capital flight. The movement of funds out of a country because of political risk in that country.

Caps. Interest rate contracts that enable a borrower to pay a premium as insurance that the floating rate of interest on a debt instrument never exceeds a specified ceiling.

Cedel. One of the two principal clearing systems in the Eurobond market. It is based in Luxembourg and was established in 1971.

Chicago Mercantile Exchange (CME). Futures exchange where Eurodollar and currency futures contracts as well as options on these futures contracts are traded. *See* **International Monetary Market (IMM).**

Clearinghouse. A division of an exchange or independent corporation through which all trades must be confirmed, matched, and settled daily until offset.

Clearinghouse Interbank Payments System (CHIPS). A New York-based computerized clearinghouse used by banks to settle interbank foreign exchange obligations between members.

Closed-end fund. A fund with a fixed number of shares. New shares cannot be issued without shareholder approval and old shares cannot be redeemed. Such funds can be traded on stock markets and their value may be different from the net asset value of the fund.

Collars. Floating rate debt contracts with two caps: one on the maximum interest rate, and one on the minimum interest rate.

Collateralized Mortgage Obligation (CMO). A catch-all for securities derived from pools of government-backed mortgages. Each CMO is divided into classes each with its own set of potential risks and rewards.

Comanager. A bank that ranks just below a lead manager in a syndicated Eurocredit or international bond issue. Comanagers may assist the lead manager bank(s) in the pricing and issue of the debt instrument.

Commercial risk. The risk that a foreign debtor will be unable to pay its debts because of business events, such as bankruptcy.

Commodities Futures Trading Commission (CFTC). The U.S. regulatory agency that regulates all exchange-based futures and options trading.

Contango. A futures market in which more distant delivery month contracts trade at higher prices than near months. Such prices typically reflect the time premium—the cost of holding the position and the perceived risk of price volatility over time. Futures markets are generally in contango.

Controlled Foreign Corporation (CFC). A foreign corporation in which U.S. shareholders own more than 50 percent of the combined voting power or total value. Under U.S. tax law, U.S. shareholders may be liable for taxes on undistributed earnings of the CFC.

Convertibility. The degree of freedom to exchange a currency without government restrictions or controls.

Correspondent bank. A bank that holds deposits for and provides services for another bank, usually located in a different geographic area, on a reciprocal basis.

Country risk. The risk from unexpected events within a host country that influence a client's or a government's ability to repay a loan. These include currency inconvertibility, violence, contract interference, and expropriation.

Coupon. The periodic interest payment on a bond.

Covered interest arbitrage. The process whereby an investor earns a risk-free profit by borrowing funds in one currency, exchanging those funds in the spot market for a foreign currency, investing the foreign currency at interest rates in that foreign country, selling forward, at the time of original investment, the investment proceeds to be received at maturity, using the proceeds of the forward sale to repay the original loan, and having a remaining profit balance.

Crawling peg. A foreign exchange rate system in which the exchange rate is adjusted very frequently to reflect the prevailing rate of inflation.

Cross-hedging. The hedging of an asset with a futures contract of a different asset.

Cross rate. The exchange rate between two currencies, neither of which is the U.S. dollar. Such a rate is usually constructed from the individual exchange rates of each currency with the U.S. dollar.

Cumulative Translation Adjustment (CTA) account. An entry in a translated balance sheet in which gains and/or losses from translation have been accumulated over a period of years. The CTA account is required under the rules of the Financial Accounting Standards Board (FASB-52) No. 52.

Current account. The account in the balance of payments, which includes exports and imports of merchandise trade and goods and services.

Currency basket. The value of a portfolio of specific amounts of individual currencies, used as the basis for setting the market value of another currency. It is also referred to as a currency cocktail.

Currency swap. A contractual obligation entered into by two parties to deliver a sum of money in one currency for a sum of money in another currency at some stated interval or according to stated circumstances.

Current account. In the balance of payments, it is the net flow of goods, services, and unilateral payments between one country and all other countries.

Current/noncurrent method. A method used to translate the financial statements of foreign affiliates into the parent's reporting currency by translating all current assets and liabilities at the current rate and all noncurrent items at the historical rate, or the exchange rate in effect at the time the items entered the financial statements.

Current rate method. A method used to translate the financial statements of foreign affiliates into the parent's reporting currency by translating all items at the current exchange rate, the rate in effect when the books are closed.

Default risk. The risk that an issuer will be unable to timely meet interest and principal payments.

Delta. Option delta is the ratio of a change in the option price to a small change in the price of the asset on which the option is written.

Delta hedge. A dynamic hedging strategy using options with continuous adjustment of the number of options used, as a function of the delta of the option.

Derivatives. Securities bearing a contractual relation to some underlying asset or rate. Options, swaps, futures, and many forms of bonds are derivative securities.

Devaluation. A decrease in the official value of a currency with respect to a second currency or real asset.

Dirty float. A system of floating exchange rates in which the government occasionally intervenes to change the direction of the value of the country's currency.

Discount (in the foreign exchange market). The amount by which a currency for future delivery trades less than the spot exchange rate.

Domestic International Sales Corporation (DISC). A type of subsidiary once allowed by the U.S. tax code to export U.S. produced goods. The company that established a DISC was allowed to defer a portion of the income of the DISC from U.S. tax liability.

Down-and-in option. A barrier option that is activated only if, during the life of the option, the spot rate falls to some level specified in the option contract.

Down-and-out option. A barrier option that becomes worthless if, during the life of the option, the spot rate falls to some specified level.

Edge corporations. Specialized banking institutions, authorized and chartered by the Federal Reserve Board in the United States, which are allowed to engage in transactions that have a foreign or international character. They are not subject to any restrictions on interstate banking. Foreign banks operating in the United States are permitted to organize and own an Edge corporation.

Eurobank. A bank that regularly accepts foreign currency denominated deposits and makes foreign currency loans.

Eurobonds. Bonds that are simultaneously in the capital markets of several nations and that are issued outside the normal regulatory restrictions that apply to domestic issues in each of those capital markets.

Euroclear. One of two principal clearing systems in the Eurobond market. It began operations in 1968, is located in Brussels, and is managed by Morgan Guaranty Bank.

Euro-commercial paper. Short-term notes with maturities up to 360 days that are issued by companies in international money markets.

Eurocredits. Intermediate-term loans of Eurocurrencies made by banking syndicates to corporate and government borrowers.

Eurocurrency market. The money market for borrowing and lending currencies that are held in the form of deposits in banks located outside the countries of origin of the currencies issued as legal tender.

Eurodollar. A dollar denominated time deposit in a bank outside the United States or at International Banking Facilities (IBFs) in the United States.

Eurodollar bonds. Eurobonds denominated in U.S. dollars.

Euro-note. Short- to medium-term debt instruments sold in the Eurocurrency market.

European Currency Unit (ECU). A portfolio currency used in the European Monetary System as an average exchange rate for the European Union. It is used as a currency of denomination of lending, borrowing, and trade.

European Monetary System (EMS). An exchange arrangement formed in 1979 that involves the currencies of European Union member countries.

European Union (EU). An economic association of European countries founded by the Treaty of Rome in 1957 as a common market of six nations. It was known as the European Community before 1993 and is comprised of 15 European countries. Its goals are a single market for goods and services without any economic barriers and a common currency with one monetary authority. The EU was known as the European Community until January 1, 1994.

European-type option. An option that can be exercised only at expiration.

Exchange controls. Governmental restrictions on the purchase of foreign currencies by domestic cit-

izens or on the purchase of the local domestic currency by foreigners.

Exchange rate. The price of a unit of one country's currency expressed in terms of the currency of some other country.

Exchange Rate Mechanism (ERM). The methodology by which members of the EMS maintain their currency exchange rates within an agreed upon range with respect to the other member countries.

Exchange risk. The variability of a firm's value that results from unexpected exchange rate changes or the extent to which the present value of a firm is expected to change as a result of a given currency's appreciation or depreciation.

Exercise. The use of the right given by an option to purchase if a call or to sell if a put of an asset at the strike price stated in the option contract.

Exercise date. The last day on which an option may be exercised.

Export-Import Bank (Ex-Im Bank). The U.S. Federal government agency that extends trade credits to U.S. companies to facilitate the financing of U.S. exports.

Expropriation. The official seizure by a government of private property. Any government has the right to seize such property, according to international law, if prompt and adequate compensation is given.

FASB-8. A standard issued by the U.S. Financial Accounting Standards Board that required U.S. companies to translate their foreign affiliates' accounts by the temporal method. Gains and losses from currency fluctuations were reported in current income. It was in effect between 1975 and 1981 and became the most controversial accounting standard in the United States. It was replaced by FASB-52 in 1981.

FASB-52. The accounting standard in the United States that replaced FASB-8. U.S. companies are required to translate foreign accounts by the current rate and report the changes from currency fluctuations in a cumulative translation adjustment account in the equity section of the balance sheet.

Federal Reserve System. The central bank of the United States, established in 1913, and governed by the Federal Reserve Board located in Washington, D.C. The system includes 12 Federal Reserve Banks and is authorized to regulate monetary policy in the United States as well as to supervise Federal Reserve member banks, bank holding companies, international operations of U.S. banks, and U.S. operations of foreign banks.

Fisher effect. A theory that nominal interest rates in two or more countries should be equal to the required real rate of return to investors plus compensation for the expected amount of inflation in each country.

Fixed exchange rates. Foreign exchange rates that are tied to the currency of a major country, to gold, or to a basket of currencies such as the Special Drawing Right or the European Currency Unit.

Floating exchange rate. An exchange rate whose value is not constrained by central bank intervention to remain within a fixed range. It is determined by trading in the foreign exchange market.

Floating rate note. Bond issued with variable quarterly or semiannual interest rate payments, generally linked to LIBOR.

Floor. A contract that protects the holder against a decline in prices below a certain point.

Foreign bonds. Bonds issued by nonresidents in a country's domestic capital market. Foreign bonds are subject to the securities regulations of the domestic market and are primarily underwritten by banks registered in the country in which the bond is issued.

Foreign Credit Insurance Association (FCIA). A private U.S. consortium of insurance companies that offers trade credit insurance to U.S. exporters in conjunction with the U.S. Export-Import Bank.

Foreign currency translation. The process of restating foreign currency accounts of subsidiaries into the reporting currency of the parent company in order to prepare consolidated financial statements.

Foreign direct investment (FDI). Purchase of physical assets in a foreign country to be managed and controlled by the parent company.

Foreign exchange broker. A company or individual that arranges foreign exchange transactions between two parties but which does not act as a principal in the transaction but settles the transaction for a commission.

Foreign exchange controls. Various forms of controls imposed by a government on the purchase

(sale) of foreign currencies by residents or on the purchase (sale) of local currency by nonresidents.

Foreign exchange dealer. A firm or individual that buys foreign exchange from one party and then sells it to another party. The dealer makes a profit from the difference between the buying and selling prices, or spread.

Foreign exchange market. The market in which currencies of different nations are bought and sold with respect to each other.

Foreign exchange risk. The risk that an unexpected change in exchange rates will alter the home currency cash payments expected from a foreign source or that the unexpected change will alter the amount of home currency needed to repay an obligation denominated in a foreign currency.

Foreign sales corporation (FSC). A type of foreign corporation allowed U.S. companies under the U.S. tax code which provides tax-exempt or tax-deferred income for U.S. persons or corporations having export operations.

Foreign tax credit. The amount by which a domestic firm may reduce or credit domestic income taxes for income tax payments made to a foreign government.

Forfaiting. A technique for arranging non-recourse medium-term export financing used to finance imports into eastern European or developing countries. A medium-term trade credit is divided into several short-term instruments, which are guaranteed by a specialized financial institution.

Forward discount. A currency trades at a forward discount when its forward price is lower than its spot price.

Forward exchange. Foreign currency traded for settlement beyond two trading days from today.

Forward premium. A currency trades at a forward premium when its forward price is higher than its spot price.

Forward rate. An exchange rate quoted today for settlement at some future date and which is the rate used in a forward transaction.

Forward rate agreement. A cash-settled interbank forward contract on interest rates. The seller pays the buyer the difference if the interest rate rises above the agreed rate and is paid by the buyer in the reverse case.

Functional currency. Under the rules of FASB-52, this is the currency of the primary economic environment in which a foreign affiliate operates and in which it generates cash flows. Except in certain cases, it is the currency into which foreign currency accounts will be translated.

Futures contract. An obligation incurred according to the rules of a futures exchange, which results in daily cash flows that occur with changes in the futures price of a contract traded by the exchange.

Gamma. The ratio of a change in the option delta to a small change in the price of the asset on which the option is written.

Global bond. A bond, usually for $1 billion or more, issued simultaneously in Tokyo, New York, and Europe, and denominated either in yen, dollars, or marks.

Gold standard. An international monetary system in which currencies are defined in terms of their gold content and payment imbalances between countries are settled in gold. It was in effect from about 1870–1914.

Group of Five (G-5). The five leading countries (France, Germany, Japan, United Kingdom, and United States) that meet periodically to achieve some cooperative effort on international economic issues. When currency issues are discussed, the monetary authorities of these nations hold the meeting.

Group of Seven (G-7). The G-5 countries plus Canada and Italy.

Hard currency. A freely convertible currency that is not expected to depreciate in value in the foreseeable future.

Hedging. The process of reducing the variation in the value—from price fluctuations—of a total portfolio. Hedging is accomplished by adding to an original portfolio items such as spot assets or liabilities, forward contracts, futures contracts, or options contracts in such a way that the total variation of the new portfolio is smaller than that of the original portfolio.

Herstatt risk. The risk of loss in foreign exchange trading that one party will deliver foreign exchange but the counterparty financial institution will fail to deliver its end of the contract. It is also referred to as settlement risk. The term is derived from the 1974 failure of Bankhaus Herstatt in

Germany as a result of overextended trading in foreign exchange.

Historical exchange rate. An accounting term that refers to the exchange rate in effect when an asset or liability was acquired.

Hot money. Money that moves across country borders in response to interest rate differences and that moves away when the interest rate differential disappears.

Hybrid. A package containing two or more different kinds of risk instruments that are usually interactive. A change in the market value of one component of the hybrid can also change the value of others. A hybrid enables the CFO of a multinational company to hedge back into the home currency all the variables, including receivables and inventory costs of an operation that, for example, exports products from one foreign country into another for finishing and then ships the finished product into still another country. A hybrid might also be used by the portfolio manager of, for example, a global bond fund with an uncertain forecast of the direction of interest and exchange rates. The hybrid forms protective hedges across the portfolio.

Indirect quotation. The price of a unit of a home country's currency expressed in terms of a foreign country's currency.

In the money option. An option that has a positive value if exercised immediately. If the option is a call, the strike price is below the spot price of the underlying asset. If the option is a put, the strike price is above the spot price.

Interest equalization tax. A measure proposed by the Kennedy administration in 1963, which became law in 1964. It imposed a 15 percent tax on portfolio investments by U.S. citizens and eventually was amended to cover some bank loans. It was repealed in 1974.

Interest-only strip (IO). A security based solely on the interest payments from a pool of mortgages, Treasury bonds, or other bonds. Once the principal on the mortgages or bonds has been repaid, interest payments stop and the value of the IO falls to zero. It is a bet on high interest rates, since lower rates would encourage bond or mortgage repayments that would end interest payments, and the IO's value.

Interest parity. An equilibrium condition under which a borrower (lender) is indifferent between borrowing (lending) in the domestic currency or in a foreign currency, when the need to convert currency now through the spot market is considered, with exchange risk covered by a reverse transaction through the forward market. When the interest parity condition is restated, it yields the forward exchange rate as a function of the spot rate and the interest rates on the two currencies.

Interest rate swap. A contractual obligation entered into by two parties to deliver a fixed sum of money against a variable sum of money at periodic intervals. This usually entails an exchange of interest obligations on fixed and floating rate debt.

International Banking Facility (IBF). An IBF is a division of an existing U.S. banking operation, either owned by a U.S. bank or a foreign bank operating in the United States, that is allowed to conduct Eurocurrency business but is prohibited from issuing negotiable certificates of deposit. They were authorized by the Federal Reserve Board in 1981 as a means of gaining some control over off-shore banking operations of banks located in the United States.

International bonds. A collective term that refers to global bonds, Eurobonds, and foreign bonds.

International Fisher effect. A theory that the spot exchange rate should change by an amount equal to the difference in interest rates between two countries.

International Monetary Fund (IMF). An organization founded in 1944 by the United Nations members and located in Washington, D.C. Its objectives are to oversee exchange arrangements of member countries and to lend foreign currency reserves to members with short-term balance of payments problems.

International Money Market (IMM). The IMM, located at the Chicago Mercantile Exchange, is the world's largest market for foreign currency and Eurodollar futures contract trading.

International Securities Market Association (ISMA). An association formed in 1969 as the association of International Bond Dealers to establish uniform trading procedures in the international bond markets.

International Swap and Derivatives Association (ISDA). An association of swap dealers formed in 1985 to promote uniform practices in the writ-

ing, trading, and settlement of swaps and other derivatives.

Intrinsic value. The value obtained on an option if it were to be exercised immediately.

Inverse floating rate note. A variable rate security whose coupon rate increases as a benchmark interest rate declines.

Jumbo loans. Loans of $1 billion or more.

Lag. Payment of a financial obligation later than is expected or required, as in lead and lag.

Lamda. The ratio of a change in the option price to a small change in the option volatility. It is the partial derivative of the option price with respect to the option volatility.

Lead. Payment of a financial obligation earlier than is expected or required, as in lead and lag.

Lead manager. The commercial or investment bank with the primary responsibility for organizing a syndicated bank credit or bond issue. The lead manager recruits additional lending or underwriting banks, negotiates terms of the issue with the issuer, and assesses market conditions.

Letter of credit (L/C). An instrument issued by a bank in which the bank promises to pay a beneficiary upon presentation of documents specified in the letter of credit.

London Interbank Offered Rate (LIBOR). The rate at which banks in London will lend Eurocurrencies in the interbank market.

London International Financial Futures Exchange (LIFFE). A London exchange where Eurodollar futures as well as futures-style options are traded.

Lookback option. An option that allows the buyer to choose as the option strike price any price of the underlying asset that has occurred during the life of the option. If a call, the buyer will choose the minimal price that has occurred during the option's price, whereas if a put, the buyer will choose the maximum price. This option will always be "at" or "in the money."

Managed float. *See* **dirty float.**

Management fee. The part of total investment banking fees accruing to the managing banks in a bond issue. In a syndicated credit, it is the fee paid to the managing bank or banks for organizing the loan.

Margin. The amount of money and/or securities that must be posted as a security bond to ensure

performance on a contract. In the futures market, both short and long positions post margin. Margin may be initial margin, the minimum deposit a futures exchange requires from customers for each futures contract, and maintenance margin, the minimum equity a futures exchange requires in a customer's account for each futures contract subsequent to deposit of the initial margin.

Mark-to-market. The revaluation of a futures contract or a security to reflect the most recently available market price.

Market risk. The risk of loss from changes in the market price of assets.

Merchant bank. A bank that specializes in financial assistance to corporations and governments using a number of techniques. They usually combine commercial and investment banking activities.

Monetary/nonmonetary method. The accounting method for translating foreign currency accounts in which all monetary items in the financial statements are translated at the current rate and all nonmonetary items are translated at the historical rate. It has been referred to as the temporal approach in the United States.

Money market hedge. A hedge that uses foreign currency borrowing to reduce transaction or accounting foreign exchange exposure.

Nominal exchange rate. The actual foreign exchange quotation in contrast to the real exchange rate that has been adjusted for changes in purchasing power.

Note issuance facility (NIF). An agreement by which a syndicate of banks indicates a willingness to accept short-term notes from borrowers and resell these notes in the Eurocurrency markets.

Offer. The price at which a foreign exchange trader is willing to sell foreign exchange, securities, or commodities. It is also referred to as the "ask" price.

Official reserves. The amount of reserves owned by the central bank of a government in the form of gold, Special Drawing Rights, and foreign cash or marketable securities.

Off-shore finance subsidiary. A foreign financial subsidiary owned by a corporation in another country, usually located in a tax-free or low-tax country, which enables the parent corporation to finance international operations without being subject to domestic tax liabilities.

Open interest. The total number of futures contracts for a particular asset that have not been liquidated by an offsetting trade or that have not been fulfilled by delivery.

Open position. A net long or short foreign currency or futures position whose value will change with a change in the foreign exchange rate or futures prices.

Operating exposure. The potential for change in expected cash flows and, thus, company value, of a foreign affiliate because of unexpected changes in foreign exchange rates. Also referred to as economic exposure.

Option. A contract, traded on or off an exchange, which gives the purchaser the right, but not the obligation, to buy (call) or sell (put) an asset at a stated price (strike or exercise price) on a stated date (European option) or at any time before a stated date (American option).

Option premium. The price of an option.

Out of the money. A term used to refer to a call option whose strike price is above, or to a put option whose strike price is below, the current price of the asset on which the option is written.

Parallel loan. A process whereby two companies in different countries borrow each other's currency for a specific period of time, and repay the other's currency at an agreed maturity for the purpose of reducing foreign exchange exposure risk. Also referred to as back-to-back loans.

Participating fees. The portion of total fees in a syndicated credit that go to the participating banks.

Philadelphia Stock Exchange (PHLX). A securities exchange where American and European foreign currency options on spot exchange are traded.

Plain vanilla. A term that refers to a relatively simple derivative financial instrument, usually a swap or other derivative that is issued with standard features.

Planned amortization class CMO. One class of CMO that carries the most stable cash flows and the lowest prepayment risk of any class of CMO. Because of that stable cash flow, it is considered the least risky CMO.

Points. The smallest unit of price change quoted or one one-hundredth of a cent or percent or other smallest unit of a currency.

Political risk. The risk that political events in a particular country will have an adverse effect on the foreign operations of a company. Also referred to as sovereign risk.

Possessions corporation. A type of corporation permitted under the U.S. tax code whereby a branch operation in a U.S. possessions can obtain tax benefits as though it were operating as a foreign subsidiary.

Premium. The price of an option agreed upon between the buyer and writer or their agents in a transaction on the floor of an exchange.

Principal-only strip (PO). A security, sold at a discount, based only on the principal payments from a pool of mortgages or bonds. It is a bet on low-interest rates, since the lower rates go, the faster mortgages will be repaid or bonds called and the faster investors will be paid back.

Purchasing Power Parity (PPP). The notion that in equilibrium the market exchange rate for any two currencies will exactly reflect the relative purchasing power of the two currencies.

Put option. A contract that gives the purchaser the right, but not the obligation, to sell a particular asset at a stated strike price on or before a stated date.

Quantos. Currency options with a guaranteed exchange rate that enable buyers who like the asset, German bonds for example, but not the asset's pricing currency, to arrange to be paid in a different currency for a fee.

Quotation. In foreign exchange trading, the pair of prices—bid and asked—at which a dealer or trader is willing to buy or sell foreign exchange.

Real exchange rates. Exchange rates that have been adjusted for the inflation differential between the two countries.

Real interest rate. The market interest rate as commonly quoted (nominal interest rate) minus the rate of inflation of the price level.

Registered. The term used to refer to bonds or stocks that are recorded in the bond or stock issuer's books in the name of the owner. Ownership of such securities can only be transferred by a formal transfer of the ownership name in the issuer's books.

Reinvoicing center. A central financial subsidiary used by an MNC to reduce transaction exposure by having all home country exports billed in the

home currency and then reinvoiced to each operating affiliate in that affiliate's local currency. It can also be used as a netting center.

Rembrandt bonds. Bonds issued within the Netherlands by a foreign borrower, which are denominated in Dutch guilders.

Repurchase agreement (REPO). An agreement by one party to sell a security with an agreement to buy it back at a specified price on a specified date.

Reserve currency. A foreign currency held by a central bank or monetary authority for the purposes of exchange intervention and the settlement of intergovernmental claims.

Revaluation. An increase in the foreign exchange value of a currency that is pegged to other currencies or to gold. It is also referred to as appreciation.

Samurai bonds. Yen denominated foreign bonds issued in Tokyo.

Secondary market. A market in which securities are traded following the time of their original issue.

Section 482. Regulations of the U.S. Internal Revenue Service that govern transfer prices.

Selling group. All banks involved in selling or marketing a new issue of bonds.

Shogun bonds. Foreign bonds issued in Tokyo and denominated in currencies other than the Japanese yen.

Sight draft. A bill of exchange that is due on demand, when presented to the bank.

Singapore International Monetary Exchange (SIMEX). A leading futures and options exchange in Singapore.

Smithsonian agreement. A revision to the Bretton Woods international monetary system, which was signed at the Smithsonian Institution in Washington, D.C., in December 1971. Included were a new set of par values, widened bands to ± 2.25 percent of par, and increase in the official value of gold to $38.00 per ounce.

Society for Worldwide Interbank Financial Telecommunications (SWIFT). A computer network cooperative based in Belgium comprised of banks worldwide, which provides a funds message transfer service between member banks worldwide.

Soft currency. A currency that is expected to drop in value relative to other currencies.

Sovereign risk. The risk that a government may default on its debt.

Special drawing right (SDR). An artificial reserve asset created and held on the books of the IMF. An SDR is defined in terms of the U.S. dollar, German mark, French franc, Japanese yen, and British pound.

Speculator. An individual or firm that attempts to anticipate price movements and attempts to profit from them by taking appropriate long or short positions on market-traded assets.

Spot exchange. Foreign currency traded for settlement generally two business or working days from the trade date.

Spread. The difference between the buying and selling rates of a foreign currency or a bond, or the difference between borrowing and lending rates on Eurocurrency deposits.

Strike price. The price at which an option buyer may purchase (if a call) or sell (if a put) the asset upon which the option is written.

Subpart F. A type of income defined by the U.S. Internal Revenue Service that is taxed under certain conditions in the United States even though it has not been remitted to the United States.

Sushi bonds. Dollar denominated Eurobonds issued by Japanese companies, managed by Japanese banks, and purchased primarily by Japanese investors.

Swap. In the interbank foreign exchange market, the simultaneous purchase and sale of identical amounts of a currency for different value dates.

Swaption. The purchase of the right, over an agreed period, to enter into a swap at specified terms.

Syndicate. A group of banks that acts jointly, on a temporary basis, to loan money in a bank credit (syndicated credit) or to underwrite a new issue of bonds.

Synthetics. Customized hybrid instruments created by blending an underlying bond or note with a future or option contract. These are generally used to change the effective yield or maturity of bonds or note.

Systemic risk. The risk that a failure of a large bank or other financial institution in one country will cause a failure of a financial institution in the same

or another country. Also referred to as contagion risk.

Tax haven. A country with no tax rate or very low tax rates that uses this system to attract firms for the purpose of international financial transactions.

Temporal method. A term used in the United States to refer to a foreign currency translation method that is quite similar to the monetary/non-monetary method.

Theta. The ratio of a change in the option price to a small change in the option term-to-maturity. It is the partial derivative of the option price with respect to the option term-to-maturity.

Trade balance. The balance of a country's merchandise exports and imports.

Transaction exposure. The risk of change in the value of outstanding financial obligations entered into prior to a change in exchange rates but not due for settlement until after the exchange rate change.

Transfer pricing. The setting of prices to be charged one unit of a multi-unit firm by another unit, i.e. a foreign affiliate by the parent corporation, for goods or services sold between such related units.

Unbiased predictor. A theory that spot prices at some future date will be equal to today's forward rates.

Underlying asset. The asset, reference rate, or index whose price movement determines the value of the derivative. Its theoretical value is referred to as notional value.

Underwriting syndicate. The banks, in a new bond issue, that agree to pay a minimum price to the borrower even if the bonds cannot be sold on the market at a higher price.

Unilateral transfers. Items in the current account of the balance of payments that correspond to gifts from foreigners or pension payments to foreign residents who once worked in the country whose balance of payments is being considered.

Volatility. The standard deviation of changes in the logarithm of an asset price, expressed at a yearly rate. The volatility is a variable that appears in option formulas.

Warrant. An option issued by a company and generally attached to bonds.

Withholding tax. A tax levied by a country of source on income paid, usually on dividends remitted to the home country of the foreign company.

World Bank. A multilateral development finance agency created by the 1944 Bretton Woods, New Hampshire negotiations. It makes loans to developing countries for social overhead capital projects, which are guaranteed by the recipient country.

Writer of an option. An individual, bank, or company that issues an option and consequently has the obligation to sell the asset (if a call) or to buy the asset (if a put) on which the option is written if the option buyer exercises the option.

Yankee bond. A dollar denominated foreign bond issued in New York.

Index

Budgeting, 442
Bugnion, J.R., 171
Business Environmental Risk Index (BERI), 126, 127
Buying hedge, 335

C

Callable step-up note, 378
Call options, 350–54, 377
Calvet, Louis, 164–65
Capital budgeting
  cost of capital and financial structure, 182–83, 184–86
  cultural problems, 179
  discounted cash flow models, 179–82
  factors that affect affiliate's financial structure, 183
  function, 174–75
  literature, 171–74
  management application, 178–79
  methods, 173–77
  parent versus local perspective, 181–82
Capital exports, 41–42
Capital gains, taxation of, 457
Capital management, long-term. *See* Capital budgeting
Capital management, short-term, 389–518
  international cash management, 391–415
Carter administration, 46, 88
Cash disbursement system, 401–2
Cash flow
  analysis, 443
  See also International cash management
Cash management
  in Germany, 403
  See also International cash management
Cash manager, 402–4
Cash receipts system. *See* International cash receipts system
Caterpillar company, 425
CBOT. *See* Chicago Board of Trade
Cedel, 298–99, 501
Centralization, 109, 201
  of foreign currency accounts, 413
Central securities depositories (CSDs), 509–10
CFO. *See* Chief financial officer
CFTC. *See* Commodities and Futures Trading Commission
CHAPS (Clearing House Automated Payments System), 394, 494, 496
Chase Manhattan Bank, 260, 503
CHATS (Clearing House Automated Transfer System), 495, 496
Chemical Bank, 259
Chicago Board Options Exchange, 346, 360
Chicago Board of Trade (CBOT), 329, 337, 347, 357, 359, 360
Chicago Mercantile Exchange (CME; Merc), 329, 330, 346, 347, 357, 358, 359, 360, 374
Chief financial officer (CFO), 21–22, 269, 270, 281, 396
Chile, 9, 125
China, 143
CHIPS (Clearing House Interbank Payments System), 394, 494, 496, 506, 517
CIEBA. *See* Committee on Investment of Employee Benefits Assets

Citibank, 260, 405, 503
Citicorp, 327
Clearing houses, 505–13
  delivery versus payment and Herstatt risk, 506–7
  ECHO system, 508
  Eurobond, 298–99, 501
  multilateral clearing, 407
  Multinet International, 507–8
  proposed systems, 401, 508–12
Clinton administration, 44
Closed-end investment companies, 316
CME. *See* Chicago Mercantile Exchange
Commercial banks, 67–81, 100, 282–83
Committee on Investment of Employee Benefits Assets (CIEBA), 380
Commodities and Futures Trading Commission (CFTC), 339, 515
Communications networks, 394–96
Comparable profits method (CPM), 478
Comparative advantage, 3–7, 8
Competitive advantage, 162
ConAgra, 22
Consortium banks, 215
Contagion risk, 9
Continental Illinois Bank, 9
Contract(s)
  disputes, 124
  forward exchange market, 79–80
  interference, 123–24
Cooke, Peter, 223
Cooke Committee, 223
Coroporate income tax. *See* Taxation
Correlation products, 383
Correspondent banks, 214–15
Cost of capital, 182–83, 184–86
CPM. *See* Comparable profits method
Credit risk, 8, 220, 324, 491–92
Credit Suisse First Boston, 282
Cross rates, 76, 247–48, 339
CSDs. *See* Central securities depositories
CTA. *See* Cumulative translation account
Cuba, 9
Cultural variables, 13–15, 179
Cumulative translation account (CTA), 431–35
Currency
  attack of 1992, 38–39
  cross rates, 76, 247–48
  effect of knock-out options, 385–86
  fluctuations, 440
  and foreign direct investment, 155–56
  foreign futures, 329–39
  foreign options, 339–57
  and foreign subsidiary evaluations, 443–44
  functional, 430–31
  global crisis of 1995, 45–46
  interbank futures and options, 373–75
  local financing, 409
  organizing foreign accounts, 412–13
  quotations, 71, 72–74, 79
  restrictions, 122–23
  speculation, 40–41
  swaps, 366–67
  See also Foreign exchange market(s); *specific currencies*
Current rate method, 427
Czech Republic, 237

D

Daimler-Benz, 20, 43, 90, 418, 420
Daiwa Bank, 220
Debt markets
  long-term, 288–303
  risk in, 290–91
  short- and medium-term, 303–5
Decentralization, 109–10, 201
  of foreign currency accounts, 413
Decision tree analysis, 160, 161
Decomposition theory, 87
Deficit Reduction Act (1984), 465
Delivery versus payment (DVP), 501–2, 506–7
Delta, 361
Denmark, 39
Deregulation, 289
Derivative financial instruments
  clearing and settlement, 514–16
  for emerging markets, 379
  exchanges, 328–29
  exotic, 375–78, 382
  and financial theories, 327–28
  international exchange traded, 320–62
  international nonexchange traded, 365–86
  markets, 321, 322, 336
  myths about, 380–82
  notional value traded by 20 financial institutions, 321, 322
  proposed regulatory legislation, 328
  regulation of, 379–82
  risks of, 324–29
  types of, 321
  users of, 323–24
Deutsche Bank, 213, 259, 281, 282, 403
Deutsche Bundesbank, 403
Deutsche Morgan Grenfell, 259
Devaluation, 59
Development finance companies (DFCs), 284–85
Dexter Corporation, 110
DFCs. *See* Development finance companies
Diff (differential) swaps, 370–73
  correlation products, 383
  hedging and pricing, 383–85
Direct quotations, 71, 79
Discounted cash flow models, 179–82
DISC. *See* Domestic international sales companies
Dividends, 410–11
Dollar
  decline, 18, 83
  devaluation, 32
  falling, 41–42, 378, 385–86
  movement under floating exchange rates (1970–90), 38
  1994–95 crisis, 39–40, 47
  1995–96, 42–43
  world value of, 52
Domestic international sales companies (DISC), 469
Dominguez, Kathryn, 47
Dow Jones Stock Index, 312–13
Draft, 231
Dual currency floater, 378
Dunning, John, 166
DVP. *See* Delivery versus payment
Dynamite warrant, 378